# MONUMENTAL GRAFFITI

# MONUMENTAL GRAFFITI

## TRACING PUBLIC ART AND RESISTANCE IN THE CITY

RAFAEL SCHACTER

The MIT Press
Cambridge, Massachusetts
London, England

The MIT Press would like to thank the anonymous peer reviewers who provided comments on drafts of this book. The generous work of academic experts is essential for establishing the authority and quality of our publications. We acknowledge with gratitude the contributions of these otherwise uncredited readers.

This book was set in Arnhem Pro and Berthold Akzidenz Grotesk by the MIT Press. Printed and bound in the United States of America.

Library of Congress Cataloging-in-Publication Data

Names: Schacter, Rafael, author.
Title: Monumental graffiti : tracing public art and resistance in the city / Rafael Schacter.
Description: Cambridge, Massachusetts : The MIT Press, [2024] | Includes bibliographical references.
Identifiers: LCCN 2023050268 (print) | LCCN 2023050269 (ebook) | ISBN 9780262049221 (hardcover) | ISBN 9780262379793 (epub) | ISBN 9780262379786 (pdf)
Subjects: LCSH: Graffiti—Social aspects. | Memorialization—Social aspects. | Monuments—Social aspects. | Art and society.
Classification: LCC GT3912 .S33 2024 (print) | LCC GT3912 (ebook) | DDC 751.7/3—dc23/eng/20240224
LC record available at https://lccn.loc.gov/2023050268
LC ebook record available at https://lccn.loc.gov/2023050269

10 9 8 7 6 5 4 3 2 1

FOR MY PARENTS

# CONTENTS

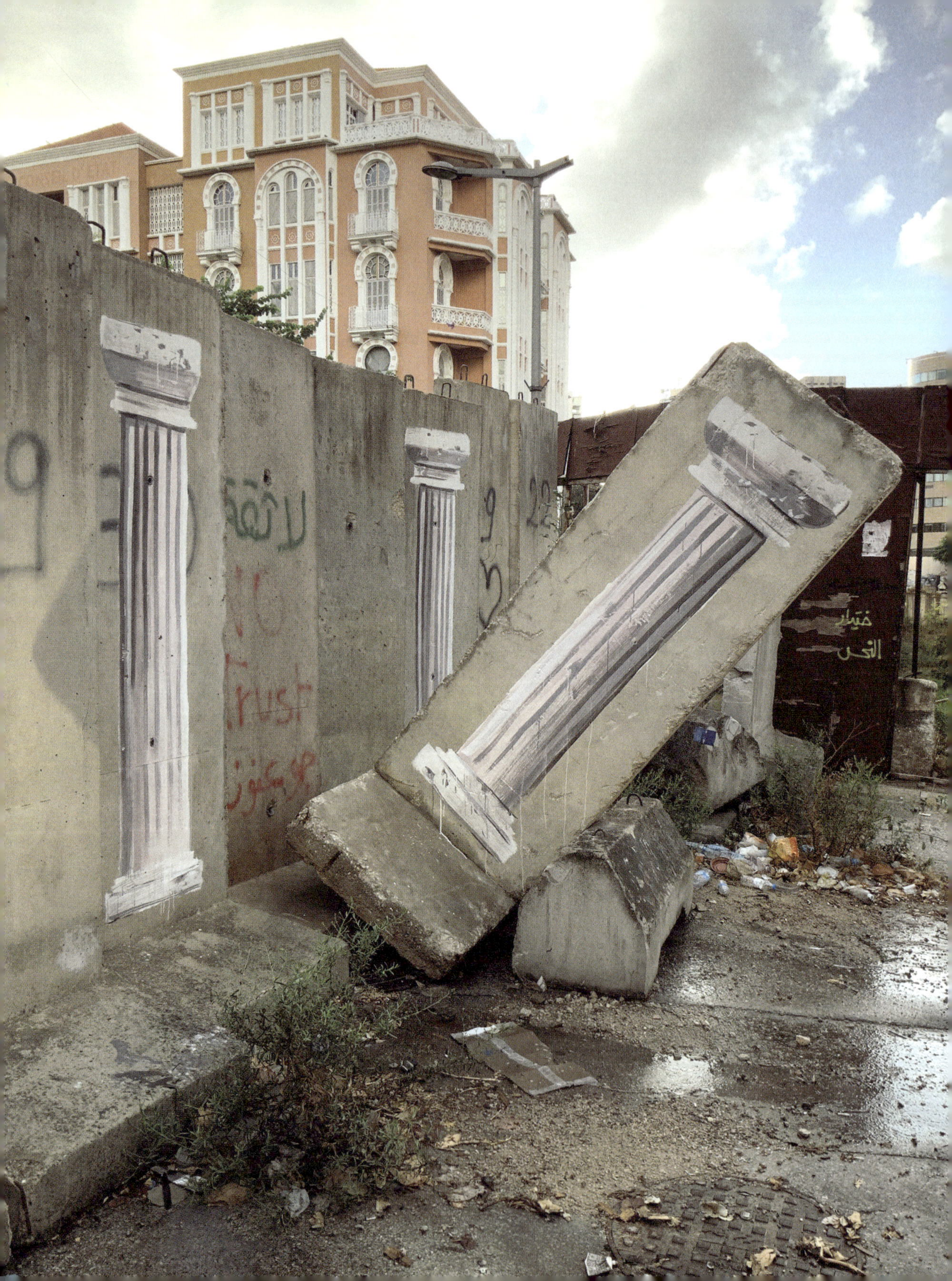
لاثقة

# INTRODUCTION

## MONUMENTAL GRAFFITI

What if we said graffiti was a monument? What if rather than dirt or vandalism, rather than ornament or even art, it was positioned as monument in the most literal of ways? What would that do to our understanding of graffiti? What, simultaneously, would that do to our understanding of monument? Focusing on the material, communicative, and contextual fundamentals of these two public forms of material culture, *Monumental Graffiti* uses monument as a lens to understand graffiti and, at the same time, graffiti as a lens to comprehend the contemporary monument. In doing so, this book aims not only to provide a new perspective on graffiti but likewise to provide a new viewpoint on public art, citizenship, and the city today. Moreover, by positioning graffiti in this way, we will unpack the doubly iconoclastic moment that sites across the globe are locked within, clarifying the wars on graffiti as much as those on institutional monuments while simultaneously challenging us to rethink what the appropriate monument for our contemporary world may even be.

Rather than understanding monument in its most contemporaneously predominant sense, as that which is permanent and large-scale, as that which is set into stone and set upon a pedestal, this book takes the term "monument" back to its etymological roots to signify a material *reminder*, *advice*, or *warning* (from the Latin *monere*).[1] Here monument emerges not via a specific style or material but through its status as a publicly positioned artifact reaching out to us on a social scale. As one of the founding fathers of art history, Alois Riegl, explained, the monument can in this way simply be seen as a marker of "human deeds or events . . . brought to the viewer's consciousness by means of the visual arts or with the help of inscriptions" (Riegl 1982 [1903]: 21). It can be seen, as literary critic John Guillory explained via the seminal iconographic work of Erwin Panofsky, as the "artifacts, events, or ideas that have the most urgent meaning for us at any present moment and that most demand our recognition or study" (Guillory 2016: 12). Monument here will hence be positioned not just as the institutionally produced forms most commonly imagined—the stony, everlasting, heroic public

**FIGURE I.1**
Escif, *Untitled*, 2021, Beirut. Acrylic paint on wall. Courtesy of the artist.

sculpture—but as an object imposing itself on our bodies and our minds. And monumental, likewise, will here be set as that which is not simply large in scale but large in scope, as an artifact containing an immediacy necessitating our attention no matter its size, material, or position in the hegemonic hierarchy of value.

With that said, the way graffiti is being defined here, as much as what I will here be calling the "institutional monument," needs to be clarified too. And rather than the overtly political graffiti recently explored by Campos et al. (2021), for example, or likewise the vernacular gang writing examined by Susan Phillips (1999), the "graffiti" being discussed here is graffiti as a specific style of public, independently undertaken name-writing first emerging from the East Coast of the United States in the late 1960s.[2] Broadly associated with the cultural world of hip hop (even though developing almost a decade before the foundation and subsequent explosion of the genre), and a practice at its outset undertaken by cross-class, multicultural, although predominantly male, youths, graffiti has been transplanted throughout the globe during the intervening half-century (via a collection of canonical books, films, and magazines) while developing in stylistically diverse and highly developed ways. Far from a monolithic culture and a practice that has always incorporated a wide range of subcultural influences (from punk and football hooliganism to situationism and heavy metal), graffiti today is one of the world's most popularly practiced art forms and as visible as it ever has been. Still, while it is in many ways hugely celebrated and commercially successful, it remains an equally controversial practice and one, as we will see, often utilized as a visual shorthand for urban decay and danger. While its practitioners are thus portrayed as antisocial criminals and inspired originators alike, the graffiti image itself has become perpetually hurled between the positions of art and vandalism (and back again) with seemingly little hope of repose.

At the other end of the scale, however, the term "institutional monument" will here act as shorthand for the dominant genre type existent within what is popularly labeled "monument" today. From the equestrian statue to the triumphal arch, from the figurative memorial to the obelisk, the institutional monument is, broadly, a hangover from the era of statumania in the nineteenth century (Agulhon 1981). This was a period in which Europe's burgeoning nation-states demanded artifacts—not only monuments but likewise flags, anthems, museums, and the like—to give material form to the immaterial state and create national homogeneity out of demographic heterogeneity. While almost always taking on neoclassical form—an artifactual style utilizing the archaeological remnants of antiquity to give these new, often precarious nation-states a temporal validity—the institutional monument does not by definition need to display these overtly classical influences. What is key, instead, is a top-down status in which power (be it political or economic) comes to assert itself publicly so as to reinforce the status quo. What is key, alongside its almost inevitably durable, spectacular, and colossal physicality, is its status as an omnipresent sign of public authority, as a marker of hegemony materialized in monumental form.

## GRAFFITI AS FORM, GRAFFITI AS MESSAGE, GRAFFITI AS TRACE

Following Régis Debray's essay on monuments, "Trace, forme ou message?" (1999), *Monumental Graffiti* will be structured through an analysis of the way graffiti operates as *form*, transmits as *message*, and discloses as *trace*. While Debray sees these three typological positions as different genres that the traditional monument can take up, here these registers will be used as three specific approaches to the monument itself. These will both align with graffiti's fundamental structure as a material, communicative, and contextual form, as well as link to the etymologic foundations of monument set out above: monument as reminder, monument as advice, and monument as warning.

Part I of the book, "Form," questions what graffiti *does* materially and is directed toward its status as a public art. It positions graffiti as a monument that, following Debray's first monumental archetype, functions through its status as an "architectural object" that "imposes itself by its intrinsic aesthetic or decorative qualities" (Debray 1999: 31),[3] a monument that creates a visual impact within its environment and that "prioritizes a space, breaks a continuum, takes centre stage" (p. 31). Sustaining this via specific chapters on "Site" (exploring graffiti's "how" or its situational features), on "Style" (exploring graffiti's "what" or its graphical characteristics), and on "Time" (exploring graffiti's "when" or its durational qualities), it will be graffiti's architectonic, figural, and temporal attributes that will be assessed here. Graffiti as form will thus here be understood through the position of the monument-*reminder*, as a marginal, corporeal, ephemeral monument formally and sensorially driven into a viewer's mind.

Part II of the book, "Message," questions what graffiti *says* as a communicative act and is directed toward its status as a practice of public citizenship. It explores graffiti as a demonstrative form that, following Debray's second archetype, displays the "civic morality of the participant" (Debray 1999: 30), a monument measured not simply by its "artistic merit" but through its ability to "stipulate a ceremony, support a ritual, challenge posterity" (p. 31). Maintaining this through specific chapters on "Speech" (unpacking graffiti as discursive act), on "Action" (unpacking graffiti as bodily act), and on "Participation" (unpacking graffiti as collective act), it will be graffiti's literal, gestural, and communal modes of production and transmission that will be examined here. Graffiti as message will thus be understood through its placement as the monument-*advice*, as a monument advising us how we can (or should) appropriate, claim, and participate in the public sphere.

Part III, "Trace," questions what graffiti *reveals* as an ecological form and its status as a particularly public artifact. It examines graffiti as a monument "enmeshed in the quotidian, in the field, in 'life,'" a monument that is part of its environment and thus "bears witness" in a "metonymic" manner to the context in which it exists (Debray 1999: 34). Maintaining this through chapters on "Publicity and Privacy" (examining graffiti's relationship to architectural and atmospheric walls), "Visibility and Invisibility" (examining graffiti's relationship to privacy and surveillance), and "Spectacularity and Temporality" (examining graffiti's relationship to the "creative" and "heritage" cities), it will be graffiti's relationship to exclusion, concealment, and the urban spectacle that will be central here. Graffiti as trace not only will be understood as the container in which "form" and "message" are able to emerge, but likewise as the monument-*warning* marking out (and alerting us toward) the transforming conditions of the urban realm today.

Yet just as the final part of the book comes to wrap together the book's first two parts through a progressive argument developing as we advance (just as the third chapter of each section likewise coalesces together its preceding two), there is an equivalently important lateral argument taking place throughout the text. While "Form," "Message," and "Trace" split the book materially through dividing graffiti via its status as public art, public act, and public artifact, the lateral approach enables a thematic reading that focuses on space and appearance (in the first chapter of each part, chapters 1, 4, and 7), on the body and visibility (in the central chapter of each part, chapters 2, 5, and 8), and on temporality and sociality (in the final chapter of each part, chapters 3, 6, and 9). As seen in figure I.2, the book can thus be read forward or sideways, materially or conceptually dependent on the choice of the reader. What remains key within both readings, however, is a position placing the production, consumption, and circulation of graffiti at center stage, that examines graffiti not only as monument but as material image, as technique of citizenship, and as urban trace combined.

## POSITIONALITY AND SCOPE

Based on nearly twenty years of research[4] and curation[5] within graffiti, street art,[6] intermural art,[7] and public art more broadly, the data presented in this work has emerged from a long-term ethnographic engagement within the material and social environments that together make up these related aesthetic worlds. Conducting more than two years of embedded fieldwork with graffiti independent public art practitioners in Madrid for my PhD, as well as carrying out multisited research with artists in this field since 2006 (from London to Manila, and Hong Kong to New York), my research has widened out from an initial focus on the image-makers of graffiti to an engagement with the curators, researchers, policymakers, and anti-graffiti activists who contribute to the wider artistic ecology. Moreover, my involvement within this world has itself included professional as well as academic immersions, my own practice working alongside my interlocutors in a collaborative manner (rather than just through "extracting" "data" from them), leading to a more developed understanding of their ethics and aesthetics both. The research presented here has thus emerged from both an observational and participatory space of engagement, from thousands of conversations with practicing artists (and thousands more with those based within the wider graffiti milieu), from hundreds of instances of participant observation in both illegal and legal frameworks (and in both institutional and noninstitutional settings), and from observant participation with artists and other practitioners through collaboratively organized events (such as exhibitions, workshops, and public talks).

My position as an anthropologist working both inside and outside the academy has thus led to the empirically centered, ethnographic approach to graffiti that this study takes up. Yet while the evidence incorporated here emerges from a very specific (and subjective) set of data, in an anthropological fashion I will here concentrate on drawing out the (theoretically) general from the (ethnographically) particular, moving from the granularity of a single tag (or a single event) to the macroscopic transformations of the city and back again. In this way, while each chapter will incorporate illustrative examples from the field, it should be made clear that the basic arguments posited here have in fact *all* come from my interlocutors themselves; while I have developed these into a cohesive narrative and leaned on some of the core theoretical premises of anthropology and material culture studies that I have been trained within, the stances taken are always ethnographically substantiated ones, even if this empirical evidence remains, at points, behind the scenes. Still, this does not mean that graffiti is considered as a universalized or homogenized practice, however, or that the argument is meant to transcend all idiosyncrasies. Rather, the globe-spanning traditions and canonical norms of graffiti have created a practice that, while site-specifically enacted in each and every case, contain generalizable patterns that I will here try to address. As such, although there is a clear geographical bias (yet by no means an exclusivity) toward Anglo-American case studies (which is, as a British author working on a visual practice first established in the United States, unsurprising), the wider dynamics I discuss are aspects that can be seen in cities all over the world today. Moreover, it should also be noted that many of the examples used to sustain core arguments around both the graffiti and institutional monuments I examine come from outside the framework of the traditionally monumental. While each chapter will first focus on our two core forms—presenting case studies and examples that help to elucidate the fundamental nature of both graffiti and the institutional monument—I will also bring in examples from contemporary and ethnographic art that help to sustain or contrast these core practices. What is critical to state, however, is that just as the incorporation of comparative data from contemporary art is not being drawn on to "elevate" graffiti to the position of capital "A" Art, neither are the examples drawn from the corpus of "ethnographic" art being utilized to "denigrate" it to an "art from below." Not only is graffiti a practice set, I argue, at the tension point between these aesthetic paradigms (of both institutional "art" and ethnographic "artifact"), but the wider visual examples used are meant simply to provide more immediately appreciable evidence of the wider monumental claims being made.

Before we move to the main body of the book, however, the overall contention I hope to make here—that appreciating graffiti as monument can transform our appreciation of graffiti, of monuments, and of the city itself—is something that is critical to position in relation to one of the fundamental arguments of my doctoral monograph

|  | **FORM**<br>GRAFFITI AS PUBLIC ART<br>MONUMENT AS REMINDER | **MESSAGE**<br>GRAFFITI AS CIVIC ACT<br>MONUMENT AS ADVICE | **TRACE**<br>GRAFFITI AS URBAN INDEX<br>MONUMENT AS WARNING |
|---|---|---|---|
| **SPACE AND APPEARANCE**<br>GRAFFITI AND PUBLICNESS | Chapter 1<br>**SITE**<br>What is graffiti's position/relation/dimension/location in and to the city? | Chapter 4<br>**SPEECH**<br>What does graffiti communicate via its text, context, subtext, and linguistic structure? | Chapter 7<br>**PUBLICITY AND PRIVACY**<br>How does graffiti reveal the architectural and atmospheric walls of the city? |
| **THE BODY AND VISIBILITY**<br>GRAFFITI AND TECHNIQUES | Chapter 2<br>**STYLE**<br>What are graffiti's canonical, agonistic, disruptive, and captivative techniques? | Chapter 5<br>**ACTION**<br>What does graffiti communicate formally, visually, and sensorially? | Chapter 8<br>**VISIBILITY AND FUGITIVITY**<br>How does graffiti reveal the panoptic and bio-political surveillance of the city? |
| **TEMPORALITY AND SOCIALITY**<br>GRAFFITI AND COLLECTIVENESS | Chapter 3<br>**TIME**<br>How does graffiti's temporality emerge materially, culturally, mnemonically, and relationally? | Chapter 6<br>**PARTICIPATION**<br>What does graffiti communicate via its site, style, and discursive structure? | Chapter 9<br>**SPECTACULARITY AND TEMPORALITY**<br>How does graffiti reveal the techniques of the Creative and Heritage cities? |

**FIGURE I.2**
Breakdown of the chapters as they relate to the major themes of the book materially and thematically.

*Ornament and Order* (2014). Positioning graffiti in that case as *ornament*, as an object that is both an adjunct to an architectural surface and an embellishment of that same façade, this contention sought not to diminish graffiti as the "mere" ornament that this term today often denotes (as that which is secondary or superficial) but rather to reassert the uncanny power of ornament (and thus graffiti) to reorder and disturb their surrounds. In this book, however, I will be making an almost exactly inversive move. The conception of monumental graffiti is thus not, I want to reinforce, being undertaken to simply amplify graffiti to the "high" status of the monument, to that which is set in stone or institutionally upraised. Instead, the positioning of graffiti as monument intends to puncture the hubris of our contemporary understanding of monument while reimagining the very conception of the form itself. Unpacking both graffiti and monument in this way will thus help to clarify the resonances and capacities, affordances and vulnerabilities of these material forms while simultaneously coming to address the contemporary "crisis" over monuments and public art. It will come to defetishize and vernacularize our monuments—both our institutional and graffiti variants—in order to reexamine what they do and how they work, as much as to reassess the strange power they have over us and our cities today.

# I
# FORM

Part I will focus on graffiti as an architectural, ornamental, and durational artifact. It will address the ways in which graffiti's site, style, and time—elements examined individually but received by a viewer collectively—generate its powerful effects in the world. We will hence examine the way an artifact "controls . . . perception" and "creates the viewer's attention," the relationship, as image theorist Hans Belting has examined, between "visibility" and "mediality" (Belting 2005: 304). Chapter 1, "Site," will thus focus on the *how* of graffiti, on the way in which the image is "steered" by its primary architectural "host," before chapter 2, "Style," comes to explore graffiti's *what*, on what it "serves" or "relates" as graphic image (Belting 2005: 304). Stitching these two chapters together as the temporal container in which site and style emerge and disappear, chapter 3, "Time," will unpack graffiti's *when*, its standing as a time-based, durational artifact. Graffiti, as with all images, will hence be understood to reside "neither on the wall . . . nor in the head alone," and it will instead be the way the images "*happen*," the way in which "they *take place*" (Belting 2005: 302) that will be the focus of this first part.

Addressing the specific *position*, *relation*, *location*, and *dimension* that comprise the graffiti monument's site; the *canonical*, *agentive*, *animative*, and *distributive* factors that structure its style; and the *material*, *cultural*, *mnemonical*, and *relational* factors that encompass its time, part I will reveal a monument that radically disturbs monumental paradigms, that acts as other to the central, singular, permanent monuments that dominate our urban environments. The graffiti monument, as it emerges through its formal characteristics, will hence be seen as a marginal, distributed, transient monument, a monument set at the border not the center, working through multiplicity not singularity, ephemerality not permanency. It will be understood as a monumental-reminder that is antagonistic not consensual, dependent not independent, absent as much as present, humanely not colossally scaled, a monumental-reminder of a divergent way of understanding space, objects, and the city itself.

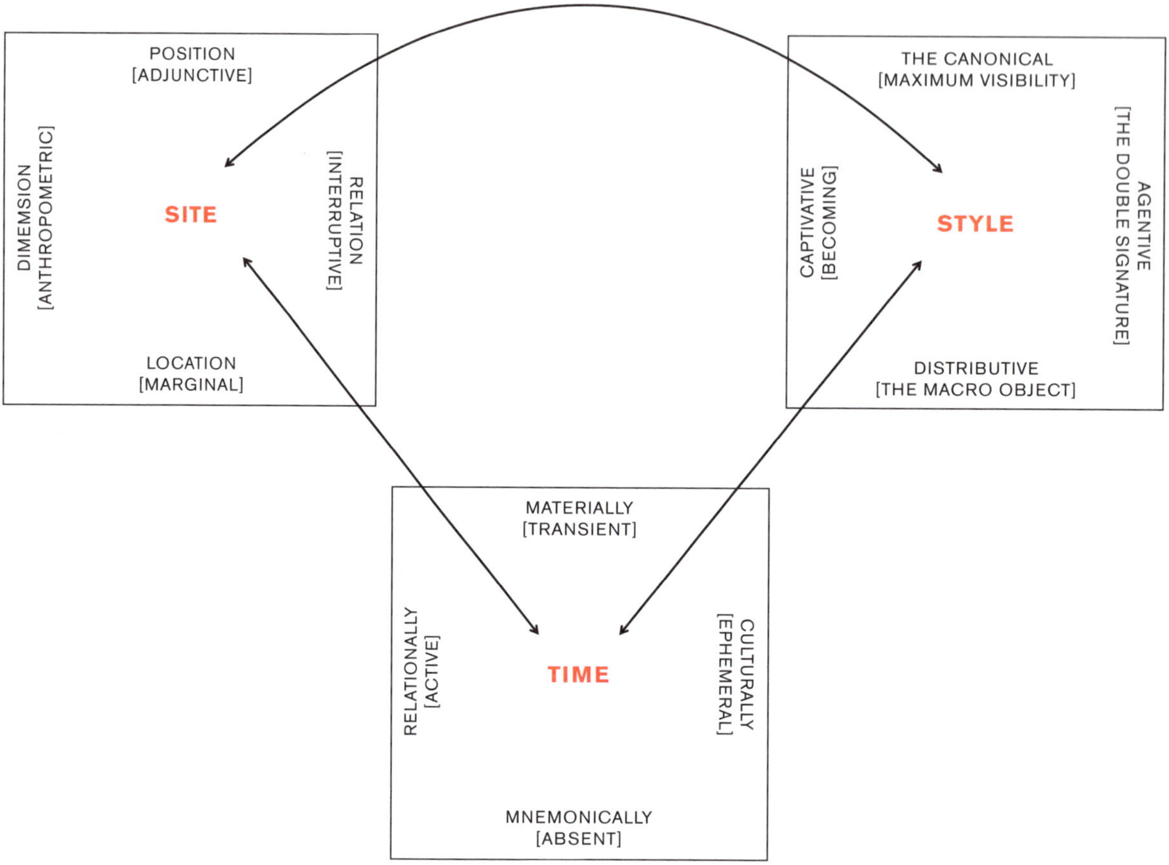


**FIGURE I.3**
Graffiti as form.

# 1
# SITE

Graffiti is a public artifact. It is not an object that exists on the page (a sketch of graffiti in an artist's sketchbook being just that, a sketch) nor on canvas (a painting of graffiti on canvas being just that, a painting) but an image that subsists *on* and *in* the city itself, an image physically attached to the fabric of the metropolis. Appearing most commonly on the city's literal boundary points, on its walls and roller shutters that divide public from private, graffiti also exists at its geographical edges, on the tracksides, overpasses, and marginal non-places that lie at our urban perimeters. Moreover, it also attaches itself to other key urban surfaces such as the city's visible forms of public infrastructure, from its street furniture (its billboards and traffic signage, for example) to its transportation systems (its buses and, perhaps most famously, its subway trains). Graffiti thus emerges through the medium of the city or not at all. And in the same way that we can never truly distinguish between the canvas and the image painted upon it (Belting 2005), the graffiti image will here be understood as an artifact that we cannot separate from the city in either conceptual or material terms; the surface and image collapse into a single aesthetic form, graffiti as artifact being inherently entangled amid the carrier in which it exists. Rather than beginning this book with an examination of graffiti's stylistic or temporal qualities, then, it is the specifically spatial attributes of graffiti that we will lead with, the specific qualities of the medium, of the surface, that turns an image into graffiti itself.

This chapter will unpack the "how" of graffiti through focusing on the four situational elements that collectively encompass it: its integrally attached physical position, its innately antagonistic architectural relation, its distinctively bodily scale, and its essentially peripheral urban locations. These four factors will together be put forward as graffiti's unique "mediality," the adjunctive, interruptive, anthropometric, and marginal means through which the image is transmitted through and with its site and onto a viewer's perception. Examining these four medial elements will then help to outline graffiti's equivalently monumental and ornamental way of being, its methods of working both within and against the city, the particularity of its scale and proportions, and the geographic and material peripheries it encounters. Moreover, these critical site-specific elements will also help to resolve key issues related to graffiti's commonly understood illegality as much as to its revelation of the tension between public and private. It will thus be a minor monument that this chapter will explore, yet a monument with the integral ability to dominate and disrupt the architectural environment in which it appears.

## POSITION *OR* THE ADJUNCTIVE

So, what makes up graffiti's "how"? What elements structure the way it is site-specifically steered, driven to a viewer via its urban medium? Well, first let's examine its primary position, the ornamental, adjunctive quality of graffiti.[1] Take figure 1.1, for example, an image depicting the exterior door of a London telephone box and the series of stickers, pamphlets, and tags that are situated upon it. In the top center of the image we have what is my key focus, a tag[2] by the writer 10Foot placed upon the glass paneling of the door. Exhibiting a left-leaning slope and drippy style (a purposeful effect achieved through holding the writing tool down upon the surface so as the liquid seeps out at a higher rate), the off-white hue of the name indicates that the image has been produced not with ink but with etching cream. A form of hydrofluoric acid produced and sold as a home craft activity,[3] and which is decanted by the writer into a secondary implement such as a shoe-polish dispenser, the acid dissolves the top layer of the glass, permanently inscribing the resultant design into it. Etch thus forms an artifact that both appears to, and actually does, dissolve into the glass on which it is set. The image here has not just been inscribed upon but also impressed *into* the surface.

The first question we need ask, therefore, is that of the *where*, in determining where exactly this graffitied image exists. And this specific image is placed not only in the city, not only on the street, but likewise in and on the glass surround itself. It is *on* it (etched upon the glass surface), it is *in* it (the fluorine atoms embedding themselves within the structure of the glass), while it is *not* it (it is not the surface but the addition). The tag seen in figure 1.1—as with an even drippier 10Foot tag produced on mirrored glass in figure 1.2—has been placed upon an already existent surface, upon the surface of the city, the surface of the street, the wall, the door, the glass. Unlike the autonomy of the institutional monument, the monument that is always and already primary, the self-governing *ergon* (or the principal work) that takes precedence wherever it is placed, the graffiti we see here is implicitly adjunctive: an addition, an appendage, a supplement to its architectural surrounds. The acid tag doesn't simply subsist on top of the glass. It exists within it, an image that cannot be wiped off or painted over, that can only be removed through grinding down the layers of glass or, more commonly, replacing the entire surface itself. While etch is just one of the many modes of inscription in graffiti, it is a technique acting as the perfect example of the adjunctive mode of *all* graffiti, the mode through which the graffiti image binds, fuses with its surrounding medium. The

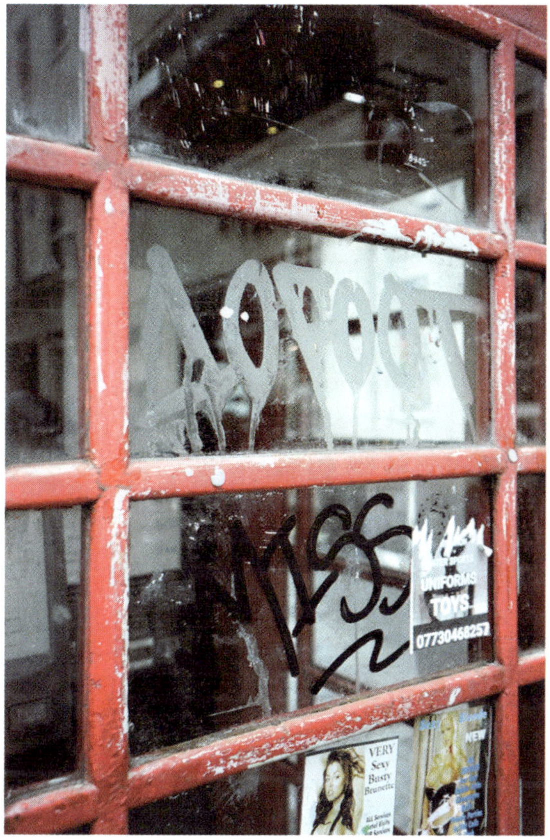


**FIGURE 1.1**
*Untitled (10Foot)*, 2022, London. Photo: Rafael Schacter.

bond between ornament and structure, between pigment and wall as much as etch and glass, creates what is the near impossibility of ever truly separating the two. And graffiti (like all ornament) must therefore be understood not as a form occurring on a pristine, untouched medium, but as one implanted within an already extant surface. It is an image integrally embedded within the living body that is the urban realm (Schacter 2014a: 21–22).

This deep-rootedness of the addition, as much as the innate porosity of the city's surface, is made most visible through the omnipresence of both "ghost tags" and "abstract graffiti." In the former case, we thus have the commonplace example of erased graffiti that bleeds back into visibility, haunting its site through the failure of the overpainting to entirely hide the original mark (as seen in the morass of overpainted tags and images in figure 1.3); the material permeability of most urban surfaces, as much

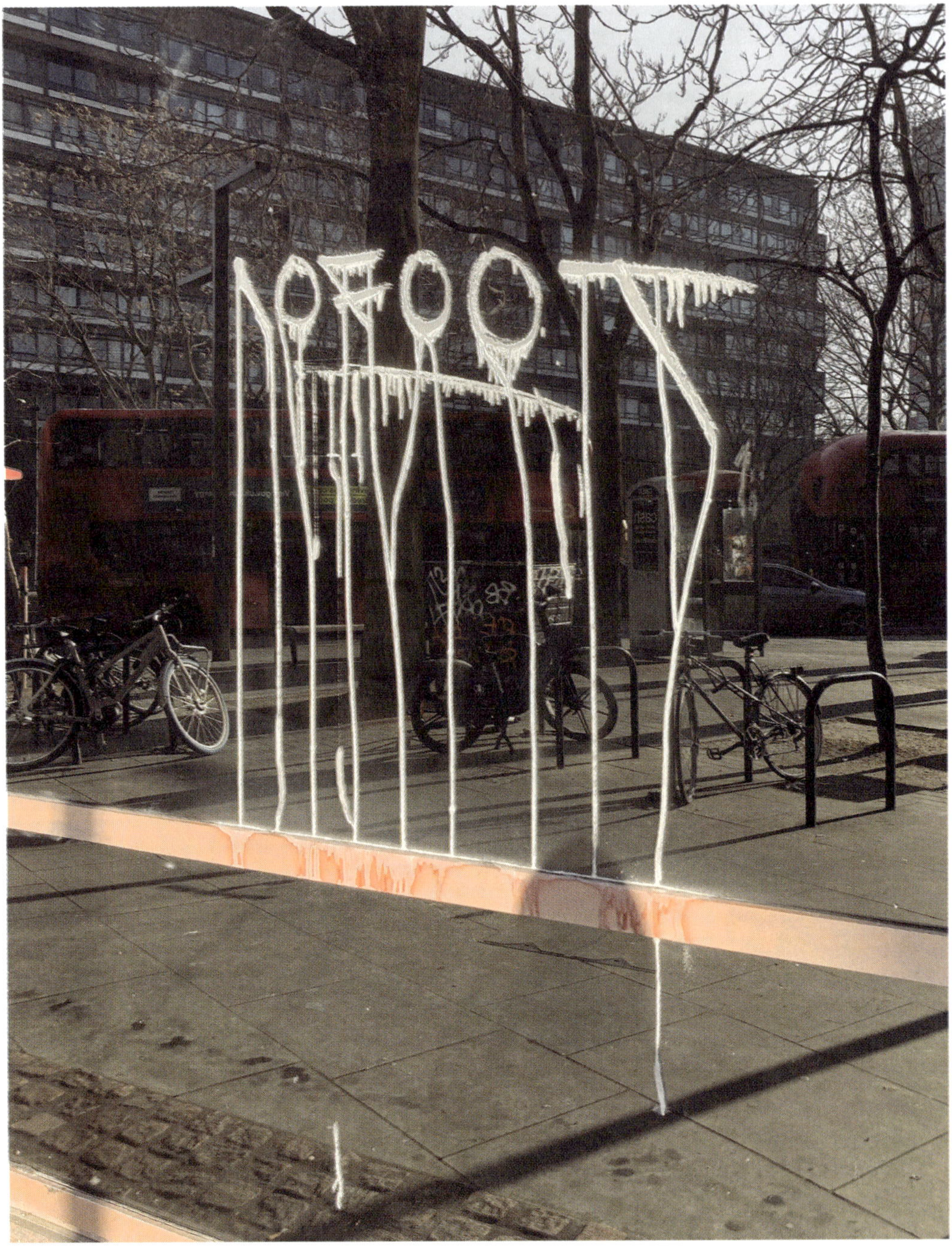


**FIGURE 1.2**
*10Foot*, 2023, South London. Photo: Alex Ellison.

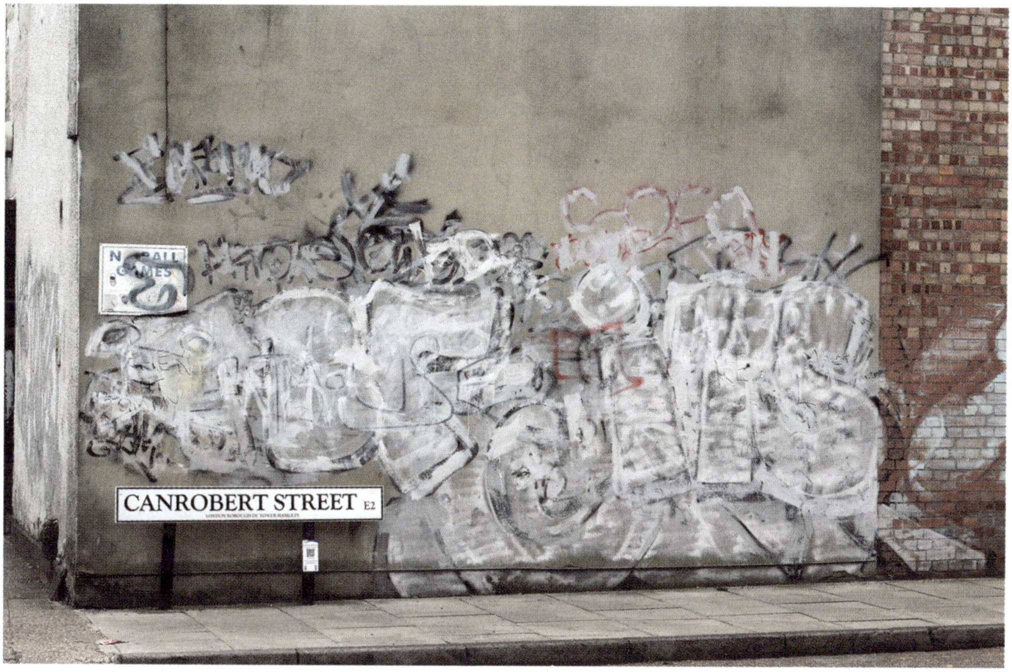


**FIGURE 1.3**
*Maltreated Buff*, 2022, London. Photo by Stephen Burke.

as the differential qualities of the materials used in both painting and overpainting, thus means that graffiti, like a tattoo, becomes only skin-deep in the most deep-set of ways. In the latter case, however, we have the cubist quadrilaterals in which graffiti has been overpainted with a color different (only subtly so) from its surrounding surface, accidentally creating the appearance of a geometric abstract art (as seen in figure 1.4's multicolored cubism); here the graffiti, even if occluded, remains ever present via its overt absence. Like a palimpsest, the slate is never truly wiped clean, the initial inscription remaining visible as an uncanny trace peering through the surface, repressed yet inescapably present. As such, while all public art can be understood as an imposition, graffiti is especially so. It is not something merely "placed upon" a resultant surface (from the Latin *impōnĕre*), but an image emergent through the "action of attaching, affixing, or ascribing" (OED), an image attached to, affixed to, *written into* the city itself.

The innately adjunctive position of graffiti has two key effects: first, upsetting the distinction between primary and secondary, between wall and image; and second, overwhelming the normative order of site itself. The fear emergent from graffiti's adjunctive location thus emerges through it muddying the border between structure and

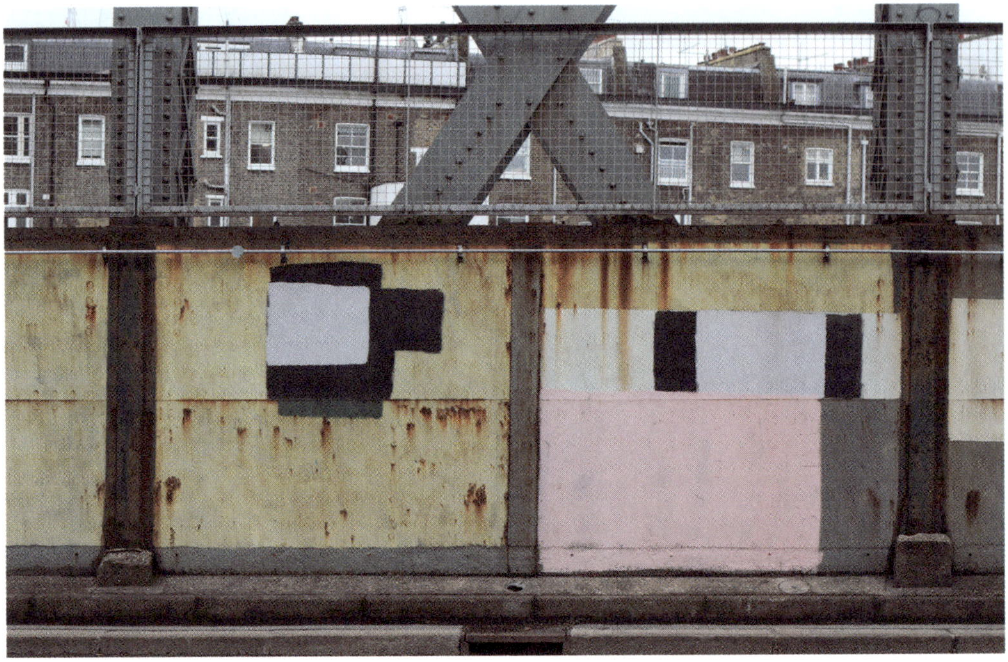

**FIGURE 1.4**
*Conservative Buff*, 2022, London. Photo by Stephen Burke.

ornament, intrinsic and extrinsic, figure and ground. The ornament envelops its medium, fastening itself upon it, sullying its originary purity and cohesion. Yet not only does this position situate graffiti as the archetypal pollutant, the matter out of place made famous by Mary Douglas (2000 [1966]), but it likewise situates it as a prime example of the *parergon* explored by Jacques Derrida (1979), the primary form that can only be understood through its structural relationship to its addition, the primary form whose *inseparability* to this addition defines it. Like bodily decoration and tattoos (artifacts often placed in a relational continuum with graffiti), to (re)move these ornaments is to *destroy* them, a destruction in which the primary structure becomes collateral damage. Graffiti, like all site-specific sculpture, like all ornament, must therefore be understood as a child of its surface, to be born of it, to be a product of it, while simultaneously acting as the constituent outsider overcoming its habitat. As such, the tags seen in figures 1.1 and 1.2 (as well as every example of graffiti we will see over the forthcoming pages) come not only to destabilize the notion of primary and secondary but to destabilize structure and milieu combined. The adjunct becomes a threat, confounding and exceeding its structure. The addition becomes a danger, convoluting and displacing its surround. And graffiti's locational attachment thus comes to infect the entire body of its host, spreading to the entire site no matter its location of entry. Like all ornament, it reorders (or disorders) that which is already ordered.

While the victory column, the equestrian statue, and the triumphal arch are not adjunctive but autonomous, placed *in* not *with* their locales, produced purely for themselves rather than responding to their site specifically,[4] graffiti is an artifact always functioning in relation to and with its site, a monument that cannot physically separate itself from its encompassing surface. This adjunctive modality can be seen in other modes of artistic intervention too. The American artist Brad Downey's work *Making Illegal Permanent* (2009), for example (see figures 1.5 and 1.6), a work that transformed a graffitied wall into a patterned mosaic depicting the identical scene first encountered, not only played with graffiti's latent ephemerality (as discussed further in chapter 3), but disturbed any clear distinction between ornament and structure. Reproducing the entire façade in what could be considered as a mosaicked trompe-l'oeil, here what is often (and mistakenly) believed to subsist on top of the surface (the graffiti image) becomes unmistakably embedded in its core (the structural foundations). Both pattern and surface simultaneously, not only is the mosaic an image that is structure and a structure that is image, but, like graffiti too, the attempted removal of this ornament inevitably leads to the destruction of the surface itself. In the French artist Olivier Kosta-Théfaine's series of ceiling interventions (as seen in figures 1.7 and 1.8), however, the adjunctive inseparability of graffiti is reinforced through the artist's utilization of a classic writing technique in which one's name is burned into a surface using a cigarette lighter. Creating ornamental embellishments that, as seen in the work's title, reference the classical *soffitto* of the Italian Renaissance, the resultant works can be seen not simply as placed on the surface but to enmesh themselves within the molecules of the material they are burnt into. Like graffiti, the images Kosta-Théfaine produced are thus surface "decorations" that intertwine deep within the surface itself.

10Foot's tags, Downey's ceramic graffiti, and Kosta-Théfaine's burnt ceilings thus each act as the foreign disturbance to their site, the secondary form that purposefully overwhelms its structural surrounds. Here we find an ornamental monument (or a monumental ornament) working through a technique of attachment, not separation, through a supplemental rather than archetypal mode. In this way, then, it must be seen to be the city itself, the wall, the glass, the building, the *site* that becomes of critical importance to us here. What truly "constitutes" graffiti, as literary theorist Roland Barthes beautifully outlined in his seminal text on the artist Cy Twombly, is thus "neither the inscription nor its message but the wall, the background, the surface" (Barthes 1991 [1979]: 167). It is graffiti's status as the constitutive addition (whether emergent via acid, fire, or spray) that turns it into that which is "*in excess*, supernumerary, out of place," as that which will always be an "enigmatic surplus" (p. 167). The graffiti image thus appears not via the philosopher's tabula rasa or the artist's pristine canvas but via the dirt and grime of the city. It appears on a site that is unclean but on which an aesthetic overturning can

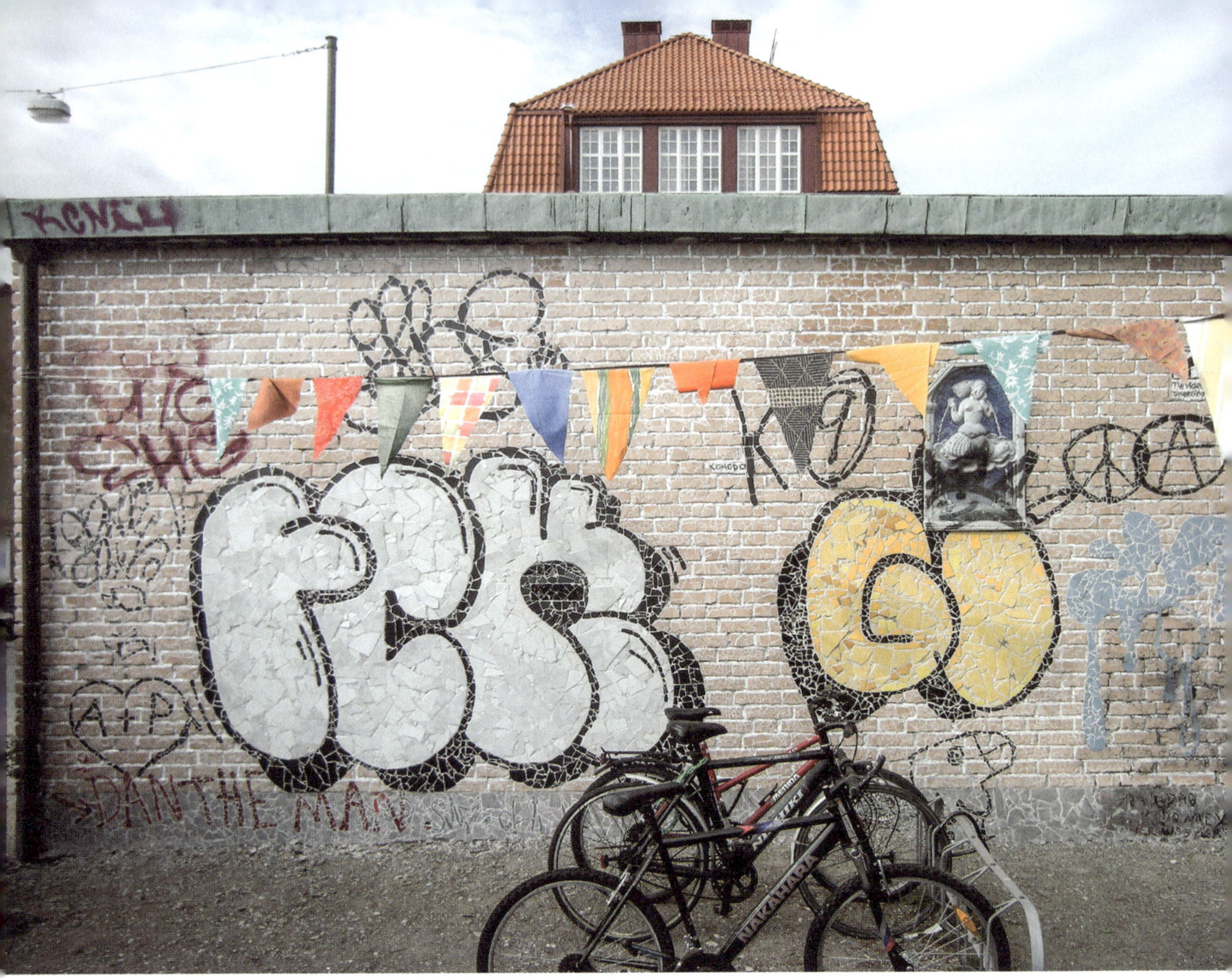
A+P
DANTHE MAN
NAKAHARA

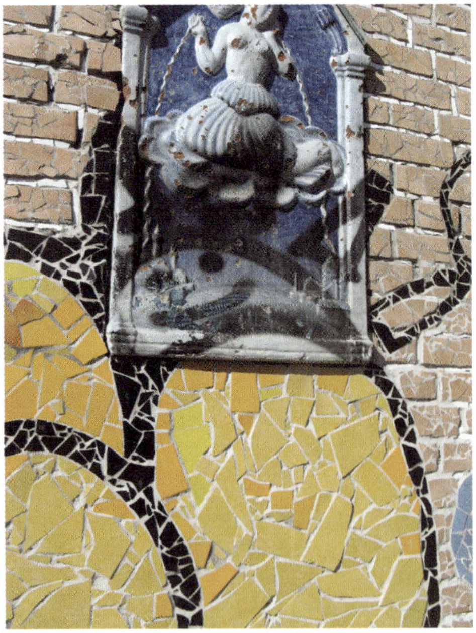

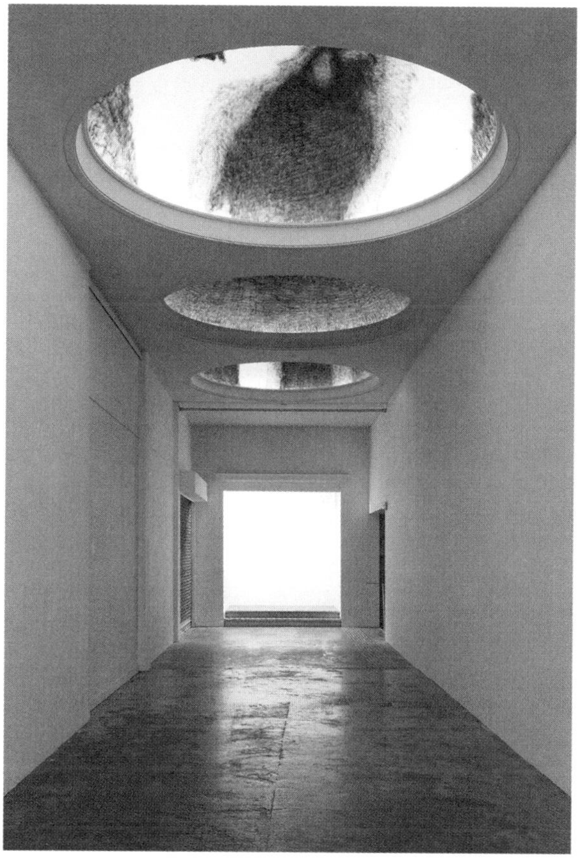

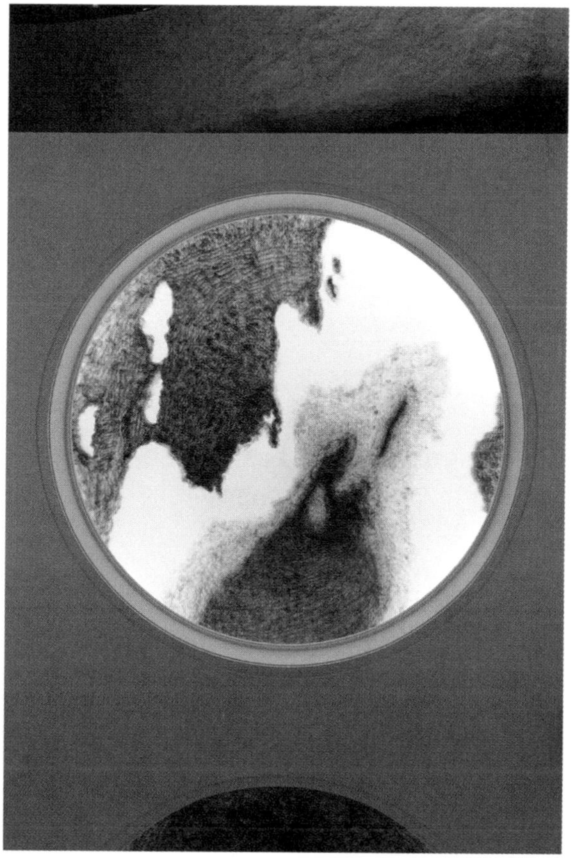

**FIGURE 1.5**
Brad Downey, *Making Illegal Permanent*, 2009. Ceramic tiles and grout. Malmo, Sweden. Courtesy of the artist.

**FIGURE 1.6**
Brad Downey, *Making Illegal Permanent* (detail), 2009. Ceramic tiles and grout. Malmo, Sweden. Courtesy of the artist.

**FIGURE 1.7**
Olivier Kosta-Théfaine, *Soffito*, 2016. Flame of a cigarette lighter on ceiling. Installation view, Palais de Tokyo, Paris. Courtesy of the artist.

**FIGURE 1.8**
Olivier Kosta-Théfaine, *Soffito* (detail), 2016. Flame of a cigarette lighter on ceiling. Installation view, Palais de Tokyo, Paris. Courtesy of the artist.

develop, its ornamental positioning and ability to overwhelm the primacy structure being that which is of equally primary importance to us here.

## RELATION *OR* THE INTERRUPTIVE

Graffiti's adjunctive position thus explains its "how" through its where, yet its *relation* to site emerges through the antagonistic approach it exhibits to its surrounds. Consider figure 1.9, for example, an image centering on a four-letter, two-color throw-up[5] by the writer Depo produced using a simple white fill-in and thick black outline. Painted continuously over what I count as twelve different surfaces—traversing its first doorframe, glazing, side jam, casing, before moving onto a tiled surface, a wooden box frame (and its various posters), and then back to a second tiled surface, doorway, glazing, side jam, casing, before finally hitting another tiled surface and then the neighboring building—it refuses, at any point, to formally conform or adapt to its context. It travels through, over, across these surfaces. It works not to highlight or respect the façade's geometry but to interrupt its contours and configuration, transgressing and defying its

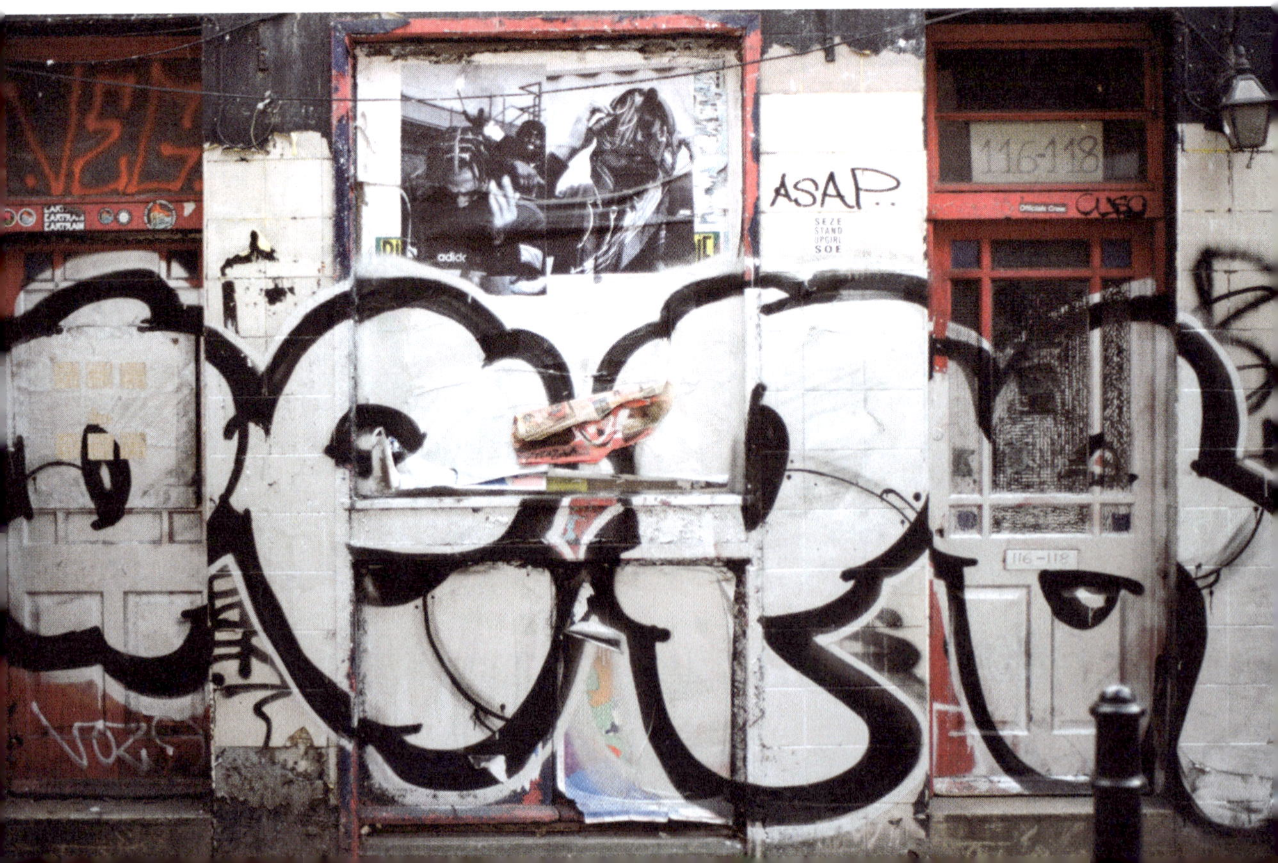

architectural borders. As such, while we now know that graffiti acts adjunctively upon an already present medium (here the various doors, walls, posters, and panels that make up the surfaces perpendicular to the pavement), here we can see the way graffiti contravenes these architectural elements too: it does not integrate (or ingratiate) itself within its material environment, does not adapt to the geometry of the structure or support its existence through its addition, but instead *bulldozes straight through it*. Graffiti is thus a doubly interruptive addition, intervening in both a material and formal manner.

This transversal approach is not the only way in which graffiti interrupts its site, however. A single tag, for example, often needs to work within the physical confines of structure to become discernible. Working with a pen rather than a spray can, and thus needing to remain directly on the surface rather than hover over it, writers will work to hijack structure through a pertinent positioning that creates a graphic contrast and visual prominence. While this may not overwhelm the border of the structure itself, the resultant image still works to interrupt the structure's *function* (as much as being legally forbidden and socially taboo). The series of tags seen in figure 1.9 (by Neg, Asap, Voz, Cuso, Festa, et al.), as much as the array of stickers also present (from Cartrain, Seze, Stand, Upgirl, Soe), disturb their site through refusing both social and material norms. Without needing to interrupt the boundary of their surface layers, they thus still reject spatial norms through an innately interventional approach. As such, although not all graffiti pieces engage in as extensive a process of interruption as Depo, many will still edge over their borders, even if just by an inch (or two) as seen in figure 1.10, let alone over the multiple angles and materials seen in Egs's work in figure 1.11. Not only done to more than fill their surrounds, as a formal technique that works to expand the overall impression of the specific piece, this interruptive aesthetic likewise makes clear that the surrounding structure has been consciously overturned. It makes clear that the surface does not take precedence over the practice. The larger interruption seen in figure 1.9 thus simply represents the most emblematic and visible way that graffiti intervenes with site transversally, the way it refuses to abide by the structural norms of site and overtakes the rigidity of its architectural frontiers, the interjection and interruption that contravene not just legal codes but so too architectural ones.

The institutional monument, on the other hand, can be seen to function through an explicit assimilation with its surrounds. While it may stand separate from its milieu through its untouchable singularity rather than its status as ornament, it simultaneously seeks to bolster (rather than disrupt) the architectural and social order in which it resides. Most commonly seen through the institutional monuments' references to antiquity, a stylistic approach at the heart of the state-down aesthetic, this monumental classicism not only replicates the classical education that still persists within elite (private) schools,[6] but sets the state into a deep historical time, no matter how temporally

**FIGURE 1.9**
*Untitled (Depo)*, 2021, London. Photo: Rafael Schacter.

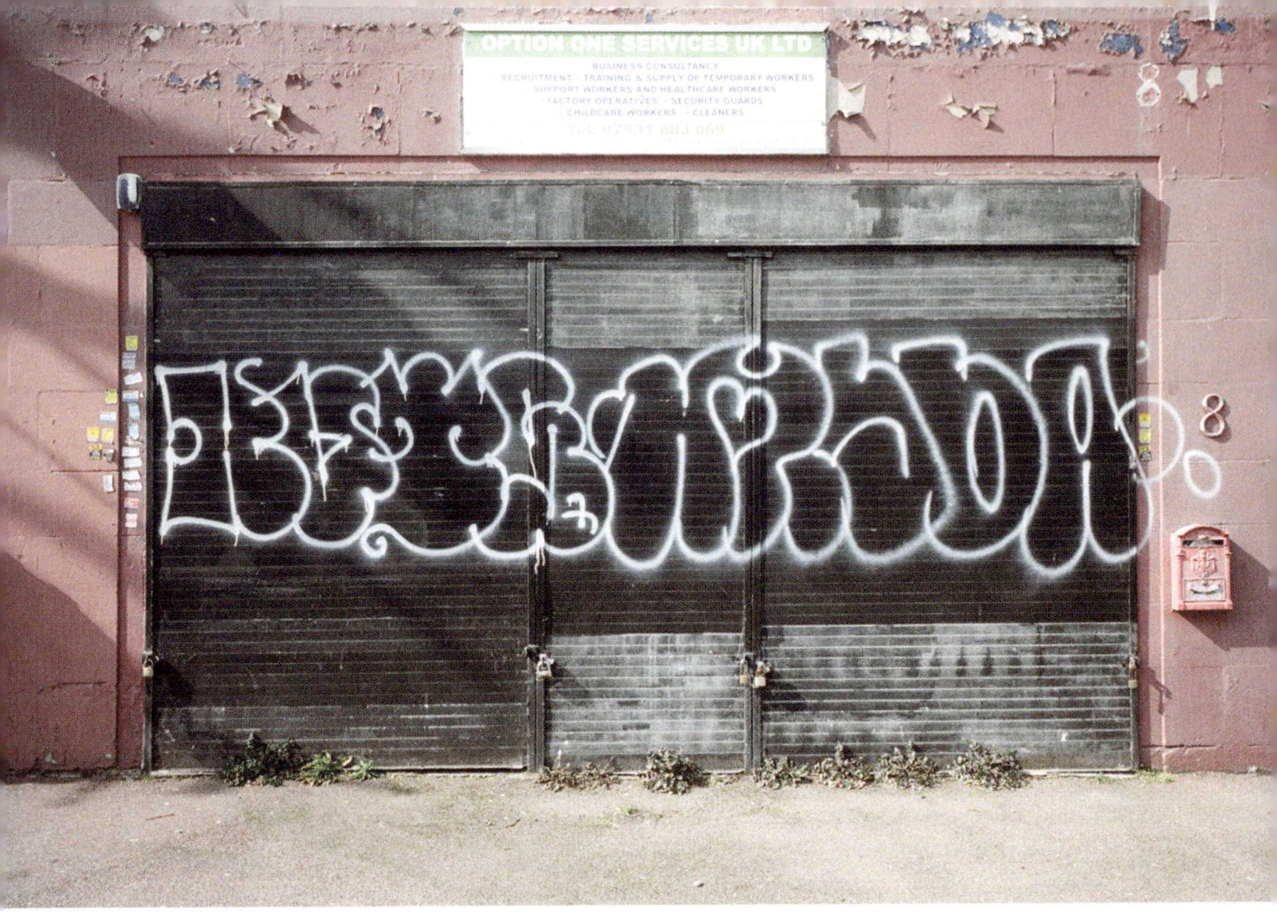


**FIGURE 1.10**
*Untitled (just by an inch)*, 2022, London. Photo: Rafael Schacter.

precarious it may in fact be. The institutional monument thus functions, as art historian Benjamin Buchloh suggested, as an "affirmation of the actually existing order of things" (Buchloh 2003: 123), upholding the histories, the needs, the regulations of the state as much as the city itself. It may be materially independent, but it acts as the ultimate ornament of power, the monument sustaining, not interrupting, its milieu. The graffiti monument, however, can be seen to more closely align with the traditions of site-specific art emergent in the mid-1970s that developed in contradistinction to the then dominant modernist paradigm in which architectural autonomy reigned. Site-specificity was here not only always produced explicitly for the environment in which it was set (and thus, like graffiti, could never truly be moved) but meant to always interrupt this same environment in which it was set. As the key theorist of the practice, Rosalyn Deutsche, wrote, truly "radical site-specific art" aimed to "disrupt, rather than secure, the apparent coherence of its new urban sites" (Deutsche 1996: xvi). It was an art

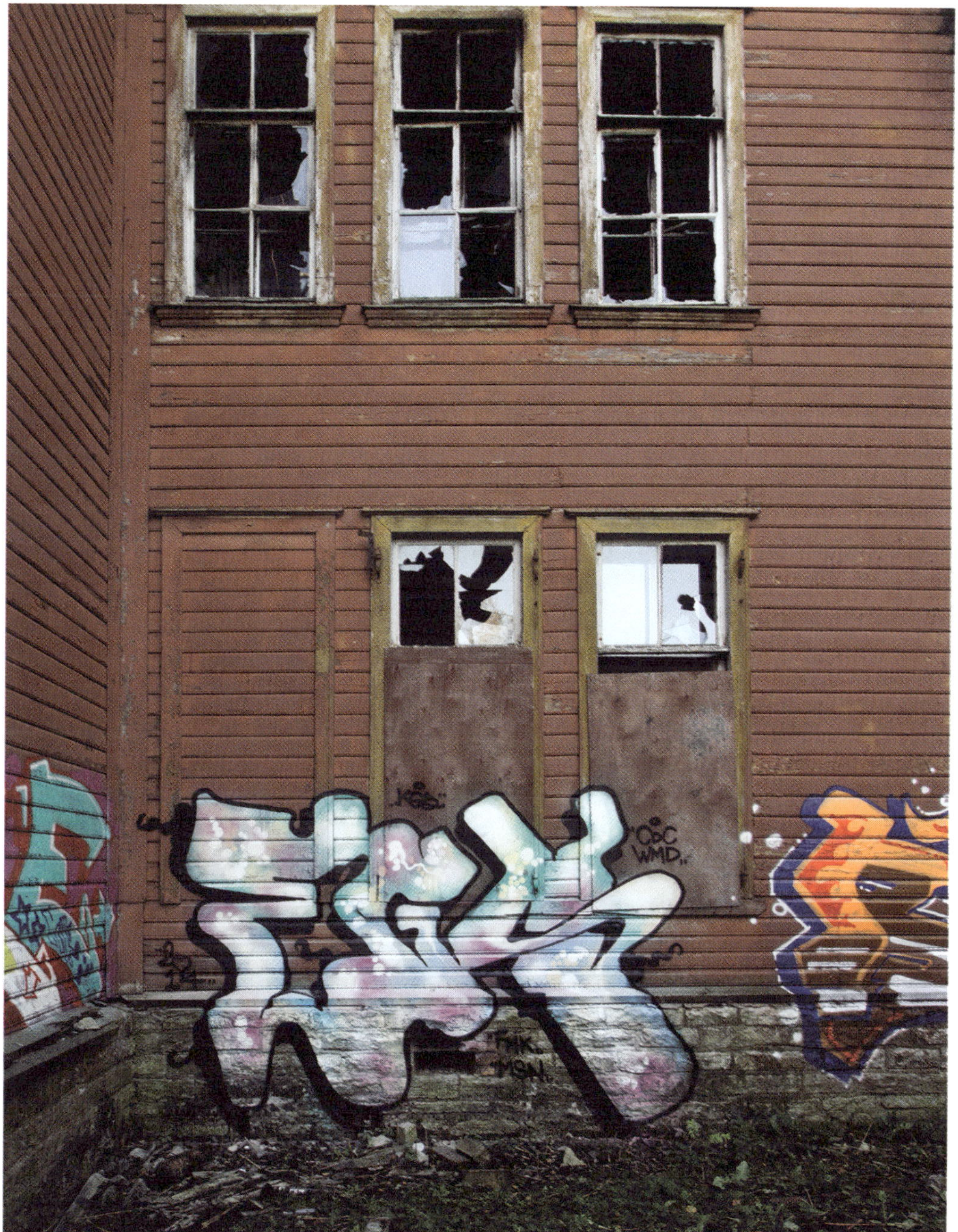

**FIGURE 1.11**
*Egs (acid-house)*, 2014, Tallin. Courtesy of the artist.

that was as much about its immersion in, as its disturbance of, its physical surrounds. It was a practice, like graffiti, in which the normative hierarchy of public art (as that which must be subservient to a wider political discourse of order) was site-specifically rejected, a practice in which disruption of the city's sleek flatness was the aim.

The renowned "building cut" works of Gordon Matta-Clark—as seen, for example, in his masterpiece *Day's End (Pier 52)* (1975) (figures 1.12 and 1.13)—can similarly be seen to have disrupted the basic regulations of architectural form. Slicing and lacerating the outer wall of Pier 52 while creating a series of holes in both the floor and ceiling of the warehouse, *Day's End*, like many of Matta-Clark's works, aimed to dislocate the normative relationship between inside and outside, floor and ceiling, figure and ground. Striving, as he wrote, to work through "PASSING THROUGH THE BOUNDARIES," through "PASSING THROUGH MOVING IN AND GETTING AWAY WITH IT," through "DESTRUCTURAL PUNCTUATION" (Matta-Clark in Bessa 2017:

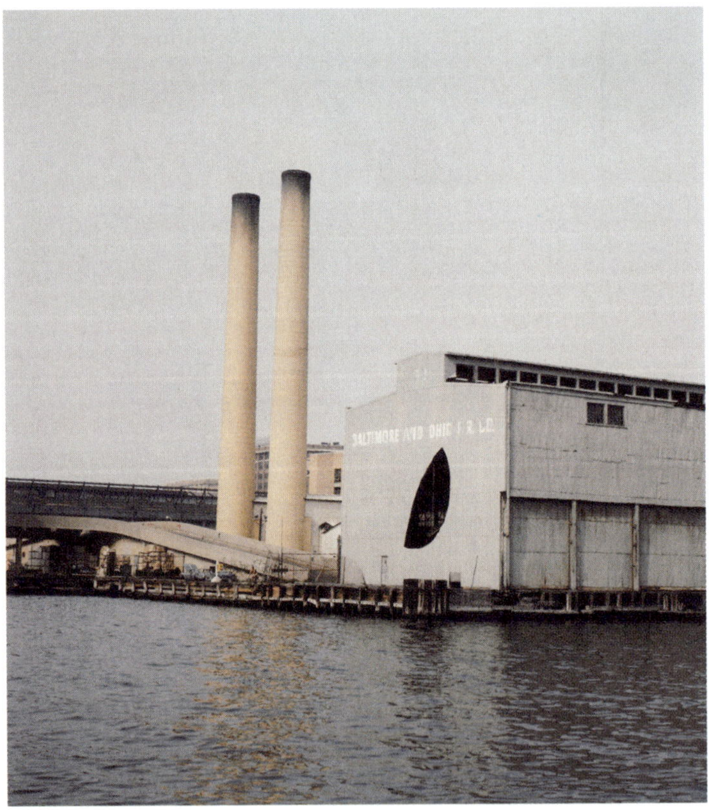

**FIGURE 1.12**
Gordon Matta-Clark, *Day's End (Pier 52)*, 1975. New York. © Estate of Gordon Matta-Clark, ARSNY.com, DavidZwirner.com.

14), his *non-umental* practice destabilized the basic principles and rationales of architectural space. Like the nascent graffiti images Matta-Clark likewise revered (and so too archived),[7] what we find here is an interruption that rejects the spatial conformity of the institutional monument, that highlights site through refusing its canonical use and form. Taking a parallel approach, the architecture-spanning productions of Katharina Grosse likewise function through interrupting their surfaces, here through a very literal form of surface transgression (a crossing over or a passing through). As seen most prominently in her public projects, such as that seen in figure 1.14, a work entirely subsuming the walls and windows of the abandoned warehouse it lies upon (along with the adjacent rubble and fallen trees that lay along the train tracks), Grosse's adjunctive works function through their status as ornamental imposition, breaking down physical borders and rejecting their quotidian functions simultaneously. The materiality of paint thus treats all surfaces equally; the wood, the metal, and the brick

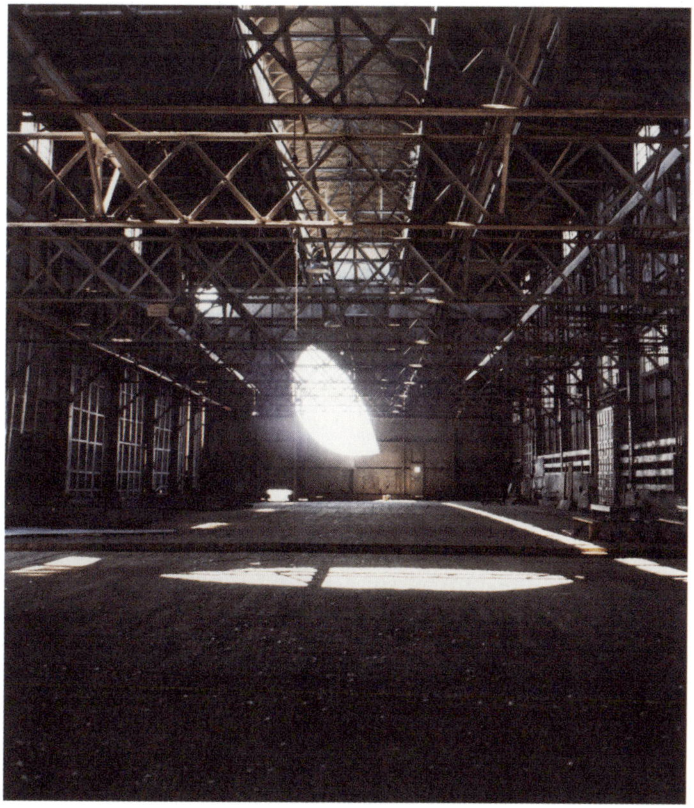

**FIGURE 1.13**
Gordon Matta-Clark, *Day's End (Pier 52)*, 1975. New York. © Estate of Gordon Matta-Clark, ARSNY.com, DavidZwirner.com.

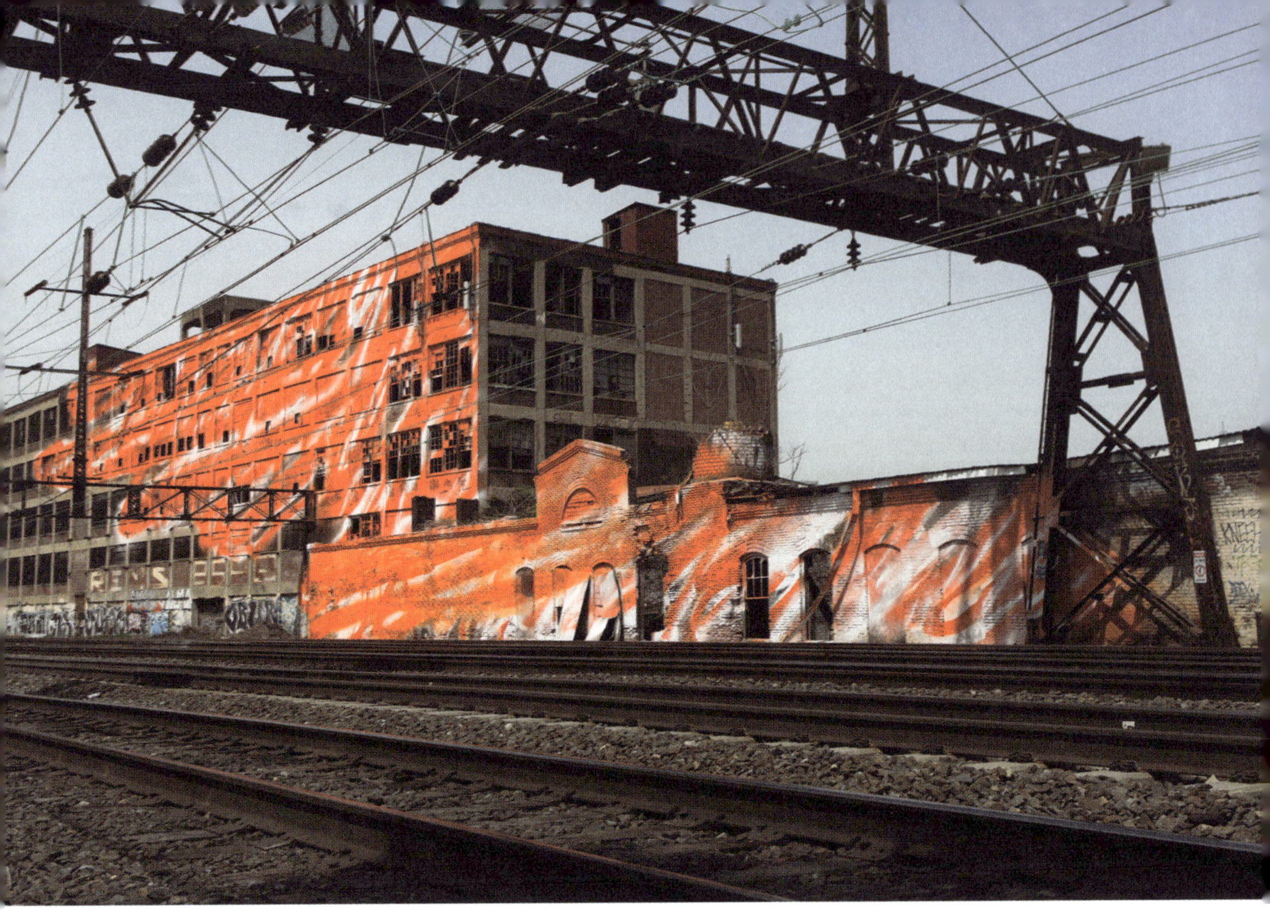

**FIGURE 1.14**
Katharina Grosse, *psychylustro—The Warehouse*, 2014, Philadelphia, acrylic on wall and various objects, 2,100 × 14,500 cm. Commissioned by the City of Philadelphia Mural Arts Program. Photo: Steve Weinik. Courtesy of König Galerie, Berlin. © (2023) Katharina Grosse and DACS, 2023.

structures of the warehouse in figure 1.14, as much as the steel beams of the surrounding railway architecture, are each diminished, or perhaps amplified through Grosse's installation, the pigment containing an equally dramatic and penetrating capacity.

Like Grosse's and Matta-Clark's works, graffiti must be seen as a deconstruction, rather than simple destruction, of architectural space. It functions not solely through its immersive emplacement within the dense gravity of the city but through techniques of rejection and resistance to that same emplacement: Here we thus find a rejection of the material coherence of its medium, a resistance to the structural and functional rationales of its surface. Here we find an approach to public art in which disruption of the apparent harmony of public space and dissension to spatial rules remains paramount. As such, the second spatial element I want to uphold in this chapter is the graffiti monument's innately interruptive relation to its surrounds, its agonistic approach to the city's spatial surfaces. Rather than graffiti treating the city as canvas, graffiti ruptures its frame, ruptures the city both physically and functionally. Whether small-scale or large, it materially rejects assimilation, integrally interrupting site.

## DIMENSION *OR* THE ANTHROPOMETRIC

Attached to and structurally hostile to its location, graffiti also functions through what I term an anthropometric proportion.[8] Figure 1.15, for example, an image of the writer Mosa producing a series of vertical tags on the side of a truck, not only is implicitly adjunctive and interruptive (taking place on, and intruding upon, a secondary surface), but directly indicates the artist's own bodily measurements. Standing on his tip-toes, his arm extended almost to its maximum, the tags here show not only movement but

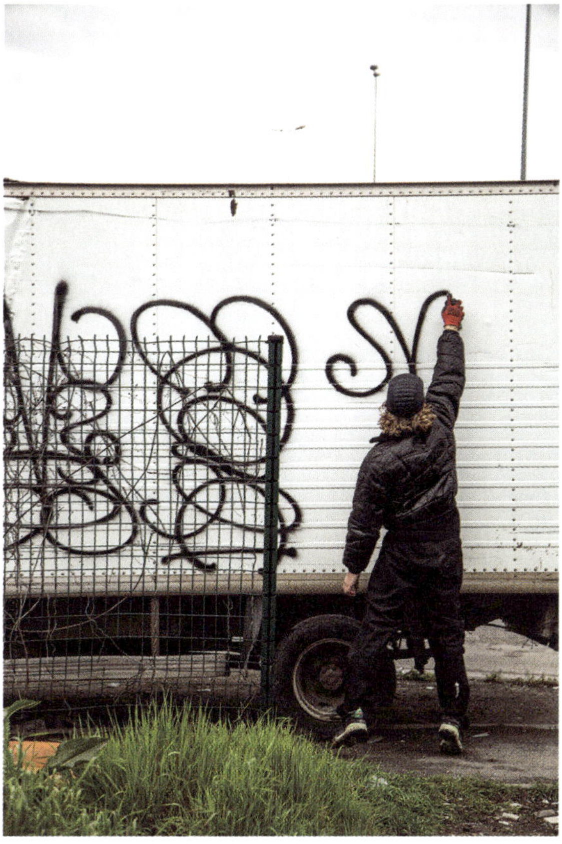

**FIGURE 1.15**
Mosa, *Untitled*, 2022. Courtesy of the artist and *Tramontana Magazine*. Image by Elliot Sitbon.

*scope*. Like a boxer's jab, they show reach, mirroring the wing-span of the writer even when the writer themself cannot be seen. As such, aside from moments in which specific tools are used to extend one's natural proportions, in the use of a modified fire extinguisher or extendable paint roller, for example,[9] the graffiti image reveals the bodily scale of its author, whether in the wide arcing of an arm or the narrow movement of a wrist. Graffiti thus takes up a Vitruvian rather than Herculean dimension. Even when using adjacent structures to extend one's natural height (such as an upturned bin, a bicycle, a fellow writer's shoulders), the image itself remains bound to the magnitude of the body. Circumventing the (supposed) heroism of the "monumental," graffiti thus retains the dignity of the human scale. Moreover, set within an environment in which the individual is increasingly eclipsed—dominated by both the mass presence of vehicular traffic and a continually elevating urban architectural topography—the innate anthropometricity of graffiti can come, antithetically, to stand out. The resulting image is thus not only anti-"monumental," but dimensionally idiosyncratic. It is not only an image of a perceptible body in evident movement but an image graspable and relative through our own physical proportions.

The basic size of all public art—whether the relatively small, bodily-sized tags and throw-ups produced by Remio in figure 1.16, or a gargantuan, plaza-spanning sculpture—can thus be understood as something that we comprehend through the body first and foremost, through the body as our primary tool of measurement. As anthropologist Christopher Tilley has suggested (following the work of the phenomenologist Maurice Merleau-Ponty), our "lived body allows us to know what space, place and landscape are because it is the author of them all. From the body we learn what is near, what is far, that which is above, that which is below" (Tilley 2004: 3). Magnitude and proportion are hence determined through a sensuous bodily relationship with our surroundings rather than a distanced, scientific gaze. A monument's size, the heady mass and dominating presence of a free-standing Corinthian column or the intimate proximity of a small-scale tag, are thus always experienced somatically.

This corporeal relationship to our artifactual surrounds is one, however, that innumerable architects have chosen to exploit. For Albert Speer, the chief architect of National Socialism, the colossal was utilized as a weapon of the sublime, as a tool to both empower (the singular) and overpower the (collective) human body. The design of the Nazi party rally grounds in Nuremburg, as Sharon Macdonald has explained, was formed through a "calculated Nazi ideology of dwarfing the individual, and [thereby] subsuming individual identity to the collective project" (Macdonald 2006: 111), a technique in which what was explicitly coveted was the "violation of human scale" (Speer 1995, in Macdonald 2006: 111). The overwhelming immensity of this totalitarian landscape, its embracement of the *kolossal* and the "überdimensional" (p. 111), was even understood by Hitler himself to have the ability to affect our "sensory organs and emotions, unmediated by language," to be able to directly influence the populace via its "impact on the eye" (p. 109). Sheer size thus not only subjugated the individual but

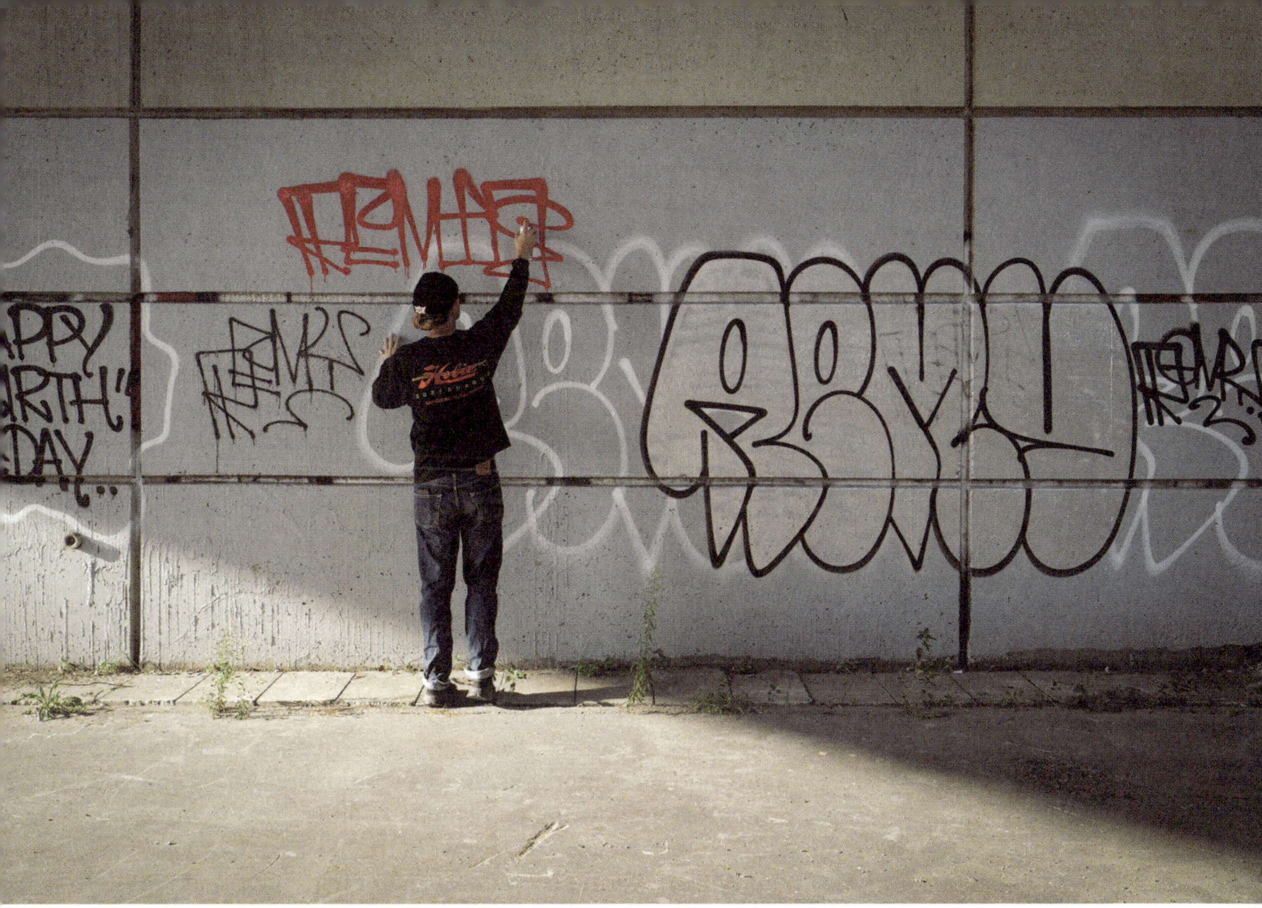

**FIGURE 1.16**
*Untitled (Remio)*, 2022, Paris. Photo: Gökhan S.

transformed the mode of corporeal apprehension Tilley discussed above from a multisensory to more singularly scopic dimension. Terming this technique of gigantism the "Wagner effect" (Morris 2000: 482), the artist and theorist Robert Morris likewise argued that this maximalist regime altered sensory apprehension from one that engaged with objects that were "in your space," objects that "you had to confront . . . with both body and eye," into one in which the vastness of size created a purely optical response (pp. 478–479). This was an art in which endlessness created a distanced vision functioning through a pomposity that titillated and dominated simultaneously. While large works could still, for Morris, function within a bodily scale—creating artifacts that could be appreciated through touch or bodily inhabitation, for example—size and tonnage were for him almost impossible to enlist without falling into both kitsch and the spectacle. The monumental-monument not only subjugated and undermined the human body, but could only be seen, not felt. The large-scale thus held within it both the danger of wanton idolatry as much as an implicit rejection of the bodily itself.

This totalitarian transcendence of the human scale is something often seen within the space of the institutional monument, within the laddish pissing contests that are the phallic shafts standing so proud and erect in the public sphere. From London's Nelson's Column—not only the 18-foot sandstone statue of the man himself but likewise the 170-foot pillar he stands upon—to the mammoth victory arches and the well-endowed horses (and their oversized riders), the epic presence of these gargantuan forms ensures a particular physical subservience, an enforced gestural reverence and a very visible, corporeal hierarchy (our necks crane, our gaze climbs, our bodies wilt before thee). Our graffiti monument, however, remains fixed to the realm of the anthropometric, taking place in the mundane intimacy of the everyday. It belies the grand heroism of the institutional monument, being set within an always conceivable bodily scale. Even when placed high up on a building or upon a freeway spanning overpass, the image remains bound to the human form that produced it (a body upside-down, a body precariously balanced over the side of a rooftop or bridge). It remains physically sensible even whilst the evident danger of its production visibly persists.

This rejection of the oversized and the engagement of the anthropometric can be illustrated through more official public art too. In Do Ho Suh's installation *Public Figures* (1998), for example (see figure 1.17), it is the classic tool of material hierarchy—the stony plinth atop which our grand rulers (and their trusty steeds) traditionally stand—that becomes the focal point of the artist's work. Positioning a set of miniature figures underneath, rather than atop, a classical stone plinth, Suh's work not only focuses on the individuals whose the traditional hero's boots rest upon but inverts the techniques through which these martial figures are "placed upon a pedestal" at the detriment of those who they unquestionably (and violently) displaced. The triumphs of the disappeared hero are thus shown to have been supported by the many unnamed who now physically support rather than stand upon the stony platform itself. Here, the plinth as technique of power, as technique of physical ascendency and vertical hierarchy, is made overt. Here, the proximity of the small scale, rather than the pretension of the large, is adopted. Similarly, in Mark Wallinger's *Ecce Homo* (1999), a statue of Jesus Christ produced, as seen in figure 1.18, to a "life-sized" scale, we are presented with a figure of god as everyman (standing in stark contrast to his colossal Brazilian counterpart, the famous *Christ the Redeemer*). First exhibited on the Fourth Plinth in London's Trafalgar Square alongside the abovementioned and overlooking Nelson, who massively dwarfs Wallinger's sculpture, the work demonstrates a modesty of scale even in its life-sized state. In a context in which the body is normally portrayed at double or triple its true size, the human scale thus comes to illustrate a basic (our basic) vulnerability. Wallinger's Jesus thus takes on a conspicuously marginal, minor position. It stands humbly, meekly, rejecting the overtly celebratory defiance of the marble and bronze men surrounding him.[10]

While rarely taking on the overt humility integral to Suh's and Wallinger's monuments (something easier to do, it must be said, when officially validated), the graffiti

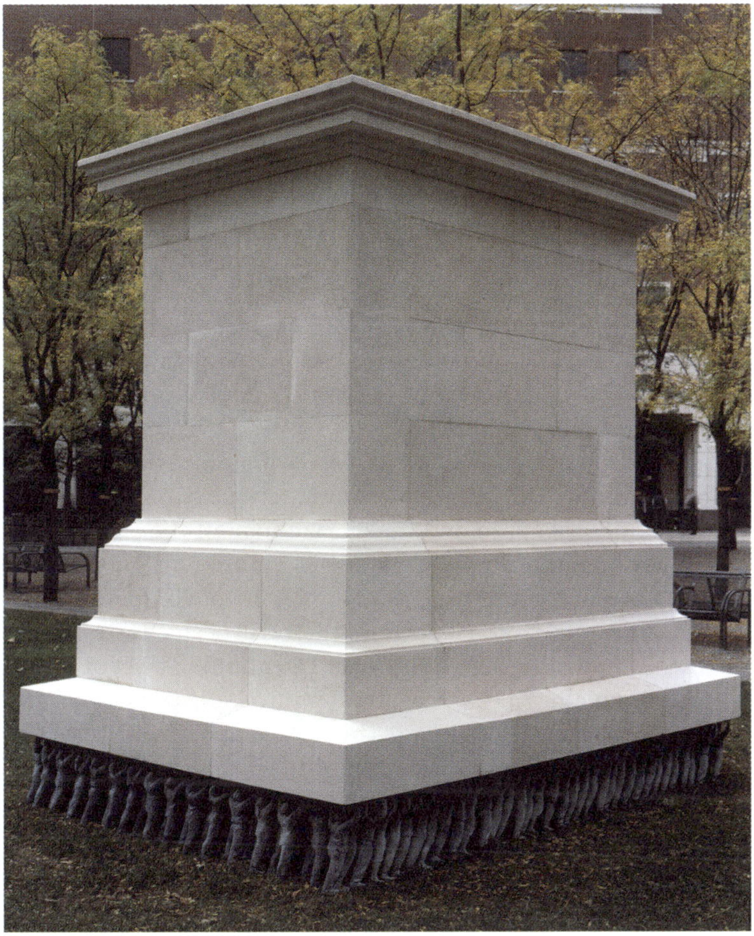

**FIGURE 1.17**
Do Ho Suh, *Public Figures Installation at the Metrotech Center Commons, Brooklyn, NY*, October 1998–May 1999. Fiberglass/resin, steel pipes, pipe fittings. 120 × 84 × 108 in/304.8 × 213.4 × 274.3 cm. © Do Ho Suh. Courtesy of the artist and Lehmann Maupin, New York, Hong Kong, Seoul, and London.

monument mirrors these artists particular approach to scale and hierarchy, espousing a dimension not of the titanic but the anthropometric. Fixed to the measure of the body, to the maximum extensions of its physical frame, it venerates rather than violates bodily capabilities, creating a work of a sensorially tangible and intimate scale. Acting through a human measure, not inhuman size, it rejects the "will to power," the "police-like machismo," the "masculine brutality" of verticality (Lefebvre 1991: 144). Graffiti thus forms a somatic monument, one constructed from and with a conceivable human scale.

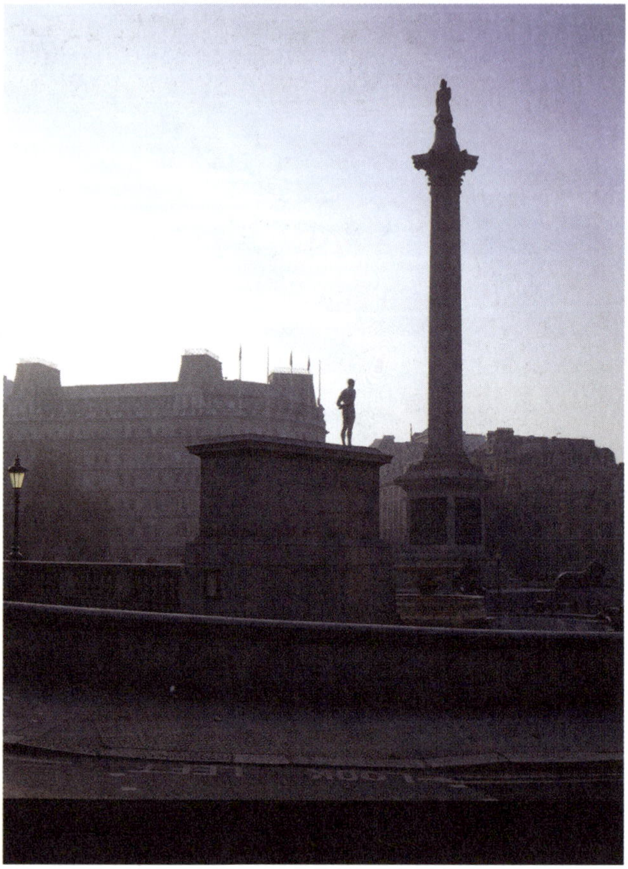

**FIGURE 1.18**
Mark Wallinger, *Ecce Homo*, 1999–2000. Trafalgar Square, London. © Mark Wallinger. Courtesy of Mark Wallinger. Photo: Peter White.

## LOCATION *OR* THE MARGINAL

The physically marginal position of Wallinger's monument, not only its comparatively diminutive stature but its position at the very edge of its plinth, can also be seen to link toward the final element of graffiti's site-based qualities that we will discuss in this chapter, to the final "how" of its spatially peripheral location. Take figure 1.19, for example, an image taken adjacent to a railway trackside in Hackney Central, London. Not only displaying a whole range of tags and throw-ups—a partially occluded yellow tag displaying the name "Nigel" and a two-letter throw-up of the same writer's name "NI," two conjoined throw-ups from "Ofske" and "Noe," and a large outline stating

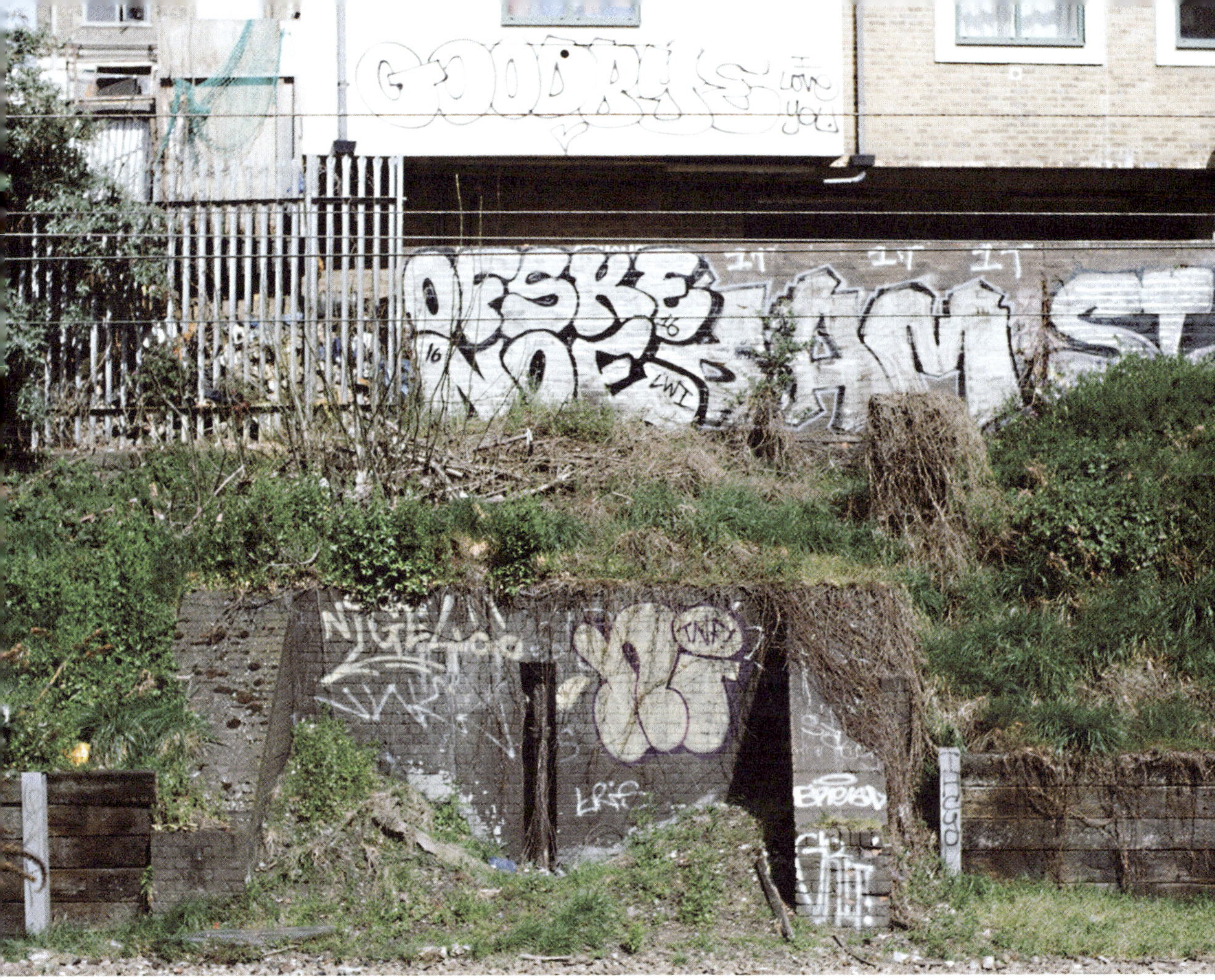

**FIGURE 1.19**
*Untitled (Hackney Trackside)*, 2021, London. Photo: Rafael Schacter.

"Goodbye (I love you)" among a series of other smaller and occluded pieces—what is likewise visible here is the wild, overgrown wasteland that these various graffiti images appear within. We find a field of unkempt grass and bushes, piles of old wood, alongside a section of palisade fencing with an overflowing mountain of refuse pushing through its metal stakes. We have a setting in which renegade weeds have taken back control, a marginal landscape acting as the marginal ground to the marginal graffiti figure. Invisible within my image, however, is both the metal fencing that my camera lens is poking through as well as the double set of train tracks hidden just beneath the edge of the frame. Signaling them, however, one can see the five overhead power lines cutting across the center of the image, as well the ballast at the bottom edge of the shot, holding the wooden sleepers and metal rails in place.[11] Judging by the height of the adjoining wall at the top of the image, however, it seems likely that there is a fairly unproblematic point of entry for the writers whose work is visible here. Even as the site is a clear no-go zone, then, the numerous tags and throw-ups—as seen not only here but on railway lines throughout the city—provide the viewer with clear knowledge that trespass has taken place, that trespass is possible, common even. It may be a marginal site, but these are margins that are evidently utilized rather than empty voids.

What figure 1.19 thus shows is not only a set of adjunctive images, a group of interruptive, anthropometric graffiti pieces, but likewise a set of works produced on a marginal border (the walls/barriers/façades), in a marginal territory (a gray space/an urban edgeland), in a marginal site (a nonprincipal/peripheral location of the city). Spatial marginality thus emerges in three distinct ways here, revealing the liminal surfaces between public and private, the liminal frontiers beyond the control of the city, and the liminal fringes of graffiti's everyday, suburban sites of practice. Within a classic core-periphery dynamic, then, graffiti remains set firmly within the zone of latter, at the periphery, even when appearing in the very core. Rather than the dominant centrality of the classical monument, a monument traditionally placed in the heart of the city, a monument set in major not marginal sites, a monument that reinforces the geographic hierarchies of the city, these three situationally marginal attributes outline some of graffiti's most foundational aspects.

First, then, graffiti's appearance on our peripheral *borders* functions to unsettle one of the key divisions of the city, that set between the private and the public. Placed, as we see in figure 1.20, for example, on the diaphanous border between intimacy and exposure, on the surface of the city's entry points, on its doors and roller-shutters, windows and structural edges, graffiti thus highlights the ambiguity of the threshold: the marks placed upon the superficial veneers of the city, on the millimeter-thick substrate that are its painted or raw surfaces, come to signal not simply a territorial marking of "ownership" (as so often assumed), but a form of encroachment that questions the delineation of this separation itself. Marginality, following the work of Anna Tsing, can thus be seen here not only as a "geographical, descriptive location," not only as a site of "deviance from social norms," but as a placement that creates "zones of unpredictability" (Tsing 1994: 279). The marginality of the border disturbs where the common space of the pavement ends and the private space of property begins. It becomes a space of instability, of permeability, a space "where contradictory discourses overlap . . . where discrepant kinds of meaning-making converge" (p. 279). As such, rather than the threshold acting as a boundary—the space, in Richard Sennett's terms, that "establishes closure through inactivity"—these zones can instead be seen to act as the archetypal border—as an "active zone of exchange," that is both "porous and resistant" at the same time (Sennett 2017: n.p.).[12]

Second, graffiti's position on the city's borderline *territories* reveals a space outside the control of the center, an edge in which the routine structures of our contemporary

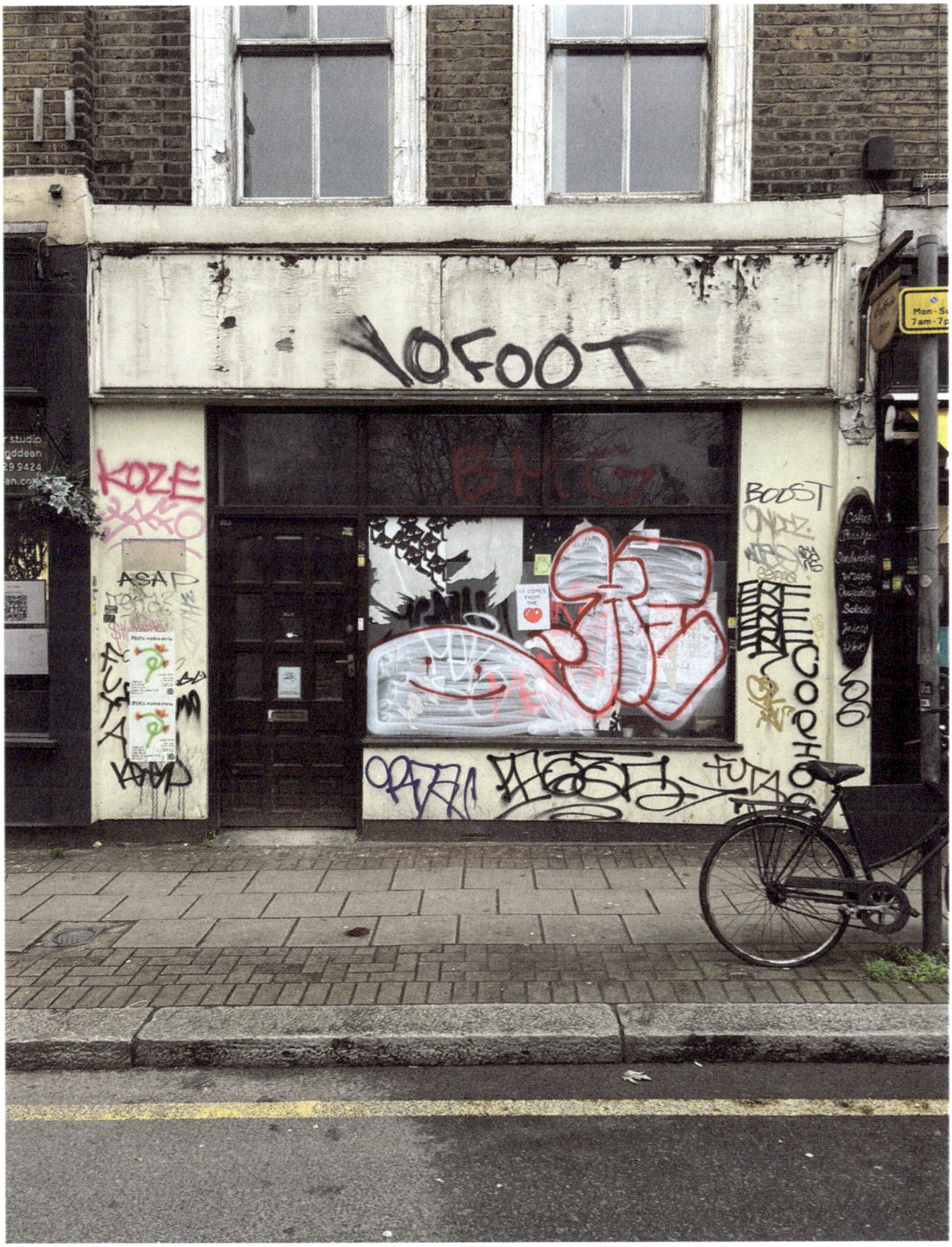


**FIGURE 1.20**
*Untitled (Bethnal Green Road)*, 2022, London. Photo: Rafael Schacter.

world are fleetingly displaced. These backstage or interstitial zones, the spaces below (the tunnels and catacombs) or above (the rooftops or railway bridges), the sometimes abandoned, sometimes disregarded, marginal wastelands of the city (as seen in figure 1.21, for example), not only encroach upon the spatial and legalistic conventions of the city, but offer a site of potential autonomy. Termed "*terrain vagues*" by the architect Ignasi de Solà-Morales Rubio—"terrain" here linking to the francophone (rather than anglophone) notion of an undefined territory, "vague" to that which is "empty, unoccupied" but also "free, available, unengaged" (de Solà-Morales Rubio 1995: 119)—these liminal sites were understood to "exist outside the city's effective circuits and productive structures," to emerge in the margins "where the city is no longer" (p. 120). What remains crucial to the structure of *terrain vagues*, however, is their standing at an edge in which the "absence of use, of activity, and the sense of freedom, of expectancy, is

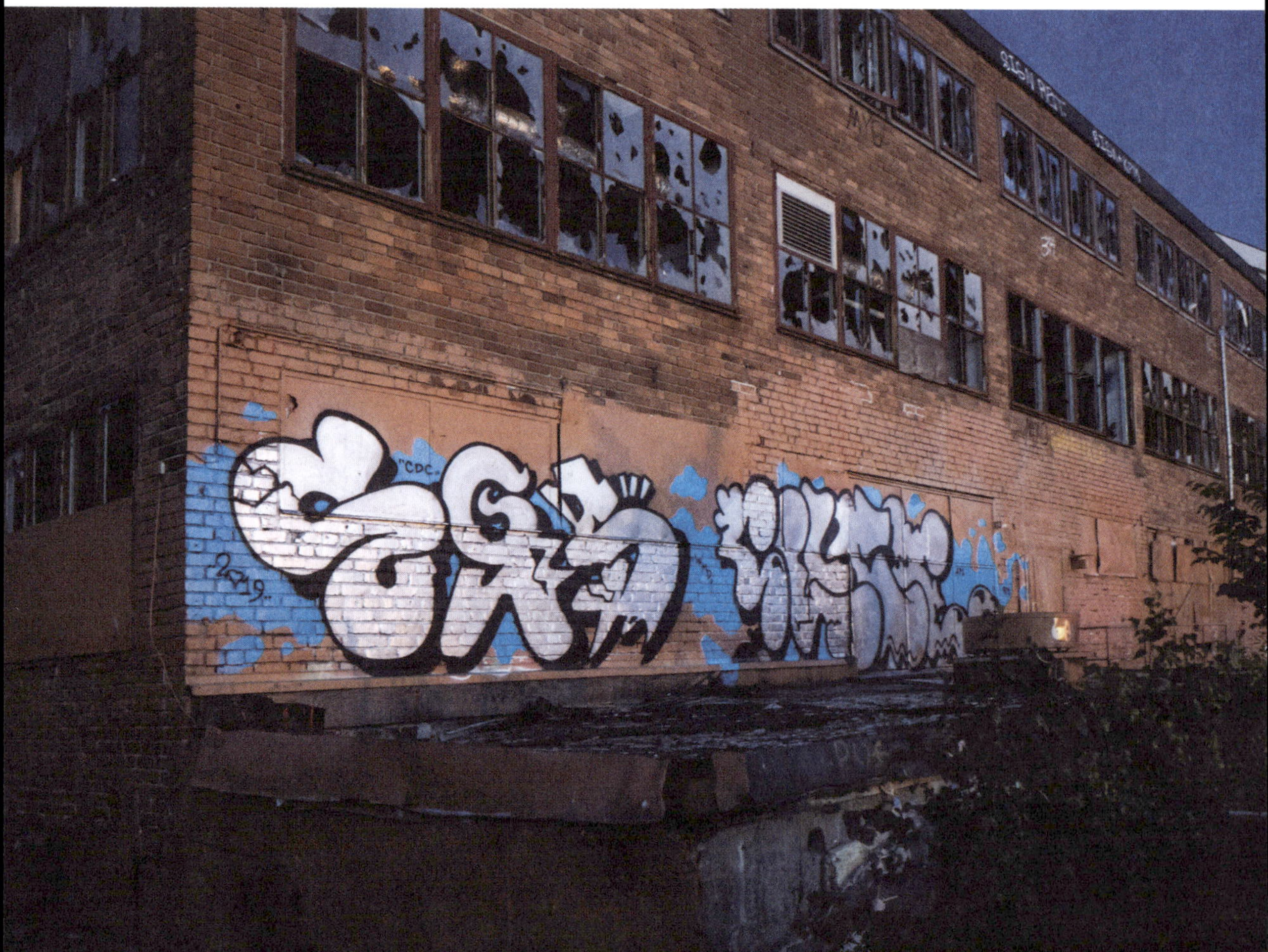

fundamental," as much as their being "mentally exterior in the physical interior of the city" (p. 120). What may thus first appear as the space in between space, as the discarded leftovers of the city, can here be understood as sites of play, of experiment, of adventure. What may first seem, as de Solà-Morales Rubio continues, as a space of "absence" and "void" can also be seen as one of "promise," as a space of both "critique" and "possible alternative" (p. 120).[13]

Third, graffiti's placement at the city's marginal *localities* reveals a visual culture implicitly at home within the city's daily, mundane, commonplace sites, within its outer, rather than central or touristic locations. This more classical marginality, set at the literal peripheries of the urban realm (as seen in figure 1.22), can be seen to expose a commonly held (and deeply suspect) binary in urban life, that set between the traditionally derided suburban periphery and the commonly venerated metropolitan center.

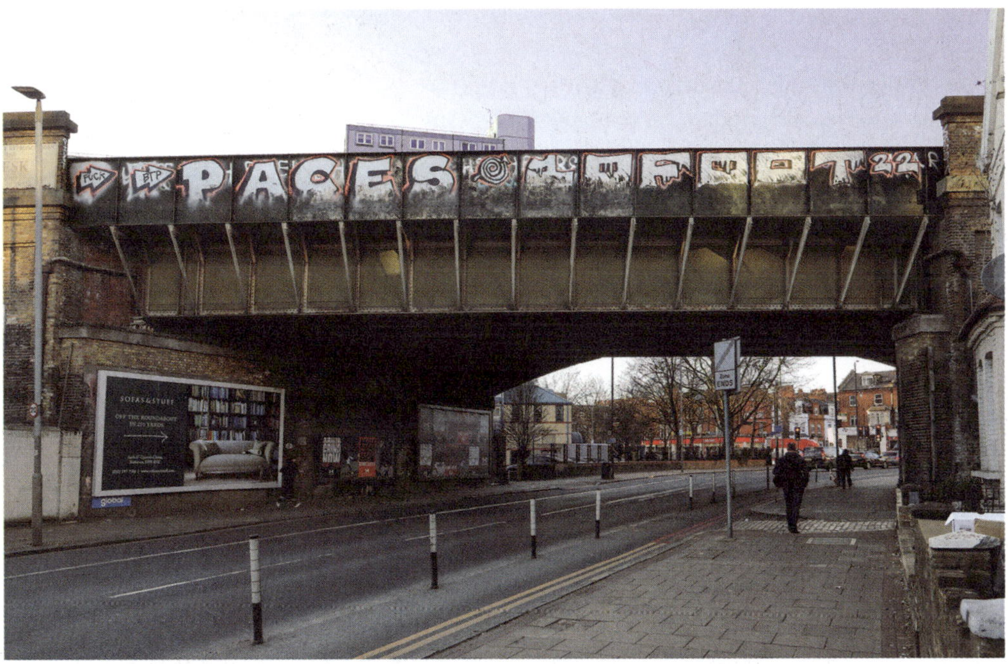


**FIGURE 1.21**
*Egs/Slice*, 2019, Stockholm. Courtesy of Egs.

**FIGURE 1.22**
*Paces/10Foot,* 2022, South London. Photo: Alex Ellison.

Standing in contradistinction to the crushing blandness and touristified flatness of our increasingly privatized and spectacularized cityscapes (as discussed more in part III of this book), the margins can be understood as spaces in which one can act free from the economic imperatives of the corporatized center, spaces in which a vernacular creativity can emerge and thrive (Edensor et al. 2009). Whether witnessed in the creative evolution of subcultural music genres (think grime and jungle in the United Kingdom or suburban punk in Los Angeles) or subcultural fashion styles (think the British Mods or Congolese Sapeurs), the favelas, banlieues, and suburbs are spaces in which a burgeoning creativity is always ready to explode.[14] The margins can thus, as philosopher Edward Casey noted, be seen as the space in which human action "comes to happen in the most effective or significant sense," to be not a "zone in which human action gives out or comes to an end" but rather the space "where it intensifies" (Casey 2007: 508).

While graffiti thus emerges from and so too embodies the margins of the border (between public and private), of the territory (between backstage and front), and of locality (between center and periphery), we can see this marginal mode within more recognized public art too. Jenny Holzer's *Truisms* series (1978–present), for example, a text-based body of work often pasted illegally onto city walls (as discussed further in chapter 3 and seen in figure 3.5) as well as being displayed on the entrance structures of movie theaters in the series *Marquees* (1993) (see figure 1.23), questions the border in which public and private both start and stop in the city. While, like graffiti, the intimate, fiercely individual thoughts and propositions being proclaimed in Holzer's works could be argued to be deeply private ones, by independently taking over traditionally commercial (and thus privatized) sites, the space on which they appear becomes transformed into a relational zone utilized for non-instrumental, civic means. Calling out to us as public citizens rather than private consumers (in contradistinction to the neighboring shop signage), they destabilize the notion of public space and public speech alike. In Olivier Kosta-Thefaine's project *Flore de Compagnie* (2015) (see figures 1.24 and 1.25), however, it was the margins of our urban non-spaces that he set out to explore, along with the hierarchies of value set up in both the horticultural, artistic, and social worlds. Creating bouquets of flowers from the wild vegetation growing at the marginal edges of the city, Kosta-Thefaine sought not only to document and map the urban realm via its flora but also to reveal the vibrancy and possibility of the edge. Giving full attention to the city's overlooked beauty, the artist here rejects traditional urban value systems and gives weight to spaces outside of the city's management and control. In Ian Strange's work, however, it is the margins of the *sub*urban world that he has recurrently come to examine. Focusing much of his practice on this culturally maligned part of the city, Strange's documentation and site-specific installations in these areas—such as seen in the project *Suburban* (2011–2013) in which he painted, illuminated, and intervened within classical suburban abodes—come to both transform these peripheral sites into monuments in themselves (as seen in figure 1.26, for example) while likewise reclaiming suburbia as a site of artistic practice and investigation in itself. Here, as with Holzer's

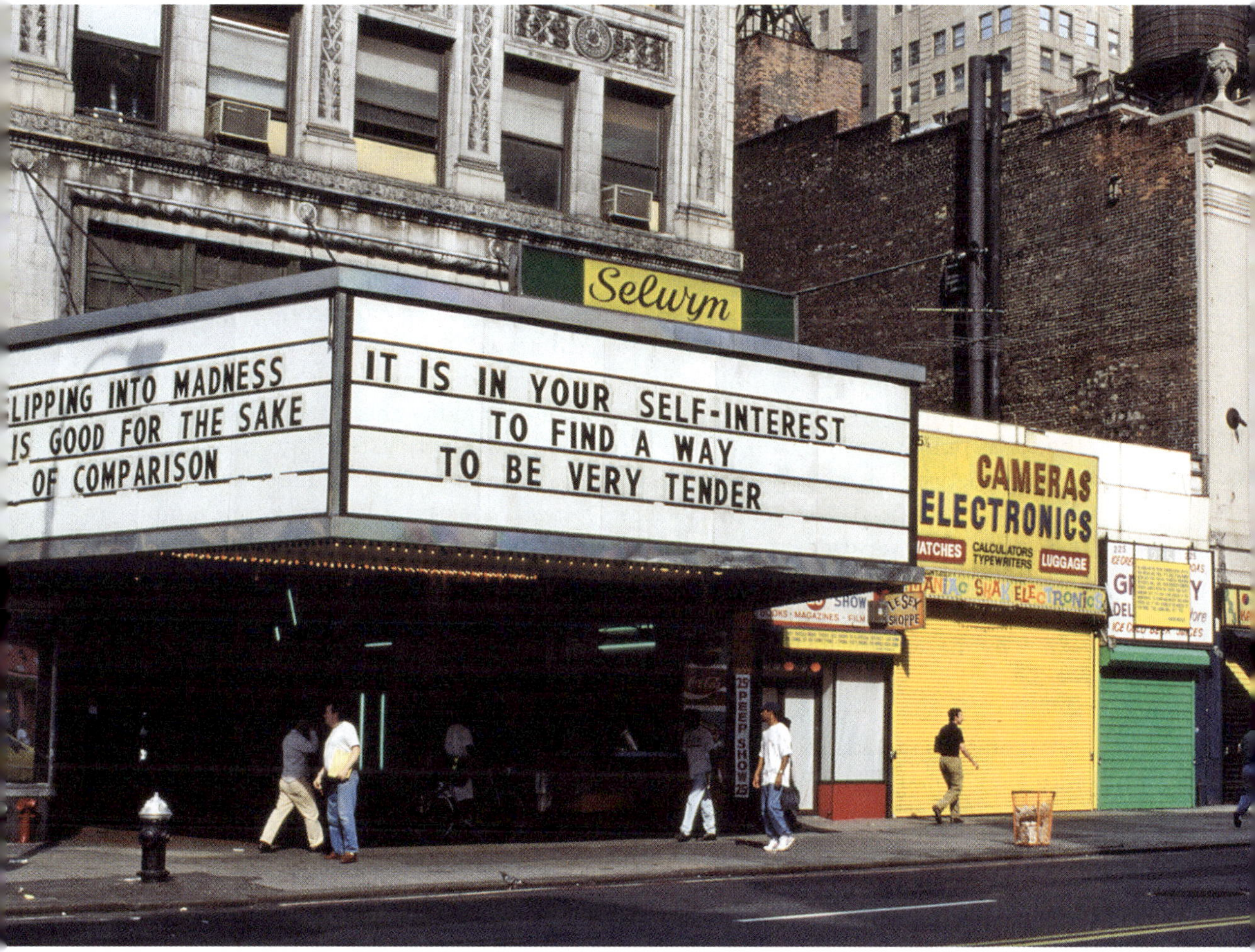


**FIGURE 1.23**

Jenny Holzer, from *Truisms*, 1977–1979; *Survival*, 1983–1985. Theater marquee. Installation: Forty-Second Street Art Project, Times Square, New York, 1993. Photo: Maggie Hopp. Photo credit: Courtesy of Jenny Holzer/Art Resource, NY.

and Kosta-Thefaine's interventions, marginality signifies much more than lack. Here, the edge can come to act, as bell hooks so powerfully argued, as a "site of radical possibility, a space of resistance," as a space that offers a "radical perspective from which to see and create, to imagine alternatives, new worlds" (hooks 1989: 20). Marginality can thus reveal itself not only as a space in which monuments emerge in direct opposition to (the authority of) the center but a site through an outsider, peripheral, minor status is valued in and for itself.[15]

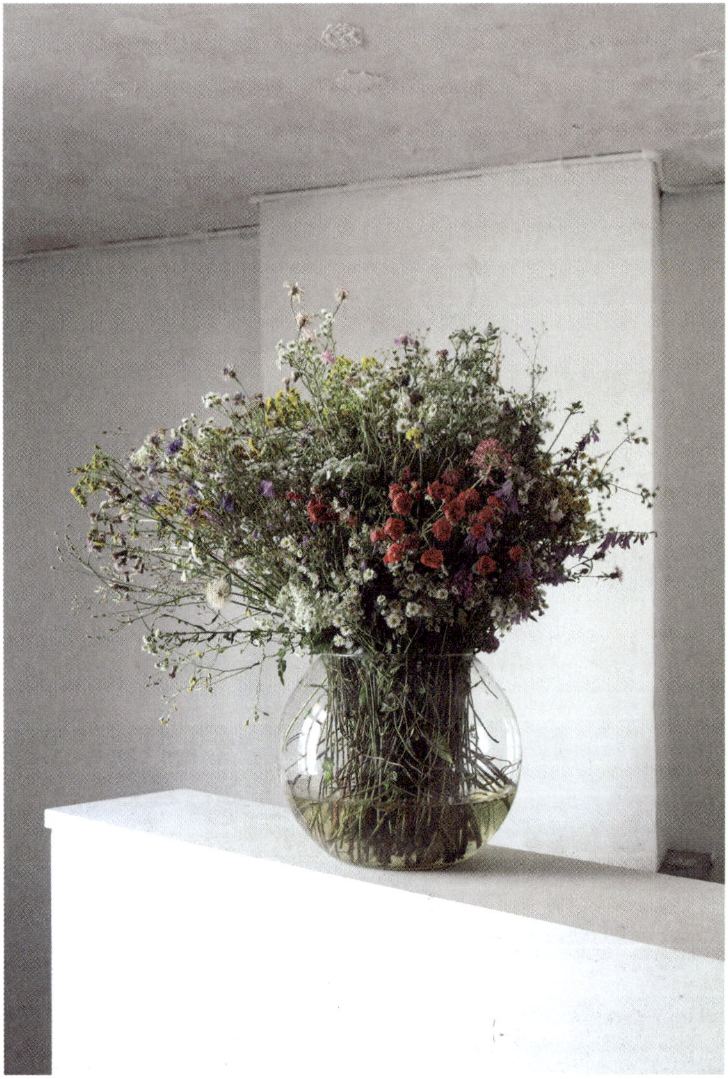

**FIGURE 1.24**
Olivier Kosta-Théfaine, *Flore de compagnie*, 2015. Besançon, France. Photo by Elisa Murcia-Artengo. Courtesy of the artist and Bien Urbain.

**FIGURE 1.25**
Olivier Kosta-Théfaine, *Flore de compagnie* (process), 2015. Besançon, France. Photo by Elisa Murcia-Artengo. Courtesy of the artist and Bien Urbain.

**FIGURE 1.26**
Ian Strange, *Corrinne Terrace*, 2011. Archival digital print, documentation of site-specific intervention. Selected work from *Suburban* (installation). Mountainside, NJ. Courtesy of the artist.

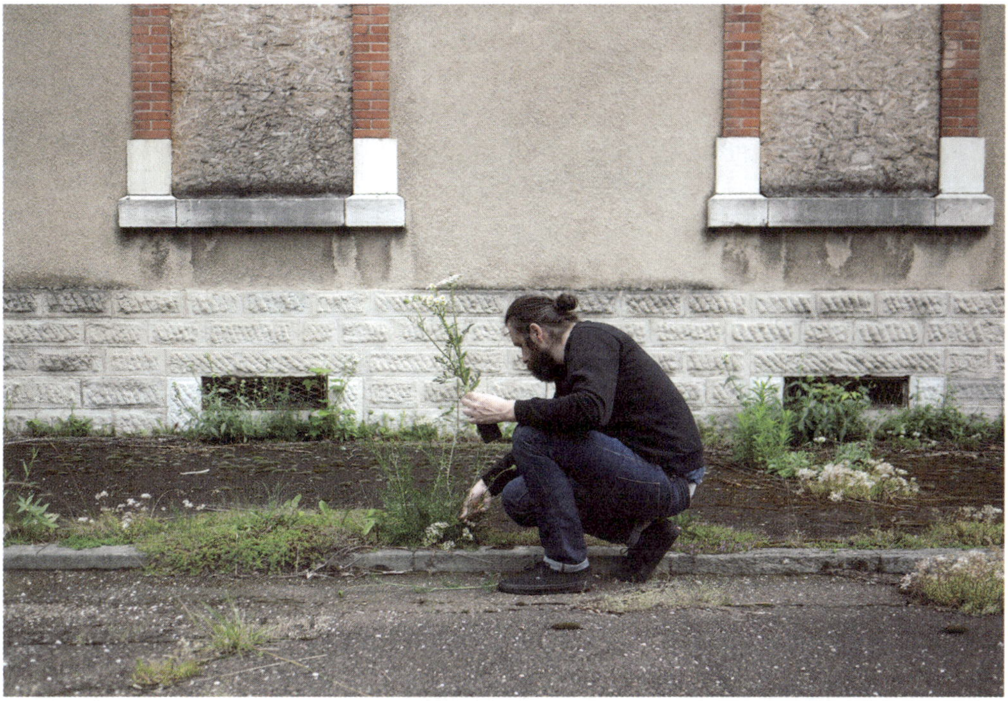

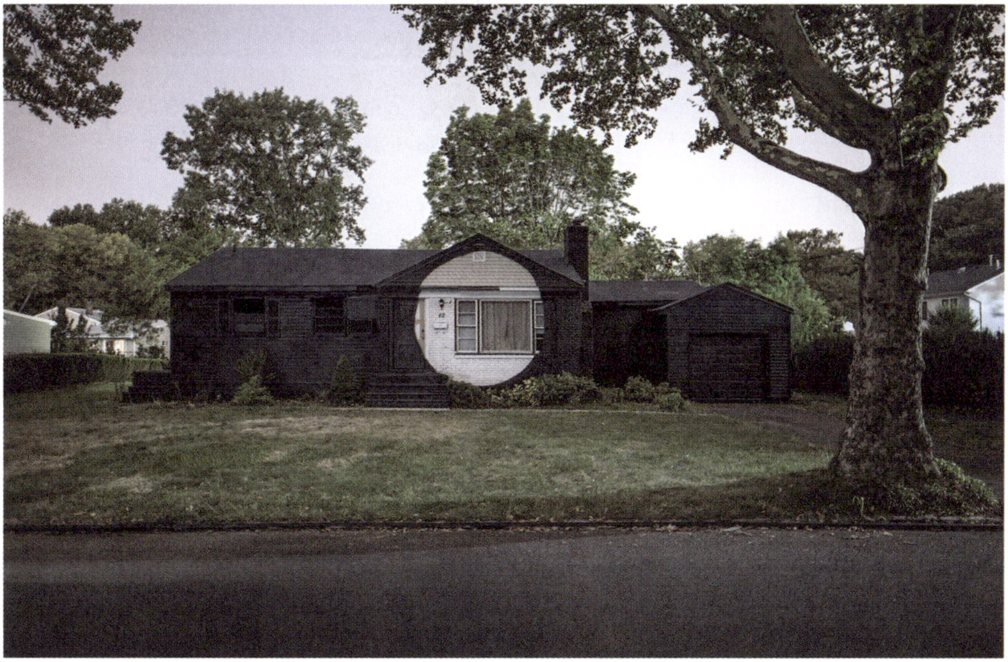

## CONCLUSION *OR* THE ISSUE OF (IL)LEGALITY

Graffiti's site-specific position, relation, dimension, and location in the city can thus together be seen to create its unique mediality. The specific qualities of adjunctivity, interruptivity, anthropometry, and marginality that it reveals are critical to the way it emerges and is received in the city, the constitutive "hows" that, in relation with a specifically stylized image, come to turn a text into graffiti itself. Without any of these four elements, an image's status as graffiti falls into doubt. Without its adjunctivity, graffiti reverts back to the merest of images; it may be a sketch, a drawing, a painting, but it remains an image split from its requisite host. Without its interruptivity, graffiti serves to uphold, rather than reject, spatial norms; treating the city as canvas, not site, it becomes superficially submissive, its spatial assimilation placing it within the traditions of the institution. Without its anthropometricity, graffiti becomes *kolossal*, Wagnerian; losing its bodily scale it turns from intimacy to enormity, from haptic to spectacle. Without its marginality, graffiti becomes domineering; it rejects the plural boundary and becomes part of the singularized border; it becomes a practice of power, of the hegemonic, the center. Still, this is not to say that one cannot find examples of graffiti that disregard one of these medial qualities (as seen in the large-scale graffiti pieces produced with modified fire-extinguishers, for example, as seen in the work of Christian Falsnaes in figures 6.15–6.20). These four elements are norms rather than hard and fast rules, and their occasional subversion could be seen in many ways to reinforce them. What is key to uphold, however, is the way in which these four elements act as the spatial foundations from which graffiti can emerge, as the site-specific core through which a canonical image becomes graffiti itself.

With that said, there is an issue of site that I have yet to unpack here, that being graffiti's customary illegality. While often placed at the center of any discussion of graffiti, illegality is a factor that, I argue, lies in a subordinate position to the four site-specific elements that have been analyzed in this chapter thus far. Although an aspect directly focused on by some writers—linked to a wider aesthetic related to vandalism and "damage," providing a link to the necessary level of performative commitment and risk, as well as being linked to the mode of interruption explored earlier in this chapter itself—graffiti's four site-specific fundamentals do not place it in an *inevitably* illicit state in itself. While graffiti's adjunctive location in the city is thus commonly illegal, its integrally attached position is not necessarily so: like a gargoyle on a cathedral or a sgraffito wall decoration, graffiti may always act through the status of the constitutive outsider, but its illegality—as with a graffiti image on a legal graffiti wall—may be of secondary importance. While graffiti's interruptive relation is, in the same way, often illegal, its fundamentally antagonistic position is not necessarily so: like a large-scale sculpture impeding passage through a plaza or a series of agonistic projections on public monuments, graffiti may always work to upturn architectural norms, to refuse assimilation, but its illegality—as with a work produced with a building owner's consent—may be up for question. And although graffiti's anthropometric dimensions have in themselves no *direct* relation to the illicit—aside from a small-scale work being able to be produced quickly, independently, and surreptitiously, and a large-scale work being almost necessarily legal due to the difficulty of making it without plant machinery (and thus institutional backing)—its marginal position within the urban realm is, like its location and relation, often illegal, yet not essentially so; like a memorial produced in a suburban street or an ornamentally patterned doorway, graffiti may always function through a marginal site, through a physical or embodied peripherality, but its illegality—if produced in an urban wasteland or an abandoned factory, at sites with no clear structure of ownership—may be subject to doubt. Producing work in and on public space, producing human-scaled work that interrupts its margins, simply takes precedence over producing work for the sake of illegality itself. And while something prized by many artists for the sheer thrill of the chase, for the primal enjoyment of destruction, for the rejection of norms and sensation of resistance it engenders, illegality is a factor evolving through graffiti's four key site-specific prerequisites rather than an innate prerequisite in itself: the *how* of graffiti thus makes it a commonly but not constitutively illicit act.[16]

Moreover, the site of graffiti that these four elements outline—the adjunctive position and relational intervention, the dimensional anthropometricity and locational marginality of all the different forms of graffiti witnessed in this chapter—not only points toward the innate publicness of graffiti, its status as an image whose public exhibition and visible existence is critical, but likewise begins to test the very conception of "private" through which its legal prohibition emerges. 10Foot's adjunctive acid tag in figure 1.1 could thus be seen to occur on the public facing edge of a collectively owned (and often collectively disregarded) piece of street furniture and a space neither purely public or private in itself. Depo's interruptive piece at figure 1.9, likewise, could be seen to occur on a seemingly abandoned site, on a surface in which the legal owners are either nonexistent or missing. Remio's human-scaled writing at figure 1.16 could be seen to occur on a roadside wall, a wall that may officially be owned by the local council, but whose surface is directly adjacent to and in fact an implicit part of the public sphere. And the marginal wasteland in figure 1.19 could be seen to occur in a site in which ownership, if denoted by care, seems to be implicitly renounced, a site that, while officially managed by Network Rail, exists within a hazy or gray space.[17] While the majority of our legal systems make the actual realities of property ownership very clear (even more so when it comes to judicial sentencing), for graffiti practitioners, these remain spaces in which individual (rather than collective) ownership is a debatable point. Within the internal graffiti regulations around appropriate sites of practice we thus find very clear distinctions between types of sites deemed acceptable or unacceptable for practice, distinctions that make clear the dividing line between public and private rather than a rejection of the concept itself. Differentiating between what are regarded as "private" spaces—such as home residences, memorials, private vehicles, and religious sites, which should never be touched by committed practitioners—and what were recognized as fully "public" zones—the shopfront shutters, the walls, the street furniture, and the other forms of "public" property understood as acceptable hosts[18]—the sites in which artists work contain a very important delineation between public and private, a delineation that clearly differs from legal codes, but one in which the personal and the common are quite clearly (and literally) marked out.

The four key factors of site-specificity outlined above thus intersect directly with issues of legality and illegality, publicity and privacy, yet more than anything provide us with a starting point to understand graffiti as both form and monument; they help outline a practice that is supplementary rather than separated, that is agonistic rather than integrative, that is human not colossal, that is peripheral not predominant in the public sphere. They help us to fix not only the way in which graffiti as monument functions spatially—as an adjunctive, interruptive, anthropometric, marginal monument, as a site-specific reminder of our own site-specific realities—but so too the way graffiti as monument perfectly mirrors the spatial mode of the institutional monument that it remains in opposition toward: to the detached, the assimilative, the large-scale, the central monument that has today become the monumental norm. They help to define the distinction between monuments that are dependent or independent of their sites, that are conflicting or conformative to their surrounds, that are modest or titanic in their scale, that are set at the exterior or interior, the boundary or border, at the edge or the core of the urban realm.

# 2
# STYLE

Graffiti is an object existing only via its style. Style is what makes graffiti discernible among a sea of other urban artifacts, what enables it to attract and fascinate, to circulate and produce effects in the world. While site defines graffiti's *how*, the "how" of its emergence through and with the medium of the city, style is here positioned as its *what*: the "what" that makes up graffiti's necessary graphic qualities and compositional characteristics, the "what" that comes to create a visually apprehensible and demarcated form. The city may be that which turns an image *into* graffiti, but style is what dictates the appearance of that image itself. Unpacking the "what" that makes graffiti graffiti, this chapter will delineate the textual and figural foundations, the ornamental and monumental elements that turn one of a thousand public inscriptions into something perceptible as graffiti itself.

First addressing the way in which graffiti style developed as a cohesive visual canon, the chapter will then focus on what this canonical status comes to provoke as these images move through the city. Doing this via the three key themes that graffiti stylistically engages—agency, animation, and distribution—the chapter will thus lean heavily on the work of anthropologist Alfred Gell, whose seminal writing on style will be used to unravel the visual affordances of this image world. As such, examining what the image *is* as much as what it *does*, this chapter will unpack the equally visual and relational ways graffiti functions. Style will hence be seen not only as the indispensable tool through which graffiti artifacts become perceptible and create effects, but, as the chapter will conclude, as a way individual capability and group commitment are revealed and resolved, as a way value is created and consolidated in public and monumental ways.

## STYLE AND GRAFFITI *OR* THE CANONICAL

A term often used yet rarely defined, style, as Margaret Conkey has explained, can be understood as the particular "formal attributes" and specific "design conventions" (Conkey 2006: 358) that together create the boundaries of a visual system. A technique ensuring that "common difference" is established and that some graphic principles are "cultivated" while "others are suppressed" (p. 361), style is hence a mechanism through which coherence is formed and idiosyncrasy formally demarcated. As such, style forms a structure through which a set of grouped artifacts can remain comprehensible while often undergoing radical transformation. The structural logics that style forms, as Susanne Küchler and Timothy Carroll suggest, thus generate a "set of immediately recognisable images that measure (or 'rule') the aligned set" (Küchler and Carroll 2021: 86), a canon that can be "spread across genres of artefacts" (p. 86) because the artifacts themselves all remain within the wider canonical style. So, what determines graffiti's common differences and, as Gell termed it, its "axes of coherence" (Gell 1998: 167)? What is canonical style within graffiti and how did this canon emerge?

The first appearance of graffiti in the late 1960s materialized through the name-plus-street number signature formulation such as inscribed by the early writer[1] Taki183 (Taki a diminution of his given name, Dimitraki, 183 indicating his 183rd Street city address), as seen in figure 2.1. Witnessed mainly on urban walls and produced using the most basic of writing implements, name-writing at this early point was a game, a children's game like tag or hopscotch (Birzin 2019) in which *visibility* was the overarching

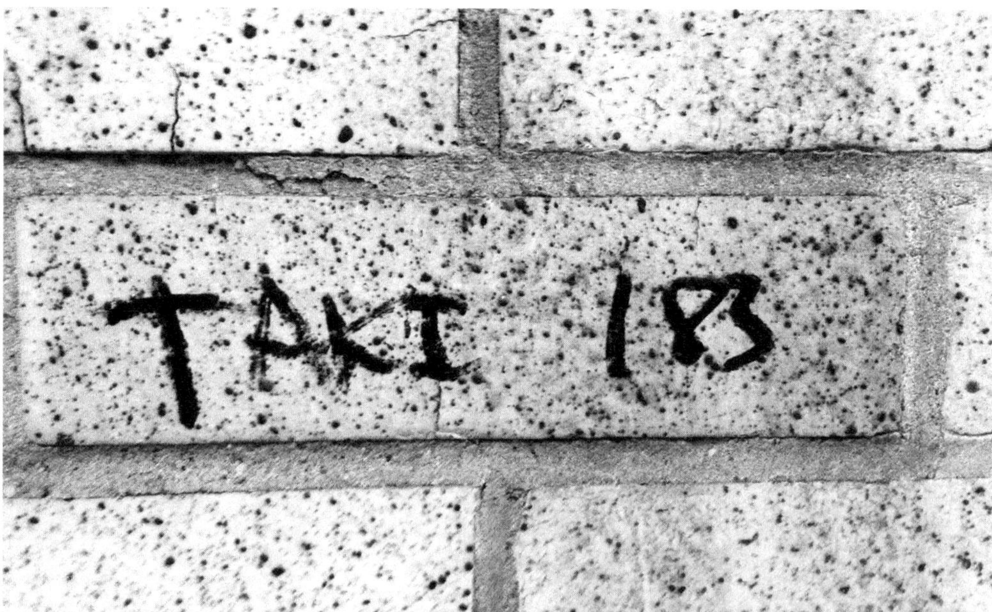


**FIGURE 2.1**
*Taki183*, 2011. Photo: Underdestruction. Attribution-NoDerivs 2.0 Generic (CC BY-ND 2.0).

goal. One wrote to be seen. One wrote to spread one's personhood over the world. But *how* one wrote was still a broadly undefined quality of the game, the practice being grounded by the visible quantity of one's epigraphs and practitioners using only rare and minimal embellishments such as the still omnipresent three-pointed crown and five-pointed stars seen in figure 2.2 (in the former case embedded in the letter form itself). As the number of graffiti practitioners themselves began to escalate, however, thanks in part to the 1971 *New York Times* article "'Taki 183' Spawns Pen Pals,"[2] the players of the burgeoning game began to search for new techniques of gaining prominence beyond the stripped-back purity of the name, or increasingly the chosen pseudonym, alone. At the same time, with the movement of the focal graffiti surface from the city's public walls to its subway carriages (in which one's output was often seen only at speed and from a distance), as well as the increasing utilization of more specialized tools[3] such as spray cans and modified homemade markers (in which one's work could both be produced *at* speed and made visually prominent *from* a distance), the scope of the writers' productions began to develop in increasingly elaborate ways. As seen in Gordon Matta-Clark's hand-tinted and hand-colored photographs in figures 2.3 and 2.4, the three- to six-letter name, the artistic pseudonym[4] that soon became completely

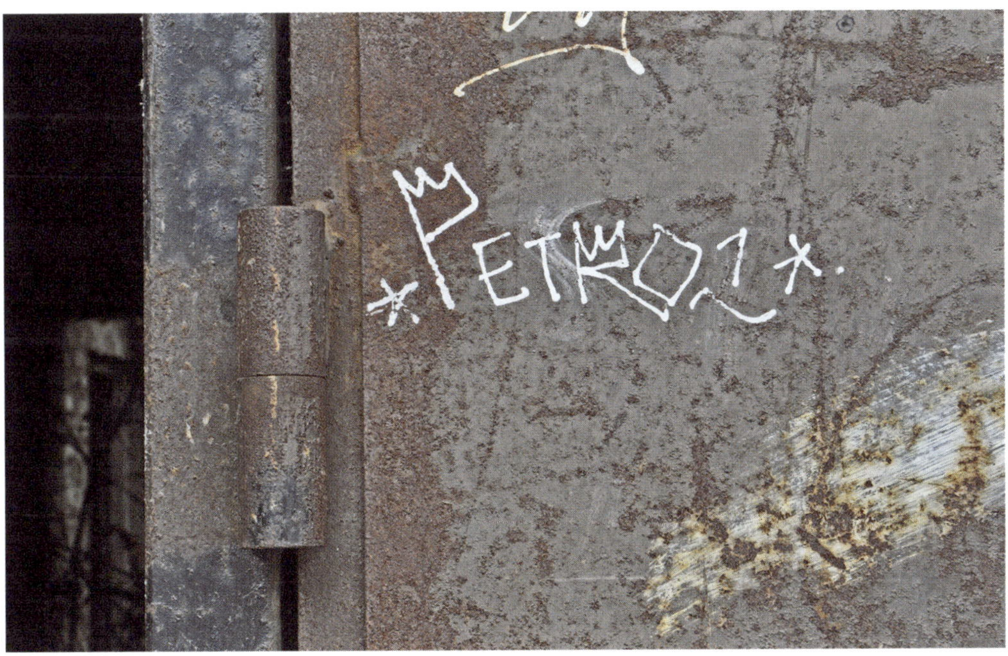


**FIGURE 2.2**
*Petro*, 2013, London. Photo: David Stuart.

interchangeable with the writer's own *birth* name,[5] still remained at the center of the practice. Yet the necessity for visual apprehensibility, to follow the fundamental tenet of graffiti style—*of being seen*—led toward the pursuit of the progressively elaborate principles and increasingly formalized structure that graffiti soon obtained.

By the mid-1970s, then, the small-scale, embryonic signatures had metamorphosed not only into more intricate calligraphic directions but likewise into large-scale, incredibly complex "masterpieces" that depicted the chosen name in multiple colors and embellished them with manifold ornaments and decorative forms, amplifying a work's visibility while exhibiting a practitioner's skills and techniques. Utilizing new graphic techniques (such as high contrast, shading, three-dimensional illusions, and complex textures), new typographic influences (taken from public signage, corporate advertising, TV shows, and underground comics, for example), as well as taking on a horizontal, strip-like formal structure (that both followed the natural shape of the railway vehicles they were designed to be written upon while also following the natural proportions of the body, which could cover more space laterally than vertically), the innovations that were cultivated during this early era led to the creation of a series of ground-breaking alphabetical orders that were as technically sophisticated as they were structurally

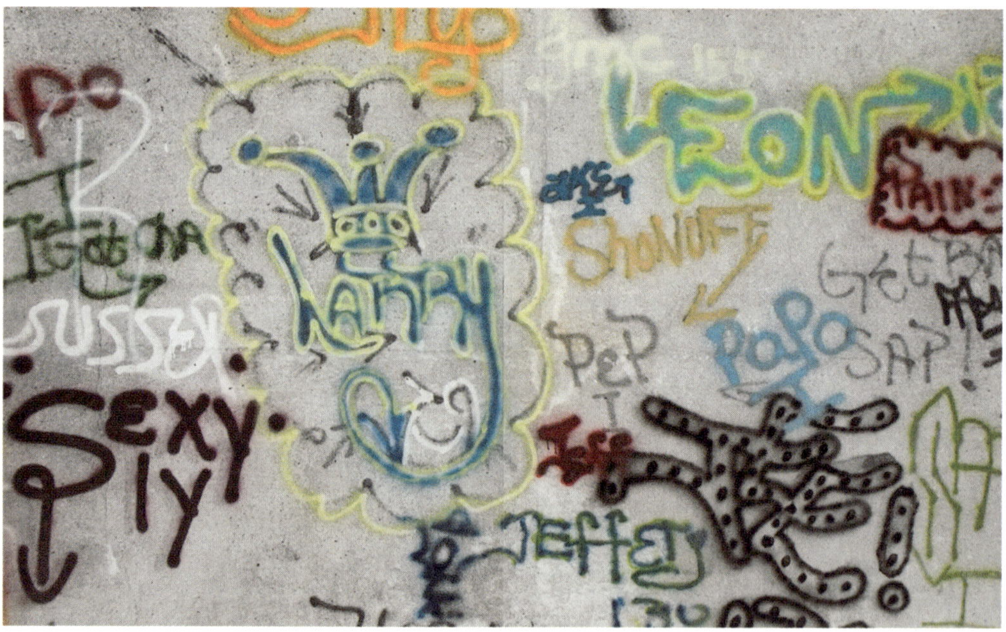


**FIGURE 2.3**

Gordon Matta-Clark, *Graffiti: Leon*, 1973. Gelatin silver print with hand coloring. © Estate of Gordon Matta-Clark, ARSNY.com, and DavidZwirner.com.

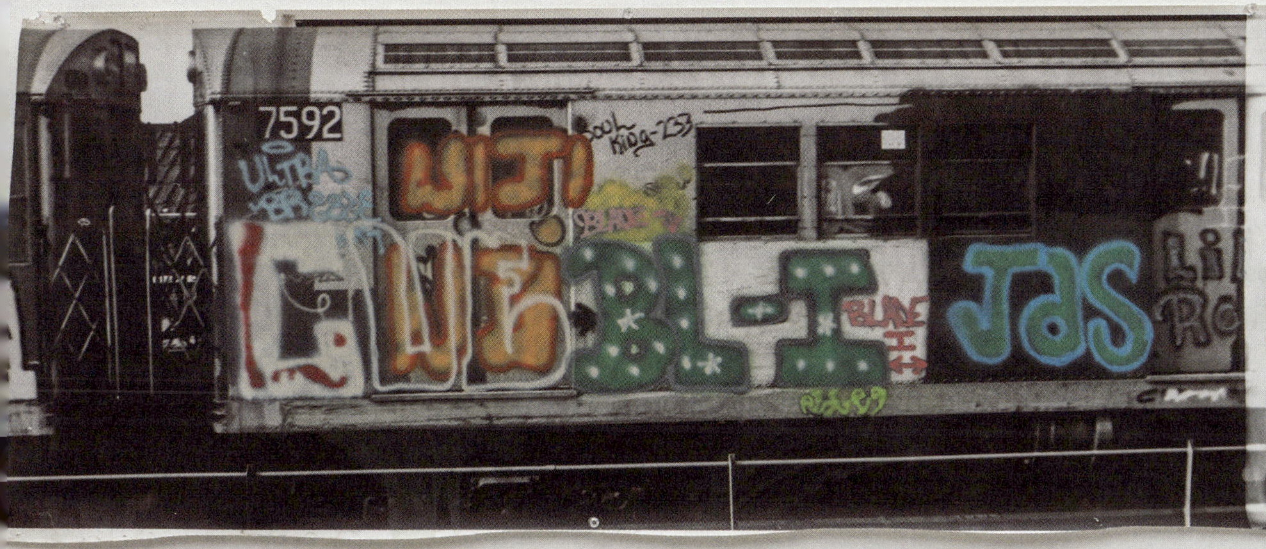


**FIGURE 2.4**

Gordon Matta-Clark, *Graffiti*, 1975. Gelatin silver print with hand coloring. © Estate of Gordon Matta-Clark, ARSNY.com, and DavidZwirner.com.

consistent. As detailed by Anssi Arte in his graphical dissection of classic graffiti typography (2015), they led toward a series of named, codified, locally categorized writing systems—techniques such as Broadway Elegant, Platform, Soft Letters, and Hi-Tech, seen in figure 2.5—that moved far beyond the letter form alone: the virtuoso figures that formed the creative vanguard of the culture codified a range of stylistic alternates (such as the cuts and cracks, the humps and feet that Arte illustrates in figure 2.6), decorative fills (from the early polka dots and candy stripes to an increasingly abstracted and technical use of color), graphic backdrops (the block colors and fluffy clouds, the fire-scapes and star-scapes that the names would sit upon), attendant characters (the Disney icons, the cartoon B-Boys, and the Vaughn Bode characters who would flank the names), as well as supplemental texts (the crew acronyms, the calendar year, and the tagged maxims and messages that each piece would also incorporate), which together came to form the foundational elements sustaining the canon. The young writers of the 1970s thus created a baseline typographical structure—a clearly defined understanding of balance, hierarchy, proportion, contrast, and unity—as much as the critical criterion of where one should reproduce this structure, which future writers were then able to twist and turn into a set of infinitely mutable arrangements, changing the key and the rhythm of a piece while still remaining within the harmonic configurations of the overarching style.

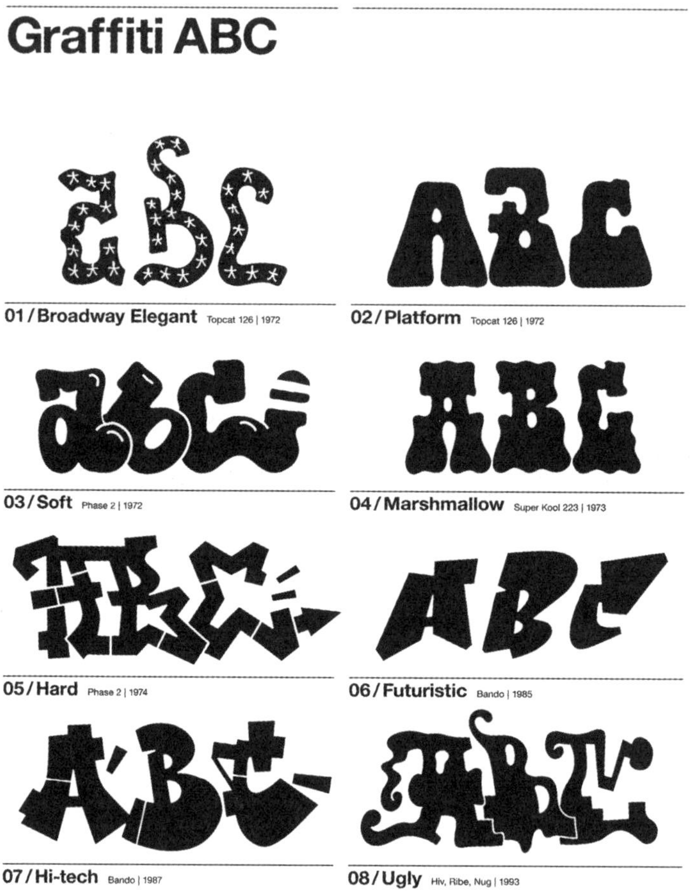


**FIGURE 2.5**

Anssi Arte, *Graffiti ABC*, 2015. From *Forms of Rockin'* by Anssi Arte (author/designer), published by Dokument Press.

It was through the dissemination of two critical graffiti documents that these conventions become officially canonized, however. Henry Chalfant and Martha Cooper's legendary book *Subway Art* (1984), colloquially called the "bible" within the graffiti scene, alongside the equally celebrated documentary film *Style Wars* (1983), co-produced by Chalfant and directed by Tony Silver, together transformed graffiti from a marginal subcultural practice to a major global aesthetic. These two documents (alongside a range of others that followed them)[6] spread and circulated the stylistic stipulations and technical traditions of this early era to aficionados across the entire world. It helped to move graffiti beyond the traditions of pen pals and writers' benches,[7] beyond word of mouth and in-person witnessing, and into a sphere of mass production that enabled the images to travel on a previously unimaginable scale. The key stylistic techniques

**Stylistical alternates**

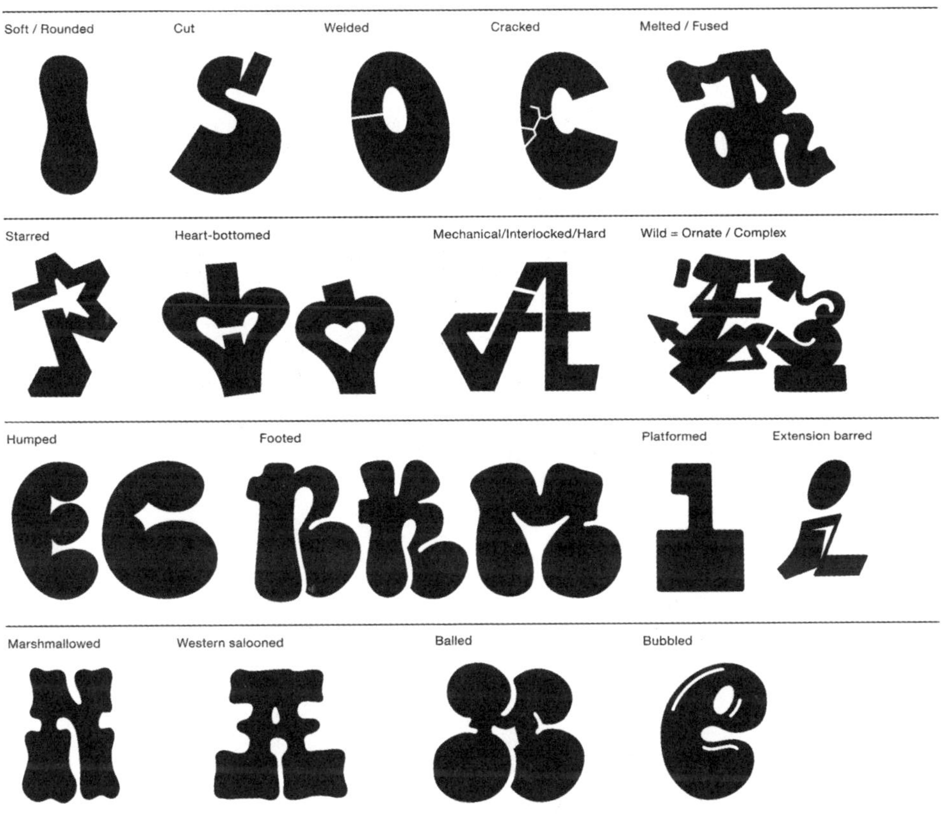


**FIGURE 2.6**

Anssi Arte, *Stylistical Alternates*, 2015. From *Forms of Rockin'* by Anssi Arte (author/designer) published by Dokument Press.

and graphic templates, the key artists and collective principles of "New York" graffiti (of just a few hundred key practitioners in just over a ten-year period of intense aesthetic creativity), thus became disseminated throughout the world via these critical canonical artifacts. *Style Wars* was thus not simply a film nor *Subway Art* a book. They were *manuals*, how-to guides for both a visual and a cultural world.

The British artist Duncan Weston's project *The World's Most Stolen Book*, a series of original paintings reworking the entirety of *Subway Art* page for page (the front cover of which can be seen in figure 2.7), begins to show the painstaking way the book was seen by its adherents. Every single image, no matter how small or apparently marginal, was examined in microscopic detail by its readers, every single image a guide to a world of alphabetical possibilities. Weston's "reproductions" thus not only become

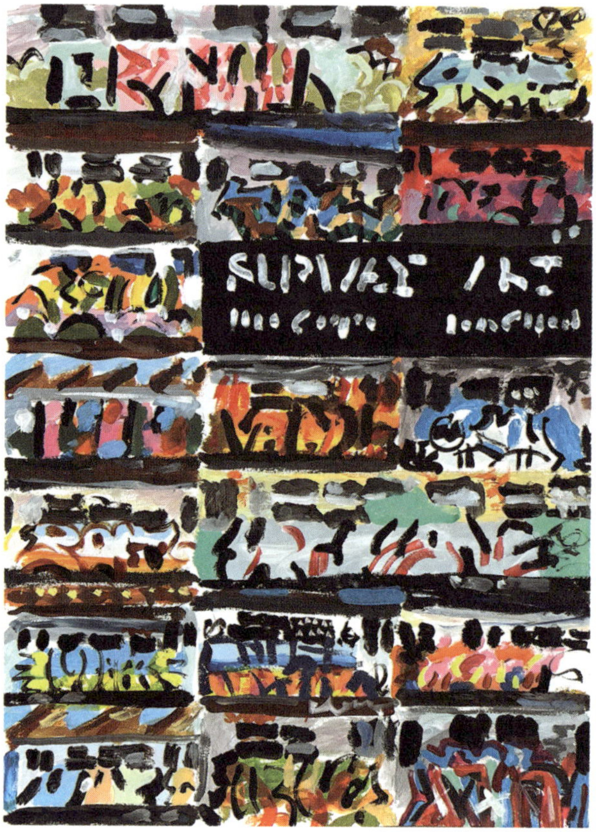

**FIGURE 2.7**
Duncan Weston, *The World's Most Stolen Book* (cover), 2021. Oil on paper. Courtesy of the artist.

a monument to both *Subway Art* and the canon-defining works produced during this era, but also try to recreate the energy and feeling that each of these images themselves contained, the explosive creativity and explosive performance held inside every photographic reproduction. The New York group Slavery Collective, however, has shown the importance of these same works through a project in which the original pieces became templates for odes to historical figure (from Gandhi to Spinoza and Laozi). Their work *Joan of Arc* (as seen in figure 2.8), for example, is an homage to "Hand of Doom," a piece produced by the renowned writer Seen in 1980. Reproducing Seen's letter shapes and shading, his backdrop and imagery, as well as the famous central dagger and fist, but transforming the letters to proclaim the eponymous name of the martyred saint, the final piece acts as tribute to both Seen's canonical work and the famous "Maid of Orleans" herself. Not only revealing the manner in which the works featured in *Subway Art*

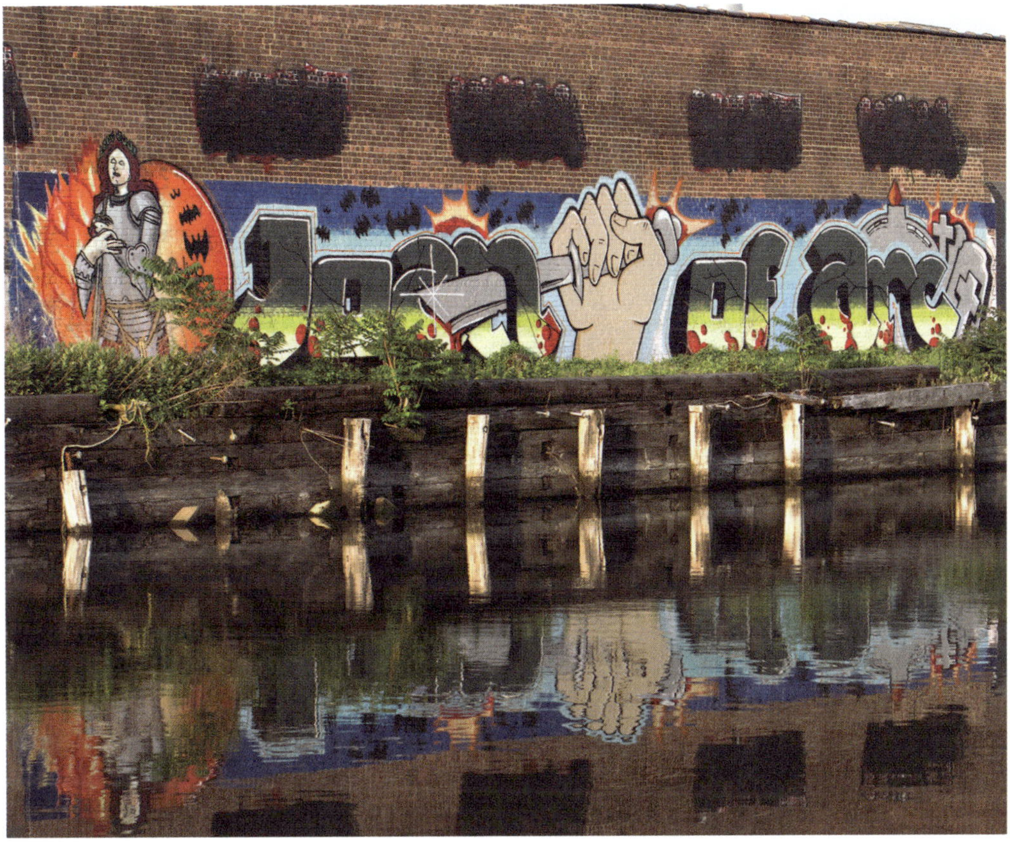

**FIGURE 2.8**
Slavery Collective, *Joan of Arc (Hand of Doom)*, New York, 2010. Courtesy of the artists.

have become sanctified in a way entirely unanticipated by the original producers, the piece—alongside other productions such as Know Thyself (a Delphic maxim), seen in figure 2.9, a reproduction of a classic work by Kell and Futura 2000—comes to reveal the basic structure of every canonical graffiti masterpiece: the signature name, the letter extensions, the backdrops, characters, and supplements that a fully-fledged masterpiece would contain, the customary hierarchies and balance of a canonical work.

Still, while *Subway Art* and *Style Wars* consecrated the graphic conventions of the aligned set, the veneration of quantity and the goal of becoming "all-city" (of being present on every subway line or in every borough) remained a clear stylistic prerequisite in these documents too. Whether one focused on stylistic *quality*—on a form of graphical embellishment vernacularly termed "style"—or stylistic *quantity*—a focus on mass[8] vernacularly termed "bombing"—the key in both cases was perceptibility and

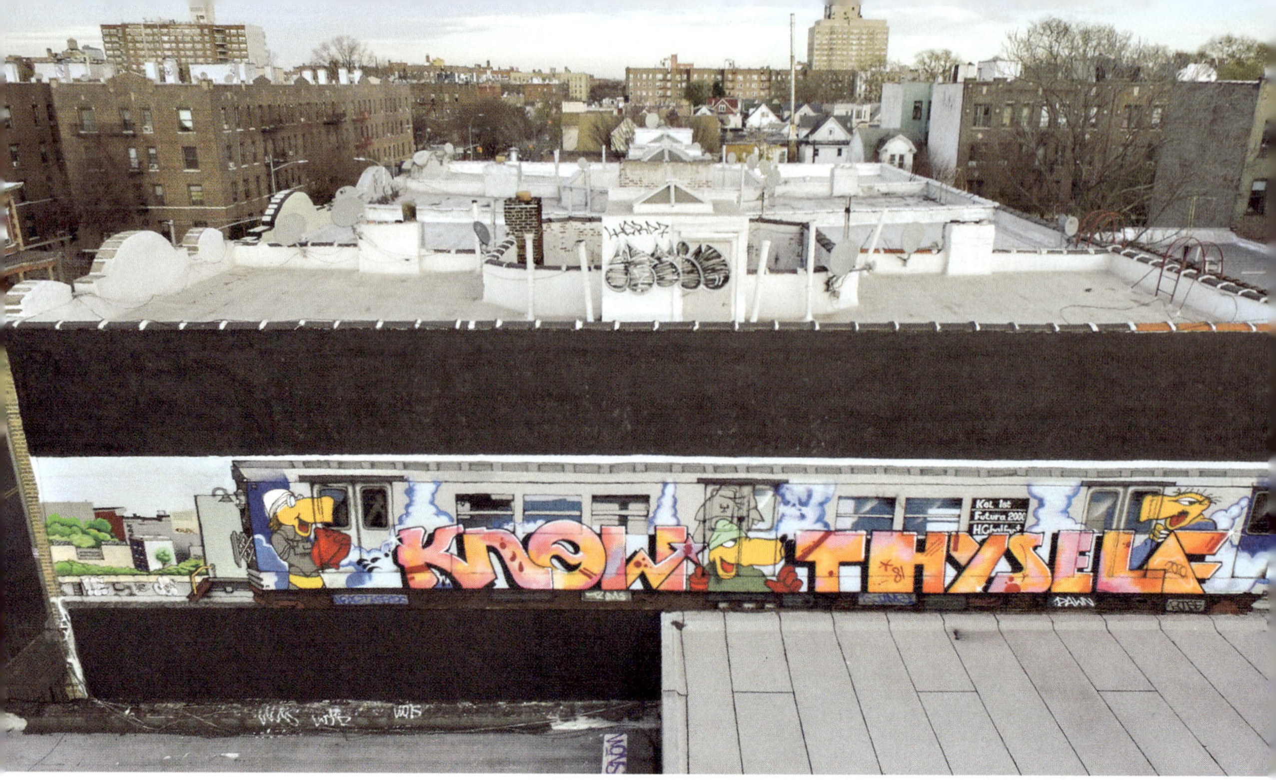


**FIGURE 2.9**
Slavery Collective, *Know Thyself*, New York, 2010. Courtesy of the artists.

captivation. Style must therefore be understood as a twofold term here: as a technical notion indicating the basic structure that enabled an image's recognition as one participating in the graffiti game and as a vernacular label that indicates an image developing beyond these fundamentals in formal terms. Whichever specific technique a writer chose to focus on, however, the goal was still to bring the name to the viewer's attention. The denominational options outlined in the canonical documents thus followed the core graffiti principle of maximum visibility, the need to be seen amid the mass of surrounding images (graffiti and nongraffiti alike); both quality and quantity were hence stylistic choices, even if the latter approach can be seen to forsake traditional aesthetic conventions of "style" in itself. The key here was a technique enabling a practitioner to take part in the visual system, to become known by their fellow participants (and thus to become in many senses alive). The key was to distribute the name within the community and the commons alike, to get up and to be *seen*.

The stylistic regulations formed within the emergent graffiti canon thus created a very clear palette of potential actions, a clear boundary of what could be produced and how improvisation could occur while an image still remained recognizable to the genre. True masters of the practice could thus link and cohere not only the letters of their own name but the letters and names of others; could create coherent, harmonic compositions and demonstrate unforeseen, unexpected linkages; could exhibit new solutions to ever-present alphabetical and architectural conundrums, all the while remaining true to the fundamentals of the canon itself. Within the basic stylistic framework we thus find artifacts that remain the same while being entirely distinctive, images set genealogically within the ancestral form while still pushing at the edge of common difference. As in all creative practices, style in graffiti thus remains implicitly derivative (the weight of the canon, as depicted in Escif's work in figure 2.10, often hanging heavily on a participant), yet within these canonical derivations lies an almost infinite improvisatory potential, an endless mediation between restrictions and possibilities. The basic rules of graffiti that developed in this early era were thus very simple (as they remain so today): one needed visibility to be publicly recognized (in both the spatial and social realm). One needed visibility to move from the social position of "toy" (a neophyte) to

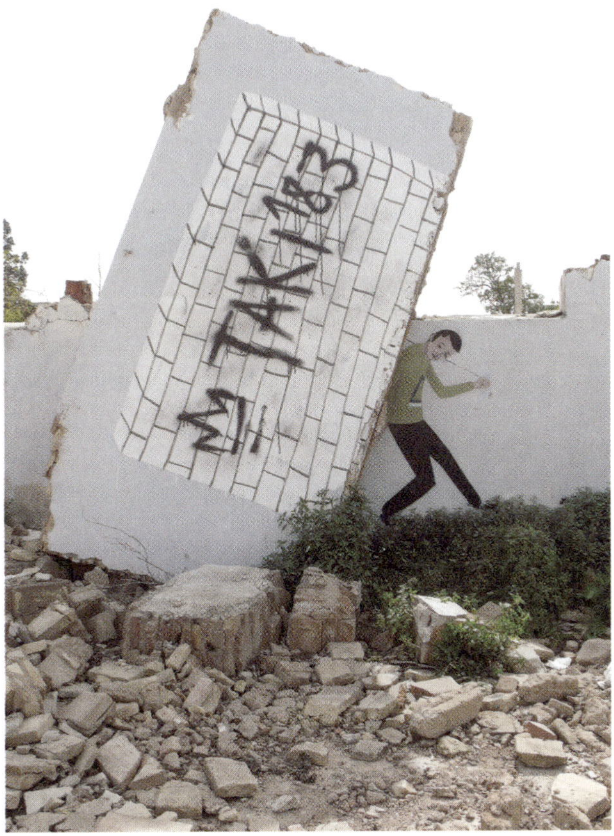


**FIGURE 2.10**
Escif, *Untitled*, Valencia, 2010. Acrylic paint on wall. Courtesy of the artist.

"king" (an expert). One needed visibility to move from the surface of the city to the surface of people's minds. And how did one obtain this? Through both the saturation and animation of the image alike.

So what does this brief sketch of the stylistic conventions of graffiti begin to reveal? I have so far elucidated the basis of graffiti's common difference, unpacking a decorative system in which the search for discernibility (molded by specific virtuoso figures and regulated by specific canonical documents) led to a graphic development of the image from an initially minimal text to a wildly complex and/or widely disseminated one, to a practice in which visual coherence remains clear (for insiders at the very least) even when stretched to its outermost limits. Yet, and critically for us here, style must be seen as something that does more than just "classifying objects as sharing, or not sharing, stylistic attributes with one another" (Gell 1998: 155). Rather, a specifically anthropological approach to style aims to unpack the way the internal structure of an image can come to echo the "unity of thought which binds members of social groups together" (p. 163). Style, what Gell terms as the "harmonic principle which unites works of art into groups, into collectivities," can thus be understood to contain a direct relation to the core anthropological concept of culture as a particular "configuration of intersubjective understandings" (p. 156). As such, beyond purely iconographic explanations, material form will here be understood to "thematize and make cognitively salient essential cultural parameters" (p. 159). A stylistic analysis of graffiti can thus tell us much more than what it looks like. It can explain the relationship between the visual and the social, between aesthetic and cultural patterns. It can explain how the production of the name (enacted via a decorative and agentive signature) and the desire for visibility (enacted through a mode of animation and distribution) connect us to the relationship between the individualized tags and the communal environment in which these culturally regulated styles are later circulated (and judged, ignored, or revered). The basics of the graffiti image thus link us to a set of classical anthropological themes, to issues of agency, objectification, distribution, captivation, animation, ambiguity, and fame, to issues the image graphically articulates through stylistic means.

## PERSONHOOD AND AGENCY *OR* THE DOUBLE SIGNATURE

Let's return again to the fundamental basis of all graffiti, *the name*, the unique name put up, the unique name emerging from the unique individual inscribed in a unique space at a unique time. This is what style in graffiti is ultimately about: the selection of the name, the placement of that chosen name onto an urban surface, the scripting of that name utilizing the typographical and ornamental foundations of the graffiti canon. From the single color tag (as seen in figure 2.11) to the two color throw-up (as seen in figure 2.12) to the multicolor masterpiece (as seen in figure 2.13), this signature-signature is fundamental to graffiti, no matter how spare or how embellished it may

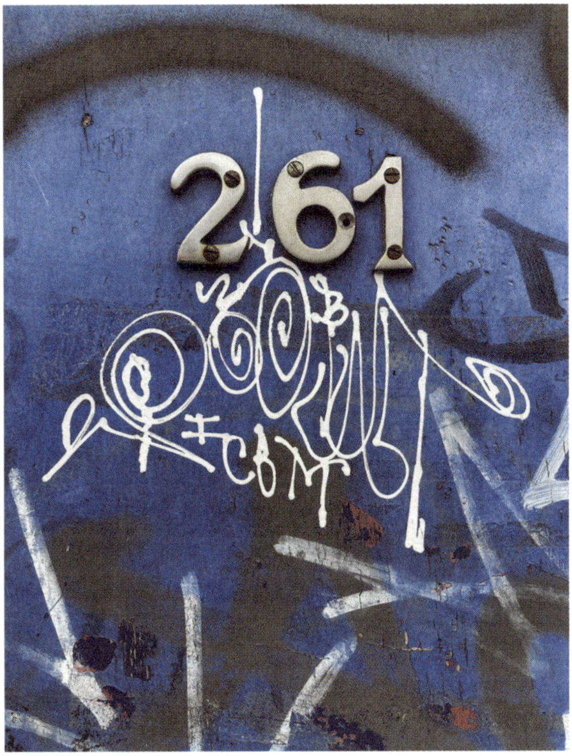


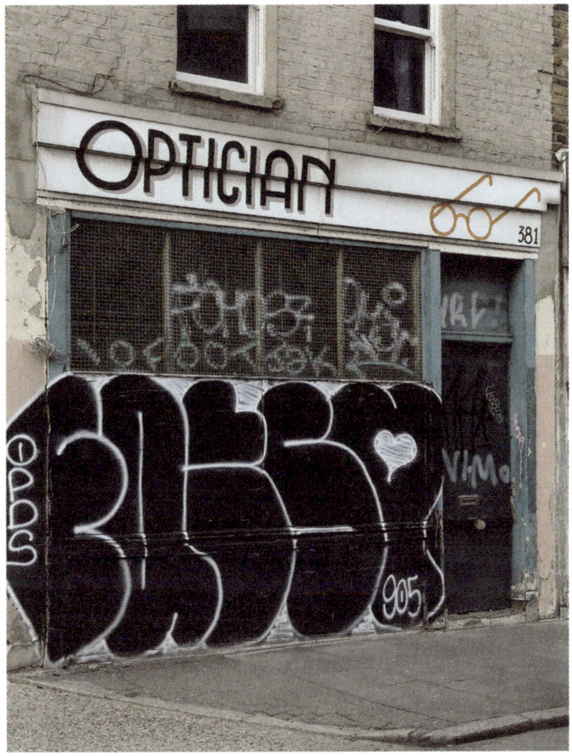


**FIGURE 2.11**
*Wombat*, 2023, London. Photo: Alex Ellison.

**FIGURE 2.12**
*Fatso*, 2014, East London. Photo: Alex Ellison.

be. Graffiti style thus *is* this signature, a signature artifact that, like all signatures, acts both as a material remnant of the absent writer and a material verification of their agency too. While all signatures are alike, then, they must also be understood to be irrevocably unique, their recognizable uniqueness being that which enables the signature to successfully function. The signature in its classical form thus acts as a marker and authorization of identity, an inscription securing an irrevocable identity claim. In a parallel manner, the artistic signature—first recognized in the movement from collective to individual authorship seen within post-Renaissance art—can likewise be seen to both confirm and corroborate the artist's prior *presence*. As Horst Bredekamp argued, the signature is here understood as a "witness to the self" (Bredekamp 2018: 45), a form

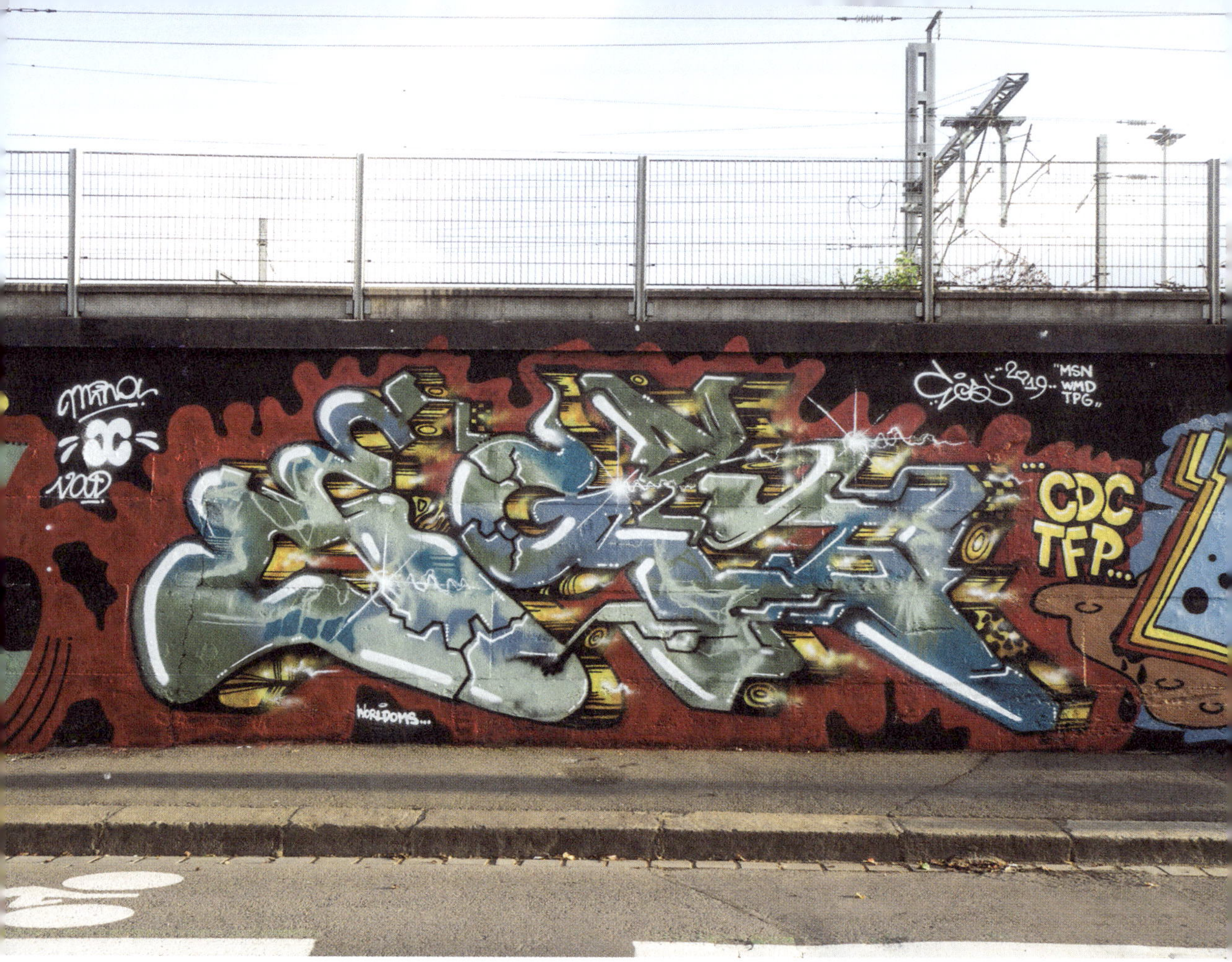


**FIGURE 2.13**
*Egs*, 2019, Rennes, France. Courtesy of the artist.

of inscription that authenticates itself through the "first person singular" (p. 51). It is hence an image that is both created *by* and speaks *for* the artist, that speaks through the "I" of the "maker who speaks of his product" as much as the "me" of the object "that speaks of its maker" (p. 62). In this way, then, the artistic signature—as seen in the works of Jan Van Eyck that Bredekamp analyzes—both proclaims the name of its producer while simultaneously announcing itself to us in the first person; it asserts "Remio Me Pinxit" (Remio Painted Me) while likewise declaring "I Remio" at the same time (as seen in figure 2.14). Each tag a writer forms thus becomes more than just text, more than just image. It affirms the existence of a work that is "both created object and autonomous subject" (Bredekamp 2018: 58–59), of a set of works that consist of "anorganic material and yet function as if they were alive" (p. 53).

This concept of artifactual personhood (Gell 1998)—an idea giving selfhood and agency to artifacts, not just people—may at first appear to be entirely at odds with the "rational" distinction between subject and object/active and passive that exists within "modern" societies. Yet this way of regarding the graffiti image is entirely dominant among its practitioners, a truism so true it remains taken for granted. As the legendary New York graffiti writer Lee explained to cultural historian Ivor Miller, the "letters" he and his fellow writers produced were "actually images of people" (Miller 1994: 165). Moreover, as style developed, Lee continued, the images went beyond mere letters, became "not words . . . not a name anymore" but "more of a living thing that you have created" (p. 166).[9] Lee thus here outlines Bredekamp's argument precisely. He sketches out the "me"/"I" paradox in which the image both *is* the artist and is an agentic object in its own right, is both portrait and living creation simultaneously. We thus have a set of works that, like Jackson Pollock's drip paintings discussed by Gell, both act as a set of "(non-representational) self-portraits" (Gell 1998: 17), while also coming to act as a "person, or at least a partial person," in their own right, a "congealed residue of performance and agency in object-form" (p. 68). Here, then, we have a set of works that are not only commonly anthropomorphized—as in Remio's grimacing and giggling letter Rs in figure 2.14 and Veks's beaming tag in figure 2.16—but commonly understood to

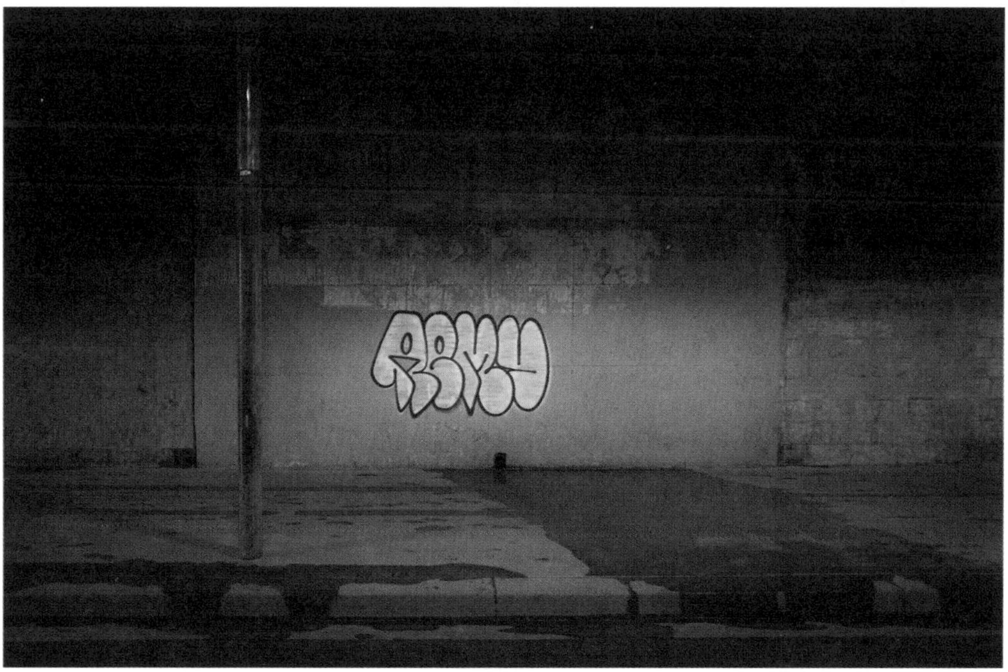

**FIGURE 2.14**
*Untitled (Remio)*, 2022, Paris. Photo: Gökhan S.

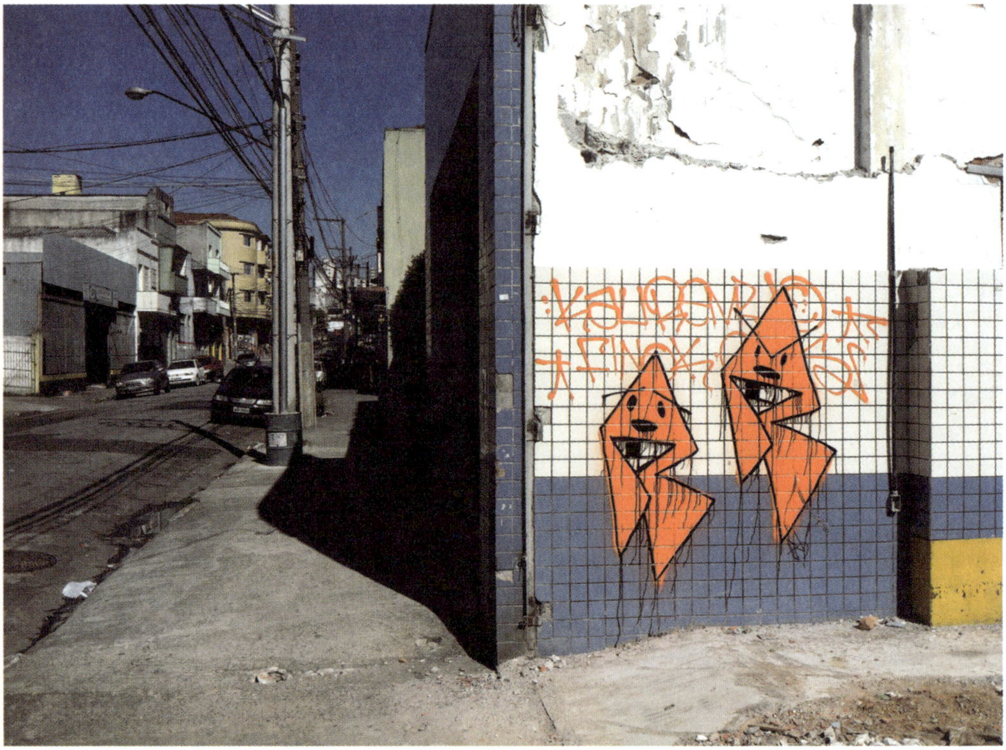

**FIGURE 2.15**
*Remio*, Sao Paulo, 2009. Courtesy of the artist.

imitate body forms too. The anatomy[10] of each letter—its links and loops let alone their shoulders and spines—can thus come to replicate the movement of a (break)dancing body with its arms twisted and legs splayed. The body of the writer and the body of the letterform thus intertwine and mirror one another, the text manifesting as a form that has been caught by a photograph in the tenth of the second as they bend on the spot, sway from left to right, pop and lock like a living breathing body. From the hard and angular texts to the soft and bubbled ones, the graffiti image can thus be seen to carry a bodily energy, a cartoonish feeling of flesh and blood (as seen in Honet's characterful piece in figure 2.17, for example). Graffiti thus not only comes to stand out (in a gestalt figure/ground reversal) as something artifactual, three-dimensional, but here takes on a lifelike character itself, acting as a still life of the writer while also taking on a unique life and agency of its own.

Not only containing the visceral remnant of their producers, however, the classical signature also contains the residue of their actions and objectives too. It functions not only as a marker of personhood but as a functional tool that, when placed in the

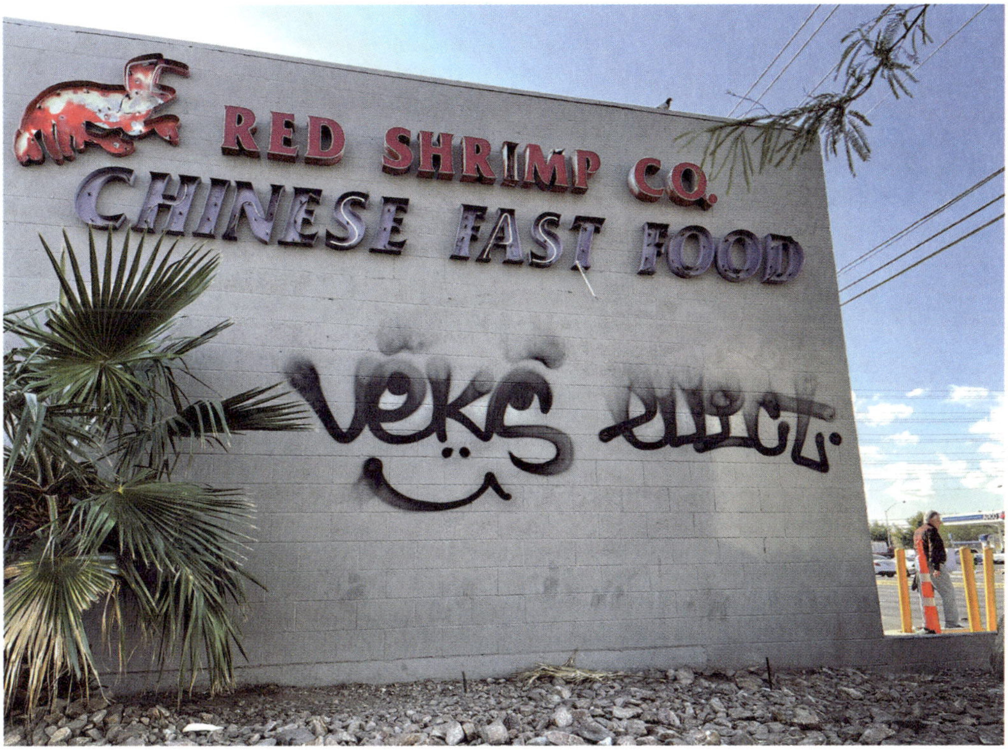


**FIGURE 2.16**
Veks and Evict (KYT), *Untitled (Red Shrimp)*, 2022. Las Vegas, Nevada. Courtesy of the artists.

correct location, acts both *for* us and *as* us. The signature thus carries not only identity but intent. It can legally evidence intent, in fact, authorizing that within which it is set, declaring it as true and original, as that which we sanction and approve. The signature thus does not just say something but *does* something in the world (containing, as an illocutionary act, the power to authorize marriage, divorce, even death). As such, the graffiti signature must be understood to contain an agency founded on the presumption of this intent, an agency able to then impress or disgust us, to compel exaltation or destruction, to enjoin us to replicate or digitally capture it. Much more than just "I was here," then, it is "I committed here" that the signature also affirms, verifying its commitment to the action in which it was produced. The "meaning" of graffiti is this commitment to action in itself, its affirmation of the very act through which it comes to life. The canonical graffiti image thus not only traces the movement of an unseen person, leaving a part of that person on the material surface, but so specifies their material intent, a pledge turned from flesh into stone. It authorizes the self and their intentions. It acts as witness not just to the presence of the writer but so too their promise.

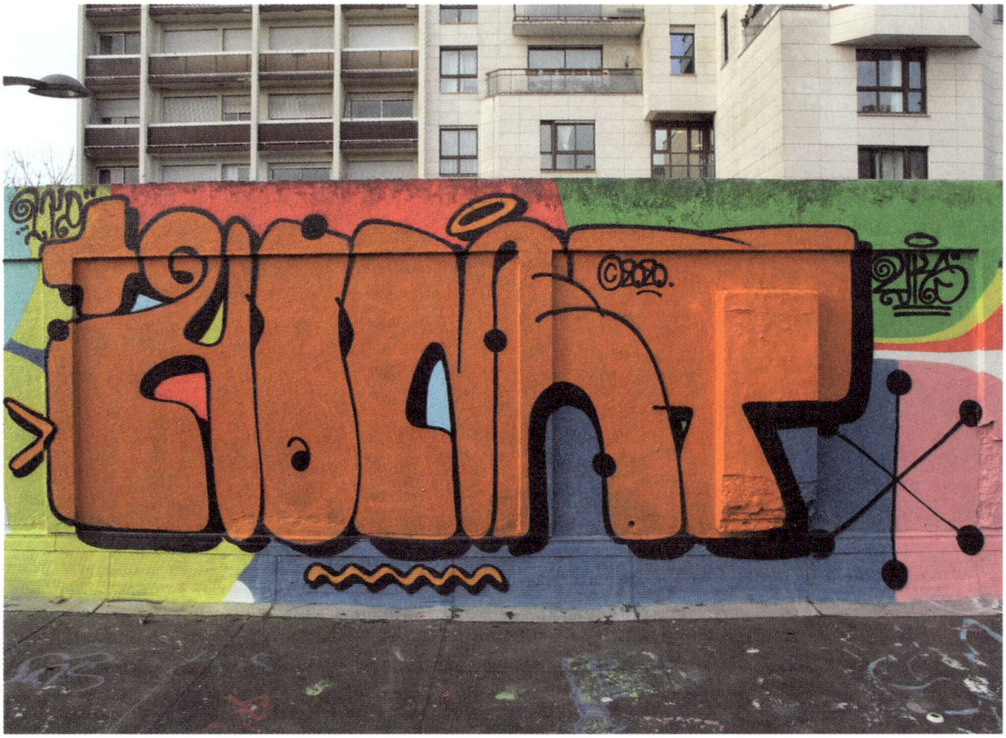

**FIGURE 2.17**
*Honet*, Paris, 2020. Courtesy of the artist.

Just like our doubly powerful signature, graffiti likewise reveals a dual mode of artifactual attachment, a mode in which the producers of the image first attach themselves to the things that they decorate (a bond between marker and site), before which these objects attach *them*selves onto further actors in the social field (a bond between site and spectator). The initial mode of objectification (from person to object) is thus transferred onward in the social chain (from object to viewer). Like the ornamental art Gell describes, the graffiti signature can thus be understood as a social technology through which "access to other persons can be attained" (Gell 1998: 68), a technology that forms an "attachment between persons and things . . . mediated by surface decoration" (p. 74). Just as with painting, as Christopher Tilley has explained, the viewing of the graffiti signature can be understood not simply as "an act of pure vision" but rather as one that establishes "bodily contact between the painter . . . and the painted" (Tilley 2004: 18). The marker of identity present in the signature image clings to those who witness it, coming to "diffuse out into the ambience" before being "incorporated by the onlooker in the process of perception" (Gell 1998: 223). Like a name penciled on the inside of a book, let alone the scribbled marginalia that adorns and embellishes it, the handwritten marking turns the mass-produced into the personal (engaging some people, disturbing others). It places a remnant of the human actor directly onto the space in which the image now resides, alarming as much as it delights, excluding as much as it includes. The agency held within the graffiti signature thus attracts and absorbs us, willingly or not. It compels a relationship between viewer and artifact, dispersing agency amid both cultural and material environments. It acts as an intermediary set in the space between producer, artifact, and viewer, an image tethered to the unique personhood of its producer luring the beholder into its relational form.

## ANIMATION TO AMBIGUITY *OR* VISUAL DELIGHT

The graffiti image can thus be understood as a sign of personhood and agency, as a signature marking intent and promise, and an intermediary attaching the body to the city and the image to the viewer. Yet what is missing in this discussion so far is the crucial factor of what will be called *animation* (following Gell once more), the affective power of the image to captivate via the generation of visual delight (or disgust). While, as we will see in our next section, the saturated image can stylistically captivate using the most rudimentary graphic techniques, the captivating quality of animation emerges directly through the ornamental virtues of the image and its ability to attract through its innate graphical composition. The visual delight harnessed here can thus generate a sensory pleasure via the optical experience of the decorative. The ornamental is perceptible, and its perception contains an affective potential far beyond the base meaning of the word. The ornamental is sensible, and the sensibilities it awakens emerge whether they are overtly desired or not. The ever-present danger (and potential) of the image is its ability to create these relations through which, as Tilley has noted, in "looking at something, I am 'touched' by that which I look at" (Tilley 2004: 17). The rhythm and balance, the harmony and poise, the technical and imaginative prowess that an image exhibits can hence be understood to contain a figural power to move its viewer: The unexpected passage of the pen, the humorous or bewildering movement of a line, thus incorporates a dangerous, visceral impact addressing us through the level of the felt. It contains an animative potential that, in graffiti, emerges through at least three specific (and often conjoined) ways: through the choreography and purity of the line, through the engulfing impact of complexity, and through the unstable impenetrability of ambiguity.

In our first case, then, we have the captivating qualities of *simplicity*. Take one of the most minimal of images within the graffiti canon, a simply stylized tag. In figure 2.18, which shows two large-scale tags produced by Mosa, we can find an innately rhythmic set of works that swiftly pierce and slickly arc through their various letter forms. We find two tags in which the letters take on differing shapes and positions (the low "v" on the first "m" compared with the high one on the second, the severe peak of the first "a" compared with a flattened bar on the second) yet in which each creates a balanced and poised totality. There are no power lines or contrasting colors here. No backgrounds or characters. Nothing added save a sharpened underscore on the first tag and a set of inverted commas on the second. As likewise seen in the tags of figure 2.19, what becomes apparent here are a set of clean strokes tracking from left to right, a set of individual forms turning single parts into conjoined wholes. We have a set of cutting lines and sweeping curves that are about purity, coherence, rhythm, that test out the possibilities of the letterform but that elaborate nothing but the letter itself. Here, then, it is subtle eloquence rather than wild exuberance that is displayed, the "elegant simplicity" emergent via "economy of color and certainty of line" (Grabar 2009: 23). The wandering track and passage of the line are still critical, the creation of a gestural dynamism, an energy and palpable tension in which, as Oleg Grabar has said, our senses become affected by the "languid elongation of a loop or the daggerlike precision of a hasta [a cross stroke

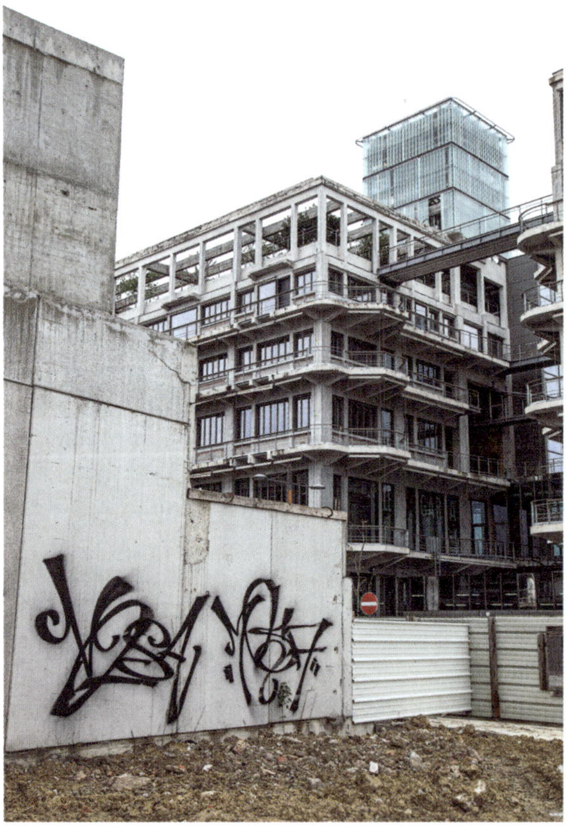

**FIGURE 2.18**
*Mosa*, 2022. Courtesy of the artist and *Tramontana Magazine*. Image by Elliot Sitbon.

as seen here in the letter As]" (Grabar 1992: 107), in which an image's speed and flow captivate us through its visceral motion. Yet here the gesture works in relation to the balance formed through its unifying cadence, the perfect scale, the perfect control, that together create the perfectly discernible artifact. Impact here thus emerges through an image concentrated to a state of clarity, captivation via the witness of a "hand drilled to perfection in the practice of a skill," through the "consistency of linear movements" and the "rhythm . . . compelled by the repeated beat of the vertical parts of letters" (Grabar 1992: 103). Impact comes through a gestural purity in which nothing more than is strictly necessary is added.

At the same time, the knowledge that the production of the image is a onetime affair, an image produced "live" with no retakes allowed, likewise transforms the way the signature is appreciated. The perfect "hand style" thus balances the harmonic beauty

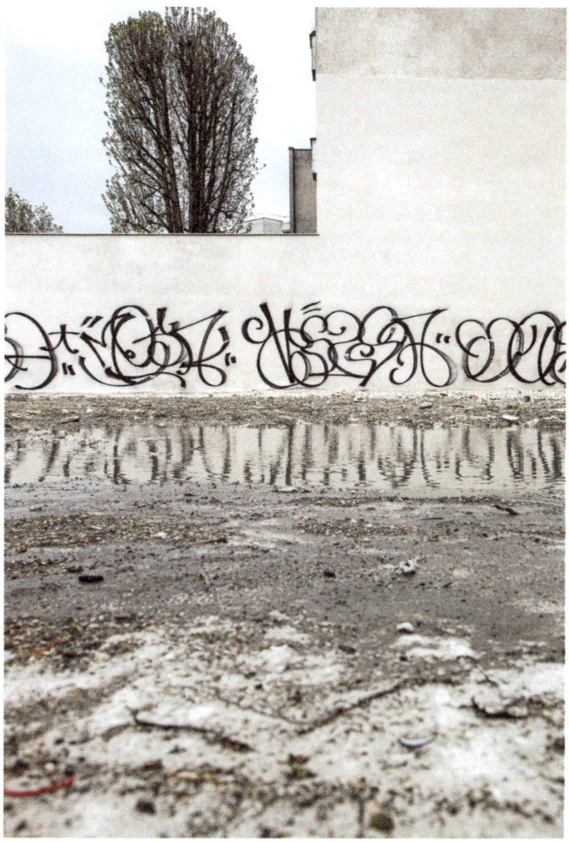

**FIGURE 2.19**
*Mosa*, 2022. Courtesy of the artist and *Tramontana Magazine*. Image by Elliot Sitbon.

of the proportionate with the charged charisma of the performative. It creates a distinct energy in which we follow the movement like a dance (as discussed in more detail in chapter 5). This is hence a graphic style that embraces the "utmost simplicity" because any unnecessary embellishment, as suggested by the critic John Martin in his discussion of the work of choreographer and dancer Mary Wigman, "would only defeat its purpose of expression" (Martin 1983 [1933]: 27). Captivation here thus emerges from a simplicity that "establishes its rhythms with great clarity and thereafter touches only the high spots of its design, leaving it to you to fill in the space and complete the form" (p. 27). Here, then, simplicity is never simple, is, perhaps, the hardest thing to achieve. Here simplicity means that the bare bones of the object must stand up by themselves, a return to purity that only one who has mastered complexity can truly assemble. The distilled elegance of an expert tag thus gives us the freedom to *see* the rhythm, the room to visually apprehend the flow.[11] Virtuosity thus emerges through a "discriminating" minimalism in which "the more simple the shape the more careful must be the handling of the surface" (Gombrich 1984: 31). Virtuosity generates visibility through the expert choice of the right space, the right tool, color, scale, through a condensed subtlety and an expert completion of a rhythmic dance.

While simplicity creates a particular feeling of captivation through the witness of visual grace, *complexity*, in terms of both technique and thought, functions through a striking visibility that traps us within the dense materiality of the image. A fully elaborated masterpiece, a text-image with intersecting dimensions and perspectival shifts, with innumerable embellishments and ornaments, fades and shines—as seen in Egs and Trama's emblematic piece in figure 2.20—generates an animative quality in which the individual parts can never be fully separated from the whole, a "mazy dance in which our eyes become readily lost" (Gell 1998: 76). The name, the signature, thus here becomes supplemented by the ornamental, overpowered by its additional form. Rather than the monochrome tag or throw-up—a minimalism of color that enables a focus on the flow of the letters themselves—here the classic chrome-and-black is exchanged for a kaleidoscope of color. Simplicity is thus overtaken by a virtuosity in which the writer is able to form a coherent piece from a multitude of elements, is able to hold complexity together before it explodes into chaos. While, at its very basis, every complex piece could be reduced down to the tag that sits at its core—the raw name here being fleshed out into a larger bodily form—the material density of the image works to both draw in and repel sight. As in Egs's solo piece seen in figure 2.21, a piece's optical illusions can turn surface into depth, figure into ground. We become enmeshed by a surplus in which the image builds up alternating hierarchies and sequences, in which it bifurcates and radiates in unexpected and dramatic ways. Yet the compositional convolution that the viewer observes comes not only via *technical* complexity but so too via the *conceptual* density emergent through the shock of novel movement. Here, the unexpected (and thus often witty) arrangement, the graphic repositioning that goes beyond the expected script, becomes exhilarating. These works confound us not via geometric

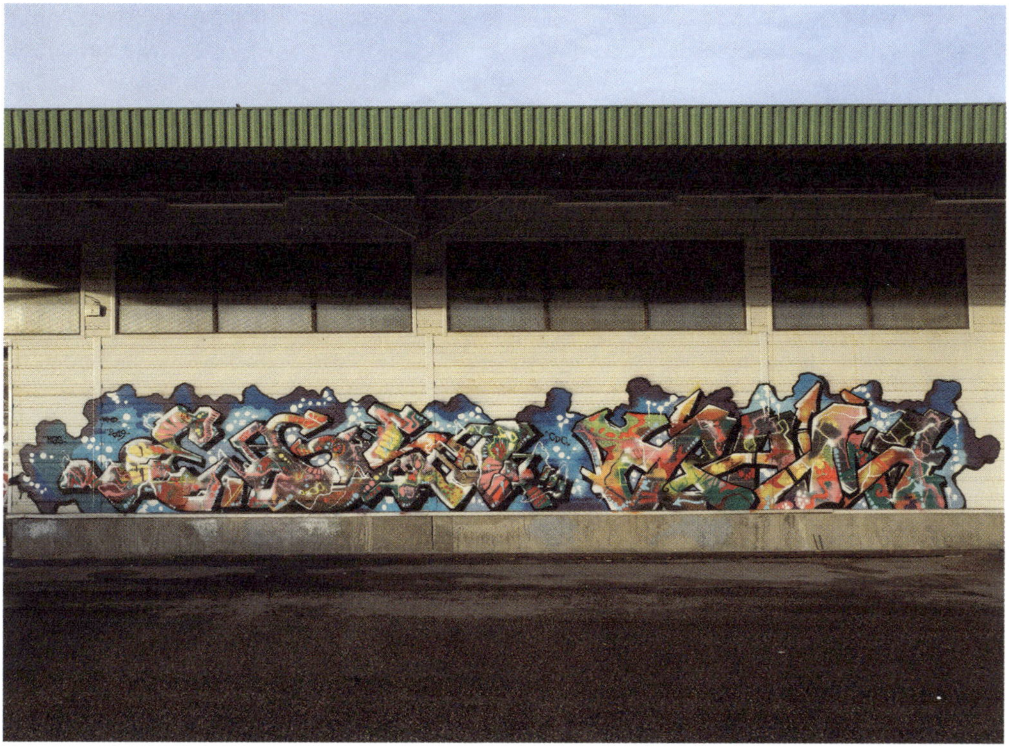

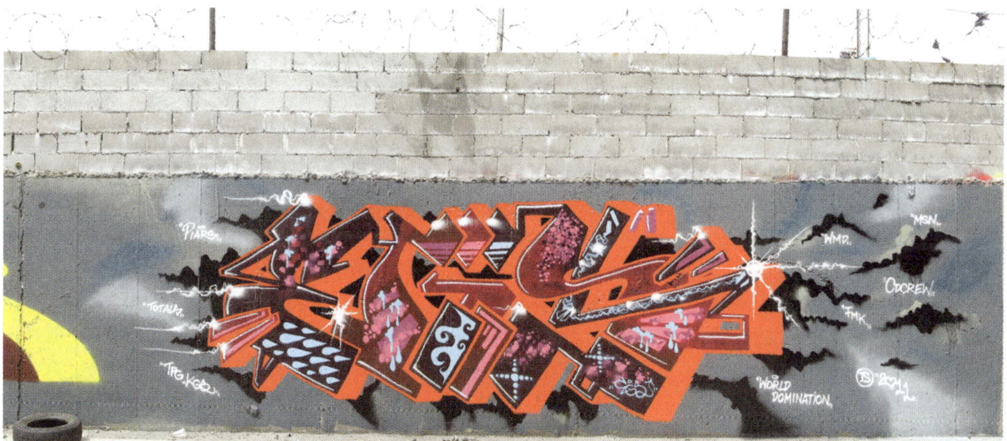


**FIGURE 2.20**
*Egs & Trama*, Helsinki, 2019. Courtesy of the artists.

**FIGURE 2.21**
*Egs*, New York, 2011. Courtesy of the artist.

intricacy but through unexpected movements that defeat our expectations, by startling linkages that, as with a labyrinthine pattern or a visual pun, could never have been foreseen. Honet's piece in figure 2.22, like his earlier work in figure 2.17, for example, does not contain the intricate complexity of Egs's earlier works, but rather contains connections (the "N" to the "E" in both cases, for example) that I still find incredibly satisfying even after having seen them a hundred times. Its complexity thus emerges through an animative complexity whose movements and internal rules we simply cannot begin to anticipate. Its complexity emerges through the witnessing of an expert playing against themself (and somehow still winning).

Complexity thus morphs between these poles, between the games of ornamental density and compositional intricacy. Both approaches, however, work to generate the "pleasurable frustration," as Gell termed it, through which we become "drawn into the pattern and held inside it, impaled, as it were, on its bristling hooks and spines" (Gell 1998: 80). Both harness the frustration in which we are unable to "follow the sequence of steps in the artist's 'performance,'" an inability to untangle the image that forms a "delay, or lag" in their visual comprehension (p. 81). The rotating of angles and axes, the

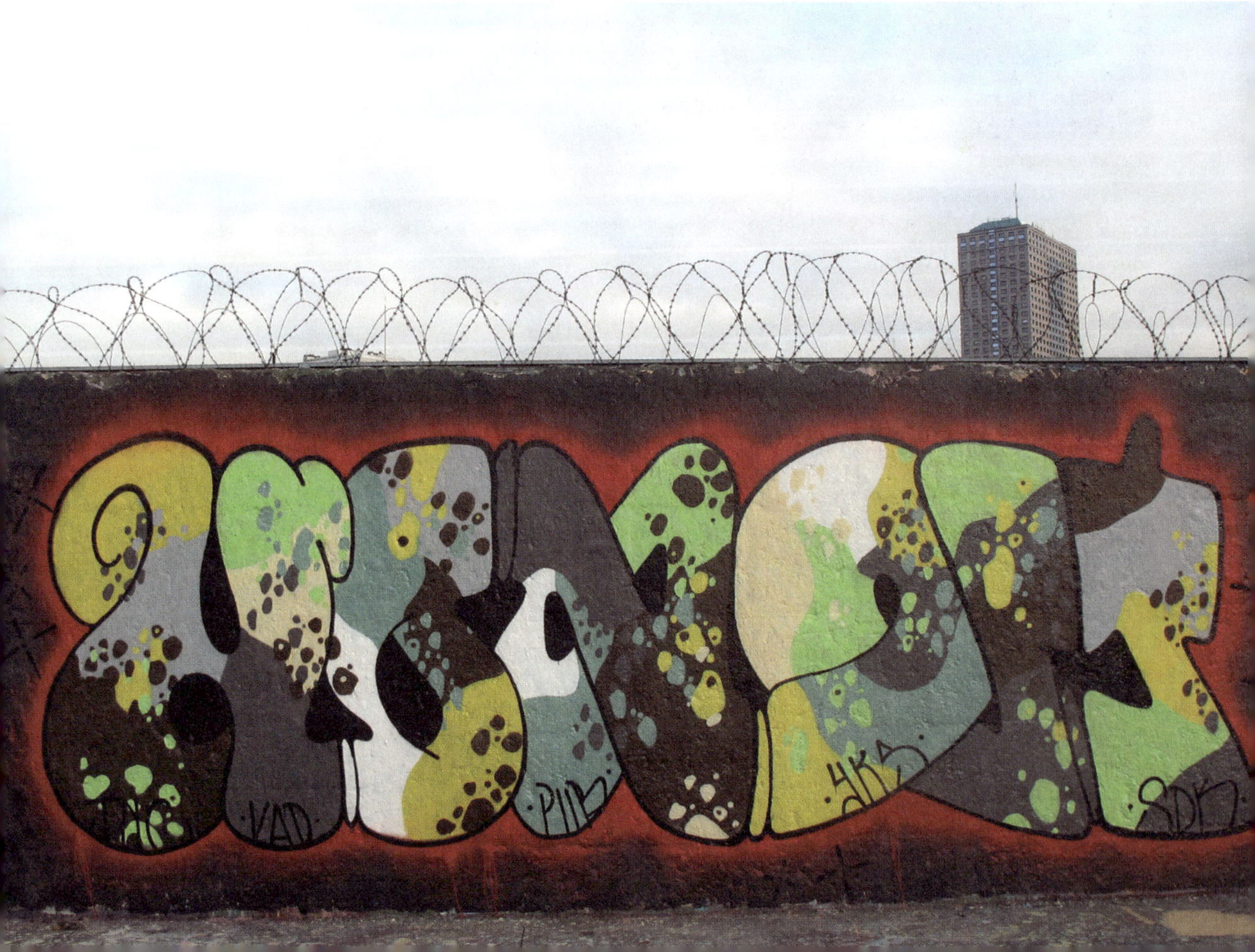

intersection of figure and ground, or the baffling intermixing of forms can thus come to form an uneven exchange, an "unfinished business" in which the viewer is forever entangled in the "cognitive resistance" of pattern (pp. 81–82). It can create a feeling in which an object is "never fully possessed" but always "in the process of becoming possessed" (p. 81). In this way, then, the complex graffiti image comes to function through what Grabar terms a "monoptic" style, a writing whose reading is "complex and time-consuming" and involves "rotating the object or being rotated around it" (Grabar 1992: 103). Like the classical maze patterns Gell also discusses, complexity thus creates "obstacles" or "sticking points" in which our eyes are caught, "impassable frontier[s]" in which we become trapped (Gell 1998: 90). It creates a captivating optical blockage that we fight to turn back into flow.

Whether taking on simple or complex approaches, however, graffiti often adopts a further animative quality too, that of the captivative power of *ambiguity*. Here the image pushes into a space of almost (and often) total indecipherability. Here, whether embracing the gestural purity of the line or the ornamental complexity of the convoluted, the ambiguous creates a work that almost entirely resists its own apprehension. As seen in Delta's pieces in figures 2.23 and 2.24, for example, here the graffiti image seems to reject the primary rule of the graffiti aesthetic itself, that of its participation in the fundamental game of visibility. Something is being revealed and concealed simultaneously. We see the piece but the name is hidden, veiled.

While much of this urge toward the illegible can be seen to have arisen from a classic subcultural desire to restrict accessibility for the sake of purity, to produce work that could be seen but not *read* by outsiders, the level of visual erudition developed by insiders means that aficionados will often be able to recognize an artist's style regardless even of the existence of visible letters themselves. Delta's three-dimensional puzzles may thus contain a level of graphic distortion, refusing a status as either text or image, confounding categories and shattering their own name, yet this mode of ambiguity must in fact be understood to function as not merely a tool of obfuscation but one of attraction, a mode of constitutive ambiguity that makes us look. Here, then, we become attracted not via *what* is written but by the sensation that an encounter with the writing itself provides. As Anthony Forge wrote regarding the art of the Abelam people of Papua New Guinea, what we find is the creative ambiguity of "poetry, not the lack of clarity of poorly written prose" (Forge 2017: 104). What captivates is hence not the inability to see but the feeling that there is more contained in the image than can ever be seen in itself. As Ludovic Coupaye has argued through his own ethnographic research with the Abelam, the power of ambiguity emerges from the particular mode of engagement that the equivocal image enforces, an agency that comes not only from the "aesthetic effects" these images produce but from the "interpretation processes they demand" (Coupaye

**FIGURE 2.22**
*Honet,* Paris, 2022. Courtesy of the artist.

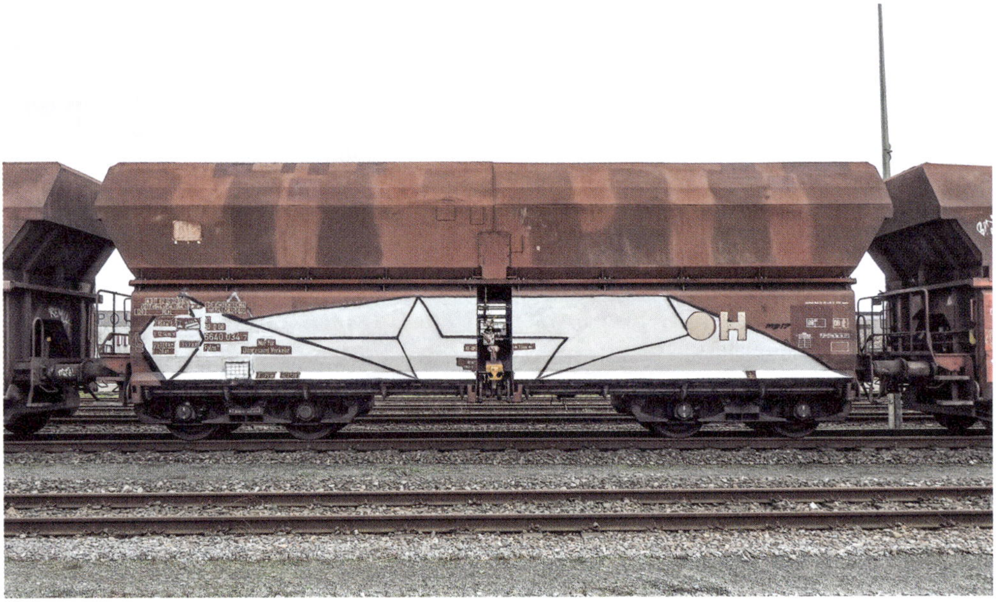

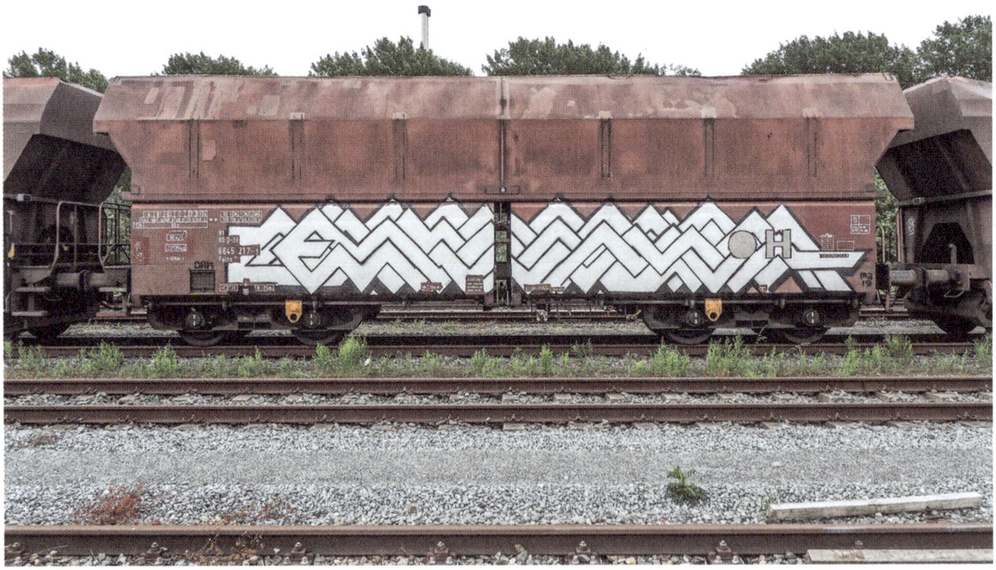

**FIGURE 2.23**
Boris Tellegen/Delta, *Untitled (Freight Project)*, 2017, Amsterdam Westpoort. Courtesy of the artist.

**FIGURE 2.24**
Boris Tellegen/Delta, *Untitled (Freight Project)*, 2019, Amsterdam Westpoort. Courtesy of the artist.

2017: 252). An image with clear content and materiality can thus become all too easy for us to digest and cognize, and hence become literally *un*remarkable, slipping down with dangerously silky ease.[12] The ambiguous image, however, traps us through its resistance to both evaluation and comprehension, through a need to interpret we can never come to fulfill.[13] It forces us to attend to it. The common disparagement of graffiti as "incomprehensible" can thus be seen as a fundamental power rather than failing of the style. Ambiguity, as Jakub Stejskal has likewise explained in a critical appraisal of Forge's work, forms "a referential instability that creates an aura of mystery around the objects" (Stejskal 2016: 90), a "striking visibility" that comes to increase the object's "authoritative presence" (p. 85). Like the pleasurable feeling of clarity engendered by the witnessing of simplicity, like the bodily convolution engendered by complexity, the ambiguous image creates a sensation through which we become struck by or sucked into the image. It creates a visible virtuosity activated by the density of an image's animation, a captivation inherent within the graphic qualities of the form itself.

## DISTRIBUTION TO SATURATION *OR* THE MACRO-OBJECT

Graffiti can hence be considered as the signature that stands and acts for the self (that contains both identity and intention), that captivates us through its relational density (the intermediary conjoining producer, artifact, and viewer), and as an animative image captivating via simplicity, complexity, and ambiguity. Yet more than perhaps any other form of art, graffiti also functions through distribution and mass, not through the singularity of the single tag but through its disseminated multiplicity. As I hope should now be clear, the fundamental aim of graffiti style is to spread one's signature-signature throughout the social and spatial milieu. And distribution spreads the primary artifactual attachment of personhood over both time and space, forming a set of objects "indexing a distributed person" (Gell 1998: 232), a set of finished works produced in different places and at different times that together circulate and multiply the self. Take figure 2.25, then, a screenshot of a few of the tens of thousands of graffiti works produced by the writer 10Foot.[14] The disseminated graffiti signature we see defies the physical restrictions of the artist's body through the production of artifacts that act as disposable, separable parts of the artist themselves. The painted surface can thus be considered as a "physically detached fragment" of the artist distributed "beyond the body-boundary" (Gell 1998: 104). The dispersed objects we leave within the world multiply the self and enable an expansion outside our brute corporeal limits. In this way, then, the graffiti signature becomes a distributed part of the self that, like the "tombs" or "memorials" of the Western canon, extends individuals "beyond the confines of biological life" (Gell 1998: 223). Graffiti thus creates a body materially distributed in both time and space. It creates a body of work functioning through scale, accumulation, magnitude.

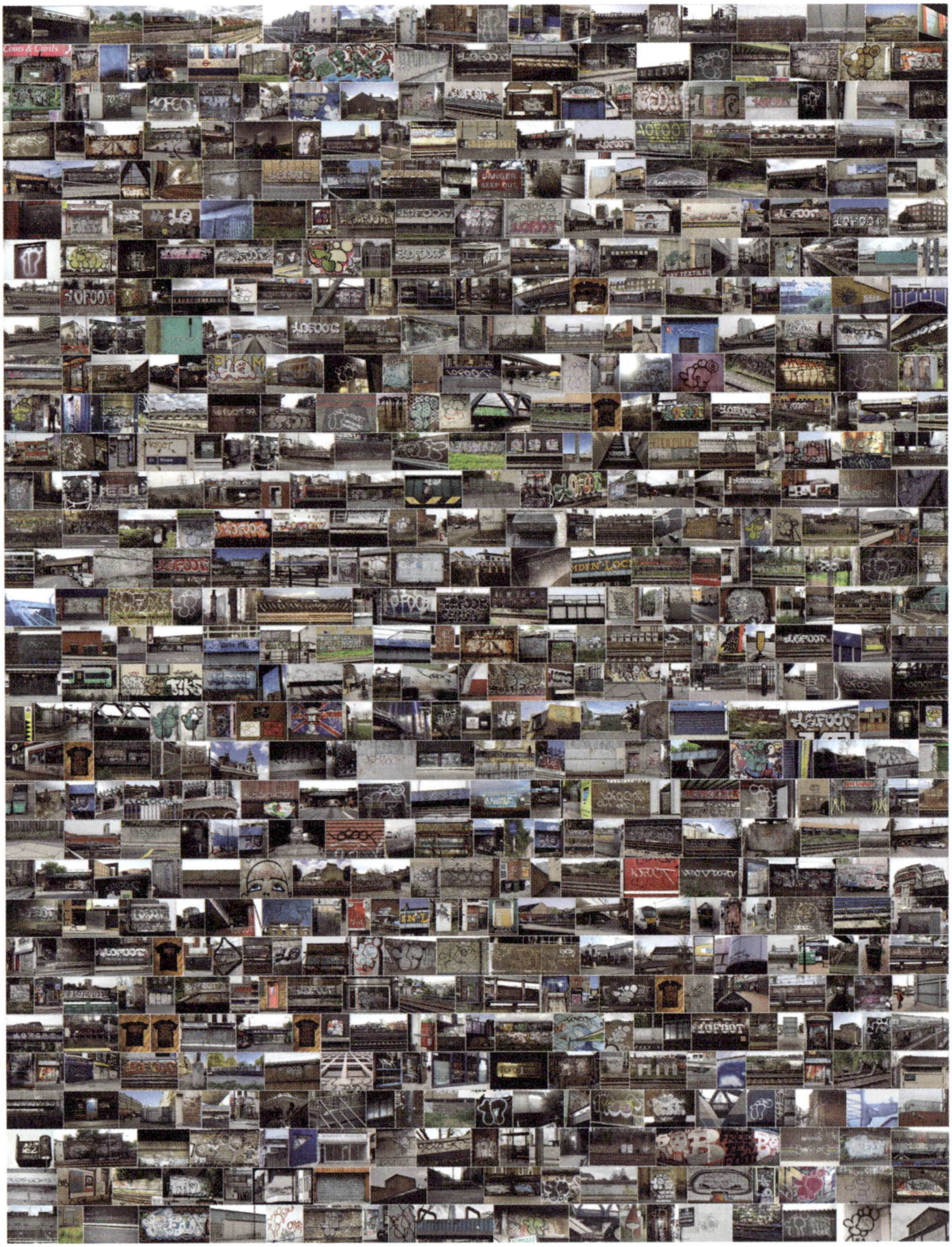

**FIGURE 2.25**
*Ten Feet of Mass*. Screenshot by author of the search term "10Foot" on Flickr. March 31, 2023.

This concept of distribution pushes us toward an understanding of art in which totality rather than singularity becomes key, and hence connects us straightforwardly with the notion of the artistic oeuvre prevalent within Western art. As a concept in which it is the total works of an artist that are significant—the set, as Gell says, of "early works, middle-period works, late works" that are "disseminated in various collections" (Gell 1998: 232)—the oeuvre helps us to situate the innately cumulative nature of graffiti. The single tag, in this understanding, never simply stands for itself but forms part of the opus that is the entire body of one's output. The image a writer produces can hence together be understood, as Gell continues, as "an independent chunk of space-time, which can be accessed via each work individually, each standing, indexically, for all of them and the historical-biographical context of their production" (p. 232). As such, a graffiti writer's distributed pieces—whether collated in photographs hidden in shoeboxes or still visible on the street, whether accessed via the digital reproduction of a now destroyed work or a physical encounter with a piece so fresh it still smells—together come to form a "macro-object or temporal object" that "evolves over time" and further expands an artist's personhood (p. 233). They create an oeuvre in which the various artifacts exist not as a "collection of separate objects, but just *one* object with many parts distributed in many different places" (p. 167). Graffiti can thus never be understood through the singular image, the single signature alone. It is mass that defines it, quantum. Proliferation is hence as crucial a part of graffiti style as innovation, extending the self and showing prowess through the capacity for self-extension itself. Just one image is never enough (as Fatso, here Fatzoo and Fatsoo, shows in figure 2.26). One image may show quality, but without mass it shows no reach or extension, no quantifiable dedication. Captivation thus emerges here through the raw power of abundance, style emergent through the enchantment of scale and the scale of enchantment (Gell 1992).

Beyond the relationally potent appearance of the signature alone and the animative potency of its design, distribution thus facilitates the stylistic prerequisite of saturation within graffiti, the technique emergent through *making the name known*. And being that the knowing of the name can only emerge through its bodily reproduction, stylistic saturation captivates through the bodily commitment that this diffusion necessitates. It emerges through the knowledge of the energy and intensity it takes to successfully produce this macro-object, through the risk and fearlessness that inundation requires. It emerges through an awareness of the performative process that remains sensible in *every* work of art, that remains "present and accountable in the object, yet abstracted from view" (Küchler and Carroll 2021: 88). The stylistic captivation of distribution can thus be seen to emerge through two specific routes (both developed further in chapter 5). In the first case, as a duty that only a committed body can truly achieve—a body willing to commit to the time and drive necessary to saturate, to write all night every night (and then a little bit more)—saturation captivates through the sheer torrent of images, creating a sense of bewilderment in the mind of the viewer, through the inconceivable

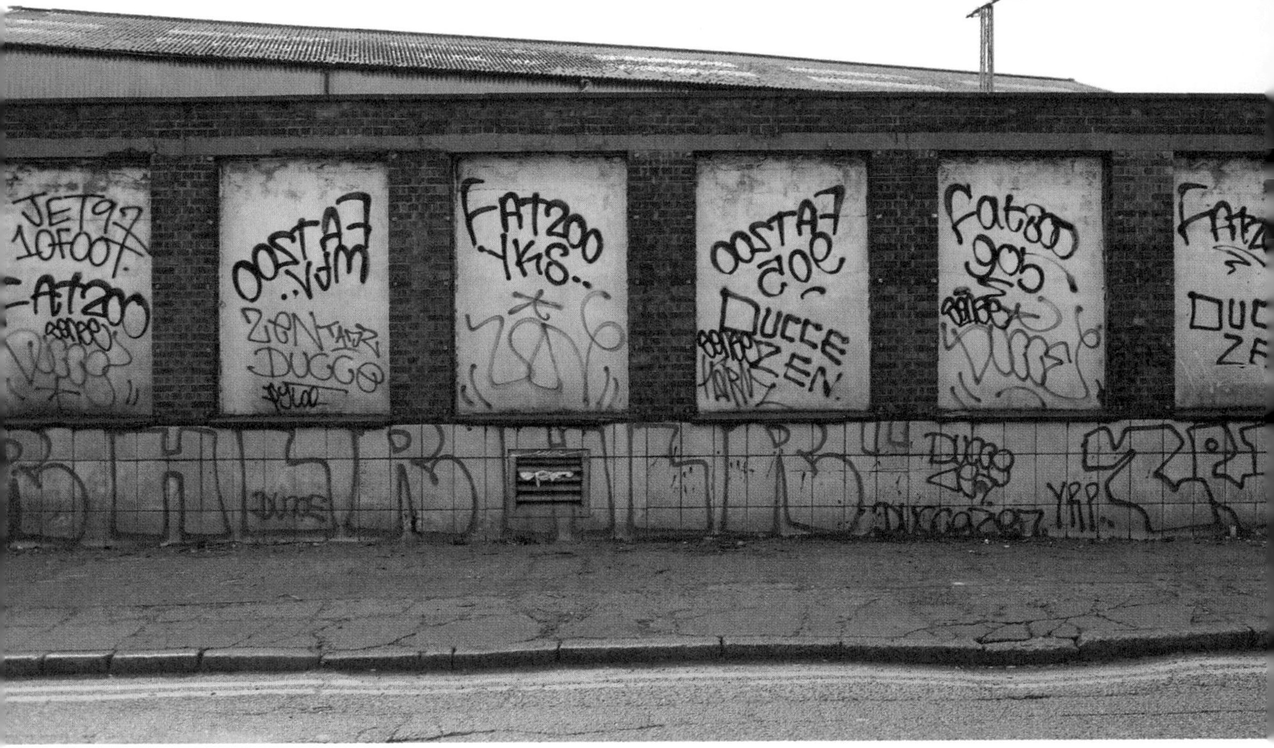


**FIGURE 2.26**
*Fatso/10Foot/Jet97*, 2022, East London. Photo: Alex Ellison.

temporal commitment that has been made. In the second case, however, as a task that only committed action can produce—the action of a body scaling up and over walls, below and through tunnels, a body placed literally at the edge—captivation surfaces from the abstracted witnessing of a body willing to take risks to achieve its task. Positioning images in sites that garner attention through an architectural audacity, the success of an artist's output comes to be judged far beyond its animative style alone. Physical daring thus gives a piece as much stylistic force as any graphic flair. Skill here becomes entrenched in the image through the invisible yet still discernible trace of a practitioner successfully completing their task. As such, a purposeful spareness, as seen in the grouping of tags and throw-ups displaying 10Foot and Tox in figure 2.27, reveals a stylistic minimalism in which visibility (and virtuosity) emerges through spatial techniques, through location and saturation both.[15] Style in graffiti can thus never be separated from medium or location, is as innately related to its surface as it is site-specifically attached. Style must be understood as a corporeal as much as an artifactual property, virtuosity residing in the conjunction of image, medium, and body rather than in the image itself alone.

While the single graffiti signature affirms and commits, the macro-object thus cannot lie. Saturation proves authenticity and sincerity. Efficacy and captivation increase in direct correlation with stake. The various levels of bodily commitment revealed within the graffiti image thus become a fundamental warranty of allegiance and faith: "I write to show that I write come what may," each work announces, "I write to prove my fidelity without doubt." The spatiotemporally scattered macro-object thus captivates due to both its physical prowess as much as its cognitive inconceivability. The halo effect of technical enchantment (Gell 1992) in graffiti thus emerges due to the impossibility of imagining how works such as these could come into being. How could the artist have produced this? How could an individual have committed to this? The "source of the power such objects have over us," as Gell argues, emerges through "the way an art object is construed as having come into the world," through "their becoming rather than their being" (Gell 1992: 46). It is hence not just the *what* but the *how* that is crucial to style here, not simply the "look" of an image as would be conventionally understood in

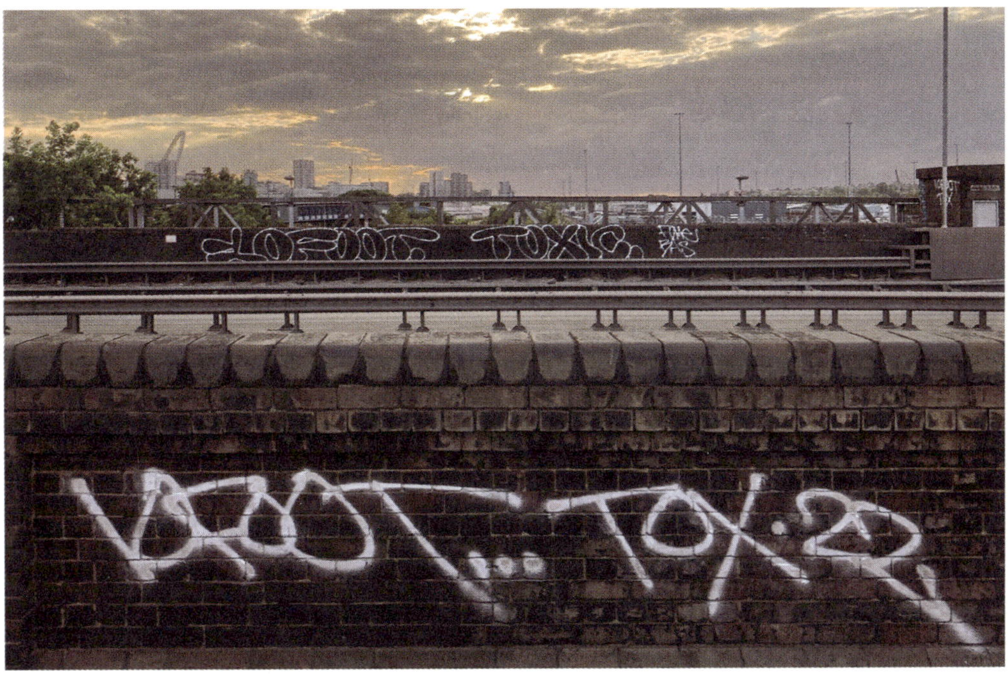

**FIGURE 2.27**
*10Foot*, 2022, North West London. Photo: Alex Ellison.

terms of its composition or graphical animation, but rather the knowledge of what the productive process itself necessitates. Distribution hence comes to captivate through the witnessing of the material control necessary to produce the graffiti oeuvre; through the witnessing of the way in which an expert ritual actor masters their tools, their bodies, their surroundings; through the way they master the extrinsic and intrinsic dangers in order that the macro-object be disseminated in the world. Style here thus develops far beyond the pure instantiation of the name, far beyond even its animation. It becomes about the production of an image that may not be monumental in size but is monumental in scale. It becomes about a human dimension in which bodily commitment is revealed, a macro-object captivating its viewer through its mode of becoming rather than its being alone.

## CONCLUSION *OR* VIRTUOSITY TO FAME

This, then, is the "what" of graffiti. The "what" of its graphic qualities and their consequences, of its distributive characteristics and their effects in the world. This is the canonical structure of the signature-signature, the patterned signature and the signature pattern that attracts in multiple, intersecting ways. The signature thus carries a captivating personhood. Yet the pattern carries that personhood too. The signature captivates through its graphic animation. Yet the pattern is graphically animative too. As the material attachment attaching the body to the wall and the image to the body, as the circulating ornament captivating through its palpable commitment and tangible risk, the signature, as seen in the numerous tags present in figure 2.28, becomes a dense visual trap. Whether through its engagement of scale or oeuvre, its reduction to purity, the intricacy of its becoming or its elaborate abstraction, it is the entrapment of a viewer that is graffiti's stylistic goal.

Beyond mere beauty, then, style in graffiti can best be understood through the concept of "efficacy," through a work's ability to capture our attention and its "capacity to accomplish tasks" (Gell 1998: 94). Evaluating an image through what Nicholas Thomas has called "judgements of what is strong and weak" (Thomas 2001: 3), through an image's ability to create a visceral response, can thus provide us with a much more effective way of comprehending how graffiti functions than through ideas of the "beautiful" or the "ugly." "Ugliness" can here be considered "beautiful" if a necessity for a work's effectiveness, the "unsightly" considered "pleasing" if successful in fulfilling the basic desire for visibility (through pushing to the maximum extent of its anthropometric scale, through pushing against the traditional limits of an image's material life span). "Beauty" thus arises through efficacy, virtuosity emerging not only through the calligraphic animation discussed above—from an image's visually gratifying or surprising movements—but through a "beauty" in which "damage" can be aesthetically treasured as a route toward visibility. Beauty in graffiti thus emerges through quantity and quality

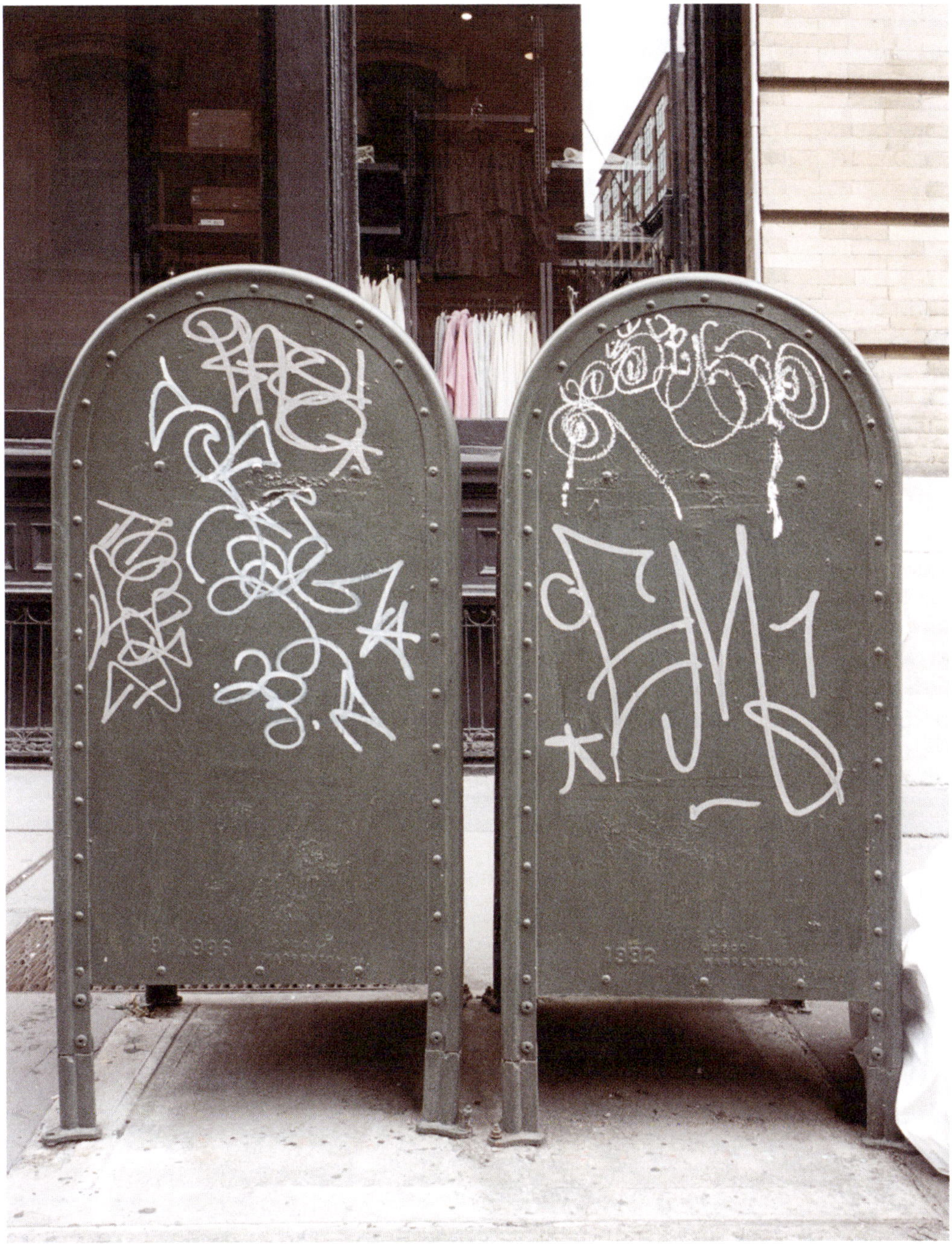

**FIGURE 2.28**
*Twins (Em1/Wombat et al.)*, 2023. New York City. Photo: Rafael Schacter.

but likewise through the visible revelation of a practitioner holding complete mastery over their tools, their medium, their task. It emerges through the skilled revelation of an act in which visibility is the ultimate aim.

The renown of the name is thus entirely critical to style, the fame of the graffiti writer a result of this fundamental desire for perceptibility. Fame thus means success. Fame means that one's material and bodily techniques—*one's style*—have captured the eyes of one's viewers. As rooted in the Greek term *fama* (meaning not only fame but rumor, report, or reputation) as well as linked to the term *kleos* (meaning renown or glory), fame is hence created through *what others hear about you*, through heroic acts that places one's name in the mouths and minds of others. As such, while this open desire for fame is commonly used to disparage graffiti from those outside the subculture, a critique denigrating fame as a childish desire, as antithetical to "true" art, the need for renown is the stylistic glue that holds graffiti together. Without fame—as argued by Nancy Munn in her classic ethnography exploring value creation among the Gawan society in Melanesia—an individual's "influence would, as it were, go nowhere: successful acts would in effect remain locked within themselves" (Munn 1986: 117). Without fame, style becomes stuck. The fame that emerges (via what Munn suggestively calls the "circulation of names") thus enables a participant's "virtual influence" to spread in the world (p. 117), enables a person to enter "in the mind of another who may then know of him and positively evaluate him irrespective of whether he has ever seen him or not" (p. 115). The writer whose "name is known in distant communities," as Gell continues in a discussion of Munn's work, thus becomes "more than a merely incarnate man," becomes an "expanded and disseminated being, present here, there, and everywhere because his name is attached to circulating objects" (Gell 1998: 230). Fame, in this reading, is visibility in quantitative and qualitative terms.

Yet fame not only gives freedom to the image (and the person) but also, as Munn continues, enables a community to become "the *agent of its own value creation*" (Munn 1986: 20). It lets communities create their own self-sustaining and self-regulating forms of significance. As likewise seen in graffiti, then, fame places power into the hands of those who, by dint of age, of race, or of class, are otherwise unable to accrue normative social value (or simply reject it for this more substantive value form). It creates a world in which value is not economic but aesthetic (and in which commitment is the most important currency of all). Furthermore, fame must here be understood to be about the social just as much as the individual. In the Melanesian context that Munn explored, for example, fame created a site from which egalitarian and individualistic desires could be balanced, in which the tensions between "hierarchizing and equality" and "autonomy and social encompassment" were publicly resolved (p. 20). Fame thus not only lets one come to know themself "as someone that is known by others," reflecting the "influential acts of the actor back to himself" (p. 117), but helps to form a "generative potency" for the wider community (p. 118). It enlarges the social as much as the singular body, the "climbing fame" of each individual constituting a "sign of the positive value state of the community and its internal transactive potentialities" (p. 118). The question of how idiosyncrasy and the canonical are stabilized within graffiti, how innovation and tradition do not tear the culture apart, is here brought to the fore. Yet rather, as in Munn's case, fame being collectively contained by the negative value (and fear) of witchcraft, here it is the negative value (and fear) of co-optation, of "selling out" to perceived instrumental values that, I argue, acts as the boundary point ensuring members remain bound to one another. Selling out is the ultimate cultural depravity. Selling out means one is committing purely to oneself rather than to one's collective or one's (sub)culture. This is why writing one's own name alone is never enough. This is the why one's crew name must be put up, why deceased writers' names must be proclaimed (as we will see in the next chapter).[16] It is the "fame of graffiti" as much as the fame of the self that is desired. Graffiti, in this way, becomes an ornament not just of the city and of the letter but of the individual and culture too. It becomes, as Munn described in the Gawan case, a "metaphorical body décor" (p. 111) or "cosmetic adornment" (p. 105). It becomes a virtual beautification constructed by the power of the name.

Unlike the institutional monument, then, the monument in which the agency of the maker is largely invisible and instead housed within the individual(s) depicted (in either the figurative monument or the mass memorial), here the graffiti monument is a monument to the personhood of the producer themself. Unlike the institutional monument that captivates through its size and expense, through its references to the ancient stylistic archetypes that dominate the formal conceptions of monument, here the graffiti monument captivates through animation and distribution. Unlike the monumental singularity of the institutional monument, here the graffiti monument captivates through a monumental oeuvre, a macro-object that engages both quality and quantity alike. As with the kula decorations discussed by Munn (1986) and the tattoos considered by Gell (1992), the graffiti image must be understood to speak to notions of both the individual and the social, to form a set of images that commemorate and circulate their producers—that speak of names, times, relationships—as much as commemorating and circulating their canonical grounds—proclaiming lineages, denominations, techniques. What we thus have is a set of ornamental forms that embellish the self and the society, that attach the self to the society and the society to the world. And much like the kula, then, much like the tattoo, graffiti can be understood not only as a quintessentially public form (only existing through its circulation within the public as people and place), not only as a quintessentially artistic form (as something "difficult to make, difficult to 'think,' difficult to transact" [Gell 1998: 23]), but so too as the quintessentially monumental one: a visual reminder of the committed practitioners who produced it, and a monument to the social environment from where it is formed.

The tag, the tattoo, the kula may each be minor, marginal, mobile artifacts and remain formally other to the conception of the monumental within Western public art, yet they each stylistically intertwine the person with both the culture and environmental milieu. Canonical graffiti is thus not only a monumental aesthetic achievement and a form of visual culture that has become monumentally revered by adherents across the world, but a monument singing out the expanding fame of the individual and the intensifying renown of their collectives both. It is a monument emergent not through centrality (as seen in chapter 1) nor through permanence (as will be seen in chapter 3) but rather through the decorative creation of an ornamental attachment; through the agentive import of personhood and identity; through the animative techniques of simplicity, complexity, ambiguity; and through the distributive circulation of a monumental macro-object emergent via a relational, animative, and distributive signature form.

# 3

# TIME

Graffiti is a time-based form. It is an object whose transient rhythm, compressed chronology, and accepted evanescence are entirely critical to its way of being. Complementing the *how* of graffiti's site-specificity discussed in chapter 1 and the *what* of graffiti's canonical style explored in chapter 2, it will be the *when* of graffiti's inherent fragility, the *when* of its violent disposability, the *when* of graffiti's haunting fleetingness we will now examine. From this temporal perspective, the *terrain vagues* of de Solà-Morales Rubio examined in chapter 1 will be understood as zones in which time becomes marginalized as much as space, in which the domination of clock time can be evaded by "the flows, the energies, the rhythms established by the passing of time and the loss of limits" (de Solà-Morales Rubio 1995: 123). Likewise, the first-person signatures described by Bredekamp in chapter 2 will here be grasped as "generator[s] of simultaneous temporal epochs . . . endowed with the capacity to invoke the dynamism of diverging temporal spheres" (Bredekamp 2018: 49–50). As Georges Didi-Huberman suggestively noted, "to stop before the painted surface [be it a framed canvas or an urban wall] is not only to question the object of our gaze. It is also to stop before time" (Didi-Huberman 2003: 35). And it is graffiti's distinct durational dynamics, its monumental brevity, expendability, and fugitivity, that we will thus now go on to examine.

Proceeding through a set of three key temporal themes, chapter 3 will explore graffiti's material precarity, its culture of erasure, and its mnemonical absence. Unlike the preceding chapters, however, here we will first focus on graffiti's monumental counterpart, unpacking the institutional monument's perfectly contrary status as that which is long-lasting (rather than short-lived), conserved (rather than effaced), and ever-present (rather than evanescent). This chapter will thus present graffiti as a monumental form whose rhythms run in an entirely contrary direction to the institutional monument, let alone to those of Western art. And while we will still explore a monument that, as Debray says, "catches time in space and traps the fluid by the hard" (Debray 1999: 28), here what will also be determined is how long it takes before this temporal snare is sprung. This chapter will thus uncover a monument to decay, a monument to flux, a monument to the fleeting. It will uncover not simply an anti- or counter-monument but rather a monument to a differing conception of time itself.

## DURABILITY AND TRANSIENCE *OR* MONUMENTAL MATERIALITIES

The basic material nature of the institutional monument is that of durability. It is a state in which permanence (as opposed to precarity) and hardiness (as opposed to fragility) are not only desired but fundamental to its functioning. The monument of the state, of the monarchy, of the military, must be as unwavering and resolute as these institutions themselves, must be made of materials that tangibly convey this robust endurance. It is thus granite, limestone, marble, and bronze that are most commonly utilized here, honored and prestigious materials whose tensile strength and solidity, as much as their natural patterning and patina, have today come to denote power, wealth, and authority.

Within the monumental architecture of England, it is Portland stone that has come to dominate the urban scene. Witnessed not just in London's great monuments (such as the iconic Cenotaph, seen in figure 6.1), but so too in its cathedrals (such as St. Paul's), palaces (such as Buckingham), and museums (such as the British), here we have a material whose solidity is a marker of status, its resistance a marker of power, its patterning a marker of distinction. Not just a raw building block, then, without its hardiness, and without its projection of these resilient characteristics, Portland stone would simply be unfit for the purpose. As with the other traditional materials mentioned above, the stone here becomes understood as beautiful because of this ceaseless temporal density. Yet the fixed, material obduracy of these forms can also be understood to mirror an attempt to establish a similarly fixed and obdurate understanding of the social and political world around them. The monument, as Kirk Savage has explained, endeavors to stabilize "the physical" as much as "the cognitive landscape" (Savage 2018 [1997]: 4). Its rigidity strives to project "an image of permanence on to a landscape," to "fashion a stable image of the past," and, as Michael Rowlands and Christopher Tilley conclude, to deny the "realities of change" (Rowlands and Tilley 2006: 500). Physical intransience can thus often mark out a conceptual intransigence, monumental "imperishability," as Henri Lefebvre remarked, bearing the "stamp of the will to power," the "wish for mastery, the will to will" (Lefebvre 1991: 221). The hegemonic monument hence turns to stone not only what or who it represents, but likewise the entire cultural world around them. How could the world be any other way but this? How could something this solid, this stable, this pure, be anything other than fact? The monumental temporal presence of these stony forms thus moves beyond time as merely measurable, beyond "history" as a series of calendrical dates. It moves the monument from the merely mortal to the immortally divine, placing it beyond the presumptions of meager man and coming to naturalize the ideals and narratives of those who formed them.

One could take almost any institutional monument as an example here, but let's briefly return to the key British example, to Nelson's Column in London's Trafalgar Square (see figure 3.1). More than just the giant sandstone statue of the Viscount in his full naval regalia (at over three times his living height), Nelson stands upon the

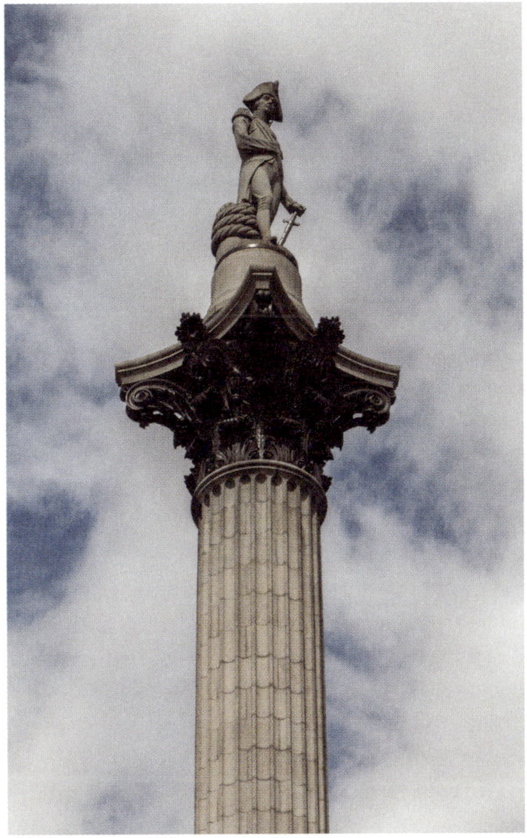

**FIGURE 3.1**
*Nelson's Column* (detail), London, 1843. Designed by William Railton. Statue by Edward Hodges Baily; bronze relief panels by John Edward Carew, John Ternouth, Musgrave Watson, and William F. Woodington; bronze lions at base designed by Sir Edwin Landseer. Photo: Diego Delso, delso.photo, license CC-BY-SA.

enormous, almost comedically high granite Corinthian column that bears his name (at 169 feet over double the height of the largest known ancient column). At the base, above the tiered, triple-stepped platform, the giant pedestal that the column rests upon is embellished with four huge bronze reliefs (cast, apocryphally or not, from captured French cannons), each portraying a key battle fought during Nelson's reign and each revealing a distinctive quality of our archetypal leading man. Flanked, finally, by the four "Landseer Lions" placed at the intersections of the pedestal (that are themselves some of the largest bronze monuments in the United Kingdom) we collectively find a narrative told on both symbolic and material levels. The lions, the reliefs, and Nelson himself personify the mythic, storybook hero—unwavering, resolute, serenely calm even within the fiercest storm—while the monument's physical form emphasizes its weight and significance (let alone its triumphalism). What is marked out here is thus an unyielding solidity not only authenticating the historical narrative figuratively, but making it materially irrefutable. The dramatic majesty of bronze (an exceptionally strong material almost entirely immune to corrosion and decay), alongside the 350-million-year-old Craigleith sandstone and the 295-million-year-old Dartmoor granite, reveal a set of incredibly durable materials that stand both so deep and so perpetual in time that they seem to lie beyond it. Moreover, the stylistic usage of the Corinthian column generates a direct visual link between Lord Nelson and the ancient world, an ancestral relation to the era in which Western civilization was purportedly born.[1] Not only bringing the memory of the past into the present and setting history into stone, Nelson is here placed on a pedestal and positioned as Greek god; like his physical form he is everlasting, transcendent, elevated into the sacred space of the epic. Here, then, we have a range of specifically temporal, specifically material maneuvers that reaffirm that which they depict. Like the archetypal institutional monument, it is the "mass and size," as Benjamin Buchloh notes, the "awe inspiring physical presences" that these forms display that come to create the impression of a "seemingly unchangeable status quo" (Buchloh 2002: 123). They act as the perfectly self-reflecting forms that make their argument through material as much as figural means. In this way, as Lefebvre has noted, the institutional monument comes to be understood as "beautiful" through its "imposing . . . durability," achieving a "monumental beauty because it seems eternal, because it seems to have escaped time" (Lefebvre 1991: 221). Beauty and durability, the monument and hardiness are thus here integrally intertwined.

The graffiti monument, however, functions in an almost entirely contrary temporal manner. It emerges (in the vast majority of cases) through a material made not of stone or of metal but mere paint, an inherently fragile, incredibly thin film of pigment, a single coat of which is just a tenth of a millimeter thick. While paint solidifies into a tight, compact layer, drying and then fusing with its surface, it is prone to a whole series of natural degradations. Paint can peel, blistering due to moisture within its surface. Paint can chalk, powdering through overexposure to light. It can crack, flaking through an uneven expansion of the pigment itself, can wrinkle via heat, weep via humidity, soften via chemicals, fade via contact with fungal acid or ultraviolet rays. Position paint in the open air (rather than in the atmospherically controlled space of the museum) and it becomes subject to the force and whims of nature, to bleaching by the sun, buffeting by the wind, soaking by the rain, perishing by pollution. Take figures 3.2 and 3.3, for example, depicting a set of graffiti images whose bodies have become broken, have crumbled and decomposed. The paint here not only has become discolored and washed out but has cracked and flaked to leave its form in a state of deconstruction. Unlike marble, then, unlike granite or bronze, paint simply weathers away. Stone may discolor, metal tarnish, but paint will almost entirely disappear. It becomes subject to what Zoe Strother has termed *passive* iconoclasm, a "destruction by proxy" emerging from "natural forces" (Strother 2002: 458). In this way, then, graffiti can be seen to be "programmed

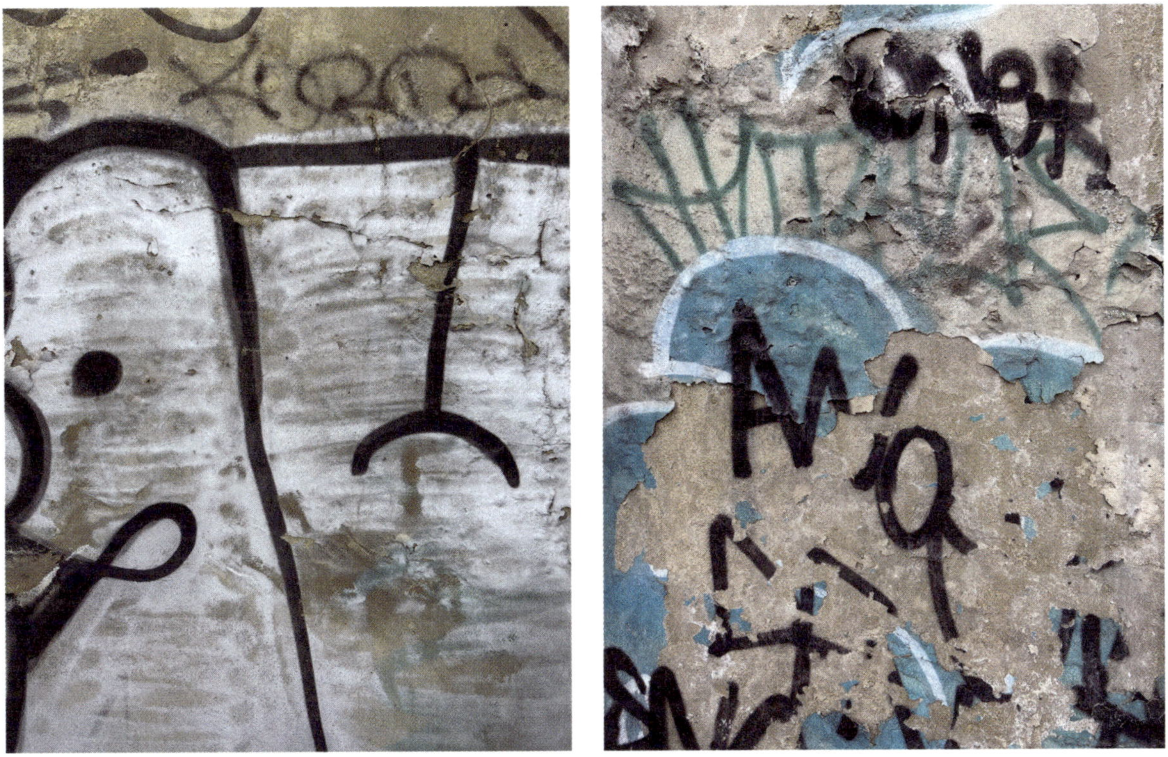

**FIGURES 3.2 AND 3.3**
*Broken Bodies*, London, 2021. Photos: Rafael Schacter.

to self-destruct" (p. 458), becoming a victim not of the termites that Strother discusses, but rather of the inherent poverty of paint.

While graffiti writers will often employ materials that elongate their piece's natural life span (home-mixed paint being made to last longer, for example, and acid, as earlier discussed, being the exception to the rule), true material durability is rarely part of a writer's vocabulary. Yet unlike the entrenched fear of deterioration we see within the sphere of the normative monument, these processes of decay, of what we could call graffiti's *natural* erasure, are not understood in a negative way within the subculture itself. While the degeneration of the institutional monument is understood to both indicate and generate the *de*generation of the idea or memory the monument sustains, in the world of graffiti material transience is understood not only as undeniable (and thus neither intrinsically good nor bad), but to carry aesthetic value in itself. The manner in which graffiti fades and bleaches can thus be seen not as a transformation linked to "loss," as the geographer Caitlin DeSilvey has explained in terms of architectural decay (DeSilvey 2017: 3), but rather as an alteration that can be "additive as well as destructive"

(p. 20). Demise here is part of the process and life of the work itself, reaffirming the basic acceptance of the precarity of *all* form and the fact that decay can never truly be repelled. Moreover, the process in which the graffiti image comes to decompose and decline can be seen to give it its particularly organic ruggedness. Rather than looking as perfect and pristine as the moment it first appeared, the subtle degeneration of the image—as can be seen in Rainman's throw-up in figure 3.4, in which the basic instability and material limits of the pigment that formed it can be witnessed in the bleed-through of paint from the image it has been placed above—allows it to fit more naturally within its site. Termed "age-value" by Riegl, here the dissolution of "shape and color" is valorized not feared, "imperfection" and "lack of completeness" generating "aesthetic satisfaction" (Riegl 1996 [1903]: 73). Visual pleasure here thus emerges "not from the stasis of preservation but from the continuous and unceasing cycle of change in nature" (p. 73). Permanence denies the basic realities of change, forswearing its site-specific realities. Perfection is hence an insincerity, erosion adding to an image's stylistic presence and enabling the image as living organism to live out its own life.

The public poster works of Jenny Holzer (whose marquee work was discussed in chapter 1) become a helpful example here, going through a pattern of decay similar to

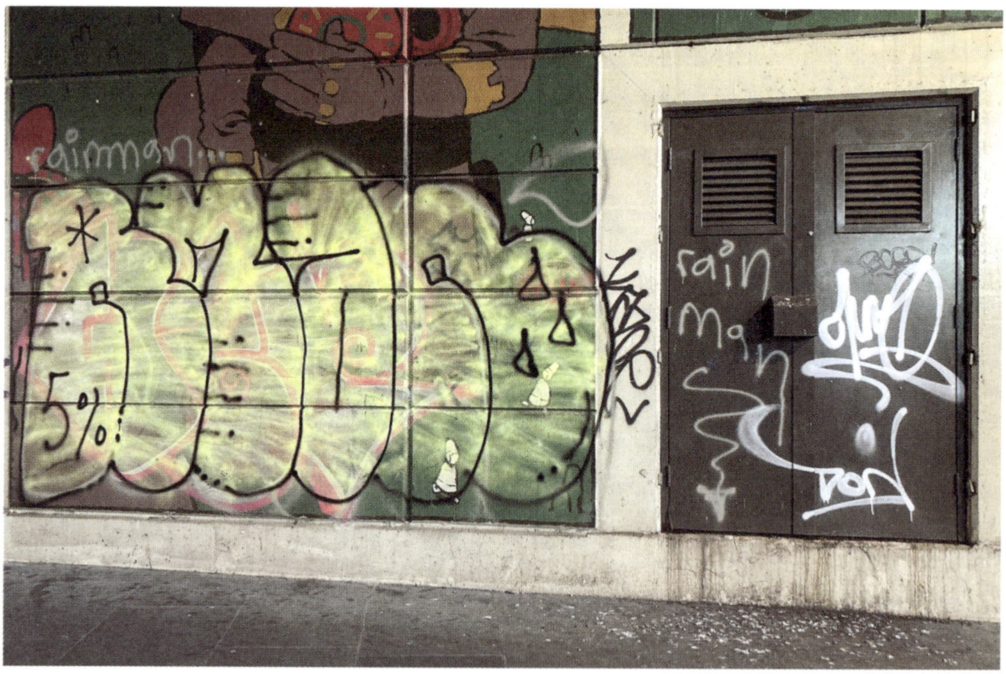


**FIGURE 3.4**
*Rainman*, North West London, 2023. Photo: Alex Ellison.

that of graffiti.[2] Illicitly pasting her work within the dirt and grime of the city, Holzer's *Inflammatory Essays* (as seen in figure 3.5) became torn and weathered, commonly commented on and revised by passers-by. They became naturalized within the grit of the street, became, like graffiti, a part of, not apart from, the city. They may have appeared disheveled, yet they looked in place, part and parcel of the street. Placed within an institutional site, the posters become excised from a medium that enforces a processual life and death, losing their organic vivacity (if gaining a different audience). Like the faded graffiti, however, the decay of Holzer's street works marks out a process of deterioration in which the image is always transforming and never staying still. The image thus reveals the environmental realities of its specific space and time within the waning granularity of its very materiality.

Still, the binary of decay versus durability presented here is less clear-cut than so far presented. The true permanence of the supposedly permanent, of that literally set in stone, is subject to its own cycle of material precarity. Not only subject to the iconoclastic instability of human agency, the institutional monument is likewise subject to the vagaries of the natural world. Without care, the permanent too falls into disrepair, to the inevitability of discoloring and tarnishing mentioned above and to the damages

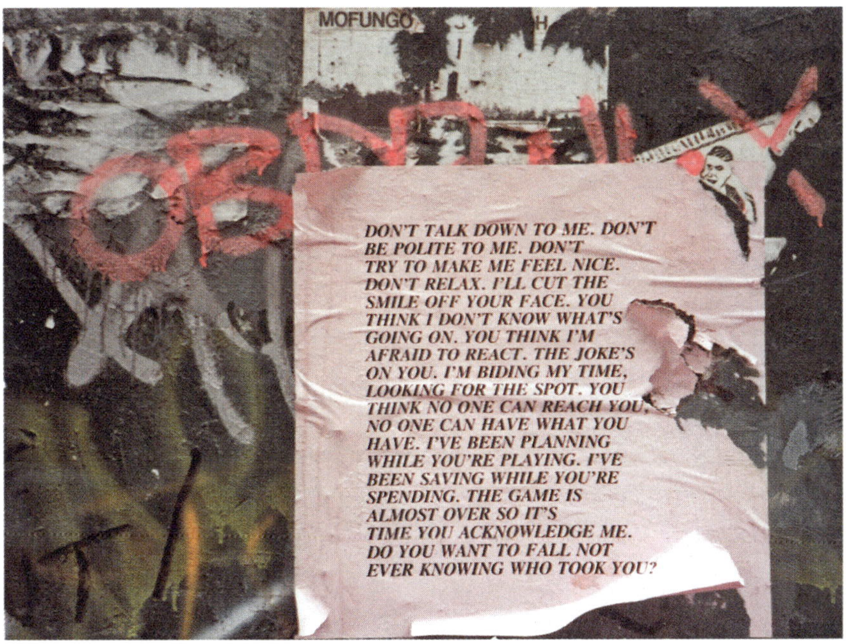


**FIGURE 3.5**

Jenny Holzer, from *Inflammatory Essays* (1979–1982), 1983. Courtesy of the artist. © 2019 Jenny Holzer, member Artists Rights Society (ARS), NY/VEGAP. Photo: Jenny Holzer.

wrought by a basic neglect.[3] As observable in any local cemetery, without the lineage to maintain them, these intimate monuments can become damaged to a point beyond the possibilities of restoration. Moss and ivy defeat even stone. Nothing, as historian David Lowenthal has noted, can thus be "preserved forever," and every "inanimate object, like every living being, undergoes continual alteration, ultimately perishing" (Lowenthal 2019: 17). As such, while, as Diana Young has shown, a certain "[t]ime-worn patina is . . . generally valued in European art," an aesthetic of authenticity that, like our decaying graffiti, "resides in the faded surface" (Young 2006: 174), this is a managed notion of decay, not a constant movement toward actual ruination but a constructed appearance of longevity in which preservation is still obligatory. This is not the interminable decay of Riegl's age-value but rather the suspension of "future decay" via what he termed "historical value" (Riegl 1996 [1903]: 77), a value based on the disciplined suspension of time's passage. Simultaneously, however, just as the permanent reveals its integral precarity, so too the "transient" reveals its resilience! The *graffito*, the "little scratch" as per graffiti's etymological origins, can be understood as a technique of writing that permanently marks its surface through incision. This is a process, as seen in so-called scratchiti,[4] in which the possibility of removal is radically reduced and thus a form of permanence created. How can one ever remove something that is already itself removed? Moreover, and as seen in figure 3.6, even the incision's natural decay (here through rusting) can often serve to further highlight (and thus give more power to) the image! The usage of etching acid (as seen earlier in figures 1.1 and 1.2) likewise creates a durability that can only be eradicated by the replacement of the surface itself. Works that actively seek to embed themselves within rather than remain *upon* their surfaces are thus often directly about temporal prolongation (rather than a permanence per se), conserving themselves through a technique of additive destruction.

While the inherently transient graffiti image may thus reveal ways of transcending its own temporariness, the permanence of the monumental must likewise be seen as a pretension that its sheer hardness can never truly evade. The graffiti monument thus here becomes a monument of and to decay. It becomes a monument to transformation, not loss. It becomes a monument refusing to deny the degenerative future of all material form. Whereas the "irreducible foundation" of the institutional monument, as Lefebvre says (1991), transmutes the "fear of the passage of time, and anxiety about death, into splendour," the graffiti monument upholds decay as "a release into other states, unpredictable and open" (DeSilvey 2017: 3). Material transience thus gives the image an aesthetic power reveling in the time (and space) of the image itself. The site-specific imperatives of graffiti mean that age-value must be accepted, that the image is inevitably subject to change. It is hence a monumental form in which the "reign of nature, including those destructive and disintegrative elements considered part of the constant renewal of life, is granted equal standing with the creative rule of man" (Riegl 1996 [1903]: 73). Still, while both age and historical value can be understood as "commemorative values," they "diverge decisively," as Riegl concludes for us, "on the critical

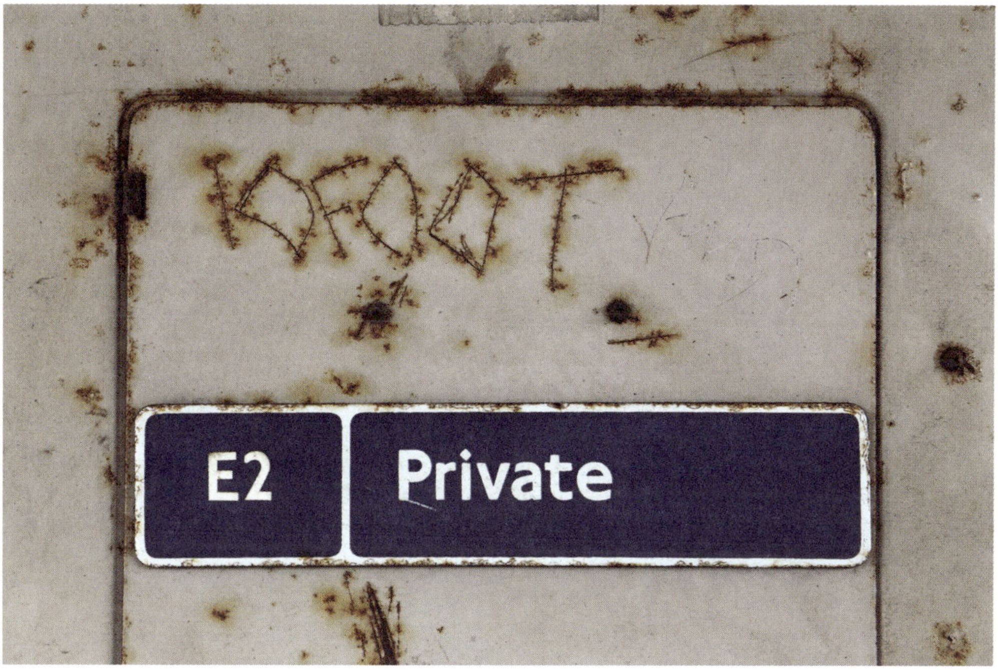


**FIGURE 3.6**
*10Foot*, West London, 2018. Photo: Alex Ellison.

issue of monument preservation" (p. 76). As such, it is the critical theme of conservation, toward a cultural, rather than natural, mode of destruction, that we will now move on to discuss.

## PRESERVATION AND EPHEMERALITY *OR* MONUMENTAL ONTOLOGIES

The institutional monument functions not only through a paradigm of durability but through an interconnected framework of conservation and care. Somewhat exposing their innate material lack, these stony artifacts must be diligently protected to sustain the façade of permanence they project. Unlike the culture of disposability present within the world of graffiti (as we will encounter below), the institutional monument is thus set within what Cornelius Holtorf has termed a "fundamentalist ideology of heritage-preservationism" (Holtorf 2006: 102); it exists within a monumental ontology in which what is predominant above all else is the interminable task of curtailing and restraining decay.

While artifactual preservation has of course been undertaken for thousands of years, the all-engulfing modality of our contemporary heritage regime evolved during the end of the nineteenth century. A quintessentially modernist concept emergent out of the rapid urbanization and industrialization of this period, this heritage ontology intertwined the Victorian era's forward-looking belief in "development, progress and change" with an idea of the past suffused by concepts of "nostalgia, identity and belonging" (Olsen 2001: 43). It thus brought together the "feeling that something was slipping away and dying, and . . . therefore had to be restored or rescued" with the burgeoning nation-state's need to create "collective experiences and stability" and to constitute "something immortal contrasting with the transitory and perishable identity of the individual" (p. 43). Heritage was, in this sense, a system both of salvage and of incorporation, a system in which the fear of a lost past (and of change more widely) was harnessed for the social needs of the present. The permanent monument was thus the indispensable tool for balancing these states, assuaging the uncertainties of a "self-liquidating modernity" through inculcating a "sense of belonging [and] civic consciousness" while so too providing the ideological framework for the "myths of national identity" (Rowlands and Tilley 2006: 501). Without the preservation of these material artifacts, then, the narratives they presented (and larger power structures they lionized) could become subject to debate. Monumental heritage was hence a system set not only toward objects but toward the surrounding social order itself, a materially conservative agenda echoing a politically conservative one.

Historic England's "Schedule of Monuments"—a listing dating back to the 1882 Ancient Monuments Protection Act, which today incorporates almost 20,000 monuments and over 37,000 "individual heritage assets" (Department for Culture, Media and Sport 2010: 7)—begins with the "presumption" that its monuments "will be handed on to future generations in much the same state that we have found them" (Historic England, n.d.). Protecting this "finite, fragile and irreplaceable legacy" from the "threats and pressures" of "human interventions" and "natural processes," let alone the dangers of "criminal or irresponsible behaviour" (Department for Culture, Media and Sport 2013: 3), is thus undertaken through a legally outlined framework in which any changes that "demolish, destroy, damage, remove, repair, alter or add to a scheduled monument" (p. 7) are considered criminal offenses subject to fines and/or imprisonment. As such, the schedule operates under the understanding that all of its monuments necessitate "conservation . . . to prolong their life" (Department for Culture, Media and Sport 2010: 12), a form of what the law defines as "maintenance," and which includes the "doing of any other act or thing which may be required for the purpose of repairing the monument or protecting it from decay or injury" (Ancient Monuments and Archaeological Areas Act 1979). Legal codes thus become critical tools to defend against both natural and/or human decay. Yet it is the armies of conservators servicing this irrepressible preservatory regime that must uphold this task, undertaking it through an inexhaustible, Sisyphean process of monumental maintenance.

It is in the museum that the ur-conservation occurs,[5] the paradigmatic preservation sheltered from the whims and dangers of the street. Described by Martin Grünfeld in an evocative account of the hidden labor undertaken at Denmark's Medical Museion, the "time-suspending" efforts in which traditional conservation engages strives to isolate its objects from the "outside world" (and the undeniable facts of organic transformation) and maintain them in a "state of *conserved permanence*" (Grünfeld 2022: 277). Placing the object within an environment "characterised by a limited flow, breakdown and exchange of matter" (p. 278), total quarantine is thus the ultimate goal, a detachment from the "flux of life" (p. 280) and an emplacement within a "hypometabolic state between life and death" (p. 279). The prime tool of the conservator, the acid-free archive box, is here conceived of as a "time-capsule" protecting objects for the future and from "sources of decay such as light, pests, climate, even humans" (p. 278). Conservation hence functions to keep the artifact out of harm's way: out of reach, out of touch, out of danger.

In public space, however, the decay-provoking qualities of the sun, the air, the wind, and the rain (let alone the pigeons and the people) disturb the Platonic preservation we find in the museum and complicate the attempt to halt the metabolic processes Grünfeld describes. Nelson, as seen in the close-up in figure 3.7, for example, reveals the battle scars not just of war but so too of plein air, the rusting on his (still existent) right arm

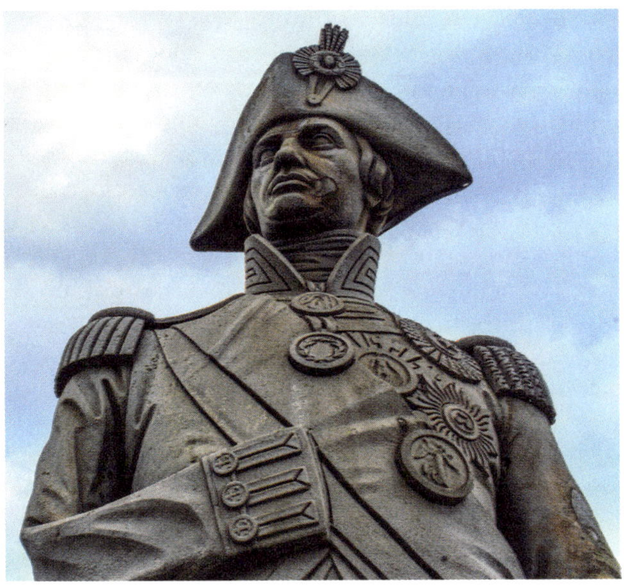

**FIGURE 3.7**
Edward Hodges Baily, *Horatio Nelson* (detail), 1843. Photo: DBR Limited. Courtesy of DBR Limited. www.dbrlimited.com.

in many ways mirroring that found on 10Foot's tag in figure 3.6, while his forehead and cheek show the disfigurements of past restoration. Going through a process of yearly maintenance (in which surveyors check for destabilizing elements and undertake running repairs) alongside a twenty-year routine of reinstatement, Nelson's last major renewal incorporated masonry indents; the repointing and filling of the column, capstan, and cap; the re-lacquering of the acanthus leaves; as well as the re-patination and hot-waxing of the bas-reliefs and Landseer lions. In the face of pollution, moss, lichen, algae, or the omnipresent pigeon poo, a whole battery of techniques—from "Nebulous Spray" to "Doff and Torc," "Air (Dry) Abrasion" to "Chemicals & Poultices" (Thomann-Hanry n.d.: 1)—are thus necessary to maintain our monumental landscape. Yet in extreme cases, the acid-free box technique is employed too. During the Black Lives Matter protests of 2020 in London, a triumvirate of figures situated in Parliament Square (just a hundred meters from Nelson) became enclosed within wooden time-capsules of their own. Boxed off into what were unique sculptural forms in themselves, the monuments to Winston Churchill, Mahatma Gandhi, and Nelson Mandela[6] remained protected not from the decaying effects of time but from potential human-led effects of physical attack (see Gandhi, or perhaps don't see Gandhi, in figure 3.8). Protected from the rain and pollution as much as the hand of anyone who wished them harm, the three entered cryogenic chambers in which the dangers of modern life could be circumvented and temporality could remain forever still.

While staticity reigns for the institutional monument, in graffiti a culture of destruction rather than protection rules. As the classical matter out of place discussed by Mary Douglas (2000 [1966]), graffiti stands as the arch pollutant that must be necessarily destroyed. As Historic England's 2021 guidance to the removal and prevention of graffiti states, these images are like "litter," environmental pollutants "creating an atmosphere of 'lawlessness' in which crime and anti-social behaviour can thrive" (p. 7). Graffiti, in this way, must be understood as the quintessential damage, the criminal, irresponsible acts of human intervention that the preservatory regime seeks to repel. It is the very shit and grime, the very dirt and decay that the heritage regime was set up to protect us from. The laws and schedules of monumental preservation thus function to purge us of these violent, pollutive images, the monumental conservation practices of the heritage industry and the monumentally destructive practices of anti-graffiti authorities[7] functioning in entirely identical ways. Utilizing indistinguishable techniques (the four broad categories, as experts from Historic England explain, of "mechanical, water, chemical and laser" [p. 34]), even being undertaken by the very same organizations and experts (graffiti removal simply being part of a conservation team's habitual activities), artifactual preservation of our official (or institutional) heritage and artificial destruction of our unofficial (or independent) one thus proceed hand in hand. Destruction here is piety, a legal form of iconoclasm considered a natural, appropriate state of affairs. Destruction, as seen in figures 3.9 and 3.10, *is* conservation (the only question being how much and how fast it destroys).

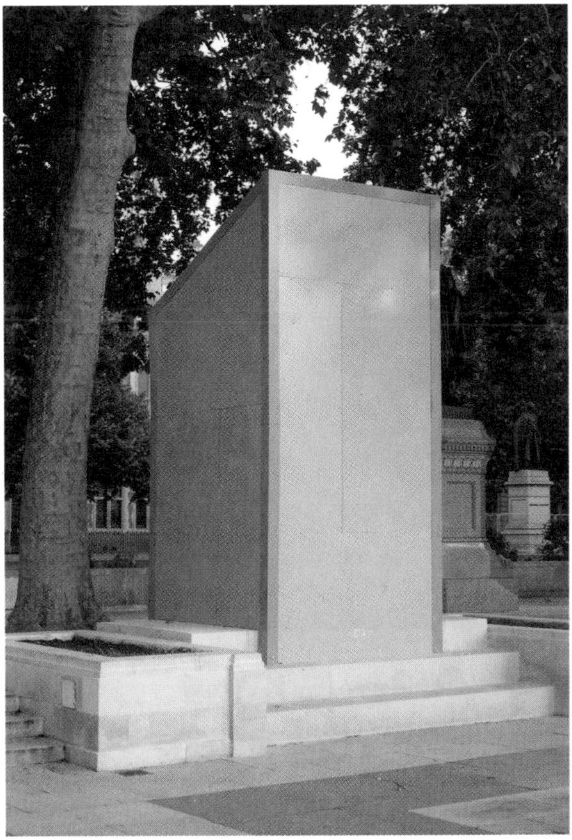

**FIGURE 3.8**
*Gandhi Entombed*, London, 2020. Photo: Rafael Schacter.

Yet the culture of disposability so present within graffiti does not simply derive from extramural bodies, through what we could call the "legitimate" destruction of vandalism,[8] but likewise surfaces from within the internal mechanisms of the graffiti subculture itself. This happens in two ways. First, graffiti will commonly be overpainted by other writers simply due to the lack of available space. If an image is in a premium location (or even just a suitable one) and an artist thinks they can surpass the already present work, or simply that the existent work has had sufficient time to be witnessed by fellow writers, they will have no reservations about painting over the image in situ (such as seen back in figure 3.4, the original piece bleeding through Rainman's latter addition). This form of erasure-through-addition is particularly common within the legal gray spaces of so-called *hall of fame* sites. In Brad Downey's video work *Searching for Something Concrete*, for example, a stop-motion video recording the work of an art

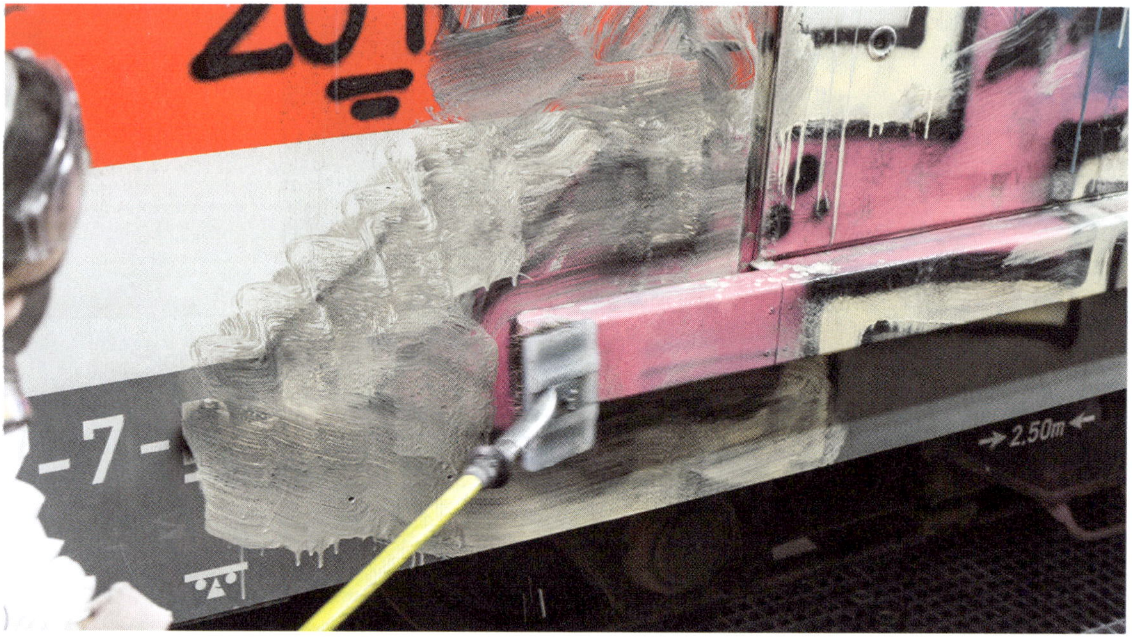


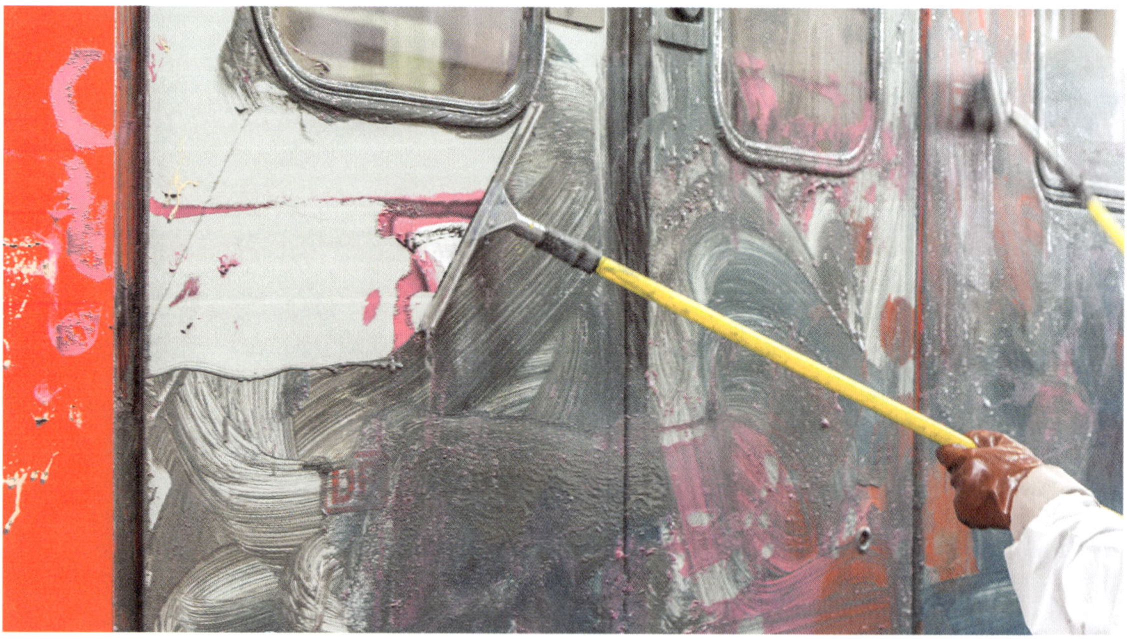

**FIGURES 3.9 AND 3.10**

Raimond Spekking, "Removal of Graffiti from a Train in a New Service Building of Deutsche Bahn in Cologne." August 9, 2016. © Raimond Spekking/CC BY-SA 4.0 (via Wikimedia Commons).

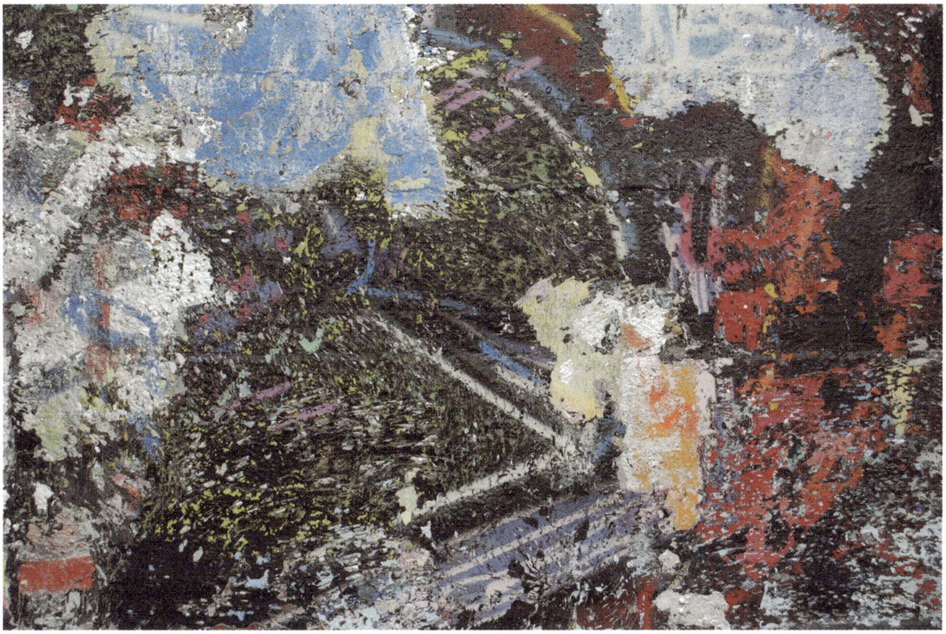

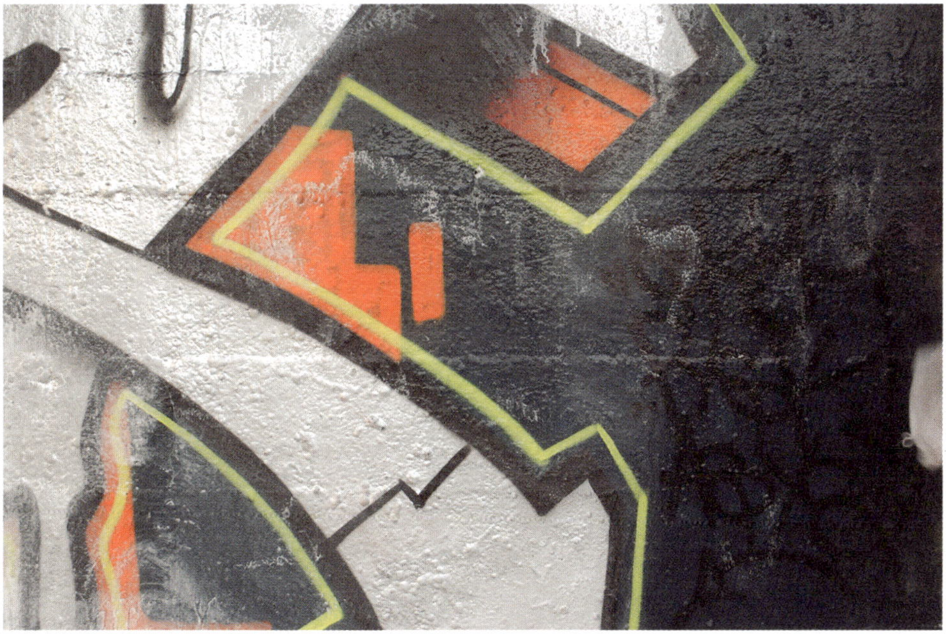

**FIGURES 3.11 AND 3.12**

Brad Downey, stills from *Searching for Something Concrete*, 2010. Digital video, 2 minutes 11 seconds. Courtesy of the artist.

restorer as they remove the layers upon layers of paint found at such a site (as seen in figures 3.11–3.12), we can appreciate what may be the literally thousands of hidden pieces that lie beneath the uppermost surface of these locations. Still, whether semi-legal or not, this form of erasure remains a norm whenever (and wherever) graffiti is produced. Second, graffiti goes through intermural erasure when there is animosity between writers—a form of internal competition often leading to increased creativity through the agonistic spirit it creates. Often descending into "cross-out wars," here opposed writers (or crews) will deface each other's "defacements," superimposing their works in a way that often shows enough of the original piece so that fellow practitioners know exactly whom they have supplanted (as seen in figures 3.13–3.15). Both practices of internal erasure can, however, only truly be understood in terms of their emergence from a milieu in which destruction is always and already inevitable. The image is never sacrosanct, is always subject to the vagaries of a world in process. Destruction thus emerges from a culture that itself understands destruction as inescapable, disposability an accepted and expected part of the graffiti game (even if offence is, perhaps unsurprisingly, often taken).

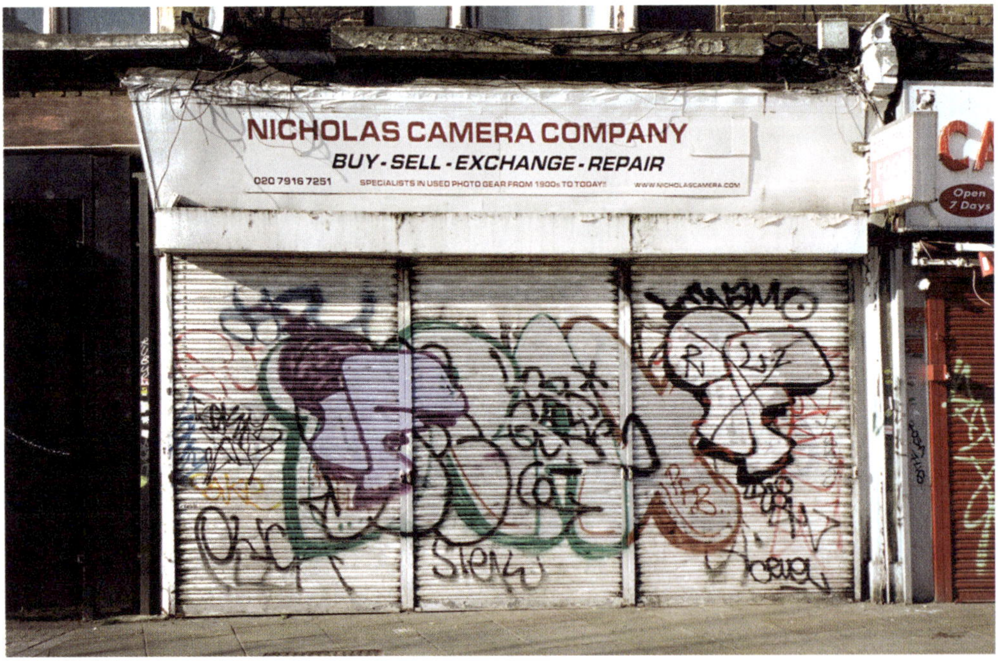


**FIGURE 3.13**
*Untitled* (Nicholas Camera/Everyone Crossed), London, 2020. Photo: Rafael Schacter.

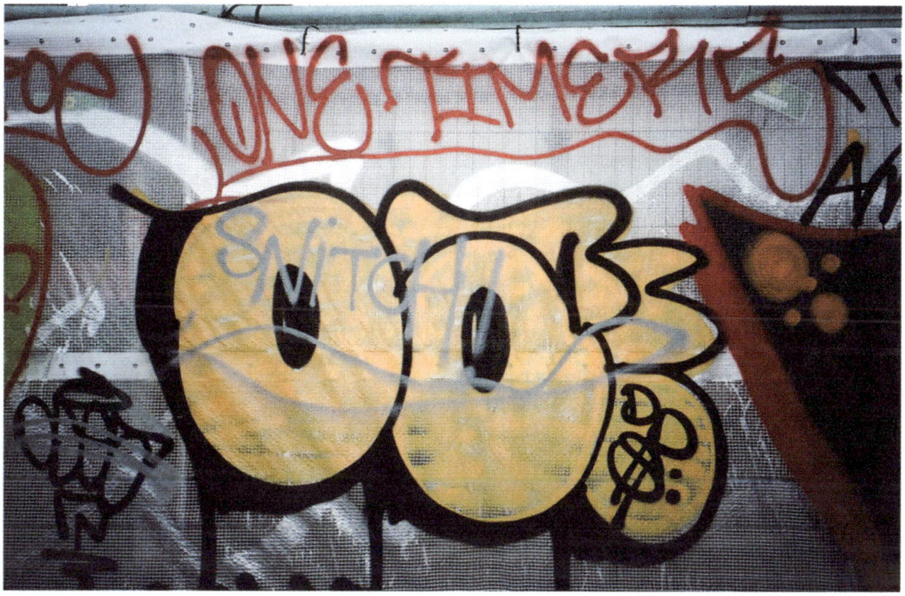

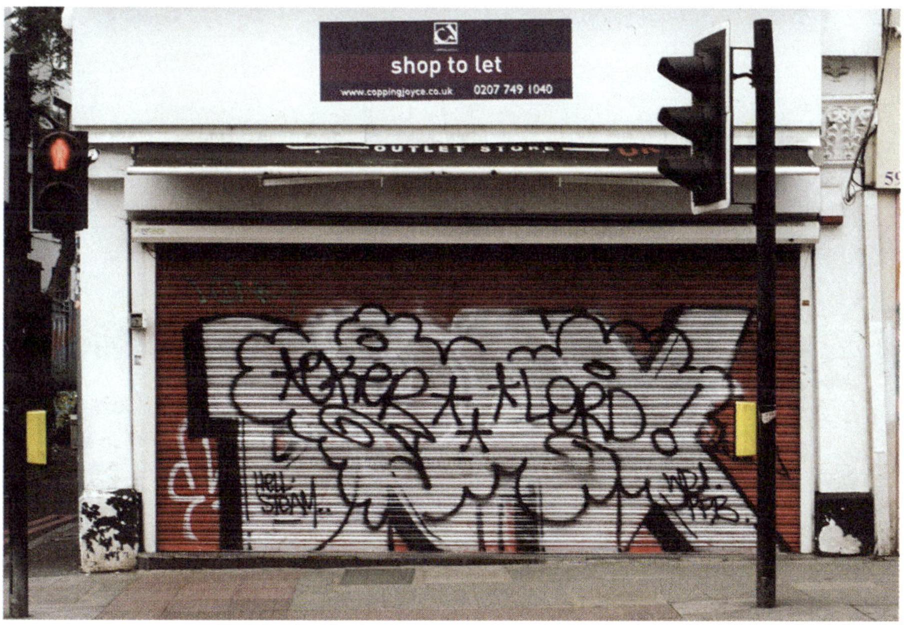


**FIGURE 3.14**
*Untitled (SNITCH!)*, London, 2021. Photo: Rafael Schacter.

**FIGURE 3.15**
*Untitled (Oker and Lord over Drax)*, London, 2020. Photo: Rafael Schacter.

The ephemerality of graffiti can therefore be understood not simply as a predictable but constituent part of the practice. Destruction alludes to the inherent power of that subject to iconoclasm, the "gesture of aggression" inherent to iconoclasm revealing itself, as Dario Gamboni describes it, to be "a gesture of reverence" (Gamboni 2002: 88). Eradication makes the image's efficacy indisputable, creating fresh space for a form often restricted in its locations and a further incentive for artists to produce more images in more places with more speed. While the graffiti image is internally revered, then, it is not perpetually worshipped but rather sacrificed to the city. The image's destruction, believed by anti-graffiti authorities to have the effect of personally wounding the artist (as discussed in Schacter 2008), can thus be seen to emancipate the producer. As per the classical "iconoclash" discussed by Bruno Latour, the annihilation of the image (whether coming from fellow artists or authorities) leads to the inevitable creation of "new images, fresh icons, rejuvenated mediators" (Latour 2002: 16–17). Erasure thus aids an artist's creative expansion, pushes the focus on doing, not simply having done. Development and progression are here dependent on the decomposition of the artifact, whether emergent from natural or artificial modes of erasure.

Graffiti writers will thus produce works with the full knowledge that they will last for only a single night, sometimes even less. The legendary Danish writer Kegr, for example, is famed for painting on trains as they are waiting to be rolled through automatic train-washing systems, while Brad Downey's video work *Buffer* (see figures 3.16

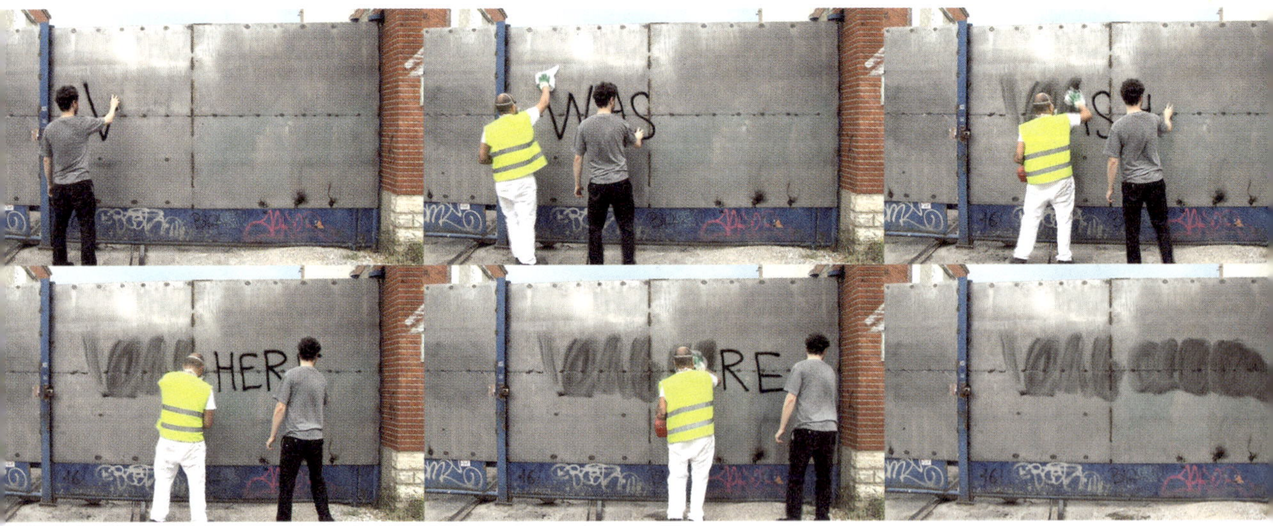

and 3.17) likewise reveals a process of eradication occurring seconds after the marking has been made (here via not an automated machine but a council worker with squeegee and power hose). The British writer Duncan Weston (also known as Petro, whose *Subway Art* paintings we saw in chapter 2) has likewise produced large-scale graffiti pieces (seen in figures 3.18 and 3.19) replicating a popular English beach-side writing technique using found chalk, only before then destroying his own works with buckets of seawater. Like the production of a sand mandala, impermanence is thus fundamental to each of these actions, the practice of writing undertaken in full knowledge that obliteration is (or could be) just moments away, undertaken for its performative and processual values rather than its artifactual ones. Why wait for destruction when it is guaranteed, come what may? Other artists, however, have destroyed their own work to prevent (or perhaps protest) its impending preservation. In 2016, the Italian artist Blu famously destroyed decades of his own murals in Bologna following the (unsanctioned) preservation of a single one of them. Removed from its public location (prior to the planned demolition of the building by its owners) in a pioneering process of preservation undertaken by globally renowned fresco conservator Camillo Tarozzi, the work was then reinstalled at the Palazzo Pepoli for the exhibition *Street Art: Banksy & Co.* (as seen in figures 3.20 and 3.21), an act seen by Blu as a radical afront. For the curators of the exhibition, the original mural was salvaged as part of a wider attempt to think through (and act on) the need to preserve site-specific practice in more general. For them, a photograph could never

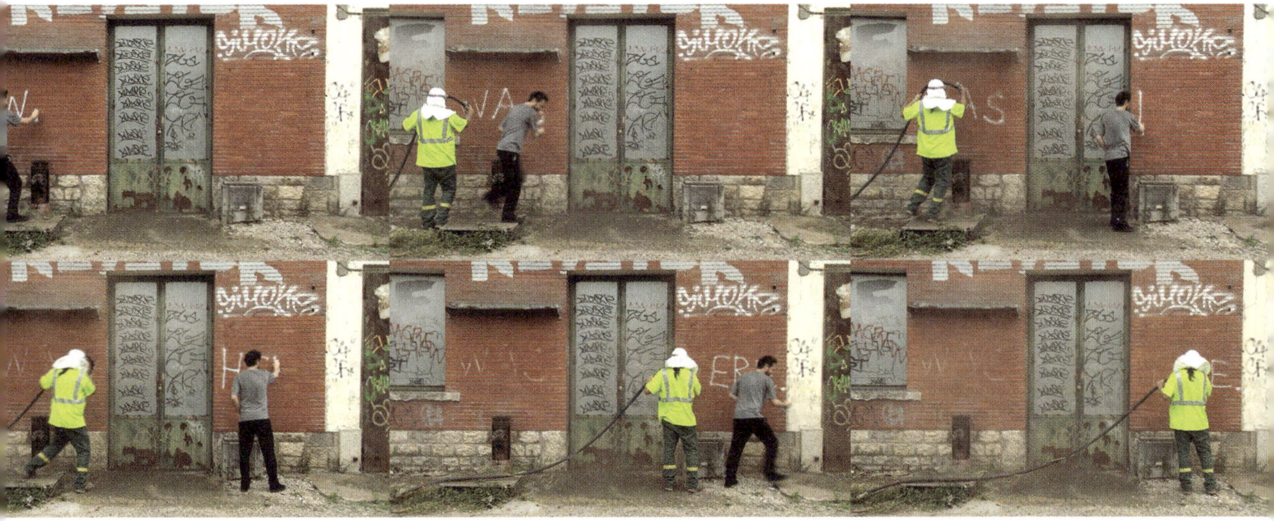

**FIGURES 3.16 AND 3.17**
Brad Downey, stills from *Buffer*, 2014. Digital video, 1 minute 58 seconds. Courtesy of the artist.

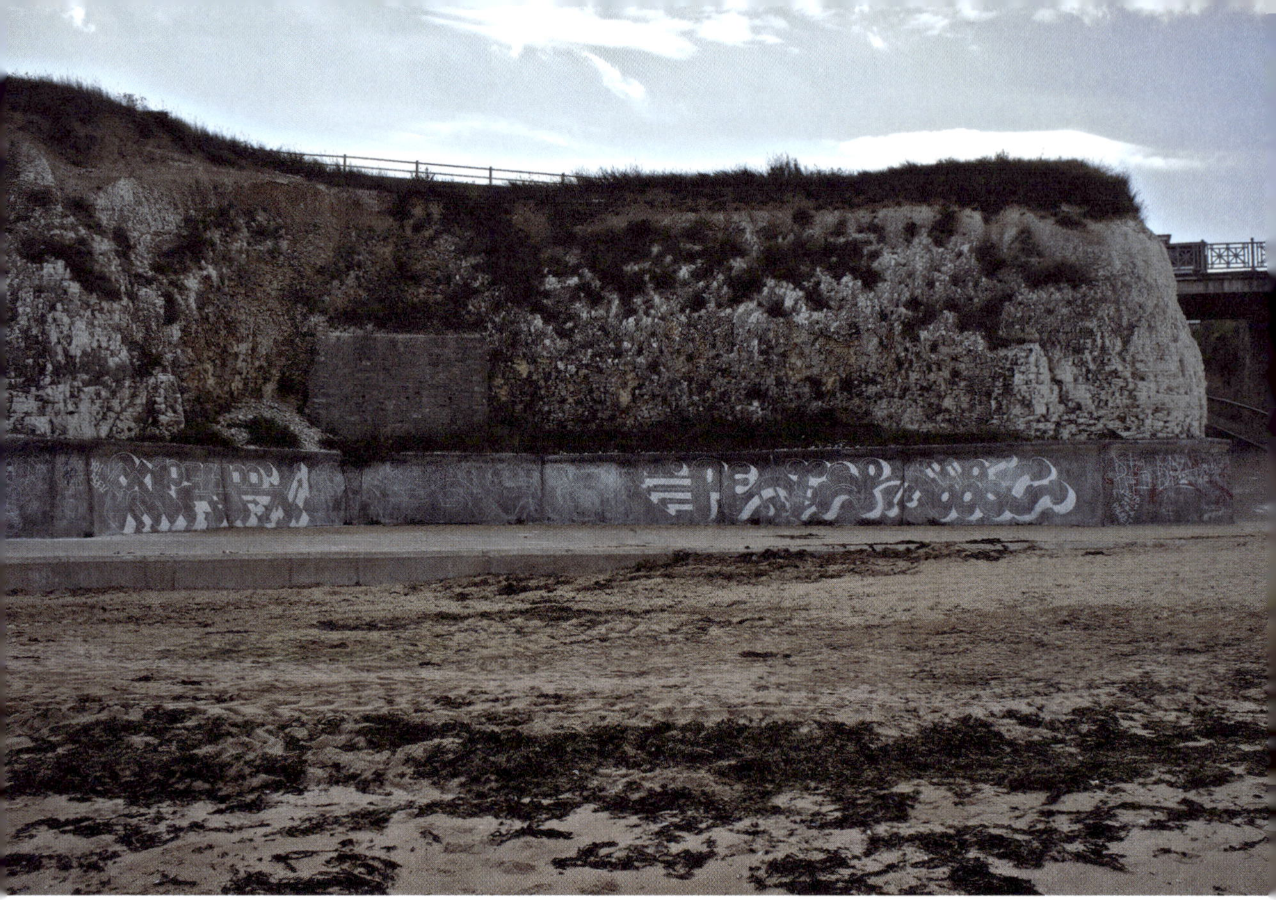

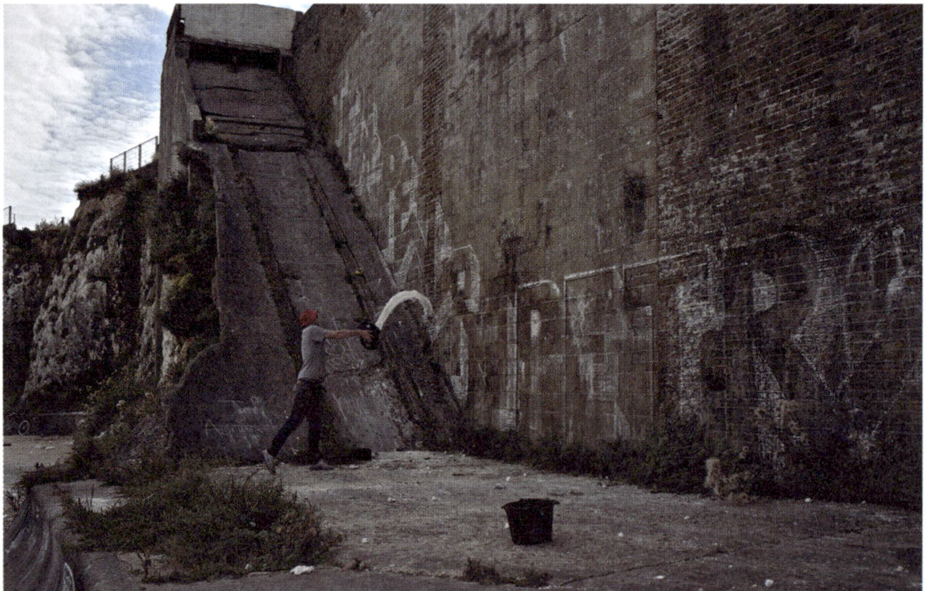

replicate the physical qualities or experience of scale when encountering a production of this size. While the museum and the curators thus saw the mural as Art, as part of a communal heritage whose survival was more important than an individual artist's personal will, for the artist the preservation of the work was believed to be part of an acquisitive, corporatist desire to own something that cannot be owned. "The only thing that's left to do," the activist collective Wu Ming wrote on Blu's behalf, is to "make these paintings disappear, to snatch them from those claws, to make hoarding impossible" (Wu Ming 2016: n.p.). Here destruction, as Holtorf has written, can thus be seen as a manner of "consuming heritage in a way that others are simply not used to or choose not to approve of" (Holtorf 2006: 104). With destruction, the life cycle of the image—its authentic heritage as considered by its producer—is assured. Destruction ensures that it stays within the realm of practice, not product, as a living rather than a dead object.[9]

The material disposability of graffiti thus begins to outline an ontology radically different not only from that inherent within the heritage regime but so too from art itself. The imposed staticity of the preservative threatens the circulation and propagation of graffiti that impermanence enables. Fixity places the focus on the image alone, curtailing a focus on performance. Conservation can hence be seen as annihilation, while annihilation itself can come to reject the "commodity logic of ownership" that, as the anthropologist Haidy Geismar has suggested, underpins most "definitions and implementations of cultural heritage" and that "converts into property or resources that which could also be chartered as inalienable" (Geismar 2015: 80–81). Debates on conservation within indigenous museological practice thus become pertinent here. As Nancy Mithlo has argued, here quoting Edmund J. Ladd of the Pueblo of Zuni, to "take care of" an artifact within an indigenous context can often mean enabling its "deterioration and disintegration," a position that is indicative not of a "misunderstanding of museum [or heritage regime] values but of an alternate ideology at work" (Mithlo 2004: 745). What emerges is thus a radically different understanding of material culture that rejects the concept of timelessness so present within Western art. Like the artifacts Ladd and Mithlo discuss, graffiti too does not fear death. Dying, whether via natural or cultural causes, via time or violence, simply makes the object more powerful. Rather than being isolated, insulated from the world, these materials must be present within the destructive processes of our natural and cultural environments to make sense. Rather than being irreplaceable, graffiti demands replaceability. Rather than attempting to prolong or maintain the image, re-formation, not restoration, is required. Grünfeld's hypometabolic state is thus an abomination in graffiti, a crime against time.

This affirmation of destruction can also be seen within a lineage of contemporary art, however. While Robert Rauschenberg's *Erased de Kooning Drawing* (1953) and Ai

**FIGURES 3.18 AND 3.19**
Duncan Weston (Petro), *Sea & Cliffs*, 2012, Margate. Found chalk, found charcoal, and seawater. Courtesy of the artist.

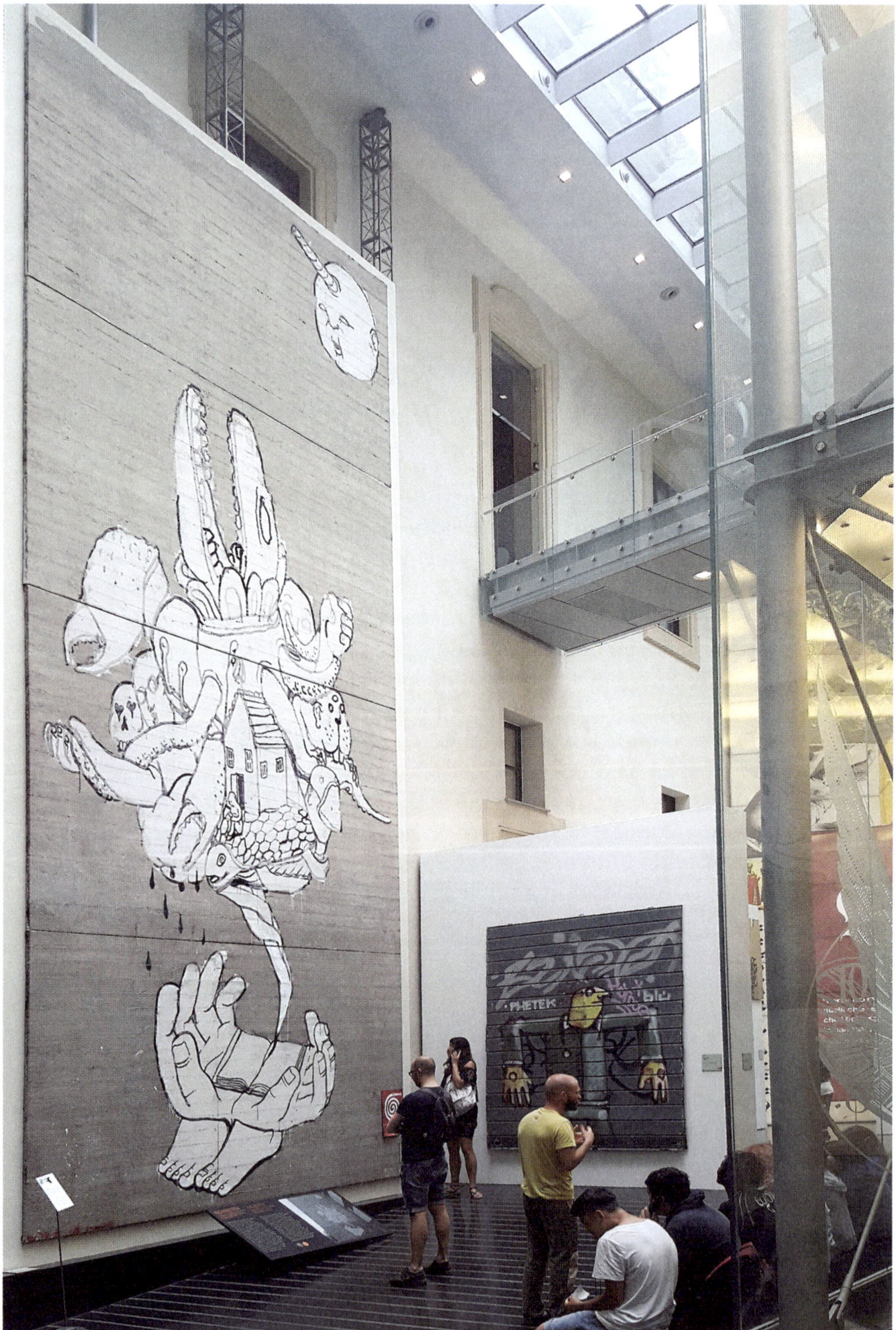
PHETEK

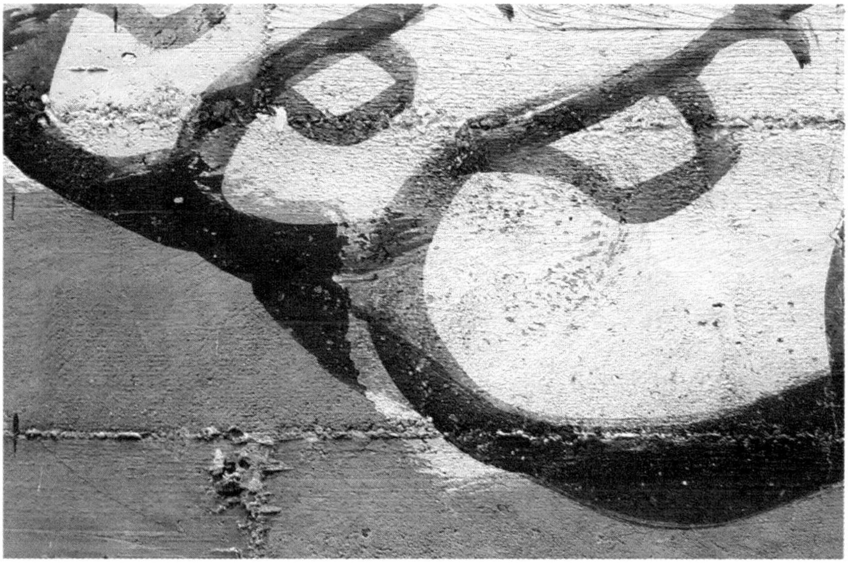

**FIGURE 3.20**
Blu, *Untitled*, 2006. Wall painting on canvas, 1,011 cm × 470 cm, four pieces. Courtesy of Collezioni d'Arte e di Storia della Fondazione Cassa di Risparmio in Bologna.

**FIGURE 3.21**
Blu, *Untitled* (detail), 2006. Wall painting on canvas, 1,011 × 470 cm, four pieces. Courtesy of Collezioni d'Arte e di Storia della Fondazione Cassa di Risparmio in Bologna.

Weiwei's *Dropping a Han Dynasty Urn* (1995) both provide key examples of an art *of* destruction, Gustaf Metzger's auto-destructive art of the late 1950s and 1960s explicitly sought to create an art that was un-conservable: "When the disintegrative process is complete," he stated, a process involving, for example, pouring acid over sheets of nylon, "the work is to be removed from the site and scrapped" (Metzger in Laurenson and Bayley 2022: 259). Yet as Laurenson and Bayley explore, Metzger's work has still been pushed through the conservatory mill that the heritage regime enforces, too important a figure for his works to be discarded to the literal scrap heap (as the artist desired). While, like Blu's mural, the material form is seemingly "saved" so as to remain materially visible to a new generation of art historians, what remains missing is not only the integral site- and time-specificity, but the "activism," "voice," and "agency" of the artist themself (Laurenson and Bayley 2022: 263). The preservation of Metzger's work destroys the "messiness, the humanity and the politics of these desperate, urgent acts of destruction," conservation functioning to "flatten, clean up, dehumanise, depoliticise and institutionalise" his practice (p. 264). Still, while we could see this case as one simply emphasizing the power of the institution to absorb all radicality into its insatiable belly, it is the paradoxes that it raises which are even more critical to affirm. It is not just that destruction can be preservative—the erasure of graffiti enabling prolongation through engendering increased productivity—but that preservation can likewise be destructive too. Conservators may have found techniques to immortalize the ephemeral, but making a "stable museum object out of something intended to self-destruct" the "maintenance machine," as seen in the Metzger case, comes to erase both the "artist and his intent" (p. 264). Conservation can thus be seen as not only a simulation, but an equally destructive process as so-called destruction itself.

With that said, alongside the way in which the acid, the scratches, and the purposefully hard-to-reach graffiti defer the speed of institutional erasure, graffiti can likewise be seen to enable preservative processes through a secondary form of documentation. The graffiti photograph (as featured throughout this book!) can be argued to act as an ancillary mode of conservation, a mode of "prolongation" in which, as McAuliffe and Iveson note, the "camera has emerged as a crucial piece of graffiti-writing equipment, every bit as important as the spray can or the marker pen" (McAuliffe and Iveson 2011: 137). Not only letting a long-erased image "circulate among friends and colleagues, be published online or in a graffiti magazine, or even make an appearance in a best-selling book" (p. 137), it can also be argued that it was photography that enabled the emergence of the graffiti canon itself! Without the documentary conservation of Cooper and Chalfant, graffiti itself may have never lived beyond 1970s New York. Still, what is clear is that these images are considered not as *art*-objects by practitioners (as documentary materials from the institutional art world have today become), but rather as records of an act completed, proleptic images foreshadowing their own death. They lack life in the same way as a photograph of a deceased ancestor may: still often venerated, still agentic artifacts facilitating narratives and stories, yet in themselves no longer considered alive. While images are thus often shared—in the late writer Tvrbo's case through Polaroids taken (and then swapped) just after pieces has been completed (seen in figure 3.22), or likewise through small batches of self-produced, photocopied zines—for the most part they have a highly delimited mode of circulation due to the dangers that images of illegally produced work can prompt. Concealed from public viewership, hidden in blackbooks (as seen in a spread from Delta's collection in figure 3.23), or kept in shoeboxes stashed under beds, access to these documents often only emerges through a highly privileged space of encounter. Still, while steadily increasing since the

**FIGURE 3.22**
*Untitled (Tvrbo/Glub)*, Madrid, 2009. Photo: Rafael Schacter.

**FIGURE 3.23**
Boris Tellegen/Delta, *Untitled*. Taken from *8697*, a compendium of "blackbook" or sketchbook/scrapbook pages produced between 1986 and 1997. Courtesy of the artist.

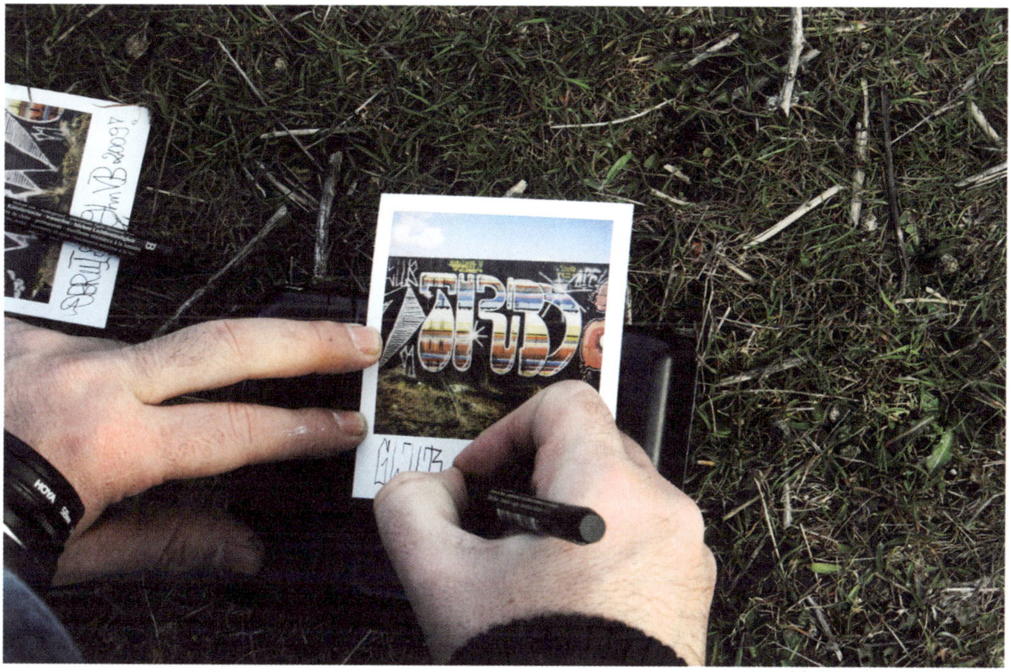

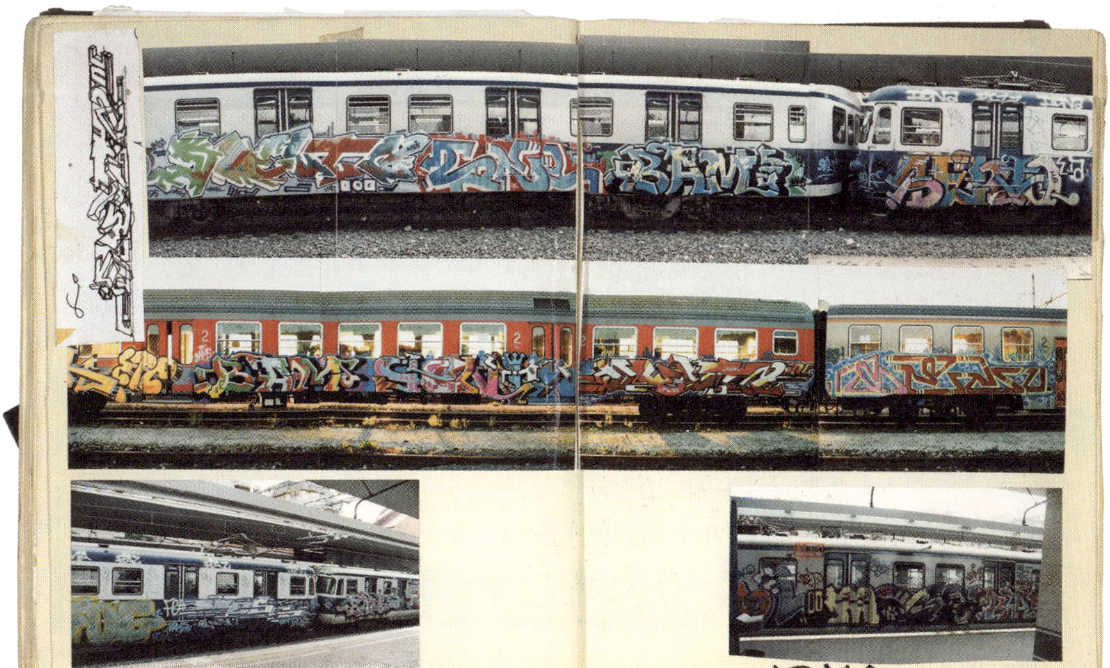
ROMA

advent of smartphones (as seen in figure 3.24), the percentage of graffiti that has been photographically preserved is incredibly small. The focus on the act above all else (as discussed in our next chapter) means that writers will often leave their piece without a second look back,[10] documentation most often emerging from aspiring photographers (or anthropologists) capturing that which the writer has left to the world. The grassroots archive[11] of graffiti images is thus understood as innately valuable, but is never a substitute for the artifact itself.[12]

The graffiti monument is therefore a monument of and to erasure, a monument to transience able to "embrace the powers and potentials of wilful destruction and irretrievable loss" (Holtorf 2006: 108). The institutional monument's techniques of conservation stand in direct opposition to the disposability of the graffiti monument, a technique of staticity opposed to one of circulation, an embracement of the singular art piece opposed to an embracement of never-ending process. What we find here are divergent material ontologies that are linked, as we will discuss in the final section of this chapter, to a mode of commemoration that engages absence and presence both. The institutional monument thus needs to be preserved not only for its material perpetuity,

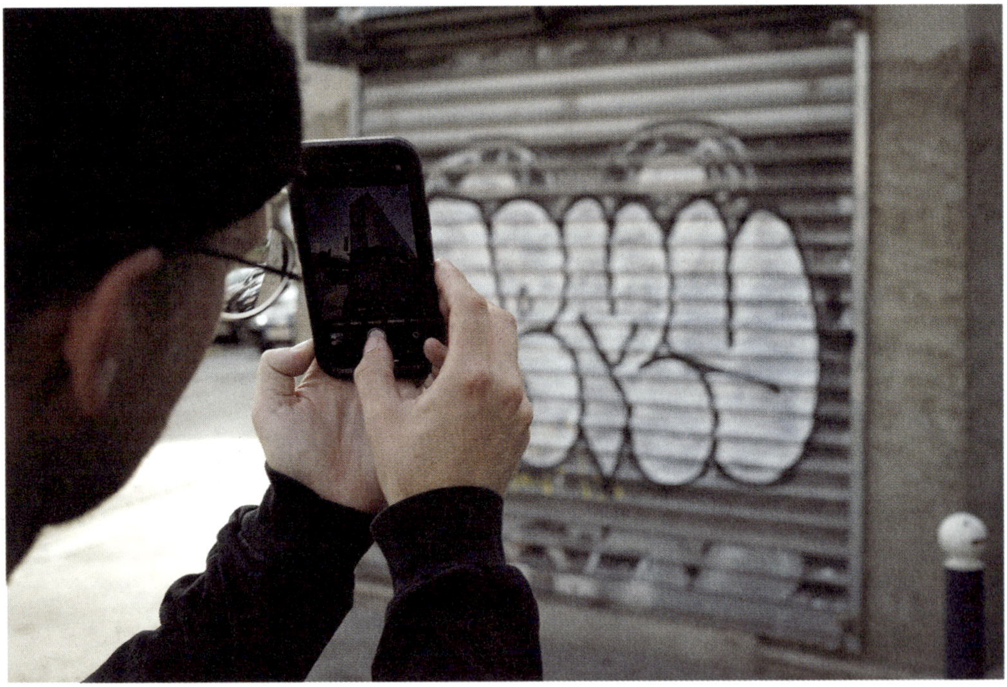

**FIGURE 3.24**
*Remio*, Paris, 2022. Photo: Gökhan S.

but for its memorial permanency too; the memory and the material, that memorialized and the monument, are, from the position of the heritage industry, irrevocably linked, and their linkage must therefore be defended at all costs.

## PRESENCE AND ABSENCE *OR* MONUMENTAL MEMORIES

The regimes of durability and conservation that the institutional monument functions through are fundamentally linked to its commemorative techniques. Its status as an aide-mémoire, a tool for *reminding*, demands an ongoing presence that only continuous protection can fulfill. As Pierre Nora famously wrote, the modern memory "takes root in the concrete," in "spaces," in "images, and objects" (Nora 1989: 9). It relies "entirely on the materiality of the trace," on "exterior scaffolding and outward signs," on the "visibility of the image" (p. 13). Here, our built environment, as Adrian Forty likewise noted, is thus believed to have the capacity to "take the place of the mental memory" (Forty 1999: 15), to "prolong or preserve" our remembrances "beyond their purely mental existence" (p. 2). The material world is hence appreciated in a mnemonical sense, the fragility of our human memory upheld by the enduring resilience of artifactual form. As such, and just as is the case with the human brain, only with protection and stabilization can the body retain the memories that come to act as the basis for that body's identity itself. The decay that emerges with advanced years—whether in physiological or architectural form—can lead not only to a state of disorientation, an instability borne from an inability to fix onto the past, but to a state in which self-identity is set adrift: just as the mind without memories becomes a mind devoid of a sense of self, total degeneration here leads to total loss. Take Nora's materiality and visibility away, then, topple these scaffolds and signs, and the mental architecture they uphold is understood to simply crumble away. Without a physical substance to hold onto them, memory of our places, our events, our *people*, is believed to become forever lost. While degradation of materiality is understood to lead to the degradation of the ideas these materials seek to project, *absence* is understood to lead to their irreversible disappearance. Out of sight (or out of site), out of mind.

While decay is a problem necessitating preservation to allay, then, destruction must be prevented at all costs. The very idea that these objects could be anything other than immovable is feared to bring the status quo they protect into question. In the UK context, in particular since the Black Lives Matter protests of 2020 and the public toppling of the statue to Edward Colston in Bristol (as seen in figures 3.25 and 3.26), the guardians of the institutional monument have been fighting aggressively (and anxiously) to uphold this position of permanence. In a now infamous letter sent to almost all of the United Kingdom's national museums and galleries by the Culture Secretary Oliver Dowden (infamous as while exceedingly polite, it contained clear threats to cut funding if adherence to its partisan line was not obeyed), these cultural stakeholders

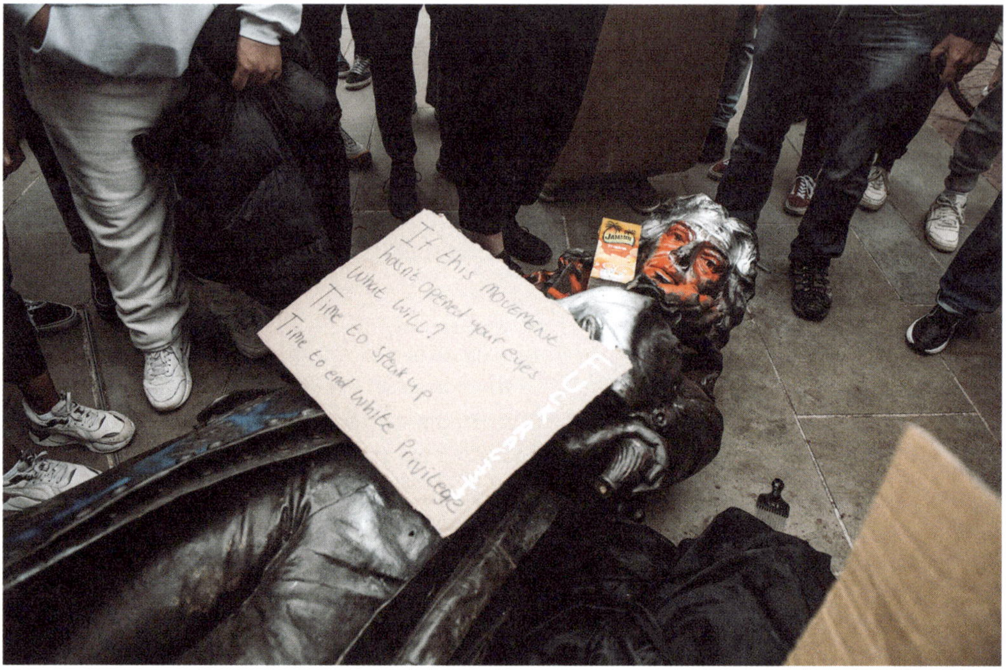


**FIGURE 3.25**
John Cassidy, *Statue of Edward Colston (toppled)*, 2020. Photo: Giulia Spadafora. Courtesy of Giulia Spadafora/Nur Photo.

were warned that "the Government does not support the removal of statues or other similar objects" and that "removing difficult and contentious parts of [our historic environment] risks harming our understanding of our collective past" (Dowden 2020). Continuing to outline his position in the *Daily Telegraph*, Dowden declared that he would not "look on as people threaten to pull down statues or strip other parts of our rich historic environment" and would instead stand up "to the political fads and noisy movements of the moment" (Dowden 2021).[13] The "duty" of the "custodians of our heritage," he continued, was "to preserve" rather than "airbrush" our material culture, to "'retain and explain' rather than 'remove or ignore'" (Dowden 2021). Going forward, not only would alterations to any scheduled or listed monuments need to go through the legal planning process (as per the existent regulations), but new laws would make the "removal of any historic unlisted statue, plaque, memorial or monument . . . subject to planning permission" (Jenrick 2021).

As such, and coming into force on April 21, 2021, the new "Town and Country Planning Order 2021" meant that "statues, memorials and monuments which have been in

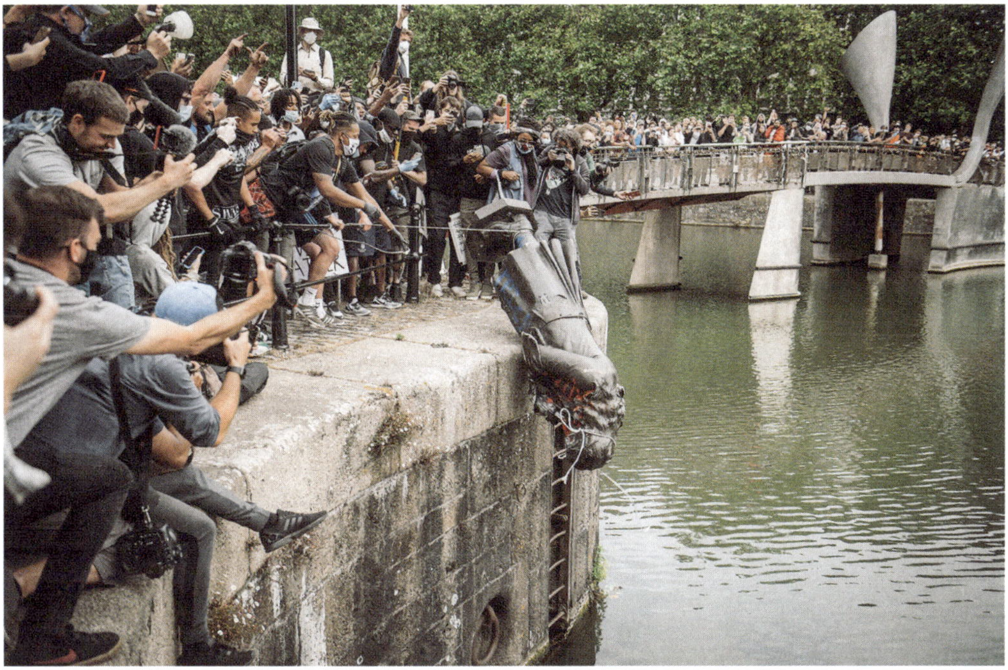

**FIGURE 3.26**
John Cassidy, *Statue of Edward Colston (tipped)*, 2020. Photo: Giulia Spadafora. Courtesy of Giulia Spadafora/Nur Photo.

place for 10 years or more" would need governmental permission to be removed. Only five categories of monuments were kept outside these new laws, "either because they are subject to other regulation, to protect the curatorial independence of museums and art galleries or to avoid everyday garden ornaments [!] being captured by the new rules" (Grimwood 2021: 6). As claimed in the government's press release, what this new bill thus meant was that over "20,000 statues and monuments throughout England" were now protected "for future generations" (Ministry of Housing, Communities and Local Government 2021). As such, even if a community convinced a local planning officer that a particular statue, monument, or street name should be removed—not only a listed but so too a *non*listed monument that was more than a decade old—the Secretary of State for Housing could simply "call in" this particular case and unilaterally refuse it. Going beyond even planning and listing law, however, the UK government likewise announced a new set of measures relating to public heritage within their controversial Police, Crime, Sentencing and Courts Bill 2021. Increasing the "maximum available penalty for criminal damage to a memorial from 3 months to 10 years' imprisonment" while decreasing the "monetary threshold for [prosecuting] cases involving damage to memorials" (Grimwood 2021: 7), the government thus made clear that public monuments (garden gnomes not withstanding) were subject to protection at the level of not only the symbolic but so too the financial and custodial. A sculpture could thus be literally *worthless* (let alone utterly offensive), but if it is damaged, significant prison time, if not a significant fine, becomes a real possibility.[14]

While it is impossible to see these legal changes outside the ongoing culture war that the Conservative government of the early 2020s clearly believed focus-grouped in their favor, the position it reveals is a coherent one. Without ongoing presence, the social constructs (and status quo) that these monuments frame and the memories they sustain are feared to fragment. Speaking in support of this (and the government's) stance, and taking up a doubly conservative position, the United Kingdom's Public Statues and Sculpture Association (PSSA) thus suggested that if

> statues are removed this will leave an historic vacuum of ignorance. We will have manipulated history in the same way these statues have been accused of doing by misrepresenting it. There will be nothing for later generations to learn from. If on the other hand, statues are retained and given full, inclusive and honest didactic labels this can help mitigate some of the cruel, barbaric acts of the past. (Harris 2021)

Leaving aside what seems to be PSSA's suggestion that history can only be learned on the street—let alone the idea that a label can ever mitigate the feeling of distress generated through being forced to look up to a man who took part in the murder of nearly 20,000 human beings, in particular for those whose ancestors were themselves enslaved by Colson—what is being said here remains quite clear: without the presence of these objects, the ideas, the people, the memories they contain will become forever absent. Without the physical immediacy of these forms, a manipulated vacuum will emerge in which we will be devoid of all knowledge. The barbarous people who enacted barbaric acts must therefore retain their (literal) positions of prominence in the public realm (albeit with updated labels). Forgetting the question of when[15] they were erected and what[16] they were erected for, forgetting the fact that the dramaturgical spectacularity of the monument will always overpower the physical paucity of its explanatory plaque, these monuments (as long as they are over a decade old) are our history and thus so too are our present and future too. Whether good or bad, as outlined in this monumental defense, without these memories we will become nations without souls.[17]

Within graffiti, however, an entirely different mnemonical pattern emerges. Here absence becomes a mnemonic structure in itself, a factor enabling, not disabling, memory. Remembering in graffiti emerges not only from the reverberations that the act of destruction generates, but through a practice of witnessing in which structural impermanence transforms the way writers physically *look*. Graffiti writers' memories are thus colossal. They are forced to remember because their images are forcibly removed. Writers are thus primed for the elimination of their own and others' work, techniques of looking structured by the knowledge that only one glimpse may ever be allowed. Structural impermanence thus necessitates a system of visual reception that is integrally different from that in which permanence rules. As such, while legacy is still critical to graffiti (and to the accrual of fame, discussed in chapter 2), it emerges not through how long a specific artifact has been up but through how long you yourself have been. Legacy emerges not through physical form but through narrative, a monument built up not only via written words but by spoken ones. It comes via an appreciation of scale that remains even when the image itself does not. While the ever-presence of our bronze men on horseback leads to their strangely amnesiatic status, prospective absence creates a different manner of re-cognizing the image: it must be mentally stored because it will be physically effaced; it must be actively remembered as it will be actively erased. Nora's (1989) position on modern memory is thus reversed: it is the image's *in*visibility that here gives rise to its remembrance. Seeing is thus critical, but seeing just once can be enough.

This style of mnemonic impermanence can likewise be seen within the New Ireland funerary carvings known as Malangan discussed by Susanne Küchler (2001). Objects that are ritually sacrificed following their momentary public revelation—through either being taken into the forest to decompose of their own volition or being sold to ever-eager foreigners and anthropologists—the destruction of the Malangan leads to the "creation of an inherently recallable image" that works through a "foreshadowing [of its] own displacement" (Küchler 2001: 63). Not only do the Malangan serve as "vessels for the transmission of names" (p. 65), which are, like graffiti, "recalled" through their "imagistic character" (p. 66), but when "attending the reveal of a malangan, everybody present is purposeful and prepared—their minds and pockets ready to attain at least a fragment of share in what is to be seen for only a matter of minutes" (p. 67). Those who witness the work before its disappearance—like, as Küchler notes, those present at the fall of the Berlin Wall or those who witnessed Christo and Jean-Claude's famous *Wrapped Reichstag*—then acquire the "right to own its memory and to use it as a source for future recollections of what was rendered absent" (p. 68). Absence thus allows us to be "'touched' by memory like an awakening from a dream," to engage with the "memory of an image seen for a brief moment" (p. 68). Just as with graffiti, then, value here is "not attributed to the objects, but to the memory of their imagery and to the right over their reproduction" (Küchler 1987: 240). The image thus becomes unforgettable *due* to its disposability. It assaults the senses, circulating through memory and materiality alike, generating a form of looking that only true adherents can then re-form and re-transmit. It creates a form of looking in which knowledge of past works become re-embedded in future ones.

Not only evident within the Malangan, this understanding of absence as *resource* can also be seen within the paradigm of what James E. Young famously termed the "counter-monument" (Young 1992: 267). As seen in Esther Shalev-Gerz and Jochen Gerz's masterpiece *The Monument against Fascism* (see figures 3.27–3.29)—a work emergent from a post-Holocaust milieu in which conventional practices of memorialization were believed to be incapable of dealing with such inconceivable loss—here the work was meant "not to remain fixed but to change; not to be everlasting but to disappear" (Young 1992: 278). While beginning as what appeared to be a broadly conventional twelve-meter-high monolith, after its inauguration in 1986 the monument went through a period of eight lowerings so that, by 1993, it was visible only through a nameplate set upon the floor. The monument not only was a participatory one—the sinkings occurring after a statement against fascism had been ratified by participants through inscribing their names on its lead surface—but exemplified the idea that the "best monument . . . may

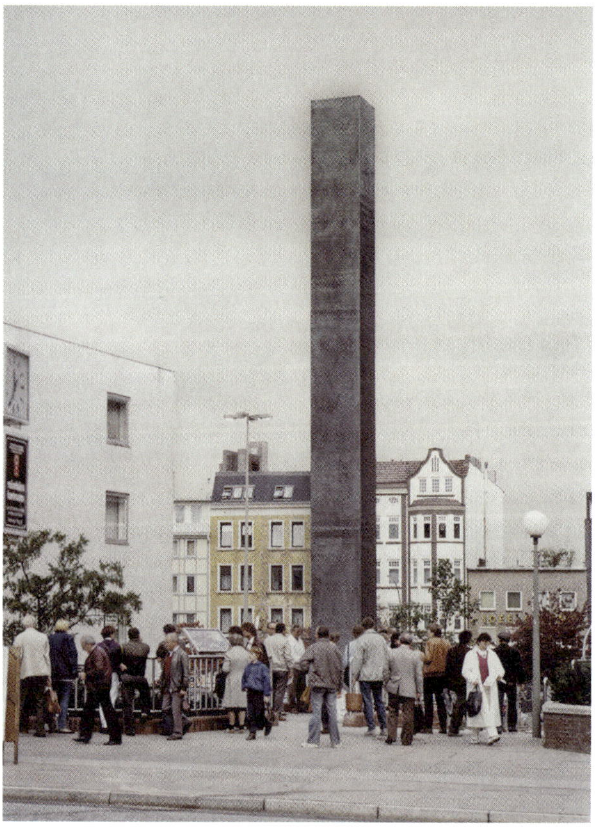

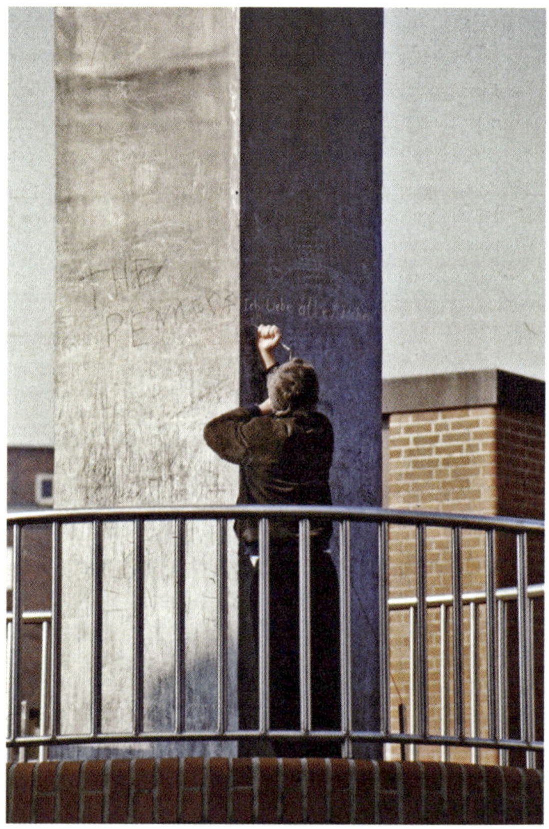

**FIGURES 3.27 AND 3.28**
Esther Shalev-Gerz and Jochen Gerz, *Mahnmal gegen Faschismus (Monument against Fascism)*, 1986. Harburg–Hamburg. 12 m × 1 m × 1 m. Column of galvanized steel with a lead coating, signatures. Courtesy of Atelier Shalev-Gerz. Photos: Esther Shalev-Gerz. © Esther Shalev-Gerz and Jochen Gerz.

be no monument at all, but only the memory of an absent monument" (Young 1992: 279). The monument, as seen in the invitation text, thus underscored not just that it was only ourselves "who can stand up against injustice," but likewise that it was only a monumental absence (rather than monumental presence) that enables memory to go "where it belongs—that is, within the people for whom it was created" (Gerz 1989 in Young 1992: 278).

The renowned public interventions of artist Krzysztof Wodiczko likewise work through a similarly powerful transience. Known for his large-scale projections that reveal the social and political realities that our public monuments often seek to conceal, Wodiczko's ephemeral performances function through the creation of images whose equally transient and ornamental nature is critical. At his legendary work in Trafalgar Square in 1985, for example—in which, as seen in figures 3.30 and 3.31, Wodiczko not only projected an image of a missile wrapped in barbed wire onto the column (to reinforce its militaristic essence), but likewise projected a swastika onto the pediment of South Africa House (in a protest again the then ruling apartheid government)—the images were not only constitutively ephemeral but all the more powerful due to that fact. While lasting only two hours before the police intervened to end the display, the works functioned via not just the image but the *afterimage* that they came to create. As Wodiczko himself said, "if one disrupts the routine perception of everyday life, one has

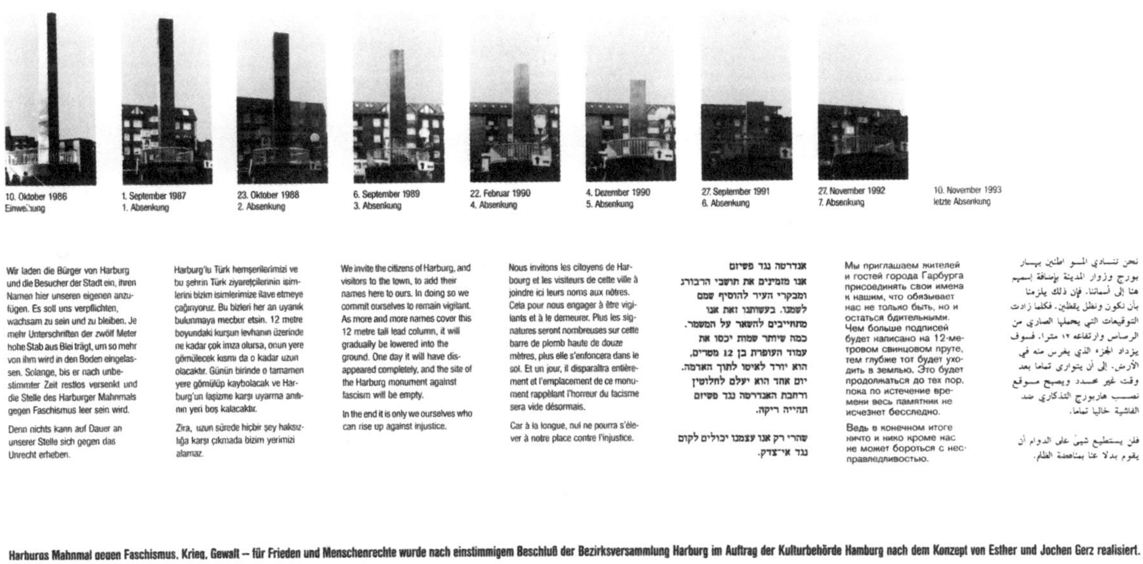


**FIGURE 3.29**

Esther Shalev-Gerz and Jochen Gerz, *Mahnmal gegen Faschismus (Monument against Fascism)*, 1986, Harburg–Hamburg. Text panel. Courtesy of Atelier Shalev-Gerz and Gerz Studio. © Esther Shalev-Gerz and Jochen Gerz.

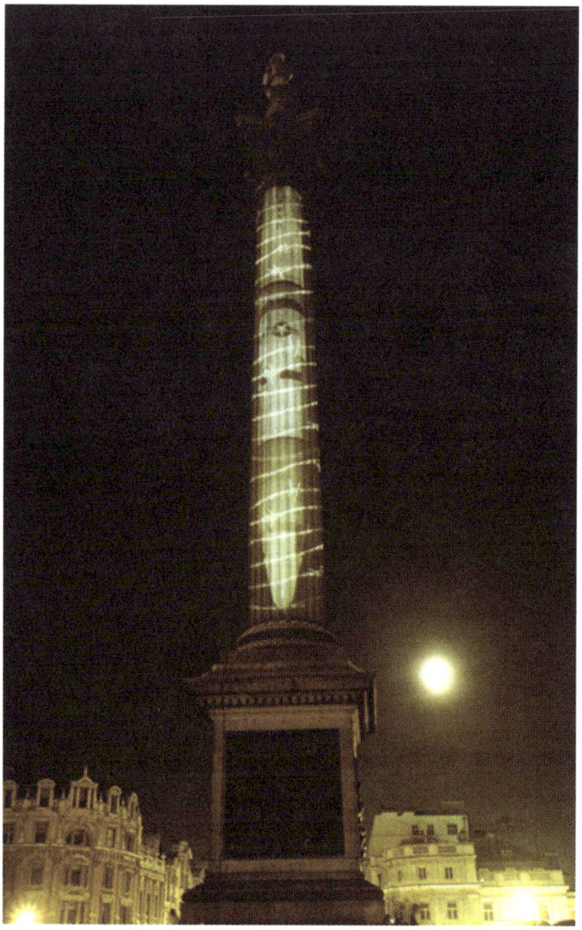

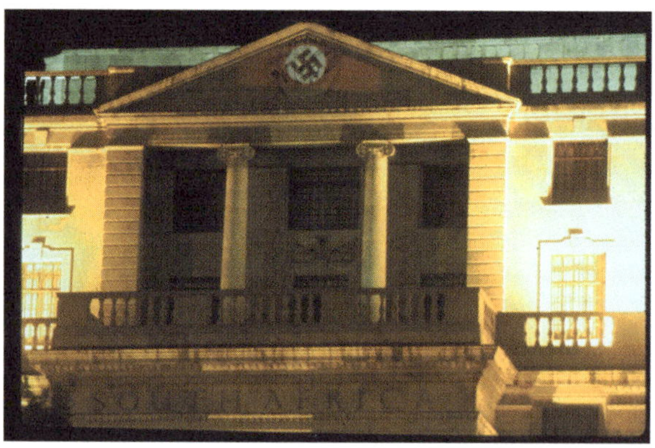

**FIGURES 3.30 AND 3.31**

Krzysztof Wodiczko, *Public Projection: Nelson's Column, Trafalgar Square, London*, 1985. Courtesy of the artist and Galerie Lelong, New York.

to be tactical and temporary by principle" (Wodiczko 1999: 208). Here, then, absence functions as a technique to remain always present in the mind.

Transience can therefore be seen as a tool that enables recollection; "less (preservation)," as Holtorf has said, often meaning "more (memory)" (Holtorf 2006: 103). The "more is more" aesthetic of the contemporary heritage regime, in which buildings today become ripe for historic preservation even before their construction has completed, becomes an exercise in numbing rather than engaging our memories. The omnipresent can thus enable forgetting, the institutional monument's shouldering of the burden of memory ridding us, as Young continues, of "the obligation to remember" (Young 1992: 273). The always-living artwork hence becomes a tool to assuage us of the need to bring back the past, the static monument an effigy in which memories are cast and then forever overlooked. While the institutional monument is almost always set toward the (idealized) past, then, destroyed or ephemeral monuments, as Rowlands has suggested, become "remembered for themselves, not for what they might have stood for in terms of remembered pasts" (Rowlands 1993: 147). The graffiti monument is thus not only an impermanent monument, but one speaking in the present tense. It reminds us of an act completed, a performance caught in pigment that sits waiting for its inevitable disappearance, yet that due to this resists the deep anxiety of our institutional structures. It is a monument that does not fear death, let alone decay. Rather than struggling to "keep everything" within what Nora termed "the imperative of our epoch" (Nora 1989: 14), the impermanent monument embraces an active memory that moves beyond the fabrications of the nostalgic. It is thus not only a monument of and to absence but an absent monument in which legacy and memory inexorably persist.

## CONCLUSION *OR* FROM THE EPHEMERAL TO THE MEMORIAL

Just as with site and with style, however, time must be considered as a pivotal formal dimension not only of the graffiti image but of the culture too. The duration of graffiti, the way the image decays, disappears, and is destroyed, is critical to the way the image is seen and comprehended, the way it is not protected but given up, is witnessed and recalled. Just as durability, preservation, and presence are integral to the way we understand the *institutional* monument—as that set in stone and placed on a pedestal, as a form protected at all costs and whose continuous witnessing is pivotal—the graffiti monument's durational patterns are just as integral. Together they form an artifact that naturally disappears through time, that is in a state of irreparable finitude, yet which gains power due to this very fact. Graffiti's material temporality thus upholds the fact not only that transience is supreme but that the transformation this generates can add as much as it takes—giving the image both age-value and stylistic presence. Graffiti's cultural temporality accepts the internal and external destruction it is subject to—understanding disposability as a factor leading to more, not less, as well as pushing attention toward action over artifact. And graffiti's mnemonic temporality comprehends absence as something inciting as much, if not more, memory than presence—something that structures the way writers look at the image, as much as the way they reproduce and recirculate it. Materially, ontologically, commemoratively, the graffiti monument is thus radically other to its institutional relative; it will degrade; it will be erased; it will dissipate. Like the veneration of the fleeting within traditional Japanese celebrations, then, "three simple principles" here likewise dominate: "nothing lasts" (graffiti will always decay), "nothing is finished" (graffiti must always be ceaseless), and "nothing is perfect" (because practice is always all) (Lowenthal 2019: 25).

Still, an inherent temporal paradox remains. With such a strong urge toward the evanescent, how is it that graffiti memorials remain such an ever-present factor within the culture (as seen in the "Rest in Paint" memorial to Trip, Aset, Lover, Kbag, and Power in figure 3.32, as well as the Robbo piece in figure 3.33, painted seven years after

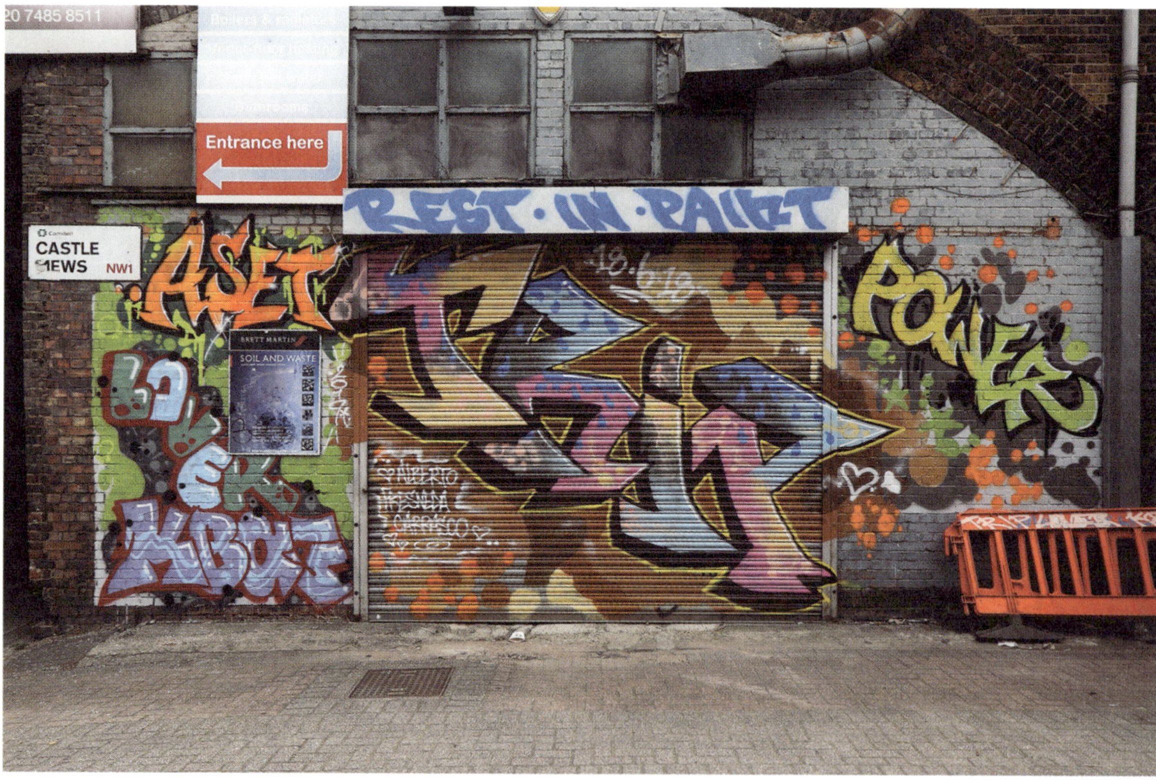


**FIGURE 3.32**
*RIP Trip/Lover/Kbag/Aset/Power*, 2018, North West London. Photo: Alex Ellison.

the writer's death)? Memorials, to be clear, are canon, featured in *Subway Art* and part of pro-social output of every writer. Yet there are two differing modes that occur, from large-scale "rest in peace" productions to the more everyday technique of tagging the names of deceased writers, a mode of memorialization through continuing circulation. Within the former approach, however, we find a much slower temporal cycle than found in the traditional graffiti piece. Working in a way that society finds rational, the clearly recognizable memorial walls are given a wider birth by graffiti-removal teams, delaying the speed of their demise (even if environmental degradation is *always* just a matter of time). Internally, too, memorials will almost never be violated as a traditional piece may be. As noted in Espo's regulations from chapter 1, worse than writing on a church or a private house, writing "on memorial walls . . . is beef beyond belief" (Powers 1999: 154–155). As seen in figure 3.34, a memorial piece for the artist OZONE still standing almost fifteen years after it was first produced, works will often survive within

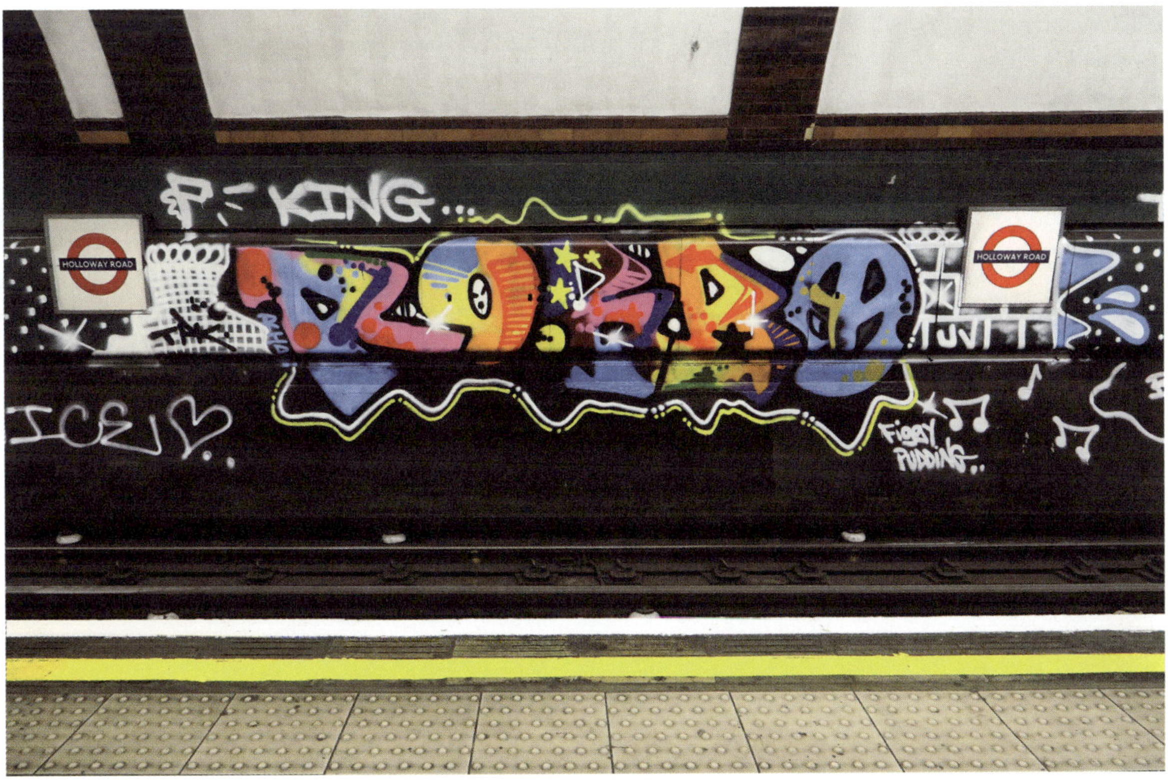


**FIGURE 3.33**
*RIP Robbo*, 2021, Holloway Road Tube Station. Photo: Alex Ellison.

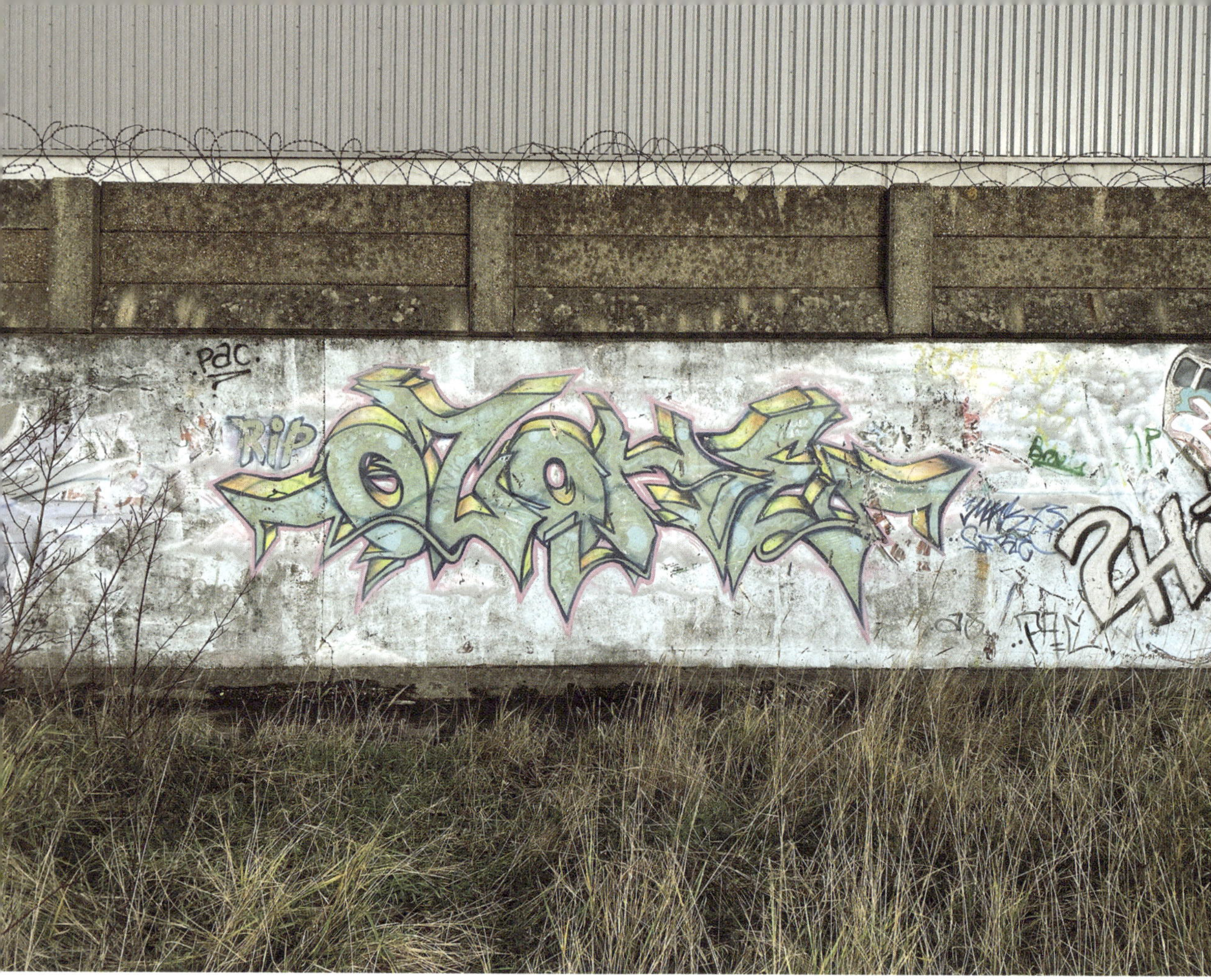


**FIGURE 3.34**
Manik13, *RIP Ozone*, 2007, London. Photo: Rafael Schacter.

a hugely expanded temporal framework to the norm. In the latter case, however, in the graffiti produced on the behalf of deceased writers often decades after their passing (as seen in the Robbo tag in figure 5.31, for example), names will be erased by institutional forces oblivious as they will be to their memorial function, while being less liable to overwriting by fellow artists (unless a neophyte is unaware of the implication of the name). In both of these cases, however, while durability and presence *are* desired, it is prolongation (*more* time) rather than perpetuity (*everlasting* time) that is key.

So how does the veneration of ephemerality and memorialization then come to coalesce? As we will come to see over the next three chapters, while form is crucial, practice, as graffiti's fleeting duration has begun to highlight, is almost always the most important thing. It is thus the key aspects of collaboration and participation that bring these seemingly contrary temporal desires back together. The social relationships developed through graffiti, developed through speaking (seen in chapter 4), through acting (in chapter 5), and through appearing together (in chapter 6), are factors that must be adhered to, even after death. They are factors that create fiercely intimate communities through which true unions of kinship emerge, bonds formed beyond the boundary of life itself. Memorials and memories must be upheld, then, yet it is *permanence of practice*, not *artifactual permanence*, that is key, the permanence of the *act* of memorialization, not of the commemorative object itself, that is of critical importance. It is the physical writing of others' names, the performative production of the memorial that burns the memory into mind, not simply the perpetuation of the physical image itself. It is the duration of the act, not the duration of image; it is the active participation that is here commemorative. The potential heritization of graffiti (discussed further in chapter 9) hence not only halts the cycle of the image, creates less not more means for reproduction and recirculation, but is a true danger to the mnemonical power of the graffiti image itself.

The graffiti monument thus brings forth an active participation in which being together in time is critical. Connectedness emerges through the durational act, through the collectively produced memory. The graffiti memorial outlined here is thus about relationality, not permanence. The object is secondary to the practice of being together, of being together *for* the deceased. As DeSilvey perfectly underscores, the focus "on heritage as physical product often does not translate well to cultures that frame their relation to the past through ongoing process and expressions of value that may (appear to) be intangible and transient" (DeSilvey 2017: 9). This is thus not an anti-heritage we are looking at but a heritage working in a directly opposite way to the institutional heritage regime. It is a heritage not of objects but of actions. Rather than remaining solely about freeze framing and isolation, about the acid-free box and the monumental encasing, heritage in graffiti is about doing, about participation, about engagement. Heritage *is* the act, the graffiti monument a mode of remembrance contained in the process, not simply in the residual artifact itself.

# II MESSAGE

Part II will focus on graffiti as a discursive, performative, and participative act. It will unpack what graffiti *says*, what graffiti *does*, and how this saying and doing are undertaken through a *collective* act. Exploring how graffiti functions via language, via gesture, and via presence, it will be the way graffiti is transmitted through the artifact and onto the viewer that we will discover, how the image maker's intentions are inferred by others who come to reason where the image came from and why it was made. Chapter 4, "Speech," will focus on how graffiti emerges as discursive act. Centered upon the city as a site of public communication, it will link to Henri Lefebvre's position on the "right of citizens and city dwellers . . . to appear on all the networks and circuits of communication, information and exchange" (Lefebvre 1996: 195–196). Chapter 5, "Action," will focus on how graffiti emerges via the body. Centered upon performance, it will link to Lefebvre's right to claim a physical presence in the city, the right to "use the space in question" through a "lived experience" (Lefebvre 1991: 137). Chapter 6, "Participation," will bring together chapters 4 and 5 through focusing on how people speak and act in concert. Centered on the relationship between appearance and assembly, it will link to Lefebvre's "real and active participation," or what he terms the right to "*self-management*" (p. 145).

Addressing the *dialogical*, *open-ended*, *illocutionary*, and *indirect* mode of graffiti's speech; the *formal* and *spatial education*, as much as the *felt* and *invisible* action of graffiti; as well as its *marginal*, *pleasurable*, *durational*, and participatory techniques of *assemblage*, part II will thus reveal a monument attending to our right to action and appearance in the city today. While as a participant it is the practice itself that will here be understood as monument, for the public viewer it is the way graffiti as "monument-message relates to a past event" (Debray 1999: 30), the way that the message linguistically and corporeally embedded in the object are sent onward to their public recipients like a "letter in an envelope addressed from one era to the next" (p. 31). The practices we see in part II will hence link to a street-level civility, a form of public opinion and counsel, that together build up an alternative vision of a possible city. It will reveal a graffiti-monument emergent as both act and advice simultaneously.

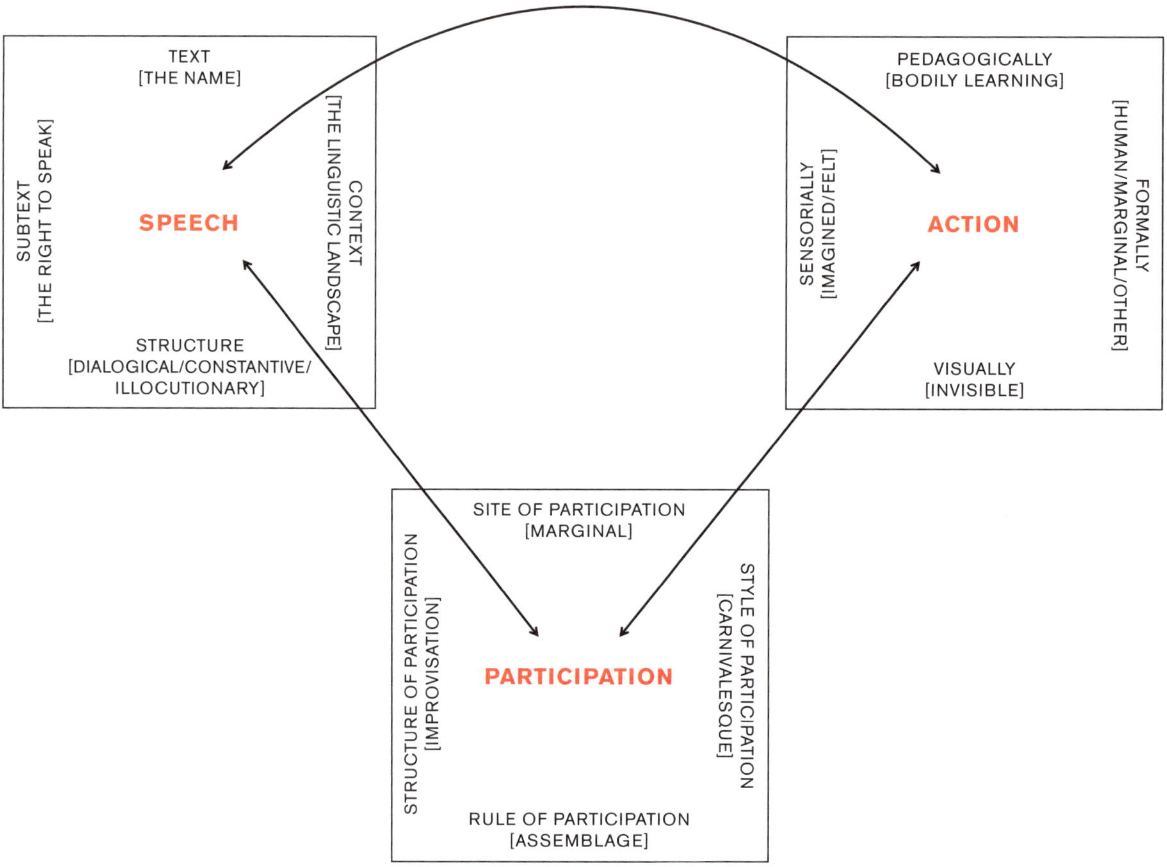


**FIGURE II.1**
Graffiti as message.

# 4
# SPEECH

Graffiti is a text. While often highly graphic and abstracted—an example of what Jean-François Lyotard termed an "imaged text," a text "haunted by the figure" (1989: 29–30)—it is an artifact always emergent alphabetically, through the material reproduction of the scripted name. It is thus an object that is not only seen but likewise read, an object publicly written and publicly said. Yet what does graffiti literally mean? A "word," as Mikhail Bakhtin argued, is a "territory shared by both addresser and addressee, by the Speaker and his interlocutor" (Bakhtin quoted in Brenneis 1986: 339). So what is it that the signature as territory, as medium, communicates from writer to reader? Is it just the name alone? Is it just telling us that Kilroy was here, that Kilroy exists, Kilroy is up? What other ideas does it communicate? What opinions does it proclaim? What beliefs does it declare?

First positioning graffiti as speech technically and exploring it as an object set at the boundary of the observed and the heard, this chapter will go on to explore the discursive context in which graffiti is performed, this being the normative linguistic landscape of the city. Unpacking the monological, imperative, and perlocutionary language techniques of this hegemonic visual register, this linguistic landscape will come to be seen as the unavoidable subtext to every act of graffiti, inescapably implicating this text-image within questions around the right to participate in the urban realm as a space of discourse and debate. As both text, context, and subtext combined, graffiti will be seen to interrogate the normative visual systems of the city through communicative indirection, through not just what it says, but when and where it says it. The witnessing of graffiti thus not only forces us to see (or to hear) that which we would not normally see (or normally hear) but pragmatically indicates toward the conditions and possibilities of public speech itself. As monument, then, graffiti's dialogical, illocutionary, and open-ended form will be seen to implicate it within issues around publicity, appearance, and visibility, issues that address not only language and speech but agency and citizenship too. Graffiti will thus be seen as an antagonistic attachment not only to its architectural landscape but likewise to a linguistic one, to act through a site-specific marginality and an equally marginal form of speech. Moreover, by emerging within a space in which both the strength and very capacity of public speech are integrally linked to economic and political power, graffiti becomes the monument-advice cautioning us of the restrictions on public speech, even while speaking in nontraditional, nonconforming, and often recalcitrant ways. Broadcasting a challenge to the linguistic status quo through its minor, marginal, and insurgent communicative form, graffiti becomes the quintessentially political speech, a monumental form of advice within an increasingly skewed public sphere.

## GRAFFITI AS TEXT/GRAFFITI AS SPEECH

Graffiti speaks. But what does it say? Or, more to the point perhaps, how does it say it? Take figure 4.1, a throw-up by the writer Fatso (contracted here to "FSO") in white fill with black outline and shadowing, a text whose body has been tightly compressed into the off-white roller-shutter it rests upon. At the bottom left of the shutter the author of this text has inscribed "905" (a crew name) while on the "O" has written "ITS [*sic*] A JUMPY PLACE"—a maxim referencing the chorus of a song (entitled "Jumpy") by local rapper Ambush, a resident of Camden where the piece in question was located. Beyond all the formal resonances discussed in part I—beyond the piece's adjunctive, interruptive, anthropometric, and marginal location; beyond its canonical, agentive, distributive, and captivative form; beyond its transient, ephemeral, impermanent, and durational temporalities—we need first address the question of whether this text can itself truly be considered as speech, before we go on to explore any other structural elements it may contain.

So, when does text become speech? And how can the two be distinguished beyond their phenomenal status? We *hear* speech, we *read* text, so would seem to be the case. But we also hear a text as we read it internally, suppressing the outward vocalization critical to the way we learn to read yet commonly retaining an inner voice, as exemplified in Wood and Harrison's sign seen (or heard) in figure 4.2. Is sign language or braille (or even Morse code) not also an example of non-oral speech? What about a text message? What about a tweet? If we argue that speech and writing are defined by presence and absence (the physical existence of the speaker in speech, the physical lack of the writer in text), have we not already seen how this argument breaks down when exploring the agency of the signature in which the self moves beyond the restrictions of the body and the image exudes a person-like presence? The rupture between these two categories can also be seen as one with a fairly recent heritage. In ancient Greece, as Charles Stewart has suggested, the categories of "'orality' and 'literacy'" were understood to be entirely interwoven, the "common mode of disseminating written messages," from those written upon tombstones to codes of law, being undertaken through "read[ing] them aloud" (Stewart 1994: 1004). In contemporary legal terms, however, speech is likewise considered to incorporate both spoken and written forms—both vocalized speech as

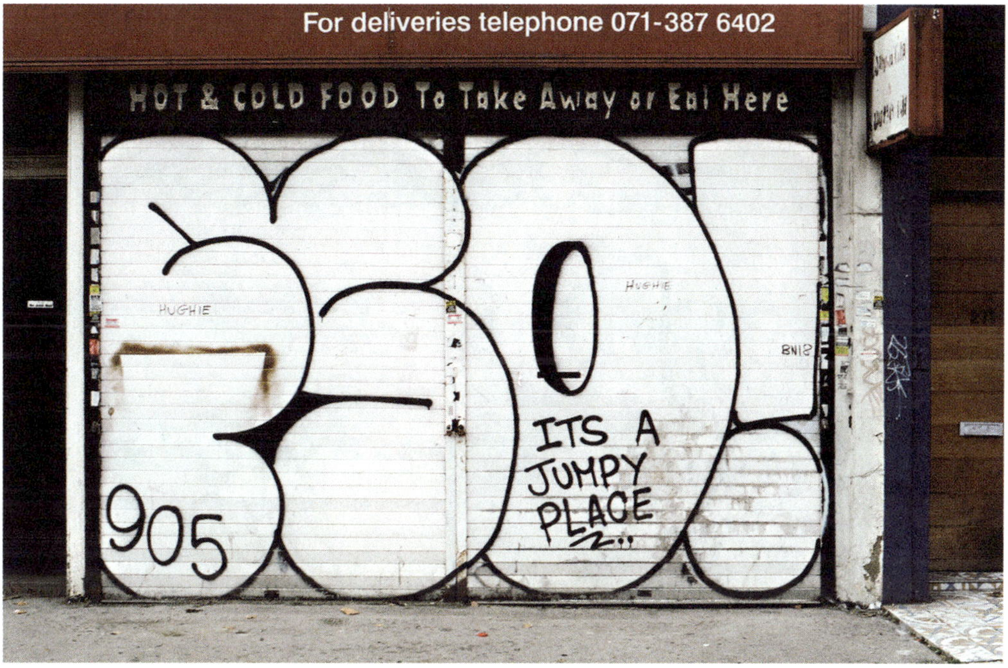


**FIGURE 4.1**
*Untitled (Jumpy Place)*, London, 2020. Photo: Rafael Schacter.

well as the printing and publicizing of the expressive ideas that this speech contains. As legal and media scholar Jennifer Peterson (2022) has argued, the very concept of speech (in Anglo-American law at the least) has always been linked more to the communication technologies that come to propagate opinions than to a specific voice alone. Contemporary free speech law has thus today come to include a whole host of mediums that express ideas and distribute information, from the classical forms of vocalized speech and print media to visual art, bodily gesture, and even algorithms and code (in what Petersen has termed a "posthuman" severance). As such, and according to the US Supreme Court, public art such as "government-commissioned and government-financed monuments speak for the government," while the "property owners" of a site in which a monument may feature are likewise considered to legally act as "the speaker" (Pleasant Grove v. Summum 2009: 8). Speech thus becomes about the pairing of a message with a medium of transmission, going far beyond the audible force of our vocal cords alone. It becomes simply about a sentiment proffered to the world through material (or even immaterial) form.

In our case in figure 4.1, however, we have a text whose human author is entirely evident, a signature image pronouncing and announcing itself to the world. We have

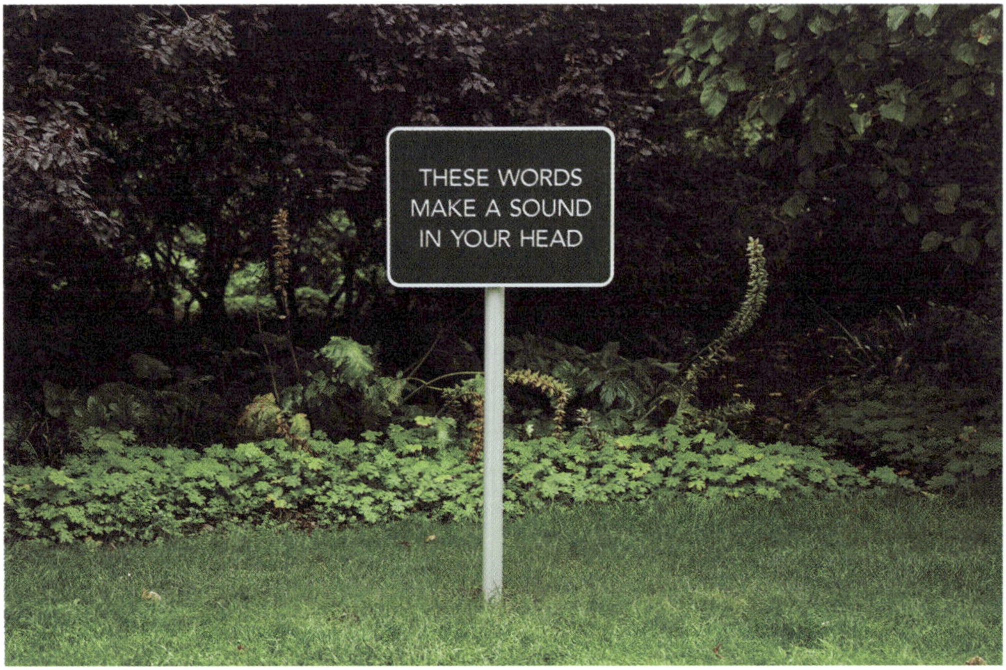


**FIGURE 4.2**
John Wood and Paul Harrison, *10 Signs for a Park (THESE WORDS MAKE A SOUND IN YOUR HEAD)*, 2022. Installation view Frieze Sculpture, Regent's Park London. Photography: Luke Walker. Courtesy of John Wood and Paul Harrison/Gallery Vera Cortes, Lisbon.

a piece of writing written by a writer, a public message using the street as its medium of transmission. The graffiti image is thus read as a linguistic unit (even if mispronounced, even if just "F . . . SO?"), read as writing, as communication, even if its overt meaning is not immediately clear. Yet it basic status as speech—as a text both read and heard—is bolstered further by the punctuating exclamation positioned at the end of Fatso's piece. Figure 4.1 reads not "FSO" but "FSO!," not only linking it to the comic book aesthetic that canonical graffiti takes inspiration from—to the KAPOW! and the CRUNCH!, the WHAAM! and the POW! so beloved by Jack Kirby and his graffiti writer acolytes—but likewise turning the name into a yelled interjection. "*F-SO!*" it says, forcefully marking out its excitement and strength of feeling, transforming the letters from what could be an acronym to a visible shout in the street. The exclamation thus not only disrupts any hard line between text and speech, makes the single word legible as a lexical unit (whether intelligible or not), but likewise gives the piece a paralinguistic quality. It is read not in a characterless monotone (as may be the case with the font such as you now read) but with intonation, pitch, volume. As such, while this signature work may be difficult to verbally enunciate due to its terminating vowel, and while the heart-shaped linking of the F to the S may potentially obscure what are still fairly lucid letters, the image's audible, gestural qualities remain. Its desire to interpellate us into its viewing/listening subject thus remains clear even if the word itself remains difficult to pronounce. Its huge, shutter-spanning letters and its visibly public site together reveal an unmistakable attempt to grab our attention. Even if discursively unpronounceable—as could be a foreign language—the formal qualities of Fatso's piece underscore the text as something meant to be read, as something meant to be *loudly heard*.

Still, even if "FSO!" alone lacks the normative orthography to provide concrete legibility, its attached maxim—which like all graffiti maxims is written in a highly legible script, not meant to be stylized or embellished because it is overt, not implicit, meaning that is the point—presents us with a clear linguistic proposition. "This place" (i.e., Camden) "is a jumpy one," an uneasy, edgy site. Here we thus have a message forming its own public yet doing so on a number of different levels; we have the public who read the maxim without grasping the reference, the more restricted community who register the intertextual meaning,[1] the practitioners and enthusiasts who read both maxim and signature, and the even more restricted in-group who acknowledge all this alongside the numerical (crew) inscription too. As in all graffiti, we can thus appreciate distinct audiences here: a primary or inner audience, as linguistic anthropologist Donald Brenneis explains in terms of all communicative events, "composed of the individual or group to whom a performance is chiefly directed, i.e., those whom the performer hopes to influence directly [here being fellow graffiti writers]," and a "secondary audience" of "overhearer[s]" (Brenneis 1986: 343–344), an outer public of passers-by and other members of the urban realm, who, while not the direct addressees, are far from simply residual either. Yet discernible here too are not just citational but temporal dialogues. We thus not only have the visible additions to the piece by "Hughie" as seen on the "F" and the "O" and by "BN18" seen on the exclamation (seemingly undertaken by nonpractitioners due to their formal lack of genre-specific qualities)—as well as the addition of the tag Heat seen in figure 4.3—but likewise the visible residue of a prior set of graffiti pieces bleeding through the white fill-in of the present work (within the body of the "O" in particular). The visible utterance is thus reacting to and has been followed by a further set of utterances. A call-and-response is apparent. Something is emerging over time, has come after a previous declaration, has been appended by a set of new expressions, and will soon be supplemented by new pronouncements too.

Fatso's piece thus fulfills a number of key linguistic qualities: it is a text whose status as an authored, broadcast announcement turns it into speech; it is an exclamatory interjection with paralinguistic qualities; it is a propositional, intertextual form in which a community is created and a dialogue enacted. Yet this status as a public proclamation and inscription, as asserted in the street rather than whispered privately in a writer's sketchbook, also turns graffiti into a prime example of what Mieke Bal has termed as "gestures of showing" (Bal 1999: 7). As a type of exhibitory cultural artifact best understood, as Bal argues, as a type of speech act, here we find an object that "shows itself,

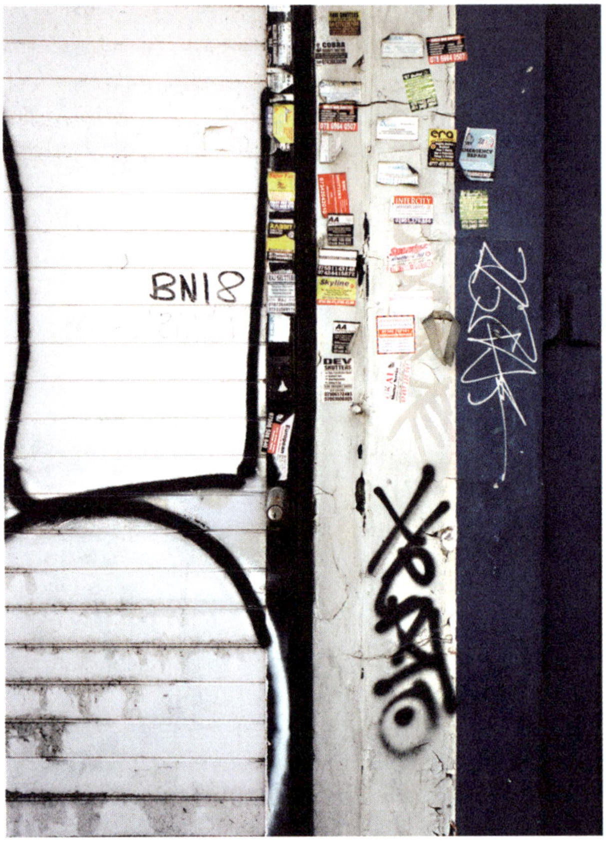


**FIGURE 4.3**
*Untitled (BN18)*, London, 2020. Photo: Rafael Schacter.

shows its hand, its presence" (p. 4), a type of object that says "'Look!,' often implying, 'That's how it is'" (p. 6). While in the first place the publicness of the gesture creates a form of propositional discourse carrying contextual information into the world, in asserting its position publicly these forms likewise become performative. They do not just say something (as a locutionary act) but *do* something (as an illocutionary one). They become acts that, in J. L. Austin's famous terms, not only convey but perform meaning, that commit their author to what they declare, that caution or inform, that remind or warn, and that enact this through the actuality of the utterance itself.

The visible pronouncement of "FSO!"—as a visible act of commitment, as a signature act that functions as a warranty of fidelity to the task of writing itself—not only asserts but performs its assertion. It says LOOK yet in doing so both performs and reveals what it says. Through the total simplicity of the proper noun, through the use of the name alone, we can hence see the signature functioning as a "performative without the operative words" (Austin 1962: 59). As likewise noted in the single-word speech act "guilty," for example, here meaning "this-court-pronounces-you-guilty-of-the-crimes-you-have-been-charged-with," here the single-word name links to a much larger performative proclamation. Rather than "I, Fatso, hereby assert my name," rather than "I, Fatso, commit to this writing," all that thus need be said is "FSO!" and the rest, unuttered, becomes evidently implied. As Austin continues, an illocutionary act "is something which is *at the moment of uttering being done by the person uttering*," something that, he helpfully states, can emerge within "written utterances (or 'inscriptions')" through the utterer "*appending his signature*" (Austin 1962: 60). The signature-signature, then, can be seen to function as the quintessential illocutionary speech act, the act that performs what it affirms, that evidences its own commitment, every time it is pronounced. The graffiti inscription states, asserts, promises, all through its signature form. Graffiti is thus not just speech but *speech act*.

While graffiti may now be intelligible as speech, then, what is it that is being asserted alongside the commitment to say the name itself? What are the views and beliefs this speech/text espouses? What are the promises being made? Well, just as much oral communication is implicitly transmitted, understood through a shared discursive ground that then enables dialogue to occur (or at least prevents perpetual miscommunications), so too this act of speech can only be understood via the contextual terrain from where *it* emerges. The metacommunicative assertions that graffiti makes can thus only become comprehensible when considering the wider environment in which this text is inscribed. The city becomes the frame that itself frames the meaning of speech, graffiti as speech as irremovably attached to its context as the graffiti image is to its architecture (and the city, in a perfect mirror of that earlier argued, acting as parergon to graffiti's ergon). Speech is never enunciated in a vacuum. And it is *where* one speaks that enables us to contextualize meaning, the subtext of any text only emergent through the *con*text in which it is set.

## TEXT TO CON-TEXT/GRAFFITI'S LINGUISTIC LANDSCAPE

In chapter 1 we laid out the case of graffiti's integral site-specificity, its adjunctive position that works to overwhelm the normative order of site. But where does this normative order emerge? Is it just the wall, the surface, the architectural environment in which the text sits? Or does it likewise concern the dominant mode of the city's visual culture, the broader linguistic landscape in which this linguistic act occurs?

Take figure 4.4, for example, a baroque barrage of letters and words that exemplify the city as a space of speech and linguistic display. First we have the most overt form of verbal communication present in the image, the text "SMART INTERNET CAFE" intoned in block capitals on bright yellow backdrop, the first word in a small red font, the second and third in a larger black one, with an icon of a computer and a cup of coffee

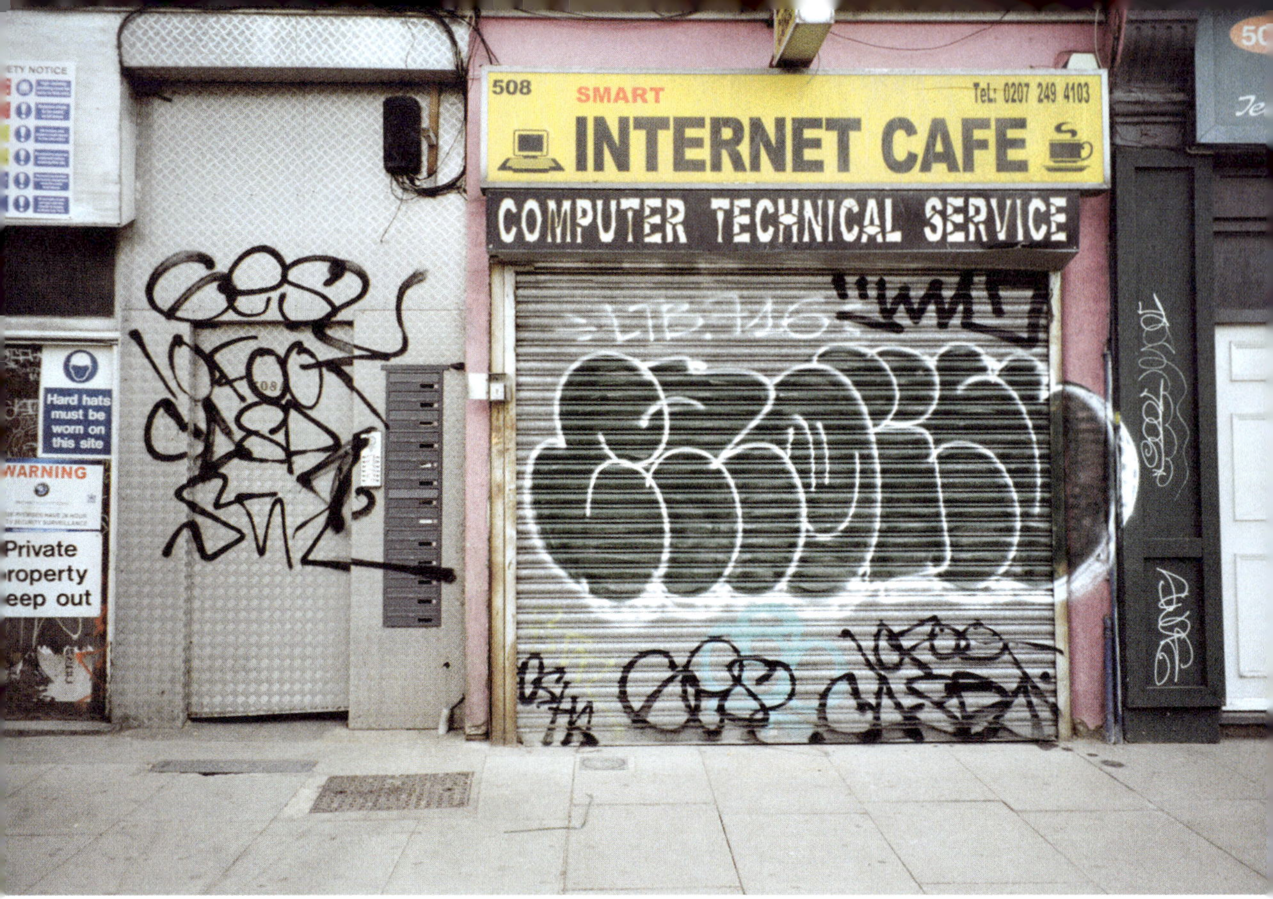


**FIGURE 4.4**
*Untitled (Eroïk et al.)*, London, 2020. Photo: Rafael Schacter.

at each edge of the sign tray. Alongside the street and phone numbers at the outer corners of the sign, the phrase "COMPUTER TECHNICAL SERVICE" has been set in white text on black background directly beneath the main yellow fascia, yet has become weathered and sun-bleached, peeling off and now appearing fragmented and bone-like. On the roller-shutter below, however, juxtaposing the two boldfaced, lucid texts above, is a large graffiti throw-up flowing across the entire shutter and adjacent wall. "Eroïk," it says, in dark green/black body and white outline—with a smiley face creating an anthropometric presence in the central "O." Standing proudly (if slightly aslant) in the middle of the shutter, the artist's crew LTB and 71SI have also been inscribed above the main piece, below which, at the very edge of the pavement, lie a series of four black tags mirroring a set produced on the neighboring corrugated metal doorway at the image's left: "Gesz," "10Foot," "Caspa," "SNZ" are placed there in a vertical order, spanning both sides of the perforated door frame and culminating with a sharp line bisecting a set of dark-metal letterboxes. Yet alongside the thin, downward-written white tags at the right-hand side of the image, at the far left we have a set of official signs complementing the direct legibility of the retail sign set in the image's center. These, a series of bold imperatives—"Private property Keep out," "WARNING THESE PREMISES HAVE 24 HOUR CCTV SECURITY SURVEILLANCE," "Hard hats must be worn on this site," "SITE SAFETY NOTICE"—have been placed upon a backdrop of tags and other ephemera and stand in direct juxtaposition to these vernacular texts. In a series of blues, reds, and yellows they caution, alert, and order their readers, commanding them to obey their directives and submit to their authority. As such, and alongside the visible graffiti, we can find two further forms of speech coexisting in this image: those of commercial retail signage and prohibitionary signage.

Retail signage, while often simple and unadorned, communicates to us in a purposeful semiotic manner. Functioning through what sociolinguist Jan Blommaert termed a technique of "*recruitment*," they "invite particular groups of people into interaction with their producers" through announcing the "kind of transactions performed in that place (selling vegetables versus performing financial services)" (Blommaert 2012: 62). More than this, however, retail signage likewise comes to structure the prevailing socioeconomic landscape, tacitly calling out to different readers through the form as much as the content of its speech. In a study undertaken in downtown Brooklyn, for example, Shonna Trinch and Edward Snajdr noted that the structure of urban sign language not only was "designed for particular audiences" but conferred "differential and competing symbolic and material values on the land" (Trinch and Snajdr 2017: 66). Shop signage could thus mark out not only a pre- and post-gentrification landscape within sites going through rapid urban change, but so too a linguistic environment of "*semiotic intrusion*" versus "*semiotic exclusion*" (p. 81). Exemplified through the division between what the authors termed "Old School Vernacular" signage—a text-dense style that explicitly delineates what the shop provides (such as our Internet Cafe seen above)—and the more contemporary "distinction-making" signage (p. 66)—a cryptic style often using just a single (lowercased) word that is almost always entirely unrelated to the services they offer—these two speech styles create an in/out group dynamic dependent on social class or economic status that is visible within the linguistic genres of the signs themselves. While both forms function through a "vocative" mode that functions to "call to those in place" (p. 66), their structural form creates a latent understanding of *whom* they are written for and thus *how* the context in which they are located is transforming. Just like the more overtly corporate logos of multinational brands, however, the logos that work through iconic recognition and hail us via their golden arches or similarly golden sea shells, both the vernacular and distinction-making signs act as public texts that seek to solicit a public. Yet whether they accomplish this via intentionally lucid, purposefully obfuscatory, or instantly recognizable communicative forms, the techniques of speech they use become as important as what they "say" themselves.

While shop signs call out to us, willing us to enter into them through their visual clarity or alluring us through their textual wit, prohibitory signage works to regulate our bodies and our public behavior. Likewise orientated toward a listener via direct address, here it is not the vocative but the imperative mode that is utilized, a style that demands we follow the instructions through verbal force. These are not warnings, however, which, as linguist Jan Svennevig has suggested, act in the addressee's "own interest," but rather "directives" constructed with the express "purpose of getting the addressees to do something . . . in the interest of the person or institution responsible for the sign" (Svennevig 2021: 166). These signs thus use the "*deontic modality*" (linked to "expressions of necessity, obligation and desirability") and hence implicitly underscore the authors' "institutionally established rights to decide about the actions of others" (p. 166). While there are different styles within this deontic mode that come to reveal different levels of privilege—"imperatives" (such as DO NOT ENTER) claiming "higher entitlement" than "modal interrogatives" (such as "could you" and "would you," for example) (p. 166)—each of them articulates its power through both the implicit and/or explicit threats of sanction they contain as much as their "fixed and non-negotiable" style of language (p. 182). They "display entitlement and seek compliance" (p. 165), bullying the reader into submission. They demonstrate an "exhortative," often "patronizing" approach (p. 171), enforcing "norms of propriety and social order" and regulating what their institutionally validated voice delimits as either "mandatory or improper" (p. 165). In figure 4.5, for example, we thus have an unknown speaker (with a strongly institutional tone) who couches their entitled imperative as a request ("please be kind"). It is not simply an illocutionary warning ("careful: security and police are patrolling"), but a deontic demand that we behave ("you are being surveilled so don't even think about it"). Ordering us (as the implicit nonlocals) to smile for their hidden camera, the sign assumes the deeply patronizing position of entitlement that Svennevig outlines, the privileged address articulating a privileged stance. It forms a didactic, entirely monological mode of speech: no discussion, no debate (and no ball games allowed). The sign is, in effect, a one-word prohibition, a schoolmasterly "BEHAVE."

Alongside retail and prohibitory signage, however, our linguistic landscape is also dominated by the omnipresent visual language of traffic signage. In figure 4.6 we can thus find a range of black, blue, purple and pink tags (Gore/BMG/Jabe/Truth/Jawns, among others) positioned on the exterior wall of a housing block and an adjacent bin store, a throw-up by Sooz (SO) containing a fanged face within the "S" and a loudly pronounced "RIP Halo" within the "O," a deontic "CCTV" warning sign in the top-right corner of the image, and, at the edge of the pavement to the left, a large, white-edged, red-filled, circular and metallic traffic sign containing a white-filled horizontal bar in its center. This sign that reads (to those versed in its international vehicular tongue) a loudly intoned "NO ENTRY" is set on a steel pole shared with a smaller, rectangular, black-edged, and white-filled sign, containing a symbolic image indicating a camera (looking amusingly like a type of folding camera that most people would have never seen in person) with the phrase "Traffic enforcement" written in bold text below. Here we thus have a language functioning through a multimodal combination of text and image, color and shape. "DO NOT ENTER," it says. "YOU ARE BEING RECORDED/

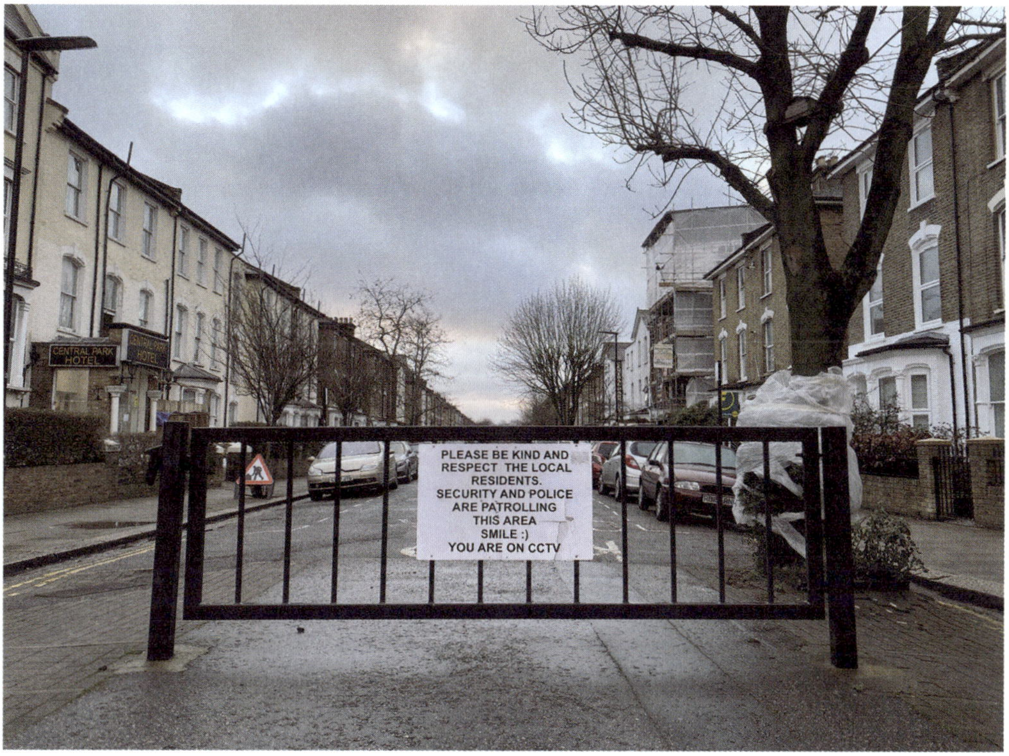


**FIGURE 4.5**
*Untitled (Please Be Kind)*, London, 2019. Photo: Rafael Schacter.

YOU ARE BEING ORDERED." This is a governmentally warranted instruction that vocatively and imperatively addresses us. It is a form of signed speech that, as seen in Brad Downey's sardonic public intervention in figure 4.7, we cannot ignore however much we try. Today a truly universal form of language present within the globally dominating vehicular city, traffic signs function through a classically illocutionary mode of "directing, informing and controlling road users' behaviour" (Department of Transport 2007: 4). They order, warn, and inform us (through circles, triangles, and rectangles, respectively), providing mandatory instructions and prohibitions both (within signs colored blue in the former and red in the latter cases) (p. 9). Similar to Austin's speech acts that function via the "primitive language of one-word utterances" (Austin 1962: 72), the traffic signs' consistent form and language-like structure propositionally command their readers through classically imperative and deontic techniques. They communicate through linguistic and iconic means, impacting their readers' conduct with all the repressive power that state authority garners.

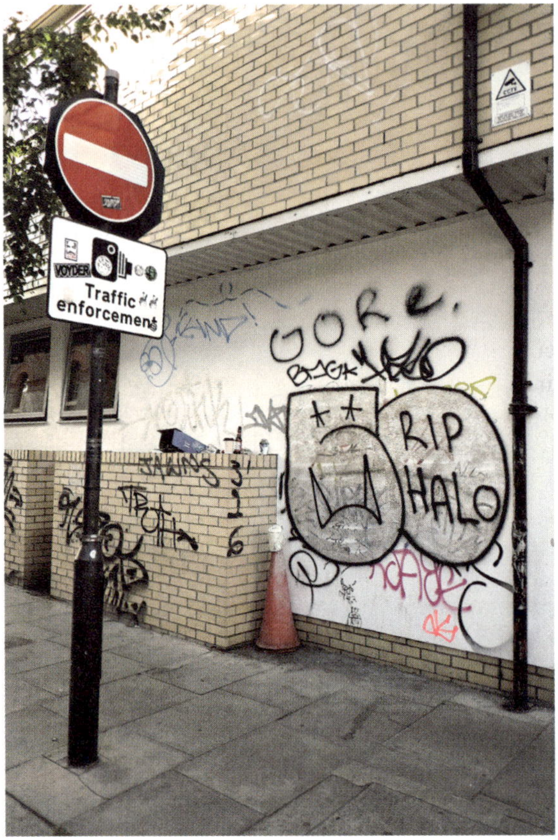


**FIGURE 4.6**
*Untitled (RIP Halo)*, London, 2021. Photo: Rafael Schacter.

The relationship between text and image seen within our traffic signs, their ability, in Roland Barthes's famous terminology (1977), to both anchor (to focus or direct meaning) and relay (to convey or complement this meaning), is taken even further within the final critical element of the linguistic landscape that makes up graffiti's context. This, the regime of public advertising, is, more than retail, prohibitionary, or traffic signage, the most overwhelming visual element of our urban environments. In figure 4.8, for example, we can find a myriad of tags; "Youts" set prominently in white on the green shopfront along with TZW, Drugz, Jask, Year1, and others; Juno (twice), CML, Know, Marx, alongside a directional poster for "Vinyl Deptford" appearing on the seemingly shuttered setting of "GEORGES [*sic*] Hair Dressing Salon," all of which are dominated, however, by a large billboard that has entirely overtaken an upper-story brick wall: "LISTEN UP LADIES, IT'S TIME TO TALK ABOUT THE F WORD" it says. "WE WANT FASHION THAT ACTUALLY FITS. YOU IN?" Along with the rest of the advertising copy and the attached brand name ("simply be.") there is a prominent image of a jeans-clad woman at the center of the picture that both anchors and relays the adjacent speech: "F-it." Here, then, we see the omnipresent corporate urban visual culture that "we accept," as John Berger wrote, as if it were "an element of climate" (Berger 1972: 130), the public "literature," as Lewis Mumford likewise claimed even earlier, that is "produced within the imprint of the metropolis" (Mumford 1970 [1938]: 230). From large to small format, billboards to posters, digital to print, static to mobile, public advertising, much like our public monuments, is today so ubiquitous that it has in many ways have entirely disappeared, so ubiquitous it has become as commonplace as the weather.

While traditional posters, such as those seen later in figures 4.13 and 4.14, function more like the vernacular shop signage earlier discussed—presenting us with information concerning their chosen performances or events (like their chosen trades), which while containing stylistic/rhetorical flourishes (bright colors/captivating aesthetics) remain at the level of the informative or constative—billboard advertising often takes on a more overtly deceptive linguistic mode. While both may try to persuade, the speech acts in this latter case are constitutionally strategic: there is an intentional message,

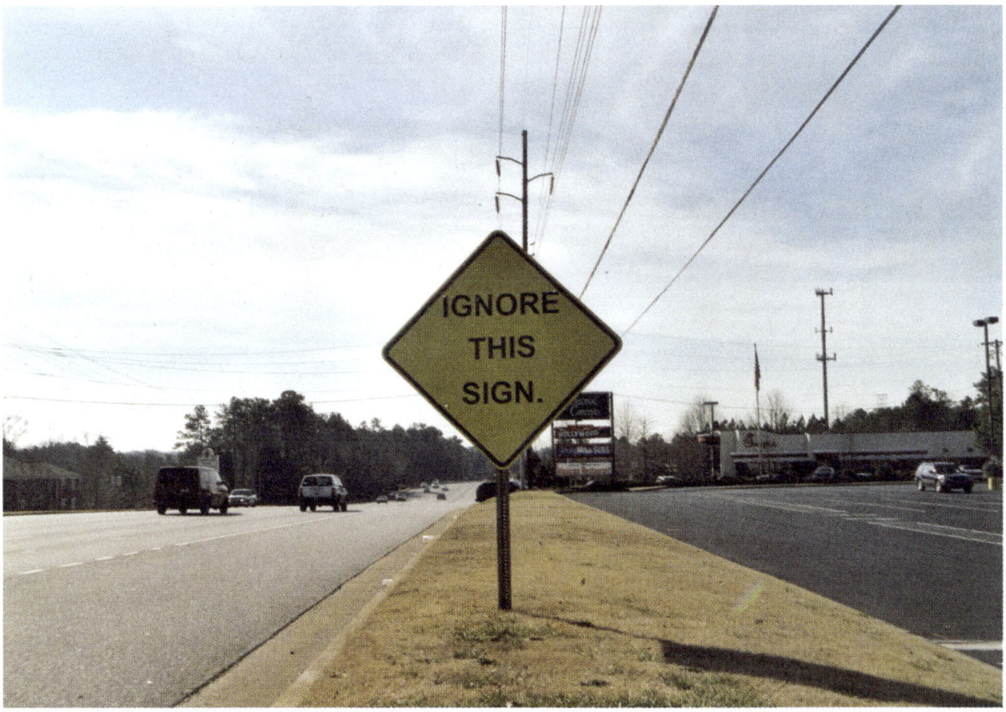


**FIGURE 4.7**

Brad Downey, *Ignore This Sign*, 2004 (duration three weeks). Marietta, GA. Paint, street sign, street pole. Courtesy of the artist.

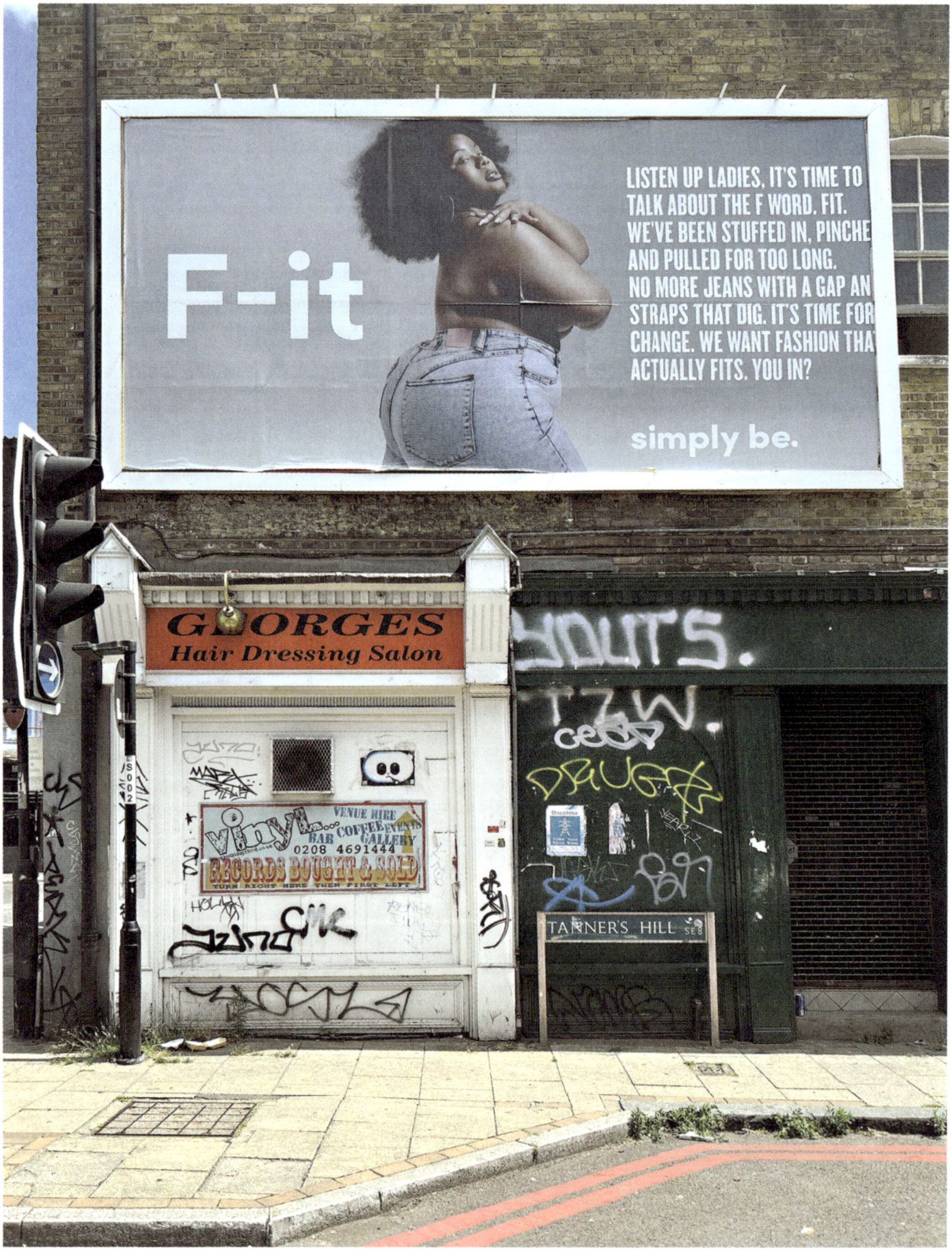


**FIGURE 4.8**
*Untitled (F-IT)*, London, 2021. Photo: Rafael Schacter.

as seen in figure 4.8, that is believed (at the minimum) to reinforce the status of the brand as something independent, authentic, approachable, the intimate language employed masking the anonymous corporate authorship that the text ventriloquizes on behalf of.[2] This is thus a type of perlocutionary language in which the "effects which our utterances have on hearers" are purposefully meant, as John Searle famously said, to "go beyond the hearer's understanding of the utterance" (Searle 1980: vii). The speaker's desire to convince or persuade is thus rhetorically occluded within the body of the statement itself ("those jeans would like great on me," you may say to someone, when actually appealing to that someone to buy them for you for your birthday). As consumer psychologists Edward McQuarrie and David Glen Mick have thus argued, when "persuasion is the overriding goal . . . the manner in which a statement is expressed may be more important than its propositional content" (McQuarrie and Mick 1996: 424). Here, then, speech style and tone strive to engage an audience to achieve the overarching goal of consumer response, a message whose real meaning is at essence a caps-locked "NEED ME WANT ME BUY ME."

As with our traffic signs, however, it is not just the text itself but the images these work in conjunction with that make advertising so powerful. Acting in a cooperative tension, as linguist Hartmut Stöckl has suggested, the image and text come to extend, determine, complement, or even contradict one another (Stöckl 2009: 11) and, in this way, either to "resolve indirectness (implicatures), trace secondary meanings of signs (connotations) [or] follow the networking of concepts (metaphor/metonymy)" (p. 3). Much like the formal techniques of captivation seen in chapter 2, advertisements thus utilize forms of cognitive trapping that "promote indirectness and delay decoding," that "highlight certain contents and hide others," or that "reduce complexity" or "provoke and shock" (p. 26). Whichever mode they employ, however, their authors "use them," Stöckl concludes, "as strategic tools to effectively develop their arguments" (p. 25), the image-text functioning to entice their core demographic target into allegiance with the brand. They thus work to captivate an audience not merely so as to present themselves but rather to motivate a feeling of desire (or lack) and thus create a consumptive aspiration. The image-text thus never says what it wants to say but rather obscures its message within formal locutions that perlocutionarily create this desire. As such, they transform the public spaces in which they appear into ones in which private interests reign, trapping us to create not a social relation but an explicitly economic one.

The informationally dense languages of retail, prohibitory, traffic signage, and public advertising are thus ones whose rhetorical modalities emerge either from an authoritative, regulatory, privileged voice or from a corporate, mendacious, spectacular one. The unauthored, vocative shop signs seek to invite and entice their viewership; the street and traffic signs to didactically and deontically assail them; the prohibitory signage to control our bodily movement; and the advertising to perlocutionary manipulate. The speech techniques of the linguistic landscape thus endeavor to tell us what to do, how to behave, what to buy. They create a public space whose dominant visual register is monological and imperative, a scopic regime that is closed, inflexible, parasitic. The public here is thus not asked to speak, only to listen (and consume). The public is not asked to participate, only to react (and conform).

## CONTEXT TO SUBTEXT/GRAFFITI'S METACOMMUNICATIVE MOOD

Let's roll back to the end of our first section on graffiti as speech, in which it was suggested that context was that which enabled us to move from text to subtext. It was the dominating ground of the linguistic landscape that graffiti is inexorably anchored to that enabled its metacommunicative content to emerge. So, what does this context create? As with all language, there is a background meaning being asserted that is left undeclared; there is a connotation that the graffiti denotation speaks through its contextual positionality. So, what are the implications of graffiti's public utterances? What are the inferences set within and beyond the proclamation itself?

While the graffiti text exclaims itself through its status as public exposition, its metacommunicative message declares its right to utter the utterance itself, to utter this utterance within the context of the linguistic landscape in which it resides. As "FSO!" is intoned, then, as "Eroïk" and "SO" are articulated by their agents when we see their written speech, what is implied is the artists' willingness to enact their speech act in a landscape in which the very enactment becomes communicative due to the architectural, social, and judicial prohibitions it challenges: "I hereby assert my right to assert," the works thus say, "I publicly assert my right to publicly assert." It is the text's communicative *indirection* that is crucial here, a form of transmission in which "by definition," as Brenneis has explained, "meaning cannot reside in the text alone" (Brenneis 1986: 345). As an example of "[e]vent-based indirection," then, here the speech act's very "occurrence," as much as the speaker's ability to construct a "public communicative context," can in itself be understood as the "most important message being conveyed" (p. 344). The "organizational features" of a speech act—that is, "who participates, how they participate and that they participate"—can thus be understood as "more important than its contents" (p. 344). In this way, a single-word utterance can communicate via who, via when, and via where it comes to speak. The speaker in graffiti thus states their commitment to state their name *here*, here in a space in which these statements are proscribed, here in a space where these inscriptions are erased. Undertaken within a milieu in which the right to speak is curtailed by economic impediments (as discussed in part III), this right to speak, this *right to write*, is publicly (pro)claimed whenever graffiti appears. "Illegal or not," each piece says, "I pronounce that I announce *here*." The overt linguistic meaning of graffiti may thus be restricted, even "impoverished," yet, as Brenneis reinforces, it is through the "fusing of meaning with emotional or aesthetic experience" that "what is communicated [becomes] understood by observers" (p. 345). It is through the heightened (speech) act and the heightened (speech) location that graffiti truly makes sense, that its right to appear on communicative networks, its right to participate in the city, is made apparent.

Still, while graffiti's subtextual content proclaims a right to speak, it also asserts a right to a particular *mode* of speech. This is an approach that rejects the anonymous,[3] monological, imperative, didactic nature of our normative linguistic landscape and instead embraces one that is authored, dialogical, constative, and open-ended. It speaks through a formal mode that, even if hard for many to directly translate, is still understood as language, as an insurgent speech subverting the supposed rationality of the city. Rather than modifying or prohibiting our movement, manufacturing or manipulating our desires, the graffiti text solely craves to be seen and heard, to exist even if disputed. The graffiti utterance is thus not only propositional (subtextually referring to its linguistic context), not only illocutionary (through its performative intention to interact with us in the world), but conveys information without attempting to parasitically modify our beliefs. Rejecting the perlocutionary visuality of the corporate city, the impersonal imperatives of the state, the reductive monologue of the linguistic landscape, it pronounces the possibility of a speech going beyond the instrumental, a speech speaking for speech's sake. Moreover, and much like the mode of stylistic ambiguity we discussed in chapter 2, graffiti not only creates a form that we are free to interpret ourselves but *captivates* through the interpretative need itself. As the very meaning of the word "clearly does not lie in the text itself," the public "audience," as Brenneis has similarly argued, is "necessarily engaged in a search for hidden meanings" (Brenneis 1986: 339–340). The formal features of the graffiti text thus signal that "more is going on than meets the ear [or the eye]," the image's "listeners [or viewers] not only allowed but compelled to draw their own conclusions" (p. 341). The constitutive indirection of graffiti thus "joins together *form*, how something is said . . . and *meaning*, the overt and covert content of what is being said" (p. 341). It makes clear that viewers must attend to more than the just the base meaning of the image. It asserts a plurality of linguistic possibilities, its ambiguity, its open-endedness, its ambivalence creating a dialogical speech in opposition to the normative speech of the contemporary city itself. It is thus not just graffiti's explicit content and its medium that are critical to understand but so too its specific linguistic structure—not just what graffiti says or where it says it but *how* it says it too.[4]

Yet graffiti does not just gain access to the (economically prohibitive) communicative platforms of the city, but hijacks and disrupts them through speaking over and against these hegemonic forms of speech. Through literally reinscribing these visual forms, graffiti's subtextual qualities become more formally pronounced. While retail signage is generally overlooked by writers (with the occasional exception of corporate logos), prohibitory signage is seen as fair game; FLY POSTING IS PROHIBITED in figure 4.9 has here, for example, been directly overpainted, stickered, partially broken off. Traffic and street signage are here targets too; the road sign in figure 4.10 and the directional sign in figure 4.11 have thus both been left entirely illegible. Yet it is to public

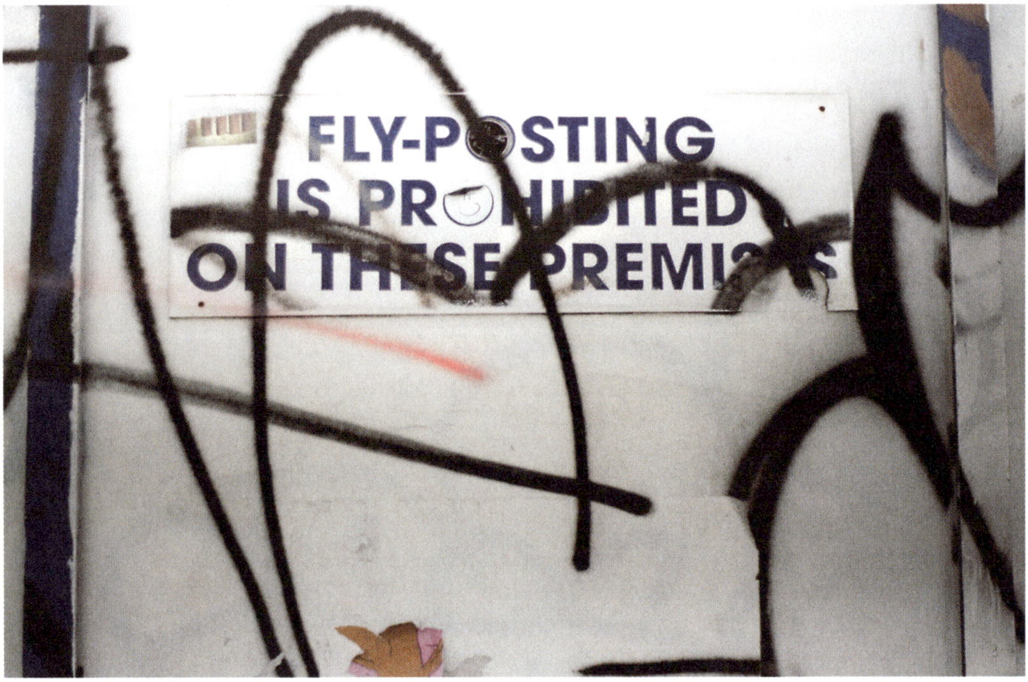
FLY-POSTING
IS PROHIBITED
ON THESE PREMISES

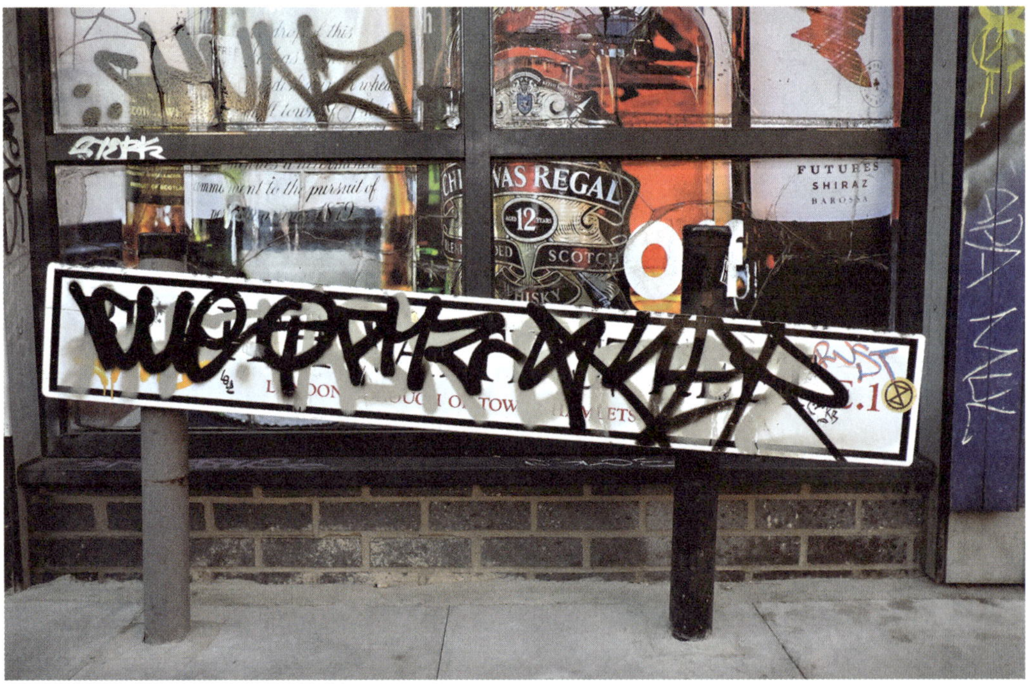
VAS REGAL
12
SCOTCH
FUTURES
SHIRAZ
BAROSSA

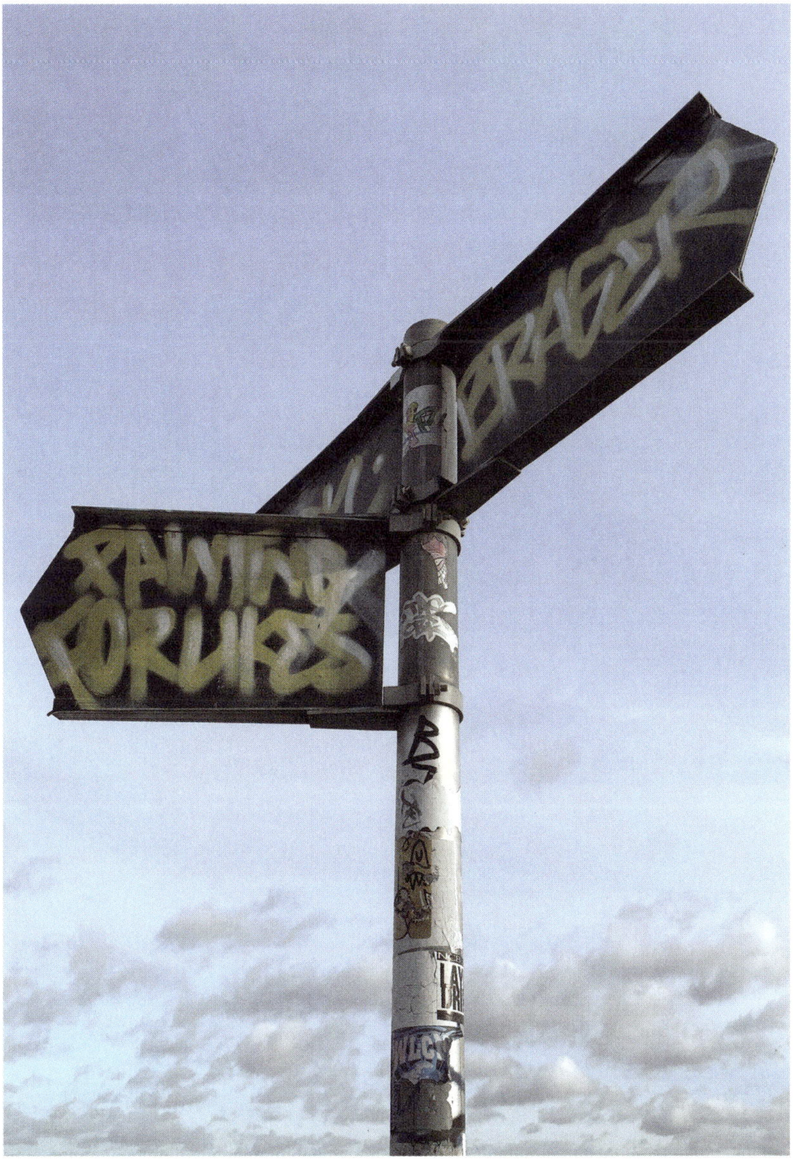

**FIGURE 4.9**
*Untitled (Prohibited)*, London, 2021. Photo: Rafael Schacter.

**FIGURE 4.10**
*Untitled (Dis-titled)*, London, 2021. Photo: Rafael Schacter.

**FIGURE 4.11**
*Untitled (Painting for Likes)*, London, 2021. Photo: Rafael Schacter.

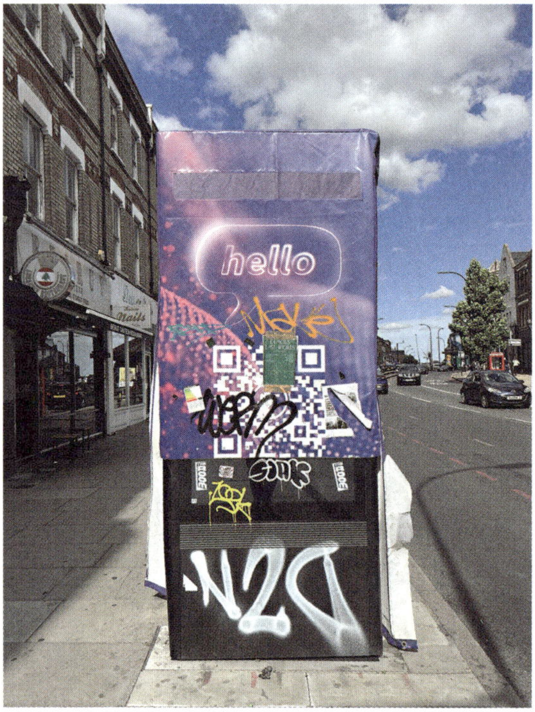


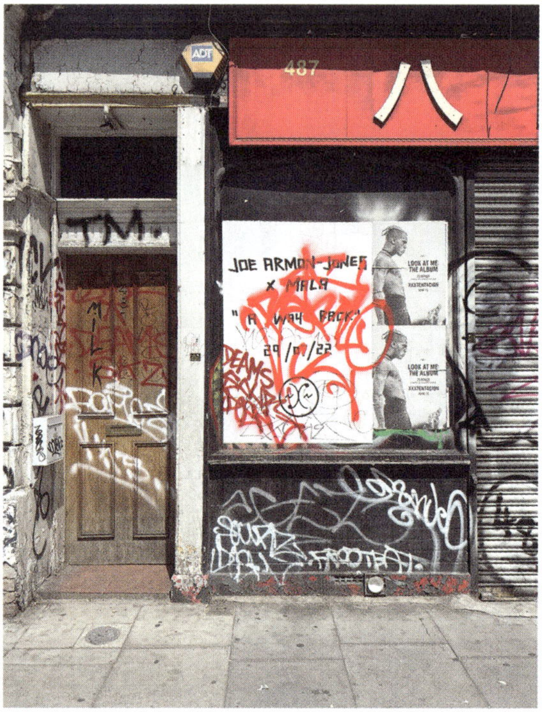


**FIGURE 4.12**
*Untitled (hello)*, London, 2021. Photo: Rafael Schacter.

**FIGURE 4.13**
*Untitled (Joe Armon-Jones)*, London, 2021. Photo: Rafael Schacter.

advertising that most disdain is shown. The plastic hoarding seen in figure 4.12 has not only been torn in half but covered in a range of tags and posters occluding the company logo and going over both the hoarding and the digital advertising board itself. Figures 4.13 and 4.14 likewise show a pair of poster disruptions: the first, a simple white poster with black text covered by two different red tags (Deams SKZ visible in the deeper red); the second, a row of posters that have themselves been placed on top of a huge graffiti piece only latterly become "defaced" themselves. It is the larger billboards that are the greatest prize, though. In figures 4.15–4.17 we can thus see two billboard takeovers by the American writer Revok, pieces commandeering the visual dominance of their corporate architecture, while in figure 4.18 we see two abstract pieces from French artist OX, whose entire public presence is based on the aesthetic reclamation of these sites.

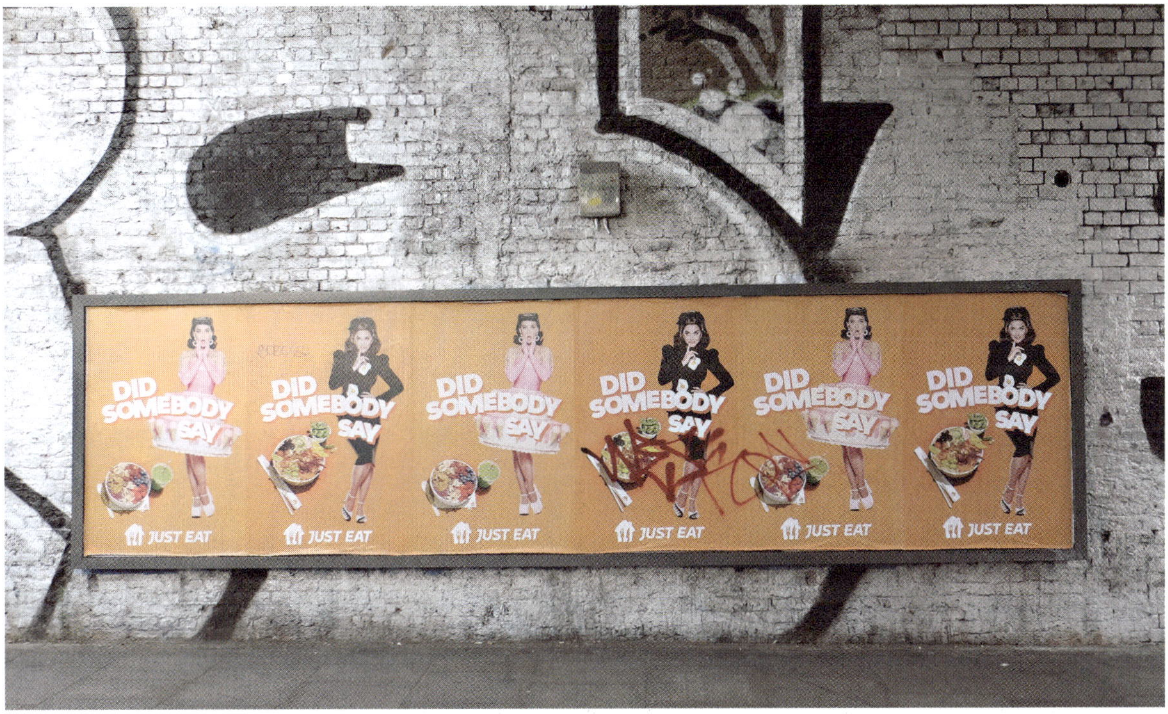


**FIGURE 4.14**
*Untitled (Did Somebody Say)*, London, 2021. Photo: Rafael Schacter.

Here, then, the normative linguistic landscape becomes a backdrop to action, a surface to appear upon rather than with. As with graffiti's interruptive modality discussed in chapter 1, then, by using these other structures as surface, by rejecting their boundaries and sacrosanct nature, graffiti makes its contempt for the linguistic landscape not just implicit but overt. It rejects their (mis)direction, their infelicity, their perlocutions, through a technique of very direct action.

It's not just graffiti writers who seek to reject the normative functioning of the linguistic landscape, however,[5] street artists, subvertisers (developed further in chapter 7; see Dekeyser 2020), and a whole range of other public artists likewise coming to destabilize the traditional functioning of our urban visual culture too. Within the pioneering practice of Edgar Heap of Birds (Hock E Aye Vi), for example, in particular within his

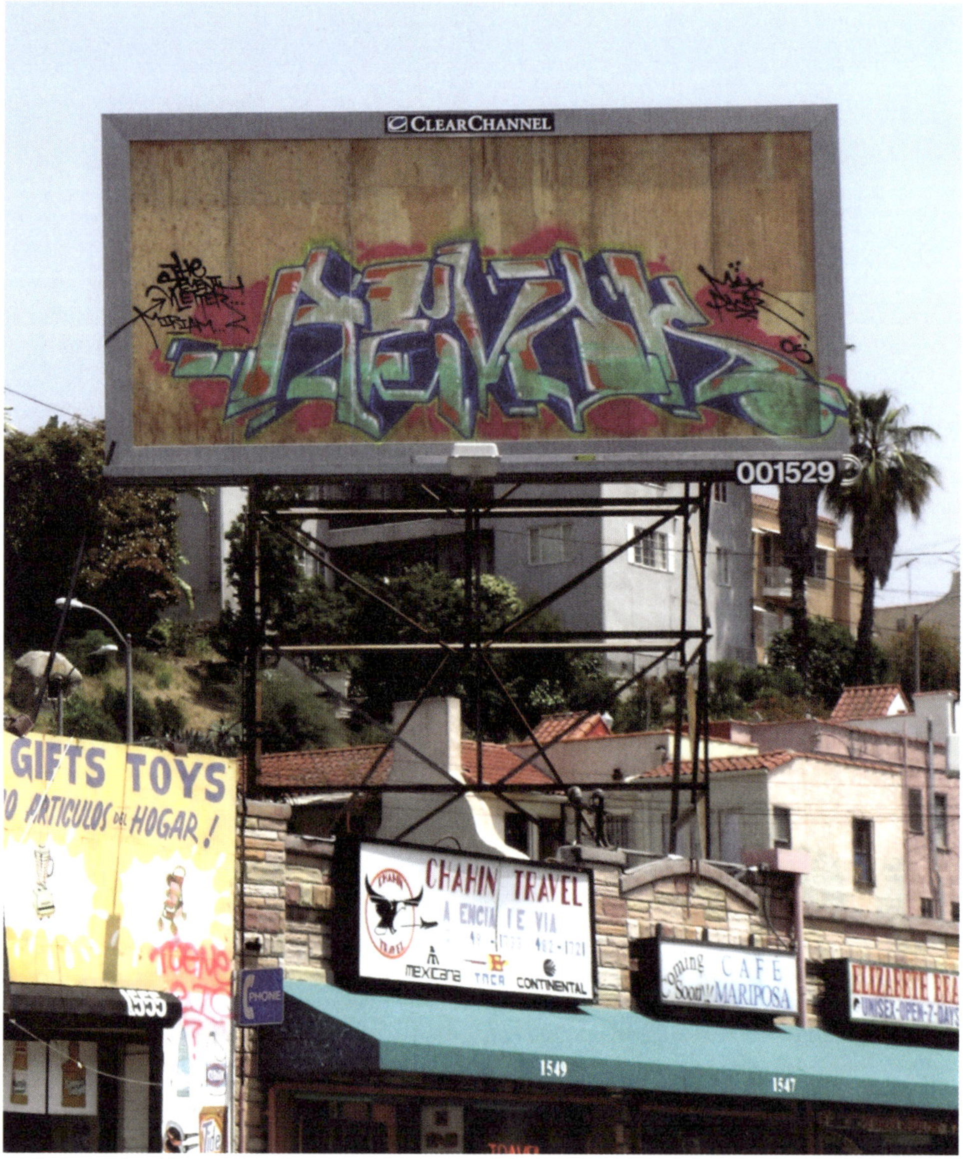


**FIGURES 4.15**
Jason Revok, *Untitled*, 2005. Spray-paint on billboard. Courtesy of the artist.

**FIGURE 4.16**
Jason Revok, *Untitled*, 2005. Spray-paint on billboard. Courtesy of the artist.

**FIGURE 4.17**
Jason Revok, *Untitled*, 2004. Spray-paint on billboard. Courtesy of the artist.

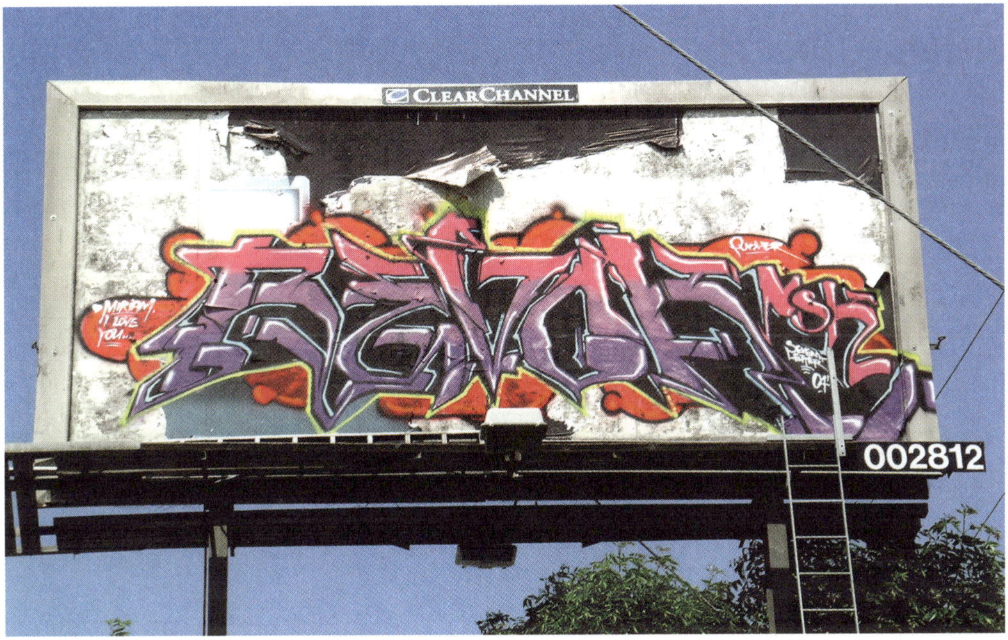
CLEARCHANNEL
002812

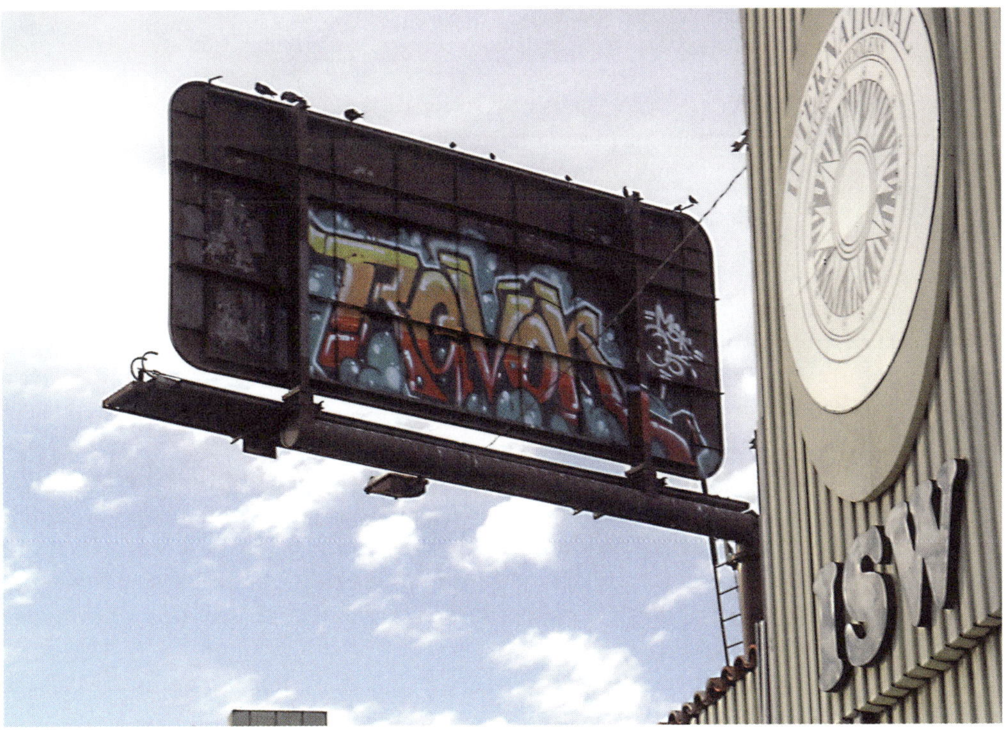
ISW

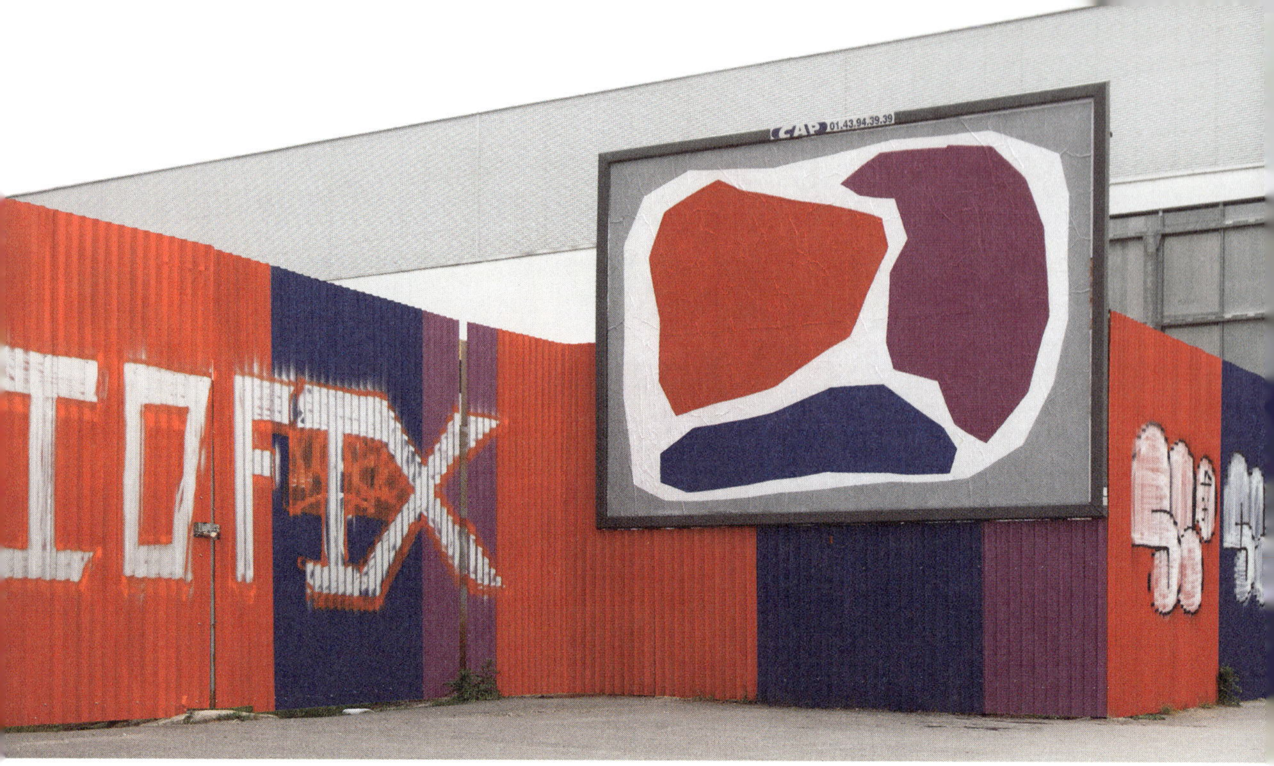


**FIGURE 4.18**
OX, *Untitled*, 2016. Paris. Acrylic on paper. Courtesy of the artist.

renowned project *Native Hosts* (as seen in figures 4.19 and 4.20), the structural formation and bureaucratic design of directional signage become a tool through which he comes to focus on issues of public address, public authority, and the hegemonic narration of American history. Appropriating the subtle power and authority of these place markers—what could at first appear to be an entirely neutral form of geographic and objective information—Heap of Birds displaces their influence through both reversing the script of the anglicized settler designations that they mark out while simultaneously (re)asserting who the rightful custodians of the land itself are. The signs thus work to both (literally) dislocate and reposition their landscapes. Reworking the imperative, declarative, and monological power of these wayfinding signs—which, Heap of Birds has noted, function much like the treaties imposed on indigenous groups—he thus appropriates their power in order to "go on record with a certain viewpoint instead of having a debate," both to issue a "change in knowledge" and to ask people to "question other 'official' signs which they may see in the future" (Heap of Birds 2004: 802). Everyday signage is thus here transformed into a powerful memorial[6] structure that utilizes the language and rhetorical power of the state to reveal what these normative speech acts so easily erase.

Other public practitioners have questioned the discursive techniques not of signage but of advertising. While we previously discussed Jenny Holzer's use of street posters in terms of their blurring the boundary between intimacy and publicity (in chapter 1) as well as the way their weathering naturalizes them within the urban locations (in chapter 3), her works can also be seen to question the normative mode of authorship in the city. While directly addressing us as a public, the diverse positionalities presented in Holzer's posters (as seen in figures 1.23 and 3.5) lead us to question where their ambiguous authority emerges from, to question whose voice is speaking and on whose behalf. Showing, as David Joselit has written, the way in which the "'possession' of language"

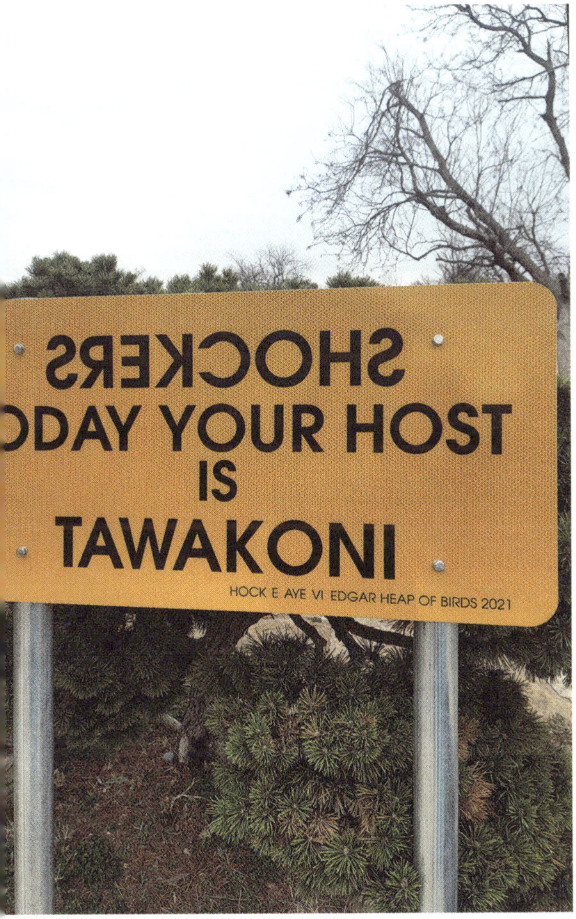


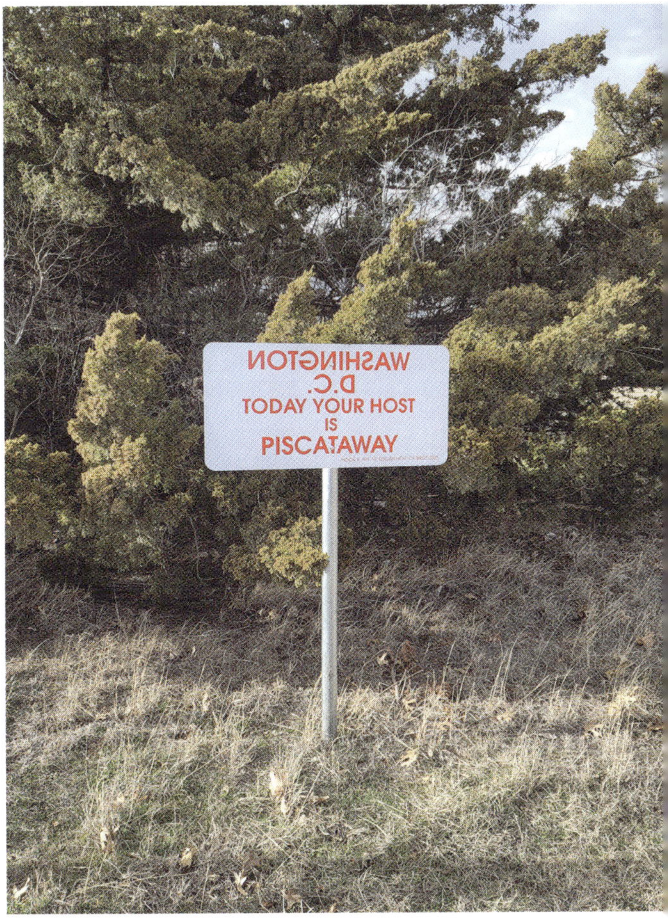


**FIGURE 4.19**

Hock E Aye Vi Edgar Heap of Birds, *Native Host for Wichita*, 2022. Mylar on aluminum sign panel, 18 in × 36 in. Collection of artist. Photo: Shanna Heap of Birds. © Hock E Aye VI Edgar Heap of Birds.

**FIGURE 4.20**

Hock E Aye Vi Edgar Heap of Birds, *Native Host for Washington DC*, 2022. Mylar on aluminum sign panel, 18 in × 36 in. Collection of artist. Photo: Shanna Heap of Birds. © Hock E Aye Vi Edgar Heap of Birds.

can be understood as a "profoundly gendered privilege," the posters undermine this "patriarchal authority" (Joselit 1998: 46) through both their constitutive inconsistencies and conscious lack of fixed political position. For Barbara Kruger, however, an artist often paired with Holzer due to both the location and text-based foundations of their practice, it is the language of corporate advertising that structures her mode of address. Using techniques similar to that described by Stöckl above, Kruger's work uses the spaces and techniques of advertising—most famously that of the billboard—to expose the industry's clichés, redirecting its form and interrogating its structure while simultaneously using its dense power against itself. Providing a commentary on issues such as consumption (as seen in figure 4.21) or housing (as seen in figure 4.22), Kruger rejects the perlocutionary structure of advertising while utilizing a form of direct address that could, as she suggested, both "make space for another kind of viewer" and come to "construct another kind of spectator who has not yet been seen or heard" (Mitchell and Kruger 1991: 435). Rather than attempting to seduce the eye of the passer-by in order to persuade or sell to them, Kruger presents the viewer with open-ended meanings and open-ended content that can then lead them, she hopes, to question wider social and spatial norms.

Still, while the works of all the artists above utilize overtly textual forms to question the city, speech acts can likewise be seen to emerge through nonlinguistic public forms too. Eltono and Nuria's multisited *Signs* project, for example, experimented with ideas of ownership and authenticity, value and context, public and private, while likewise taking aim at the didactic and corporate visual culture of the city. Installing a series of hand-painted signboards (of a size and shape reminiscent of estate agents' "For Sale" or "For Rent" signs) throughout a local neighborhood—while a text on the reverse of the signs asked their finders to claim and then return them to the artists who would sign and then gift the works to their new keepers—the project sought to question not only the relationship between independent and institutional public art, but so too the overbearing urban linguistic landscape that sought push and pull us in multiple directions. The signboard's abstract indirection and palpable ambiguity, as seen very clearly in figure 4.23, not only speaks to and reflects off the official signage it mimics but its public positions questions the linguistic clutter of urban space, the way the city confronts and commands us, all while doing so in purely nonlinguistic terms. In a similar way, Steinbrener/Dempf and Huber's *Delete!*, as seen in figures 4.24 and 4.25, sought not to

**FIGURE 4.21**
Barbara Kruger, *Untitled (Shopping)*, Schirn Kunsthalle/Kaufhof department store façade, Frankfurt am Main, Germany, 2002. Courtesy of the artist and Sprüth Magers. Photo: Norbert Migulez.

**FIGURE 4.22**
Barbara Kruger, *Untitled (Who Is Housed When Money Talks?)*, 2020. Mural for Housing Is a Human Right, the housing advocacy division of AIDS Healthcare Foundation, 6500 Sunset Boulevard, Los Angeles, CA. Courtesy of the artist, Sprüth Magers, and AIDS Healthcare Foundation.

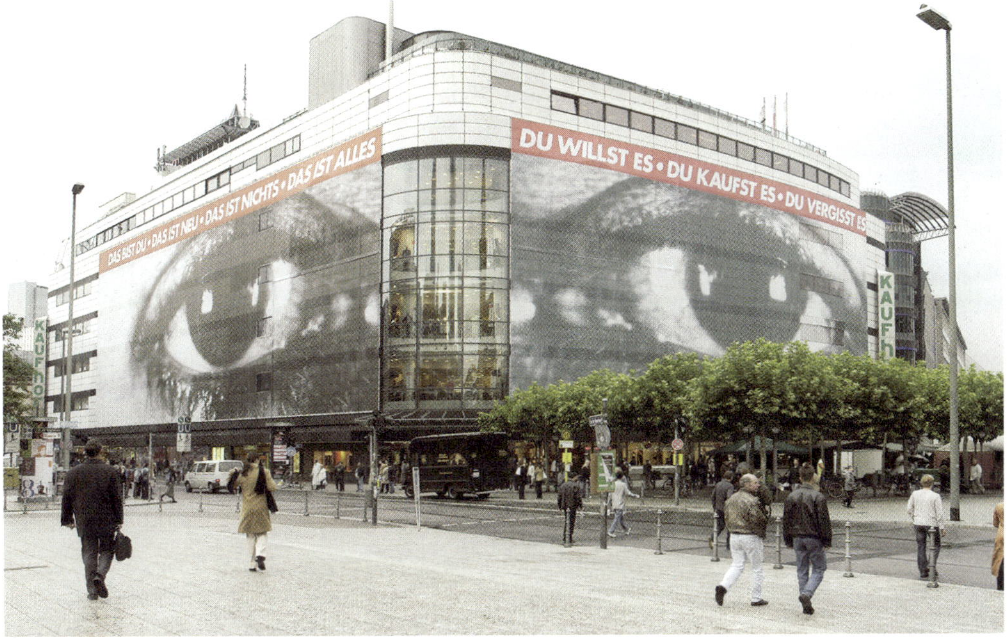
DAS BIST DU • DAS IST NEU • DAS IST NICHTS • DAS IST ALLES
DU WILLST ES • DU KAUFST ES • DU VERGISST ES

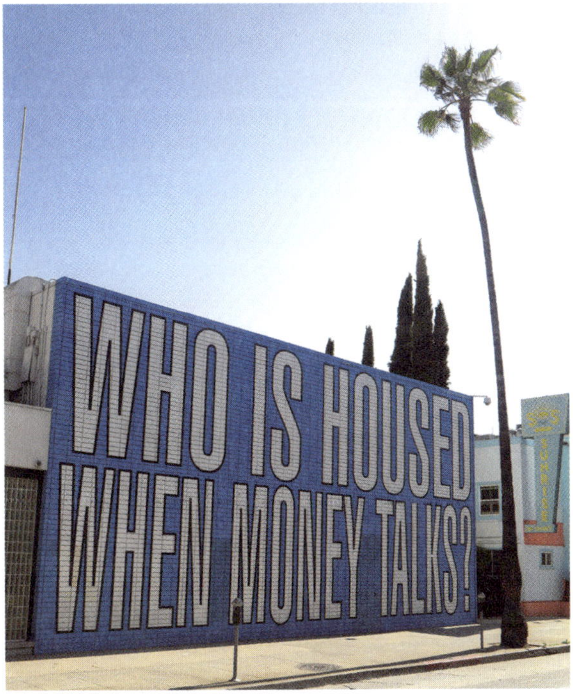
WHO IS HOUSED
WHEN MONEY TALKS?

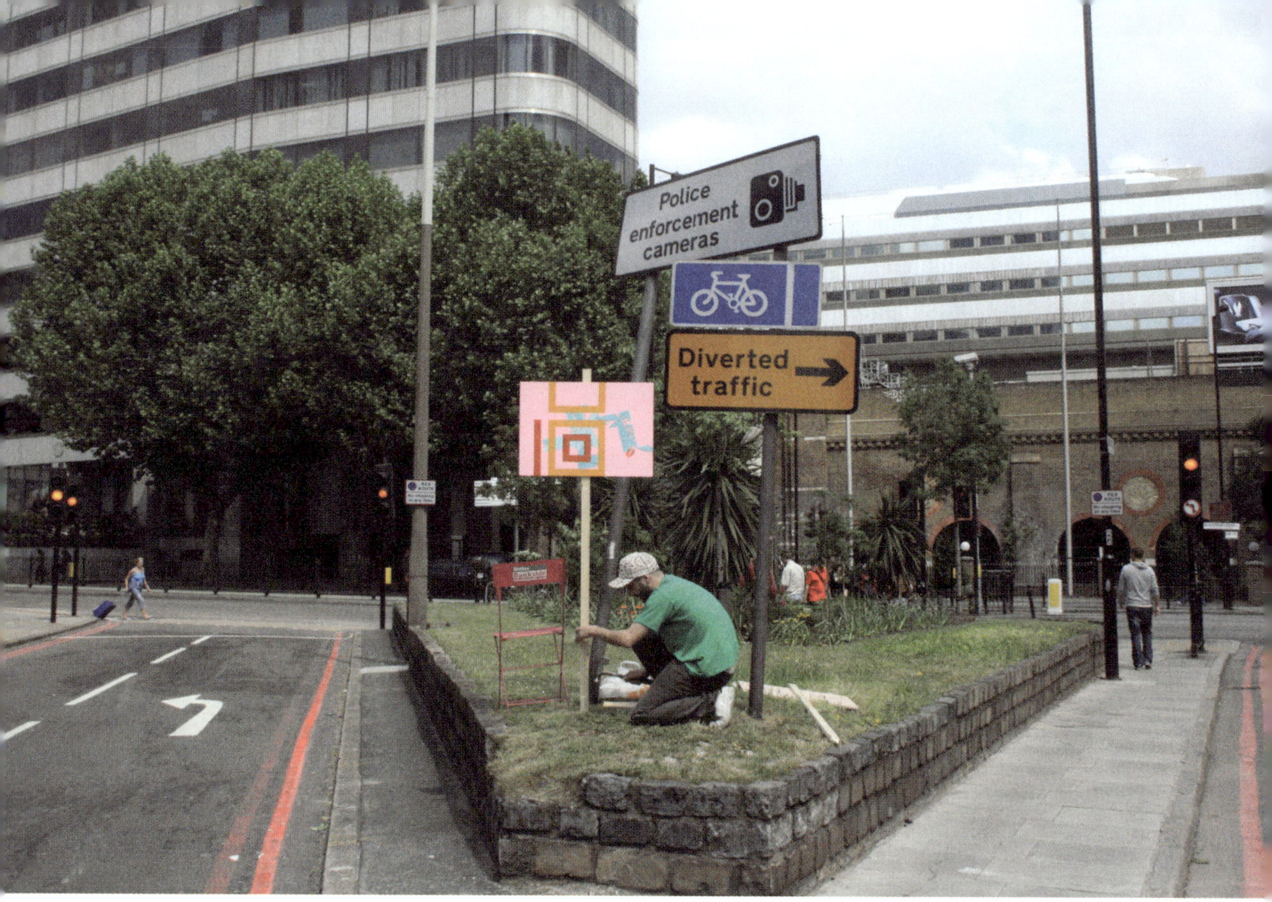


**FIGURE 4.23**
Eltono and Nuria, *Signs*, London, 2008. Fifty hand-painted signboards. Part of the *Walking Tour* for the exhibition *Street Art* at the Tate Modern, London. Photo: Rafael Schacter. Courtesy of the artists.

**FIGURES 4.24 AND 4.25**
Steinbrener/Dempf & Huber, *Delete! Delettering the Public Space*, 2005. © Steinbrener/Dempf & Huber.

just question but to entirely erase the linguistic landscape itself. Removing all visible inscriptions within a street in Vienna's 7th district through wrapping them in a plastic yellow coating, the collective created a space in which the attention-seeking invocations and cacophony of the street were emptied out and abstracted. Not only highlighting the density of linguistic forms so normalized within the public sphere, the public deletion also brought the sculptural presence of the architectural environment to the fore. Seeking aesthetic enhancement through aesthetic negation, *Delete!* thus propositionally rejected the dominant language of public space, saying something and making a public pronouncement without the use of words.

While graffiti may not directly address issues of settler-colonialism or explicitly question inequitable housing laws, then, still it speaks. Like Heap of Birds, graffiti produces

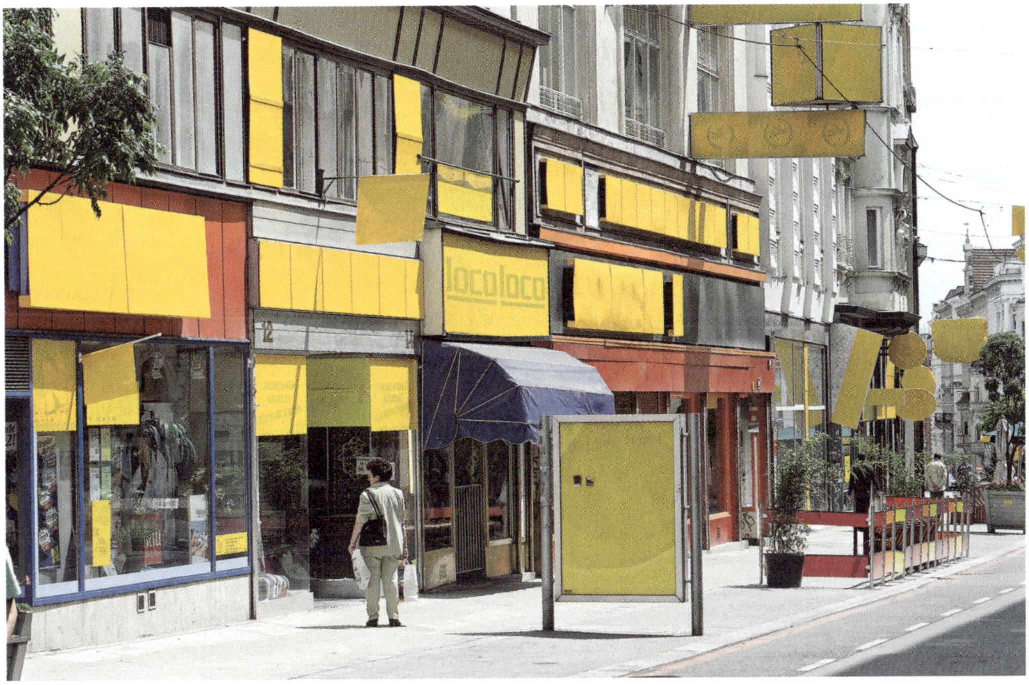
locoloco

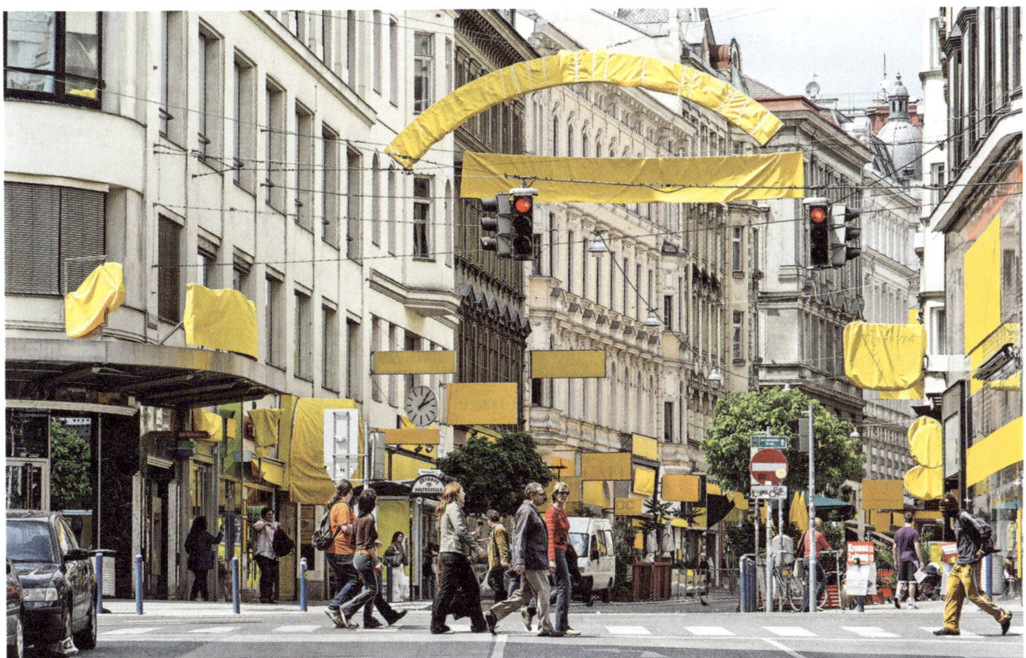

marginal modes of writing (including similarly reversed letter forms, as seen in figure 4.26), addressing the way modes of speech can proclaim rights to geographic space. Like Holzer, graffiti attacks the hegemonic control of language, pluralizing public speech and mocking the power of institutional discourse. Like Kruger, graffiti creates space for a different kind of viewership, creating a speech that is open-ended and seeks a discursive, not commercial, relation. Like Eltono and Nuria, graffiti questions the commands of the city, generating ambiguity within its didacticism, being legible even while taking a nonlinguistic approach. And like Steinbrener et al., graffiti brings the abnormal normalization of our linguistic landscape into focus, making it visible through negation and abstraction both. Graffiti's subtextual propositions thus reject and reinscribe our linguistic landscape to offer an altered communicative modality for public space. It

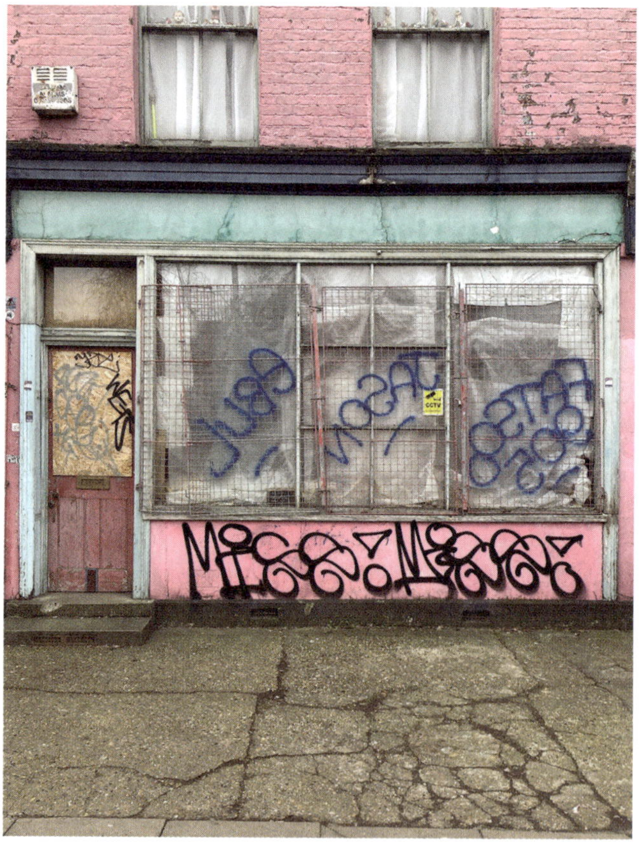

**FIGURE 4.26**
*Fatso/Jason/Ebul/Miss*, 2023, North West London. Photo: Alex Ellison.

uses absurdity and incongruity to refuse the solemnity, the functionality, the taciturn address of the linguistic landscape. It ridicules and repossesses the language of authority, inserting the emotional into the bureaucratic and reclaiming the public as a space of non-instrumentality and joy. Graffiti thus says something that is visibly audible. It proclaims its name and proclaims its right to proclaim this name. It uses the margins of the city as a space for marginal, non-instrumental communication. It rejects the city as a space of the monological, the imperative, the perlocutionary, and inserts a dialogical, constative, illocutionary mode of speech into the heart of the public sphere. Explored subtextually, then, graffiti questions where we are allowed to speak, where public starts and private stops, and does this through speaking on public and private space alike. Explored subtextually, it makes a claim toward its right to communicate while questioning the communicative validity of our normative linguistic landscape too.

## CONCLUSION *OR* THE MONUMENT SPEAKS/A MONUMENTAL COUNTERPUBLIC

Now that graffiti's text, context, and subtext have been laid out, what about that of the institutional monument? What does it pronounce through its stony-faced form? As a classical speech act functioning through its status as reminder, advice, and warning, the monument can be seen to have been explicitly built so as to speak. But in what mode and through what techniques does it come to do so?

Let's return to Trafalgar Square and Nelson once again, for Nelson can be seen to speak to us in numerous different ways. As text, as monumental reminder, Nelson's overt function is as grand eponymous commemoration to the man himself. He memorializes his own final, heroic victory at Trafalgar, memorializes his life as valiant life and venerates his death as most valiant death. His size and solidity reinforce the immensity of the man and immensity of the loss. Here stands a man of incredible power; worship him. Here stands a hero at the level of a god; look up to him. As the *Illustrated London News* put it at the moment of its inauguration, Nelson's Column is thus a tribute from "the citizen to the warrior," a "funeral record" that "is raised in a sacred spot, and is consecrated by religion," and that possesses interests "of a higher and more sacred kind" (*Illustrated London News* 1843: 289). The surrounding bas-reliefs of his great deeds—Nelson graciously accepting the surrender of the Spanish at St. Vincent, Nelson courageously injured in Abu Qir Bay on the Nile, Nelson sternly marking his seal before the Battle of Copenhagen, Nelson mortally wounded at Trafalgar—likewise reveal a narrative and framing of a man beyond mere man, a man of integrity and gallantry, of character and valor, war and sacrifice. The overt content as speech act and the joint linguistic structure thus set in place a hegemonic mode of one-way veneration, a statement that necessitates no response: Nelson reminds us through a didactic technique (he teaches, we absorb); he advises us via a monological frame (he speaks, we listen); he warns through imperative means (he instructs, we obey). There is no dialogue here, no

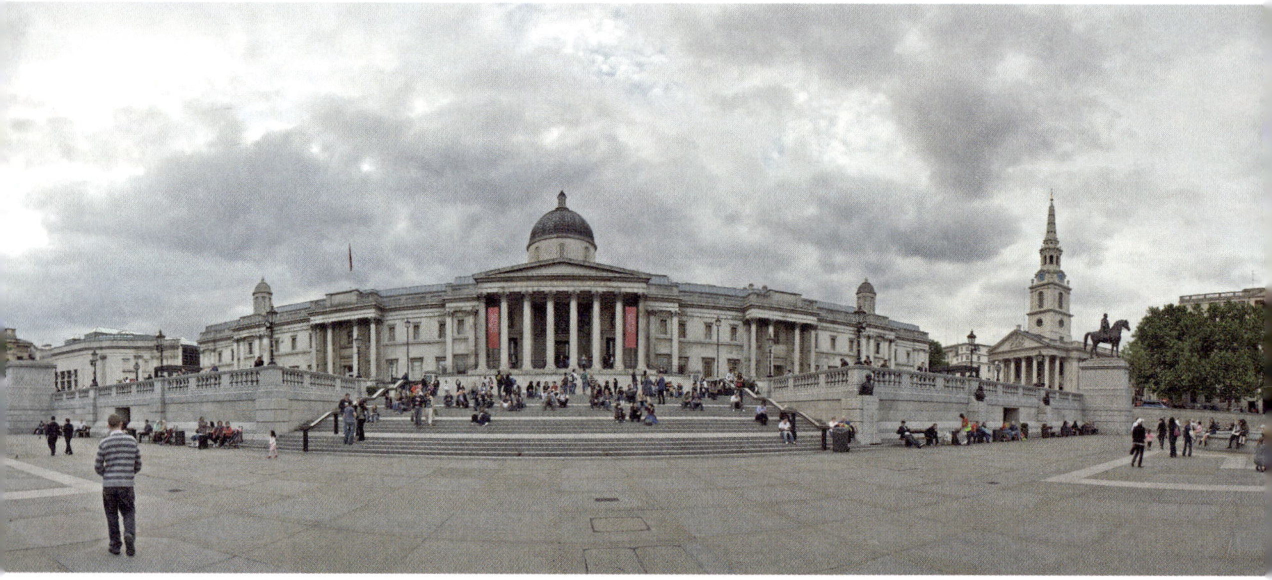

questions allowed. The size and strength, the height and depth of the monument make its statement incontrovertible.

But what of the wider context in which Nelson sits as seen in figure 4.27? Here we have not only a singular monument but a monumental mise-en-scène, a highly staged architectural ensemble. Nelson thus not only stands in a square named after his great victory but, as described in chapter 3, is flanked by his four huge lions, his triple-stepped platform, his enormous pedestal and outlandishly high column. Moreover, he has been placed adjacent to both the Palace (the King's chief residence just off to his right down the Mall) and Parliament (which he looks out upon down Whitehall), as well as in front of the hugely significant National Gallery (built just a few years before the column's construction). Nelson thus stands in the ultimate site of the nation-state, the literal and metaphorical mile zero of the capital. He dominates, in Rodney Mace's terms, the nation's "front room," the site existent in every capital city that attempts to most palpably express its "host's social historical and political aspirations" (Mace 2005: 11). The importance of this contextual location, as much as Nelson's total control of this site—piercing the sky and permeating the ground, both deific and ever-present—places the monument in an unparalleled public context. Nothing could be given more supreme affirmation. As such, while a monument's purposeful "readability," as Lefebvre terms it, "embodies and imposes a clearly intelligible message" (here lies a great man), it "hides a good deal more" (Lefebvre 1991: 143): like all monumental forms, it implies a "certain

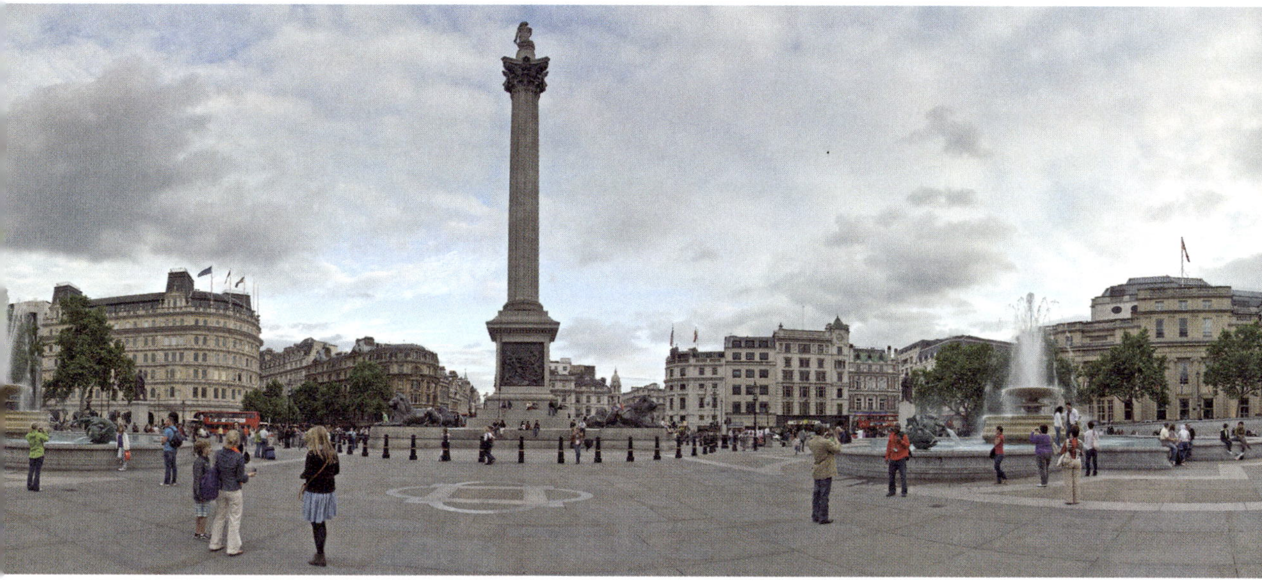

**FIGURE 4.27**
*Trafalgar Square*, 2009. Photo by David Iliff. License: CC BY-SA 3.0.

order . . . commands bodies, prescribing or proscribing gestures," while it "mask[s] the will to power and the arbitrariness of power beneath signs and surfaces which claim to express collective will and collective thought" (p. 143). Nelson's contextual position thus communicates to us far beyond its literal meaning alone.

Yet context develops beyond space alone here. To fully comprehend Nelson's subtext, we need to examine his *temporal* status too. Unlike graffiti, a speech act whose ephemeral existence means that its temporal frame is almost always one of immediacy—a speech act almost always spoken in the "now" as it commonly endures for little more than the present—the institutional monument's initial moment of enunciation can lie not just years but literally centuries in the past. While stone persists, sound decays, and an utterance that was clear to those in its vicinity contemporaneously may today have become subdued. What the monument says now and what it initially may have said can thus be entirely different. In our case here, at the time of the column's erection in 1843, at the very onset of the wild era of statumania taking place over the whole of Europe, public monuments were still an emergent public form. Rather than the habitual urban presence that they are today, as normalized as advertising or traffic lights, the era in which Nelson first spoke was one in which these artifacts were only just moving out of the intimate private sphere (of the aristocracy) and into the more communal public sphere (of the emerging bourgeoisie) (Mace 2005: 48–49). This was likewise an era in which there was a firm belief that patriotic fervor needed to be stirred, in which a hegemonic fear existed not just of the foreign other but likewise of the internal one represented by the "infant Chartist movement and the burgeoning trade unions" (p. 57). It was an era in which the appeals of "tradition" and nostalgia, thirty-five years after the death of the hero in question, marked out Nelson as the ultimate Victorian champion who could best espouse the period's "muscular, male and Christian values" (p. 13). As such, and emergent during an era in which monuments were artifacts consciously utilized, in the words of Eric Hobsbawm, to "teach, inform, and inculcate a state's value system" (Hobsbawm 1995: 13), Nelson would have had a very different contextual meaning from that which today adheres.

While today Nelson's Column stands subtextually as a symbol of London and of Britain—a center point for tourism and national heritage, a historically estranged, yet symbolically powerful metaphor for the nation-state and its grand Imperial past—during the Victorian age the statue's relationship to the monarchy (for whose enrichment Nelson battled), to the aristocracy (for whose property he fought), to the admiralty (for whose dignity he served), and to the wider country (for whose safeguarding he died) would have been more audibly present. Nelson's subtext would have thus gone far beyond the "In Memoriam" that its public text most openly states. While it is the monument's location and physical form that create its dominant (yet indirect) meaning today, for the original audience the monument clearly spoke of patriotism (if not jingoism), of an attempt to bring Crown and country together. Nelson thus comes to commemorate much more than himself or his victory at Trafalgar. He comes to anchor the collective ideals of the nation, securing its physical and psychic perpetuity. He comes to instruct and cohere his geographic and societal surrounds, to construct past, place, and populace through perlocutionary means. "Rule, Britannia!" the column thus subtextually exclaims, "Britannia, rule the waves." Nelson's Column thus obligates not just remembrance and memorialization but consensus and concord. It functions as a technological device to sustain power, to foster national pride, to generate a polity of citizens from a mass of disconnected individuals. The work's single formal linguistic utterance, reading "ENGLAND EXPECTS EVERY MAN WILL DO HIS DUTY" (as seen at the outer base of the south-facing bronze panel in figure 4.28), thus acts synecdochally for the entire structure. Speaking through not only the imperative mode but so too the deontic, acting as the expression of necessity and obligation that Svennevig noted above (2021), it is "England" that here stands in the position of power, that makes

**FIGURE 4.28**
John Edward Carew, *The Death of Nelson*, 1843. Bronze relief. Photo: Rafael Schacter.

**FIGURE 4.29**
Antonin Mercié, *The Robert E. Lee Monument*, 1890–2021, Richmond, VA. Photo: Martin Falbisoner. License: CC BY-SA 3.0.

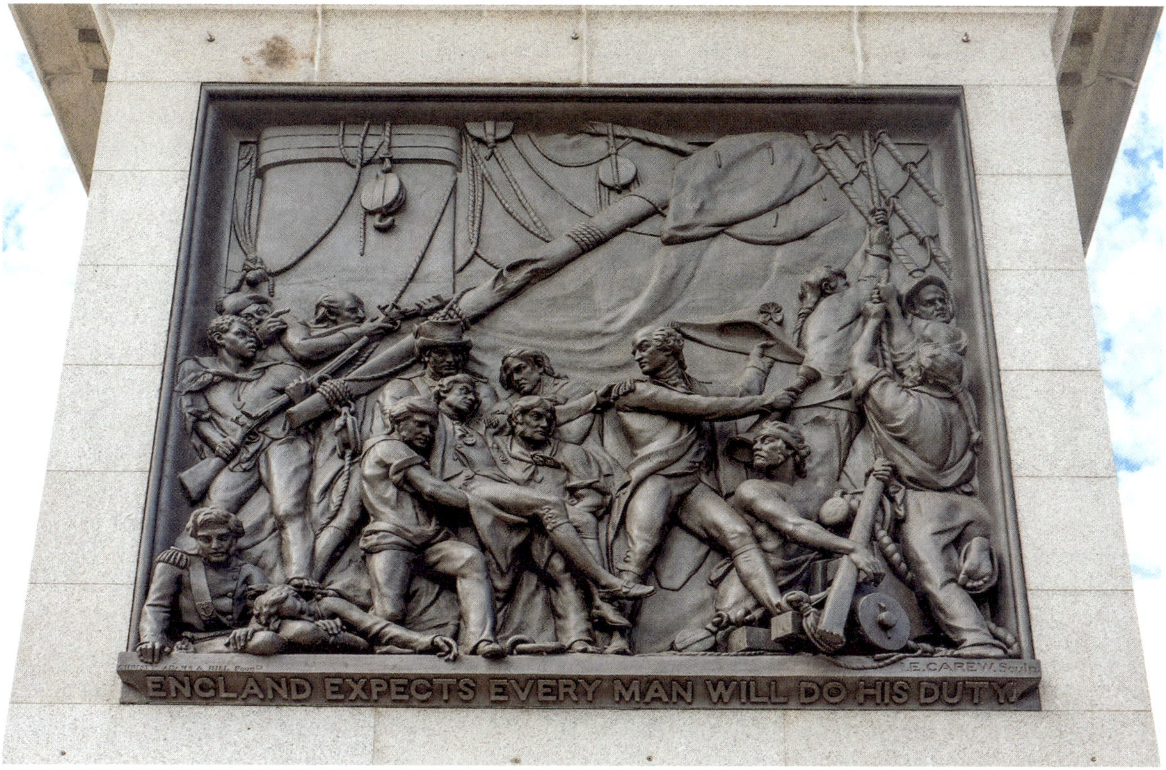
J.E. CAREW. Sculp.
ENGLAND EXPECTS EVERY MAN WILL DO HIS DUTY.

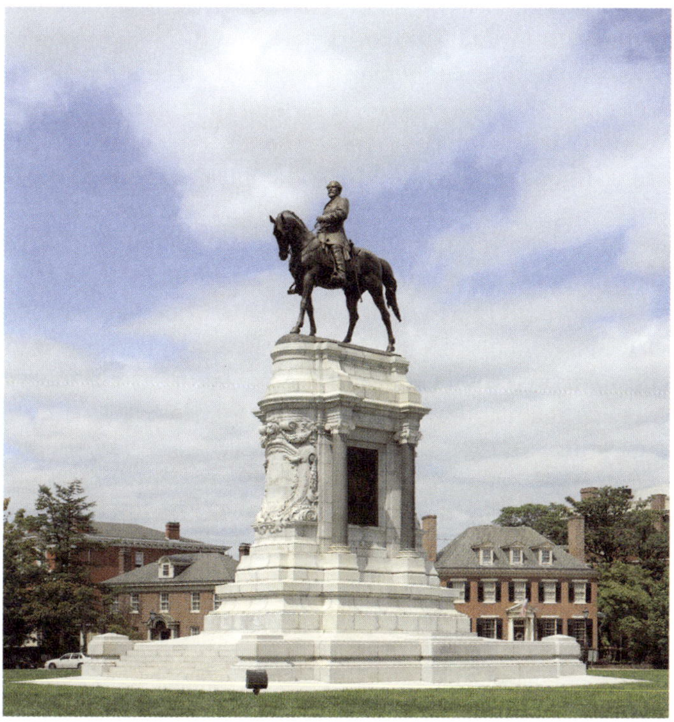

decisions about the actions of others. It is England that Nelson is ventriloquizing. It is both he and England that expects.

Taking this focus on text, on context (spatial *and* temporal), and on subtext into the fold, the anxious debate over what has been termed "difficult heritage" (Macdonald 2009) can become a much more straightforward story. Take the obdurate issue of Confederacy monuments, for example. Their overt status as text today, as either monuments to the Civil War or memorials to the specific military leaders who participated within it (as seen in the Robert E. Lee memorial in figure 4.29, for example), is subtextually redetermined by the spatial and temporal contexts in which these artifacts first spoke (and still speak today). And where and when did they emerge? Well, as made clear by the Southern Poverty Law Center, there were "two major periods in which the dedication of Confederate monuments and other symbols spiked" (Southern Poverty Law Center 2019: 11), these being in the early 1900s, as the Jim Crow laws disenfranchised African Americans through upholding state segregation (following the *Plessy v. Ferguson* case in 1896), and during the 1950s and '60s, as the civil rights movement emerged and the Supreme Court outlawed segregation in schools (following *Brown v. Board of Education* in 1954). Like the heightened temporal context of their erection, the spatial context in which these monuments were situated—appearing on courthouse grounds in the former case (a public reminder of the case that was won) and on those of public schools in the latter (a material bulwark against the case that was lost)—site-specifically endorses the perlocutionary message the monuments enunciate. These artifacts do not simply look back into the past but speak directly to a supremacist present. They work not to revere a great loss but to set in stone a segregationist future. The individual depicted or the battle recounted is thus entirely overwritten by the contextual strength of the monument itself. "Here Lies Robert E.," the monument may overtly pronounce; "Here Stands a Monument to Exclusion and Segregation," it subtextually sustains.

While what Arianna Shahvisi (2021) has termed the "slurring speech acts" of these "difficult" monuments still persist—even as their "derogatory pedestalling," as Ten-Herng Lai termed it, honors "individuals or ideologies that can only make sense when members of a targeted group are taken to be inferior" (Lai 2020: 604)—it is our graffiti monument that is still the monument subject to overwhelming institutional condemnation and destruction today. And just as the subtext of our institutional monuments is silenced, the graffiti monument's metacommunicative message is likewise suppressed. It is simply much easier (and more hegemonically beneficial) to read both of these monumental forms through their direct texts alone, even while, as Brenneis argued, the sole focus on a "literal message" is often "inadequate or misleading in itself" (Brenneis 1986: 341). The graffiti-monument, the monument-*advice*, the indirect speech act comprised of text, context, and subtext combined, thus states much more than its name alone. It suggests a way of thinking about the city, a way of *acting* within it. It advises us through its visible presence on the city's communicative networks, a presence working against social, legal, and linguistic regulations. In this way, then, graffiti reveals the artificiality of the city's seemingly "natural" state, of a linguistic landscape that did not just grow but that was tended, cultivated. The radical acts of cities that have, for example, rejected the constitutively private speech of "public" advertising—as famously undertaken in São Paolo with their Clean City Law, but also in cities such as Grenoble and Chennai—thus come to show the extraordinary nature of our "natural" urban scopic regime, a space not only in which private interests dominate public space, but in which graffiti can be removed from *privately* owned space (and fines levied) even when appearing with the express permission of the property owners themselves![7]

Still, graffiti continues to speak, to question *who* gets to be present in public, *what* forms of speech are deemed acceptable, *where* one can conduct public discourse. It creates a community of readers and listeners who, as seen in Warner's counterpublic, are brought into being "by virtue of being addressed" (Warner 2002: 413). It creates a structure of speech that, while first and foremost spoken to other speakers of the language, "promises to address anybody," that "commits itself in principle to the possible participation of any stranger" (p. 422). It formulates a mode of communication that—through the "pragmatics of its speech genres, idioms, stylistic markers, address, temporality, mise-en-scène, citational field, interlocutory protocols, [and] lexicon" (p. 422)—renounces the structural frameworks of hegemonic public discourse itself. The speech enacted here thus seeks to make visible "different assumptions about what can be said or what goes without saying," to call into question not just "ideas or policy questions, but the speech genres and modes of address that constitute the public" (pp. 423–424). The graffiti counterpublic, as Warner continues in terms of all counterpublics, thus not only comes to "characterize the world in which it attempts to circulate" but attempts to "realize that world through address" (p. 422). The reduction of graffiti to "vandalism," to "scrawl" (a terminology as senseless as labeling an unfamiliar language "babble"), can thus be seen to emerge constitutively through its refusal of the dominant modes of public address and its refusal of the normative location of speech. "The urban space of the street," as Lefebvre proclaimed, is a site "given over as much to the exchange of words and signs as it is to the exchange of things. A place where speech becomes writing. A place where speech can become 'savage' and, by escaping rules and institutions, inscribe itself on walls" (Lefebvre 2003: 19). Graffiti is exactly this "savage" speech, this speech from the edge refusing control. It is a monumental speech that appears on communication networks regardless of legal sanctions. A monumental speech that speaks for itself through the magical power of the single-word utterance alone.

# 5
# ACTION

Graffiti is a practice. It is a performance transforming the city into a domain of action. While a fact often left unrecognized due to the characteristic invisibility of graffiti's production, process is not only formally fundamental to graffiti but habitually valued more than the resultant image by practitioners. Graffiti not only emerges *via* performance (as the material residue of a prior action) but is a performance itself. It is a dance, a gestural art, that becomes more than a merely necessary act. As an artifact that is, as described in chapter 3, inherently precarious, the transience of the graffiti image empowers a focus on process over product, the inevitable annihilation of the object meaning that it becomes not the end point but rather the result of practice itself. It becomes a way of enabling practitioners to publicly commit to the act and to the culture while generating pleasure from the experiential encounters it generates. Exploring the way graffiti writers appear in public space and use their bodies as their primary artistic tool, this chapter will thus examine graffiti as an achievement that speaks louder than its words. Here, then, it is Hannah Arendt's "doer of deeds," rather than just her "speaker of words," who will be focused on (Arendt 1988 [1958]: 179–180): the doer whose actions create uniqueness, the doer whose actions produce the unexpected, the doer whose actions create new beginnings yet are likewise ends in themselves.

This chapter will first position graffiti as a praxis through which the graffiti canon becomes embodied. Exploring the formal and social techniques that a graffiti education instills, the first section will unpack the way the body becomes sculpted by skill and style becomes written into the skin. The second section explores not just formal but spatial ways of knowing. Creating a form of (sub)cultural belonging as much as marginal bodily resistance, the graffiti body will here be seen to dissent through acts of exploring, walking, and mapping the city. The final section explores the way bodily risk becomes critical to the way the graffiti image is later read: beauty and efficacy, commitment and belief become embedded within the image through the absent presence of the performing body. Not only will style and action be seen as in many ways indistinguishable, but the performed image will be positioned as a form of advice on how to act in the city and how to embed oneself within its living fabric. As such, while the previous chapter focused on a subject's ability to appear on networks of communication and exchange, this chapter focuses on the right, as Engin Isin maintains, following the work of Lefebvre, "to claim presence in the city" (Isin 2013: 14). This chapter will thus explore the way in which the graffiti body inhabits and appropriates the contemporary city, the way in which, as Susana Torre has written, a recalcitrant body can introduce "direction, rotation, orientation, [and] occupation" into a landscape and organize space "through gestures, traces, and marks" (Torre 1996: 249). It will explore the way the city is made through performance and the way bodily action comes to speak in the most monumental of ways.

## EMBODYING THE CANON/A BODILY PRAXIS

Graffiti is a practice that is not just performed through, but learned via, the body. It is a gestural practice whose skilled techniques come to create the self and the social alike. Learned through an informal educational environment and most commonly emerging through the wider social hierarchy of a graffiti crew, these classically paternalistic[1] and homosocial spaces of training (Marchand 2008) embed the canon corporeally through the disciplinary conventions of the genre as much as the disciplinary conventions of the didactic system itself. Whatever way one learns, however, the absorption of canonical style is only ever accomplished through an intense period of bodily education and an even more intense dedication to practice. Only this can lead to one becoming a fully-fledged member of the social body, developing into a unique individual and a subcultural citizen at the same time.

Cultivating the formal sensibilities of novices (or "toys") in order to transform them into full members of the aesthetic community, graffiti pedagogy functions via both master-apprentice and peer-to-peer relations, the cooperative maxim of "each one teach one" acting as an overarching and general rule. Knowledge acquisition emerges through the collective unpacking of classic works and canonical artists,[2] the examination of specific letter forms and styles, the discussion of specific techniques and approaches, alongside a constant critique of each other's practice in a manner no different from (and no less intense than) an art school "crit." Yet while knowing is critical, knowing does not turn you into a writer; only *doing* does that. Methods for controlling specific tools (from spray cans to fire extinguishers), materials (from ink to acid), and substrates (from aluminum shutters to steel trains) can be verbally explained, but it is only through an "active, perceptual engagement," as Ingold argues is necessary within all craft activities, that a participant can truly "fine-tune his own movements so as to achieve the rhythmic fluency of the accomplished practitioner" (Ingold 2000: 353). Younger artists thus gain technical and embodied knowledge from more senior crew members through the classical apprenticeship techniques of "assisting, observing, engaging in mimesis, and repeatedly practising" (Marchand 2008: 254), while mentors also gain from the relationship—not only from the esteem of having a school of adherents but through being forced to critically reflect on their own knowledge (p. 255). Self-discipline is thus still critical—the drive to improve and to be accepted as a member of the community quickly separating the committed from the fleeting—yet the crew system creates communities of practice focused on communal as much as individual development, focused on the energy and encouragement of teamwork and the collective push for improvement. They create a drive, a (healthy) competition pushing each member to be the best that they can, a painting *for* (for oneself, for one's crew) more than just a painting *against* (against rivals, against norms). The educational system within graffiti thus trains not only skills but how to "think and act as a team member" (p. 255), forming a community as focused on technique and expertise as they are on the specific practices of one another. Style hence surfaces through gesture just as gesture is stylized through the hours of training and collective refinement that practitioners undertake.

Yet the "fidelity to tradition" that any apprenticeship system creates, something that is, as Downey, Dalidowicz, and Mason have noted, an "extraordinarily demanding, not inevitable" achievement (Downey et al. 2015: 185), has its own transcendence written within it. While cultural continuity is guaranteed through classical structures such as "teacher authority and charisma, practical constraints (such as genre rules, the materiality of instruments or even the human body itself), and disciplining institutions (like audience expectations, group performance, and obligatory exercises)" (p. 185), the knowledge gained prepares adherents' bodies so as to create a baseline from which a practitioner can progress beyond themself. Yet it is only through breaking and amending the rules of the canon that one can ever truly develop into the role of an expert (or "king"). As in many craft practices, the structure of graffiti is thus able to accommodate "improvisation, thoughtful innovation and personal ambition" while still reproducing "stable communities and enduring practices" (Marchand 2008: 250). Just as the stylistic basis of the canon balances egalitarian and individualistic desires through the taboo of instrumentally motivated public action (and the collective rejection it elicits), here the crew system helps to structure the structuring boundaries of not just the formal but the social world. As such, while practitioners learn where and how one writes, *whom* one should write with is also tacitly imparted (and one should write with any committed practitioner, no matter their level of skill or fame). While when and what one writes soon become a given, *why* one writes is likewise materially demonstrated (and one writes not only to distribute the self but likewise to distribute one's kin, to act morally to the city and one's culture in equal terms).

The apprentice system thus not only teaches technical proficiency but so too how to act bodily in the world—something reflexively revealed through the image itself. A perfectly written tag, then, a tag whose economy of line shows a total control of bodily movements, whose balance and symmetry shows total command of materials and medium (such as seen in Mosa's tags in figure 5.1, for example), reveals a devotion to practice (and *the* practice) impossible to simulate. Yet the associated names a practitioner writes, the crew names they exhibit, the dedications they offer—all of which are a staple of graffiti practice that every practitioner must adhere to—together show a writer's fidelity to their teachers and cohort, show an adherence to the social through the material residue of the bodily (as seen in the dedications to Osha, Sepy, Caspa, and Meth in figure 5.2 and to 10Foot, Flash, Tox, Drax, and Serva in figure 5.3). Graffiti pedagogy thus teaches a form of communality without which one's success in the practice would be unachievable and one's tie to the community short-lived. Writing graffiti entirely on your own is not only tough, but more than anything it is unenviable. What could thus first appear as a purely bodily method of learning thus soon reveals itself to be a critical "site for establishing an education for social citizenship," a site in which individuals are turned into "valued and responsible agents within their communities of practice" (Marchand 2008: 267). It reveals a form of knowledge transfer in which what is taught are not just formal skills but likewise the "social knowledge, worldviews and

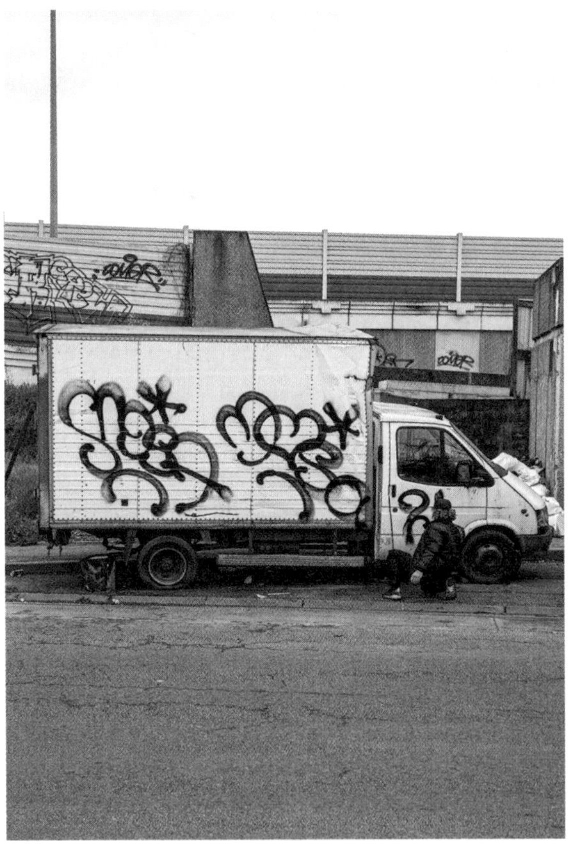

**FIGURE 5.1**
Mosa, 2022. Courtesy of the artist and *Tramontana Magazine*. Photo: Elliot Sitbon.

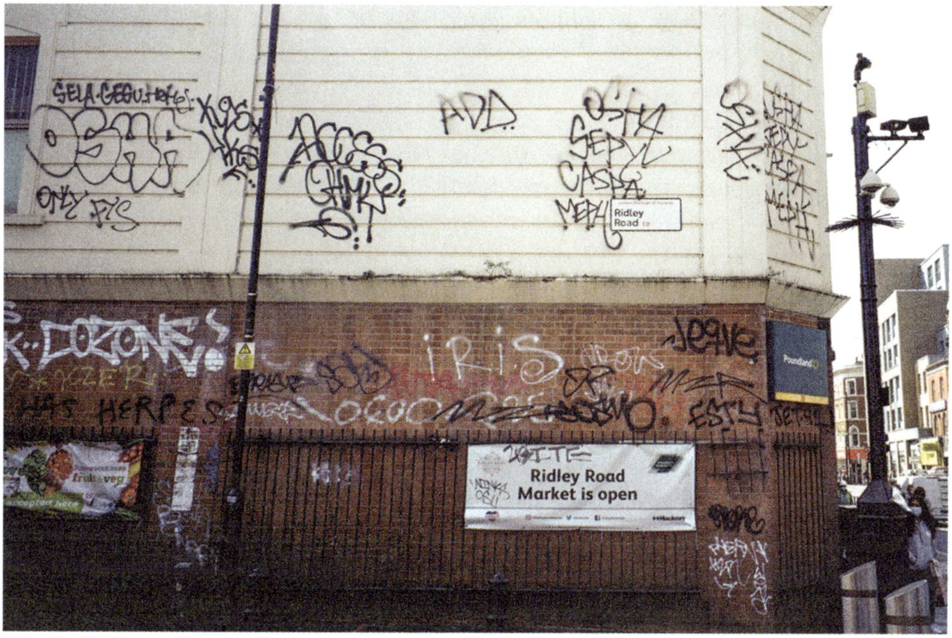


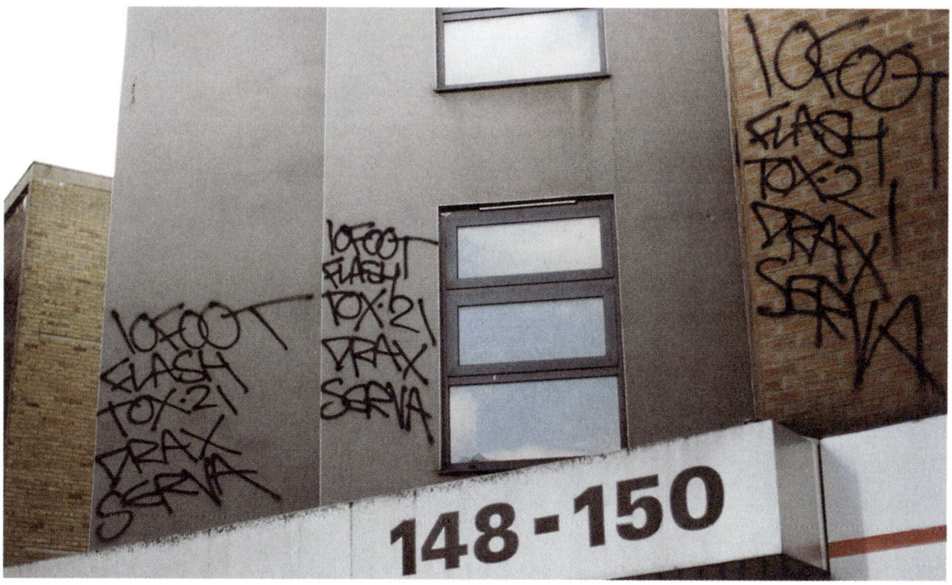


**FIGURE 5.2**
*Untitled (Ridley Road)*, 2021, London. Photo: Rafael Schacter.

**FIGURE 5.3**
*Untitled (148–150 Mare Street)*, 2021, London. Photo: Rafael Schacter.

moral principles that denote membership and status" (p. 246). Like all learned bodily techniques, then, graffiti must be seen to socialize through enskilling, to facilitate both formal and cultural systems of knowledge in the same moment.

Learning in graffiti thus creates a body that is trained formally and socially, a body in which knowledge is embedded deep within the skin. It creates a gestural body underscoring the always bodily nature of inscription. The art of writing, as Ingold has suggested, not only "emerges through a continuous process of bodily modification" but through postural techniques in which our whole body engages in a form of "dextrous movement" (Ingold 2000: 402–403). As he continues to describe via the bodily deportments of Sumerian scribes and Chinese calligraphers, writing materializes not only via the "controlled movement of the hand" but through "the way in which the hand together with the tool it holds is brought into a certain angular relation with the surface of the material to be inscribed, which in turn affects the writer's entire comportment" (p. 403). Graffiti is thus doubly inscribed, engraved onto the surface of the city and the surface of the body. In the artist Evan Roth's series *Graffiti Analysis* (see figures 5.4–5.6), the embedded and highly controlled physical movements emergent in writing have been both digitally and sculpturally reproduced. Transforming the writer's processual flow into a three-dimensional chrome-dipped thermoplastic sculpture that itself casts a two-dimensional shadow re-rendering the original design, each piece shows bodily movement through both time and space while likewise visualizing the complex motions that go into the creation of a seemingly simple graffiti piece. Yet it is

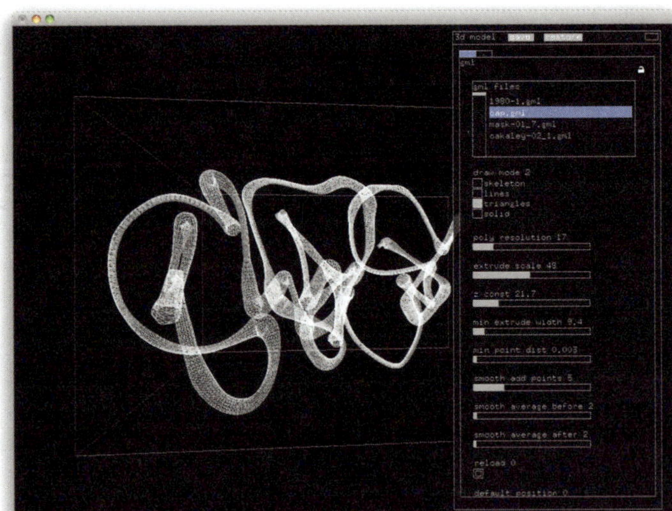


**FIGURE 5.4**

Evan Roth, *Cap (Graffiti Analysis Series)*, 2012. Software screen capture. Courtesy of N2 Galeria and the artist.

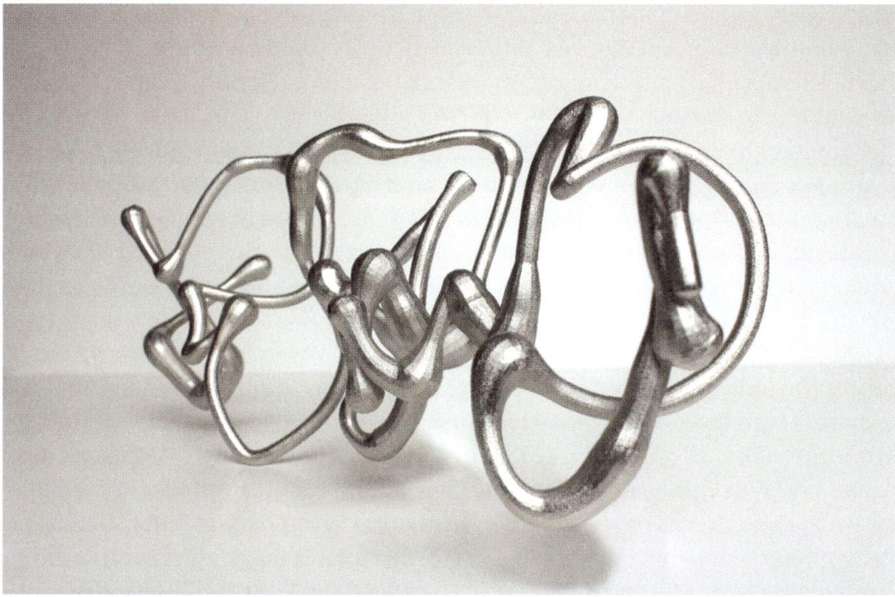

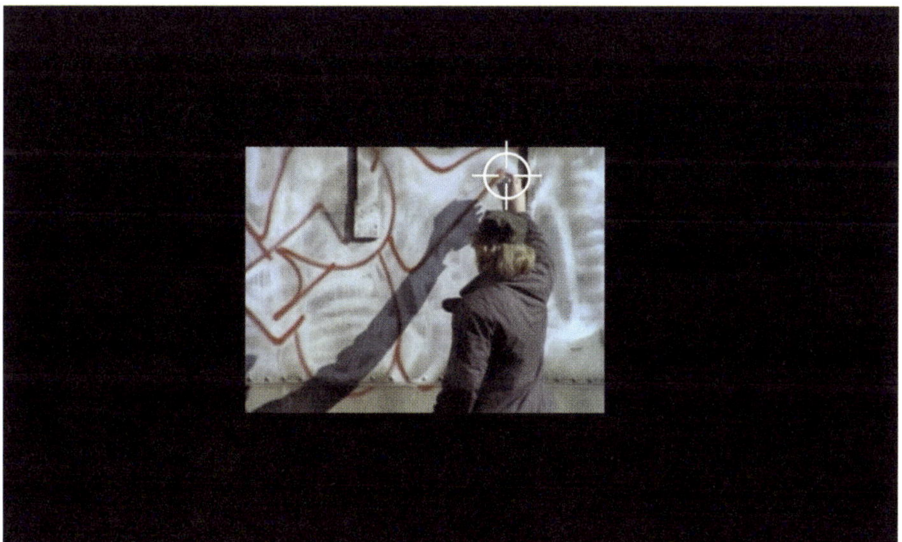

**FIGURE 5.5**
Evan Roth, *Cap (Graffiti Analysis Series)*, 2012. Chrome-dipped ABS thermoplastic, 37 cm × 39 cm × 24 cm. Courtesy of N2 Galeria and the artist.

**FIGURE 5.6**
Evan Roth, *Cap (Graffiti Analysis Series)*, 2012. Still from *Style Wars* (1983) footage. Courtesy of N2 Galeria and the artist.

in the motion-capture video that the bodily micro-techniques a writer uses (here of the legendary bomber Cap) can likewise be performatively unpicked: here, then, we see Cap not sitting upon a chair and leaning on a table (as is traditionally taught within Western writing) but in a standing position facing a huge steel train. Here we see the way he holds and controls the spray can with the entire hand rather than with his thumb, index, and middle finger alone (as we might hold a pen). Here we see the way this writing implement becomes an extension of his wrist and his arm, we see the relationship between head and hand as Cap gazes not at the can but at the position it will next be taking up. Here we see his arm reach to its highest extent, see him furtively glance to the left while continuing to paint to the right. Here we see the way he engages not just his five senses but so too his somatic sixth, the sense, as Marchand explains, that comes to monitor the writer's bodily "position, location, orientation, movement and muscular tensions" (Marchand 2008: 261), the sense that enables him to balance and change weight while making the hundreds of tiny adjustments necessary to complete his task. The dense bodily training that graffiti writers undertake, the thousands of hours of writing in blackbooks, the thousands of hours of writing in the street, thus creates a knowledge that comes to "lodge itself," as Carrie Noland has suggested in her reading of the work of Marcel Mauss, "in the very tissues of the body," a knowledge emergent through a form of "sensual apprehension" that "renders the body at once culturally legible (socially useful) *and interoceptively available to itself*" (Noland 2009: 21). In this way, then, the graffiti body not only becomes the artist's primary tool but becomes sculpted by skill, both corpus of knowledge and artwork simultaneously.

Just as the images go into the body, however, so too the body goes into the image. Every act of writing, as Noland continues, must be understood as a performance that can reveal the "tempo and quality of the body's movements," a performance that registers "types and quantities of physical force" (Noland 2009: 131). The arcs and cutting lines, the drips and jets of paint thus reveal a rhythm, reveal the bodily pressure going into the production of every image. They reveal a body pressing its weight against a surface, dragging themself across it or perhaps trailing down. They reveal a bodily act in which the production of the image becomes a dance. Alexandre Bavard's performance work *Bulky—Study of the Body in Space* (2017) systematically illustrates this concept, revealing a choreographic body that has been schooled and transformed by the process of production. Producing what he terms as a "system of notation of the movement generated by the tag," the work, in both its performative (see figures 5.7 and 5.8) and diagrammatic forms (see figures 5.9 and 5.10), uses the "vocabulary of body expression" to explore the "dialogue between the body and the urban material induced by the calligraphic stage."[3] Donning an outfit that, like the invisible graffiti writer, veils the identity of his performing body, Bavard creates an action that unveils the balletic shifts traditionally concealed from public view, the elegant realignments, the dramatic pirouettes and reverse turns that together bring the tag as image to life. In its diagrammatic form, however, the artist created a score in which the traditionally hidden movements are exposed in graphic form. Splitting the gesture into four core elements—the "rhythm" (representing the head, chest, torso, and lower legs), the "letter" (here drawing inspiration from "the Georgian alphabet and arabesques"), the "movement" (in which the body is divided into twelve points, each represented by a letter), and the "partition" (a method of scoring that reveals a body that is "stretched, flexible, [or] round")[4]—*Bulky* annotatively re-presents the kinetic flows that together create the shadow dance of the image. In this way, then, Bavard's project comes to reveal the echoes between graffiti and the works of action painting, in which the final canvas was considered as the outcome of the true work of art, the processual act of production itself. Here the artist's action was always understood to exceed its visual remainder, the artifact a visual remnant of the physical actions that created them. As Roland Barthes described in his discussion of the work

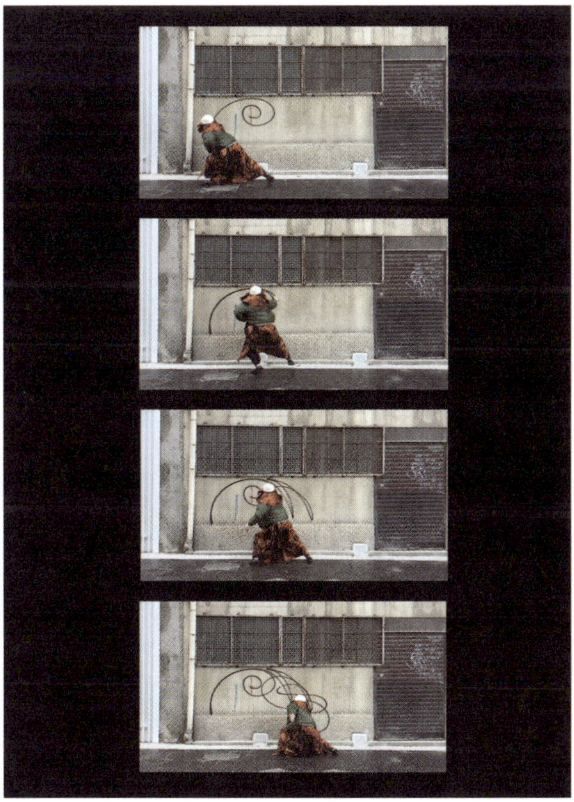

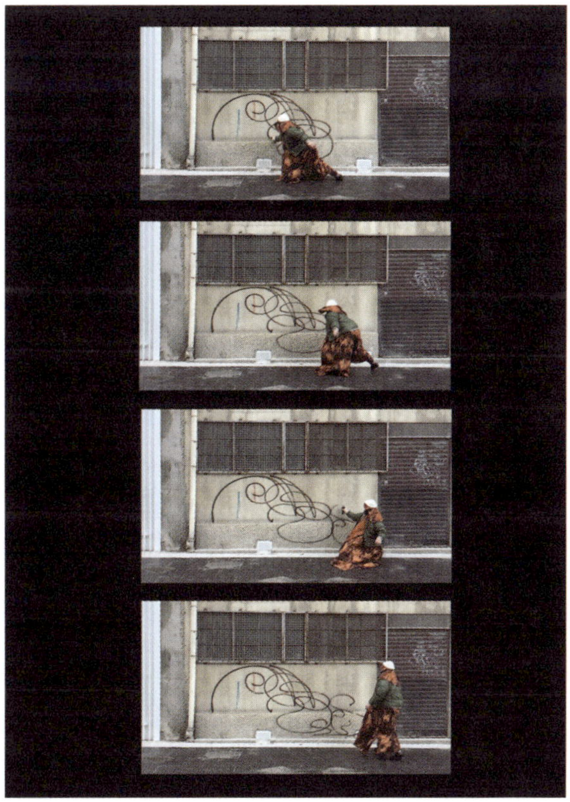

**FIGURES 5.7 AND 5.8**
Alexandre Bavard [Mosa], stills from *Bulky—Study of the Body in Space (Slowmomom)*, 2016. Video, 4 minutes 32 seconds.

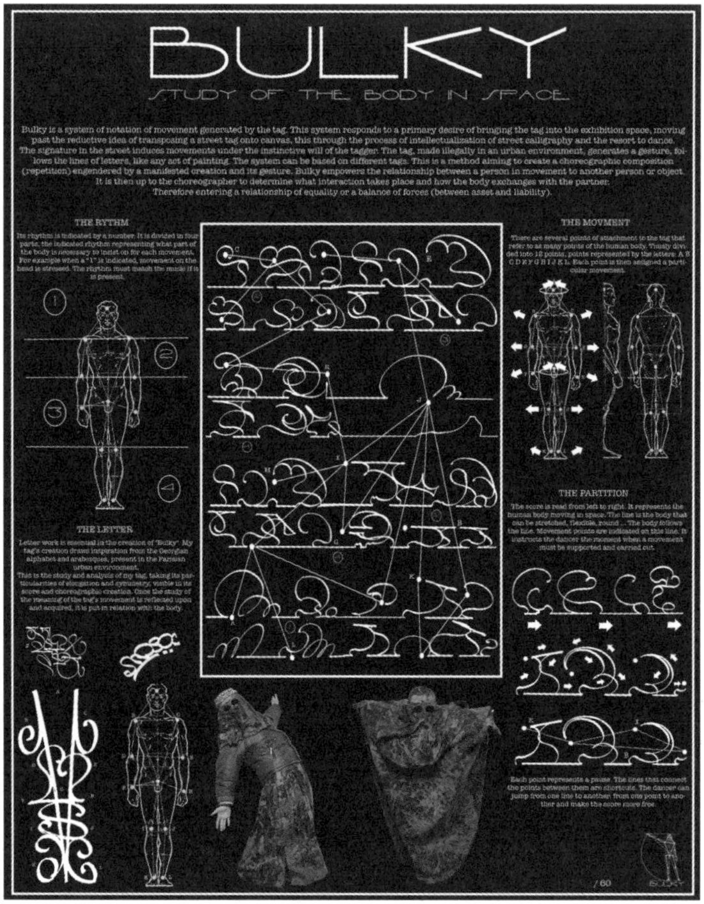


**FIGURE 5.9**
Alexandre Bavard [Mosa], *Bulky—Study of the Body in Space*, 2016. Silkscreen print. Courtesy of the artist.

of Cy Twombly, the final image "*shows* the gesture. We are not asked to see, to conceive, to savor the *product*, but to review, to identify, and so to speak, to 'enjoy' the *movement* which has ended up *here*" (Barthes 1979: 164). Twombly's (literally) sensational, urgent acts of writing (as seen in figures 5.11 and 5.12) thus reveal not propositional content but the pulse of the body, its radius and scope, poise and breath. As seen in the dense inscriptions of Twombly as much as the dense inscriptions of graffiti, then, the "essence of writing is neither a form nor a usage but only a gesture" (p. 158). The text here, the writing, the *tag*, is not just movement or performance. It is energy. It is dance. It is action.

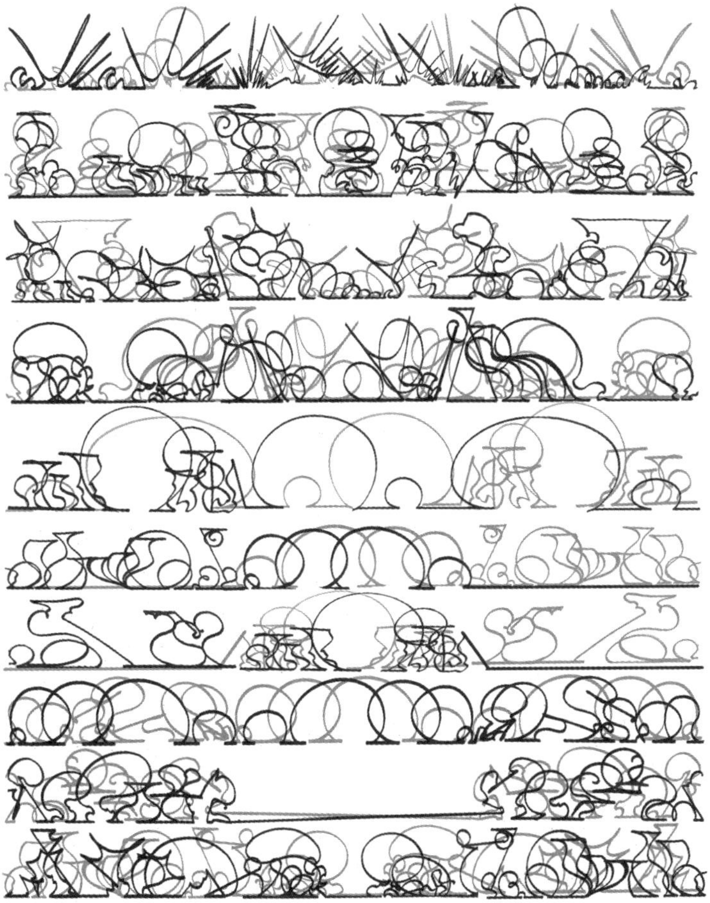

**FIGURE 5.10**
Alexandre Bavard [Mosa], *Bulky—Study of the Body in Space (Partition)*, 2017. Courtesy of Palais de Tokyo and the artist.

## EMBODYING THE MARGINS/A BODILY PHENOMENOLOGY

While the embodied relation between the graffiti image and the physical frame of the writer is key, as educational platforms graffiti crews train bodily skill in terms of not only the formal and calligraphic but so too the spatial and cartographic proficiencies of a writer. This technical urban know-how, this "streetwise" disposition that an apprentice must obtain, is critical to their success. Teaching yourself how to paint a complex piece, to navigate the complex geographies of the alphabet, is difficult enough but possible with sufficient commitment; learning to navigate the complex geographies of the

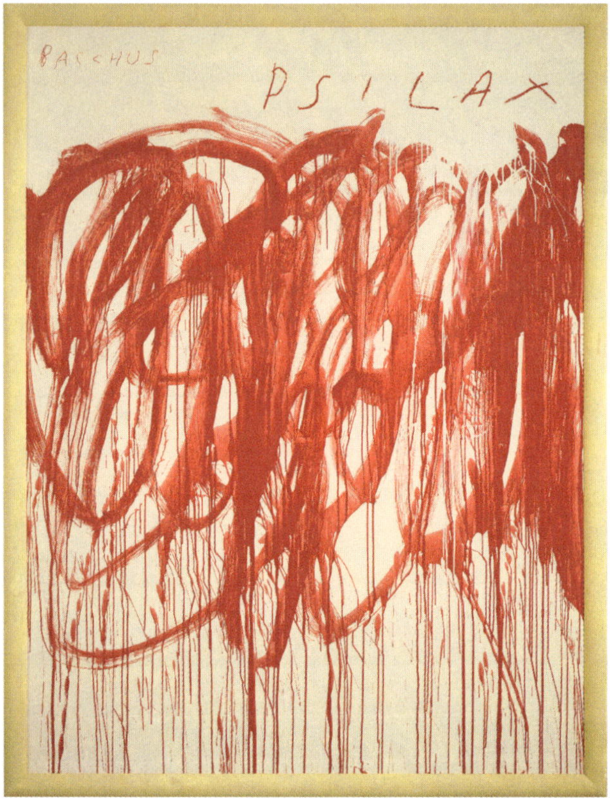


**FIGURE 5.11**

Cy Twombly, *Untitled (Bacchus 1st version III)*, 2004. Acrylic on wood. 104⅜ × 78¾ × 2½ in, 265.1 × 200 × 6.4 cm. © Cy Twombly Foundation. Courtesy of Gagosian.

city, however, to gain the spatial and environmental awareness necessary to one's practice as a writer, is *impossible* without the knowledge that apprenticeship and collaboration imparts. The production of the letter is thus the tip of a much larger iceberg. Below the visible level are all the elements a writer must undertake to successfully reach the point of writing those letters themselves (as well as finishing and departing from those letters without injury or arrest). Learning how to enter a guarded train depot (let alone knowing where the depots are, which trains are stored there, how they are secured and surveilled), learning how to complete a complex piece in the center of the city (becoming invisible within the hyper-visibility of the contemporary city), let alone learning how to successfully evade the police (or any other form of institutional authority), necessitates another type of bodily knowledge and bodily technique altogether. In this way, then, embodied skill, as Ingold continues, must be understood not simply as an

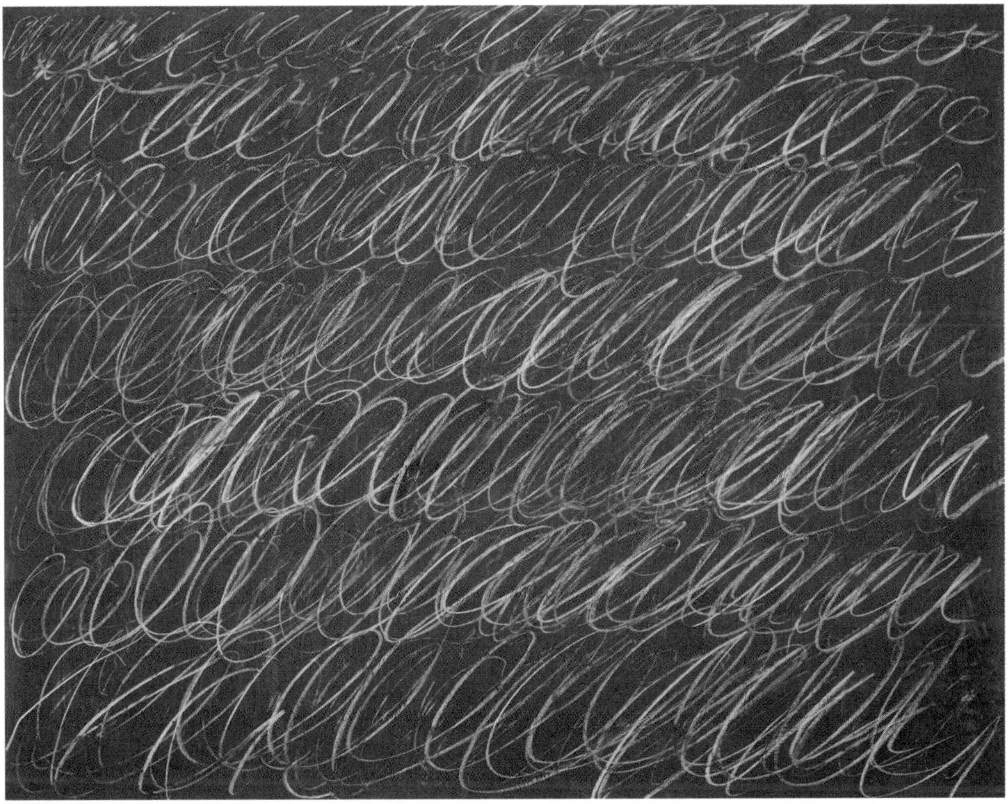

**FIGURE 5.12**
Cy Twombly, *Untitled*, 1969. Oil and crayon on board. 27⁹⁄₁₆ × 34¼ in, 70 × 87 cm.


"attribute of the individual body in isolation but of the whole system of relations constituted by the presence of the artisan in his or her environment" (Ingold 2000: 291). Skill thus emerges through the synergistic relation between writer, tool, and environment, becomes a technique not simply of the body but of a body engaging in space.

To write one must thus learn to travel above and below the city, inside and outside its traditional routes. One must learn how to distribute the body within its margins and borders, its tunnels and sewers, rooftops and overpasses, back streets and back alleys. One must learn to move in between the city, to navigate beyond its deontic no-entry signs, and to do this while leaving no trace but your image itself. Moving vertically as much as horizontally, beyond not just through the city, the writer thus gains a physical and mental knowledge of the urban surface that very few urban dwellers have. The tools an expert writer must use thus go far beyond paint and spray alone, and how to conceal those tools—the bolt cutters and pliers, the manhole keys and torches revealed by Klara Liden in her work *Self Portrait with Keys to the City* (2005) (in figure 5.13)—is an achievement in itself. The disciplinary bodily habitus that normative societal structures aim to generate (through both social and familial, material and architectural forms), a way of acting in the city that enables our bodies to be acceptable and permissible (not acting in any way out of the putative "norm"), is thus subtly circumvented. Graffiti apprenticeship creates subcultural citizens whose bodily behavior necessitates acts deemed normatively "immoral" so as to fully participate within the moral norms and regulations of the community of practice itself. In this way, then, it is the spatial choreography that writers must undertake, more than their formal, calligraphic outputs, which places their bodies in an oppositional position to the standards of society at large and to the "rationality" of urban space. Graffiti writers thus not only paint on the margins

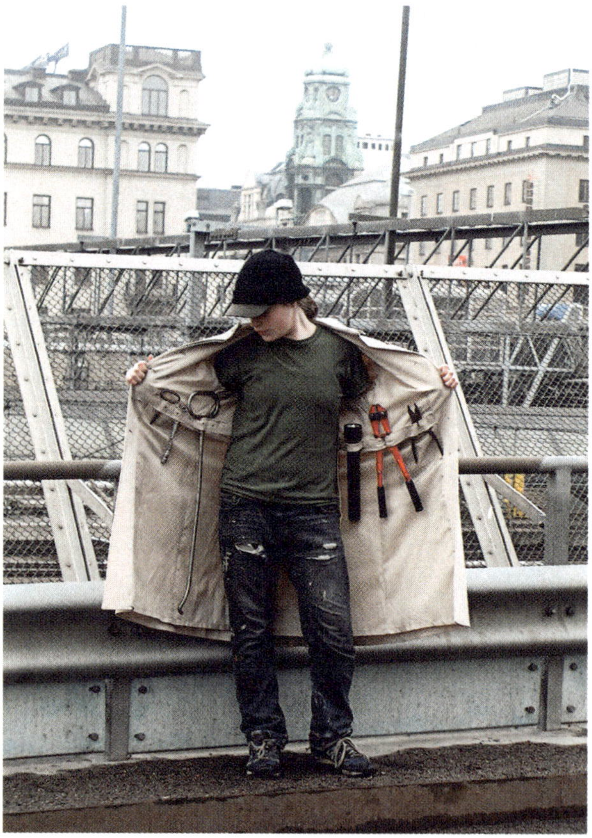

**FIGURE 5.13**
Klara Liden, *Self Portrait with Keys to the City*, 2005. C-print. 60.5 × 42 cm, 23.8 × 16.5 in.
© Klara Liden. Courtesy of the artist.

(and utilize a marginal speech) but physically engage these margins themselves. Their bodies become tools of both action and resistance (as seen in figures 5.14 and 5.15, for example), dissenting bodies undertaking dissensual bodily acts. What Michel de Certeau thus termed "delinquency"—in his famous discussion of the minor bodily tactics of resistance in the contemporary city—can thus be understood to begin with what he called "the inscription of the body in the order's text," with the subtle power of the "body in movement, gesticulating, walking, taking its pleasure" (de Certeau 1984: 86–87). Without a bodily engagement with the city, a writer cannot write. Without engagement at the very edge, a writer cannot be part of the community of practice. Bodily resistance thus takes place not simply for the sake of itself. Bodily resistance takes place for the sake of the crew and the canon.

The stylistic imperative to produce, to distribute oneself and one's name, thus results in a bodily relationship with the city that, for many writers, becomes an end itself. The canon creates a connection to site that, while a by-product of graffiti's formal goals, becomes as deeply intimate as it is engaged, becomes gratifying in and of itself, a practice that is not just against but *for*. Moreover, navigating the city, climbing it, exploring it, touching it (before one even gets to painting it) creates an active intermixture of self and site in which the participant becomes indelibly embedded in their environment. It creates an encounter that emerges through multisensorial, not merely ocular, sensations, an encounter working in total juxtaposition to the look-don't-touch sensorial regulations of the contemporary city. While the calligraphic gesture emergent through the production of the graffiti writes itself back into the body, the choreography of the *distributive* gesture forms a phenomenological relationship in which writers engage in a bodily mapping of the city, a corporeal cartography that writes the landscape into the body of the writer too. Moreover, the normative acceptance of and necessity for trespass gives writers access to the untold expanse of marginal urban space that we rarely see let alone inhabit, the untold hundreds (if not thousands) of square miles of the city that normally remain out of reach. The city thus explodes in size and scope, transforming from the monotony of our two-dimensional passage into a multifaceted, three-dimensional arena. The graffiti writer, like the hacker, thus gains access to clandestine, backstage worlds that lie behind the superficial veneer of the desktop. As such, while graffiti is almost always defined by its visual remainder, for many writers voyaging becomes the true goal of painting.

For the Parisian writer Honet, for example, the city's famous catacombs have become not only a thematic influence on his artistic practice but a key site of exploration itself. Fascinated with the unseen and hidden elements of our urban surroundings, his journeys into this huge network of urban tunnels—as seen in figures 5.16–5.18—have become a link to the ancient heritage of Paris as much as a space in which he and his friends can play and explore beyond the eye of the state (as we discuss further in chapter 8). The travels into the catacombs thus become as much of an end as the production of graffiti that takes place within them, a site in which the mapping of space becomes a

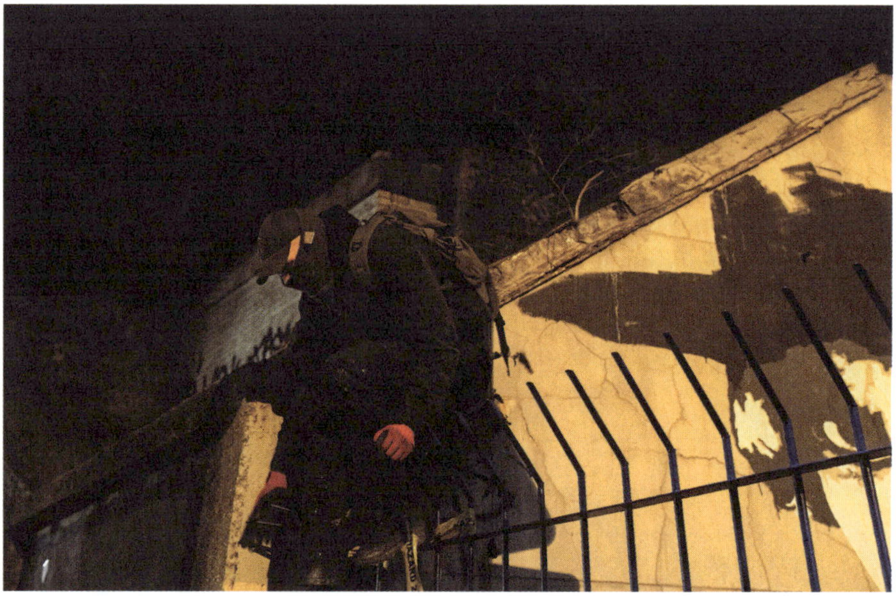

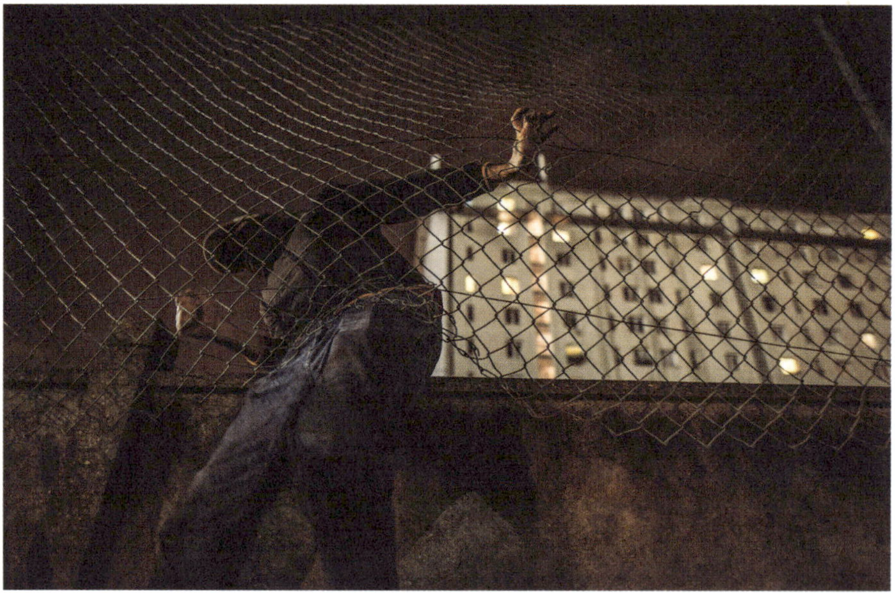

**FIGURE 5.14**
R Seventeen | sory.world, *10Foot*, 2022, London. Courtesy of the artists.

**FIGURE 5.15**
Enrique Escandell, *Barcelona Subway 2013*. Taken from *Subterráneos* by Enrique Escandell. Courtesy of the artist.

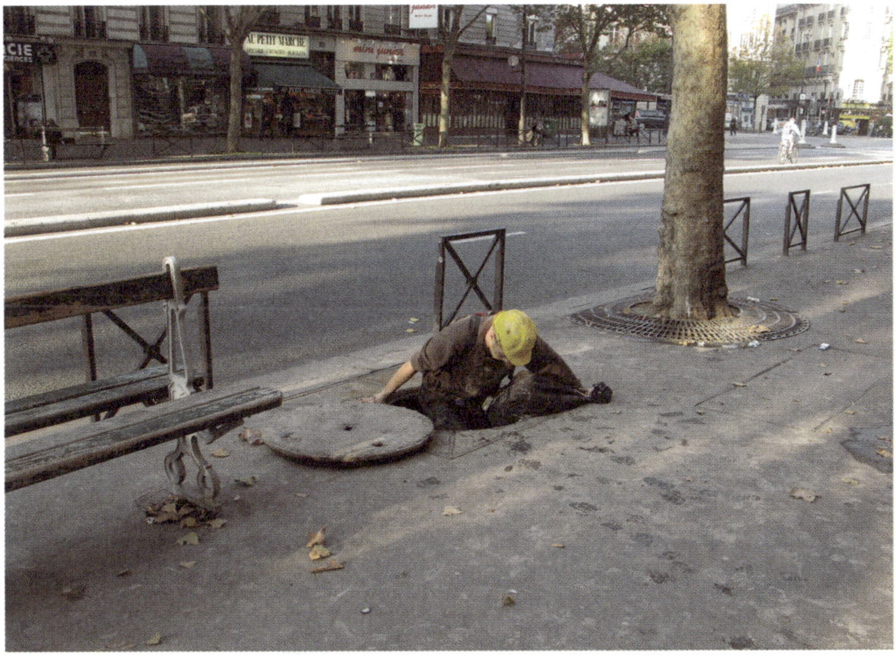

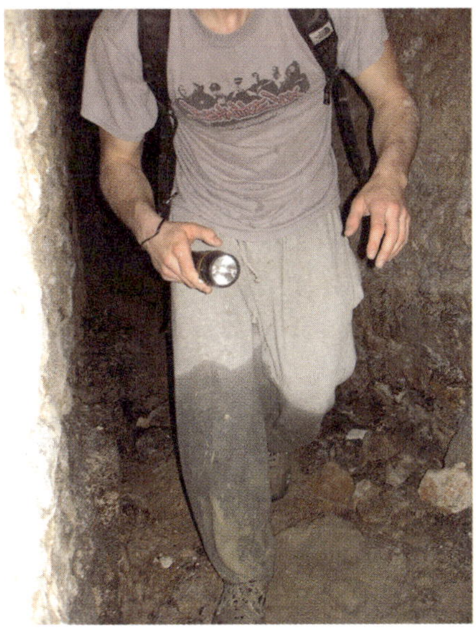

**FIGURE 5.16**
Honet, *KTA17*, 2004–2023. Paris. Courtesy of the artist.

**FIGURE 5.17**
Honet, *KTA2*, 2004–2023. Paris. Courtesy of the artist.

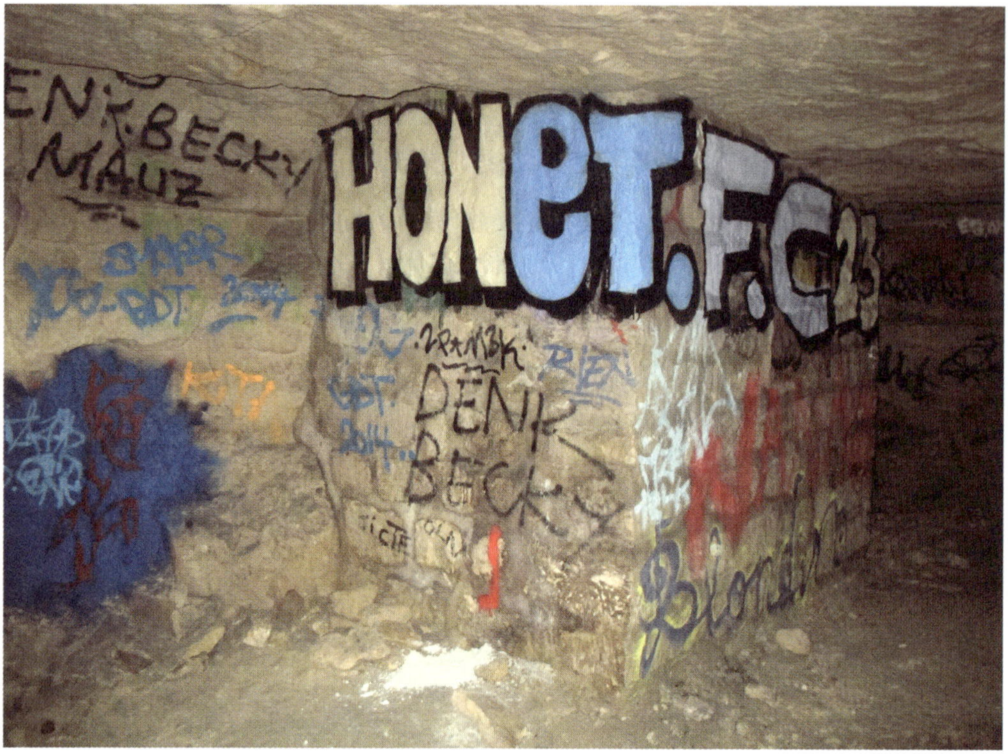


**FIGURE 5.18**
Honet, *KTA23*, 2004–2023. Paris. Courtesy of the artist.

pleasure in itself. In artists Matthias Wermke and Mischa Leinkauf's practice, this intuitive, impromptu technique of flowing through our urban interstices—and doing so in a manner beyond the instrumental aims of the commuter body—is likewise critical to their urban performances. While also conducting experiments and interventions in the city's subterranean worlds, it is in their journeys *over* the city in projects such as *Drifter* (2012) that we see their intense engagement with its urban fabric (an engagement that, like Honet's, also emerged from their influential experiences within the graffiti subculture). The elegant architectural encounters we see in the artists' video installations—in which we as viewers are often forced to climb into the installations themselves—position the city as a natural space we are meant to explore, a concrete jungle that our body can scale and engage with. In figure 5.19, for example, we see a figure strolling in the early morning along the uppermost section of a bridge trailing over Gleisdreieck Park in Berlin (having climbed a secret ladder beside a railway yard to get there). In figure 5.20, we see the body in the air straddling the architecture in Tokyo (in a work reminiscent of Philippe Petit's high-wire walk between the Twin Towers in New York).

In figure 5.21, we see a figure on the roof of a flak tower in Vienna in a work dedicated to the philosopher Vilém Flusser (and for which the artist had to climb a fence and cut a chain lock with an electric grinder before climbing itself could even begin). And in figure 5.22, we see them back in Tokyo drifting atop the now demolished Nakagin Capsule Tower (for which they had to access a nearby building and climb over a sheer gap, all the while navigating not just the architecture but so too a minor earthquake). Rather than searching for the spectacular—as often seen in the testosterone-fueled practices of (social-mediatized) urban exploration—Wermke and Leinkauf's works instead aim to show the possibilities existent for all of us, to show the way in which the seemingly impenetrable parts of the city (that form a part of the graffiti writer's commonly navigable realms) can become part of our geography too. The pair's projects thus are not about the decorative or the monumental but are motivated through a resistance to the restrictions of the city, to the spirit of graffiti practice in which participation and exploration is all.[5]

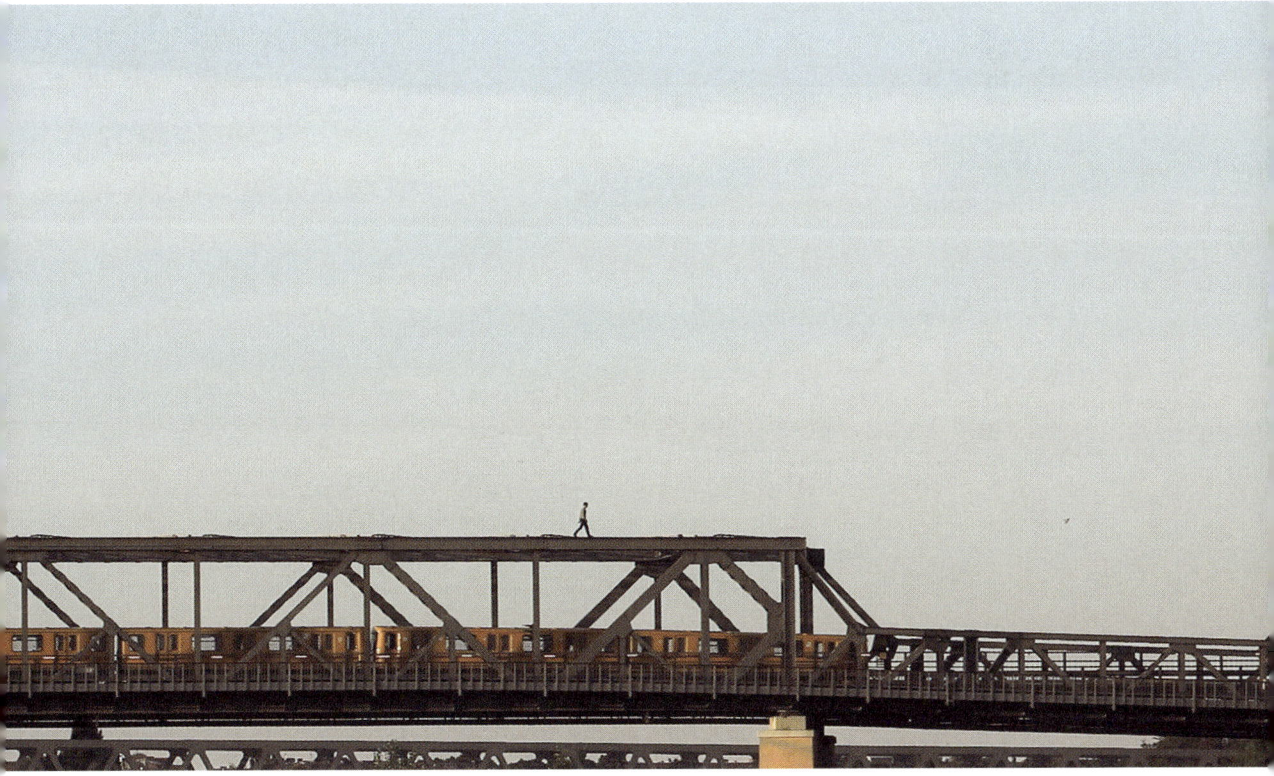

**FIGURE 5.19**

Wermke/Leinkauf, still from *Drifter*, 2012–2014. Berlin. HD/SD video. Courtesy of the artists.

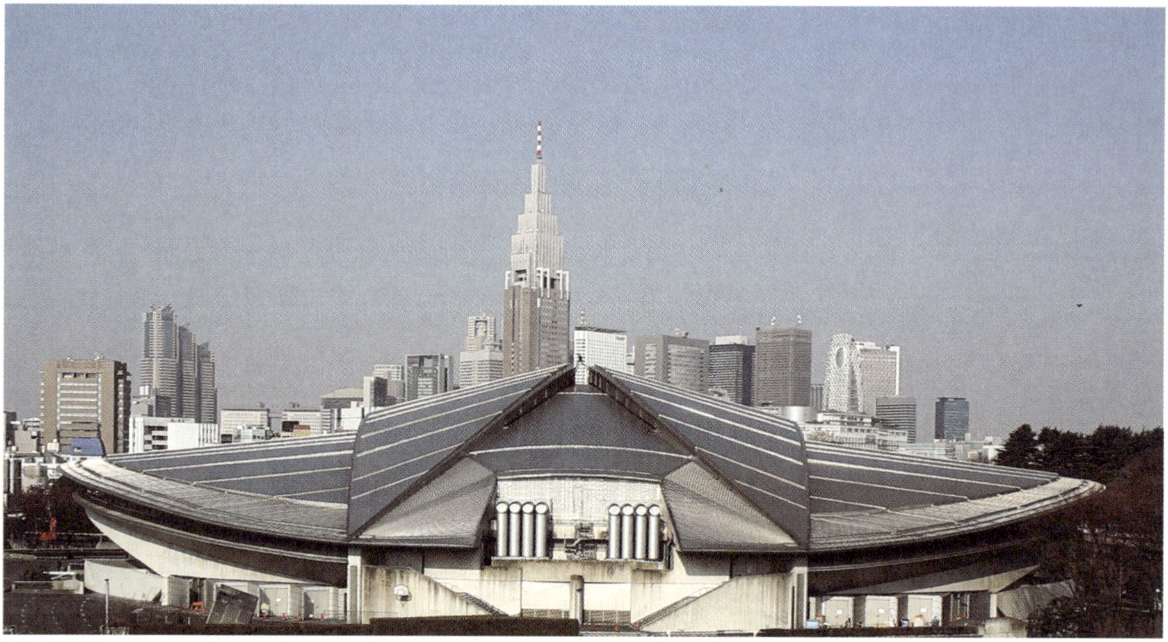

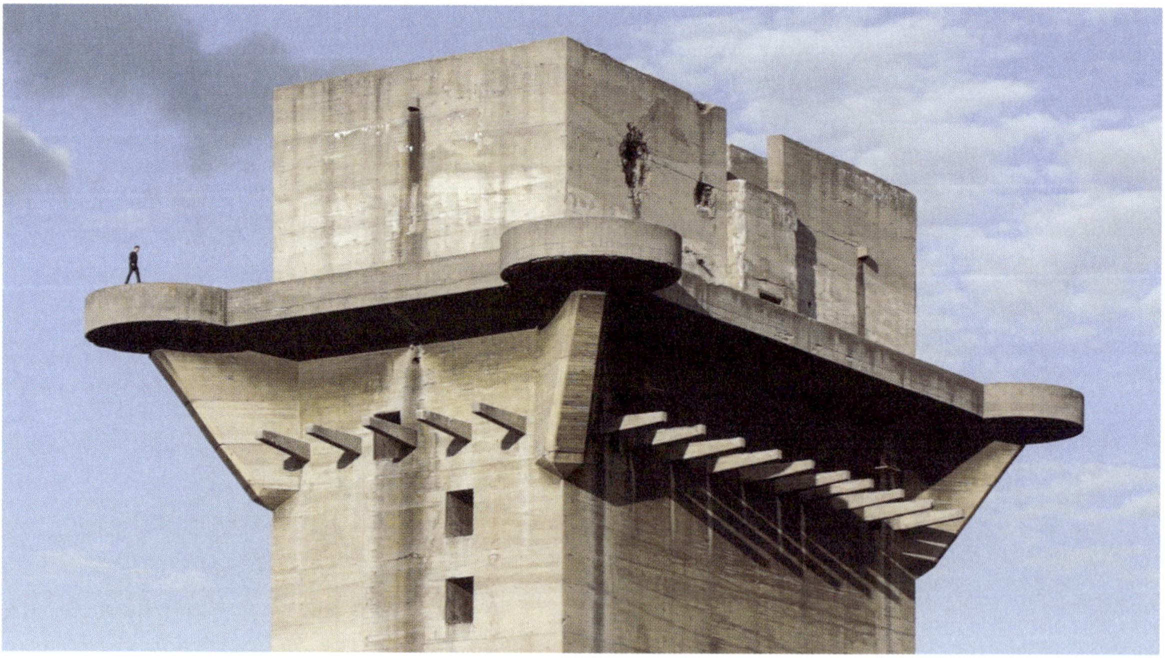

**FIGURE 5.20**
Wermke/Leinkauf, still from *Drifter*, 2012–2014. Tokyo. HD/SD video. Courtesy of the artists.

**FIGURE 5.21**
Wermke/Leinkauf, still from *Drifter*, 2012–2014. Vienna. HD/SD video. Courtesy of the artists.

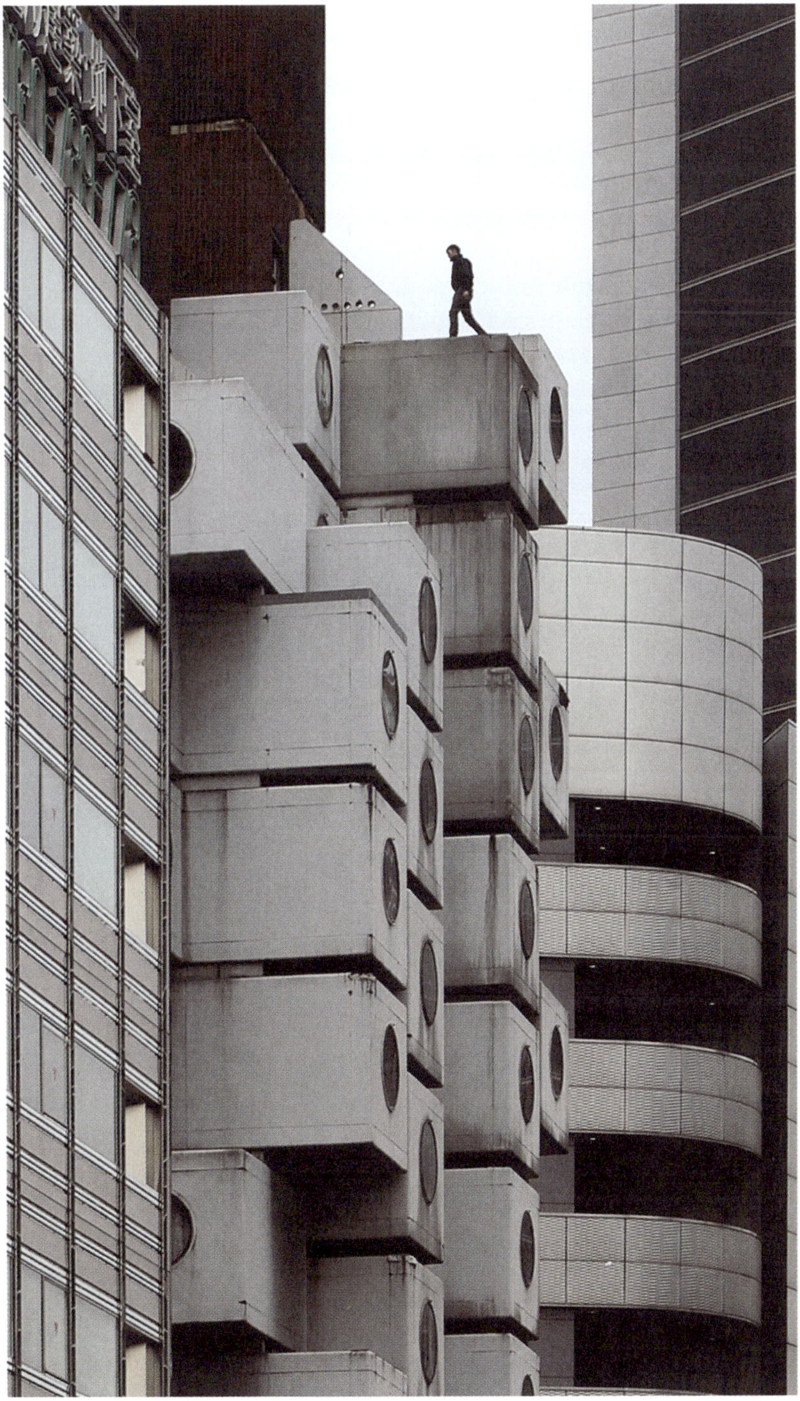

**FIGURE 5.22**

Wermke/Leinkauf, still from *Drifter*, 2012–2014. Tokyo. HD/SD video. Courtesy of the artists.

Beyond what are often extreme acts of voyaging, however, beyond the reaches that seem impossible to reach, a much more seemingly mundane form of urban practice—the simple act of walking—can likewise be considered as central to the spatial choreography of the graffiti writer. Writers are ambulatory creatures. They walk, for *hours*, for nights on end (as seen in figure 5.23). They walk from one end of a tube line to the other, from the center to the periphery of the city. Distribution is impossible to undertake via any other channel (save for the bicycle, which often acts as a tool not only of movement but of physical extension, taking the writer both up and across the city). The writer thus learns to walk in a way in which others do not walk, to walk not focused on destination but attentive to what is happening just out of view or just out of reach. Rather than the bodily techniques of walking famously explored by Marcel Mauss, then, here it is a technique of what Erving Goffman would have called *pedestrianism* that is key. As explained by Nick Crossley, our physical engagement in the city emerges through the "crowds we have to wade through [or silently slip within], the dark streets we avoid [or perhaps engage], the kerbs we trip over and manhole covers we swerve past [or lift up and duck beneath]" (Crossley 1995: 136–137). Walking is thus not just a movement through the city but a movement with and against it. Moreover, and as de Certeau famously suggested,

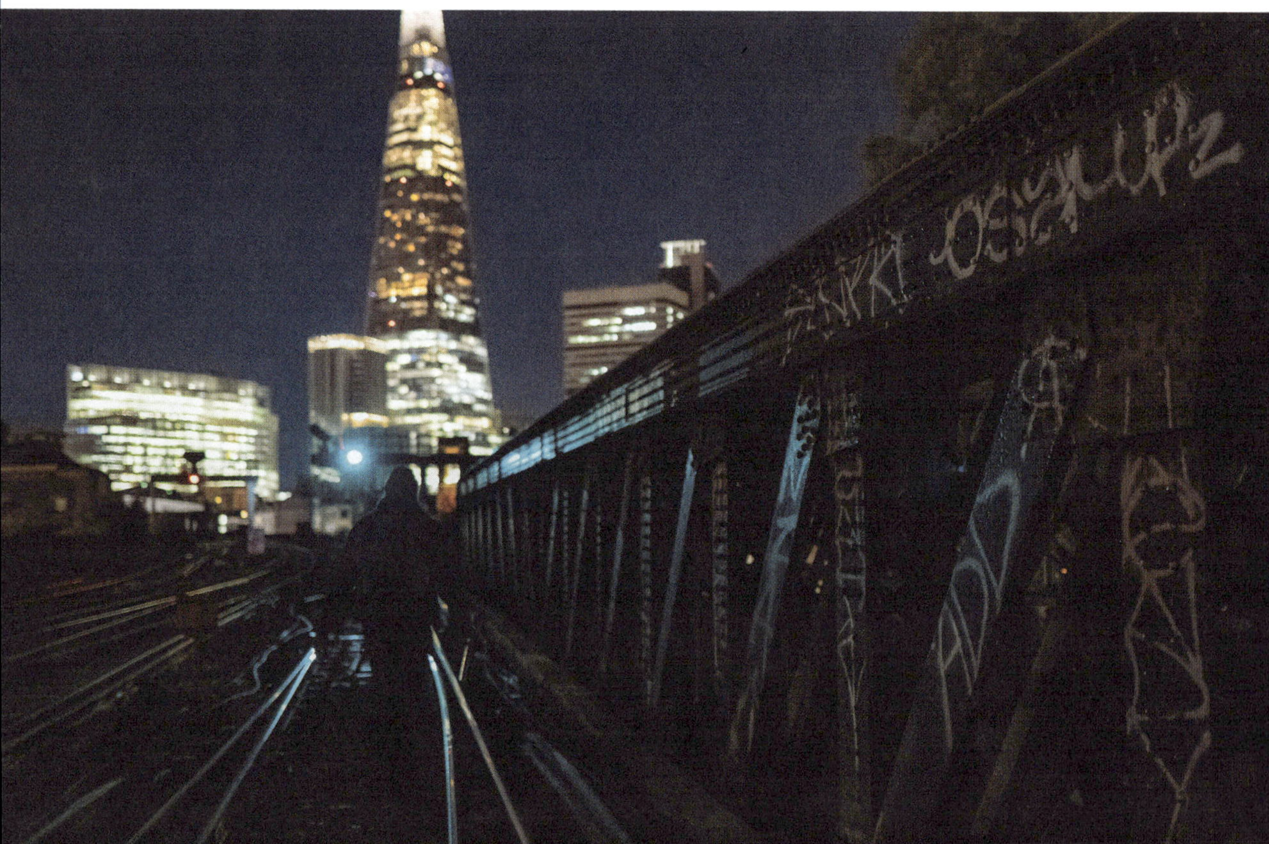

through “creating shortcuts and detours,” through “crossing, drifting away, or improvisation,” walking here becomes a practice through which “interdictions” (such as the walls that block our path) can be surpassed (de Certeau 1984: 98). It becomes a mode of “clandestine . . . dispersed, tactical, and make-shift creativity” (p. xiv), an “appropriation of the topographical system” or “spatial acting-out of the place” (pp. 97–98) that creates not texts but “anti-texts, effects of dissimulation and escape, possibilities of moving into other landscapes” (p. 107). Walking can thus be seen to contain both an “ethical, esthetic, and practical character” (p. 75). It becomes not only a form of movement necessary for the production of the graffiti image but proof of engagement with the city’s surface, a practice of endurance in which one’s duration in both space and time becomes visibly proven. What could appear as a rudimentary act of passage, then, as an act that simply takes the artist where they want to go, must be seen as a practice through which one learns as much about oneself as the city, a practice rooted through play and opposition both.

The Belgian artist Francis Alÿs has utilized techniques of walking in a number of his seminal public interventions. Most famously employed in *Paradox of Praxis 1* (1997), in which he walked for nine hours through the streets of Mexico City pushing a giant block of ice (until it completely dissolved into the city’s fabric), and in *The Green Line* (2004), in which he traced a 24km margin through Jerusalem by walking through it with a leaking can (in fact, several leaking cans) of paint, Alÿs’s many walks seek to map the city in a nonrepresentational manner, in a way that focuses on narrative and juxtaposition over the expected and accepted. Within his series *A Personal Repertoire of Possible Behaviour While Walking the Streets in London Town* (2004–2005), however, his work *Railings* (seen in figure 5.24) addressed issues of private and public space through a technique enabling one to not just see but *hear* a city’s architecture. Engaging in the time-honored children’s game in which a stick is run along a metal railing to create a rhythmic sound, the game not only upset the normative behavior expected of an adult (and rational) urban dweller, but took pride in its own seeming childishness and pointlessness. As with Alÿs’s other urban walking practices, then, the very fact of just “drifting, or strolling,” as he himself has said, can become a form of resistance “within the speed culture of our time . . . there can be a certain wisdom involved in the act of walking. It’s more an attitude . . . a state where you can be both alert to all that happens in your peripheral vision and hearing, and yet totally lost in your thought process” (Cuauhtémoc, Fisher, and Ferguson 2008: 31). Like the renowned urban tactics of the Situationist International, in particular their famous urban technique of *dérives*, or *drifts*, the freedom of walking thus enables one to encounter a space’s tempo and atmosphere, to explore the intertwined relationship between body and space through

**FIGURE 5.23**
R Seventeen | sory.world, *10Foot*, 2022, London. Courtesy of the artists.

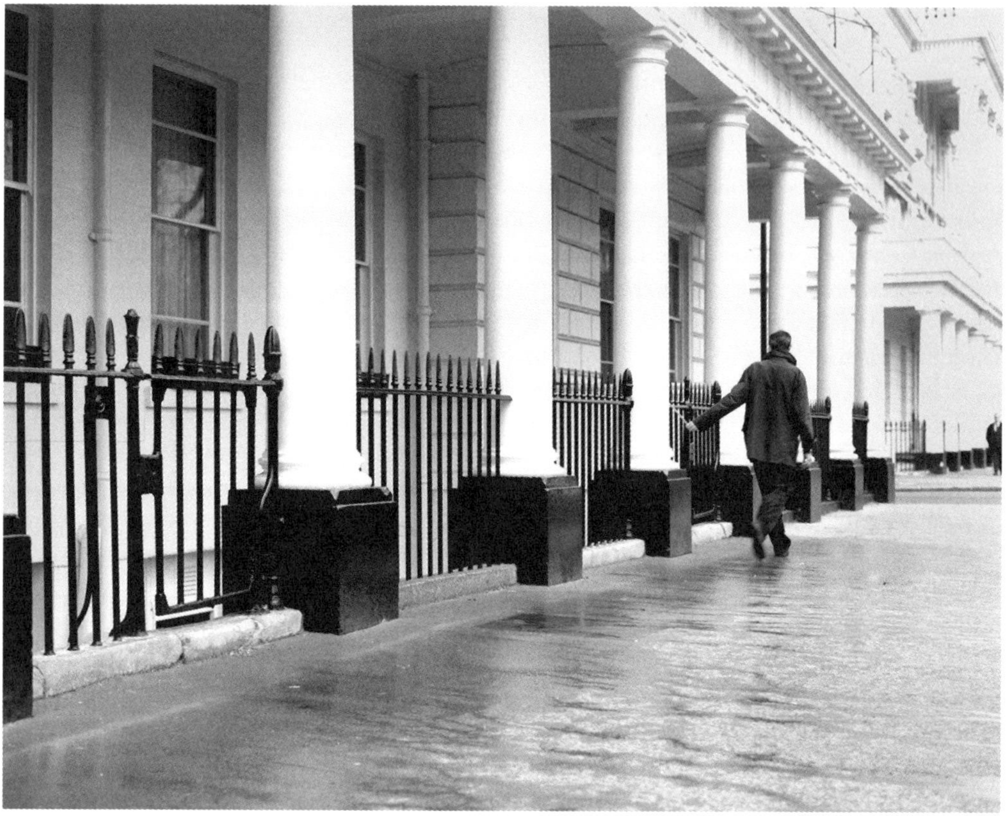

**FIGURE 5.24**
Francis Alÿs, *Railings*, 2004, London. In collaboration with Rafael Ortega and Artangel. Video documentation of an action, 6 ft 57 in. *Upon arriving in London, pick up a stick, run it along the architecture and listen to the music of the city*. Courtesy of the artist.

an open encounter with its surface. It enables a relationship to the city that rejects the "logical" use of the urban surface and instead engages in child's play, an encounter that rejects speed and embraces pleasure. The seemingly mundane act of perambulation, as the architect and theorist Francesco Careri has explained, can thus turn the city into "an immense aesthetic territory, an enormous canvas on which to draw by walking" (Careri 2017: 131). Like a "wayfarer," walking thus "registers the events of the journey, the sensations, obstacles, dangers, the variations of the terrain" (p. 131) and in doing so helps us to subjectively map our urban terrain.

Still, while the graffiti body must be considered as a marginal body, a body rejecting the reduced, goal-driven movements of the commuter, a body rejecting the speed and instrumentality of the city, a body rejecting the city as a "productive" space in economic terms alone, it is an abled body that is the norm here,[6] let alone almost always a *masculine* body that we see in action. Graffiti, it must be said, is an infamously gendered practice.[7] In both the stereotypical perception from outside the subculture as well as within the actualities of the practice itself, women are in a huge minority, almost always involved to some extent (as attested by the critical presence of the writer Lady Pink in the canonical texts, for example), yet peripheral figures at best. As Nancy Macdonald wrote in her monograph on youth and masculinity in the graffiti subculture, on the "'diehard' masculinity" in which writers come to "play the warrior or superhero" (Macdonald 2001: 222), the "notions of power, control, independence and freedom" celebrated within graffiti come to directly "interface with cultural definitions of youthful masculinity" (p. 225). "No one," Macdonald continues, is "going to question Superman or Actionman's masculinity, and no one is going to miss it either. . . . It screams testosterone, making sure it gets the attention and recognition it needs to be validated" (p. 222).[8] As such, while bodily norms can be subverted by graffiti, many of these actions could be seen to reinforce a quite normative notion of masculinity itself, a notion of a masculine body that runs and jumps, that extends and encompasses its environment; a masculine body that climbs and clambers, that dominates and colonizes its space—"Boys will be boys."[9] Rather than the act of writing itself, then, it is the spatial aspect of graffiti that is gendered, not painting but rather just being in the city that enforces this overly male dominance. The practice of graffiti thus links very clearly to the learned habitus of our society in which gender roles are violently policed: the street is a site made for men by men, and being able to comfortably inhabit that space is a gendered (and in many places an able-bodied, white-bodied, cis-bodied) privilege. As David Pinder has warned, we must always "consider how ostensibly 'radical' explorations [of the city] may themselves depend on privileges of power," and how these privileges can neglect to highlight the "specific identities through which people negotiate their passaging the city" (Pinder 2005: 402). Space and place, as Doreen Massey famously wrote, in particular, "our degrees of mobility," are thus "gendered through and through" (Massey 1994: 186), graffiti here acting as both reflection and rejection of urban norms.

Still, this does not mean that female bodies cannot appropriate and affect public space (as innumerable female graffiti writers have done and continue to do). As Susan Torre has argued, the political performances of the Madres de la Plaza de Mayo in Argentina, for example, the mothers protesting the thousands of "disappearances" undertaken during the military junta of the 1970s and '80s, worked "not merely to inhabit but also to transform the public realm" and, like many other female activists, to construct themselves as "subjects altering society's perception of public space and inscribing their own stories into the urban palimpsest" (Torre 1996: 141). While women are thus often described in urban literature as "passive agents rather than engaged subjects," as "unintentional agents of a collective social project, acting out assigned scripts" (p. 140), this ignores, Torre continues, the appropriations of spaces such as also seen at "the Washington Mall (in favor of abortion rights) or in the display of intimacy in very public settings (such as the private offerings and mementos that complete Maya Lin's Vietnam Memorial and compose the monumental Names Quilt honoring AIDS victims)" (p. 141). Rather than the figure of Alÿs, then, the radical yet very male, very white, very tall figure seen whistling as he strolls through Mexico City with a loaded gun in *Re-Enactments* (2000), we can think instead of the figure of Mona Hatoum (seen in figure 5.25) as she shuffles through Brixton with Dr. Martens boots tied to the back of her bare feet in her performance *Roadworks* (1985); walking here is not solely about imagination and exploration but about the fragility of the body, not simply about "potential"

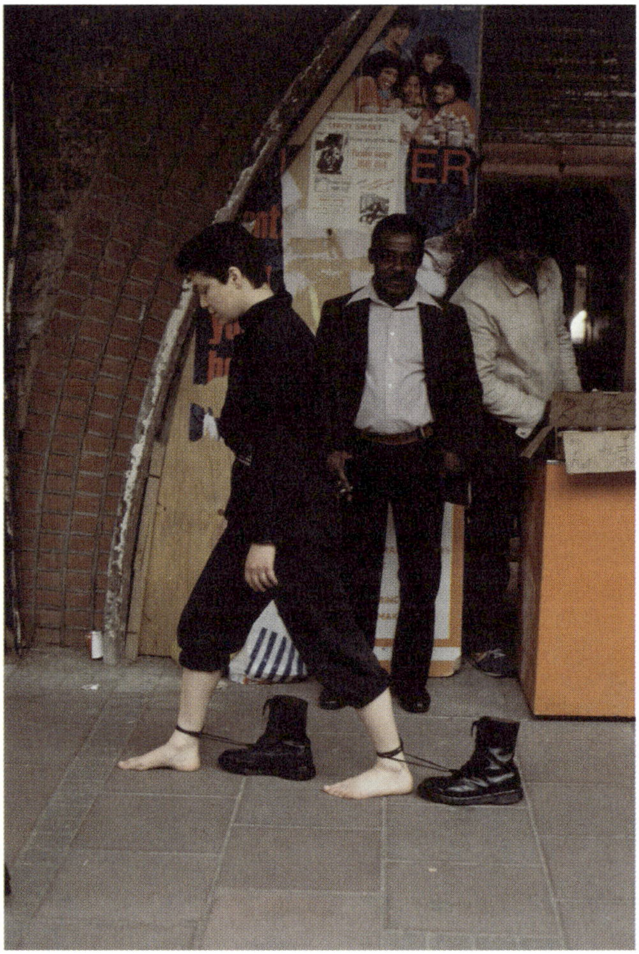

**FIGURE 5.25**
Mona Hatoum, *Roadworks*, 1985. Live action with Dr. Martens boots. Performed in Brixton, London. © Mona Hatoum. Courtesy of Brixton Art Gallery. Photo: Patrick Gilbert.

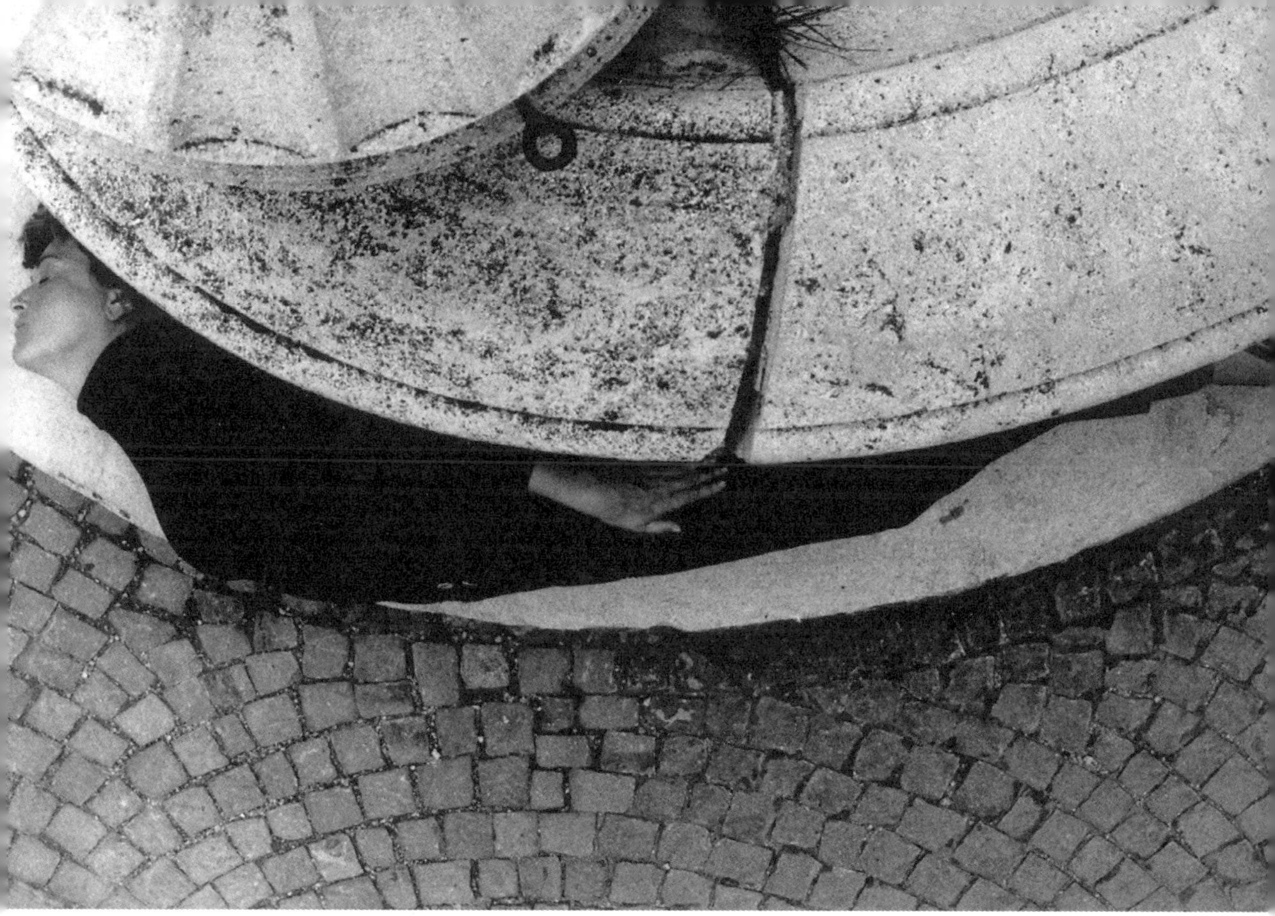

**FIGURE 5.26**
VALIE EXPORT Kumetrie II, *Body Configuration*, 1982. © VALIE EXPORT, Bildrecht Wien, 2023. Photo © Hermann Hendrich. Courtesy of Galerie Thaddaeus Ropac, London • Paris • Salzburg • Seoul.

but about potential danger and (sexual/racial) violence; walking here is about a slowness that comes not through choice but through struggle, a walking that is about commitment as much as solidarity. Likewise, rather than Wermke and Leinkauf's journey to the top of the city or Honet's journey to its foundations, we can think of VALIE EXPORT's attempt (seen in figure 5.26) to integrate the female body with Vienna's classical architecture in her series *Body Configurations* (1972–1976); mimicking the architectural forms of the city, EXPORT's bodily occupation of space sought to rupture its domineering material status, to transform its rationality and power by her bodily presence alone; it not only exceeded the traditions and norms of the city, but turned stone into flesh, the cold of the city into the warmth of the physical form. Performance and intervention are thus still possible in the city, exploration and endurance still achievable. Yet the embodiment of the margins and the marginal phenomenology we have seen are practices still too often couched within masculine bodily norms.

## EMBODYING RISK/A BODILY COMMITMENT

As seen in the urban projects of EXPORT, the graffiti writers' bodily action in the city is about a visceral engagement with its fabric and a rejection of its normative use—even as these acts of writing, of exploring, of walking, are themselves often enabled by the actors' normatively masculine frame. Yet the *risk* that the body engages (be that a male or female body), the risk embedded in the formal and spatial acts of graffiti, is central to the way in which the image and act are understood by writer and viewer alike. Risk is central to graffiti's stylistic power and techniques of captivation. The attraction of the balletic gestural dance, as much as the allure of the committed physical act, thus comes to intertwine through themes of chance and its control, linking beauty and efficacy with the unexpected and the uncontainable. In this way, then, style and action become analogous, ritual and artistic performance one and the same.

In our first case, the formal act of graffiti is an act in which predictability and constancy are literally impossible to realize. The signature-signature is unavoidably unique, unavoidably affected by the surrounding milieu each and every time it is produced. The endlessly indeterminate possibilities of the city, its lived cacophony that acts in total contrast to the neutral vacuum of studio or gallery, thus comes to exist in the materiality of every image. From factors of the environmental (such as the buffeting of wind or rain) to those of the social (such as the sudden appearance of police or passers-by), from issues of the material (be it the drippiness of ink or the changing porosity of the substrate) to those of the emotional (be it excitement or tiredness, agitation or elation), true uniformity, true iterability becomes physically impossible to achieve. The street one writes in (like the river one steps in) is never the same twice. Risks are thus managed but never allayed within graffiti. And like all public performances in which there is only one chance to prove oneself, the management of these "extrinsic dangers"—as anthropologist Leo Howe has termed the outside risks that "accompany the enactment of a ceremony" and the "uncertainties" that could lead to failure or "incorrect performance" (Howe 2000: 68–69)—are not just critical to one's performative accomplishment but a space in which an actor can show their virtuosity and expertise. As every instance of graffiti is publicly visible to the world, then, the innate risk of practice is that of "gambling [with] one's status" (p. 69), every act of writing becoming a game that one must "dare to conduct" (p. 76). Unlike the work of a studio artist, one's output cannot simply be hidden from the public eye, cannot be burnt or thrown away. The perils of public performance in graffiti thus are not just of managing risks but likewise of taking them. Graffiti's allure is, in this way, found in the successful control of risk, a control in which beauty is itself revealed.

Alfred Gell's discussion of Malakulan sand art—a form of ephemeral pattern making from the Vanuatu archipelago produced by tracing a maze-like pattern on the ground with a single finger in one continuous motion (as seen in figures 5.27 and 5.28)—contains many resonances with this mode of performed risk. Similar to graffiti,

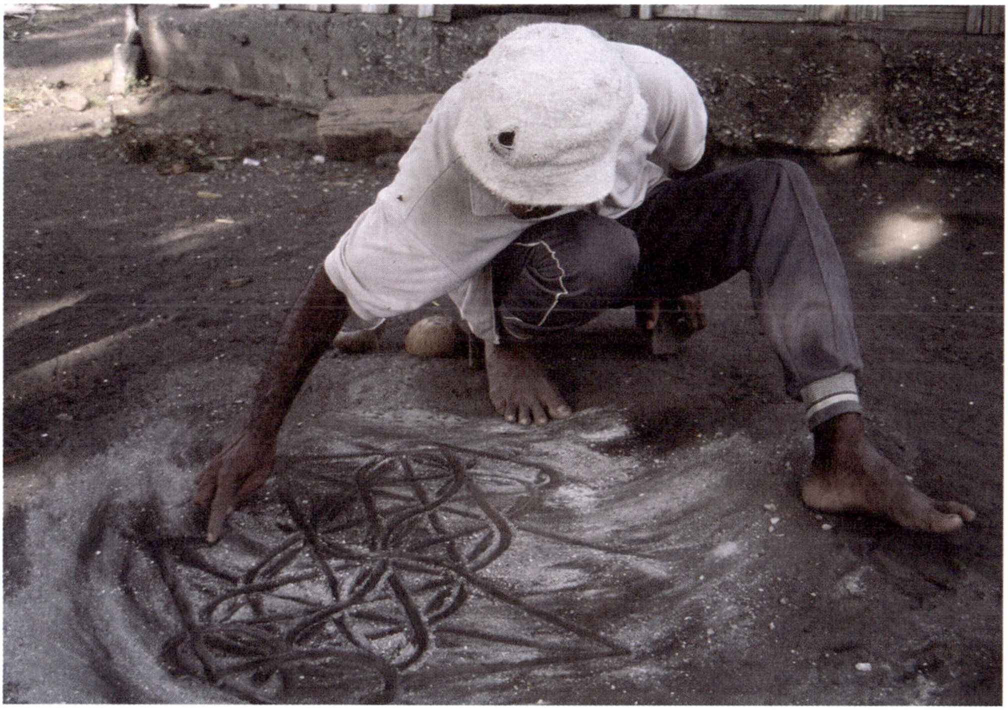

**FIGURE 5.27**
John Teungkon performing a sand drawing, Craig Cove, Ambrym, Vanuatu, 1999. Photograph by Stephen Zagala.

what captivates here is the gamble in which one's control of the live performance, of the unforeseeable dynamics and dangers of public practice, is made visible to all. What captivates, as likewise seen in Mosa's analogous floor inscription in figures 5.29 and 5.30, is thus not simply the "artefact produced, but the 'performance' aspect of the procedure, the way in which an expert could delineate a complex figure . . . without hesitation of deviation, in a single continuous movement from start to finish" (Gell 1998: 93). What captivates is the perfect gestural control, the complex twists and turns that so gracefully and artfully transform themselves into their final graphic image. Virtuosity here thus emerges through the way in which complexity becomes simplicity, through what we know to be convoluted being made to appear effortless. Beauty, or "efficacy," as Gell submits, hence materializes through the "capacity to accomplish tasks," the final designs (whether sand drawings or tags) understood by their makers not as "independent visual objects" but rather as "performances, like dances, in which men could reveal the capability" (p. 94). Here we thus see a gestural action rather than a graphic

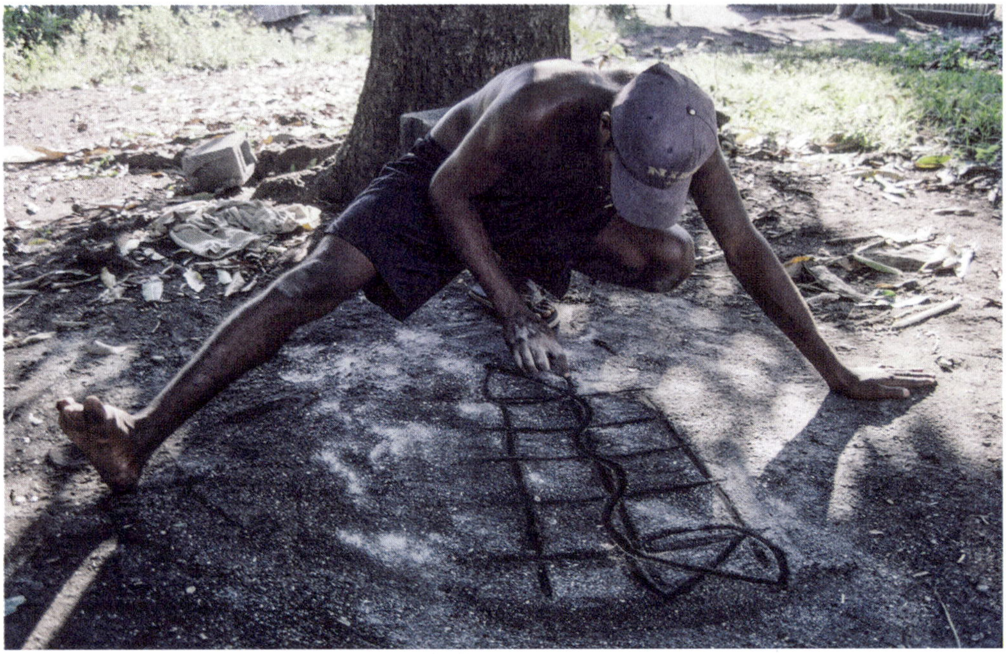

**FIGURE 5.28**
Unidentified artist performing a sand drawing, Craig Cove, Ambrym, Vanuatu, 1999. Photograph by Stephen Zagala.

form alone, a performative image that captivates through the performative control of formal risk. Here we can see not *just* a dance, but a choreographic display in which an expert's calligraphic and bodily control is exhibited.

For insiders, then, for those who have an embodied understanding of the act of production, what is read in the graffiti image is not only the bodily movements of the writer as they encounter the world but the bodily "know-how" of others (Marchand 2008: 261). What is read is the embedded knowledge that emerges within the "coordinated integration of mind, body and tool" that enables an expert, as seen in the improvisatory spontaneity of a dancer, to undertake the "quick and confident recalibration of position, force and movement" necessary to successfully perform one's task (pp. 260–261). Learning how to simultaneously manage one's body and one's environment is thus what becomes beautiful. In this way, then, one can "never grasp the meaning of calligraphy simply by looking at it and wondering what it might express or reveal" but, as Ingold has suggested, one has to enter *into* it and to join in the process of its production—in other words, to be reunited with the calligrapher in his or her 'inked traces'" (Ingold 2007: 50). While outsiders have the knowledge that the image was at the least produced by a body engaging in corporeal risk, for insiders what is read in these traces is movement, is the chance of the dance. It is painting read as gesture. Painting read as control. Painting read as the active engagement and bodily management of risk.

Yet it is not just in graffiti's formal production but likewise in its spatial actions that risk and chance come into play. Here it is a gamble with the body rather than a gamble of personal status that is key, not extrinsic but intrinsic risks that come to the fore. Here the hazards become "integral to the rite itself, part of its very essence" (Howe 2000: 69), and hence create the dangers of not just poor but *non*completion. Here the hazards are not of shame but of bodily harm. To produce a work as seen in figure 5.31, for example, a piece produced by Wombat on the Golden Jubilee Bridge in central London, requires one to travel along the edge of a train track (in one of the busiest parts of the city), to scale a bridge, climb down its reverse side, before jumping over the partition that

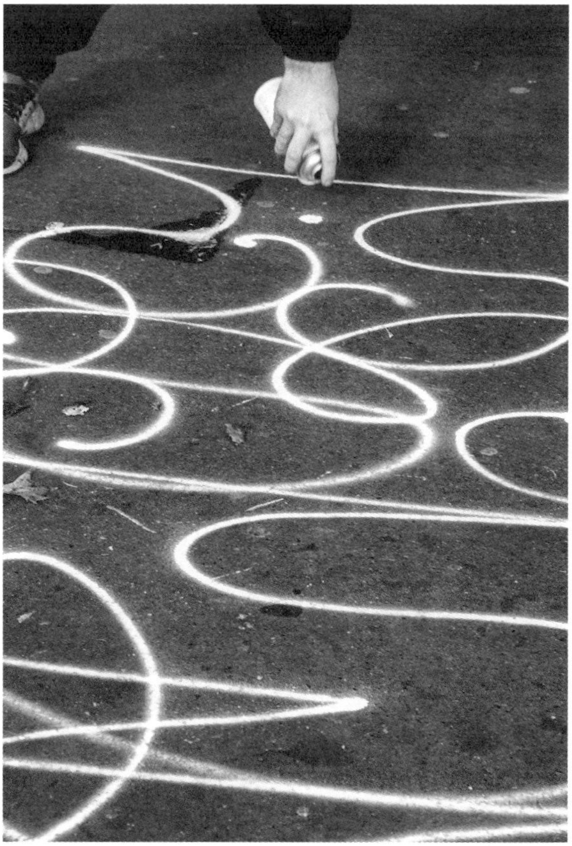

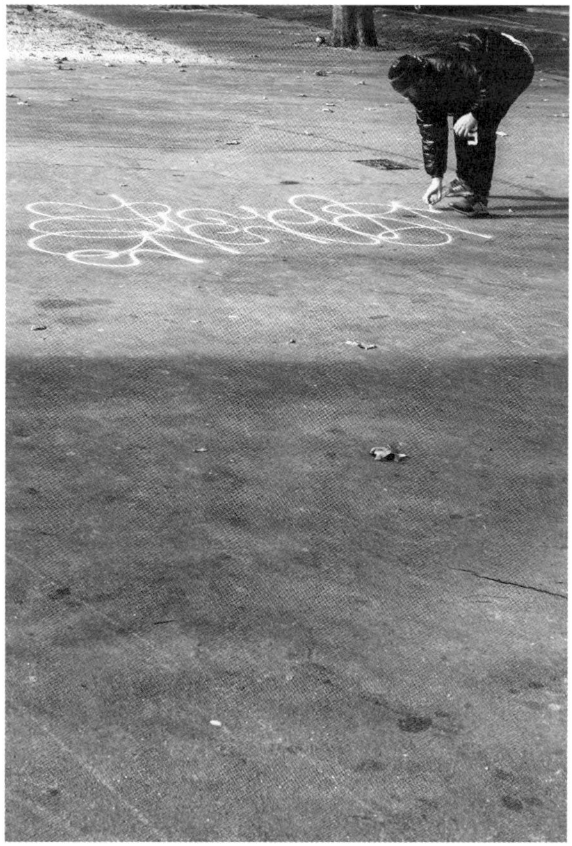

**FIGURES 5.29 AND 5.30**

*Mosa*, 2022. Courtesy of the artist and *Tramontana Magazine*. Photos: Elliot Sitbon.

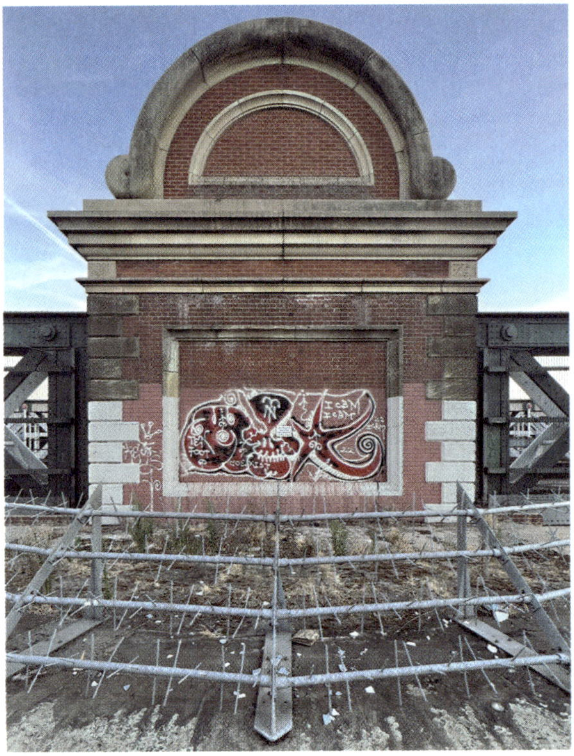

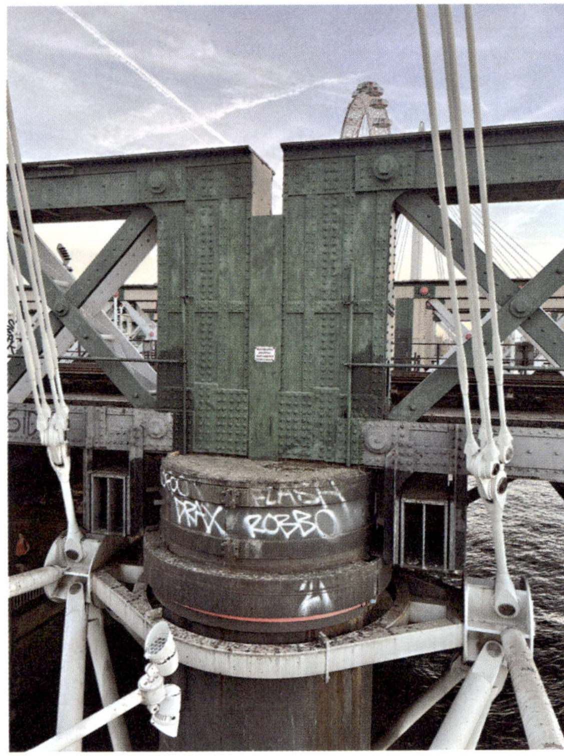


**FIGURE 5.31**
*Untitled (Golden Jubilee Wombat)*, 2022, London. Photo: Rafael Schacter.

**FIGURE 5.32**
*Untitled (Golden Jubilee 10Foot/Drax/Robbo/Flash)*, 2022, London. Photo: Rafael Schacter.

separates it from its adjacent pile cap (around thirty feet up from the Thames and its dense currents). Only then is one given the opportunity to paint, standing in full view of the public with literally nowhere to hide while doing so! In figure 5.32, one has to do all of this while standing on a one-foot-wide ledge, with little to hold onto above. In figures 5.33 and 5.34, however, we get a rare glimpse of the performative charge that goes into many productive processes. Shimmying across a one-foot ledge above four lanes of moving traffic and with a moving train careening past their head, painting with their right hand as they hold onto the top and side of the bridge with their left, the writer here can be seen (seen as subject to rare photographic capture, seen as producing this in the middle of the day, at even greater risk!) to show prowess through their bodily actions alone. For the internal graffiti audience, then, the "motor-based understanding" that a fellow producer of the image has via their own knowledge of "engagement and

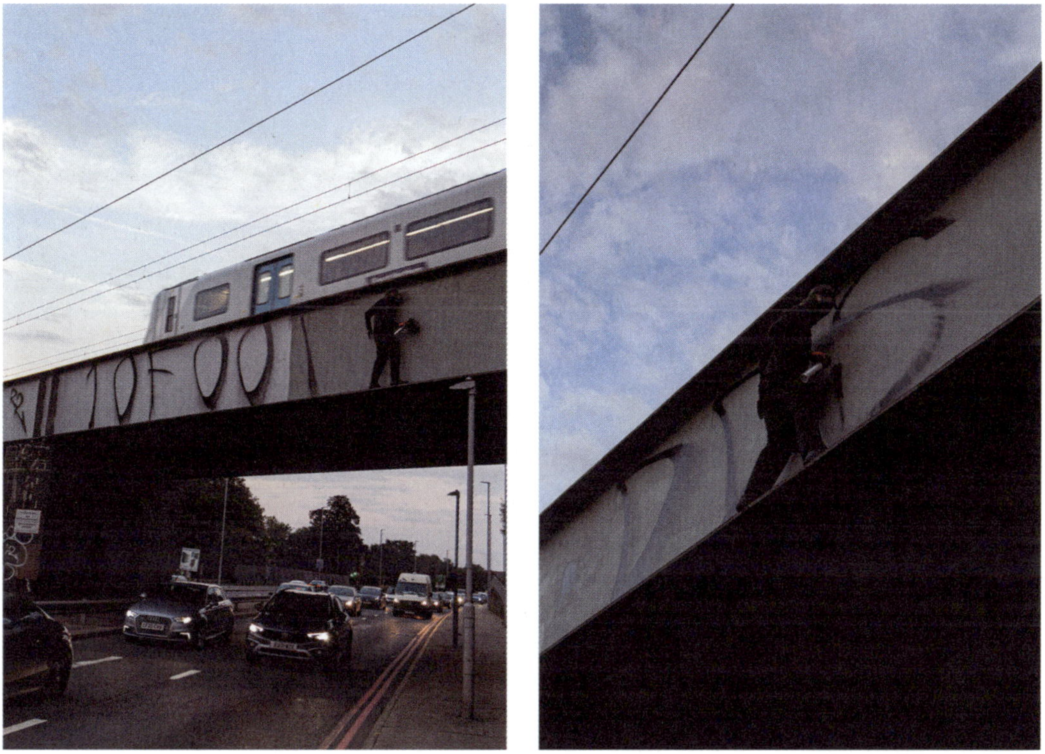

**FIGURES 5.33 AND 5.34**
R Seventeen | sory.world, *10Foot*, 2022, London. Courtesy of the artists.

experience" (Marchand 2008: 263–264) creates a second layer of legibility. The piece is read not just linguistically but bodily. It is read via the "kinaesthetic information" encoded within it, the information that "represents the corporeal sensation associated with that action: the feeling of muscular extension and contraction; the feeling of muscular relaxation and tension; the feeling of flow, disruption and vibration in action" (pp. 264–265).

As such, while very few people will observe what we see in figures 5.33 and 5.34, they may imagine what we see in the artist and writer Clement Gelly's images in figures 5.35 and 5.36. Part of a larger series of stop-motion composites that reveal the way a writer gained access to a specific graffiti location, the subcultural viewer will mentally plot the way a writer moved and contorted their body in the completion of their piece in the same way as Gelly's images photographically recount. Graffiti thus becomes an object

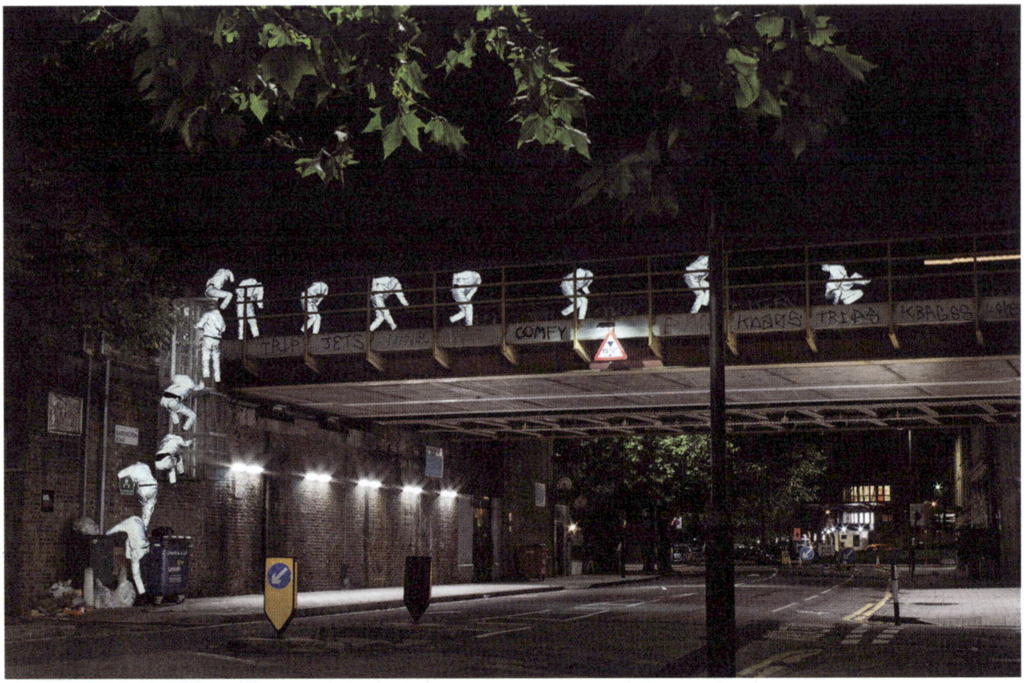
COMFY

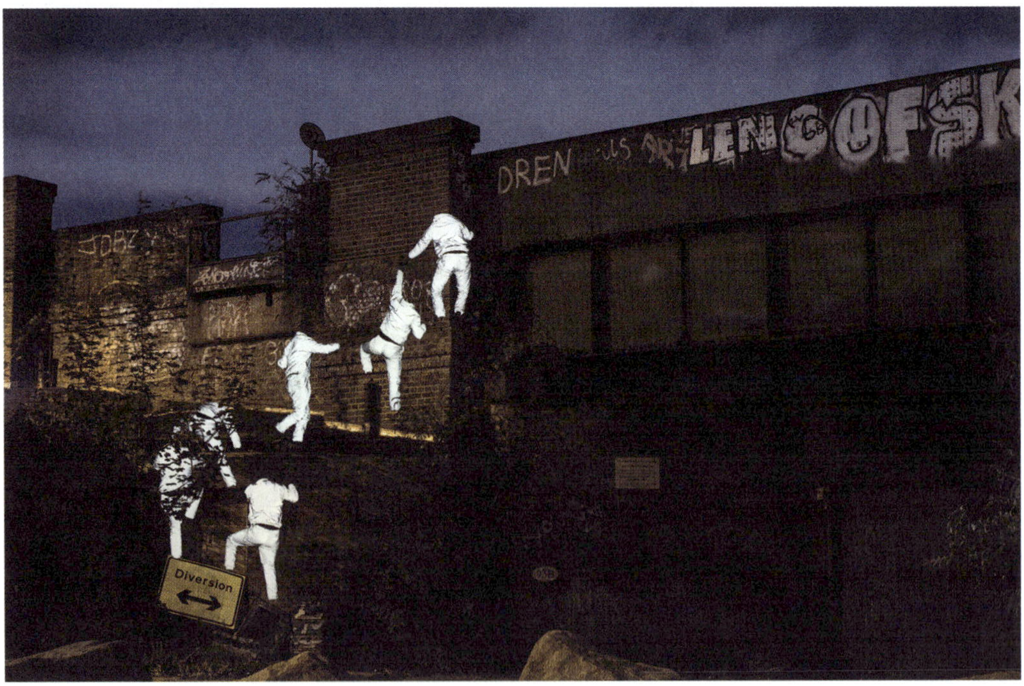
DREN
Diversion

that, as Debray noted in terms of monument more generally, "materializes . . . absence in order to make it visible and meaningful" (Debray 1999: 27), here not the absence of the soldier or ancestor but the absent body of the graffiti writer. The visceral presence of this absent body means that co-producers don't just see but *feel* the image, the management of the sensations that went into the writing of the piece not only coming to be legibly engraved into the image but being reincorporated by the insider-viewer themself. While the outsider may experience what I have previously termed "corporeal illicitness" (Schacter 2008: 39), a knowledge (and an internalized feeling) of a body engaged physically and illicitly while never truly being able to reconstruct the actions that went into the image's production (hence the image's magical captivation), performative precarity is kinesthetically transmitted to those who themselves practice. Risk is thus felt, danger reembodied by the insider in a tactile transference of heat.

It is not the image alone, then, but the commitment, the endurance necessary to the fulfilment of the marking that is here key, the doing of graffiti not only outlasting the image but lasting in the body of the doer themselves. One puts one's body in jeopardy for the task of writing, submits to a bodily wager with the self. Only by fully investing in the performance does the image truly gain efficacy. Only by having something to lose can something be gained. Greater risk can thus here be understood to demonstrate greater power, demonstrating an expert's ability to encounter and surmount great dangers. The inherent difficulty of production (let alone the very real hazards emergent from judicial punishments themselves) thus leads to an increase in a work's value functioning in direct proportion to the difficulty itself. Risk demonstrates expertise and fidelity both. It becomes a visible representation not just of a performing body but of a committed one. It publicly proves that one accepts and adheres to the canon, proves one's allegiance to public action. What thus becomes visible here is not just the dance and the danger but so too endurance and *belief*.

This form of bodily commitment can be seen within other forms of public art practice too, however. In the performances of artist William Pope.L, for example, in particular within his renowned "crawl" projects, bodily fortitude and stake are, as in graffiti, entirely critical. In his inaugural *Times Square Crawl* (1978), as seen in figures 5.37 and 5.38, Pope.L dragged himself through New York's most famous public arena, engaging themes of homelessness and visibility but so too of exhaustion and perseverance. His horizontality, however, his visible and purposeful abjection, can be seen to work in parallel to the fortitude and perseverance necessary to accomplish his task. The crawl works thus become not simply about what the artist appears *not* to have—i.e., verticality

**FIGURE 5.35**
Clement Gelly, *Lewisham*, 2020. From the series *Hi-Viz*. Courtesy of the artist.

**FIGURE 5.36**
Clement Gelly, *Lambeth*, 2020. From the series *Hi-Viz*. Courtesy of the artist.

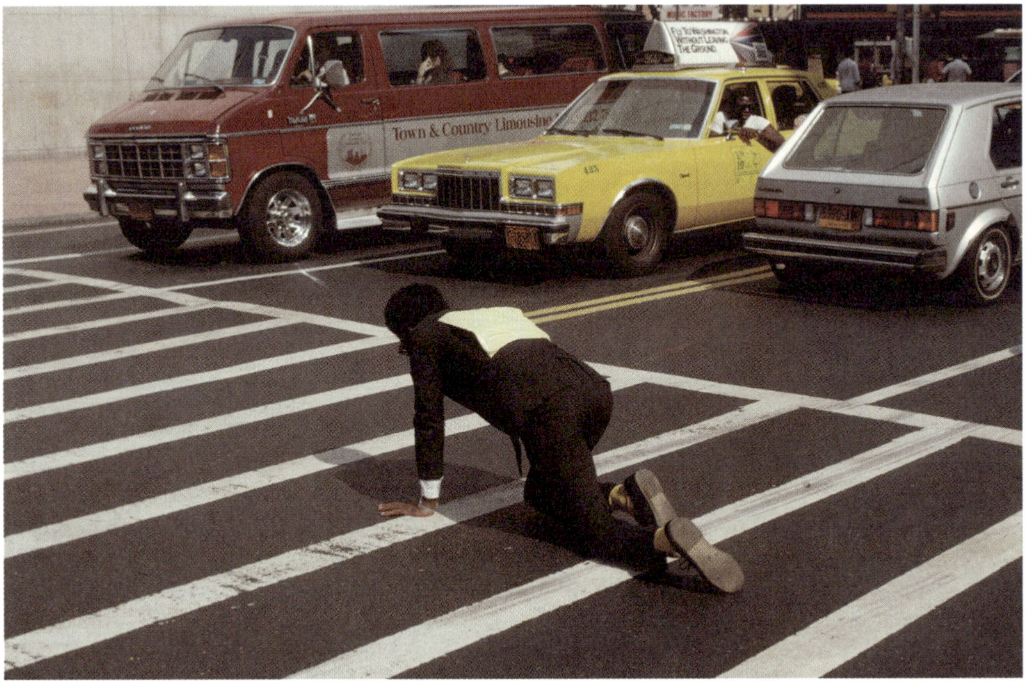
Town & Country Limousine

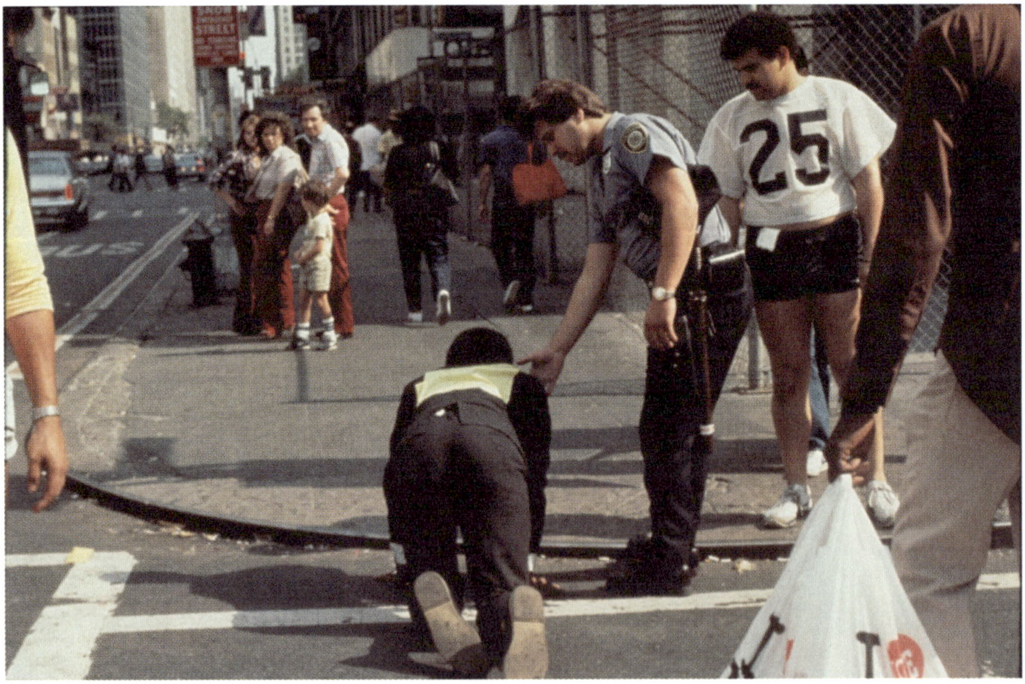
STREET
25

or power—but about what he *does* have: a form of strength, will, resolve, to push the body beyond its physical and conceptual limits. As a viewer, a viewer who Pope.L sees as an unwitting participant, we likewise cannot help but project ourselves bodily into his practice, to start (and then fail) to imagine how one could withstand that level of discomfort and (literal) exposure, that level of physical risk. Performance thus becomes captivative here through the management and control of unimaginable tasks (like the management and control of a complex pattern). And, as with graffiti, rather than being about pain or suffering, it is commitment and perseverance that are key. Even as the graffiti performance remains invisible, what persists in the image is the dedication to action that only a truly committed actor could undertake. What persists is an act that is about the body, the city, and the control of the uncontrollable too.

## CONCLUSION *OR* SET WITHIN THE SKIN

Graffiti, then, is a performance, a gesture, a dance. It is a mode of training the body, of inculcating formal and social skills. It is a way of sculpting the body and embedding learning into the skin, a mode of exploration, of endurance, and of commitment to one's community of practice. The body, the now absent but still ever-present body, is thus critical to understanding graffiti. Through the singular spectacularly located piece as much as the durational necessity for spectacular distribution, the acts of the body ensure that one's dedication to practice is placed beyond critique. As such, while in our last chapter we claimed that graffiti is speech, a form of indirect speech directed by its context (Brenneis 1986), here I want to argue that the meaning of this speech is guided by the bodily act itself. Its "literal message," whether announcing "Wombat," "Osha," or "Cap," is thus not what it means—the text alone, as mentioned in our last chapter, being "inadequate or misleading in itself" (p. 341). While the image may convey expertise, may be enjoyed for its purely figural qualities, the name in itself *means* nothing, simply making clear who undertook the act that brought the name into existence and how they specifically engaged. The meaning is the process. The meaning is the act. The meaning is the choice to write, the choice to engage the city and the self. Rather than any "idea it expresses," the meaning of the object is, as Ingold has pronounced, held within the "current of activity to which it properly and originally belongs" (Ingold 2000: 346). Graffiti does not represent something; it does something. It shows bodily skill and bodily knowledge, bodily risk and bodily commitment. It reveals an action in which the artifact is just one bodily act in a much larger bodily process, an act emergent before

**FIGURES 5.37 AND 5.38**
Pope.L, *Times Square Crawl a.k.a. Meditation Square Pieces*, 1978. Digital C-print on gold fiber silk paper. 10 × 15 in, 25.4 × 38.1 cm. © Pope.L. All files courtesy of the Artist and Mitchell-Innes & Nash, New York.

and after the life of the artifact in much larger cycle of production. Here, then, there can be no confusion, no linguistic obfuscation. Here the bodily act speaks for itself.

The body in action in graffiti is hence a marginal body, a gestural body producing marginal images while employing marginal physical techniques. But what of our institutional monuments? What are the bodies that the institutional monument espouses if not embodies? Well, here we of course have the omnipresent military bodies. We have the able and upper-class bodies. We have the white bodies, the Christian bodies, the *male* bodies. The institutional monument thus displays what types of bodies our society esteems, what types of bodies are considered the norm: the martial men on horseback, the elite men on plinths, the domineering men that dominate us in physical and geographical terms. When almost 90 percent of monuments in the United States[10] are of white men (a figure that moves down to "just" 80 percent in the United Kingdom[11]) and when there are ten times more monuments of mermaids than of congresswomen in the United States and *double the number of sculptures depicting animals than depicting named women in the United Kingdom*, it is unsurprising that public space feels gendered male. Not only very male and very white (London has only has two monuments to women of color, the earliest being erected in just 2012), there are only a handful of monuments to members of the LGBTQ+ community, almost none of which relate to the history of prejudice they faced or fought. At the same time, while men may be allowed to be elderly or physically impaired (Churchill in Parliament Square, for example, being both hunched and leaning on a stick), women should be young, beautiful, and preferably nude.[12] Even when those with disabilities *are* depicted, as seen in Marc Quinn's sculpture *Alison Lapper Pregnant* (2000), for example, these often fall into the heroic mode in which one needs to be *super*heroic to be accepted as fully human at all. Here, then, the normative body (and thus the irregular one) is made explicitly clear. Women are acceptable if naked, but animals (mythic or not) are preferred. Heterosexual is the preference but, if not, please don't ask or don't tell. Public space is thus monumentalized as a white, male, cis-gendered zone.

Still, today more representative representations *are* beginning to take presence in the public sphere. We could think of the monument to the Suffragist campaigner Millicent Fawcett by Gillian Wearing in Parliament Square (2018), for example (see figure 5.39), not only the first monument to a woman to be included at this critical site of public memory but also the first monument at the site to be sculpted *by* a woman too. Including images of fifty-nine women and four men who supported women's suffrage across all four sides of the plinth, the work likewise displaces the singular heroic archetype of the traditionally masculine and individual monumental form, disrupting the conventions of masculinity in conceptual and figurative ways. We could think too of Kehinde Wiley's equestrian monument *Rumors of War*, a work based on a monument to the Confederate General J. E. B. Stuart in Richmond, Virginia, in which the military leader is replaced by a hooded and dreaded African American figure sitting in the same pose as the original statue. Creating a monument that, as the artist himself said, "looks

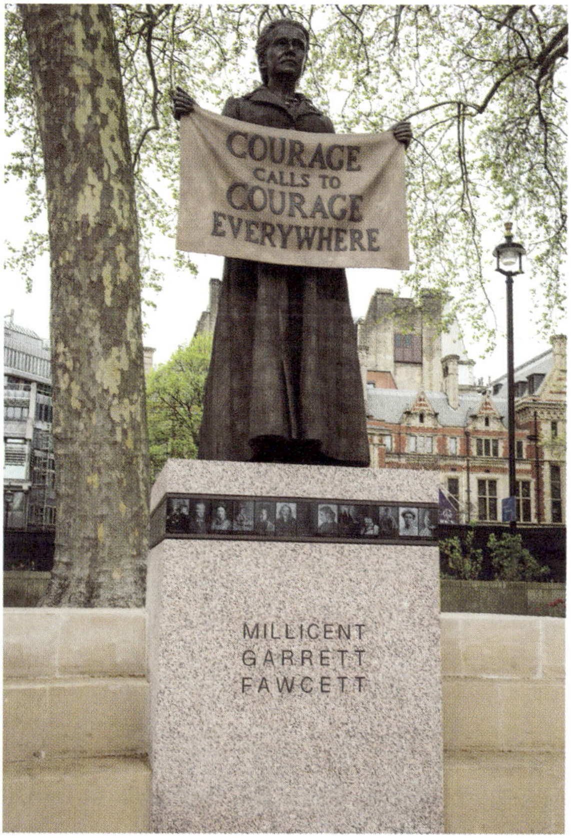


**FIGURE 5.39**
Gillian Wearing, *Millicent Fawcett*, 2018. Bronze on marble plinth. The statue has been commissioned by the Mayor of London with 14–18 NOW, Firstsite, and Iniva to commemorate the centenary of the Representation of the People Act 1918, through the government's national centenary fund. Photo: GLA/Caroline Teo. © Gillian Wearing, courtesy of Maureen Paley, London/Hove, Tanya Bonakdar Gallery, New York/Los Angeles and Regen Projects, Los Angeles.

like us," Wiley's monument addresses the "sense of dread and fear" that segregational monuments contain while saying "yes to broader notions of what it means to be an American" (Ugwu 2019: n.p.). While it's clear that both of these more representative monuments function within the broader framework of the institutional monument (of the putting on a pedestal, of the setting into stone), they still come to broaden the canonical norms while working within its canonical forms. Yet other artists have sought to rupture and challenge the bodily paradigms and structures of the institutional monument itself. In Rafa Esparza's 2015 piece *Bust: A Meditation on Freedom* (see figure 5.40), for example, a performance undertaken adjacent to the Twin Towers Correctional

Facility in Los Angeles (one of the largest prisons in the United States), the artist first encased himself within, then chiseled himself out of, a concrete plinth. Seeking to honor (as much as simply display) the queer and working-class bodies of color so often left out of (if not oppressed by) public space and art space alike, Esparza's ephemeral, public action positioned his own restrained body—like the bodies of those interned in the Twin Towers facility—as well as his own liberating actions—the meditative, physical, exhausting, yet unstoppable process of release—as both monument and monumental itself. As similarly enacted in a more recent work, *Bust: Indestructible Columns*, undertaken in Washington, DC, in 2019 and seen in figure 5.41, he sought to deconstruct the monumental edifices of our contemporary cities (be they the prison system or the veiling architecture of the state) while simultaneously rejecting the material forms they most commonly function through.

Bodily actions themselves must, in this way, be seen to house the potential of the monumental. And just as with Malakulan sand art—the bodily practice that, like Western memorials and monuments, allows "access to the world of the dead and of the ancestral spirits" (Geismar 2014: 108)—graffiti too must be understood as a bodily practice in which memory becomes set within the skin. Like Esparza's and Pope.L's monumental acts of endurance, graffiti too must be understood as a practice in which the relationship between body and space, body and time are brought to the fore, in which the elasticity and durability of the body is made into monument itself. Rather than only being held within stone (be it placed upon or produced of it), the body becomes a site from which memory is renewed, a site from which messages can be sent to others via bodily action itself. Rather than separating the ephemeral from the archival, here knowledge and memory can become inscribed within bodily performance, the body writing itself into the hegemonic text of the city, the body communicating and memorializing public culture itself.

It is thus not just that the letters in graffiti have bodies, act like bodies, are the representations of bodies, but that the gestural graffiti body itself acts as monument and monumental advice. The act of writing, of exploring, of walking the city becomes a monument in itself, even while the artifactual remainder it leaves behind (the stories of the exploits, the documentation, the ephemeral artifact) likewise acts monumentally too. The material residue of the performance becomes the monumental advice on a

**FIGURE 5.40**

Rafa Esparza, *Bust: A Meditation on Freedom*, 2015. Performance outside the Twin Towers Correctional Facility, Los Angeles. Photo by Nancy Popp. Courtesy of the artist.

**FIGURE 5.41**

Rafa Esparza, *Bust: Indestructible Columns*, 2019. Performance in Washington, DC. Photo by Natalia Mantini. Courtesy of the artist.

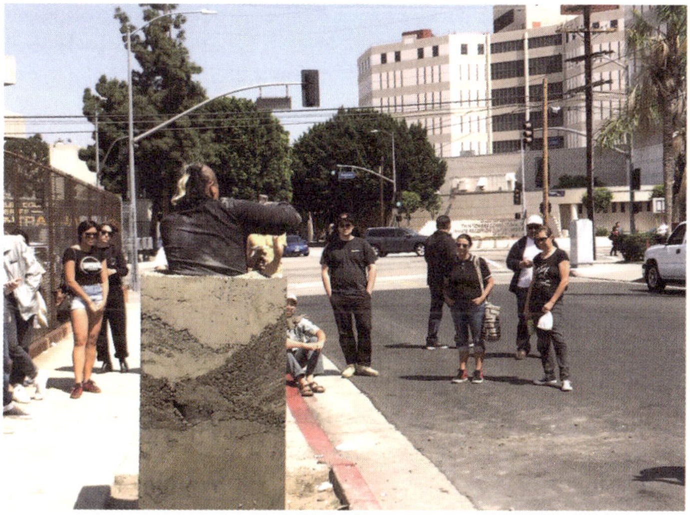

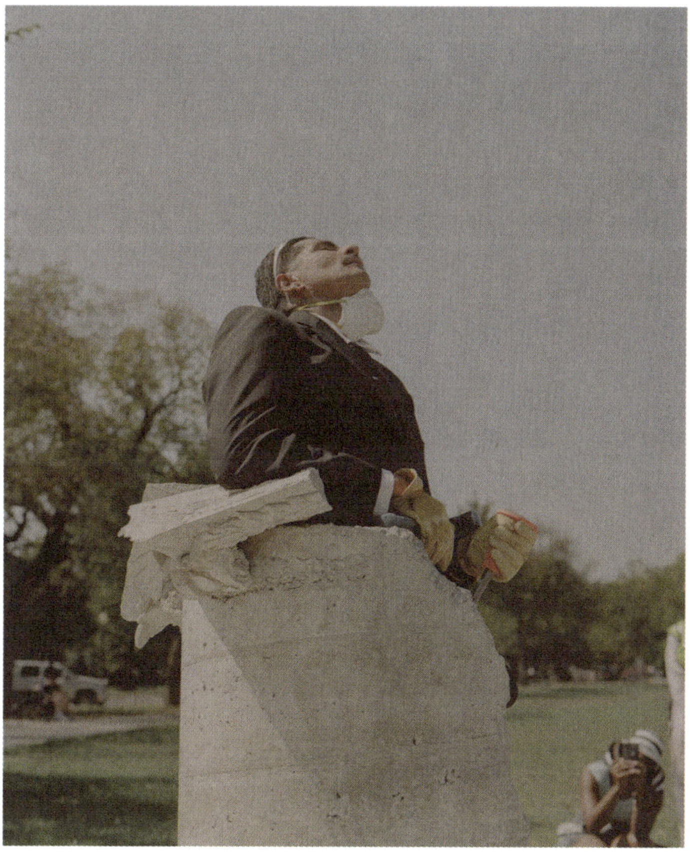

mode of civility, on a mode of urban practice that venerates action, that espouses not just the *right* but the *need* to (re)produce locality. The action and the belief that graffiti as monument indexes thus reveal a particular understanding of publicity and citizenship, in which it is physical, corporeal performance that creates the true communal bond. Monumental graffiti thus questions the idea of the normative body that the city expects, utilizing embodied performance to reinscribe the manner in which the body is produced in and by space. It exposes a bodily endurance working not only spatially but so too temporally, a walking body distributing itself over time in a way that multiplies the gamble through its duration, an exploratory body willing to place itself at bodily risk through architectural and geographic encounter. It becomes a bodily monument to bodily dissent, to the marginal bodies that stand in opposition to the martial bodies that surround us. It becomes monument to exploration and endurance, not just a monumental rejection of the normative way of experiencing the public sphere but a monument advising of an engaged mode of doing this itself.

# 6
# PARTICIPATION

Graffiti is a participatory act. It is a practice undertaken by not just a body intertwining with its material environment but a body intertwining within the web of a wider social world. Rather than the individual whose unique voice is heard through something *said* or the individual whose specific actions emerge as something *done*, this chapter moves graffiti from the one to the many as something said and done *together*. It realigns our focus from what graffiti accomplishes to the self—be that artist or viewer—and toward what it accomplishes collectively—to its joint participants or public at large. Like all monuments, then, the graffiti monument (even if a marginal, distributed, ephemeral monument) becomes a hinge from which community is created, a site where people come together in the plural yet unite together in the singular. The popular image of the graffiti writer as a lone, male, hooded, disaffected, violent youth will thus here be positioned as a total fallacy (except, possibly, for the hoodie), a fallacy belied through the mutual and relational status of the practice. This chapter will hence focus not just on the right to appear on communication networks or to claim spatial presence in the city but on the right, as Lefebvre has said, "to participation and *appropriation*" (Lefebvre 1996: 174), to a mode of urban participation that incorporates pleasure, play, and the political in equal measure.

Starting first with the participatory mode of the classical monument (as likewise undertaken in chapter 3), this chapter will then examine collaboration in graffiti in relation to its site-specific position (its liminal rather than central location), its stylistic and bodily techniques (its carnivalesque rather than ritualesque methods), and its temporal and discursive status (its improvised rather than composed procedures). Both the institutional and the graffiti monument's participatory grammar, its potentially emancipatory or disciplined agencies, will thus be unpacked through the structuring themes developed within this book so far. In this way, then, Hannah Arendt's focus on both speech (as action) and action (as speech) will here come together with her equal focus on plurality, commonality, and collectivity, on her concept of the *polis*—the ideal site of citizenship and participation—as not just a "physical location" but a space arising "out of [people] acting and speaking together . . . no matter where they happen to be"

(Arendt 1988 [1958]: 198). The graffiti monument will thus be seen to generate a power that only people coming together in concert can generate, an active and volitional practice that, as Barney et al. argued following Arendt, is "not validated instrumentally by the ends it achieves but is sufficient unto itself," a participation whose very enactment becomes "its own reward" (Barney et al. 2016: xiii).

## INSTITUTIONAL PARTICIPATION

The participation centered around London's Cenotaph monument (see figure 6.1), the United Kingdom's principal memorial to the two world wars of the twentieth century, presents us with a prototypical example of collective practice at the institutional

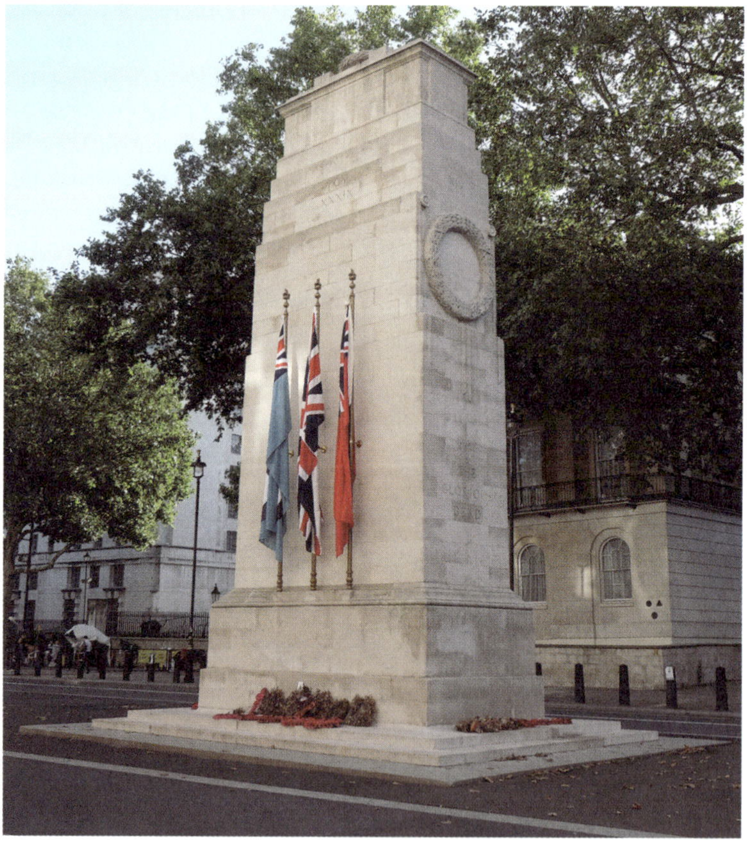

**FIGURE 6.1**
Sir Edward Lutyens, *The Cenotaph*, London, 1920. Photo: Rafael Schacter, August 2020.

monument.[1] In site-specific terms, the Cenotaph acts on our bodies in the most immediate of ways. Bordering the key seat of political power that is 10 Downing Street (the home and office of the UK Prime Minister), while standing in the vicinity of the monuments to Nelson (a two-minute walk down Whitehall) and Churchill (outside the Houses of Parliament, another two minutes away in the other direction), and so too Westminster Abbey (the coronation site of almost every English monarch), it is positioned in the heart of England's capital as one of the fundamental pieces of the state's memorial mise-en-scène. Surrounded too by the Ministry of Defense, the Cabinet Office (the government department with the most senior decision-making powers), as well as the Horse Guards (the barracks for the monarch's personal bodyguard, the Household Cavalry), the entire site in which the Cenotaph is located impresses and dominates its public in spatial and symbolic ways: it is palatial, set in Portland stone and designed in a classical Palladian manner, housing the political, religious, and military elite of the nation and doing so in a purposefully assertive architectural fashion. The Cenotaph thus resides in a site not of daily encounter but of rare distinction, in a site of the privileged and powerful elite. What envelops it, and envelops us as we stand beside it, is thus a material space of authority and hegemony, a site, whether meant for local citizens or international tourists, that generates a mode of hegemonic sociality through its monumental centrality. Our participatory encounter with the Cenotaph is thus first and foremost an encounter with site. The physical position of the Cenotaph establishes it in a literal position of power. We are subjugated by its setting, by a monument that is not just in the center but is the center itself.

While site is paramount, however, for the majority of the year the Cenotaph in fact endures as a strangely positioned, monolithic traffic island. Set in the middle of Whitehall, a prominent London artery with buses, taxis, and traffic careering past it, its visibility is of a highly variable nature. The monument is only truly brought to life on the annual event that is Remembrance Sunday (the Sunday closest to Armistice Day, on November 11), a yearly moment in which its perceptibility is unbracketed and iconic standing publicly substantiated. On this day, not only does the Cenotaph become a focal point of national attention, but its particular stylistic structure comes to explicitly intertwine with the mode of bodily action it likewise generates. The understated, severe classical style that the architect Sir Edward Lutyens employed within the Cenotaph's physical architecture can hence be seen to reflect the similarly understated, similarly severe bodily architecture that is established during the annual Remembrance even itself: nothing over-the-top, nothing over-ornamented must be witnessed on that day, just perfect classical order and perfect classical structure in material and corporeal form. As contemporaneously described by John W. Simpson, the president of the Royal Institute of British Architects at the time of the Cenotaph's installation, the monument's simplicity, its "austere yet gracious" perfection, its "technically perfect" construction, can be understood to have reflected its status as the "very expression of repressed emotion" (how perfectly English!), the memorial's physical qualities mirroring the personal

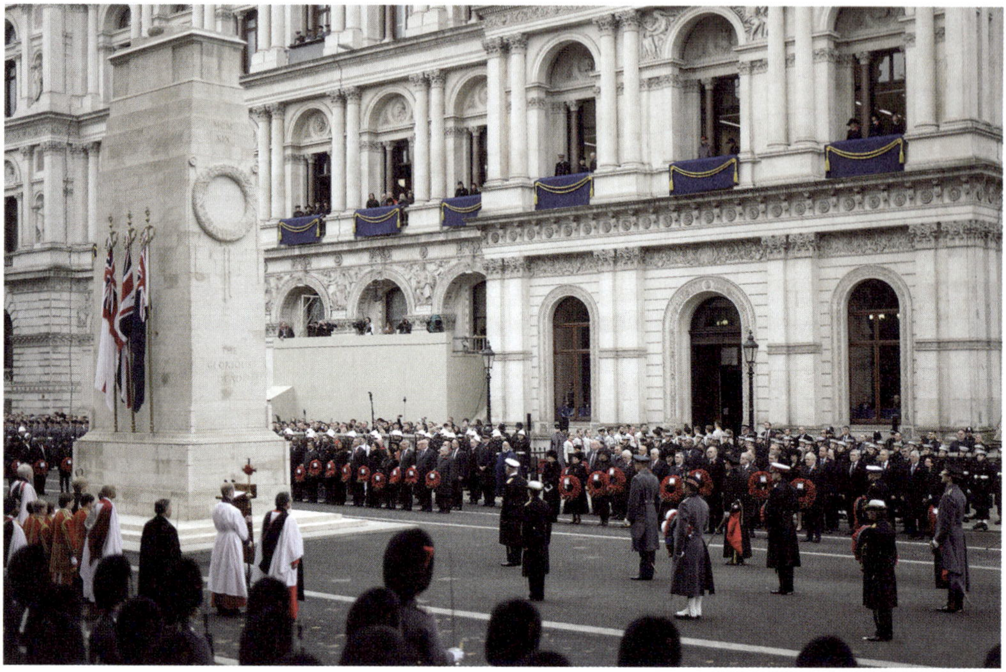

**FIGURE 6.2**

*Prime Minister Boris Johnson—Remembrance Sunday at the Cenotaph*. November 14, 2021. London. Prime Minister Boris Johnson and members of the Cabinet join members of the Royal Family at the Cenotaph for Remembrance Sunday. Picture by Andrew Parsons/No. 10 Downing Street. Attribution 2.0 Generic (CC BY 2.0).

qualities of both those "whom it commemorates and those who raised it" (Simpson in Greenberg 1989: 11). Within the highly structured formalism, the tight system of regulations, and more than anything the absolute *invariance* of the ritualized performance that occurs at the Cenotaph on Remembrance Sunday (as discussed more below), both body and monument are austere and gracious, both body and monument technically perfect, both body and monument embodying the classical and traditional.

At the same time, however, while the Cenotaph's notably abstract design (as much as the anonymity of the unknown soldier metaphorically housed at its pinnacle) presents us with a monument embodying collectivity rather than singularity, the commemorative performance is likewise one in which all distinctiveness and individuality is cast aside: not only deeply somber, as a memorial to mass death would always be, the ritual acts reinforce the communal rather than singular nature of the monument too. While those outside the honored elite enact a participation of passivity—we watch and listen immovably, we participate through an active submissiveness exemplified by our (two-minute) silence—the intensely choreographed actions of the privileged leaders who perform the rituals (on our behalf) mean that each member, even the monarch themself, becomes an innately interchangeable representative of the state. Here, then, all attendees must look the same, if not in their matching military uniforms then in dark clothing, dark overcoats, in formally discreet clothing that ensures one remains a figure, not an individual.[2] Agency is thus rejected here in both stylistic and bodily terms. Total adherence to tradition, total deference to the nation is required. Collectivity is King. In this way, then, not only is participation at the Cenotaph created through a negative principle, through an active and committed bodily submission, but monumental style and monumental performance are entirely inseparable.

But what does the participatory mode of the Cenotaph itself *say*? Well, in the first case, the order of service performatively (re)constructs and (re)presents the hegemonic structure of the nation. The choreographed performance seen in figure 6.2 demonstrates the religious, monarchic, political, and military authority of the realm, perfectly enacting the order of state power. Commencing with a square of military bodies that forms around the Cenotaph, "Rule Britannia" inaugurates a sequence of traditional martial music performed by military bands (representing each of the four nations of the United Kingdom), following which a short religious service is conducted by the dean of the Chapel Royal (traditionally the Bishop of London). The Royal family then emerge, shortly before the famous two-minute silence that begins as Big Ben chimes at 11 a.m., following which the gift of wreaths is made to the Cenotaph. First laid by the monarch and other members of the Royal family (in hereditary order), these are then followed by presentations from the Prime Minister, the leaders of the other principal political parties, the Foreign Secretary, Commonwealth High Commissioners, and finally representatives from the Army, Navy, Royal Air Force, Merchant Navy, and the Civilian Services. Only then do veteran service personnel get to march past the Cenotaph, saluting it as they do. The monument thus exhibits not only whom this society should valorize (its deceased soldiers) and how they should be remembered (through stony and invariant means), but so too who has precedence to the memory itself (the monarchic, political, and military elite). Yet alongside these metacommunicative announcements, the Cenotaph also speaks to us directly: "THE GLORIOUS DEAD," it pronounces in its sole linguistic inscription (seen in figure 6.3), set alongside the dates of the two world wars (written, reiterating its classical form, in Roman numerals) as well as the monument's stony wreaths (a symbol of heroism and victory used since ancient Greece). The Cenotaph thus speaks to us of bravery, duty, patriotism. It seeks not to forewarn us of our own mortality, but, working in perfect synergy with Nelson's "ENGLAND EXPECTS," to remind us of the equally glorious sacrifice that each of us is expected to one day make.

What the Cenotaph says, however, works in close relation to the temporal mode in which it says it. The hegemonic social and political structure that its architectural structure reinforces functions through a configuration in which permanence and the archival are critical. While originally constructed from wood and plaster and meant to

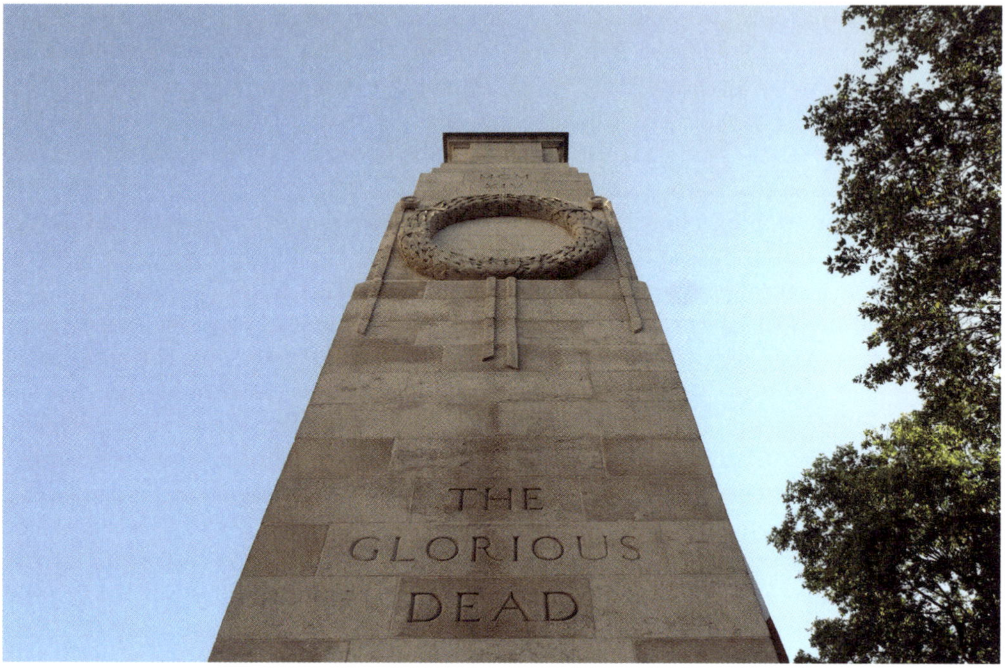


**FIGURE 6.3**
Sir Edward Lutyens, *The Cenotaph*, London, 1920. Photo: Rafael Schacter, August 2020.

be present solely for the Peace Day Parade of 1919, the Cenotaph's transformation into permanent form the following year (as seen in figure 6.4) led to its reformulation in Portland stone. The monument thus functions through a classical mode of heritage in which physical intransience is understood as critical to public memory, in which the monument's material being must remain fixed to the moment in which it was very first formed. Moreover, participation at the Cenotaph comes to be not only about continuous and never-ending tradition but about *becoming* the past. Bodily actions here are set into a deep time, a time of the monument's original erection. To act, we must here be not in but out of time; to act we must enter into an eternal not just annual temporality. Nothing is improvised at the Cenotaph. The ritual text that is performatively recited is a text that must be *re*-performed and *re*-enacted in total invariance year on year. It is total replication of the past that is critical. While the deep history embedded in the Cenotaph's stylistic form—its Grecian name alluding to the classical influences that can be witnessed within all of Lutyens's work, never more so than through the Cenotaph's use of *entasis*—speaks of a structure of time that exists beyond the ravages of our own mortal frame, its physical and participatory presence mean to preserve history

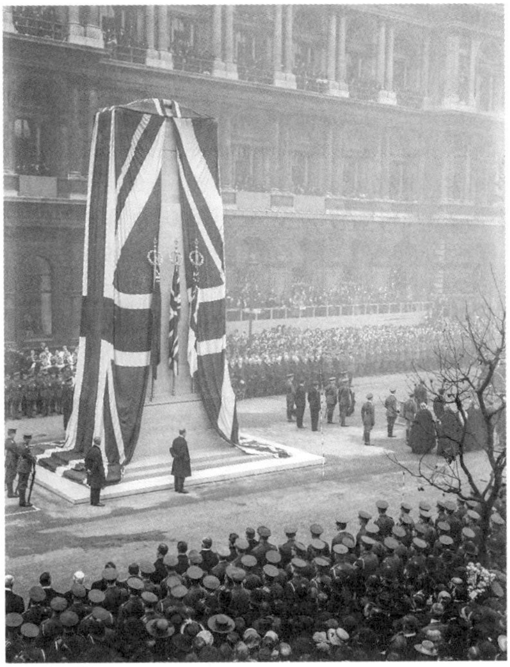

**FIGURE 6.4**
*The Cenotaph at Whitehall*, 1920 (the unveiling of the permanent Cenotaph at Whitehall, by King George V, November 11, 1920). Photo: Horace Nicholls.

and the status quo forever. The monument's physical and performative invariance thus perfectly mirror its archival and monumental temporal aims. Its ritual re-performance is hence a "performance" in only the very weakest of senses, a performance in which participants are automata with barely no agency at all.

The site-specific, stylistic, performative, discursive, and temporal modes of participation that the Cenotaph generates thus form a mode of engagement that fixes not only the past and the future but so too social structure itself. Our participation is proscribed and prescribed here, the public's role one that is restricted, delimited, pacified. Participation here is thus about an outward mode of public action in which collectivity must be witnessed. The sheer spectacularity of the event—as an archetypal example of the "large scale 'crowd choreography' in public spaces" noted by Brian Osbourne—creates a very particular mode of hegemonic sociality. It turns the overwhelming majority into either "spectators" or "distanced participant-voyeurs" (Osbourne 2001: n.p.), a choreographic mode in which the accepted inequality of our participation reinforces the accepted inequality of the nation itself. The "highly formalized," highly "restricted code" that the participatory mode utilizes creates a collective modality we cannot refuse and are structurally forced to commit, a ritual mode, as Maurice Bloch famously described (1989 [1974]: 24–25), in which we are compelled into an ideological structure that permits no alternative: the dead here thus died not in vain but in glory. They died, like the nation's religious figurehead himself (be that Jesus or Nelson), for *you* (if not for your sins).[3] Yet just as the monumental mode of participation defines how, what, and whom we remember, it likewise defines whom we choose to forget. The 70,000 civilian deaths during the world wars in Britain are not remembered here—they were collateral damage and hence disregarded as inglorious. The two million British men left physically disabled by the war are not considered—they were instead relegated to the outskirts of society, not manly enough to have died when they should have and later treated as only partial men themselves. Nor are the tens of thousands of war widows recalled—often left impoverished by the meager war pensions they were left with—who were in fact barred from participation at the Remembrance Sunday service (despite continual protest) until 1982! What is reinforced as the Cenotaph performance is a collective understanding of our place in the nation, our role within this sacred institution. Dissenting opinion is believed to disrespect the lives of those lost, to disrespect an idea that cannot be touched. Participation here thus not only creates a very palpable, powerful, collective relationship, a relation to the nation that compels us into martyrdom, but keeps everyone fixed to their social place. It is a participation without control, without agency. A participation in which a dense bond to the imagined nation is formed, a relation for which we must be willing to make the ultimate sacrifice.[4]

## MARGINAL PARTICIPATION

Participation in graffiti, however, emerges through an active, not passive mode.[5] While those outside the subculture can participate only visually (and vicariously) through looking or through capturing the images photographically, participation among subcultural members is an active process of engagement and encounter, an act of *doing*. At the Cenotaph, even the elite few participate through a passive mode of reperformance, yet in the case of graffiti, as we will now see, production, not mere consumption, is a must.

In the first case, while the site-specific participation undertaken within the space of the institutional monument is dominated by centrality, the graffiti monument engages a participatory structure in which liminality is the principal mode and in which geographic marginality the overarching rule. Here the liminal (literally, a space of the threshold) provides a space in which participants can engage outside the power (and eye) of the state, a space on the margins in which relations, not just images, can be formed. A topic famously explored by the anthropologist Victor Turner, what he termed the *liminoid* events of industrial society were understood as not "cyclical but intermittent" events that we entered into "voluntarily" rather than hereditarily, events seen to develop “apart from central political and economic processes, along the margins, in the interstices” (Turner 1979a: 492). Like the traditional rites of preindustrial groups that Turner also examined, the condition of marginality created here was understood to have the power to form an “alternative and more ‘liberated’ way of being socially human, a way both of being detached from social structure . . . and also of a ‘distanced’ or ‘marginal’ person’s being more attached to *other* disengaged persons” (Turner 1979b: 49). As such, what was critical about participation at the limen was not only the geographic and conceptual separation from the everyday and the voluntary, horizontal status, but likewise the affective qualities that the space at the edge could generate. The margins thus not only enabled social experimentation, but formed spaces from which what Turner termed *communitas* could come to develop. This was a state of being whose maxim was “each for all, and all for each” (Turner 1967: 101), a state in which collectivity and intimacy were generated between one’s proximate companions (rather than to an imagined nation), a sense of fellowship that could then flood “across structural boundaries” (p. 188). While there may still be a ritual leader present in these scenarios, leadership is of a lay, not authoritative, structure, a structure in which leadership denotes not hierarchy but simply a guiding role in the wider organization of the event itself. At the edge, then, what emerged was a “comity of comrades” rather than a “structure of hierarchically arrayed positions” (p. 100), a space in which each member becomes responsible for one another, becomes a part of one another. At the edge, the intensity of collective practice, of people freely gathering together to engage jointly outside the norms of the literal and metaphoric center, could come to reject not only the hierarchical structure of classical participation but likewise the social and political norms of society itself. Rather than ritual as a mechanism of societal maintenance, as a tool of hegemonic legitimacy and control, liminal forms of ritual were understood by Turner to cohere collectivities while also containing the power to form new cultural norms and social relations. They could engage a space at the margins in which marginal ways of being together could be pursued, yet then flow back into the everyday and transform society itself.

Within graffiti, the margins and the marginal are entirely critical to the participatory mode. Not only an act transpiring on the city’s literal thresholds (its doorways and walls, its bridges and tunnels), graffiti likewise occurs at the city’s borderline territories outside the control of the center. It emerges in the *terrain vagues* of de Solà-Morales Rubio, as discussed in chapter 1, in the city’s elusive, unoccupied sites positioned outside the power of the urban realm’s political and economic drivers. Here, at the city’s interstices, graffiti writers not only can remain hidden but can experiment in social as much as visual terms. Here it is not just what is seen (by others) but what is done (by members) that is key, not just one’s material output but one’s engagement with the collective that counts. Still, there are varying levels of collective intensity and affectivity that come to emerge. On a daytime sojourn to an abandoned brownfield site where legal regulations are less strictly enforced and where there is a wall of fame on which one can (more

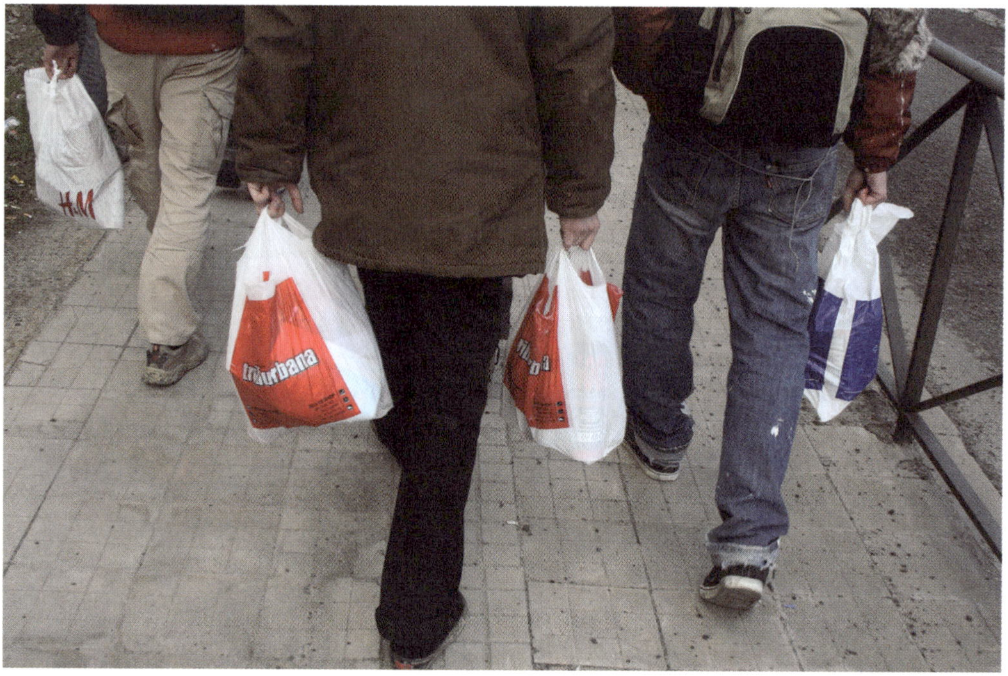

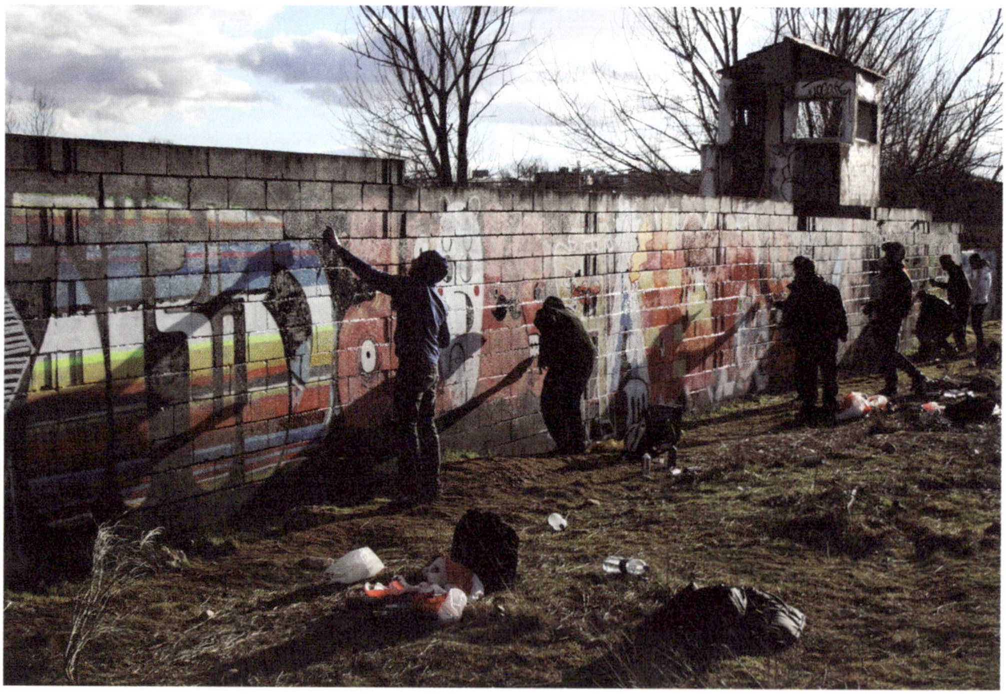

or less) paint freely for an entire afternoon (such as seen in figures 6.5 and 6.6), writers will be relaxed, able to comfortably converse and mix with one another. Subcultural sociality is thus most prominently in effect here. People are acting together, being together, socializing, and forming collective solidarity. On a nighttime mission to a train depot, however (such as seen in figures 6.7 and 6.8), intensity will be vastly magnified and the event will be experienced through an entirely different emotional mode. Writers will be more tense, alert, with conversations happening through sign or a whisper at the most. Each participant will be as bound to one another as they are bound up with their wider environment, as embedded in their human as their spatial milieu. Levels of collective affectivity thus increase in direct proportion to the dangers faced. Participation is, in this case, about sociality but so too about the *sensational*, about what is felt, not just done together. Whether containing the atmosphere of engaged hobbyists at the brownfield site (of Sunday painters if not trainspotters) or of a honed professional unit at the depot (of a military squadron if not a sports team), one becomes one with one another, engages creatively and socially with one's kin through concrete participative action. Both ends of the scale engage social horizontality, a way of being in which distance from structure, in which the voluntary and liberatory aspects of participation, enables a strengthening of bonds and of collective identity. Both ends of the scale engage social pleasure, an increased intimacy and equality with one another in which one can act together in ways entirely outside the norms of the everyday, even if affective strength exists on a sliding scale. Both create an "us" as opposed to a "them," form a kinship of choice, a comradeship, which is experienced inwardly through practice and only revealed outwardly via the visible adjoining[6] of the graffiti name.

This form of marginality, one that attempts to shift collectivity into a space beyond the scopic capabilities of the state, can be seen (or not seen) in a myriad of subcultural worlds. Within rave culture, for example, it is in the abandoned warehouses and industrial estates, in the clandestine sites at the edge of state power that communities come together, at marginal places (as seen in the artist Vinca Peterson's emblematic pair of photos in figures 6.9 and 6.10) where pleasure emerges through bodily effervescence, not bodily restraint. The feelings of "connectedness, communality, equality" that emerge within the "deviant" space of the rave (Takahashi and Olaveson 2001: 78), the feelings of an "energy or pulse which cannot be expressed or understood in words," can in fact only materialize in locations outside the spaces of consumption and leisure that the city supplies us with, being neither "socially condoned nor legally permitted in their dominant host culture" (p. 81). As seen in the United Kingdom with the infamous

**FIGURE 6.5**
*Untitled (Sunday Shopping)*, 2009, Madrid. Photo: Rafael Schacter.

**FIGURE 6.6**
*Untitled (Sunday Painting)*, 2009, Madrid. Photo: Rafael Schacter.

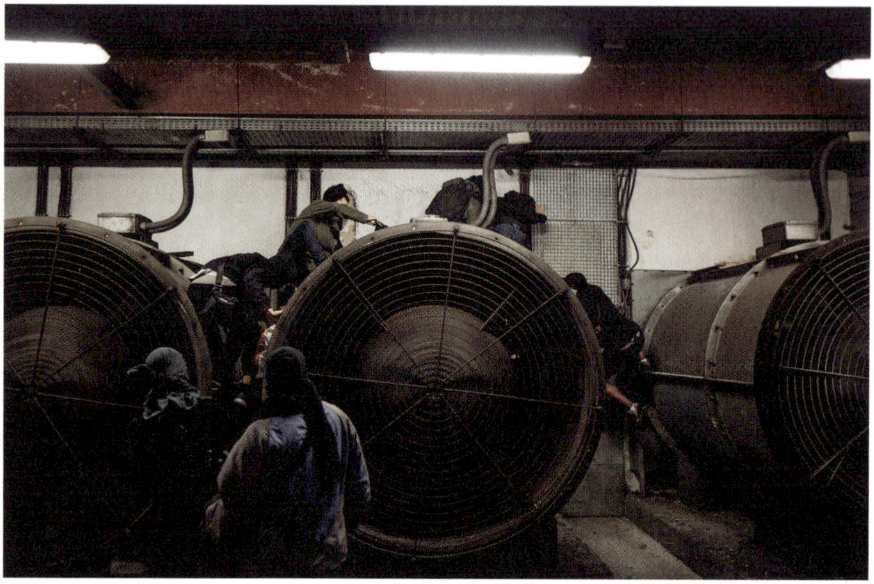

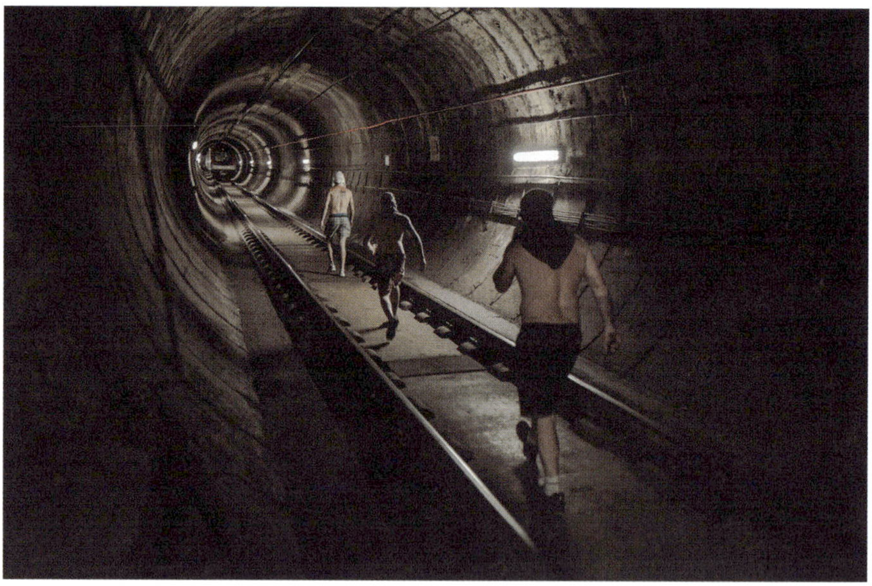

**FIGURE 6.7**
Enrique Escandell, *Barcelona Subway 2016*. Taken from *Subterráneos* by Enrique Escandell. Courtesy of the artist.

**FIGURE 6.8**
Enrique Escandell, *Barcelona Subway 2013*. Taken from *Subterráneos* by Enrique Escandell. Courtesy of the artist.

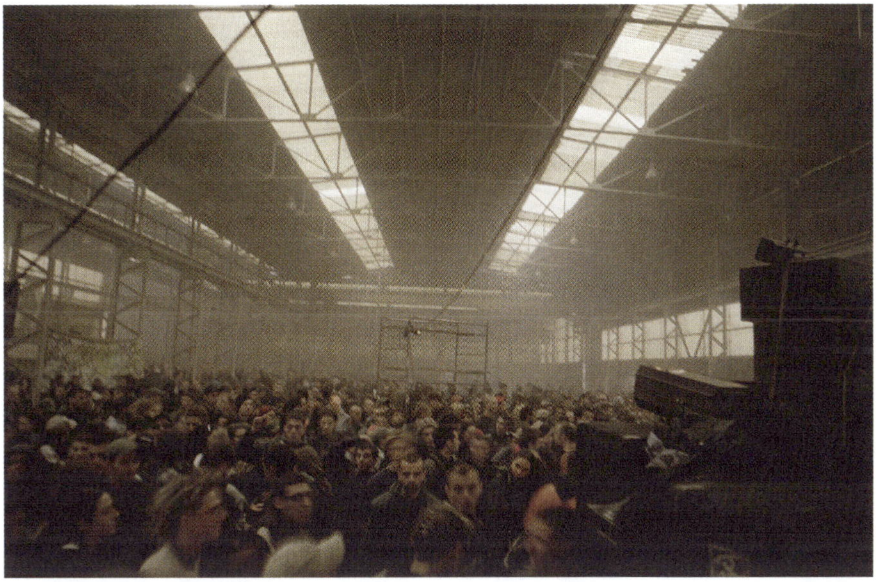

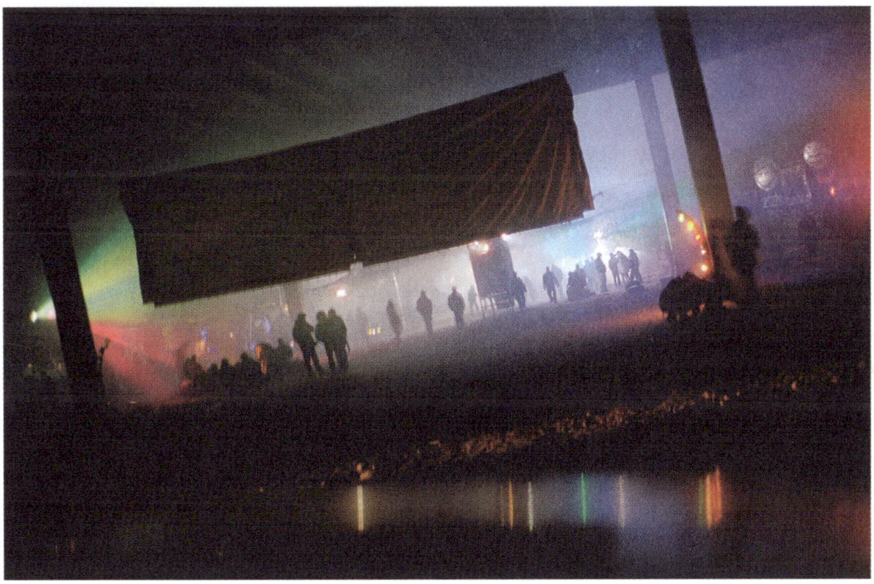

**FIGURE 6.9**
Vinca Petersen, *Warehouse Rave, France*, 2001, C-print, 50.8 × 76.2 cm, 20 × 30 in. Copyright Vinca Petersen. Courtesy of Edel Assanti.

**FIGURE 6.10**
Vinca Petersen, *Milan, New Year's Eve*, 1997, C-print, 50.8 × 76.2 cm, 20 × 30 in. Copyright Vinca Petersen. Courtesy of Edel Assanti.

Entertainments (Increased Penalty) Bill of 1990 and the Criminal Justice and Public Order Act of 1994, here the collective practices at these marginal sites were deemed so dangerous to the state that they moved to actively delimit them, proscribing the margins for communities for whom the center already proved inaccessible. This danger of proscription (or attack) means that collective practices are often forced beyond even the interstices and into the zone of the private. Outward invisibility is thus often a *necessity* for collectivity, for a space in which a public can emerge outside the omnipresence of surveillance. While in some moments public visibility becomes crucial as a means to engage the (often-hostile) center, for the well-being of a community a (safe) space set off from the everyday becomes a necessity, a space that can act as a respite from daily enmity and as a place of interpersonal freedom. The need for a space of autonomy and fugitivity thus becomes a prerequisite for true publicness for many marginalized communities. What occurs within these marginal rites is hence not simply about representation or what is *shown* (as was thought to be the purpose of public rituals traditionally), but rather about process and about what is achieved. It is what is done, not what is seen, that is critical, a way of being at the edge that the edge itself enables.

## CARNIVALESQUE PARTICIPATION

The participatory mode engaged at the edge also functions in juxtaposition to the institutional monument in stylistic and bodily terms. While the classical monument utilizes the formality of the ritualesque, at the edge it is the subversion of the carnivalesque that comes to pass. Here it is a position of irreverence rather than invariance that is assumed, an engagement of the joyful and pleasurable over the solemn and sorrowful. Here, rather than a position of consensual agreement, of submission to structure, it is an agonistic, destabilizing status that is taken, one in which it is an embracement of life rather than death that creates collective bonds.

A theme also analyzed by Turner, carnival[7] as ritual practice was understood by him not simply as the societal safety valve that Max Gluckman had taken it to be, an annual moment of release that functioned to "preserve and strengthen the established order" (Gluckman 1963: 109), but rather as a space in which "new paradigms and models which invert or subvert the old" could be formed (Turner 1979a: 474). Carnival was comprehended as "society in its subjunctive mood" (Turner 1983: 104), a mechanism of collective play in which the "messages it delivers are often serious beneath the outward trappings of absurdity, fantasy, and ribaldry" (p. 105). It was seen as a practice whose "masks, disguises and other fictions" were utilized as "devices to make visible what has been hidden . . . to let the mysteries revel in the streets, to invert the everyday order in such a way that it is the unconscious and primary processes that are visible" (p. 106). Carnival was thus not only an embodiment of the liminal in which one could move from spaces of "hierarchy to equality; from indicative mood to subjunctive mood;

from unity to multiplicity; from the person to the individual; from systems of status roles to communitas" (p. 110), but its practice of masquerading, of literally hiding in plain sight, was understood to have the capacity to place a form of liminality within the center. While commonly taking place in the heart of the city, then, carnival created a "place which is no place, and a time which is no time, even where that place is a city's main plazas, and that time can be found on an ecclesiastical calendar" (p. 103). Moreover, and as noted by another of the key theorists of carnival, the Russian literary critic Mikhail Bakhtin, rather than a "spectacle *seen* by the people," carnival was a practice in which "everyone participates because its very idea embraces *all* the people" (Bakhtin 1984 [1965]: 7, emphasis added). Carnival in this understanding is thus about the carnal rather than visual, about a "bodily awareness of another world" (p. 48). Rather than the constructed gravity and solemnity of the *parade*, of the reduced "carnival" event that is about what is witnessed, not felt, carnival was about "joyful and triumphant hilarity" (p. 38), about a subversive laughter in which hierarchy was scorned, authority rejected, normative creeds displaced.

Within the participatory practice of graffiti, the carnivalesque elements of style can be seen to mirror the carnivalesque mode of practice itself. The manner in which linguistic norms are subverted—in terms of correct spelling, correct orthography, let alone correct *location* of practice—parallels the collective subversion of *bodily* norms—the collective overturning of the normative structures of where, what, and how one should perform. Like Bakhtin's analysis of what he terms a carnivalized literature, an approach, as the German literary theorist Renate Lachmann explains, in which "techniques of mixing genres and styles" is paired with "transgressions against decorum, with the treatment of 'extreme' themes and with a parodistic, travestying orientation toward works of high literature" (Lachmann 1988: 142–143), here the image and act become similarly transgressive and perverted, the exploded letter and the explosive practice reflecting and mirroring one another. The ambivalence of the graffiti image too—the image refusing a position as discourse or figure, the image refusing to even divulge its own name—likewise reflects the ambivalence of the carnival practice too: it reveals a practice that is concealed and declared, creation and destruction simultaneously. Like the masked participants, the images too are thus masked; like the concealed names, the participants too are concealed, even as masked text and masked author act as a tool of revelation rather than secrecy alone (as developed further in chapter 8). Moreover, the visual delight held within the image, the sensuous pleasure of the figural-text, likewise corresponds to the sensuous pleasure of the act itself. The participatory mode here is thus one in which a hedonism radiates, a delight generated through the heightened collective emotions that harmonized and intensified practices can generate, an energetic experience that irrevocably attaches those who act together. The graffiti act is one in which a sensuality and carnality are central; as seen in figures 6.11 and 6.12, the anxiety, the fear, the stress of production are channeled out through a decadence and unrivaled joy in which bonds of loyalty develop. It is channeled into a

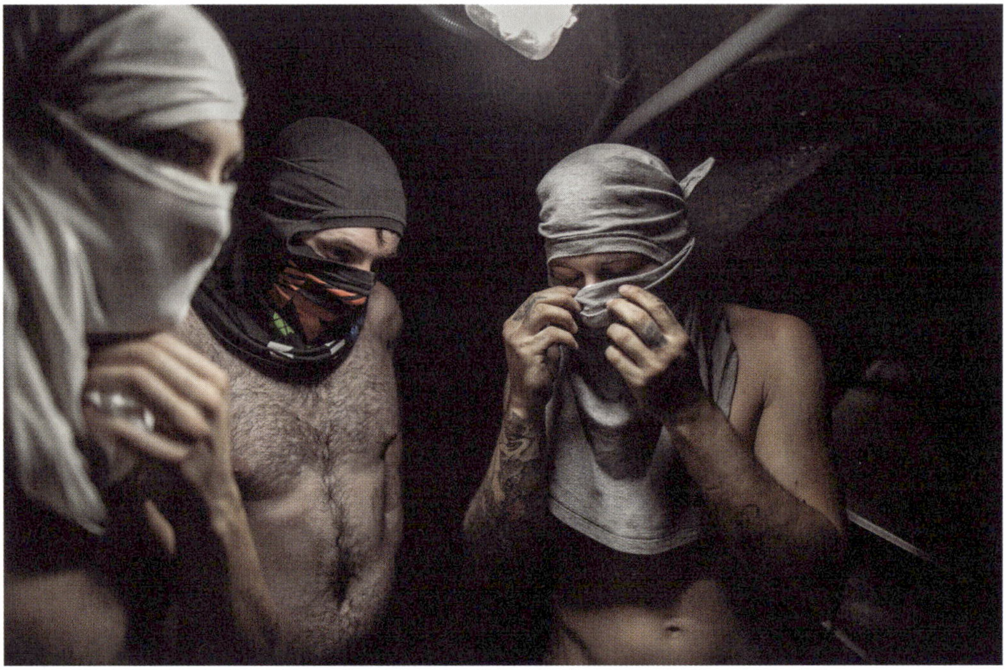

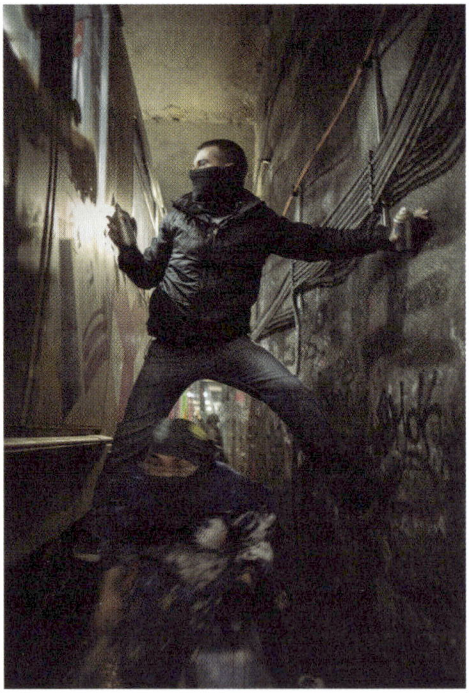

moment in which participants grasp the extremes, together expanding into a place of collective excess. The participatory act here thus becomes gratifying in itself; the collective dangers one faces, the collective energy of exploration and creativity, creating an equality, a solidarity, a subjunctive social space (no matter if one is a "toy" or a "king"). The world upside down, the world of laughter, the world of hedonism is thus emergent in both stylistic and performative terms, the masked and cryptic practice bringing both collective pleasure and collective identity to the fore.

The irreverent collectivity described here is something that can be witnessed within the performance works of Danish artist Christian Falsnaes. Engaging the transcendental potential of group action, Falsnaes's projects—in which gallery goers are enjoined by the artist to share in his self-created, anarchic rituals—come to form ephemeral moments of togetherness in which individuals who may normally be unrelated come to bond through a rejection of everyday regulations (the regulations of the white cube as much as the public sphere). As seen in projects such as *Elixir* (2014) , a performance in which the artist directs his participants through a series of ceremonies whose collective climax leads to a street parade and the illegal spray-painting of an adjacent wall (as seen in figures 6.13 and 6.14), Falsnaes engages a carnival spirit of transformation in which his audience, now his collaborators, becomes bonded through taboo breaking and inversion of normative social acts. It was through his experience within graffiti that Falsnaes's interest in these participatory themes first emerged, however, the endorphin-fueled exorbitance and pleasurable uncertainty he experienced within the collective act of writing being that which he later aimed to provoke in his institutional performances. In his 2012 viral film *Love and Security* (see figures 6.15–6.20), an intervention undertaken in Vienna alongside collaborators Søren Berner and Amos Angeles, Falsnaes tied these two worlds together. In a video piece soundtracked by the artist himself, we see three individuals furtively entering a train depot, navigating the tracks and an underground concrete bunker, before reappearing on the platform, completely in the nude, carrying brightly covered tubes of paint. Proceeding to cover a parked subway train in streams of multicolored pigment, the trio rub themselves erotically against the subway car, undertaking an Yves Klein–style *Anthropometry* painting against the canvas of the train (here using a fire extinguisher filled with blue ink to propel the paint), before being joined by three further nudists in a final anarchic festival of color. The performance shows a space of utter exhilaration. It reveals a moment in which expected patterns of

**FIGURE 6.11**
Enrique Escandell, *Barcelona Subway 2016*. Taken from *Subterráneos* by Enrique Escandell. Courtesy of the artist.

**FIGURE 6.12**
Enrique Escandell, *Madrid Subway 2015*. Taken from *Subterráneos* by Enrique Escandell. Courtesy of the artist.

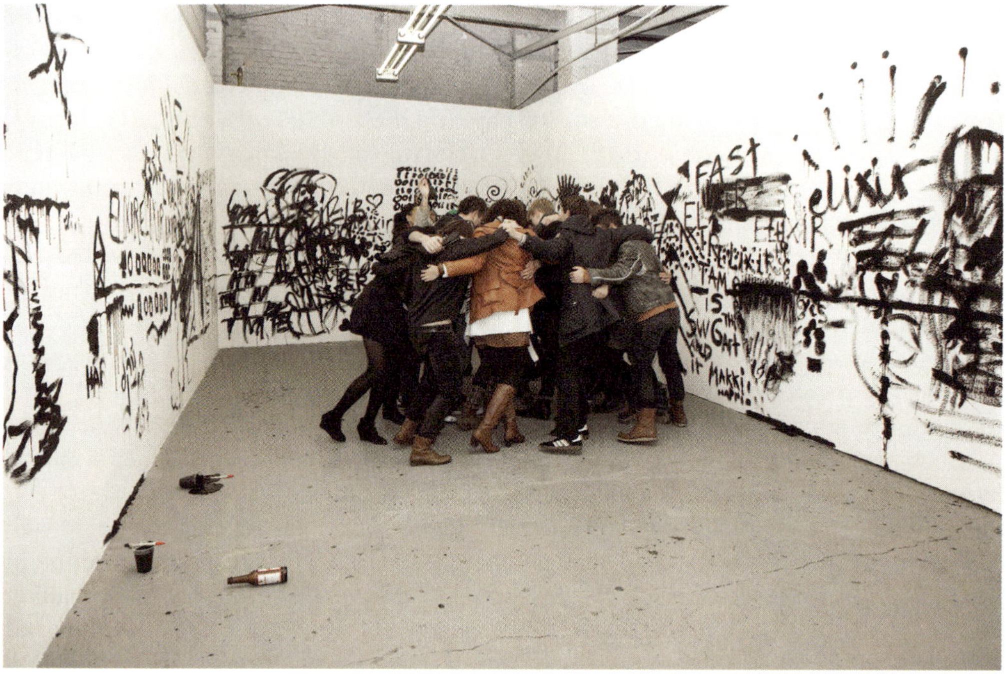


**FIGURE 6.13**
Christian Falsnaes, *Elixir*, 2011. Performance. Photo: Dirk Dunkelberg. Courtesy of PSM, Berlin.

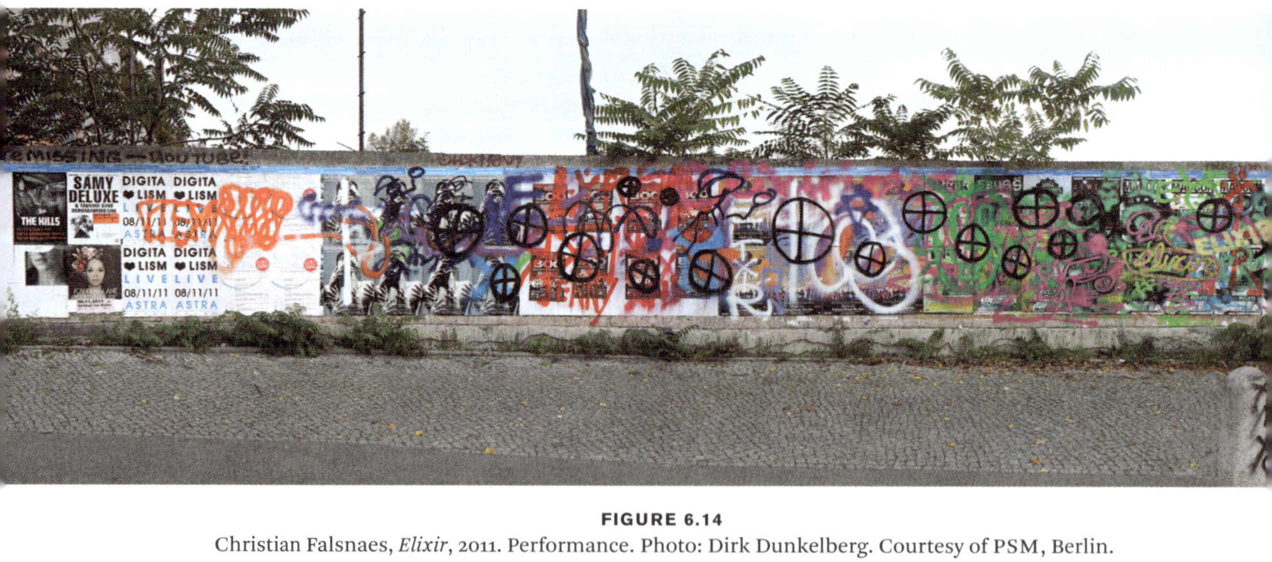


**FIGURE 6.14**
Christian Falsnaes, *Elixir*, 2011. Performance. Photo: Dirk Dunkelberg. Courtesy of PSM, Berlin.

movement and action in the city are entirely rejected, in which fears and vulnerabilities are overcome in an agonistic embracement of action and pleasure. The final refrain of the accompanying song, “it’s a pity only security see our graffiti,” highlights not only the liminality of the event, its status occurring in a site of the margins (even if in the very center), but the overwhelming importance of process, a conceit slyly pointing toward a wider truth: while the works produced in the video are visually captured and thus in many ways eternal, the scenario that Falsnaes melodically recounts is the tale of a graffiti writer who is at peace with this lack of visibility, with the knowledge that their images will (normally) never be seen by the public, will be washed off the train before it ever leaves the depot. What is done is thus done for the collective experience, for its monumental effect not just on the individual but on the group. While a “pity,” the event still takes place because it is the actions themselves that reverberate (rather than the image alone). Unlike the material image, then, the carnival act functions beyond time. It remains within the minds and the bodies of those who performed it in a way the decaying graffiti image itself can never do.

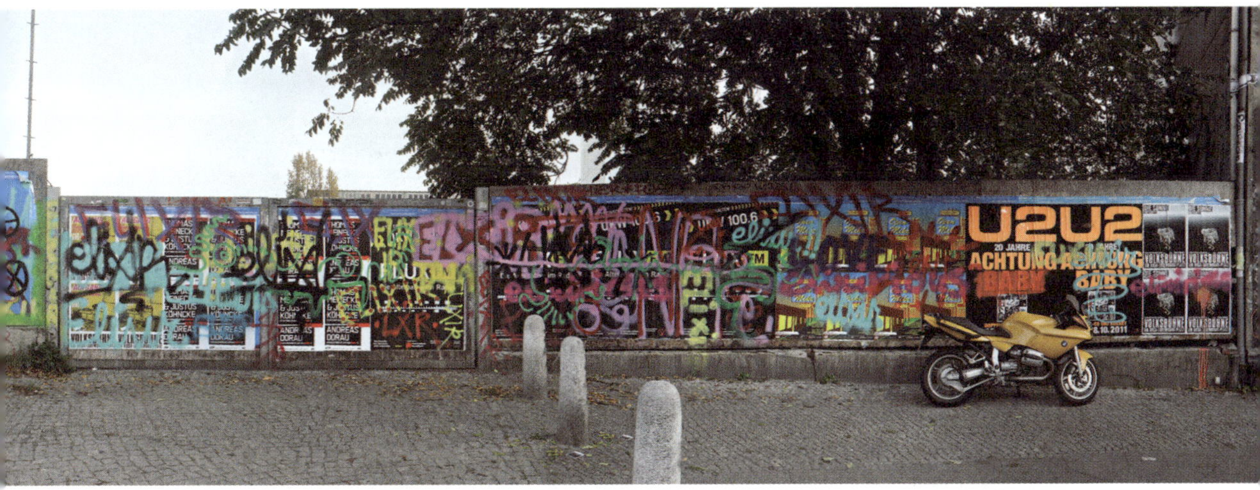

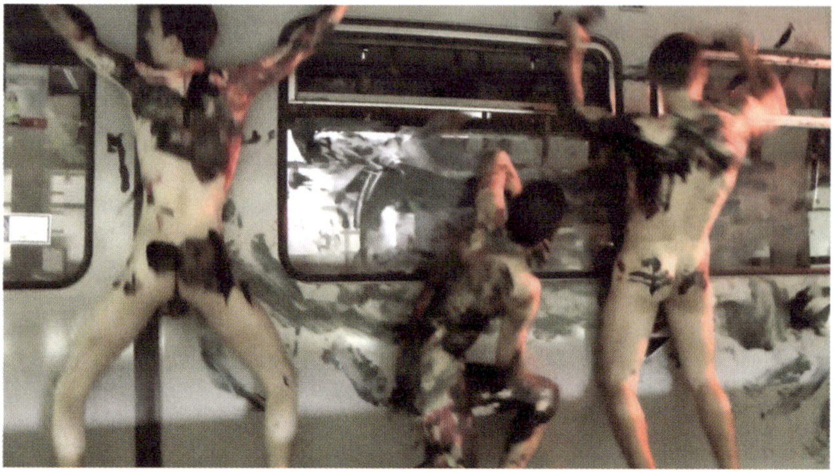

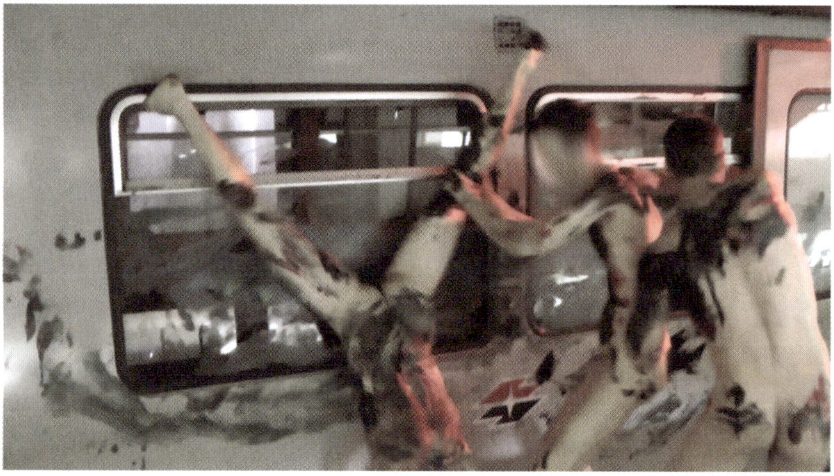

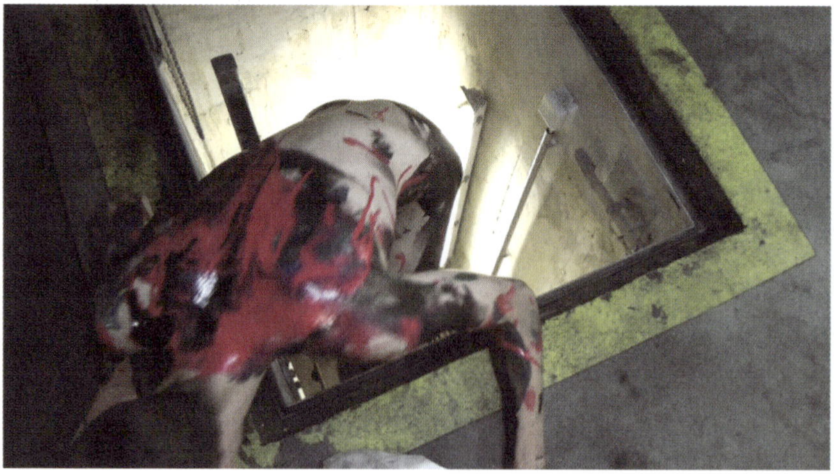

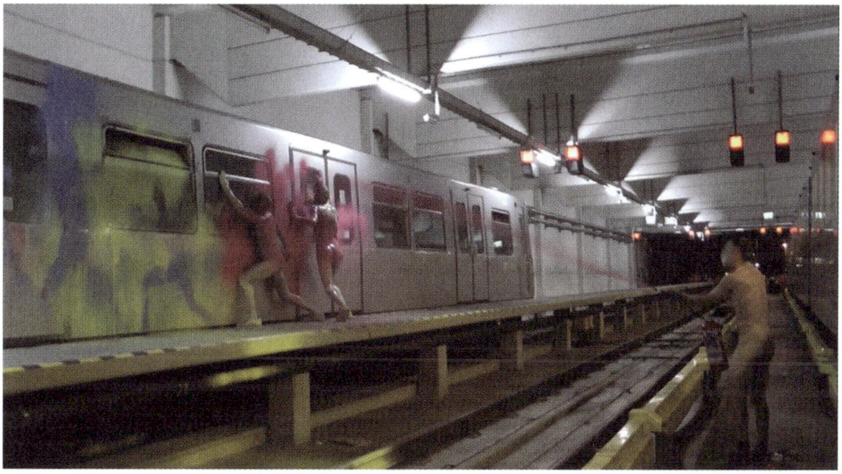

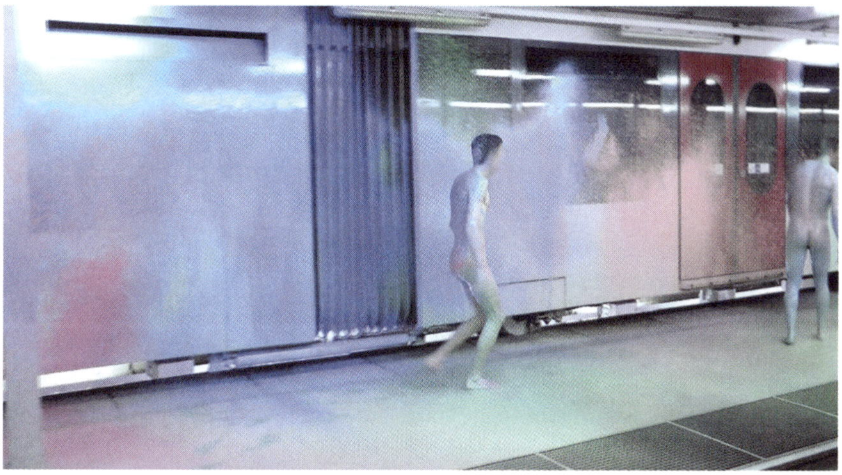

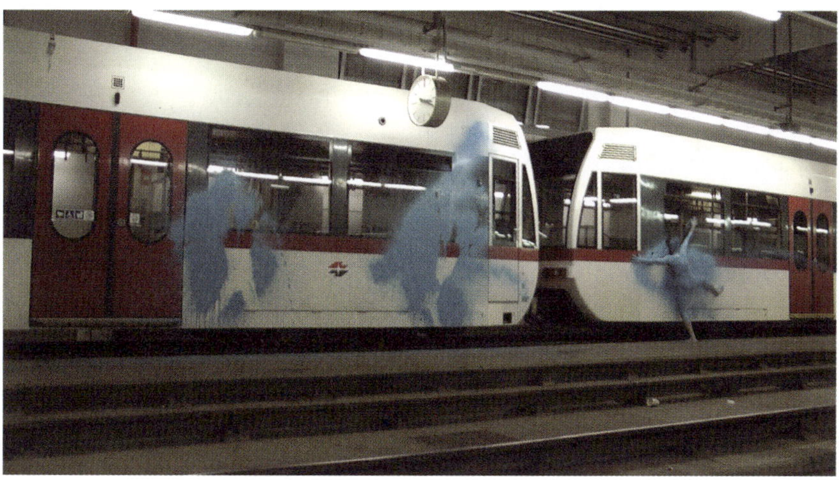

**FIGURES 6.15, 6.16, 6.17, 6.18, 6.19, AND 6.20**
Christian Falsnaes, Søren Berner, and Amos Angeles, still from *Love and Security*, 2012. Video, 3 minutes 39 seconds. Courtesy of the artists.

## DURATIONAL PARTICIPATION

While graffiti's marginal site and stylistic actions direct the way participation occurs, there is no participation outside time, outside the all-embracing element that governs all collective performance. Yet it is in the relationship toward temporality that we see the specific participatory qualities of graffiti, its functioning through a durational rather than archival temporality, through a spontaneous mode of performance rather than a theatrical mode of reenactment. Rather than attempting to enter into or reproduce historical time, to hark back to a previous era or to synthetically relive it, participation in graffiti enters into a time that can never be repeated, a time that is literally *of the moment*. Here time relates not to the invariant re-performance of a text in which exactitude to historical norms is obligatory but to the uniqueness of the collective act in which extemporaneous performance is a ritual necessity for successful completion of the textual act itself. Here, what participation in graffiti says is integrally linked to the when of when it pronounces it. Without this particular approach to time, an approach that accepts the basic impossibility of invariance and the basic necessity of the spontaneous, the graffiti text could never be produced. The mess and unknowability of the margins (of the street) compared with the regularity and stability of the center (of the military square) means that improvisation is always the rule. Instead of the passive participation that emerges through a meticulous adherence to an original composition, through the imitative or participation by rote, here we have a form of action in which performance is sui generis every time it transpires. What we find in the graffiti act is thus not replication (the habitual re-performance) but invention (the unique performance), not the fixed mode of the written archive but the unfixed presence of the now.

This concept of performance, as conceived here by feminist theorist Peggy Phelan, can thus be understood as that which contains a constitutive "inability to be reproduced or repeated" (Phelan 1993: 149), a concept honoring the "idea that a limited number of people in a specific time/space frame can have an experience of value which leaves no visible trace afterward" (p. 149). Not only does *re*-performance thus become a logical impossibility, but performance here is also able to retain a core "independence from mass reproduction, technologically, economically, and linguistically" (p. 149). Not only is it is a practice taking place at the edge of time, but its being *in* time demands its transition to a space perpetually *out* of it. Performance, as Phelan continues, thus disappears "into the realm of invisibility and the unconscious," escapes into a marginal zone from where it "eludes regulation and control" (p. 148). In this way, and from the position of the center, true performance becomes an innate danger to the status quo. The "logic of the archive," as Rebecca Schneider reaffirms, "is that which is recognized as constituting a remain, that which can have been documented or has become document," and, as such, ephemerality comes to be read simply as "vanishment and loss" (Schneider 2011: 98). The classical urge toward intransience (explored in chapter 3) is thus an intrinsically anti-performative impulse. The center needs permanency for legitimacy, requires temporal durability to retain its political authenticity. The monumental logic of the (classical/colonial) archive thus diminishes "other ways of knowing, other modes of remembering" (p. 99). It equates "performance with impermanence, destruction, and loss" rather than with a memory that can be "housed in a body," a memory "housed always in the live," a memory interwoven within a "network of body-to-body transmission of affect and enactment" (pp. 99–100). Durationality, as performance theorist Andre Lepecki has suggested, can thus here be understood not simply as time "*extended*" or "longer than average/expected" but as about time that is "*felt*" (Lepecki 2016: n.p.). Rather than being "measured, assessed, [or] inserted into an economy," durationality emerges via practices that "subvert and subdue chrono-normative time," that disrupt the time of "proper actions, behaviors, [and] perceptions," the time of "specific hours displayed by clocks (the proper time for contemplation, the proper time for consumption, the proper time for working, loving, etc.)" (n.p.). Duration is hence a qualitative time of "intensity," not a quantitative time of longevity but a form of "doing [that] is the undoing of a measured time that above all controls, mediates, and imprisons both subjects and things as objects of measure" (n.p.). Just like the physical *object* of graffiti, then, performance is set in a battle between transience and permanency, set at the margins of the archival and ephemeral both.

But what is it that these different temporal modes facilitate or inhibit? Well, just like the archival/ephemeral dichotomy, here we have a split between spontaneity and the controlled, between an improvised mode in which an unprompted reflexivity is needed and a theatrical mode in which regularity and consistency are the key techniques. Improvisation is an inherently temporal method of practice, a practice that functions, as Elizabeth Hallam and Tim Ingold have explained, not by "the oscillations of a perfectly repeating system such as a clock or metronome" but rather by the "lived and felt . . . pulsating rhythms of life" (Hallam and Ingold 2007: 10). It is thus characterized by its "processes" rather than by its "products" (p. 2), striving toward actions, not ends. As such, and as ritual theorist Catherine Bell argued, while the "least spontaneous activities, those dictated not by the current situation but by inherited or preshaped dispositions and concerns, tend to express the past," the "more spontaneous an action is, the more it is taken to express the present" (Bell 1997: 168). She continues: "Ritual repetition and redundancy, formal language and gestures, and direct and indirect references to an idealized tradition all effectively posit the existence of powerful forces understood as rooted in the past. These forces are invoked in ways that contextualize and subordinate the current moment, thereby ordering the relations of past and present and establishing a sense of continuity, security, and direction" (p. 168). Just as suggested earlier via the work of Bloch, the more constraints we find in ritual and the more set toward the past they appear, the more repressive they can be understood to be. Anachronistic style can hence be seen to go hand in hand with "traditional authority," the "ceremonial trappings of a highly formalized situation," Bloch suggested, coming to "*catch* the actors so they are unable to resist the demands made on them" (Bloch 1989

[1974]: 24). Re-performance thus can be seen not only to live in the past but to signal a societal verticality, a form of "social control" that cannot be "challenged except by a total refusal to use the accepted form" (p. 24).

While participation in the realm of the classical monument presents us with an arthritically fixed text and a staged mode of practice, the production of the graffiti text is a necessarily performative, durational, and improvisatory undertaking. Even if it wanted to, the graffiti act could never be reenacted or reperformed (it would no longer be graffiti if it was). It can *only* be ephemerally produced; its performative process can *only* disappear. The site-specific and temporal nature of the entire act—set in the intensity of the city, set in the surge of time—means that not only the image but the act too is irreproducible. As seen in figure 6.21, as a public act whose energy is forged from its status as a one-time-only event, the moment of production is one in which time resonates and reverberates at a different pace, in which the participant enters inside the time of the ticking clock. The electric feeling of *communitas*, the joyful sensation of togetherness, the collective recognition of working cooperatively on a shared goal, creates an affective, qualitative experience of time, an experience in which graffiti's social rhythms clash with societally normative ones. Yet just as in the practices of the margins, here too there is a wide variation in the range of affectivity formed. Most commonly taking place during the dark hours of the night, during a time in which one should not be awake let alone undertaking collective action, during a time in which the shadows help one's furtivity and provide a nocturnal liminality (as seen in figure 6.22), graffiti engages a temporal mode that commonly rejects the instrumental necessity of the clock. While a train-painting mission may necessitate knowledge of rail schedules and surveillance routines and thus an instrumentally motivated temporal attention, practices are still about leisure, not labor; about experiential, not financial, gain. Moreover, the drama of the act creates an animation in which every moment is intensified. It creates a collective flow, a communal feeling of intensity and a hyper-focused absorption in which time runs at a different measure. Time is charged: a second may feel like an hour (straining to hear for sounds, an hour feeling like seconds (gone before you even realize it). The hyper-focused absorption of flow means that whole nights can disappear in what seem to be less than a moment, while a moment of danger may take forever to end. Like all performance, as Phelan beautifully describes, graffiti thus "plunges into visibility—in a maniacally charged present" (Phelan 1993: 148). It is clock time subverted, as Lepecki earlier stressed, a "co-formation of endurance—a lingering in a shared plane of experience" (Lepecki 2016: n.p.). The participatory act here is thus one that is not only singular, inimitable, but one in which the experience of time is set within the flow, in the collective "experience," as Turner here explains via the work of psychologist Mihaly Csikszentmihalyi, emergent "when people act with total involvement" (Turner 1979: 487). The collective act of graffiti thus creates a temporal frame in which participation needs "no goals or rewards outside itself." To "flow," as Csikszentmihalyi concludes, is thus "its own reward: is to be as happy as a human being can be" (p. 488).

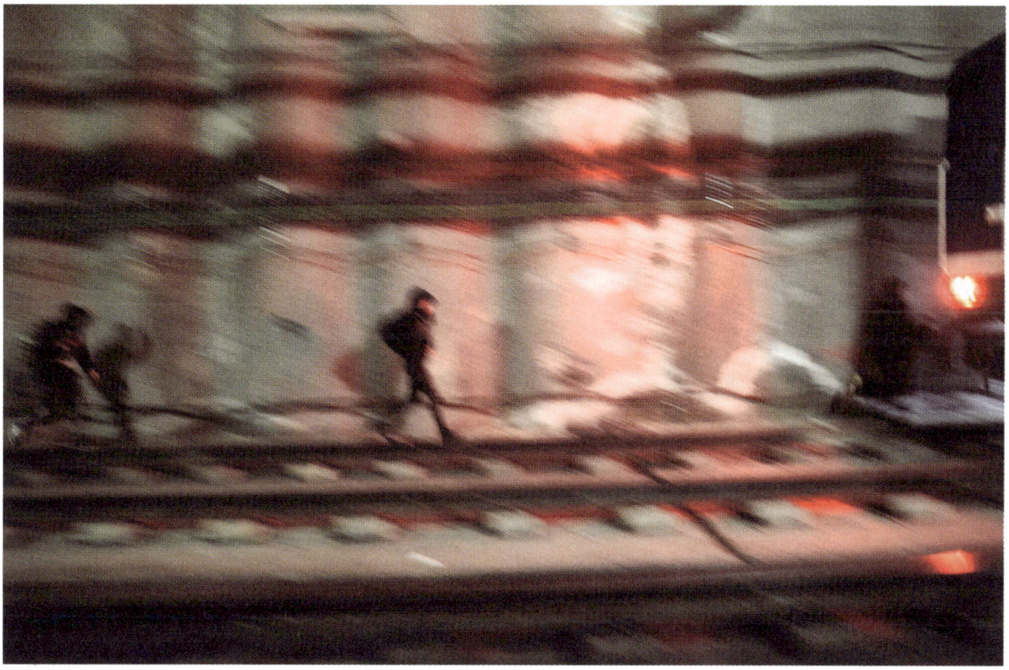

**FIGURE 6.21**
Enrique Escandell, *Madrid Subway 2018*. Courtesy of El País Semanal and the artist.

Just as temporal performativity and durational flow disrupt the fixity of the archival, of a performance in which time looks into the past, graffiti's *improvised* practice disrupts the purity of composition, the performative integrity of an iterative text. The ever-changing character of graffiti's site means that spontaneity is prerequisite for action itself. While writers will commonly start with a sketch if producing larger works and will spend hours practicing in sketch books at home, a drawing on paper can never account for the natural and human forces that determine how site-specific performance actually occurs. Writers must therefore work flexibly alongside their surrounds or work not at all. They must respond and react to the ever-changing conditions, not slavishly follow a composed text irrespective of the reality of the world around them (an approach that can only ever lead to failure). While fixed composition needs to artificially freeze time, to create a vacuum in which nothing ever changes and thus exact replication becomes (close to) possible, here the formation of a vacuum is an unviable (if ever desirable) aim. Practice is not about reaching perfection but about dynamism, about entering into the present tense. Yet true improvisation is a task not only completed by the individual body but so too by the collective one. Working together to control one's environment, working as a team yet needing to constantly modify one's own practice for the greater good, improvisation can be appreciated not only to involve a high degree

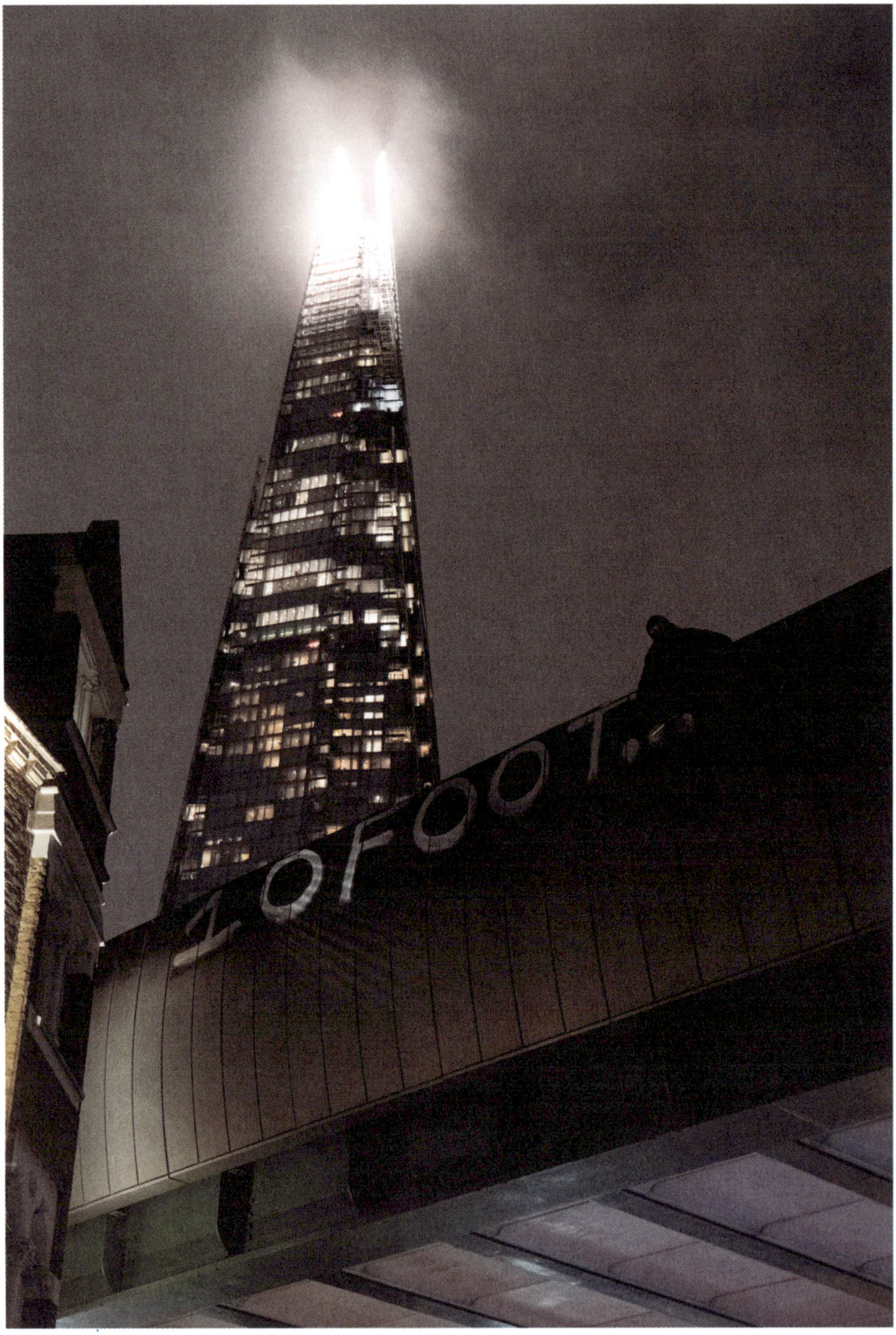


**FIGURE 6.22**
R Seventeen | sory.world, *10Foot'22*, 2022. Courtesy of the artists.

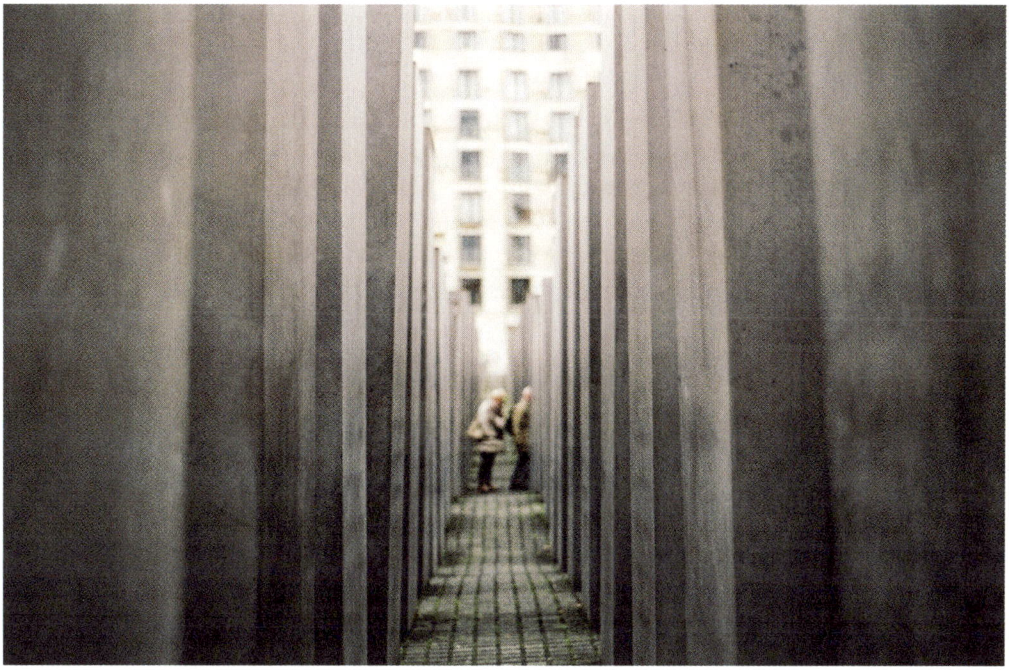

**FIGURE 6.23**
Peter Eisenman, *The Memorial to the Murdered Jews of Europe*, Berlin, 2005. Photo: Crazy Zoc. License Creative Commons Attribution-Share Alike 3.0 Unported license.

of skill and planning but to take true coevality to achieve. Time must be shared here. Like a group of musicians, each member of the collective must remain in time with one another, remain in tune, in harmony, in rhythm, or the whole structure will collapse. They not only must be attentive, alive to one another's positions and movements completely, but for the time of the performance must become as one, must act beyond the acts of the self alone. Like the skilled activities explored by Marchand, successful participation can thus only emerge through a fluid exchange of bodily knowledge, through working "in a coordinated manner, each interpreting and responding to the activities of the other" (Marchand 2008: 263). As seen in activities such as "team sports, dancing, martial arts, combat, courting and lovemaking, building and creating things" (p. 263), it is not a collective of individuals but a collective in itself that is aimed for. It is the singular "we," not the plural "I," that is desired.

Yet architectural spaces too can come to forment particular relationships to duration and participation. In Peter Eisenman's *Memorial for the Murdered Jews of Europe* in Berlin, for example (see figure 6.23), there is an explicit rejection of the stringent choreography of the institutional monument and a movement toward a space of open possibility. Attempting to shift the model of monumental participation from an arena of spectacularity (and bodily formality) to that of affectivity (and bodily autonomy), the memorial, as Eisenman himself has said, strived to "deny opticality" and rather prioritize tactility, to focus on a sensation of "pure presence" over any direct discursive idea (Blackwood 2005: n.p.). Not only is all symbolism and all representational form here denied, but the physical structure of the monument means that participation simply cannot happen through mass choreography or mass spectacle; the architecture of the space denies it. Participation is thus left entirely unstructured. There is no tradition or formalism here. There is only being, a being that exists through a bodily encounter with space. While the unbound participation at the site is for many considered sacrilegious,[8] the lack of fixity corresponds to the idea of memory itself as being ongoing rather than fixed. Participants thus do not reenact history here but live through the body in the present. As Eisenman himself has maintained, the architectural instability of the site "denotes a difference in the notion of time," a space not full of "nostalgia" or "sentimentality" but rather a "living memory, active in the present" (Eisenman n.d.: n.p.). Rather than the traditional "time of the monument," of the monument "seen and understood at the same time," what Eisenman attempted to create here was a time in which all that is available is the "vivid memory of individual experience" (n.p.). Memory here is thus set in a durational, not archival, mode.

## CONCLUSION *OR* APPEARANCE VERSUS ASSEMBLAGE

It is always hard to talk about something felt, to not destroy the magic of performance in trying to relay it in text. Yet so too images, as Claire Bishop has said in a discussion on participatory art, rarely provide "more than fragmentary evidence," and rarely convey the "affective dynamic that propels artists to make these projects and people to participate in them" (Bishop 2012: 5). The ideas that these hidden practices of participatory art often emphasize—"a group dynamic, a social situation, a change of energy, a raised consciousness" (p. 6)—are thus incredibly hard to reveal without one's own direct participation.[9] Still, and in its most archetypal state, not only is collaboration in graffiti hugely valorized within the subculture itself, but participation functions in almost total opposition to that observed within the institutional monument. Here participation occurs in a marginal, not central, site. Here its style is of the carnival rather than the ritualesque, is joyful and pleasurable, not somber and melancholy; irreverent, not invariant; agentic, not submissive. Here participation is improvised rather than pre-composed, is durational and ephemeral, not theatrical and archival. While participation within the classical monument is incredibly effective, then, its effectiveness works through overwhelming the individual, through dominance, not agency. As discussed earlier by Sharon Macdonald in her work on the Nazi rally-ground in Nuremberg, it was the "subsuming [of] individual identity to the collective project" that was here desired, a "strict choreography" and a "grouping of bodies" that generated "emotional effects on both participants and viewers" (Macdonald 2006: 111–112). The "controlled spectacle," as

Osbourne similarly notes, of "marches, pageants, mass meetings and party rallies," can thus be understood as a mechanism through which both "viewers and participants" come to act as "cogs in the collective machine of the state" (Osbourne 2001: n.p.). While imitation can thus be a powerful way of creating a link with ancestors, a way of becoming part of a historical flow, it is often harnessed as part of an unescapably domineering participatory tool.

The participatory mode created within graffiti, however, is one in which collective identity is forged and subcultural membership maintained via a form of implicitly anti-spectacular collective action. While the graffiti image functions through its public appearance—the image, like the body it physically re-presents, functioning through its visibility—the participatory act of graffiti emerges via what I term a mode of participatory *assemblage*. The image may demonstrate and point out, yet the collective practice coalesces and confirms. While appearance (an outward visibility) thus functions as a form of public exhibition (or often protestation) and moves centrifugally, assemblage (an inward sociality) functions via an act of social relationality that is figured centripetally. Assemblage is hence not about the wider public who may see the producers or their images, the outer public of fellow city inhabitants; it is about the inner group, the subcultural public who enact the practice themselves. It is not about spectators; it is about each other. The experience of gathering together is thus inward- not outward-facing. While most participatory acts thus move on a sliding scale between these two edges, between appearance and assemblage, visibility and sociality, within graffiti (and within many other liminoid rituals) the scale is a proportionally inversive one. The more visibility there is, the equivalently less sociality; the less visibility, the equivalently *more* sociality (as seen in figure 6.24). Here, then, we move from total spectacle (at the top left of the figure)—from a participatory passivity in which our bodies become a mechanized tool for others' optical consumption, a form of participation which is about mass and power—to a public invisibility that means total sociality (at the bottom right)—a *lack* of appearance that enables *communitas* and affectivity, a lack that provides a participatory collectivity and flow. It is thus inward ritual rather than outward spectacle we find in graffiti's participatory act, a form of total assemblage not meant for others, a form of being together in which real kinship can be achieved. Participatory marginality thus provides a place outside the center in which horizontal ways of being together can obtain. The carnivalesque produces a space of elation and hedonism that not only rejects the submissive tradition of the ritualesque but forges fierce moments of collectivity that remain in the mind long after their ephemeral moment has passed. And durationality creates not only an unrepeatable, spontaneous mode of performance, but an entrance into the dynamism of the present tense necessitating the discovery of the singular "we." The graffiti monument here thus becomes, as Debray has said, "the tool par excellence for community production" (Debray 1999: 28), a participatory monument in which community is sustained through social as much as material means, through hidden rather than visible techniques. As seen with our ravers (in the marginal liberation from the strictures of social structure), as seen in the performances of Falsnaes (in

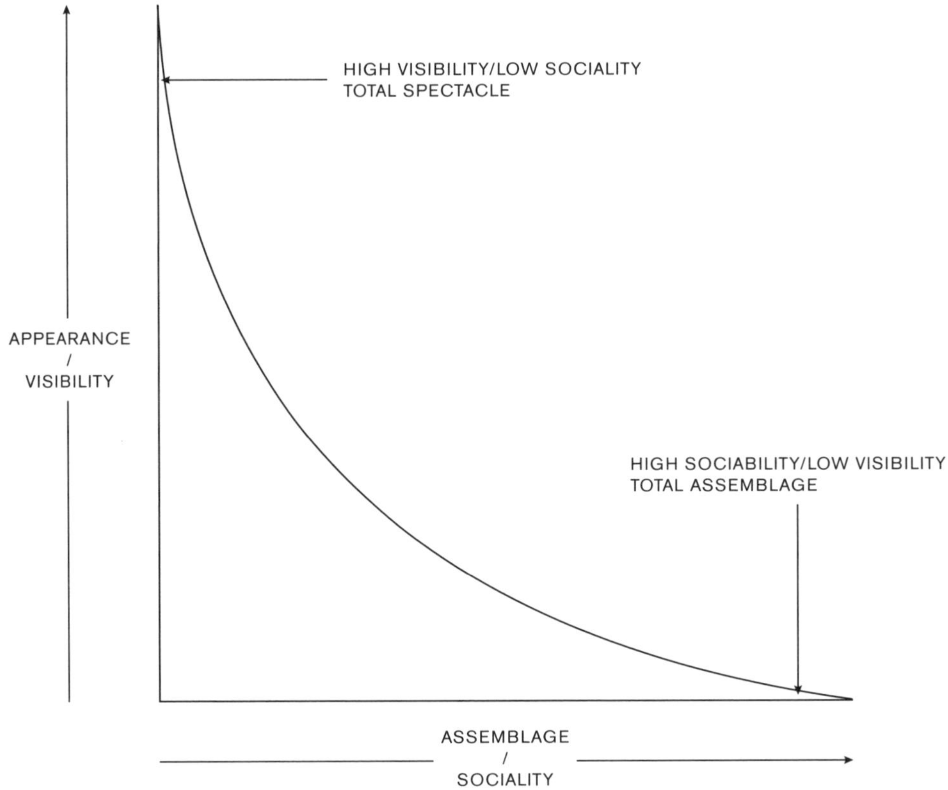


**FIGURE 6.24**
Assemblage versus appearance.

the carnivalesque, effervescent, experience), or in the architectural spaces of Eisenman (in the durational and spontaneous acts), graffiti may be fugitive, may be liminal, may be performative or ephemeral, yet it remains monumental nonetheless.

While participation in graffiti has thus commonly been understood as no participation at all, here we can see it as a "non-institutionalized, innovative, marginal" form of participation that, like the many forms of marginalized (youth) practices explored by Ilaria Pitti, Yagmur Mengilli, and Andreas Walther, not only have commonly had their "democratic potential" denied but also have been "stigmatized and criminalized" by authorities (Pitti et al. 2021: 5). Yet participation in graffiti is of an active and voluntary nature, a form of participation that can underscore, as anthropologist and information technologist Chris Kelty has discussed, not only "a sense of autonomy and equality" but likewise "a way of challenging authority . . . by emphasizing bottom-up instead of top-down knowledge and planning" (Kelty 2017: 81). Participation can thus often be seen as the "solution to our most practical concerns or even an ethical calling," yet at other moments becomes "a containment strategy designed to keep us chillingly in place" (p. 77). Participation can thus be voluntary or involuntary, can emerge with or without out control, its participatory grammar, as Kelty terms it, moving rapidly from the optative to the exploitative, from convivial to agonistic and back again. Bishop's juxtaposition of the social practice work of both Anthony Gormley and Thomas Hirschhorn is highly instructive here. For her, Gormley's 2009 project *One and Other* on the Fourth Plinth in Trafalgar Square revealed a form of participation in which spectacle and a participatory subservience were the dominant frame. While attempting to promote a more democratic form of participation through giving over the plinth space to 2,400 individual participants—each of whom was given one hour to communicate with the world (not just at the site itself but live-streamed online)—Bishop saw this as a project not of "mass empowerment" but rather of an "endless stream of egos levelled to banality" (Bishop 2012: 277). "Far from being oppositional to spectacle," Bishop argued, here "participation has now entirely merged with it" (p. 277), the bombastic individualism of the supposedly collective work mirroring the triviality and individuality of reality TV. In Hirschhorn's participatory works, however, in particular within his series of celebrated monuments, Bishop saw a "shared experience in which many different sectors of society were brought together," a space in which everyone "was there for no reason other than the desire to see and do the same thing" (p. 263). Here, then, the project was not just about the "content of what was being produced," but rather held a "meaning [that] lay in everyone's continual production and collective presence" (p. 264). Participation here was thus a temporal, durational act refusing the superficial and the spectacular both.

In Hirschhorn's most recent iteration of the series, the *Gramsci Monument*,[10] produced in New York in 2018 (see figures 6.25–6.28), we can in fact find not only the perfect participatory monument for this chapter, but likewise a radical technique of monumentality that speaks to the themes of our five preceding chapters too. Set upon the grounds of Forest Houses, a public housing complex in the South Bronx, the *Gramsci Monument* was an 8,000-square-foot public sculpture produced in partnership with the inhabitants of the project that lasted for seventy-seven days over one summer. Collectively constructing what appeared to be an overgrown treehouse, a set of sprawling pavilions made from pallets, plywood, tarpaulin, and duct tape, the monument contained a public radio station, a library, art workshop, café, bar, lounge, exhibition space, and public stage for performances, providing a space of constant activity and engagement for locals and visitors alike; a site of play, learning, craft workshops, and public lectures; a place of conversation, music, eating and socializing, drinking and debate. The Monument was set in a marginal site, its architecture both interruptive and yet integrally human-scaled. It intervened in a space while retaining an everyday, nonintimidating, provisional style. Its agency was distributed among its collection of shared authors and its temporality transient, relational, ephemeral. Its materials were subject to decay, its presence a memory burned through experience. It enabled new platforms for speaking

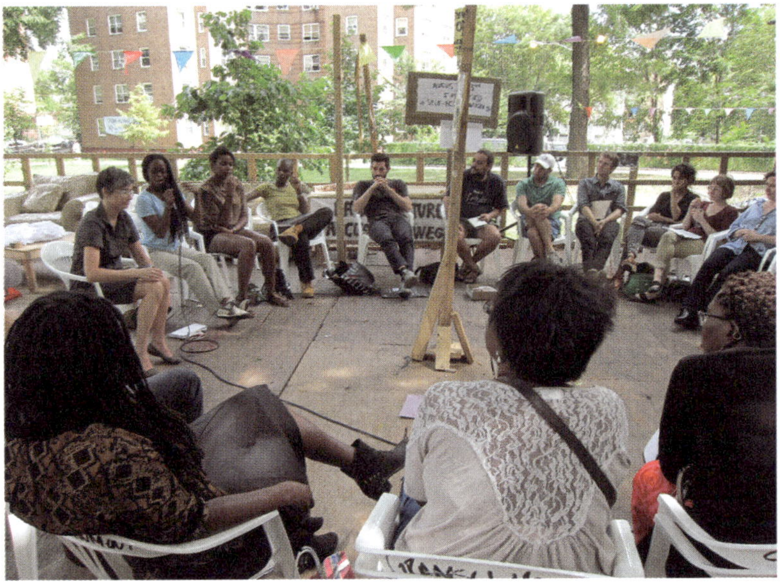

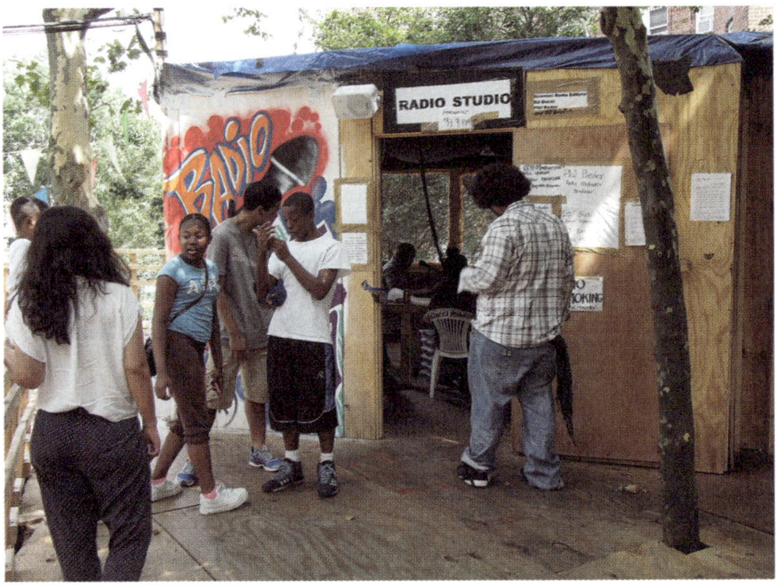


**FIGURE 6.25**

Thomas Hirschhorn, "Gramsci Monument," 2013 *(Art School: Energy = Yes! Quality = No!)*. Forest Houses, Bronx, New York. Courtesy of the Dia Art Foundation, New York. Photo: Romain Lopez.

**FIGURE 6.26**

Thomas Hirschhorn, "Gramsci Monument," 2013 *(Radio Studio)*. Forest Houses, Bronx, New York. Courtesy of the Dia Art Foundation, New York. Photo: Romain Lopez.

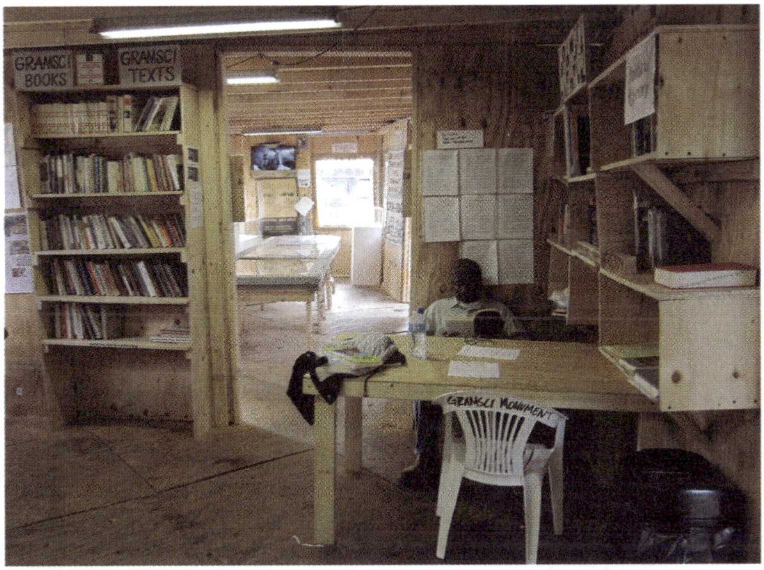


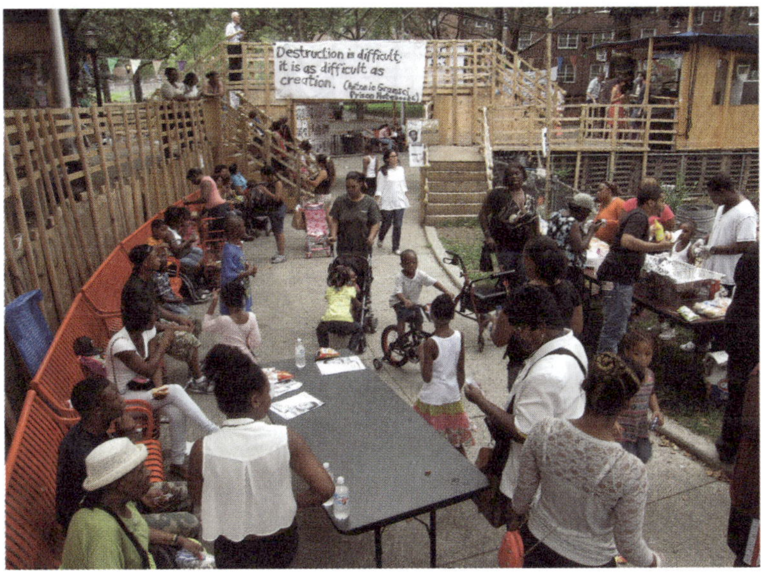


**FIGURE 6.27**
Thomas Hirschhorn, "Gramsci Monument," 2013 *(Gramsci Archive and Library)*. Forest Houses, Bronx, New York. Courtesy of the Dia Art Foundation, New York. Photo: Romain Lopez.

**FIGURE 6.28**
Thomas Hirschhorn, "Gramsci Monument," 2013 *(School Supplies Distribution by Forest Resident Association)*. Forest Houses, Bronx, New York. Courtesy of the Dia Art Foundation, New York. Photo: Romain Lopez.

and acting, for assembling together inwardly. And it formed a participation in the present tense, a participation without requisite norms of behavior, without invariant performance; a participation forming an improvised and horizontal collectivity of choice.

Hirschhorn's Monument thus privileged the experience of pleasure and enabled people to experience this coevally. Not only rejecting the traditional location, materials, temporalities, and styles of the institutional monument, the project likewise chose not to symbolize or artifactually represent the hero eponymously recognized in the work's title, to not put Gramsci on a pedestal, to set his work into stone or his life into the space of the mythic. Rather, as Simon Sheikh suggested of Hirschhorn's first three Monuments (to Baruch Spinoza, Georges Bataille, and Gilles Deleuze respectively, three other philosopher heroes of Hirschhorn's), the projects sought to "actualise the thoughts and ideas of the philosophers rather than commemorate them," to invest their "thoughts and ideas in the present . . . to give form to ideas, to make them manifest and provide them with albeit a temporary space" (Sheikh 2004: 94). The monuments thus present us with a "presence, or immanence," an ephemeral structure designed to be "there for use, for interaction rather than reverence" (p. 94). As Hirschhorn himself said, the *Gramsci Monument* not only created communal rather than just individual commitments, but acted as a "precarious form of friendship . . . beyond argumentation, beyond proof, beyond guarantee . . . a monument built in and with Friendship" (Hirschhorn and Raymond 2016: n.p.). This was a monument that was thus about encounter. About commitment, engagement, presence, *being*. Not just marginality, agency, captivation, transience, dialogue, collectivity, open-endedness, experience, but so too a bodily commitment made in time, made together, made in full view of one another. Participation is here a practice of allegiance, is a commitment visible to one another if not to the city as a whole.

The ritual of assemblage we thus see in graffiti, like the monument to collective action that Hirschhorn formed in the Bronx, is one that not only says "I commit," but also says, "*We* commit together." Participation (with full cognizance of the risks that participation entails) creates a bond between participants that cannot be achieved through any other technique. Marginality, the carnivalesque, and performativity give rise to *communitas*, to affectivity, joy, flow, simultaneity. And all these elements together forge an inward assemblage that maintains kindship and collective identity. Participation creates mutuality. Acting in concert proves rather than represents one's affiliation, publicly evidences one's responsibilities to one's crew. Participation demonstrates and performs belief. Beauty thus emerges not only via the quality of the monument or via the quantity of distribution, but via the togetherness that emerges in collective practice, in the reciprocal harmony of mutual action. Beauty comes from commitment, from sensorial collaboration and kinesthetic interaction, from the giving to one another that true commitment necessitates. Beauty comes from an affective event of the moment that speaks of the microcosmic moment of the now. Beauty comes from a participation occurring outside a space of centrality and visibility and through a monument that becomes more effective and affective explicitly due to that fact.

# III
# TRACE

Part III will focus on graffiti as a revelatory and reflexive artifact. It will explore it as a trace (from Latin *tractus*, a "drawing out") exposing the increasing privatization, surveillance, and spectacularization of the urban realm. It will thus center on the city as the ecological frame from which graffiti emerges, exploring graffiti as a monument both made by, and in turn making, the landscape to which it is ineradicably affixed.

Chapter 7, "Publicity and Privacy," will unpack the contradictions between exposure and restriction that graffiti outlines. Exploring the city as a site of borders and boundaries, it will examine privately owned public spaces, the designing-out of diversity as well as the privatizing of public space and practices alike. Here, however, the artistic reaction we will follow will be seen to encompass tactics of both trespass and amelioration, practices that seek to publicize the private and turn private spaces back into common-use. Chapter 8, "Visibility and Invisibility," surveys the way graffiti evidences the decreasing privacy of the contemporary city. Investigating the ambiguities of appearance, the public exhibition of the graffiti image and the concomitant concealment of the graffiti body, the chapter will explore the city as a surveilled, panoptic site. Here we will address the way artists engage visible-invisibility alongside tactical modes of *sous-* and *meta*-veillance. And chapter 9, "Spectacularity and Temporality," will consider the themes of both privatization in chapter 7 and visibility in chapter 8 through an exploration of the "creative" and "heritage" cities so prevalent in urban sites around the world. Examining the touristification and gentrification that these modalities enable, the focus will be on the nostalgic and kitsch relationship to the past and future they form. Here, however, it will be artistic techniques of erasure and the anti-spectacular we will find, a method of rejection over compliance enlisted to combat the spectacularized city. The monument revealed in part III will hence not emerge through a formal or a bodily structure, but rather exist through the construction of a "milieu, a know-how or a style" (Debray 1999: 34). It is thus a monument to the space of the border, to a mode of (in)visibility, to a technique of (anti)spectacularity we will see here, a monument-warning indexically marking out the prevailing conditions of the city itself.

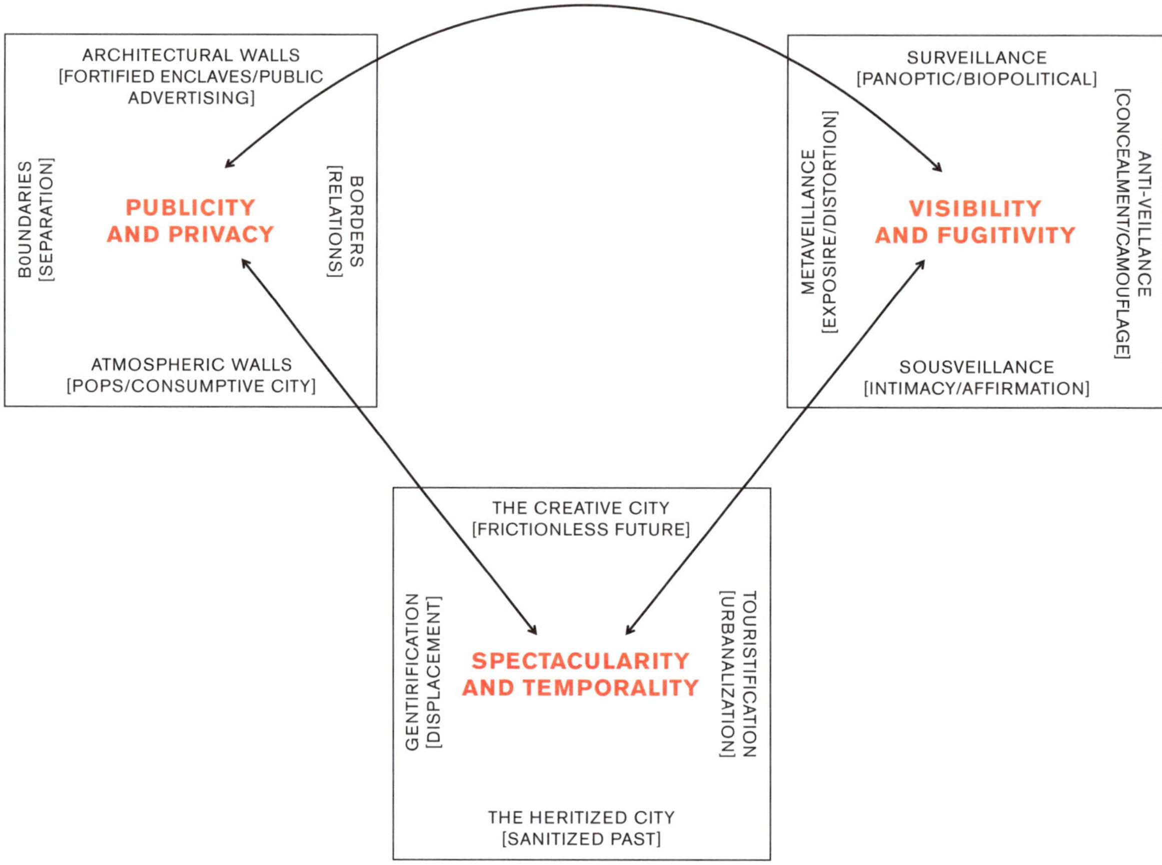


**FIGURE III.1**
Graffiti as trace.

# 7
# PUBLICITY AND PRIVACY

Graffiti plays at the edge of where private starts and public stops, tracing the ambiguities of these most fundamental of urban concepts. It positions itself in a zone that is neither/nor and both/and, in which its public or private ascription is, more often than not, determined by the beholder alone. Whether believed to be situated on a surface that is accessible or restricted, believed to insert individual interests into a collective space or communal messages into a privatized sphere, the material appearance of graffiti complicates the distinctions between what are often imagined to be diametrically opposed forms. The very understanding of public and private that graffiti writers have thus rubs up against the social norms and legal codes that dominate our understanding of this binary today. As such, through exploring the way graffiti emerges at the space set between public and private, we will here unpack the way techniques of restriction and exposure are employed (and rejected) by institutional and noninstitutional forces alike. This chapter will thus focus on both the architectural and atmospheric walls the contemporary city erects, exploring the way that the city comes to delimit heterogeneity through its fortified enclaves and hostile environments, through both public advertising and privately owned public spaces alike. At the same time, however, it is not only spatial privatization that will be examined but likewise the increasingly fluid segmentation of the public sphere. While the ability to be present in the city has always been subject to barriers of race, gender, age, and physical ability, it will be through processes of trespass and spatial appropriation that questions around publicity and privacy will here be seen to be raised. The monument, in this case, emerges not only as that which classically attempts to segregate who is able to access where (as much as who that very public is) but as a monument-*warning* tracing the ongoing transformation of the city itself.

## PUBLIC VERSUS PRIVATE

Often used as if their definitions are self-explanatory, public and private hold together a myriad of connotations, each not only historically and geographically specific, but related to particular ways of understanding our social, spatial, political, and economic worlds. While there is a general distinction made between outside and inside, collectivity and individuality, accessibility and containment (with public at the former and private at the latter part of these binaries), we likewise have interpretations that distinguish the public of the state from the private of the family, the public of the plaza from the private of the market, yet so too that which separates the public of the people (the oddly termed "general" public) from the private of the previously deemed public state! The more one unpacks the terms, then, the more interwoven they begin to appear.

In a discussion of the indefinite boundaries (and mobilities) of the terms, Mimi Sheller and John Urry outlined a set of three models that illuminate the ways "public" and "private" are commonly used. In the first case, they present a legally grounded "liberal-economistic model" that contrasts the self-motivated interests of the private sector with a public sector driven by the greater good. In the second, they present a Habermasian model of spheres in which "public" is understood as the civic space of opinion formation and rational debate set between state, market, and family. And in the third the authors explore a spatial model in which public is understood as a site of open congregation, a site of "streets, parks and plazas" in contrast to the zone of the "domestic, the familial, the personal, the bodily and the intimate" (Sheller and Urry 2003: 112). Yet each of these models exists in a state of constant flux. Just as the interests of the state can be motivated by private bodies, these same private bodies increasingly dominate our "public" infrastructure, while seemingly private individuals or organizations can undertake civically driven public acts. Spheres too are never rigid, a marginalized collective's inclusion within what is determined as "public" inevitably necessitating a fight for recognition (let alone a forcing of "private" issues into public), while the private "logics of economic commodification and state bureaucratization" (p. 111) have come to invade public and private spheres too. Spaces have likewise always been permeable: not only has the private space of the home succumbed to the "unavoidable intervention of the modern welfare state" (p. 112), but the increasingly prevalent "'property rights' approach" to public space, as argued by Margaret Kohn (2004), means that what is normatively deemed public is often legally understood as "private space owned by the government" and thus a space in which the "responsible bureaucracy has discretion to regulate or forbid citizens' access" (p. 4).

The various definitions that public and private are centered within—whether of interests, spheres, or spaces—are hence not only ineradicably intertwined and constantly shifting in relation to one another, but each likewise defined by access. As such, it is not simply their conceptual separation but our active capacity to be recognized as public in the eyes of the law, to participate in public debate, and to appear in public space that becomes critical to our life in the city. The ancient Greek sites of the *polis* and the *agora*, for example, often seen, as Neil Smith and Setha Low have argued, as the critical "prototypes of the public sphere and public space," were themselves "not defined against the ubiquity of private, capitalised space but vis-à-vis far more collective uses of space" (Smith and Low 2013: 4). The famous "publicness of the agora," they continue, was thus an "expression of prevailing social relations and inequalities," only a very "narrow and privileged social class [being] recognised as free citizens [while] many others were excluded—women, slaves, and the throng of common people" (p. 4). The *hoi polloi* of the agora, the literal *many* or *masses*, were thus in reality the few. The "public" here meant the private body of propertied citizens, and access to this space of "freedom" was entirely determined by inequitable relations of power. While "public" thus does not necessarily mean free, the flip side to its common-sense conception as "open" is the prevailing sense of it as a space of "overwhelming-vulnerability" (Bickford 2000: 358). Often set in contrast to the idea of the private as a site of "safety, and control," a site "where the unfamiliar is absent and compromise unnecessary" (Kohn 2004: 5), this pervasive binary supports a deeply inegalitarian and reductive conception of publicness. Not only is the home often a site of male violence and patriarchal hierarchy, a place, for many women, of labor and domestic employment, but likewise one's private acts in private space, especially if nonconformative to heteronormative standards, have themselves often been considered to be of "public" interest.[1] Yet the very sense of "risk, uncertainty, and incompleteness" that this concept of the public elicits can be seen to link to the "diverse perspectives" it contains, to the public as a site of "complexity or unexpectedness," a site of "that which is puzzling, different, or new" (Bickford 2000: 357). To be in public could, at the least, be understood as to be subject to difference—yet the reactions to this difference can be either welcoming or fearful ones. Yet this sense of heterogeneity and multiplicity that the city often connotes is one that can, as Bickford argues via the work of Richard Sennett, be "erected, sustained, and reflected in city design and architecture" (p. 357). Our contemporary publics thus not only trace their inequalities, but their diversity, just like their homogeneity, is physically built, created by spaces that allow no single point of view or perspective to dominate, by spaces that offer horizontal rather than vertical modes of both being and seeing. So how does contemporary urban design and architecture (including our public monuments) contribute toward these shifting conceptions of public and private? Do they demarcate the private or initiate a public? Do they promote or delimit access? Do they support or stifle debate? Do they engage or prevent participation?

## ARCHITECTURAL WALLS

The most obvious way of creating a boundary between public and private is the wall (as seen in Escif's emblematic work in figure 7.1). Like the fortification or the enclosure, walls separate in from out, here from there, us from them. Acting to control movement and regulate access, to both constrain and enfold us, the wall is at the foundation of the city itself—the ancient Greek term *polls*, as Arendt noted, originally connoting "a 'ring-wall,'" while the German term *zaun*, the origin of the word "town," meaning "a

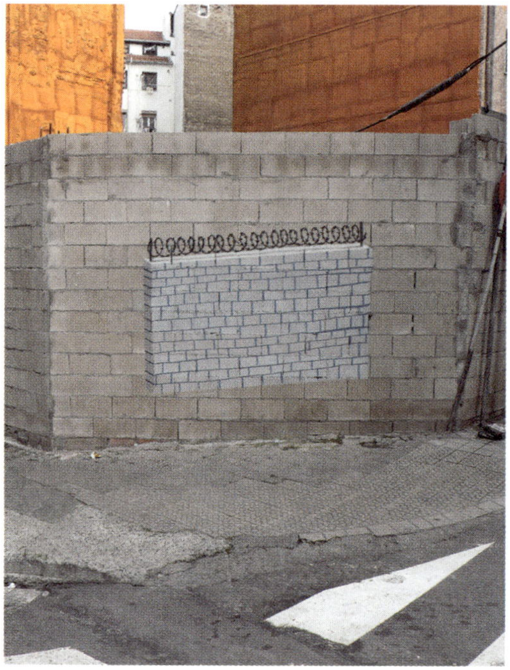

**FIGURE 7.1**
Escif, *Untitled*, 2010. Bilbao. Acrylic paint on wall. Courtesy of the artist.

surrounding fence" (Arendt 1957: 64). While architectural walls thus create boundaries in material and visible ways—both stopping us in our tracks and sealing off our field of view—more than this they act as *conceptual* frontiers, a way to close off spaces and minds both. They place a limit on the imagined community, an edge to the family or nation in concrete and cartographic terms. From the comparative modesty of Hadrian's Wall (dividing Britannia and Caledonia) to the incomprehensibly vast Great Wall of China, the wall separates more than just people; it separates us into camps of friend and enemy, civilized and barbaric, of those for whom we grieve and those we forget. While at the end of the twentieth century walls and curtains seemed to be falling everywhere, our post-9/11 world is one in which these structures have made a violent return. As such, though the Berlin Wall, the twentieth century's most famous barricade (and most famous graffiti canvas), may have been felled, others have taken on even more imposing form. While Trump's border wall incorporated only forty-nine miles of new fencing and has already been subject to erosion and legal indictments, it is the Separation Wall dividing Israel and Palestine (as seen in figure 7.2) that today takes up the foremost position in the cultural imaginary. This 440-mile barricade—for the most part

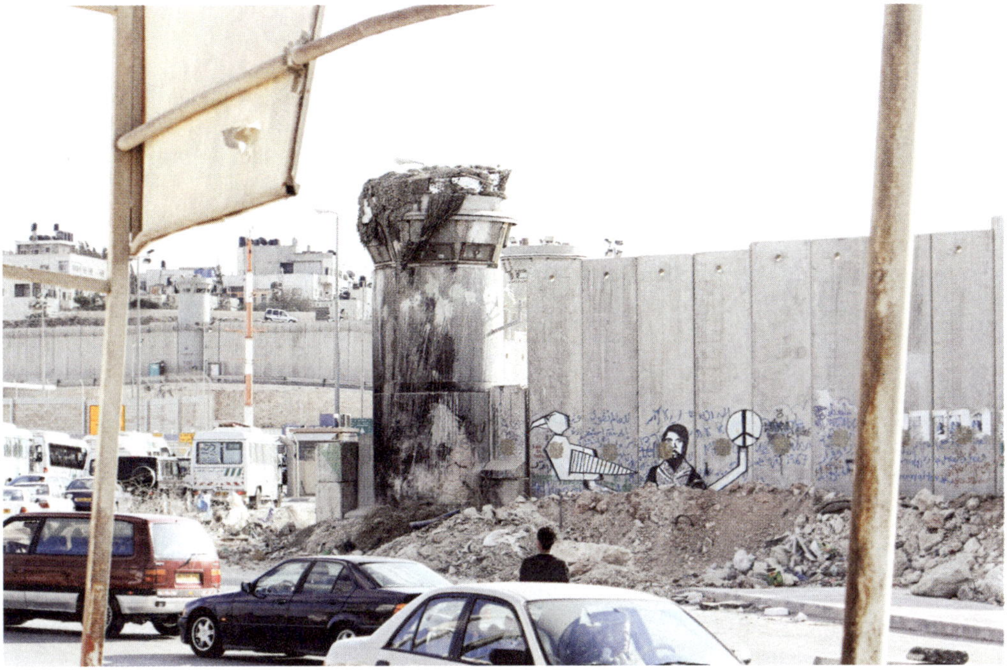

**FIGURE 7.2**
Filippo Minelli, *Untitled*, 2007. Bethlehem, Palestine. Courtesy of the artist. https://www.filippominelli.com.

following the contested Green Line but at points traveling significantly inside Palestinian territory—has today become the international gold standard of border walls. With triple-layered electrified metal fences, barbed wire and trenches, anti-vehicle ditches and 200-foot exclusion zones on either side, the snaking path of the wall not only concretizes "facts on the ground" but has trapped over 30,000 Palestinians on the Israeli side of the wall and encircled a further 100,000 who now have access to neither the West Bank *nor* Israel. The wall thus creates a boundary indicating protection for some while acting as a source of de facto imprisonment for countless more.

While the frontier borders of nation-states act as the ultimate machines of division, it is through the brick-and-mortar walls of the city, its iron railings and steel gates, its barbed-wire fences and wooden palisades, that these tools of separation most habitually manifest (as seen in figure 7.3). Life in the city is a life spent navigating these walls, moving between public and private, intimacy and exposure, dependent on what keys we hold or what privileges we access. Yet while, as Bickford suggests, a gate "that indicates safety and security to a resident of a middle-class development" can communicate "'danger-keep out' to residents of the poor neighborhood it borders," we can

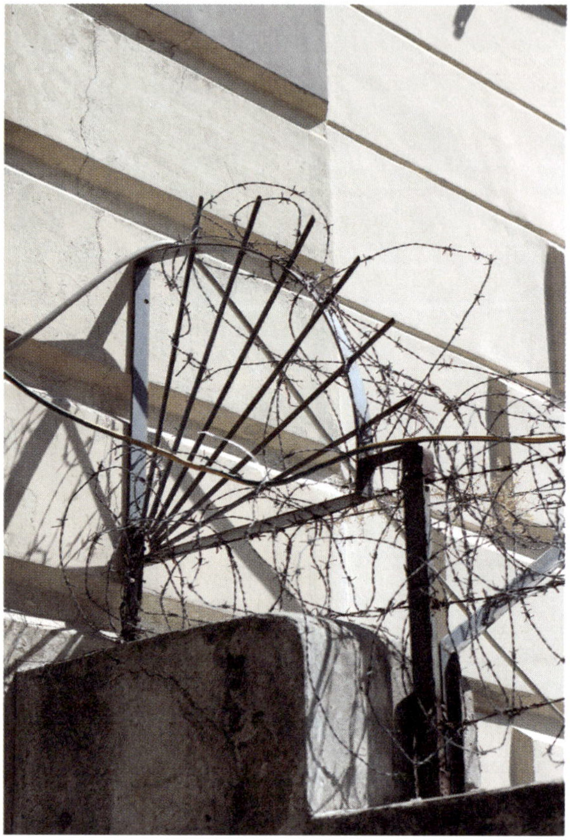

**FIGURE 7.3**
Stephen Burke, *Frites*, 2022. Document in Naples, Italy. Courtesy of the artist.

also see the way in which architectural walls function not just to exclude the *other*, but rather to "keep people on each side separate from one another—or, to put it paradoxically, to actively construct relations of separation" (Bickford 2000: 361). Not only can these enclosing walls come for many to "feel both protective and entrapping" (p. 361), but both the gated community and the archetypal ghetto function through keeping one *in* as much as others out. While the Jews in the Venetian ghetto, for example, were imprisoned within these walls on a nightly basis, the same structures enabled them to escape the persecution they faced outside them. Moreover, as Sennett has argued, the Christian community living beyond the ghetto walls was "haunted" by the "impurities of difference" that the Jewish community represented (Sennett 1994: 215), the partitions protecting and entrapping those on either side of the divide and representing a "compromise between . . . practical necessity and physical fear" (p. 216). Here, as Robert

Castel has written, we thus witness the "ambiguous relationship between protection and insecurity," the puzzling situation in which "*to be protected is also to be threatened*" (Castel 2003 in Cash 2009: 87–88).

The urge toward protectionism that we see within our contemporary landscape thus fragments both sides of the divide via what Kohn has termed an "architecture of fear" (Kohn 2004: 6). Much like the classically inward-looking architectural designs of British social housing from the 1970s (as opposed to the more utopian structures of the postwar decades) that severed their inhabitants from the wider city and wider society both, the middle- and upper-class enclave, as Teresa Caldeira argues in her discussion of the fortified enclaves of Sao Paulo, creates a space that is "physically isolated," that is "turned inwards and not to the street," that enforces "rules of inclusion and exclusion," and that is "socially homogeneous" (Caldeira 1996: 308). Rather than the forceable ejection to the peripheries as seen in the Parisian banlieue, here it is through architectural rather than urban design that separation is enforced. Either way, many of the "basic elements which constituted the modern experience of public life"—the "primacy of streets and their openness; [the] free circulation of crowds and vehicles; impersonal and anonymous encounters of the pedestrian; unprogrammed public enjoyment and congregation in streets and squares; and the presence of people from different social backgrounds strolling and gazing at those passing by"—are here architectonically denied (p. 314). The urge to separate, the very raison d'être of the fortified enclave, thus stymies some of the key organizing principles of our contemporary world. Architectural design here comes to inhibit our encounter with difference, undermining, as Kohn continues, the "feeling that people of different classes and cultures live in the same world" and simultaneously decreasing the very "opportunities for recognizing commonalities and accepting differences" (Kohn 2004: 6–7). The city of walls thus cleanses the mess of the city through separation if not total exclusion.

Apart from physically separating us, however, the walls of our city likewise speak to us, communicate to us, *advertise* to us. Be it through the use of small-scale posters pasted upon already present walls or the giant adverts placed upon hoardings specifically constructed so as to house them, our urban walls are sites of words and images, sites of speech (as we saw earlier in chapter 4). This in itself is nothing new. Outdoor advertising has been an omnipresent part of the urban fabric prior even to the invention of the industrial printing press. The London of the nineteenth century, as we see in figure 7.4, for example, was so suffused with commercial advertising that, like the graffiti of today, it was seen as a danger to public life (Richards 1991; Sampson 1874). While today there has been an increasing digitization of its materiality, the basic premise of outdoor advertising remains the same: if a public substrate exists, advertise on it. If it doesn't, build one to do the same. Denise Scott Brown, Robert Venturi, and Steven Izenour's seminal text *Learning from Las Vegas* saw public advertisement—the large-scale neon signage of Las Vegas in particular—as a visual mode that had come to overtake the architectural qualities of the buildings they themselves appeared upon. Dominating the street scene, these giant forms created an entirely new concept of place, the ornament not only dominating the monument but becoming the monument itself. The "graphic sign in space," the authors continued, "has become the architecture of this landscape" (Scott Brown et al. 1988: 13), the advertising becoming the wall, the architecture becoming the advertising.

Yet while advertising has come to exist as a fundamental element of the city's fabric, it also comes from an entirely privatized domain. The physical advert conveys a private message in a public space, emerging via a private drive and targeting a private individual. Famously critiqued by the arch theorist of the public sphere, Jurgen Habermas, the growth of the corporate mass media—first within the literary sphere of newspapers and journals before moving into the public space of the city itself—was understood to have opened a "gate through which privileged private interests invaded the public

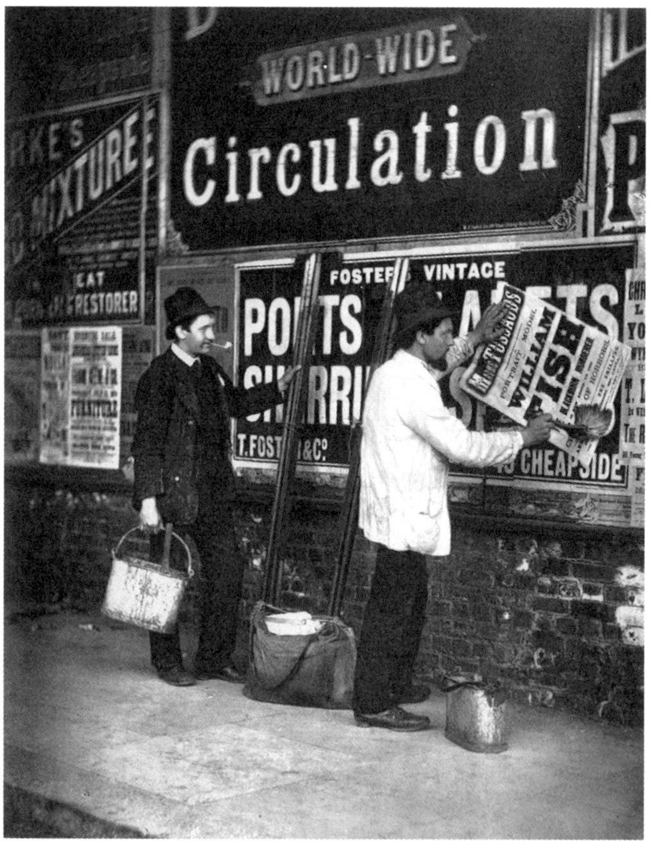


**FIGURE 7.4**
*Street Advertising*, 1877. From *Street Life in London* 1877, by John Thomson and Adolphe Smith. LSE Library, SR 1146.

sphere" (Habermas 1991 [1962]: 185). Public space was thus turned into a "medium of advertising" (p. 189), into a site where these private messages were either "directed to other private people insofar as they are consumers" or parasitically addressed to them as "citizens" through a mode of opinion formation in which the "sender of the message hides his business intentions in the role of someone interested in the public welfare" (p. 193). Our architectural walls here attempt to define not just the physical position of people but so too their views. Moreover, the economic barriers to speech—let alone the constraints placed upon messages by the private organizations who own the walls and who determine the "suitability" of message displayed—constrain the diversity of voices that public space is expected to enable. The wall thus becomes a tool to separate not merely private and public space, but likewise private and public opinion.

But what of our hero Nelson? Was he formed in the public interest? Well, just as he and his column were established and funded by the state, the naval hero can be seen to stand in the *state's* interests rather than those of the putative public themselves. The grand column, like many other consequences of statumania, was formed to adhere and solidify the nation, to create a homogenous imagined community out of flux and heterogeneity. Here the interests of the state are thus not of beneficence but of status quo. But is he then a part of the public sphere? Well, as part of the traditional sphere of the political that the Habermasian public was meant to work *against*, Nelson must be seen to be stamped with the ideological imprint of the state and subject to his own form of political instrumentalization. But so does he at the least exist in public space? Well, perhaps surprisingly not! Trafalgar Square is not even state-owned but in fact retained by the King as the possession of the Crown Estate. Like the nation's palaces and Royal Parks, the Square is the public's by monarchical magnanimity alone. While in practice Trafalgar Square does remain a space of gathering and protest, the transformations of the Square made over the last two centuries can be seen as the result of the "efforts," as Mace has argued, of "one small section of community to arrange the battlefield physically to their advantage, not only socially and politically, but so too militarily" (Mace 2005: 153). Its famous fountains as seen in figure 7.5, for example, were added to the site by chief architect Charles Barry so as to stem, he announced, the "evils of a generally objectionable character" (read: the dangers of the mob or of public rebellion) that "leaving open so large a space" were believed to have encouraged (Barry 1841 in Mace 2005: 87). In a similar way, the "Trafalgar Square Regulations" of 1892 enabled the state to "decide who should and who should not be allowed to use the square to advocate their cause" (Mace 2005: 204), forming a distinctly undemocratic right to public use. While intersubjective relations can and do still occur at the foot of Nelson, who can publicly speak and what one can publicly say under his gaze are determined by the private interests of state and Crown, and subject to violence and legal prohibition both.

Our graffiti monument is embedded within issues of private and public too, questioning the spaces, spheres, and interests of publicness. Spatially, the image is placed within a public environment, yet is almost always (perhaps inevitably) placed upon

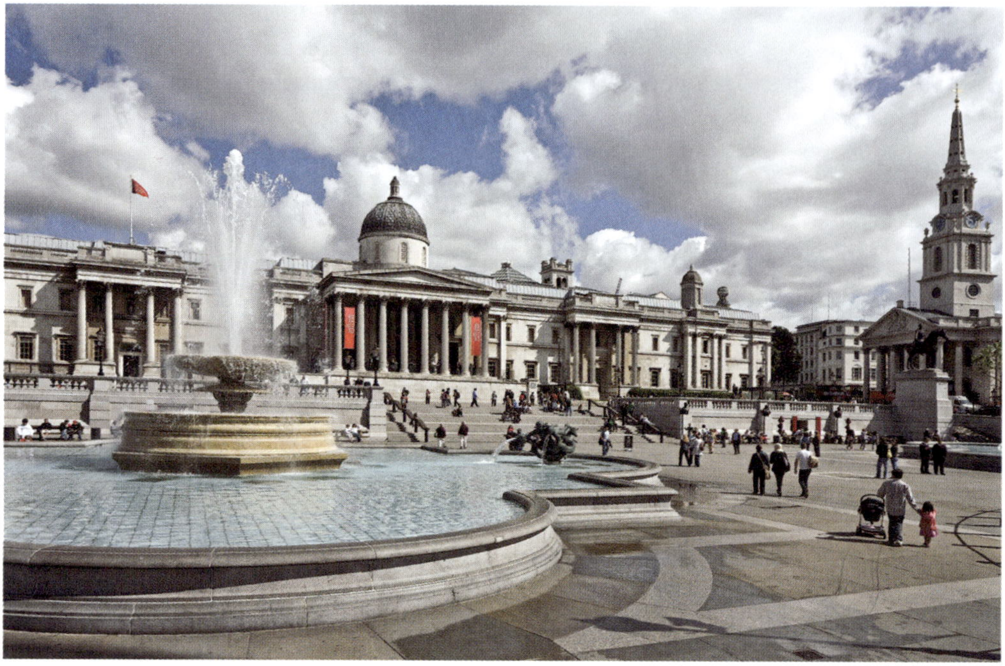

**FIGURE 7.5**
David Iliff, *Trafalgar Square*, 2009. London. License: CC BY-SA 3.0.

technically private property. While in sites where private residences are set behind front gardens or basement "moats" (as often seen in Georgian architecture), the spatial separation and front paths (that mimic drawbridges!) make public and private very clear and thus dissuade graffiti. Yet when a building directly abuts the street (be it a residential or commercial one), graffiti writers will often take the nominally private street-side surface as a public one. The millimeter-thick veneer of graffiti thus confounds its ascription as either public or private, set within a space as infinitesimal as the time of the present compressed between past and future. Graffiti thus creates a zone of porosity, its diaphanous images revealing the similarly diaphanous quality of the public/private border itself. While the status of the city's physical thresholds is thus here disordered, graffiti likewise engages its geographic borders, working at sites in which public and private are already opaque. Not only does their lack of use and activity, along with their lack of clear structures of ownership, place these vague terrains in a literally liminal position, but graffiti places them on an edge that is bent into publicness through *use*. And all this without mentioning that for graffiti to be publicly witnessed, trespass—the purposeful infringement of private space—is often a necessity too! As seen in figures 7.6 and 7.7, to engage in the city, to have your images flow through it via its walls or public

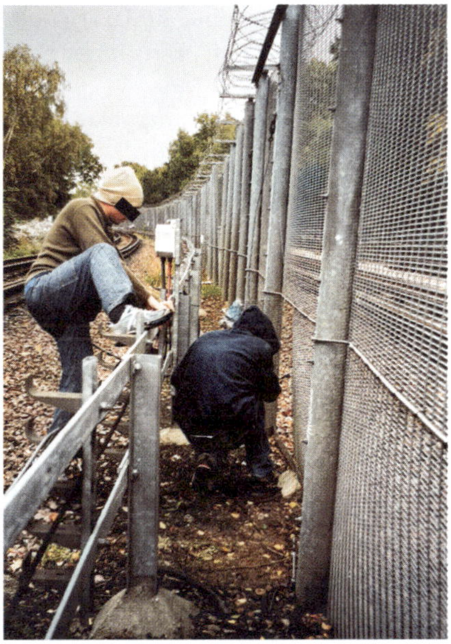

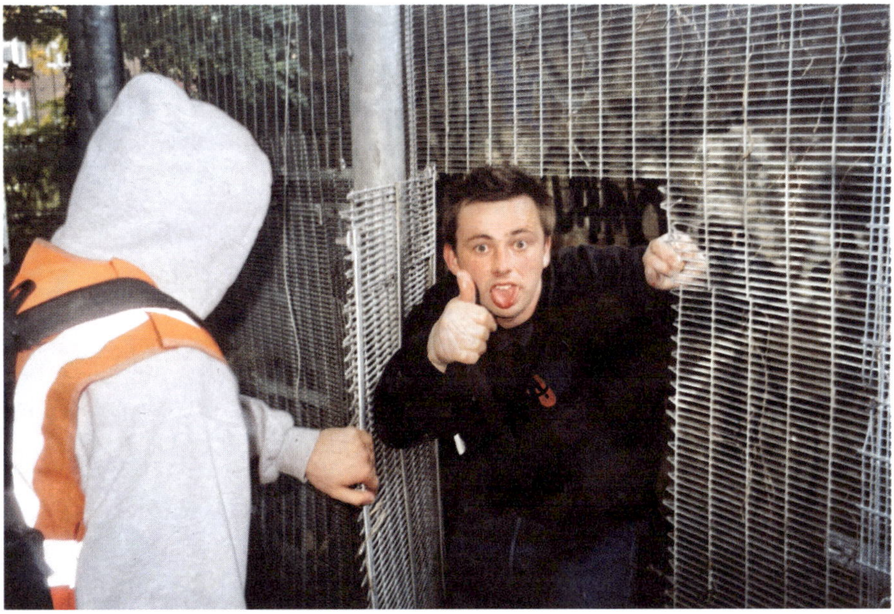

**FIGURE 7.6**
*Daytime Capers*, 2001. London Underground. Photo: Christopher Stead. Courtesy of the photographer.

**FIGURE 7.7**
*Just Doing My Job*, 2004. London Underground. Photo: Christopher Stead. Courtesy of the photographer.

transportation systems, entry into private space becomes an obligation. In each of these cases, however, what is clear is a general rejection of public/private distinctions, even as graffiti must be understood as always spatially private in legal and normative terms.

But what about graffiti's interests or rationality? Well, while many immediately assign graffiti as a speech whose interests are private, targeted toward one's subcultural kin alone, these are images made to be seen, consciously engaging with a "*public*" who, as Michael Warner claims for all counterpublics, becomes "*constituted through mere attention*" (Warner 2002: 419). By exhibiting itself in public, by working to captivate and engage us, graffiti can thus be seen to engage in a communicative act that "commits itself . . . to the possible participation of any stranger" (p. 422). Moreover, not only engaging a public *in* public, graffiti likewise positions itself outside the instrumental motivations of the private sector and the instrumental logics of the state. Even when not explicitly political, it brings opinion, argument, into the public sphere—even if this opinion rests solely on the question of one's right to speak in public itself. In this way, graffiti implicitly (if not overtly) challenges the strategic corporate aesthetic deemed so customary in our urban landscape, iconoclastically rejecting the omnipresence of advertising and placing its normative rightness into question. This is one of the very few things graffiti writers would ever agree on, in fact. Graffiti, as seen in figure 7.8, is constitutively anti-advertising. The common argument that graffiti is analogous to this commercial form thus presents an evidently false equivalence. While the aesthetics of advertising have been undoubtedly influential on graffiti (as the aesthetics of graffiti have been on advertising), their aims could not be further from one another. Both forms may try to captivate and seek recognition. Yet while graffiti addresses us as public citizen, advertising addresses us as private consumer. While graffiti's sincerity cannot be questioned, advertising is manipulative by essence. Graffiti might be publicity, an exposition to unknown strangers that is about the generation of fame, but unlike advertising, it asserts nothing but its right to speak itself.[2] The truth claims of graffiti—that public space is a site for speech, not manipulation, that the public should be a space of action, not passivity—thus exist as the indirect message of every image. The images push themselves into the heart of the public sphere, even if what they say (and what they implicitly reject) is so apparently dangerous that its creators must be incarcerated for their speech. While graffiti may thus be spatially private by essence, it is discursively public in the most fundamental of ways.

Just as with graffiti, however, many other public artists and activists have addressed the overwhelming presence of advertising in public space. While we saw the work of Steinbrener et al., Holzer, and Kruger, in chapter 4, within what has been called *subvertising*, we can find a range of tactical urban practices emerging, as Thomas Dekeyser has noted, not only through "graffiti interventions" but through processes of "supplementation, removal, reversal, cutting, digital hacking and destruction" (Dekeyser 2020: 311). While a Situationist mode of *detournement* has been seen since the late 1960s—Jill Poesner's seminal book *Spray It Loud* (1982), for example, documenting the profusion

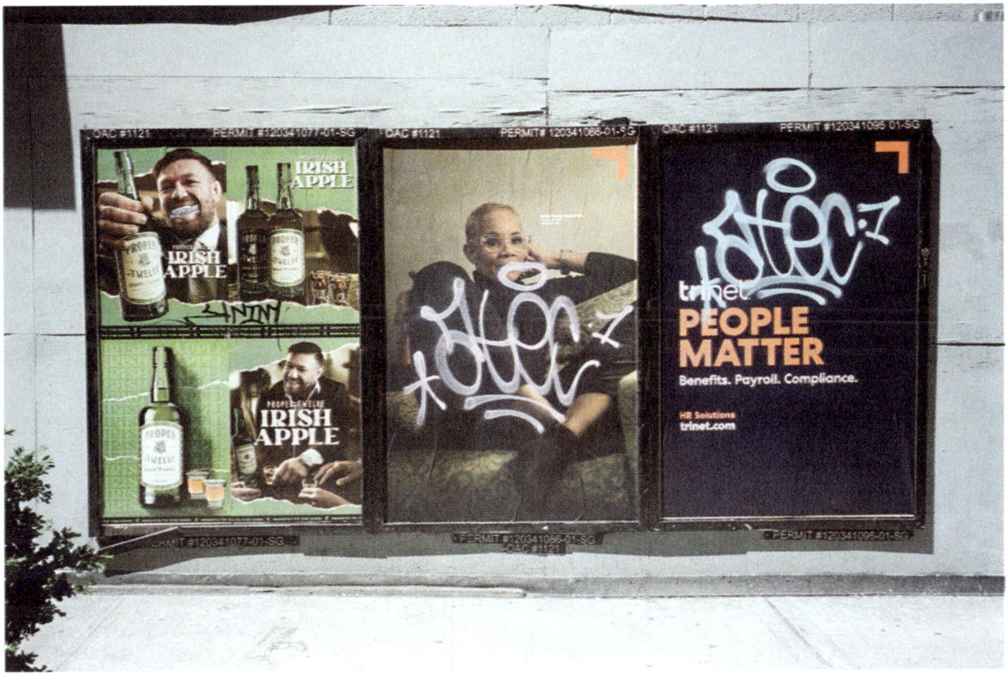


**FIGURE 7.8**
*People Matter (Constitutively Anti-Advertising)*, 2023, New York. Photo: Rafael Schacter.

of graffiti on the misogynistic billboard advertisements of the early 1980s—subvertising today attempts not only to reduce the privatization of the city but likewise to make public space more public too. The work of renowned artist and organizer Jordan Seiler is pivotal here. A key fulcrum around which much contemporary subvertising practice has flowed, Seiler not only has used advertising spaces as part of his own visual practice (as seen in figure 7.9) but has provided space for *other* artists to work too. Within his celebrated *Public Ad Campaign*,[3] for example, Seiler has organized city-wide advertising takeovers for hundreds of other artists (such as seen in Quentin Coussirat's (de) installation in figure 7.10), while within the project *Public Access*[4] he has supplied how-to guides and physical tools for countless others to engage themselves (as seen in figure 7.11). While subvertising thus works to question "who has control over the textual, affective and aesthetic landscapes of urban surfaces," it also comes to reveal the "embodied and psychic toll of an uneven access to these landscapes" (Dekeyser 2020: 312–313). Moreover, it points to the reality of advertising today as being a consecrated part of our urban landscape, which subvertising (and graffiti) seeks to "profane," revealing both "that which advertising power seeks to hide (its manufactured sacredness)" while, as

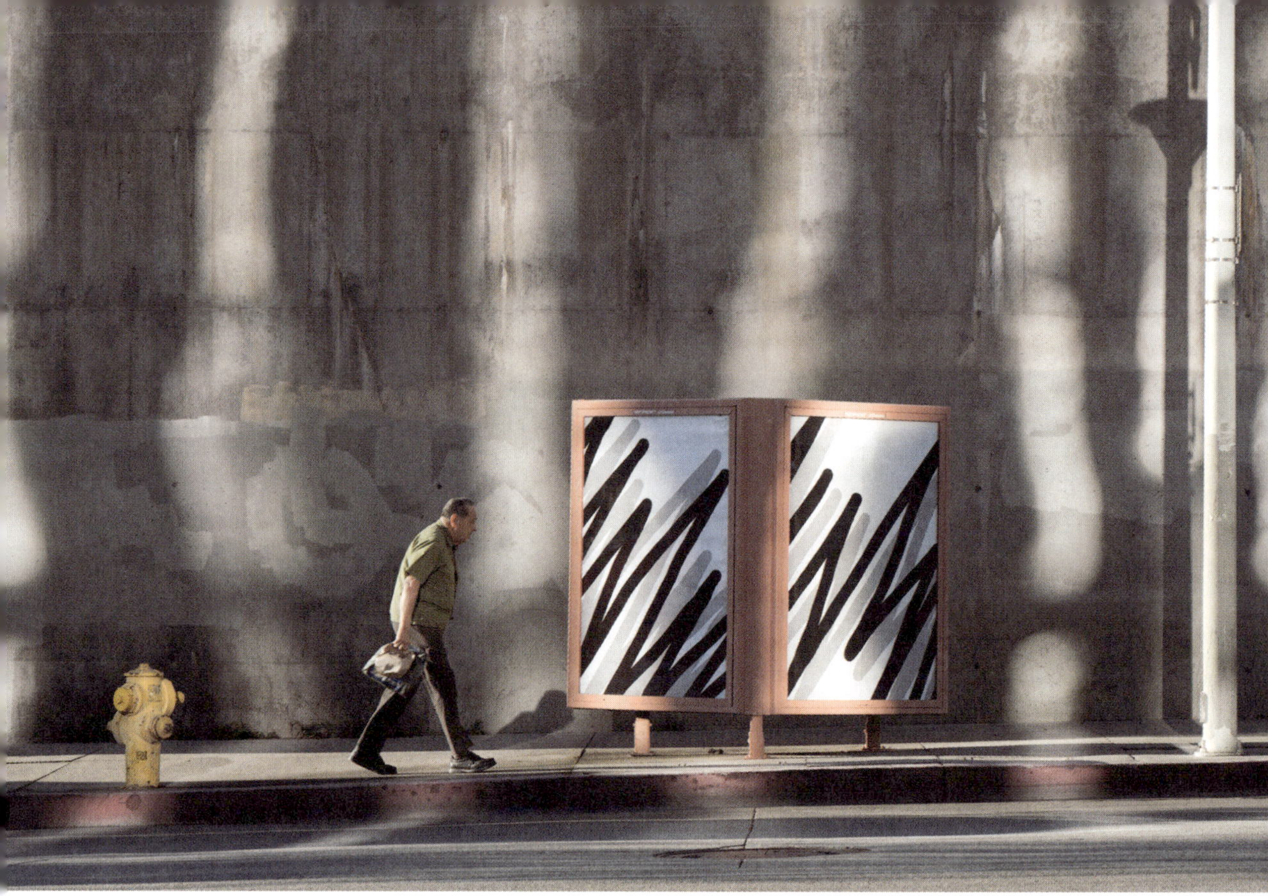

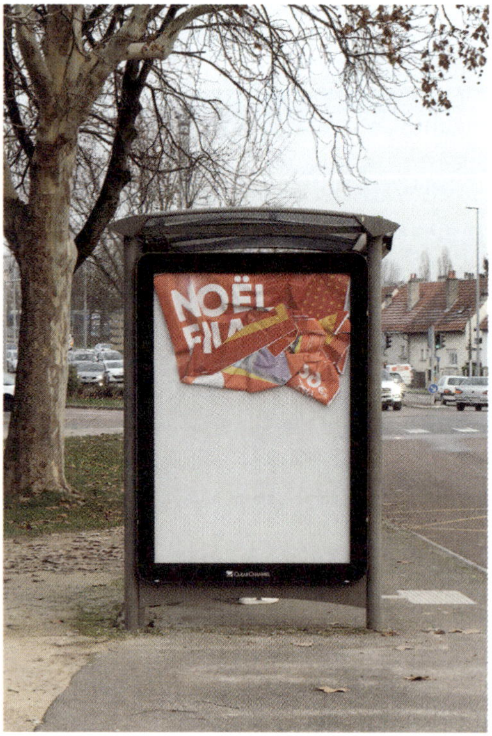
NOËL

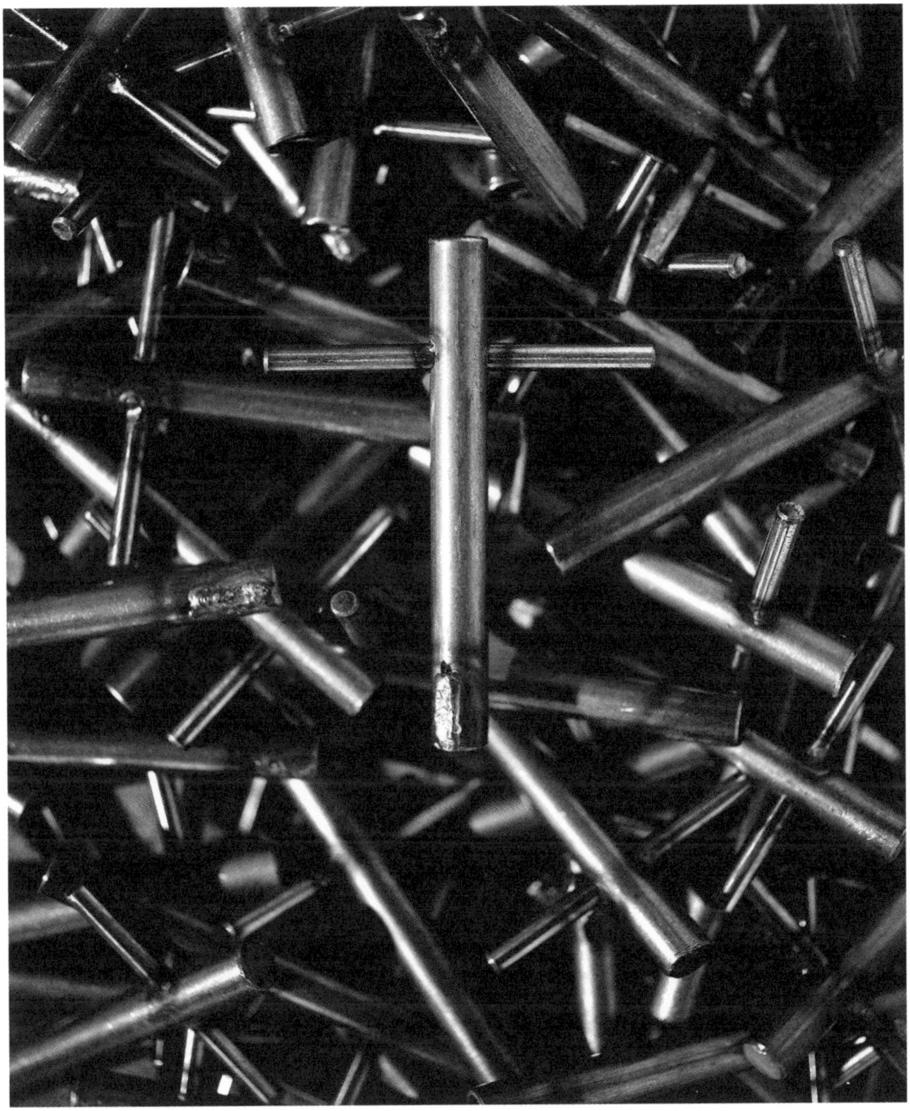

**FIGURE 7.9**
Jordan Seiler, *Collisions—Hill Street*, 2019. Giclee print with digital augmentation. Photo: Jordan Seiler. Courtesy of the artist.

**FIGURE 7.10**
Quentin Coussirat, *Untitled (Public Access Project)*, 2018. Courtesy of the artist and Jordan Seiler.

**FIGURE 7.11**
Jordan Seiler, *Public Access Keys* (*Bomb Magazine* issue 143), 2019. Giclee print with digital augmentation. Photo: Jordan Seiler. Courtesy of the artist.

Dekeyser concludes, hiding "that which advertising power hopes to reveal (its promotional material)" (p. 318).

Other practitioners, however, have addressed not the barriers to public speech but public barriers themselves. In Filippo Minelli's influential *Ctrl+Alt+Delete* (see figure 7.12) produced at the Qalandiya checkpoint on the Israeli/Palestinian Separation Wall in 2007, the artist invoked a classical idiom of the computer world (known colloquially as the "three-finger salute") that automatically reboots a PC. As part of the artist's focus on landscape and boundary zones (from the sea border between North and South Korea to the disputed territories of the Azawad in Mali), alongside his wider project on merging the digital and physical domains (as seen in his series *Contradictions*), the piece can be seen as a plea to reset or restart something, an urge to erase, to dump, to interrupt the wall's violent function. In Ana Teresa Fernández's *Borrando la Frontera* (Erasing the Border) (2011), however, the artist attempted to delete the frontier between Tijuana and San Diego through a visual eradication. Painting the steel border fence separating the two nations a bright sky blue (as seen in figures 7.13 and 7.14), the addition here becomes a subtraction, dissolving the border from the beach. Alongside questioning

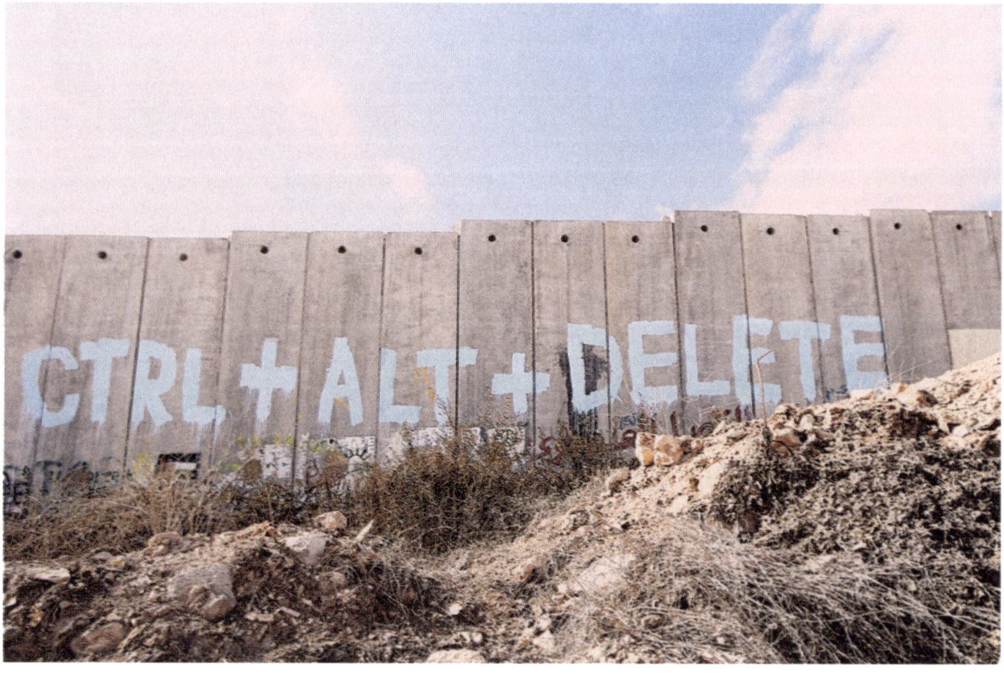


**FIGURE 7.12**
Filippo Minelli, *Ctrl+Alt+Delete*, 2007. Qualandia Checkpoint. Courtesy of the artist. https://www.filippominelli.com.

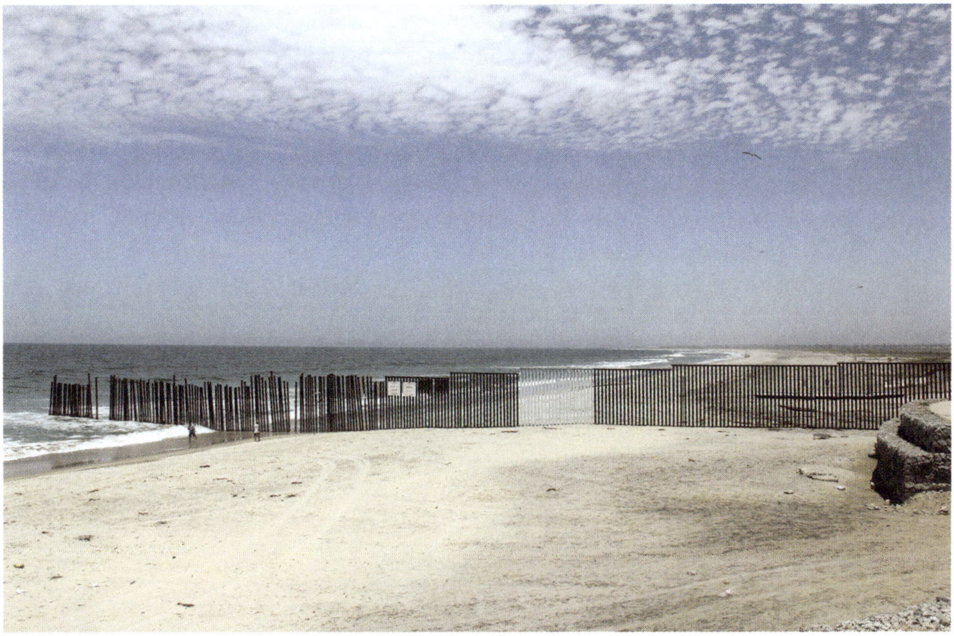

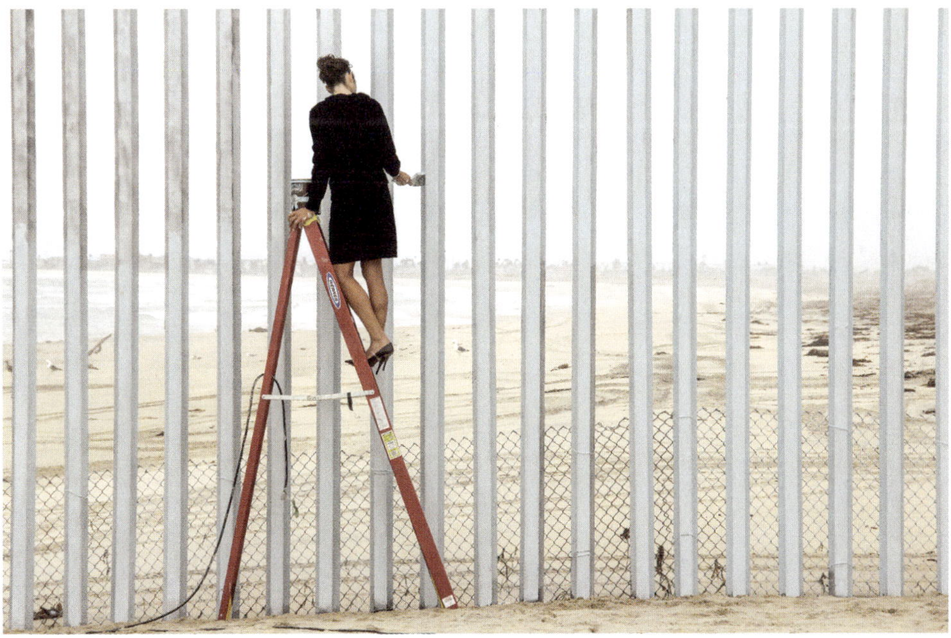

**FIGURES 7.13 AND 7.14**
Ana Teresa Fernández, *Borrando la Frontera* (Erasing the Border), 2011/2021. Pigmented inkjet prints on Hahnemuhle Photo Rag Baryta. Courtesy of the artist and Catharine Clark Gallery, San Francisco, CA.

gender roles at the border through her wearing of high-heeled shoes and a "little black dress" to compete the project—in particular at a site in which many of the women who are forced to make the crossing end up in the domestic labor market—Fernández thus enacts a project that reveals and conceals in the same moment, much like the migrants who end up on the northern side of the border themselves.

In Luce and Eltono's *Escalera Butrón* (break-in ladder) and Andrew Kass's *A Little about Lots*, however, we find a more forcefully interruptive approach to the architectural wall. In the former work (as seen in figures 7.15 and 7.16), Luce and Eltono provide public access to privatized space through a literal process of breaking and entering. Targeting a range of sealed-off city plots in Valencia left dormant while awaiting construction (by their often now bankrupt owners), the pair utilize the specific affordances of the cheap, hollow, concrete blocks that wall off the sites in order to bring these dead zones back into public use. Creating a series of zigzagging holes in these walls through the simple use of a hammer and chisel, the pair fashioned a set of foot-sized openings—often going directly through not just the wall but the uppermost layer of advertising attached to them—enabling one to comfortably scale and enter these restricted non-spaces. Here both private wall and private speech are surmounted. In a similar process

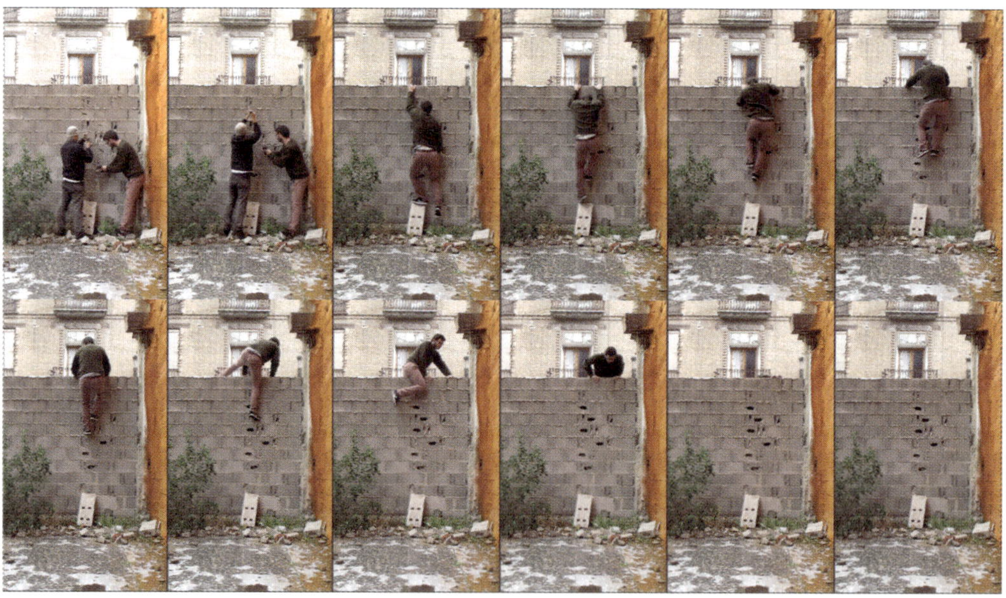

**FIGURE 7.15**
Luce and Eltono, *Escalera Butrón* (break-in ladder), 2015. Video stills from a public performance. Courtesy of the artists.

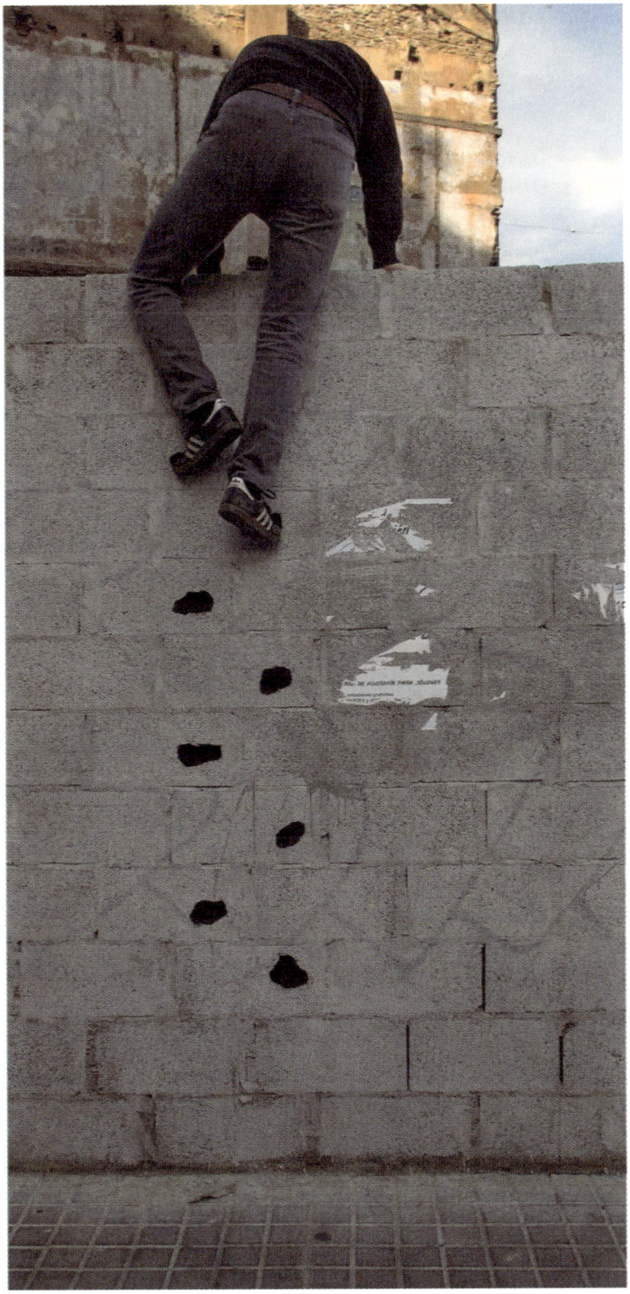

**FIGURE 7.16**
Luce and Eltono, *Escalera Butrón* (break-in ladder), 2015. Video still from a public performance. Courtesy of the artists.

of constructive deconstruction, Kass's project, seen in figures 7.17–7.19, transformed a New York City lot left vacant for over two decades into an ephemeral public park. Physically sequestered from public usage by a large green wooden fence, Kass cut a series of dramatic, curving arches into the fortification shielding this corner lot to reveal a beautifully disheveled green space—as visible through his series of elegant, rounded portals—incongruously filled with trees and wild plants in the very heart of the city's Financial District. Lasting for a period of just over seven days and reminiscent of the guerrilla/community gardens discussed further below, Kass's work, like Luce and Eltono's, questioned the public-private boundaries that the city so commonly sets up by bringing these neglected private sites back into public use. What emerges here is thus not just a communicative and utopian rejection of the border but a practice in which turning the private into public is the rule. For all the brute force of the wall, then, its very appearance becomes a challenge to be overcome. And in the same way that every monument holds

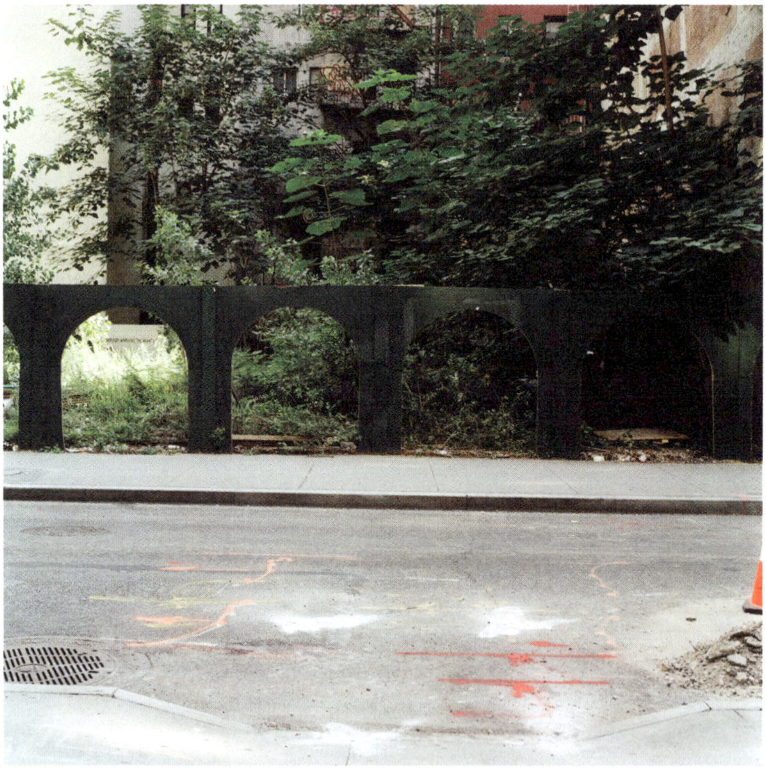

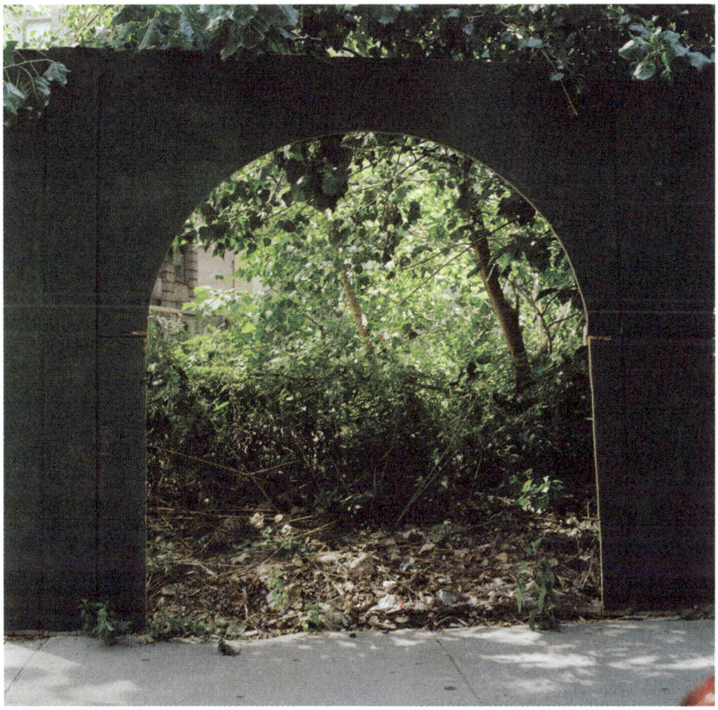

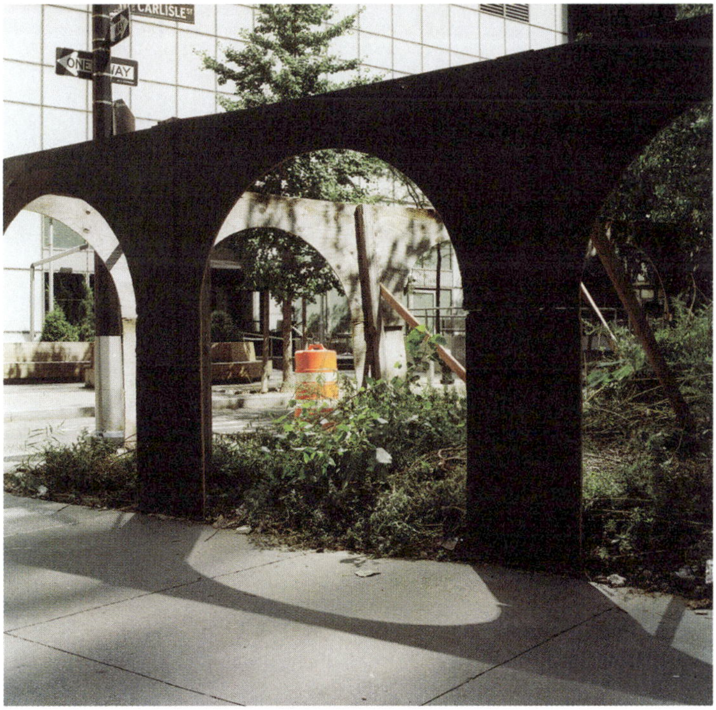


**FIGURES 7.17, 7.18, AND 7.19**
Andrew Kass, *A Little about Lots*, 2020. Courtesy of the artist.

the moment of its iconoclastic destruction in its very materiality—the moment of its first erection a countdown to its eventual fall—here too every border wall appears to holds within it the inevitable moment of its eventual breach.

## ATMOSPHERIC WALLS

While architectural walls act as the primary means of separating public and private, they are not the only way of demarcating boundaries in space. Alongside these concrete, physical structures are what feminist theorist Sara Ahmed has termed *atmospheric walls*, the intangible barriers that can obstruct just as powerfully as any material edifice. Functioning through generating a feeling of discomfort or uneasiness, atmospheric walls are systems for "making spaces available to some more than to others," techniques for "stopping something from happening or stopping someone from progressing without appearing to stop this or stop them" (Ahmed 2014: n.p.). While the method of exclusion they utilize is less overt than the wall, it is in many ways more insidious through it leading to a form of *self*-exclusion: "[Y]ou arrive, and it becomes uncomfortable. It is so uncomfortable, that you are not willing to stay. The discomfort can be tangible to you, like a thing, a wall, which you know is right there because you have just knocked into it. When you leave you do so willingly; it appears that you have left in accordance with your own will. Even if they made it hard for you . . . they do not encounter that hard" (n.p.). Imperceptible to those whose privileges make them imperceptible themselves (and who may not *want* to see these diaphanous barriers), here the ambience a space generates can have a viscerally powerful effect on those existing outside the racialized, class-based, or gendered normativities of much public space. The creation of an atmosphere here thus "becomes a polite strategy or technique of power" in which one subject to this politeness *willingly* searches for a method of "avoiding the consequences of being forced"; willingness itself thus becomes "a consequence of force" (n.p.), violence, whether physical or psychological, avoided before it is faced. While members of the majoritarian community will thus come to see public space, as sociologist Elijah Anderson has argued, as "unremarkable, or as normal, taken-for-granted reflections of civil society," members of marginalized communities (in Anderson's work the African American community specifically), may be made to feel "uneasy" at the same site or consider it "informally 'off limits'" (Anderson 2015: 10). Public space is here marked out not as a "public" space but as hegemonic space. Whether by dint of one's sexuality, religion, age, or "nonconforming" body, minority groups hence experience the ways in which difference becomes harnessed into regulatory structures determining who is allowed to feel at home in public, determining who can (or who can*not*) effortlessly pass through its atmospheric walls.

These ambient barriers are also mirrored in a city's urban design. Rather than the wall or the gated community, here the way the environment is constructed (let alone whom it has traditionally been constructed *by*) has a pivotal effect on one's levels of (dis)comfort. Atmospheres determined by factors such as lighting, ease of physical access, or the availability of public bathrooms (for the very young or the more senior, or just for one's own safety), immediately set up differential structures of conviviality. The provisions made for one's community thus indicate whether you see a place as *meant* for you. Are there benches to sit on, places to play? Is the space free or (at least) affordable? Are we questioned or welcomed when entering these sites? Our actions in public, whether our ability to walk without stopping[5] or our ability to display physical affection to those we love, are thus not only monitored and policed but *designed-in* or *designed-out* in simultaneously active and passive ways.[6] While the conventional barriers and walls discussed earlier in this chapter can thus, as defined by geographer Steven Flusty, be seen as a form of "crusty space" (and the saturated spaces of surveillance we will look at in our next chapter as "jittery space"), atmospherically hostile techniques can be understood as examples of "prickly space" (Flusty 1994: 18). This is a type of space that "cannot be comfortably occupied," a space, as Flusty continues, that is "defended by such details as wall-mounted sprinkler heads activated to clear loiterers [just like our fountains at Trafalgar Square], or ledges sloped to inhibit sitting," an unsympathetic space created via the "removal of the right amenities or the addition of the wrong ones" (p. 19). This is the space of angled, plastic bus-stop seating, of anti-homeless studs and benches as human deterrents (see figures 7.20 and 7.21). This is a space of architectural forms that are explicitly fashioned to impede usage. Atmospheric prickliness is thus designed precisely so as to "preclude interaction" (p. 19). Here, we have a space in which those outside the singular dominant community for whom public space is made, let alone those who wish to simply to take their time or occupy space without consuming it, are quickly ushered out of site.

It is thus not just social barriers or material design that can produce atmospheric walls, but likewise patterns of development that place consumption at the forefront of urban planning. What Sharon Zukin called "domestication" or "pacification by cappuccino" (Zukin 1995: xiv, 28), for example, is a result of increasing public/private partnerships emergent due to an increasingly (perhaps purposively) impoverished local government. Emergent first through business improvement districts (BIDs) while coalescing into what today have been termed privately owned public spaces (POPS), these parodic spaces have been brought into wider public focus through the work of Anna Minton. From London's Canary Wharf and Broadgate to Cabot Circus in Bristol and Liverpool One in Liverpool, the consequence of this sweeping urban privatization is, for Minton, a world in which "town and city centres are becoming little more than shopping complexes, albeit without actual walls" (Minton 2012: 19). Moreover, not only are these sites "run in a very different way to rest of the city," but the "details of how these places will actually be run, which is what determines their character" are themselves "rarely available" (p. 29). The regulations and policies determining our rights in what appears to be public space are thus not only "barely in the public domain,"

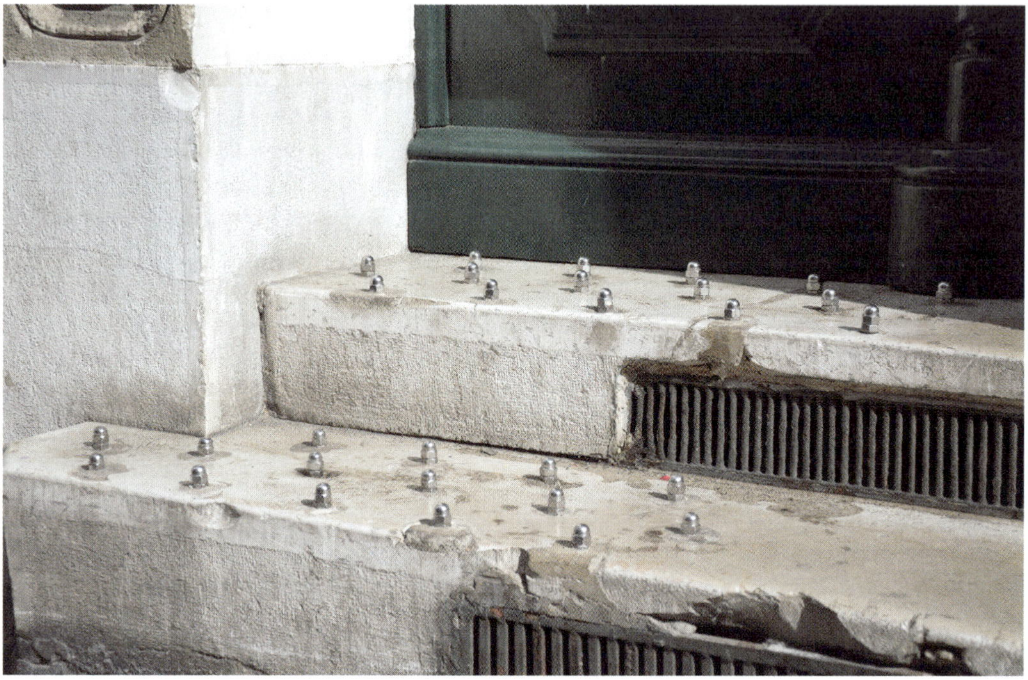

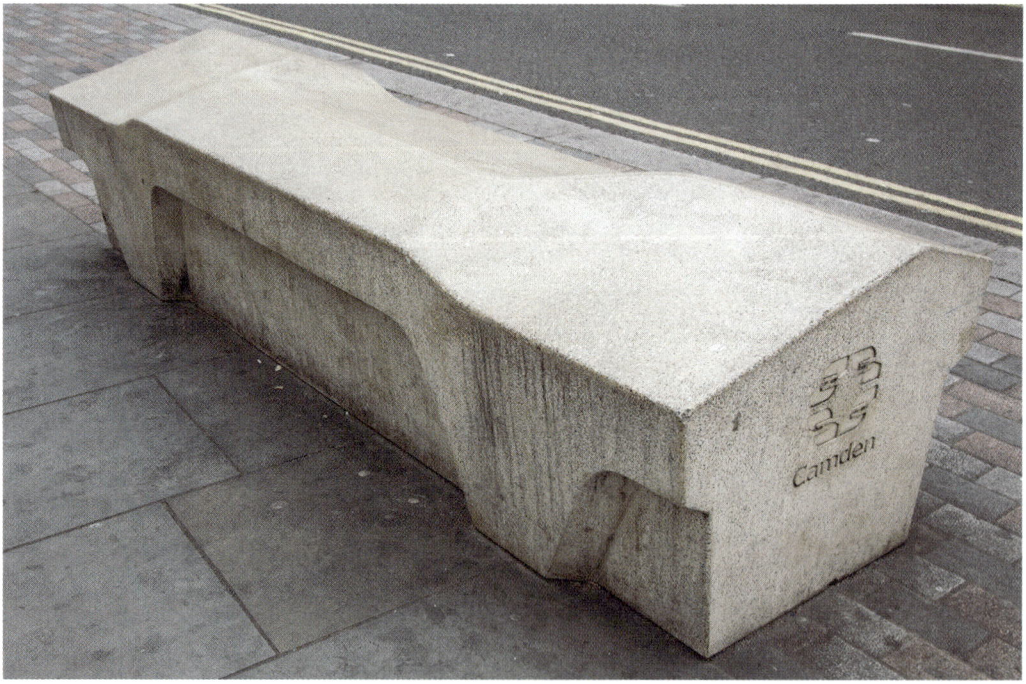
Camden

but made purposefully "opaque, mired in jargon and complex legal arrangements" (p. 29). Minton's interview with one of the developers of Stratford City (a mall adjacent to the 2012 Olympic site and the largest urban shopping center in the United Kingdom) is thus hugely pertinent for us here: "Explaining the type of atmosphere he hoped to achieve," she continues, the developer "told me he wanted to 'make sure it was up to the standard of any private office lobby,' which seemed to me to be a strange aspiration for a large part of central London marketed as a busy, diverse and 'inspiring' place" (p. 32). The perfectly clean, perfectly frictionless, perfectly ascetic aesthetic of our POPS are corporate lobbies transplanted to the site of the street. They are designed to attract consumers and consumption, to assuage us of any other thoughts bar consumptive ones. "Vitality" and "diversity" are simply a bonus just so long as they don't overshadow the main economic purpose of the site itself. Vitality and diversity may be deemed as a condition that increases this consumption. The question that still remains, however, is: who can and can't access these spaces of urban consumption?[7]

In many ways, the city has always been a privately owned space. London's famous parks and garden squares, for example, often thought of as the city's most public of locations, were first constructed for the sole use of their elite private owners. To *em*park was, in fact, to enclose, something made clear in contemporary UK park regulations as well as by their very prominent barriers to entry (in London, iron-speared fencing is the preference).[8] Moreover, many of our POPS too have emerged via the redevelopment of private sites, here often postindustrial ones. Rather than being linked, as suggested by Matthew Carmona, to a "new wave of enclosures," what is being undertaken could be argued to be the "bringing of new spaces into public use, even if it remains in private ownership" (Carmona 2022: 147). Yet the archetypal POPS that, as Carmona says, have today become "well used and highly valued," that "attempt to garner an inclusive and vibrant environment that gives back to society," and that even include a "rich programme of public events" (p. 148) are still deeply limiting and limited spaces. While a world away from the so-called bonus plazas built for the purposes of tax breaks alone (in which gathering is actively dissuaded through prickliness), and while clearly aiming to generate more cohesive public engagement (with all the marketable qualities that this creates), they are still places utterly devoid of the unexpected and accidental elements that for many define what a public space is. This constitutive lack of the spontaneous is a key part of what makes them such incredibly effective spaces. At Granary Square,

**FIGURE 7.20**
*Anti-Homeless Bolts on a Porch*, 2011. Marseille, France. Courtesy of DocteurCosmos. Creative Commons Attribution–Share Alike 3.0 Unported license.

**FIGURE 7.21**
*Camden Bench*, 2015, London. Image: The Wub. Creative Commons Attribution–Share Alike 4.0 International license.

as seen in figure 7.22, for example—part of the wider King's Cross redevelopment in London and a site that, like the comparably sized Trafalgar Square discussed earlier, will become a key counterpoint for us in this third part of the book—the space has been made to feel family-focused, to feel clean, *safe*.[9] The shops are glossy, the restaurants Instagrammable, the site's smoothness and friendly aesthetic focus-grouped (like our billboard ads) within an inch of its life. And I, as a fairly privileged, middle-class, white Londoner in full-time employment, find them all too comfortable and utilizable spaces (to my own disgust, albeit drowned in a perfect flat white). Just as with Kohn's description of the mall, what has been produced here is an "environment carefully designed to exclude any source of discomfort . . . a sanitized substitute for public life" (Kohn 2004: 62). The homogenous upscale chain stores and the same-same-unique function through a process in which predictability and control are critical. The POPS are thus sites of utter uniformity, sites in which lack of friction helps to

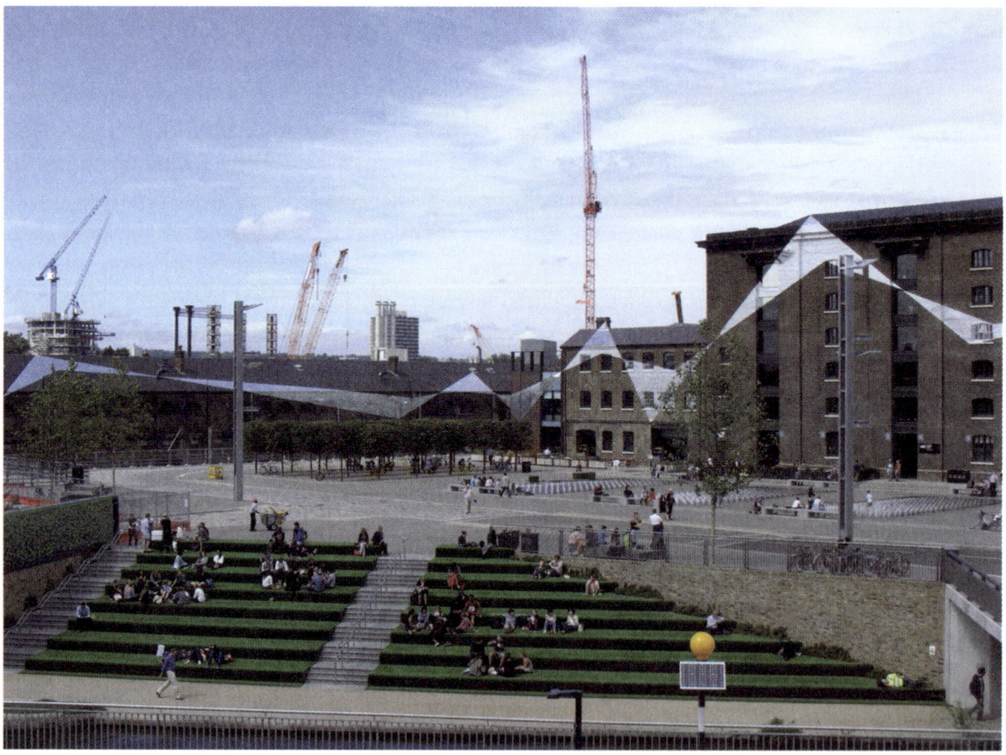

**FIGURE 7.22**
*Granary Square*, 2013, London. Image: Sludge G. ShareAlike 2.0 Generic (CC BY-SA 2.0).

encourage flow. They are not civic spaces but consumptive ones in which private, not public, acts are encouraged, in which practices that are not economically beneficial are discouraged or suppressed.

But what is the monument of the POPS, and what are the specific atmospheres that pertain to these? The key monumental element here is the spectacular (the central theme of chapter 9), a glut of inoffensive, shiny, large-scale artworks in which the "wow" factor is key. Here it is works that photograph well that are desired (publicity images of which are often taken from a height, looking better from above than from the ground), media-friendly artworks with bright colors or bright lights, as well as a selection of artists who contribute to the progressive look (and feel) that the location seeks to enlist. It is thus a heavily curated space (often overseen by star curators who work alongside their "starchitects"), a space in many ways reminiscent of an outdoor (and private) museum. Jacques Rival's *IFO (Identified Flying Object)* is one of the centerpiece public artworks in King's Cross (so successful that it was made permanent in 2014, having originally been planned as a temporary installation), and an all-too perfect example of the POPS monument. A nine-meter-high birdcage with a single swing at its center that lights up in neon at night (and is occasionally raised up in the sky), the official King's Cross webpage calls it a "framing device for the daily theater of the street" (King's Cross Estate Services 2022). Not only an incredibly lonely piece of work (perfect for a selfie on one's own or in a pair at a push), it is a space made for being looked *at*, for becoming the spectacle itself. At best it is anodyne, purposefully supporting the placelessness of placemaking. At worst, a perfect emblem of the gilded cage these theatrical spaces of consumption place us within. In their total site-specific disconnection from their sites, the POPS monument closely follows the strategies of the "plop art" of the 1960s and '70s in which total autonomy reigned. While the goal of the POPS monument is to atmospherically aid consumption, the "plops in POPS" phenomena reinscribe the attempt to move the (high) art of the corporate lobby (as described by Stratford City's developer) into the space of the plaza. This lobby art on steroids is thus once again about consumption, here a conspicuous consumption aligned to the consumptive/economic powers of their owners, yet more often than not speaks the high-art language that their cultural (as much as economic) capital requires. The monument of the POPS thus stays firmly within the design remit of the architectural, economic, and atmospheric model of the space itself: shiny, expensive, clean, and utterly bland.

The atmospheres of our institutional monuments, however, function in more classically exclusionary ways. Take our previously discussed Confederacy monuments. Like physical barriers, these are artifacts explicitly built so as to construct an "us" and "them," an insider and outsider to citizenship. They form an implicit spatial exclusion, an exclusion from the sphere of the educational and judicial, an exclusion from the sphere of the public and the political. Like our separation walls, these monuments likewise provide a feeling of security for some (a feeling of camaraderie through the formation of an exclusive, singular, racialized public) while inducing feelings of fear for others (a feeling of threat and vulnerability through one's severance from the putative "norm"), yet they trap both communities within the paradox of in/security. Still, they make their interests explicit, indicating an allegiance to one community (and their segregative beliefs) while ostracizing another and cautioning them to keep away. While atmospherically powerful, most Confederacy monuments are likewise in fact private rather than public art, often emerging, as W. Fitzhugh Brundage has written, through "private-public partnerships" between local legislatures and private interest groups (Brundage 2005: 124). The monuments not only were part of "the systematic colonization of public spaces by white elites" and an "illustration of white southerners' systematic exclusion of blacks from civic life" (p. 137), but have today fallen into the domain of public preservation groups, "thereby freezing those private decisions in place" (Brundage 2017: n.p.). Private, segregational interests are here codified into public protection, the monument not only excluding and segregating but utilizing the power of public and private simultaneously. Moreover, Confederate monuments, like institutional figurative monuments in general, present an atmosphere of exclusion through the invisible identity politics their determinedly singular positionality promotes. As discussed in chapter 5, the bodies presented here are almost exclusively male. While a representationally female body may occasionally emerge—a body symbolizing "justice" or the motherland, as well as an occasional caryatid (a female figure not only bearing the weight of its building but that famously represents maiden slaves)—just like the city's architecture, our monumental environment reinscribes this space as a city that is male by default (Nelson's 169-foot column and our city's erect edifices alike). Our monuments here thus not only act through their very physical, architectural status but as the implicit atmospheric state that presents the city as white, male, abled, heteronormative, and cis-gendered.

While many of our monuments thus design out diversity—through the exclusivity granted to spaces of consumption, through their exclusively high-art language, through their exclusive reinforcement of bodily and cultural normativity—many artists have come to challenge these atmospheric modes within their practice. Of the many critical public artworks that American conceptual artist David Hammons has produced, his influential performance work *Pissed Off* (1981)—which used Richard Serra's Cor-Ten steel sculpture *TWU* (1980) as its material base—questioned the dominant cultural aesthetic of art in public space. Confronting *TWU* through a performance in which Hammons furtively urinated on the sculpture, the intervention, as Abbe Schriber has described, worked to question "who gains the final authoritative use of the city" (Schriber 2019: 7) while simultaneously addressing the "criminalization of regular behaviors and minor transgressions if carried out by a black person" (p. 5). Noting in particular Hammons's questioning of the lack of urban amenities for those without financial capital in the exhibition text for the work when first exhibited in 1990,[10] *Pissed Off* can thus be seen as not simply a pissing contest with Serra but likewise a project making clear the artist's disgust at the "city's unequal allocation of spatial and economic resources" (p. 7). Either way, as Fusco continues in terms of Hammons's output more generally, the intervention "conjure[s] up some of the more contradictory and even painful aspects of contemporary black life" while simultaneously addressing the "pretence and commercialism of 'high' art and its exclusionary milieu" (Fusco 2001: 45–46). *Pissed Off* can hence be seen as a literally anti-monumental performance challenging the urban atmospheres formed by both institutional public art and the increasingly consumptive, inhospitable environment of the city.[11]

In a triptych of performances addressing the atmospheric functioning of prickly space, the artist Sarah Ross examined the way the body can physically resist this prohibitive landscape. In *Body Configurations Testing Resistance* (2005–2006) (see figures 7.23–7.25), a project explicitly playing off the work of VALIE EXPORT (discussed on p. 179), Ross explored Los Angeles's "Design Out Crime" initiative that used and adapted street furniture as a way of preventing (what had been deemed as) antisocial behavior. Rather than the imperial architecture of Vienna, however, here Ross's body folds itself around fences, bollards, and the now customary public bench armrests of LA, painfully (yet somehow comedically) interlocking her body within the architecture of hostile space. In *Archisuits* (2005–2006) (see figures 7.26 and 7.27), rather than the harshness of bodily resistance, Ross sought a method through which the body could find comfort within this antagonistic landscape. Designing a series of modified tracksuits—each with architectural adjustments inversely mimicking hostile structures and thus letting their users physically "lock in" to them—the suits allowed one to fit in to the sloped and curved walls, the fences and benches that deny our ability to rest or gather. Taken even further in her third project, *InAction* (2008) (see figure 7.28), here, in an ode to Paul Lafrage's 1883 essay "The Right to Be Lazy," Ross created a set of backpacks housing pre-packaged pillows and roll-out blankets designed to "facilitate public inaction" (Ross 2008: n.p.). The suits, available to loan for groups of up to twenty, were seen by Ross as a wearable form enabling their users to "host public conversations" or "contestational actions" while simultaneously helping to "soften the hardened security scapes found at nearly all sites of capitalist management" (n.p.). As with her other two projects, the work attempted to unpack the "mundane violence of architecture and urban planning, targeted at poor and unhoused people" and to examine the methods through which design acts "as an arm of the law, a form that uses the built environment to police and control raced, classed and gendered bodies" (n.p.), yet tries to assuage (or at least negatively reveal) these prickly methods.

Other artists, however, have sought not to reveal our atmospheric walls but rather to recuperate and restore them through civically minded acts. An approach, as Gordon Douglas has explained, in which actors undertake "unauthorized street improvements" as both a "reaction to and product of the structures and processes that define the contemporary city—trends such as state disinvestment, commodification, gentrification, and a general intensification of uneven development" (Douglas 2013: 10), here care is the critical concept, a care that is taken after not being received. Coming under the umbrella of what Michail Galanakis has termed "*domestication*," these insurgent,

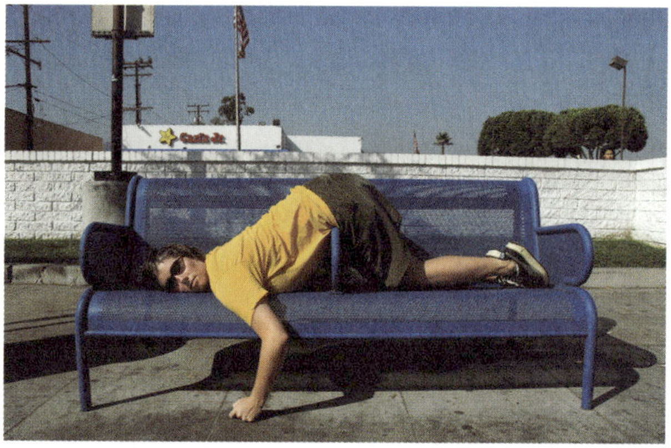

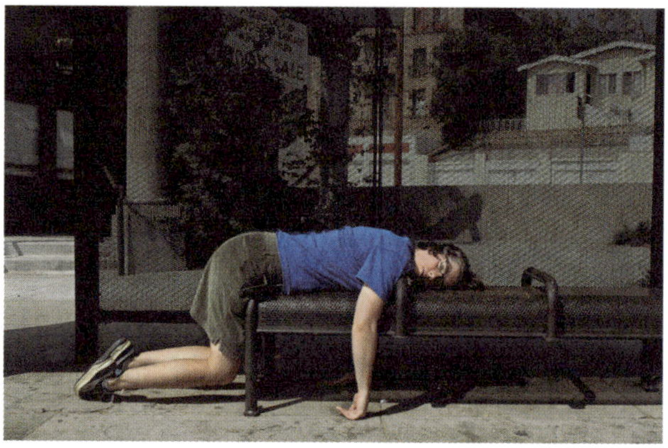

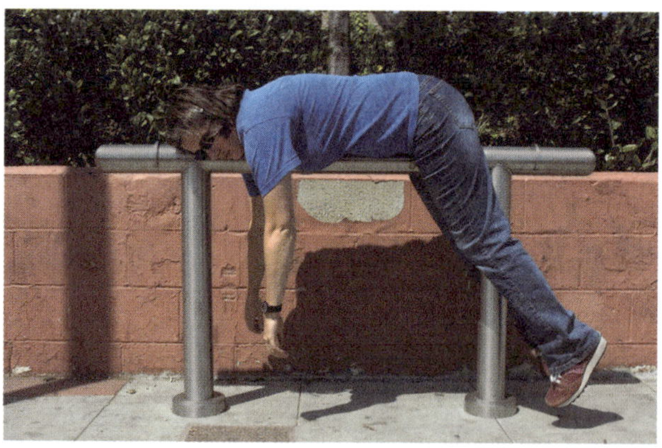

**FIGURE 7.23**
Sarah Ross, *Body Configurations—Testing the Resistance of a Bus Bench, Santa Monica Blvd., West Hollywood*, 2005–2006. Courtesy of the artist.

**FIGURE 7.24**
Sarah Ross, *Body Configurations—Testing the Resistance of a Bus Perch at 3rd and Vermont St., Los Angeles*, 2005–2006. Courtesy of the artist.

**FIGURE 7.25**
Sarah Ross, *Body Configurations—Testing the Resistance of a Bus Bench on Figueroa Ave., Highland Park*, 2005–2006. Courtesy of the artist.

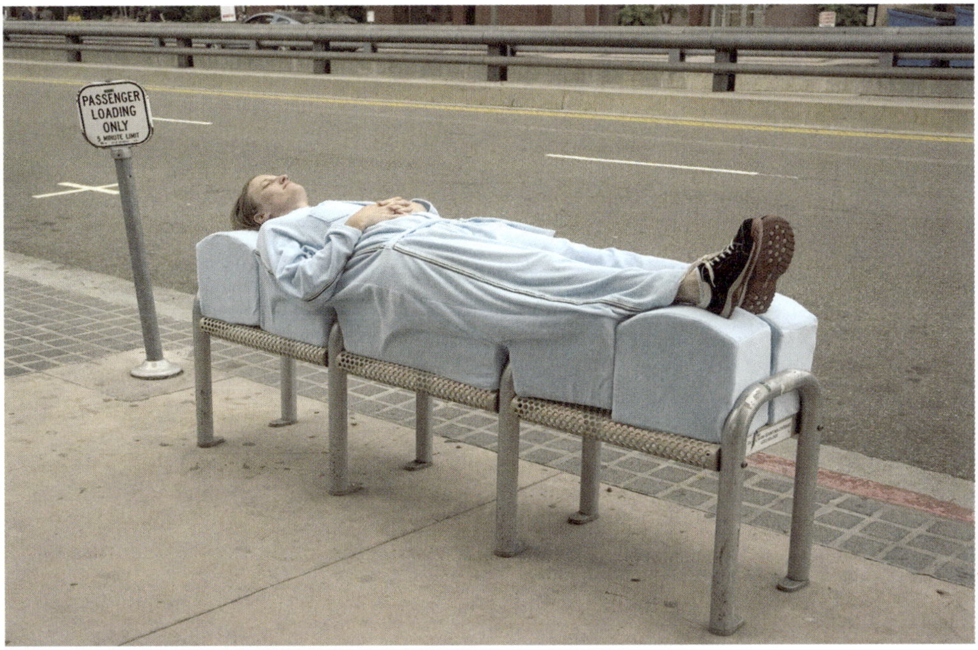


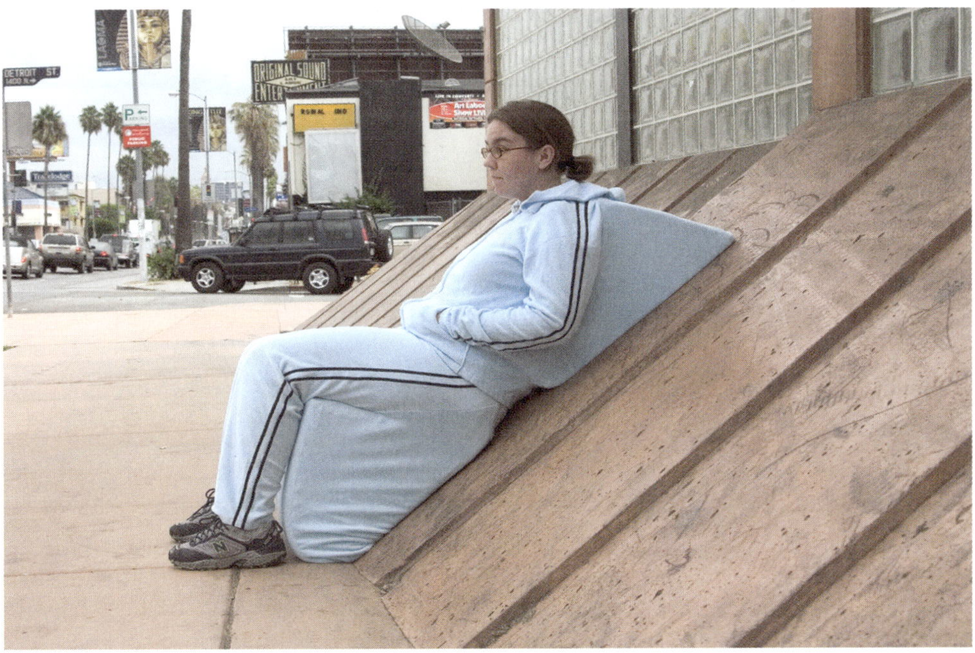


**FIGURES 7.26 AND 7.27**
Sarah Ross, *Archisuits*, 2005–2006. Fabric and foam. Courtesy of the artist.

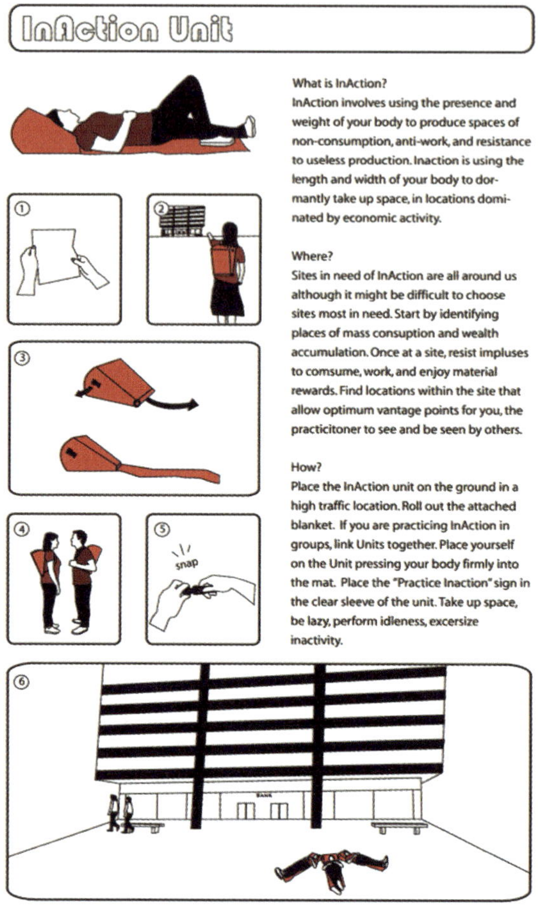


**FIGURE 7.28**
Sarah Ross, *InAction*, 2008. Courtesy of the artist.

appropriative practices emerge when "people take over public spaces and render them relevant to their own communities and cultures," when they "make a space public with their actions that has little or no relation to commercialization" (Galanakis 2013: 83–84). Rather than Zukin's domestication by cappuccino, here the consumptive city is domesticated in itself, the prickliness of public space pacified through marginal, mundane, yet often moving artistic acts. Famously seen within the practice of guerrilla gardening, here groups such as New York's "Green Guerillas"[12] undertook actions such as seed-bombing (in which seed "grenades" would be thrown over the fences of abandoned lots) or the active repossession and recuperation of private spaces in secret nighttime actions. With a long history going back to the emergence of the Diggers and Levellers following the British Civil Wars of the seventeenth century, let alone to the practices of urban farming and urban squatting emergent within 1970s New York, guerrilla gardening was about creating a relation with the environment that was otherwise withheld. In the French artist Didier Courbot's project *needs* (1999–2006), however, it is the careful maintenance not just of the earth that he undertakes, but of our urban environment more widely. In a series of delicate, restrained, elegant interventions, Courbot addressed the degradation of the street through actions that seek not to disrupt but rather to ameliorate city life. From planting flowers in the pavement to installing a pedestrian crossing and repairing a public railing (as seen in figures 7.29–7.31), from fixing a public bench to installing a picnic table and erecting an urban bird feeder,

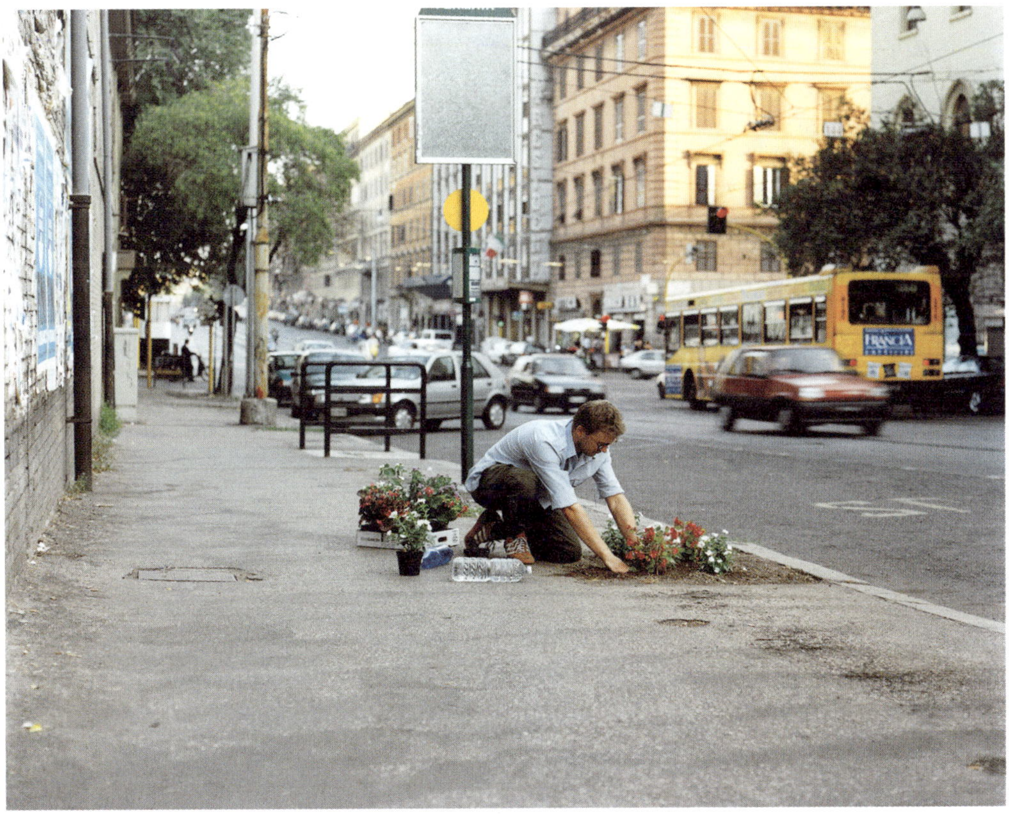

**FIGURE 7.29**
Didier Courbot, *needs (Rome)*, 1999. C-print, 120 × 94 cm. Courtesy of the artist.

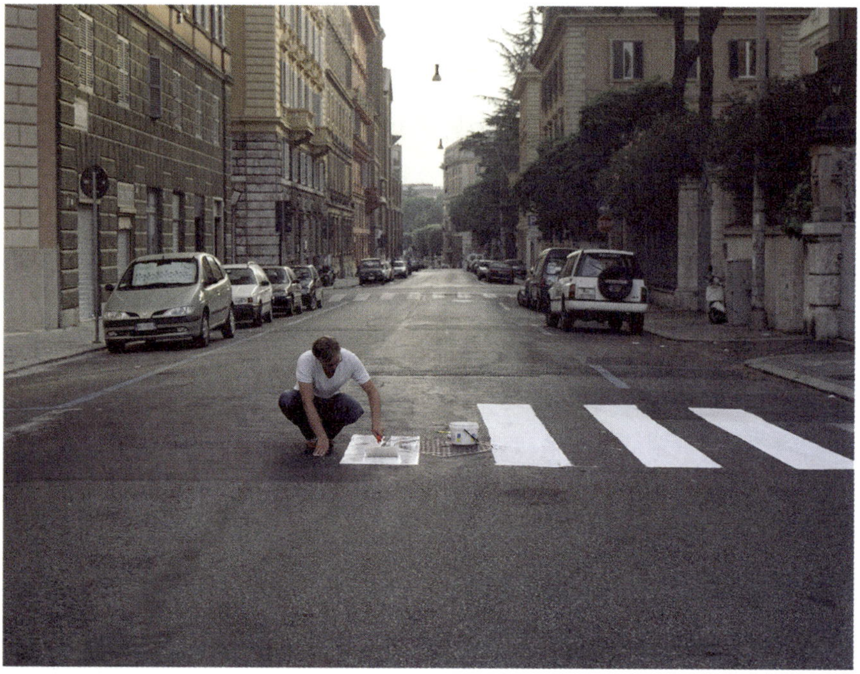

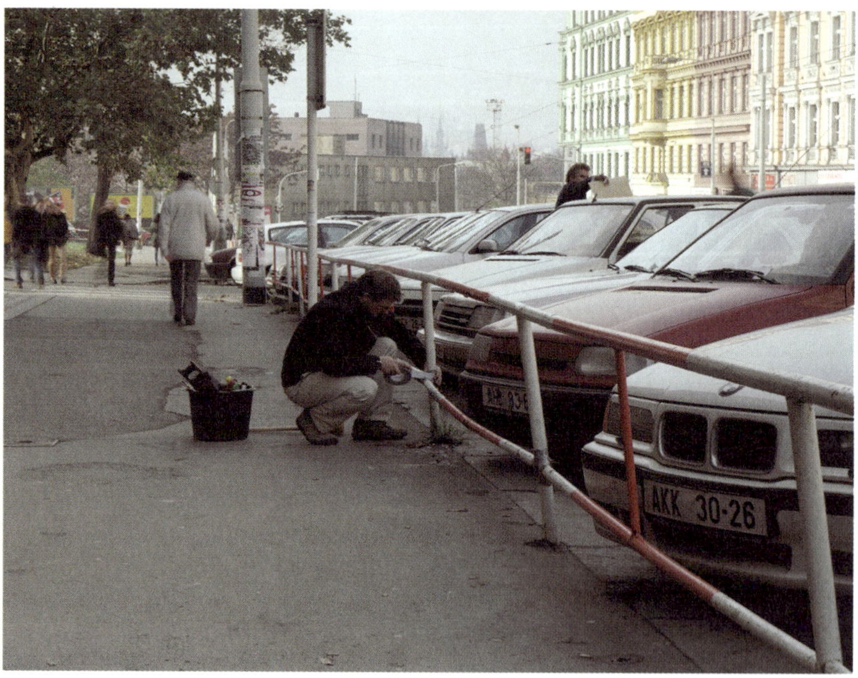


**FIGURE 7.30**
Didier Courbot, *needs (Rome)*, 1999. C-print, 120 × 94 cm. Courtesy of the artist.

**FIGURE 7.31**
Didier Courbot, *needs (Prague)*, 1999. C-print, 120 × 94 cm. Courtesy of the artist.

Courbot rejects the spectacular through minor yet poetic gestures of maintenance and repair, working through the discrete and the lowercase (as seen in the title of the series itself). The almost invisible actions that are here produced seek not the revolutionary but rather to grow in the cracks and gaps of the city, and to provide hope at the edges. They work in a space in which marginal alterations can create both a more hospitable atmospheric environment and more active (and subtly revolutionary) approach to urban life in more general.

The graffiti monument as I'm sure can now be inferred, follows many of the rationales that these atmospherically resistant projects place forward. Rather than the attempt to preclude or pacify interaction that our privately owned spaces generate, to form consumptive spaces devoid of the spontaneous with all diversity designed out, graffiti struggles against these deeply ascetic landscapes. Like the work of Hammons, then, the graffiti monument questions the dominant aesthetic of the city, questions who gets to determine its use, and why such ultimately prosaic transgressions are criminalized. Like Ross, the graffiti body interlocks itself within the prickly city, undertaking disputative actions that soften the hard and engage the hostile. Like Courbot, graffiti appropriates and domesticates the urban realm, emerging in its gaps and fissures and turning the city into a social site, not a marketplace. Still, while these may be some of graffiti's key motives, it too creates an urban atmosphere. After the years of hegemonic castigation and the innumerable "wars" against it, let alone the popular success of Wilson and Kelling's (academically discredited)[13] "broken windows theory" (1982), graffiti for many today remains a visual shorthand for decay and crime, a customarily used aesthetic portraying danger and disrepair, gangs and violence, pollution and harm. Moreover, the visual appearance of strangers (and strangeness) that graffiti could appear to connote—the existence of invisible, "criminal" actors furtively roaming through public space—speaks directly to the archetypal understanding of the public as a space of otherness, and the unknown as one of danger and distrust. Simultaneously, graffiti is also positioned as an invasion of private concerns and private desires within what should be public space. It is seen as an individual desecration of what should be a communal environment and thus a form creating an antisocial atmosphere. Graffiti thus appears both too public and too private simultaneously, too open (and hence dangerous), too personal (and hence pollutive). Yet to add to the confusion, today graffiti can be seen to generate an atmosphere of innovation and creativity too! With the triumph of street art in the media and public imagination, its older sibling graffiti has been dragged (kicking and screaming) into the "creative" fold (unpacked further in chapter 9). As such, and through its prevalence within areas deemed to be artistic, Zukin and Laura Braslow have argued that graffiti has today come to be taken as an atmospheric indicator cementing a site's "reputation as an emerging creative district," coming in this way to "attract rather than repel investors," and thus standing as one of the critical "'push' factors in the process of group migration" (Zukin and Braslow 2011: 138). Here, then, the fear that graffiti generates emerges through the fear of change that its appearance can be seen to presage.

For other communities, however, not only for its subcultural members but for those outside the normative majority, graffiti can come to create not a feeling of exclusion or danger but a sense of inclusion or safety. It can act as a material evidencing of other voices, of other ways of seeing and acting in the city. It can be seen as a visible presence that actively engages in the city through a position of passion and dedication. The graffiti monument can thus be seen to strive, as Wanda Vrasti and Smaran Dayal have said of political-aesthetic struggles and interventions in the city, in more general to "make transparent and work through the atmospheric barriers enforced by cultural and institutional conventions of manner, taste, and appearance," to reveal the way in which our cities "reflect and invite the movement of some bodies more so than others, bearing the mark of privilege like second nature" (Vrasti and Dayal 2016: 1004). Atmospheric walls, like their architectural antecedents, define who appears in the city, define who is welcome in public and who must retreat to private, who can and can't impact and affect these urban boundaries. Perhaps unsurprisingly, then, a recent study by Pablo Navarrete-Hernandeza, Arielle Vetro, and Paz Concha found that so-called tough-on-graffiti policies did little if anything to address people's actual fear of crime. The authors found that while "eliminating graffiti has a weak significant impact on perceived safety . . . removing solid walls leads to significant improvements of perceptions of safety, with the effect being stronger for women" (Navarrete-Hernandeza et al. 2021: n.p.). It was walls, they found, rather than graffiti, that increased fear. It was urban walls that became a visceral sign of public danger.

## CONCLUSION *OR* COMMON BORDERS

Graffiti is thus an image whose architectural and atmospheric status upsets the diaphanous line between public and private. It is an image whose spatial position as much as its intentions, opinions as much as its interests, exist at the very edge of these domineering binaries. Moreover, the *reactions* to graffiti—which in a circular motion form part of its very rationale—disrupt the idea of the public as open and accessible, as a place of public, not private, speech. It disrupts the idea of the city as a space for corporate not communal acts. As terms, then, as means of understanding the relationship between inside and outside, inclusion and exclusion, revelation and protection, public and private can themselves be seen as insufficient tools to aid our comprehension of graffiti, let alone of the city today. While a "pervasive spatial configuration," then, the paradigm of the "separate spheres" simply does not, as Jane Rendell has argued, "describe the full lived experience of urban dwellers" (Rendell 1998: 110). Without denying their importance as an ideological mode of framing the world, Rendell thus seeks to identify a "term which is undecidable within a binary logic—a term that includes both binary terms and yet exceeds their scope" (p. 111). What she seeks is a term that can help to explicate the "architectural spaces within the city which are neither wholly private nor public," the spaces that are neither entirely "urban nor domestic" (p. 111).

There are two terms that can come to meet this position—and thus help support a better comprehension of graffiti—these being the *border* as employed by Richard Sennett (2017) and the *commons* as formulated by Stavros Stavrides (2016). For Sennett, first, the border is a conception set in diametric opposition to the boundary. Following an ecological framing, the border is positioned as a site in which the highest organic interactivity occurs "due to the meeting of different species or physical conditions" that these environments foment (Sennett 2017: n.p.). It is thus an active, permeable space, a location such as "where the shoreline of a lake meets solid land," which becomes a "zone of exchange . . . where organisms find and feed off other organisms" (n.p.). At the territorially closed *boundary*, however, a site patrolled and surveilled by the beasts at the (literal) top of food chain, sterility is the dominant mode, and segregation inevitable. The boundary is thus a "limit, a territory beyond which a particular species does not stray," a hard edge that functions through its negative effects, "by things petering out, not happening" (n.p.). Yet for Sennett, the wall, often thought of as the hard and fast boundary, is in fact understood to exemplify the porosity of the border. Like the walled cities of the medieval era in which the edge marked out a zone not of separation but of interactivity, the extramural position can be seen as one of latent fertility, containing the potential of both transgression and integration. While the wall is thus like a "cell membrane," both "letting matter flow in and out," the boundary is like the "cell wall," a "container holding things in" (n.p.). From the highways that "cut through cities" or the "invisible walls infamously . . . used to mark off the territories separating the rich from the poor, or race from race" (n.p.), the atmospheric impediment—for Sennett an archetypal *boundary*—is thus understood as a much more domineering mode of urban separation than the architectural threshold itself. The border of the street can hence be understood as a space in which cultural contact becomes unavoidable, yet in which this proximity of difference acts as a source of renewal from which identity and community can be reimagined collectively.

For Stavrides, similarly, commons are spaces that are neither public—"created by a specific authority . . . which controls them and establishes the rules under which people may use them"—nor private—"controlled by specific individuals or economic entities that have the right to establish the conditions under which others may use them"—but rather zones created in an effort "to establish a common world that houses, supports and expresses the community they participate in" (Stavrides 2016: 54). Common space is thus a mutual space that forms a "porous world" (p. 54), a world forming "intermediary areas of crossing, by opening the inside to the outside," an edge as meeting point in which "separation is always and simultaneously an act of connection" (p. 56). Linking this conception with Victor Turner's work on liminality (as discussed in chapter 6), Stavrides sees the horizontality of the commons to link with *communitas* not as a "feeling of belonging to a specific closed community but a feeling of becoming part of a community that is potentially limitless" (p. 59). Here, then, we have a conception diametrically opposed to the sense of isolation that the bounded, walled-off community connotes. Commoning is thus about "opening the community of those who share common worlds, opening the circles of sharing to include newcomers, opening the sharing relations to new possibilities through a rethinking of sharing rules and opening the boundaries that define the spaces of sharing" (p. 3). In this way, the threshold as commons comes to "inventively threaten . . . urban order by upsetting dominant taxonomies of spaces" (p. 56). What it does, Stavrides suggests, is develop "spatialities of commoning . . . in the form of images which trigger thought," develop ways that can "imagine and express the characteristics of common space and by doing so . . . invent possible forms of space sharing and sharing-through-space" (p. 7). Neither public or private, the commons overcomes these fixed binaries through forming a space in between space, a shared, collective site that can never be closed off.

Sennett's border and Stavrides's commons are spaces, I am here suggesting, that are enacted within the materiality of the graffiti monument. Neither public nor private, neither open nor closed, graffiti is in fact constituted by its place at the edge of these binary pairs. It does not publicize or privatize its site; it occupies the porous perimeter between the two. It does not work through public or private speech; it rests at the elusive limits linking them both. It does not engage public or private interests; it exposes the site in which they meet. What the graffiti monument thus introduces in the city is the possibility of the border, the threshold in between embodying a site that is shared, that is both message to a counterpublic and offering to a public-at-large. Graffiti thus "gestures," as Stavrides himself continues, "towards a possible commoning through representations that criticizes, ironically deconstructs or, almost sacrilegiously, attacks dominant images of the city" (Stavrides 2016: 203). As 10Foot's poetic statement in figure 7.32 comes to exemplify, the act of "defacement" gives material form to "gestures of symbolic appropriation as well as to gestures of inventive inhabiting" (p. 203), and can hence "ignite practices of space-commoning through the reintroduction of repressed or violently erased common memories into the public realm" (p. 205). The graffiti monument thus questions the point at which public and private space, public and private speech, public and private opinions start and stop. Here the monument becomes the trace, the *warning*, in which access to the city becomes its monumental theme. Here graffiti becomes the border, the commons, that enacts a new form of access to the city itself.

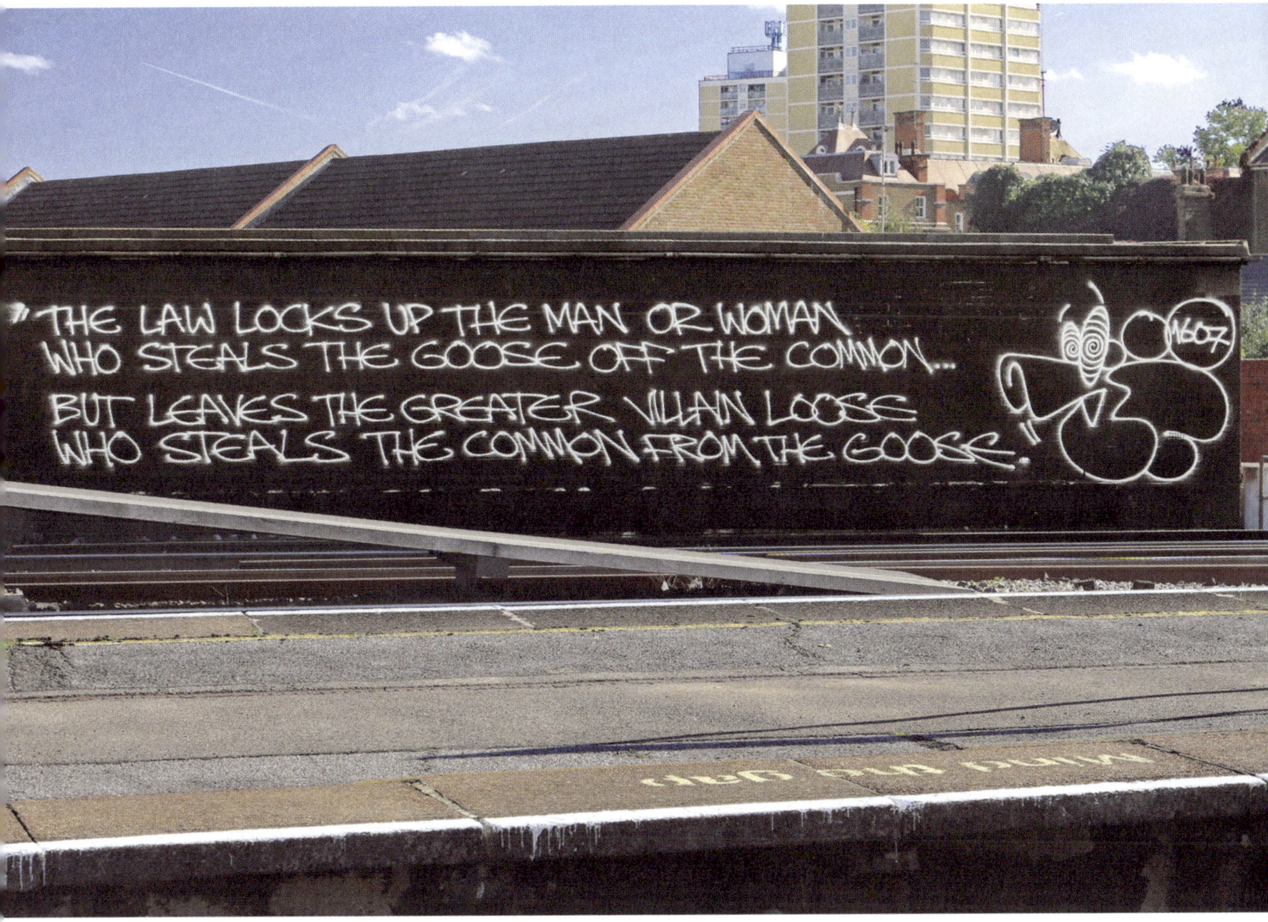


**FIGURE 7.32**
*10Foot*, 2022. Vauxhall Station, South London. Photo: Alex Ellison.

# 8

# VISIBILITY AND INVISIBILITY

Graffiti is positioned at the edge of our optical range, at once the most evident and most concealed of public arts. While the image thrives through its intense visibility—the stylistic focus on captivation and distribution in graffiti creating an object that is made explicitly so as to be seen—its performative process is one in which invisibility is critical, the participatory action necessarily hidden from the public eye. These differing scales of perceptibility—a dynamic between what I have termed "artefactual publicity" and "performative invisibility" (Schacter 2015)—are fundamental to graffiti's functioning. Without material discernibility, graffiti could not attract, could not speak. But without bodily obscurity, graffiti could not even begin to exist! Invisibility thus enables visibility. Yet in the surveillance society many of us today live within, the digital transformation of the so-called "smart city" (Townsend 2013) has led to a decreasing ability to remain private in the public sphere—a position mirroring the increasing privatization of the city noted in chapter 7. The classic site of the public protest or annual carnival is thus no longer a site of concealment but of capture, with any notion of the street as a site in which one can "fall into the crowd" extinguished. As such, the in/visible balance that graffiti has relied on—the ability to publicly proclaim the name and then physically fade into black—has gone through unimaginable change over the last decades. The all-consuming visibility of the contemporary urban body thus leads to an inversion of the perceptible norms of graffiti. Rather than the visible image and the invisible body, the always-visible-body should presage an increasingly invisible image world or, at the least, a more precarious performative process. Clarity, here, thus leads to obscurity.

This chapter will examine the tense relationship between fugitivity and revelation in both graffiti and the city through examining contemporary techniques of *sur*-veillance (our witnessing from above), *contra*-veillance (our rejection of the gaze), as well as of *sous*- and *meta*-veillance (our observation from below and our sensing of senses). It will be a means of not just observing but evading, engaging, and seeing sight that we will explore here, modes of appearance and publicity that function not just through (literal) enlightenment but through the indistinct and the opaque. The dazzling lights of the increasingly digitized and automated city has for many led toward an embracement of a space in which ambiguity becomes a technique not just of escape but of potential in an environment where anonymity is available only to the few. The monument here thus will be seen not only as that which can repel or attract attention, as something visualized and surveilled itself,[1] but as that which can reveal the dense asymmetries of visibility. The graffiti monument will in this way be understood first as a monumental achievement within the contemporary securitized city but likewise as an artifact revealing the possibilities of urban opacity today.

## CONTEMPORARY VISIBILITY (*SUR*-VEILLANCE)

Let's head back to Granary Square again. While in the previous chapter we discussed its plop art and its constitutive lack, its frictionless aesthetic engendering its private acts of consumption, what was not mentioned was the impossibility of our ever being in private within the square's atmospheric walls. This is a "public" site in which automatic facial recognition (AFR) was used between 2016 and 2018 without the consent of the site's users (and almost certainly illegally), a practice undertaken via an equally covert partnership with the Metropolitan Police (only admitted to in 2019), which handed over images of individuals to the private landowners of the King's Cross Estate Services without any processes of oversight.[2] While the usage of AFR was discontinued after an investigation by the Information Commissioner's Office (ICO), the landowners claimed that their "detection and tracking methods" had been employed solely "in the interest of public safety and to ensure that everyone who visits has the best possible experience" (Rawlinson 2019). Whom the owners of the site were looking for, what sort of experiences they were trying to create, and why they thought scanning the faces of hundreds of thousands of people without permission was an appropriate tool to achieve this is still unclear.

A contemporary tool of visualization that has today come to exemplify our pervasive surveillance culture, facial recognition software is an omnipresent fact in hundreds of cities around the world today.[3] A form of biometric technology (alongside fingerprinting and retina scans) that confirms an individual's identity through "face mapping," AFR and LFR (live biometric facial recognition) strive to extract, analyze, and classify facial features from a real-world environment before measuring them against a set of enrolled images held within a preexisting databank. As shown in Rafael Lozano-Hemmer's installation *Zoom Pavilion* (see figures 8.1 and 8.2), AFR can thus distinguish distinct individuals and map their movements and spatial relationships. Yet through developing proximity data on their targets, it can also, as seen in Lozano-Hemmer's work, examine and test the behavioral patterns of not just individuals but groups alike. While promoted as a scientifically exact tool, however, a tool moving beyond the shortcomings of mere mortals, AFR constantly fails. Using human operators alongside their human-formed algorithms, facial *mis*recognition emerges via the malfunctions both of the software (often via the inherent/unconscious biases of their programmers) as well as of their human users (in much the same way). Moreover, the watchlists that these tools utilize are commonly constructed without independent guidance and have the potential to discriminate against communities before the technology has even been introduced to a live environment. Gender theorist Shoshana Magnet, for example, has exposed the manner in which biometric systems' usage of white male bodies as the presumed norm leads to them malfunctioning when observing women, people of color, or people with disabilities (Magnet 2011: 45). As a result of incorrect identification through a process of "false acceptance" (emergent when a "person who is not you is accepted as you"), "false rejection" (emergent "when you are not accepted as you"), as much as a total failure "to be enrolled in the system at all" (p. 22), lack of representative data thus becomes a genuine danger for those outside the putative whole.

First publicly tested in the United Kingdom by the Met Police at London's Notting Hill Carnival in 2017,[4] today the main biometric tool they use is produced by Japanese conglomerate NEC, which recently refused to reveal the origins of their datasets (or even the statistics relating to gender and race) during a case brought against them at the

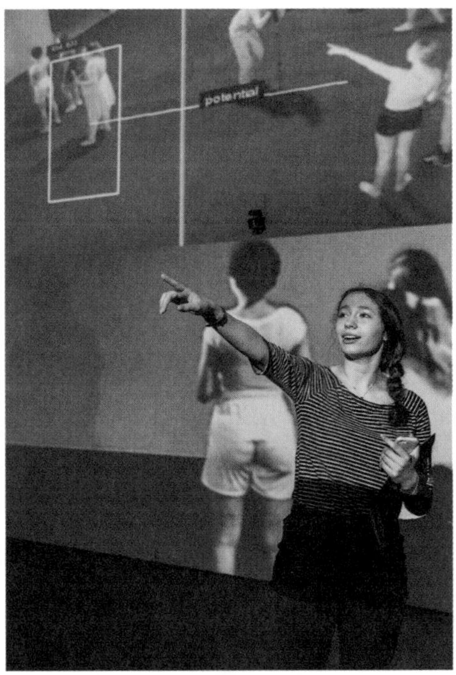


**FIGURE 8.1**
Rafael Lozano-Hemmer, *Zoom Pavilion*, 2018. Courtesy of Antimodular Research. Photo: François Maisonneuve.

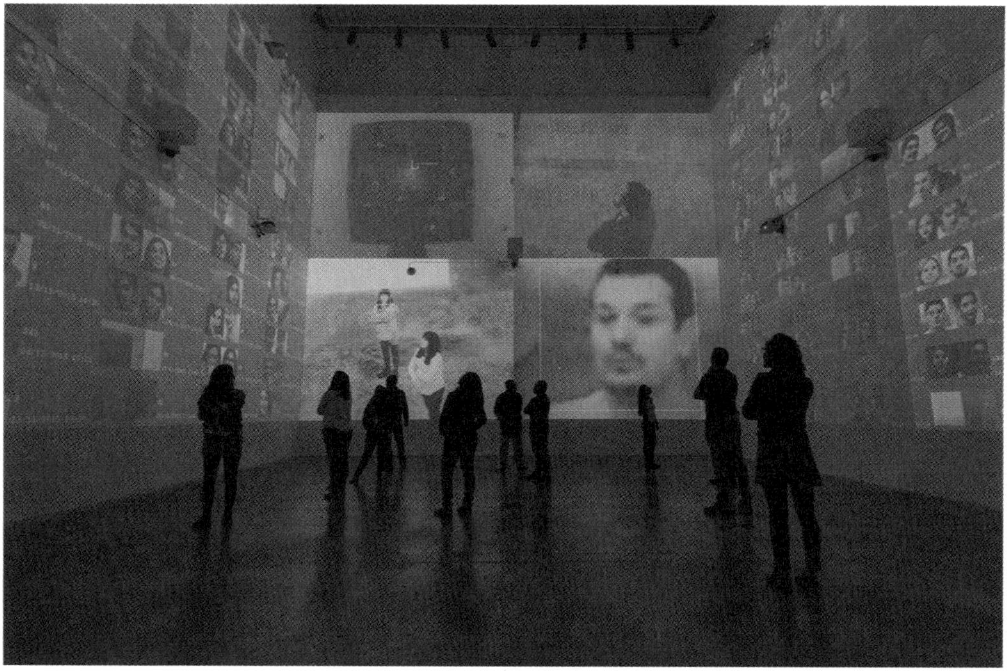

**FIGURE 8.2**
Rafael Lozano-Hemmer, collaboration with Krzysztof Wodiczko, *Zoom Pavilion*, 2015. Courtesy of Antimodular Research. Photo: Oliver Santana.

British Court of Appeal. Expert witness Dr. Anil Jain explained that while he could not prove whether the software had a "discriminatory impact" as he was denied access to the datasets on which the software was trained, the police themselves were in the same way "not in a position to evaluate" whether the software they were using contained implicit bias (Jain 2019). Prior to NEC, however, the software used in the United Kingdom was created by the infamous US-based company Clearview AI, which was fined £7.5 million by the ICO in 2022 for illegally scraping the *twenty billion* images accessible on their database from websites and social media platforms without their owners' knowledge or permission. The ICO found that Clearview breached UK data protection laws through "failing to use the information of people in the UK in a way that is fair and transparent," through "failing to have a lawful reason for collecting people's information," "failing to have a process in place to stop the data being retained indefinitely," as well as, incredibly, through "asking for additional personal information, including photos, when asked by members of the public if they are on their database," a clear "disincentive to individuals who wish to object to their data being collected and used" (ICO 2022). While Clearview's concepts of privacy (and their CEO's links to a clique of alt-right radical white nationalists)[5] are genuinely disturbing, the tools of visibility they and others use have been configured in a perfectly contrasting, perfectly opaque manner themselves. While the United Kingdom has today become an internationally leading testing ground for the technology, there remain no overarching legal regulations for facial recognition. During a recent Justice and Home Affairs Committee session, in fact, the committee warned that there was no "clear strategic plan" or "mechanisms to control the use of new technologies," and neither could it be "ascertained where ultimate responsibility lies" (House of Lords 2022: 4). "As it stands," the committee concluded, "users are in effect making it up as they go along" (p. 4).

While Granary Square may no longer be illegally scanning our faces, closed-circuit television (CCTV) is still highly dominant in the space. Here the images "captured by CCTV" or by the site's "appointed photographer or videographer" are used not only for "maintaining the safety of visitors, security of property and premises and for preventing and investigating crime" but likewise for "marketing, advertising and promotional purposes" (King's Cross Estate Services 2022). Just by being in the space, we are thus passively assenting to our bodily capture and bodily corporatization, our private movement through space turned into privately owned (and exploitable) data. As seen with its AFR, London is a city with a famous penchant for CCTV. Most commonly witnessed through its many pan-tilt-zoom (PTZ) cameras—as seen in the artist SpY's pointed installation *Cameras* in figure 8.3—these can today be moved manually as well as automatically and, unlike their fixed-view ancestors that were fixed to equally limiting analog videotape recorders, can record high-definition images and sound that can be kept as indefinitely as the hardware they are attached to. A recent study estimated that there are over a billion CCTV cameras globally, over half in mainland China, which has just under one camera for every two people (Blischoff 2023).[6] Yet CCTV is just one of a wide range of surveillance techniques utilized today. Within the larger pool of what is termed "urban informatics," we are today not just watched and listened to but so too *felt*. While our streetlights engage in sonic surveillance and our dustbins[7] track our smartphones, so too other forms of sensor data—from locational media and vehicle license plate readers[8] to purchasing data and the omnipresent "internet of things"—jointly track our movements while scanning them for unique markers (literally so, via gait recognition technology). Surveillance today is thus fully networked, biometrically multimodal, and statistically universalized through data points that have collectively come to standardize, index, and manage their set populations. Yet that doesn't mean that the human eye has lost *all* its disciplinary power. At Granary Square, for example, an array of private security personnel are employed to work alongside the AFR and the CCTV. Hyper-visible individuals in hi-visibility clothing adorned with an array of bells, whistles, and body-worn cameras, these uniformed "ambassadors" (Sleiman and Lippert 2010) are visible, mobile companions to the often invisible and static surveillance technologies these spaces otherwise use. Policing behavior through both "establishing

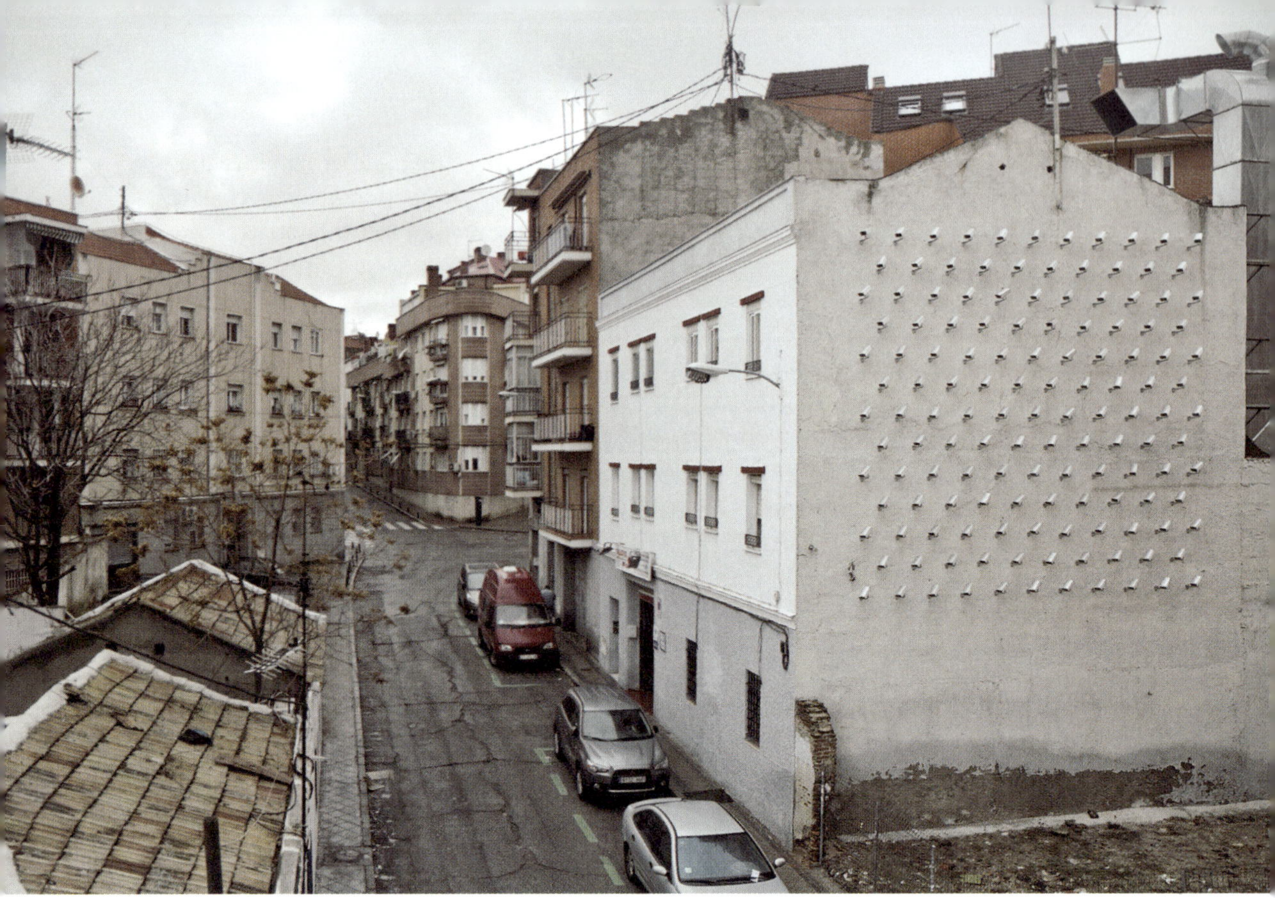

**FIGURE 8.3**
SpY, *Cameras*, 2013. Installation of 150 fake security cameras on building façade with the intention of not watching over anything. Courtesy of the artist.

a visible presence and discreetly invoking law," the ambassadors not only work to dissuade the "undesirable" (i.e., the non-consumptive) from entering the site, but likewise act as the "'eyes and ears' of police" in a vertically integrated surveillance machine (Sleiman and Lippert 2010: 318).

The "*new surveillance*" of the twenty-first century, as Gary T. Marx has described it, the surveillance enabled by both the maximalist and microscopic capacities of our digital age, has thus entirely transformed the way we understand visibility in the city today. It has come to extend our "senses and cognitive abilities" through tools that today take on both a "spongelike absorbency and laserlike[9] specificity," through sensory tools that occur from both "farther away and closer" than ever before (Marx 2005: 817). In the near field, surveillance is thus ever more intimate. From our resting heart rate to our body mass index, from our front doors to our bedrooms, we now watch *ourselves* while others watch us (and while our watches watch us too), not just consenting to our surveillance but inviting it into our own homes. Here, we willingly submit to our capture in exchange for “consumer benefits (e.g., frequent flyer and shopper discounts) or for convenience (e.g., fast track lanes on toll roads in which fees are paid in advance)” (p. 818), ease of use trumping any concerns of seemingly distant privacy issues.[10] Yet it is in the space of health and safety apps that our most personal information is freely given up. Here, as Julie E. Cohen has explored, surveillance has become not only privatized but “increasingly participatory,” aligned with “the exercise of economic and expressive liberty” (Cohen 2016: 207). The gamification of our personal data (and our whereabouts) has created an environment in which we publicly “check in” and “check out” of sites online, display the routes we’ve cycled or run, reveal the locations of our families and places of work. We track our animal companions, ultimately tracking ourselves as seen in figure 8.4. We fix ourselves (and our friends) within the panopticon-like structure of the Instagram square,[11] our online selves regulating and exposing our offline ones, the selfies of today coming to form the biometric profiles of tomorrow.[12] Any act in the city is thus today an act potentially witnessable to the entire world.

While the microscopic is freely given, however, the macroscopic emerges via an ever-present surveillance from above. Here, the god’s-eye view emergent via the power of military and commercial drones (known officially as unmanned aerial vehicles or

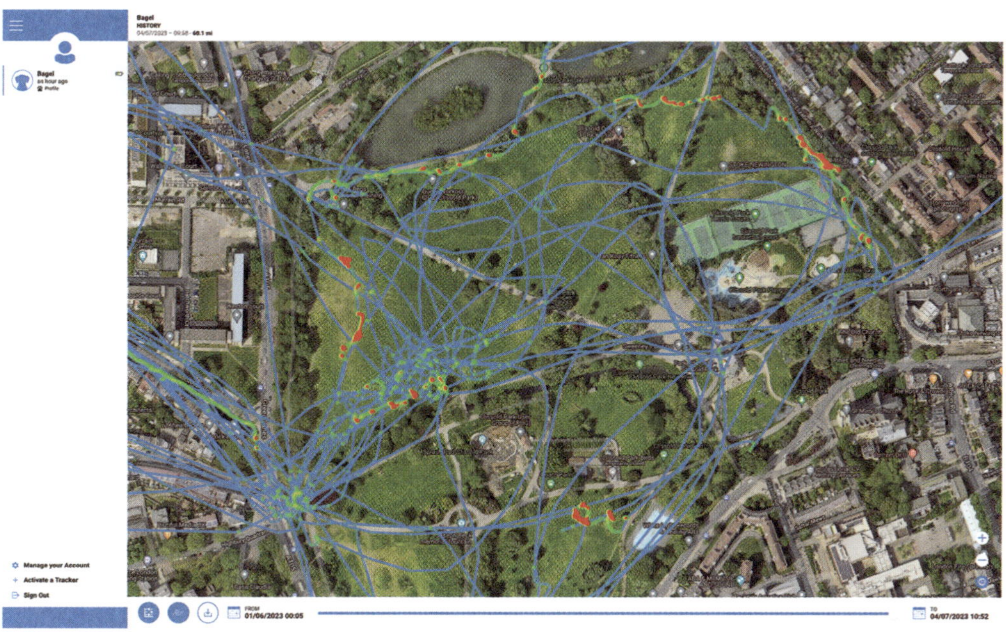


**FIGURE 8.4**
Screenshot from dog tracker (The Bagel). Image captured July 4, 2023.

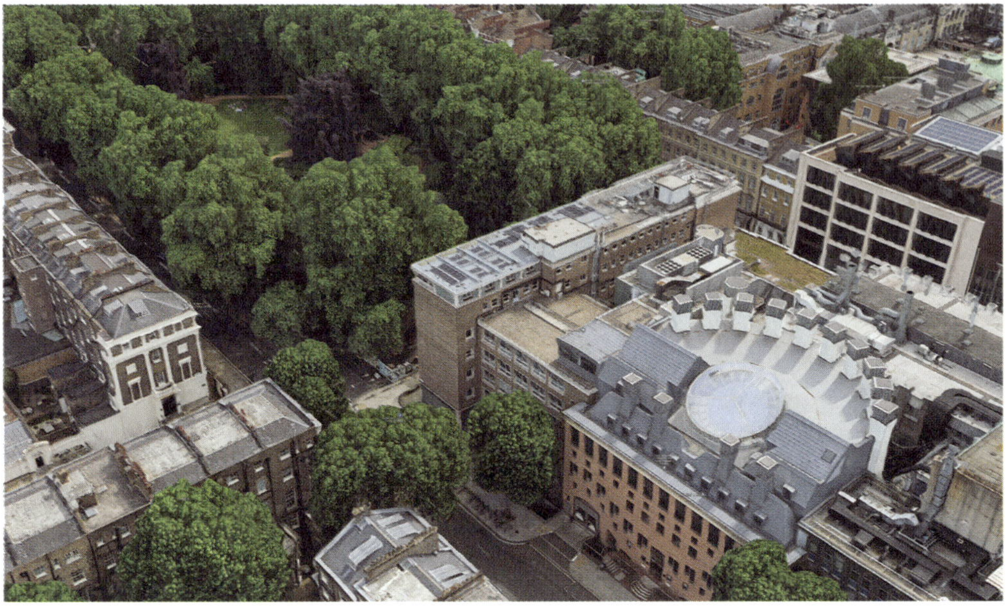

**FIGURE 8.5**
Screenshot from Google Street View 3D (14 Taviton Street, London). Image captured February 14, 2022.

UAVs) as much as from satellites and the globally dominating forms of Google Earth and Google Street View (as per figure 8.5) are slowly digitizing and monumentalizing every inch of our planet. Explored in artist Jon Rafman's *Nine Eyes of Google Street View* (as seen in figures 8.6 and 8.7)—a vast, ongoing project documenting Google's "endless quest to photograph every highway and byway in the free world," a digital surveillance of the planet which has come to appear not as a "distrusted invasion of privacy" but "made 'friendly' and transformed into an accepted spectacle" (Rafman 2009)—our cities and the activities within them have become visible in perpetuity from the comfort of our armchair. Yet these tools of visibility have also come to create what Caren Kaplan and Andrea Miller have termed the new "technology of atmospheric policing" (Kaplan and Miller 2019: 421). From the sonic aggression of police helicopters to the disconcerting buzzing of UAVs, atmospheric policing patrols the city from above so as to pervade it from below, colonizing both the literal and mental atmospheres. Moreover, the systems of "predictive analytics" that these airborne tools of visibility help to institute, via their ability to plot patterns of flow and movement, lead to both individuals and entire areas of the city being targeted by police action, whether or not a crime has occurred. Brian Jordan Jefferson's examination of predictive crime mapping, for example, has shown the way in which "spatial statistical analysis [and] geovisualization" have come to entrench and legitimize racialized policing, already existent datasets that are the

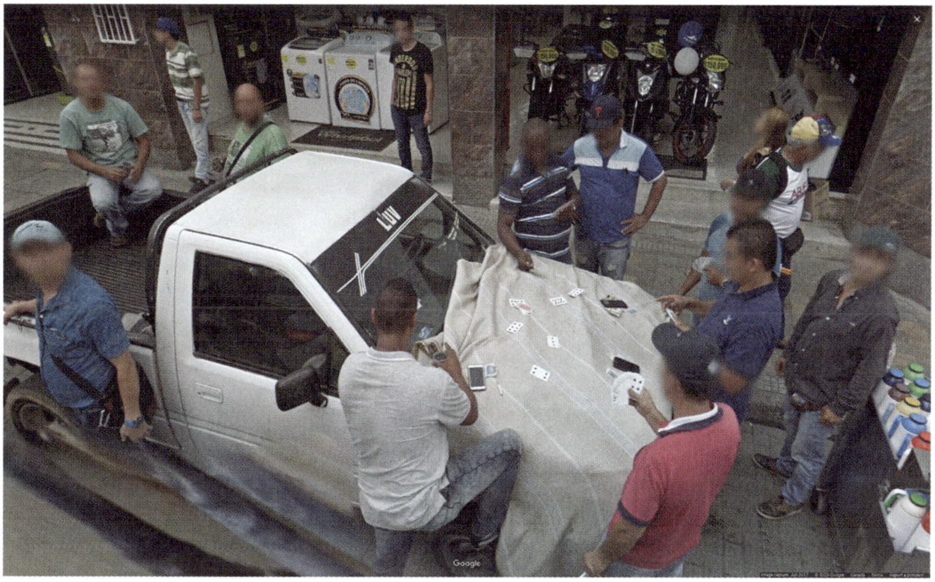


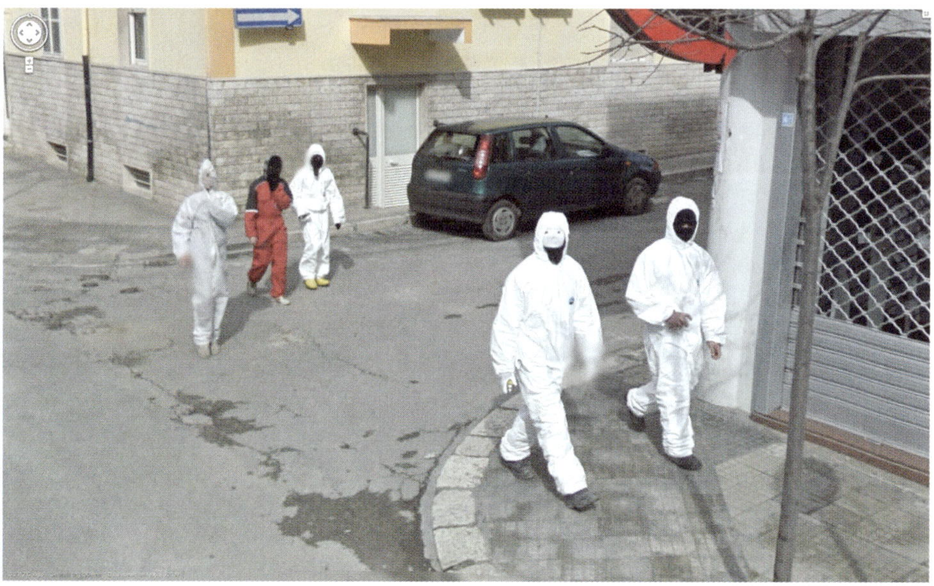

**FIGURE 8.6**

Jon Rafman, *53128 Cl. 51, Medellín, Antioquia*, 2019. Archival pigment print on dibond aluminum. 101.6 × 162.6 cm, 40 × 64 in. Courtesy of the artist and Sprüth Magers.

**FIGURE 8.7**

Jon Rafman, *Via Guglielmo Marconi, Grottaglie, Puglia, Italy*, 2013. Archival pigment print on dibond aluminum. 101.6 × 162.6 cm, 40 × 64 in. Courtesy of the artist and Sprüth Magers.

"effects of invidious law making . . . discriminatory policing policy . . . and police officer bias" ensuring that new geographic information systems simply come to "reinforce the differential policing of racialized people and places" (Jefferson 2018: 2). Surveillance from above and below thus becomes modeled into simulations that, in a self-fulfilling manner, further entrench attacks on already marginalized communities, exacerbating disproportionate policing in which the deployment of high-level violence for low-level crimes (often assisted via UAVs and helicopters) has led to an equally disproportionate impact on marginalized communities' very lives. Exemplifying the way in which the "technology of everyday policing practices," as Kaplan and Miller continue, is linked with "genealogies of colonial violence and population management"—in particular within a military-police nexus that is most visible when taking place at the border (Kaplan and Miller 2019: 423)—what becomes clear is that while surveillance today is all-pervading, not all of us are surveilled alike.

It is thus not only that the digital turn in surveillance has exacerbated (rather than ameliorated) already extant issues of racialization but, as Simone Browne has argued, that the paradigm of surveillance culture from which it emerged is itself set within a constitutively racialized frame. Browne's discussion of what Frantz Fanon termed "epidermalization" or the "imposition of race on the body," alongside what she terms the "facticity of surveillance in black life," begins to reveal a way of comprehending surveillance (both in the US setting that Browne examines and within a much wider postcolonial context) as that which not only comes to "reify boundaries along racial lines" but comes to "undergird and sustain the intersecting surveillances of the present order" (Browne 2015: 7–9). As such, whether examining AFR and UAVs or "traffic stops (driving while black) [and] stop-and-frisk policing practices" (p. 13), Browne's approach takes on board a historical perspective—going back to the surveillance techniques of the slavery era, from branding and photography to the schematic plans of slave ships themselves—in which individuals of color become conceptualized through a notion of "abnormalization" and whereby the "mere presence of blackness gets coded as criminal" (p. 20). As seen earlier in Anderson's discussion of white space (2015), here techniques of visibility become intimately intertwined with the techniques of white supremacy in which the "totalizing surveillance" and "cumulative white gaze" of the pre-emancipation period have continued directly into the "postslavery era" of today (Browne 2015: 21). Whether it is Homeland Security's "If you see something, say something" or the British Transport Police's "See it. Say it. Sorted," the everyday citizen is here deputized into the local neighborhood watch, making every set of eyes the eyes of police. As such, as Browne continues, while the "street behaviors of white men (standing still and talking, using a cellular phone, passing an unseen object from one to another) may be coded as normal and thus granted no attention . . . the same activity performed by Black men will be coded as lying on or beyond the boundary of the normal, and thus subject to disciplinary action" (p. 17).[13] The incredibly prescient work of British artist Keith Piper, in particular his installation and video piece *Tagging the Other* (see figure

8.8), can be seen to exemplify Brown's argument here. Produced as the United Kingdom was about to enter the European single market, and exploring the way in which black Britons experience of the legendarily violent stop and search (SUS) laws[14] were not only being reinforced by the digital but transmuted into a domain encompassing the whole of Europe, the work visually depicts the artist as a scrutinized target of digital visualization. Backing this with a series of audio fragments from contemporary news sources discussing increasing racist violence across the continent, *Tagging the Other* explores not only the technological fixing of the European "other," but likewise the implicitly racialized techniques of visibility that seek, as Piper has said, "to classify and codify the individual within an arena in which the logical constraints of race, ethnicity, nation, and culture are fixed and delineated in a discourse of exclusion" (Piper 1997: n.p.).

With that said (and as many do say), if you've got nothing to hide you've got nothing to fear, right? This is the constant refrain of those (from senior politicians to "the man on the street") who insist we should not be concerned by these new tools of visibility, that the hit we take to our privacy is worth the gain we make to our apparent safety.[15] If we can catch just one criminal or stop just one plot, the "minor" inconvenience of being permanently surveilled is all worth it. Yet not only does this belief privilege those at the least risk of state violence, but the maxim, as legal scholar Daniel J. Solove has argued,

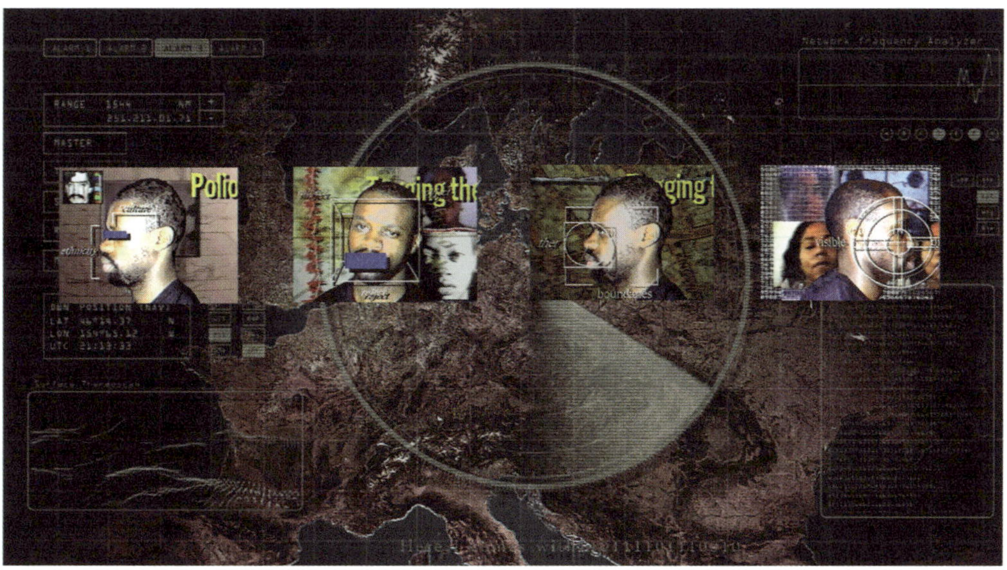

**FIGURE 8.8**
Keith Piper, *Tagging the Other*, 1992. Mixed media installation with four video monitors and slide projection. Courtesy of the artist.

rests on the assumption that secrecy is inherently immoral and privacy simply "about hiding bad things" (Solove 2007: 767). Rather than arguing about what one would or wouldn't want to hide, then, the form of uncontrolled surveillance that we today witness (or rather do *not* witness) must be understood as a tool of visibility that inhibits not only illegal activities but so too legal ones, reducing the "range of viewpoints expressed and the degree of freedom with which to engage in political activity" (p. 765).[16] Not only making people more fearful of public assembly, however, high-level surveillance also has the danger of leading to what Solove terms "aggregation," the combination of "small bits of seemingly innocuous data" that together can come to reveal things that we do not (yet) know about ourselves, while acting as predictors of future activities that, as we have yet to do them, become impossible to disprove![17] And this is all without even discussing the errors that these datasets commonly contain, the discriminately coded algorithms that skew the picture created as much as the total impossibility of our ever being able to amend or even access these errors themselves! It doesn't touch the issue of secondary use, in which "data obtained for one purpose [is then used] for a different unrelated purpose without the person's consent" (p. 767), nor the length of time our data will be kept,[18] nor the fact that the data collected is so commonly lost![19] The right to privacy here is thus not just about immediate harm, not about a supposed wrong-doing, but about a range of long-term dangers being undertaken without due process and without oversight via a (literally) warrantless[20] practice of contemporary mass surveillance. For communities that have already been subject to state and social surveillance, already targeted by discriminatory policing, there was thus always something to fear and thus always something to hide too (the body itself in most cases).

Today, then, we can see surveillance as a technology emergent through a very clear set of methodologies, through techniques in which we are captured via the vast power of the gaze and the limitless license of the algorithmic, via Big Brother and Big Data both. We can see both the strategies of Jeremy Bentham's famous panopticon—the techniques of individual control encompassed by the disciplinary conventions of the all-seeing prison famously described by Michel Foucault (1995 [1977]: 195)—and the strategies of what Foucault (2008) later described as *biopolitical* power—a bureaucratic knowledge of our most intimate data that then scrutinizes us on the scale of the predictable. While the space of limitless one-way voyeurism exemplified by the panopticon thus comes to discipline our body and self-censor our behavior through the knowledge that we are always (potentially) being observed, the regulatory control of our data produces an indirect supra-visibility far beyond the capacity of traditional surveillance alone. Together, we thus have what appears to be a form of total visibility, total exposure, total *truth*, that places the power not in the hands of those who created the data but in those who collect and control it. Our surveillance culture thus attempts to "render the previously opaque or indeterminate not merely knowable but actionable," the "observation and control of urban processes," as Adam Greenfield has argued, being a result of the "desire to observe and control citizen behavior" (Greenfield 2013: n.p.). Moreover, by reducing identity down to what artist Zach Blas calls "disembodied aggregates of data" that can only ever function through diminishing difference, individuals from minority backgrounds often become "rendered uncomputable because their difference, or alterity, cannot be digitally measured" (Blas 2013: n.p.), become dangerous because their bodies or faces or movements diverge from a supposed norm. Groups already marginalized from mainstream society thus become "excessively vulnerable to violence, discrimination, and criminalization because," as Blas concludes, "their opacity is not fully controllable" (n.p.). Here, then, the city becomes not simply the city of perfect visibility, the city of total clarity, but rather a "jittery space," a space that "cannot be utilized unobserved" (Flusty 1994: 18). It becomes a space in which the nonnormative body is a body always under suspicion, a body not allowed full entry into the public sphere yet whose privacy is simultaneously forsaken. Public space thus becomes a site of danger for all those whose movement and features place them outside its algorithmic norms. Public space becomes a space in which visibility, as Foucault said, is a *trap*.

## TOTAL INVISIBILITY (*CONTRA*-VEILLANCE)

For those set most firmly within the city's gaze, then, constant visibility comes to create a real affective presence on the body itself. Leaning once more upon the seminal work of Fanon, Browne emphasizes what she terms the "embodied psychic effects of surveillance," from physical impacts such as "nervous tensions, insomnia, fatigue, accidents, lightheadedness, and less control over reflexes" to constant nightmares such as a "train that departs and leaves one behind, or a gate closing, or a door that won't open" (Browne 2015: 6). Here, visibility becomes a constant source of anxiety through its persistently alienating presence. The artist Sarah Ross (whose work on prickly space was discussed in chapter 7) explored the affectivity of jittery space in a film entitled *Surveillance Sounds*. Produced in collaboration with artists who had each been formerly incarcerated (in locations from the United States and Iran to Australia), the film pans slowly through images of CCTV cameras and surveillance artifacts while audio recordings, developed through interviews between the artist and her interlocutors, discuss the felt experience of visibility in their post-detention lives. As seen in figure 8.9, Ross's work reveals the everyday effects that constant exposure creates, the intimate, violent, visceral nature of surveillance that creates a feeling of harassment akin to the relentless unease caused by stalking.[21] Jill Magid's seminal surveillance works have similarly explored the unnerving, unsettling nature of contemporary visibility. In her project *Evidence Locker*, produced in Liverpool with the local police's Citywatch surveillance program, the artist formed a collaborative portrait of the infrastructure of visioning itself (seen in figure 8.10). Attempting to examine the differential relations of power between seeing and being seen, it is in the culmination of the work *Trust*, in a part of the film that could have easily been cut or redacted, that these themes most revealingly emerge. While in the

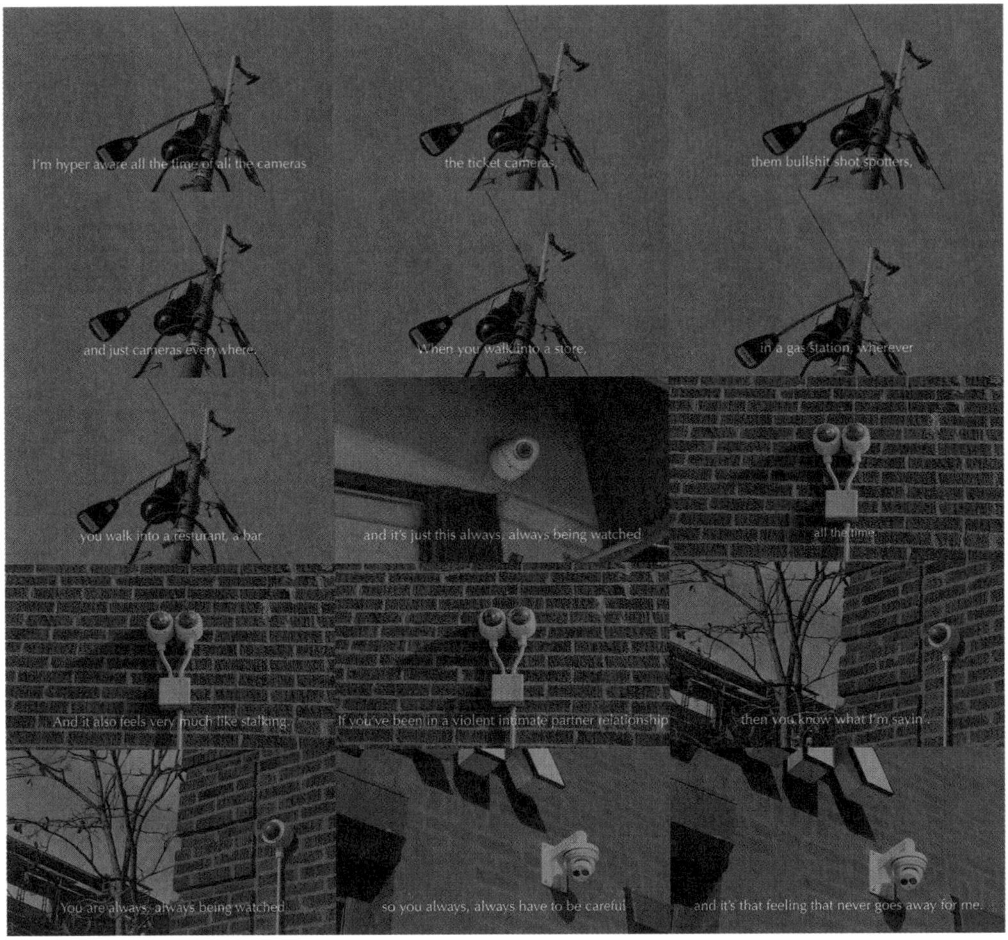


**FIGURE 8.9**
Sarah Ross, stills from *Surveillance Sounds*, 2022. Video, 7 minutes 23 seconds. Courtesy of the artist.

bulk of the film we see Magid navigating a busy urban street with her eyes shut, being directed through crowds by the off-screen CCTV operator (with whom she is connected via an earpiece), at the conclusion of Magid's blind act of trust—after what appears to be the culmination of the "work," and as seen in the video stills in figure 8.11—we see the camera suddenly shift from its fixed position and attach its gaze on a young, smart, shopping-laden woman. Focusing out from its stationary position before zooming back in to take a closer look, the camera operator tracks the unsuspecting victim walking down the street until she becomes occluded at a traffic light. As the camera struggles to capture her, the operative then pans out once again before refocusing at the near side of

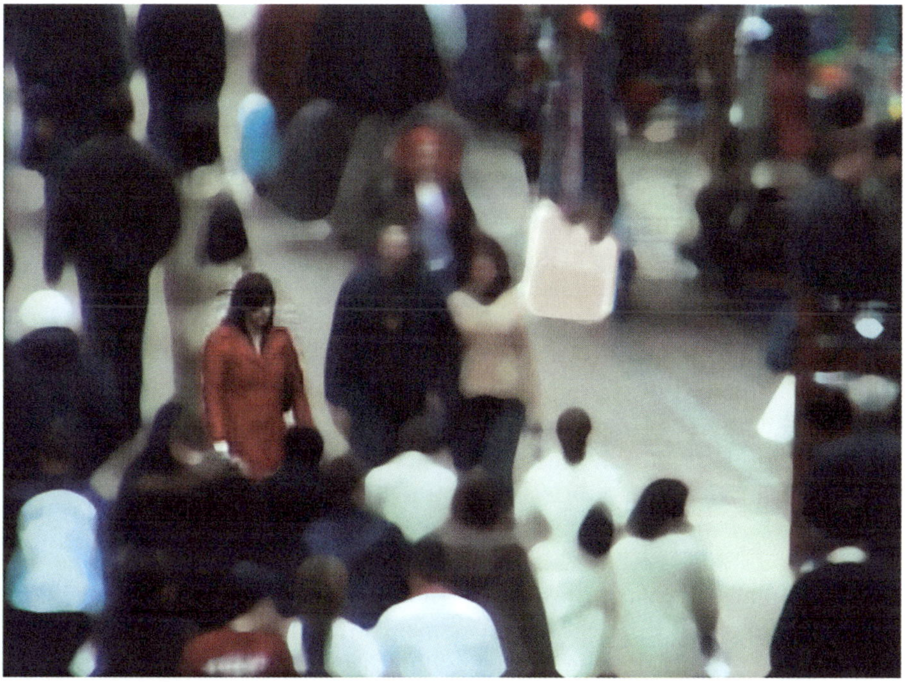

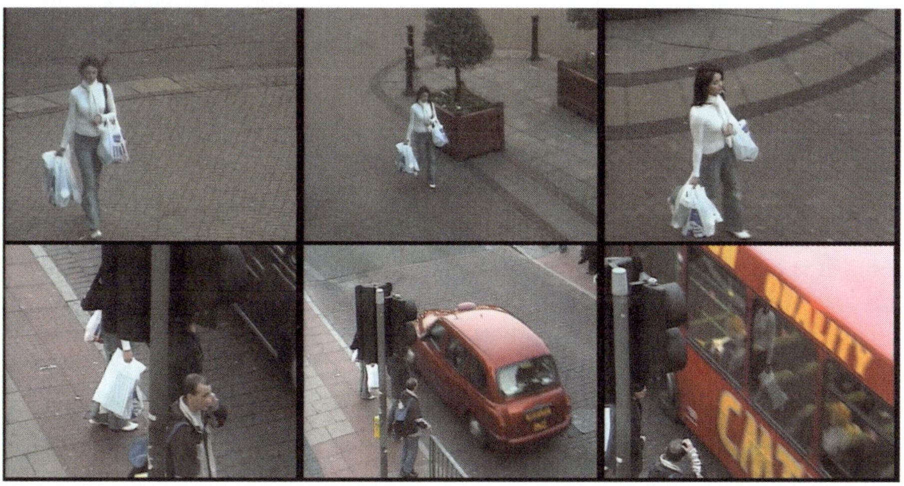

**FIGURE 8.10**
Jill Magid, still from *Trust / Evidence Locker*, 2004. Single-channel digital video, 18 minutes. Image modified by the Liverpool Police Forensic Imaging Unit. Courtesy of the artist and LABOR, Mexico City.

**FIGURE 8.11**
Jill Magid, still from *Trust / Evidence Locker*, 2004. Single-channel digital video, 18 minutes. Courtesy of the artist and LABOR, Mexico City.

the adjacent road, the new position perfectly capturing the target's image as reflected in the windows of the cars and buses that sweep by. Although just a brief moment, it acts as a highly revealing exposé of gendered voyeurism that provides an equally disconcerting and knowing end to the film.

In this space of overwhelming one-way visibility, of what engineer and professor Steve Mann (2016) has called both *univeillance*, in which we are subject to surveillance without our knowledge, and *McVeillance*, where we know we are under surveillance but are forbidden from returning that gaze (as is the case in corporate environments such as McDonald's in which we are recorded but denied the ability to record back), relief may only come through an evasion of veillance altogether. Visibility, even the desired political visibility of minoritized groups, can thus lead not only to one being heard (and hence being included within societal structures) but likewise to one being more easily surveilled (and hence trapped within them). What we must therefore acknowledge, in the words of feminist scholar Peggy Phelan, is that there may be "serious limitations to visual representation as a political goal" (Phelan 1993: 6). "[R]eal power," as Phelan continues, can thus emerge through "remaining unmarked" by the visibility that "summons surveillance and the law," unmarked by a visibility that "provokes voyeurism, fetishism, [and] the colonialist/imperial appetite for possession" (p. 6). Invisibility can hence be protective, but can also offer a space from which counter-visualities can be formed, a resistance to visibility that is itself powerfully visible. The indiscernibility of graffiti writers (as discussed in chapter 5), the critical bodily invisibility that enables the critical visibility of the image itself, must in many ways be seen as a tactic of protection that (as discussed in chapter 6) can give rise to collective ways of being that the city otherwise denies. In a similar way, for artists from marginalized groups whose visibility has always been qualified via an "otherness" from the normative white, male paradigm, this ability to entirely disappear or at least to *restrict* one's own visibility can be seen both as a strategy of safeguarding as much as a way of questioning the condition of their surveillance itself. Rather than simply using invisibility as an artistic method that could reject the "bigger is better" aesthetic that characterized much postwar art, that could refuse, as Ralph Rugoff has suggested, the "heroically-sized canvases of Abstract Expressionists, the Pop-giganticism of Rosenquist and Oldenburg, and the monuments of Minimalism and Earth Art" (Rugoff 2000: n.p.), escape and fugitivity could be understood as techniques of suppression in which one could then control the system of visibility as a whole. Invisibility can not simply be something one was passively subject to, but rather an actively adopted (or at least *exaggerated*) living tactic.

The master of this approach is David Hammons (as discussed earlier in chapter 7), an artist who has engaged concepts of suppression throughout his career.[22] Not only producing an untold amount of public works, which he left in the street never to be "officially" exhibited (works that still occasionally come to light today),[23] when Hammons *does* show, his works are often occluded in both literal and metaphorical ways. In his seminal exhibition *Concerto in Black and Blue* (2002), for example, Hammons left an entire 20,000-foot gallery space both empty of "art" and shrouded in darkness, forcing visitors to investigate the pitch-black space with a small blue flashlight they were provided on entry. Rather than simply obscuring our view, however, the darkness, as artist and theorist Glenn Ligon has suggested, could both provide a "space in which blackness can be constructed in light" while simultaneously illuminating an "unreadable" art practice that (as Ligon also suggests regarding the work of Lorna Simpson and Steve McQueen) can function through a "theater of refusal" and via a "thwarting of legibility" (Ligon 2004: n.p.). In his *Kool-Aid drawings* (2003–2007), however, Hammons's paintings may have been classically hung and lit, yet they were displayed behind an enveloping veil. The only way to truly see the painting was thus by making an official appointment with the gallery, for which the visitor was then required to enter the location via a side door! Here, then, secrecy and concealment, control and revelation, become a method not only of denying visibility (to us here too!) but of troubling it, ensuring that visibility is permitted only on the artist's terms. Still, while in many of Hammons's independently produced public works he utilized the street[24] as a site in which the surveillance (and desires) of the art world could be eluded, the street as a site of refuge and anonymity is a site of this no more. As such, while the guarding of perceptibility can be seen as a strategic move, the question is how these methods can help one escape the trap of visibility today.

To intervene within the city, then, the dangerous visibility of the urban surface must be contested through a public furtivity, through a tactic of hiding in plain sight. For the Berlin-based artist Adam Kraft, for example, the need to escape the visible led to the creation of what he and his frequent partner E. B. Itso called their "small asylums," insurgent spaces from which they could escape the claustrophobic and spectacular state of the city.[25] Kraft's most recent clandestine haven (discussed further in Kraft 2023) was formed in the very heart of historical Berlin within the Bauakademie, the original site of the Academy of Architecture that had been left partially abandoned since being destroyed during World War II and that had since become a fertile haven for wild plants and wild animals. Covered by a giant tarpaulin trompe l'oeil façade, however, a façade presaging its planned reconstruction, Kraft surreptitiously gained access to this literally veiled site, turning an abandoned workers' hut—suspended sixteen meters above the ground on a scaffold structure holding up the surrounding tarpaulin—into a secret dwelling space with electricity, plumbing, and kitchen (see figures 8.12 and 8.13). Naming it An-Bau (a building as a negation), Kraft eventually expanded this project into the bricked-up showroom set in the center of the space, turning it into an informal site of gathering and learning called the An-Akademie. Used for "screenings, meals, readings, dance practices, pirate radio broadcasts, performances, theater plays, presentations of all kinds" and for exploring "lock studies, trap door engineering, furniture making, EMP-jamming, hacking, [and] book printing" (Kraft 2023: 57), the secret site was advertised through word of mouth and accessed through a constantly changing series of secret entrances, including, for example, a hidden doorway set behind a large, framed

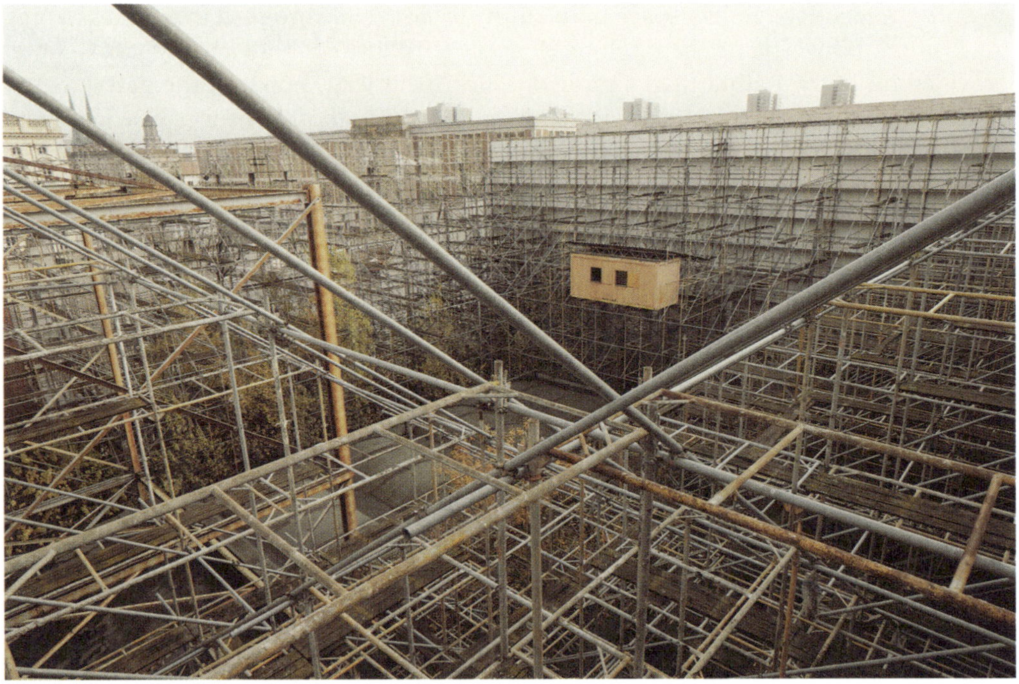

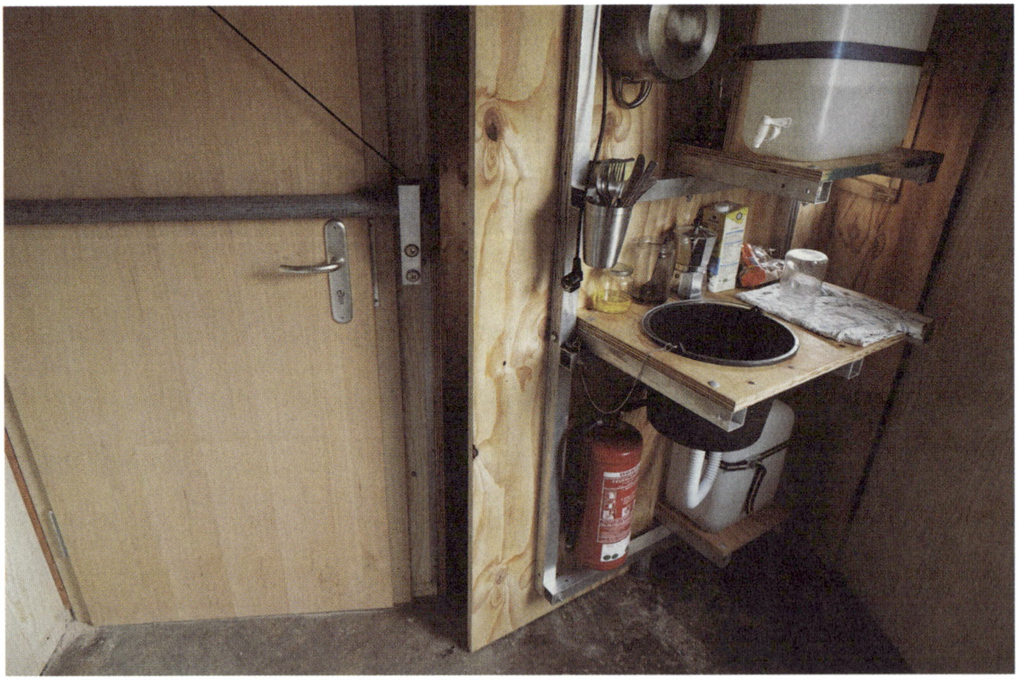

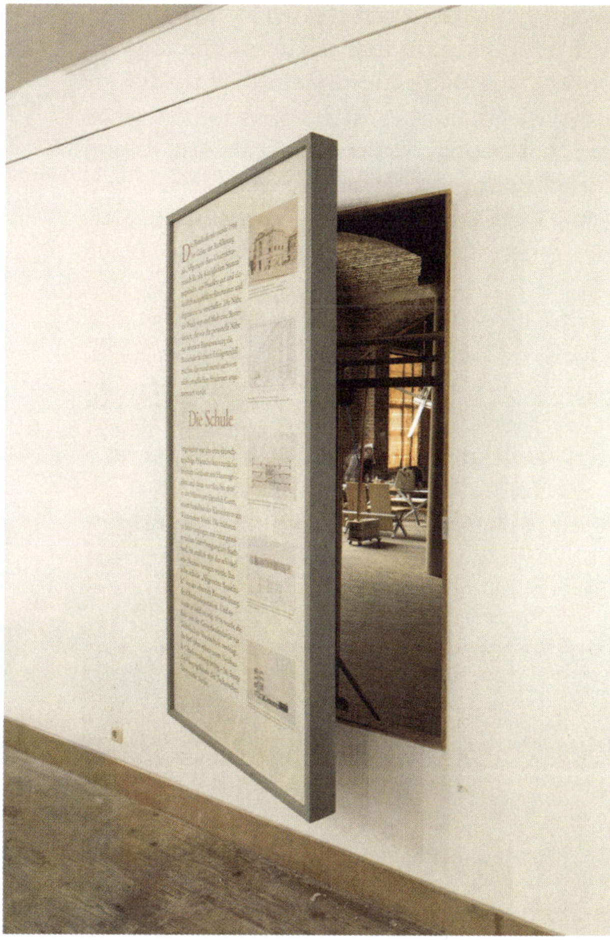


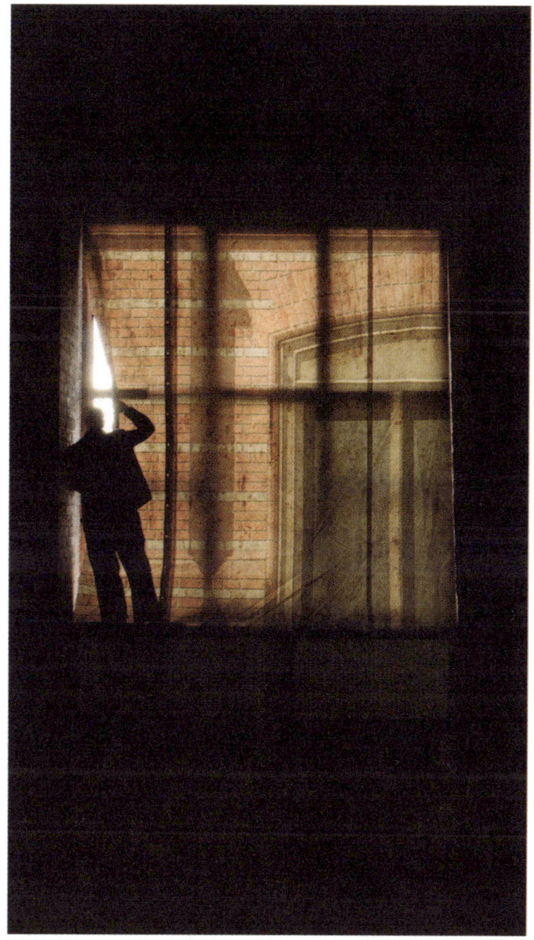

**FIGURE 8.12**
Adam Kraft, *An-Bau*, 2019. Courtesy of the artist.

**FIGURE 8.13**
Adam Kraft, *Pivoting Door (An-Bau)*, 2019. Courtesy of the artist.

**FIGURE 8.14**
Adam Kraft, *Entrance (An-Akademie)*, 2021. Courtesy of the artist.

**FIGURE 8.15**
Adam Kraft, *Window Peep (An-Akademie)*, 2021. Courtesy of the artist.

picture itself found at the site (as seen in figure 8.14). Here Kraft created a passage to an academic Narnia that existed a world away from the traditional academy. Challenging our assumptions of where the limits of both the possible and the visible are today, our assumptions of what freedom in the city now truly means, Kraft's project hints toward the outsider people and the outsider places that remain, as seen in figure 8.15, in the shadows of the everyday. Here, then, just as with our graffiti writers who actively embrace erasure, one's practice is heard but not seen, emerges through stories and narratives rather than images. Here the power of the invisible becomes its very existence beyond the power of the visible itself.

This elusive positionality and ability to quietly embrace the unmappable was also seen in the work of the late Étienne Boulanger. In his project *Plug-In Berlin* (2001–2003), for example, Boulanger mapped out over 950 sites in the city (after six months of walking through it in a peripatetic approach) that were set in its center yet outside its visible range. Working to then modify, camouflage, and inhabit these spaces—behind a destroyed advertising structure in Alexanderplatz Station (as seen in figures 8.16–8.18), behind a billboard on Joachim Strasse, or beneath the foundations of Monbijou Bridge, for example—Boulanger would make minor adaptations to the sites in order to create

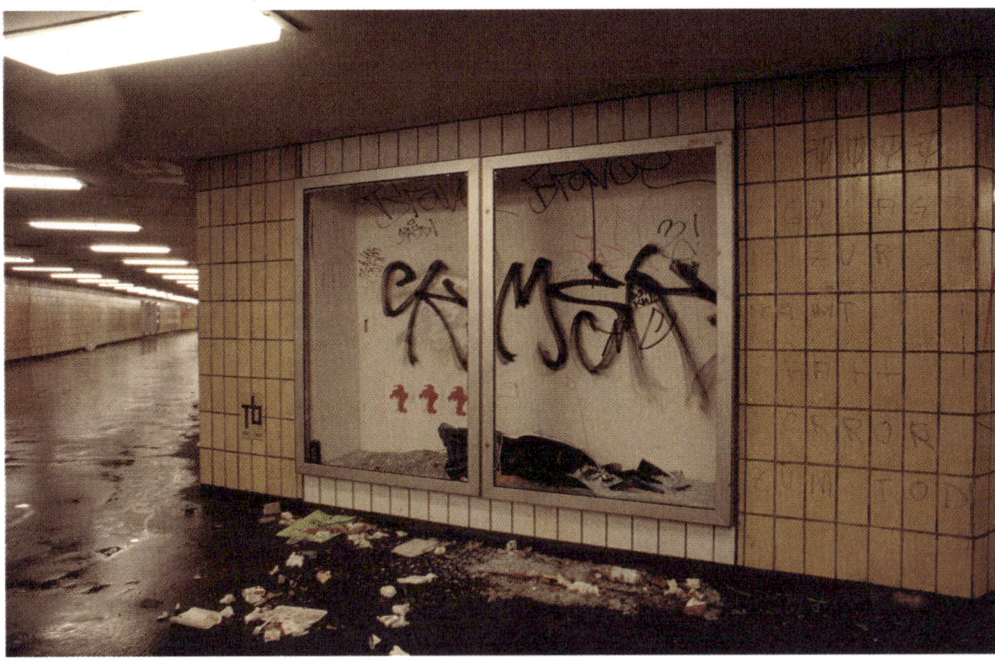

**FIGURE 8.16**
Étienne Boulanger, *Shelter #10, Alexanderplatz*. Part of the series *Plug-In Berlin*, Berlin, 2001–2003. Wood, hardboard. Courtesy of Association Étienne Boulanger.

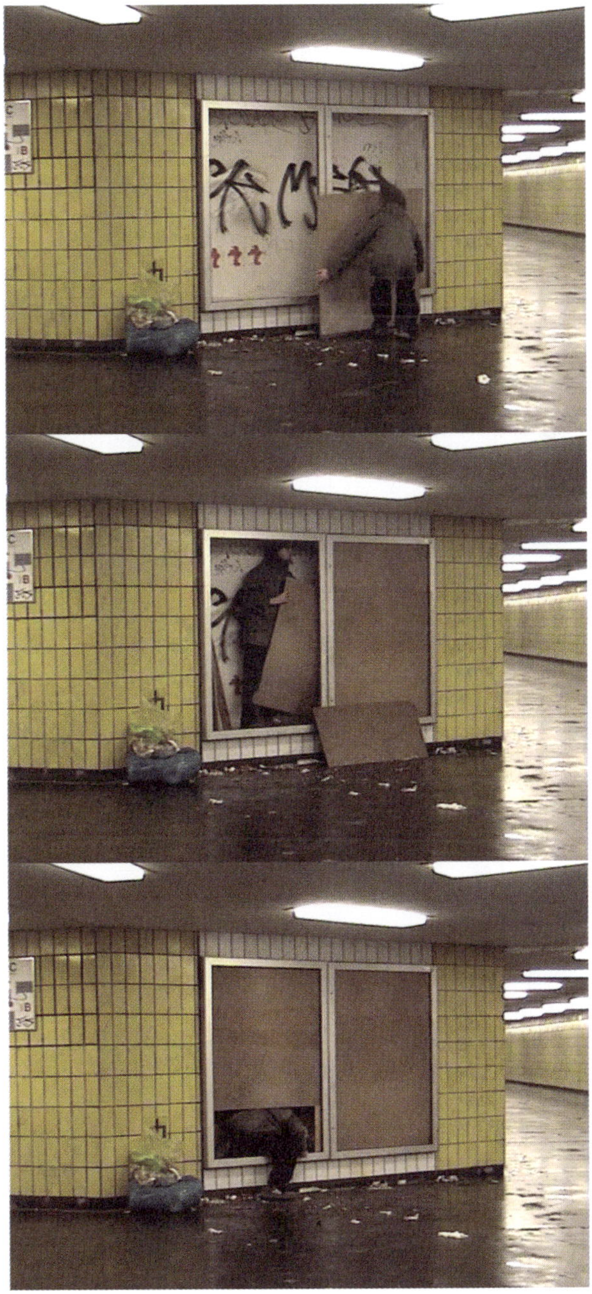

**FIGURE 8.17**
Étienne Boulanger, *Shelter #10, Alexanderplatz*. Part of the series *Plug-In Berlin*, Berlin, 2001–2003. Images of the intervention under construction, video (stills). Courtesy of Association Étienne Boulanger.

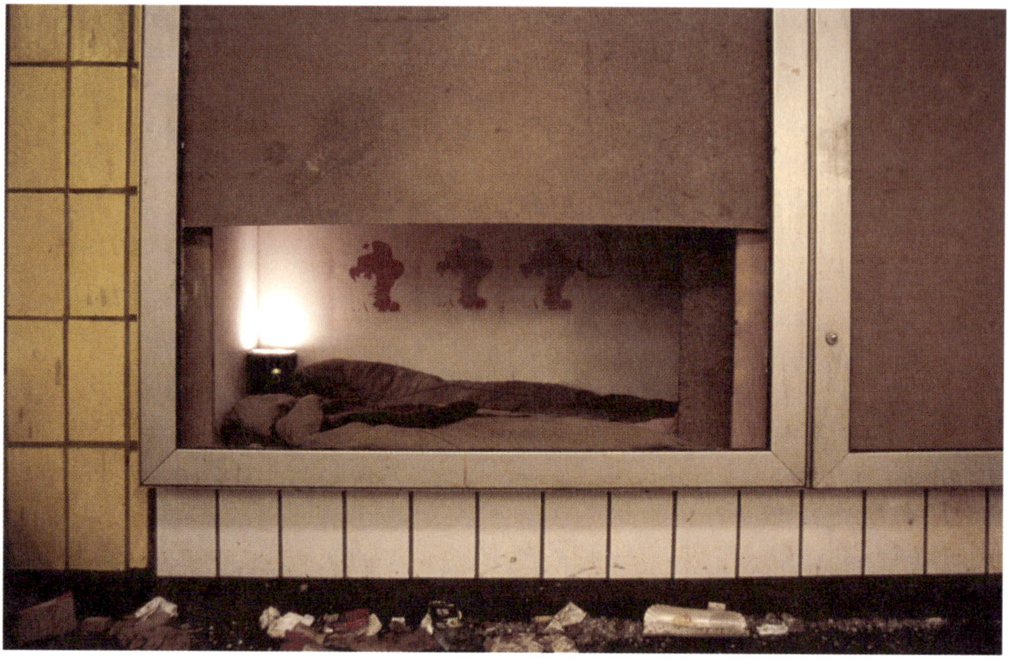

**FIGURE 8.18**
Étienne Boulanger, *Shelter #10, Alexanderplatz*. Part of the series *Plug-In Berlin*, Berlin, 2001–2003. Wood, hardboard. Courtesy of Association Étienne Boulanger.

what he termed "residual spaces" or "furtive shelters" in which to hide and subsist, shelters that aimed to merge "as much as possible with the architecture on which they leech" (Boulanger 2003: 11). Pre-constructing his architectural amendments before they were then "plugged in" to the city—being "assembled, wedged or screwed, on site in the middle of the night and as quickly as possible"—Boulanger's wish for "dissimulation and disappearance" was enabled through what he termed a tactic of "infiltration, disturbance, diversions and dispersion" (p. 10). As he continued, since "the face of the city is inseparable from that of the state, working at the limits of this territory, in the shadows, at the very point where it breaks down, is perhaps to escape its control" (p. 10). In his later project *The Single Room Hotel* (2007), however, Boulanger developed his tactical invisibility into a tactic of mimicry. Built on a disused wasteland in central Berlin that was previously part of the no-man's land or "Death Strip" of the Berlin Wall, Boulanger constructed a thirty-two-square-meter apartment—a modular space with electricity, hot water, bathroom, and double bed—within the four sides of an advertising billboard (as seen in figures 8.19 and 8.20). Making this space available for rent for members of

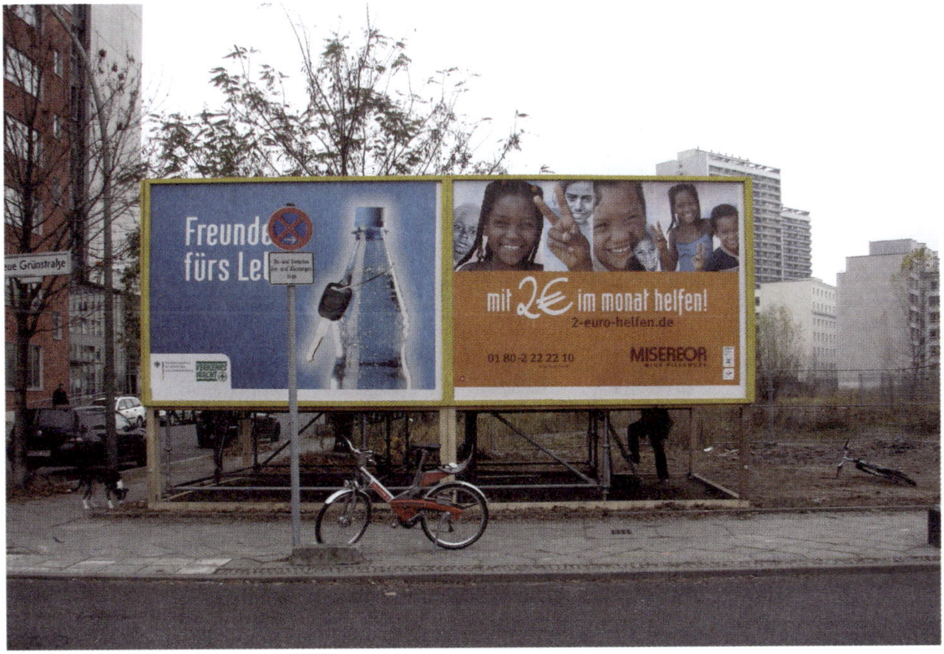


**FIGURE 8.19**

Étienne Boulanger, *Single Room Hotel*. Skulpturen Park, Berlin_Zentrum, 2007–2008. Outside views, with Boulanger. Scaffolding, chipboard panels, plasterboard, insulating materials, electrical installation, sanitary installation, advertising displays, hotel furniture. Photo: Philipp Horst. Courtesy of Association Étienne Boulanger.

the public at twenty euros per night through subsidizing it via the exterior advertising, the highly visible posters thus paradoxically enabled the apartment to remain hidden, camouflaged by this economic necessity itself. Boulanger's architectural construction thus enabled one not only to escape from the city's surveillance but to remain concealed through utilizing its most omnipresent form of visual culture.

For the graffiti writer, however, bodily visibility (as seen in figures 8.21 and 8.22) is a constant prospect that participants must work to avail themselves of: there has never been a writer who didn't need to know how to run, and a writer who hasn't run has never partaken in the canonically mandated necessity for public exposure. While for many graffiti writers a tactic of literal disappearance is thus critical, a movement into the guts and intestines of the city that enables one to work outside the surveillance gaze, the evasion of visibility also emerges through a strategy of mimicry similar to that seen within the work of Boulanger. Here, however, the graffiti writer's characteristic tactic of concealment comes through the paradoxical use of "hi-vis." A now ubiquitous urban artifact—first worn by those working in construction but today a health and safety

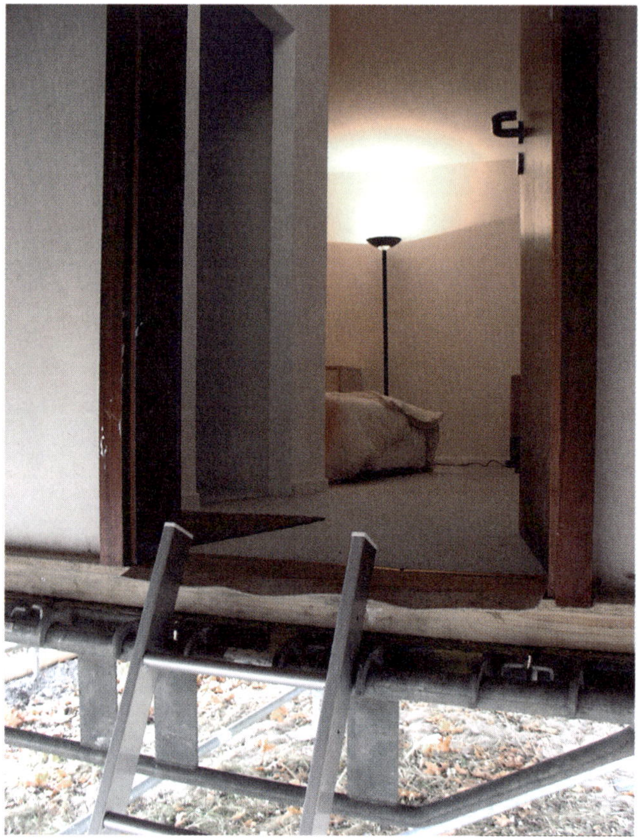

**FIGURE 8.20**
Étienne Boulanger, *Single Room Hotel*. Skulpturen Park, Berlin_Zentrum, 2007–2008. Interior views of the bedroom. Scaffolding, chipboard panels, plasterboard, insulating materials, electrical installation, sanitary installation, advertising displays, hotel furniture. Courtesy of Association Étienne Boulanger.

sanctioned uniform for almost all public service workers—high-visibility clothing has the amazing advantage of forming an appearance of anonymity and propriety, leading to an ease of disregard. Pull on your hi-visibility suit and, super-heroically, invisibility is engaged. The British artist Duncan Weston has explored this potential extensively within his practice. In 2016, for example (see figures 8.23–25), he produced a series of customized hi-vis vests as well as a full hi-vis boiler suit, playing with the in/conspicuous in/visibility they impart. While the suit incorporated the insignias of both British Rail[26] and the American fashion brand Ralph Lauren (a key figure within Weston's practice), his vests carried a series of ironic aphorisms—"In Security," "Out of Sight," "Law Abiding Citizen," "Community Disservice," "Trust Worthy," "Don't Ask," "Look Out"—that

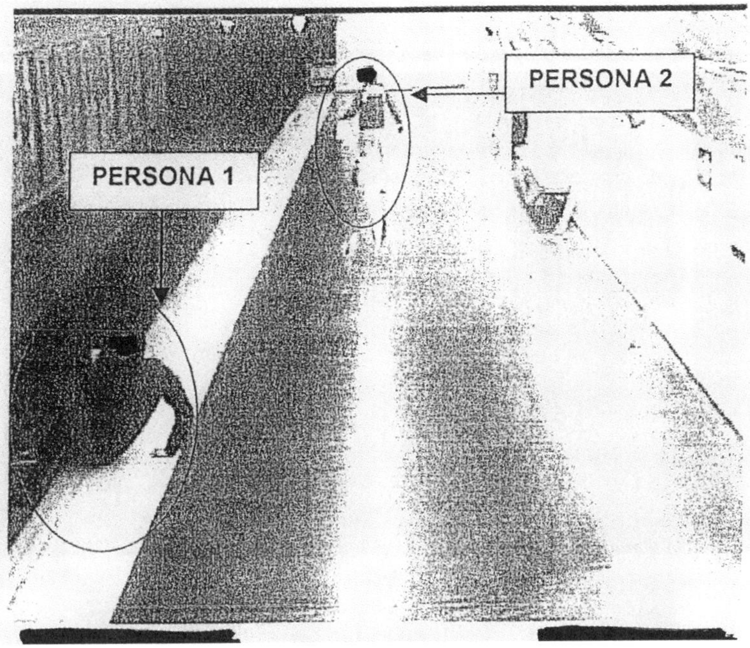


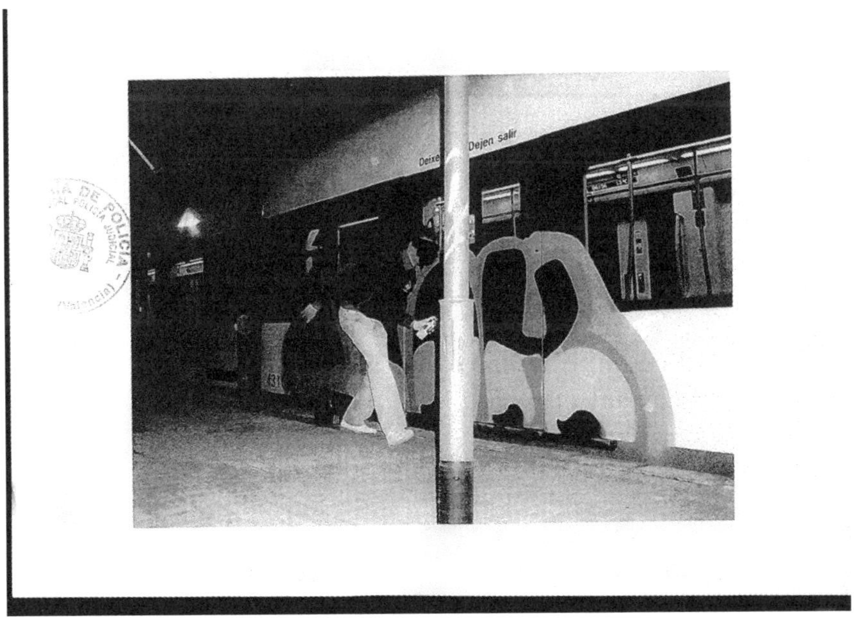


**FIGURES 8.21 AND 8.22**

Enrique Escandell, *Valencia Subway Police Investigation*, date unknown. Taken from *Subterráneos* by Enrique Escandell. Courtesy of the artist.

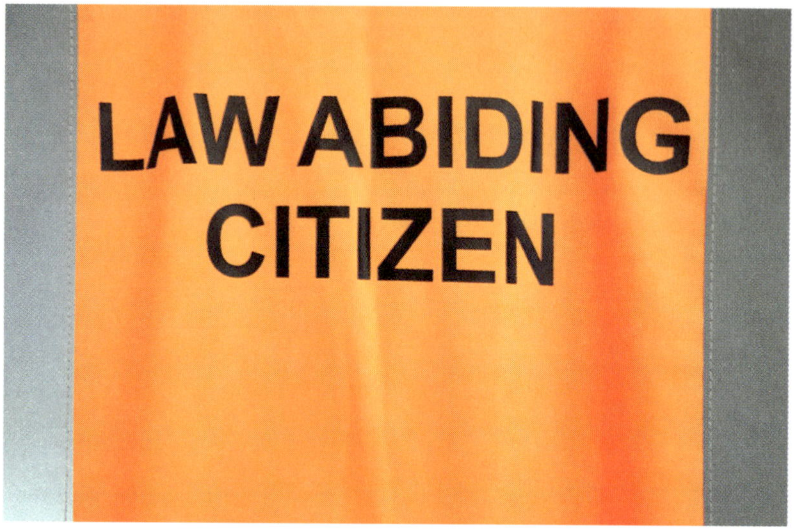


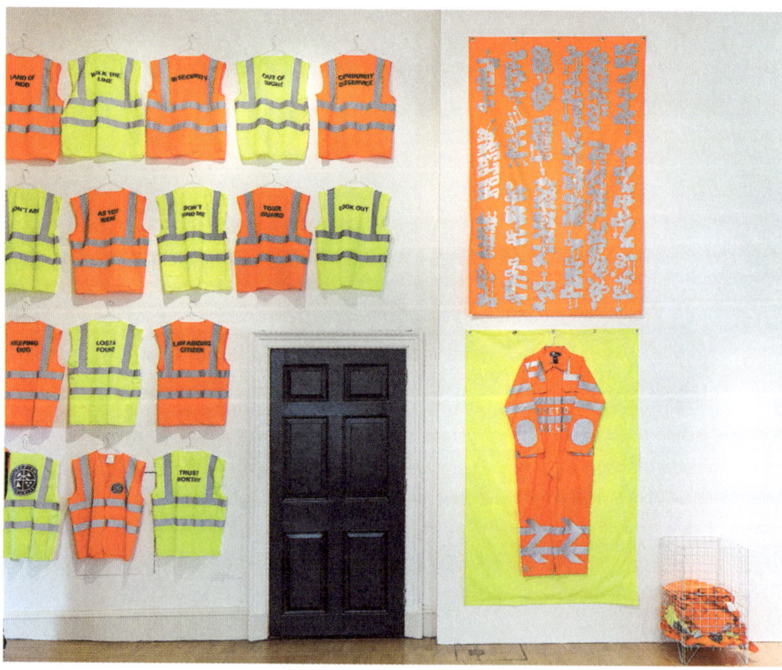

**FIGURE 8.23**
Duncan Weston (Petro), *LAW ABIDING CITIZEN (Utopian Security)*, 2016. Photo: Rafael Schacter. Courtesy of the artist.

**FIGURE 8.24**
Duncan Weston (Petro), *Utopian Security*, 2016. Photo: Filippo Minelli. Courtesy of the artist.

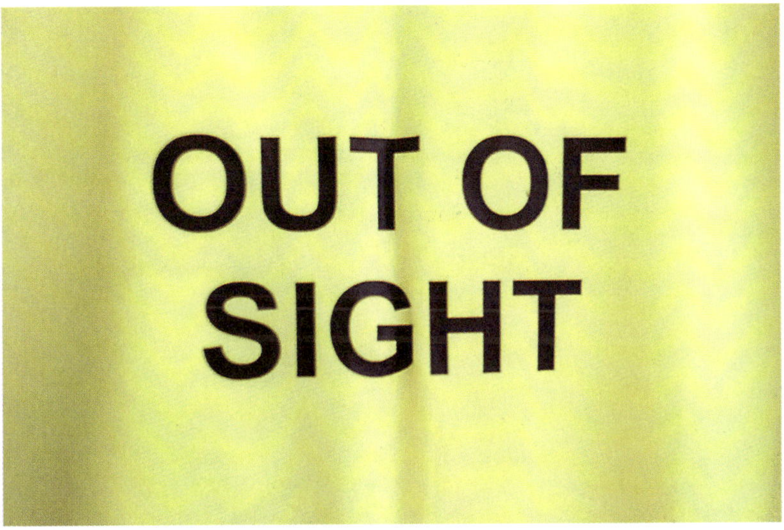


**FIGURE 8.25**
Duncan Weston (Petro), *OUT OF SIGHT (Utopian Security)*, 2016. Photo: Rafael Schacter. Courtesy of the artist.

reinforced the cloaking-device abilities that this material enables. Alongside the now equally omnipresent (and game-changing) COVID-19 masks, writers can thus fade into invisibility in the city through their personal protective equipment, a visibly invisible, banal fixture of the everyday. In the design collective Hyphen-Labs' work *HyperFace* (2017), however, in what they term a low-tech countersurveillance garment developed as part of their project *NeuroSpeculative AfroFeminism*, the veiling techniques of both hi-vis and literal masks are enhanced through a prototype textile pattern that confuses the datasets utilized by facial detection software. Speaking directly to the systems of racialized surveillance discussed earlier by Simone Brown alongside the dangers of algorithmic surveillance discussed by Shoshana Magnet, here the pattern printed on the scarf counters contemporary visioning systems through the provision of a series of "false" faces (as seen in figure 8.26) that overloads the system's processing capabilities. Like traditional camouflage (or disruptive pattern material), the design thus eludes ocular power through embracing a visual distortion that corrupts the machinic eye. Designed in conjunction with artist and technologist Adam Harvey, *HyperFace* worked in an equal and opposite way to his earlier project *CV Dazzle* (2010), which targeted the figure (the face itself) rather than the ground (the surrounding area). Through undertaking a series of simple modifications—such as the hair styling, makeup, and accessories utilized by the art collective Dazzle Club in their public protest walks seen in figure 8.27—a user's face becomes undetectable through interrupting the rules of the algorithm. Wearers

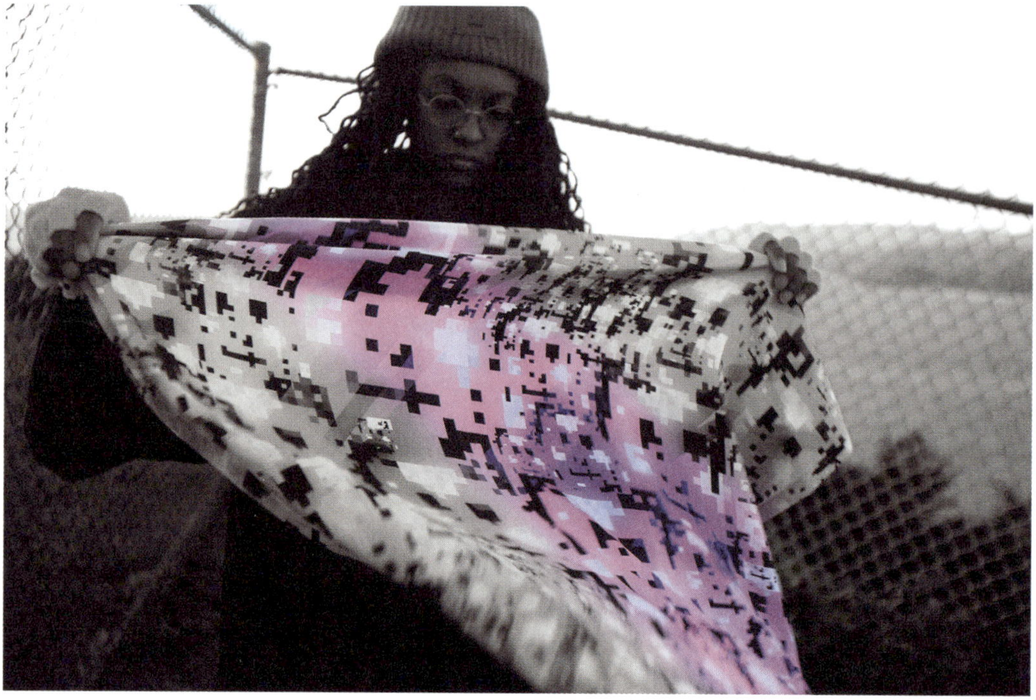

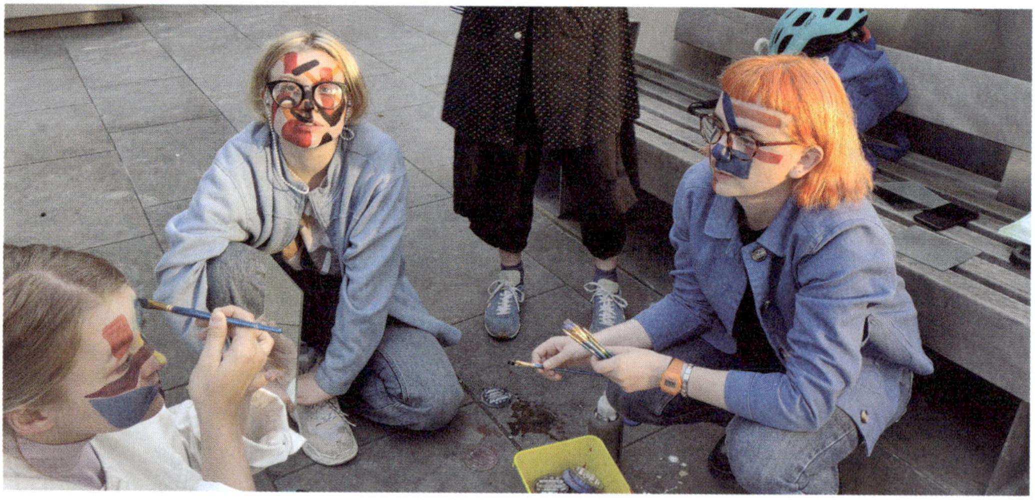

**FIGURE 8.26**
Adam Harvey × Hyphen-Labs [Ashley Baccus-Clark, Carmen Aguilar y Wedge, Ece Tankal, Nitzan Bartov], *Hyperface*, 2016. Textile print. Courtesy of the Hyphen-Labs.

**FIGURE 8.27**
The Dazzle Club, *February Silent Dazzle Walk*, Shoreditch, February 2020 © The Dazzle Club.

could thus "appear one step below the threshold of detection . . . break[ing] apart the expected features targeted by computer vision algorithms and prov[ing] that faces, or other objects, can exist in a dual perceptual state: visible to humans yet invisible to machines" (Harvey 2023: n.p.). Here, then, the bodily eye still bests the machinic one, the sensory abilities of the individual containing sensitives beyond the capacities of the algorithmic. Here the methods of refusal are as much about visibility as invisibility, methods that refuse the tools of standardization and instead form new ways of both seeing and being seen.

## WATCHING OURSELVES/WATCHING THE WATCHERS (*SOUS-/META*-VEILLANCE)

For many individuals, then, and for graffiti writers in particular, the only response to overwhelming visibility is a move to curb one's own exposure and to navigate within the shadows of the sweeping surveillance lights. Yet the techniques of anti-veillance seen above are not the only way of addressing the top-down veillancing of the city. Another, as addressed by Mann, is what he termed *sous*veillance or *undersight*, an imitative technique whereby individuals try not to hide from view but instead see back. Rather than the "few watching the many" as formed by *sur*veillance (Mann 2013: 5), *sous*veillance leads to the "many watching the few," a state, according to Mann, in which a balanced veillance (an *equi*-veillance) could mitigate the threats that univeillance presents (p. 1). While Mann's position could be seen to emerge from a space of racial and gendered neutrality and potentially lead to a further entrenchment of both participatory and self-surveillance, the basic position, as undertaken in practices such as "cop-watching," for example, is clearly powerful enough to have warranted a response from state forces. While in the United Kingdom members of the public are thus legally allowed to film police officers, it is an offense to obstruct them from carrying out their duties, a rationale often used to restrict their filming by the public. In the United States, however, several states have recently attempted to introduce legislation to legally prohibit the sousveillance of police, claiming (in an amazing exemplification of Mann's McVeillance argument) to be doing so in order to protect their officers' right to privacy. In a similar way, the writer and artist James Bridle's attempt to take a photograph of every CCTV camera monitoring London's Congestion Charge Zone (as seen in figures 8.28 and 8.29), described in an essay from 2014 entitled "All Cameras Are Police Cameras," led to his physical restraint by a private security firm and his threatened arrest by the Met Police on the grounds of "going equipped," a stipulation held within the 1968 Theft Act, Bridle explained, that "determines the imprisonment for up to three years of anyone carrying equipment which may be used to commit a burglary" (Bridle 2014). Here the simple possession of a digital camera (or today just a smartphone) could be used to justify state detainment, sousveillance so dangerous to *sur*veillance that it must be halted by repressive force.

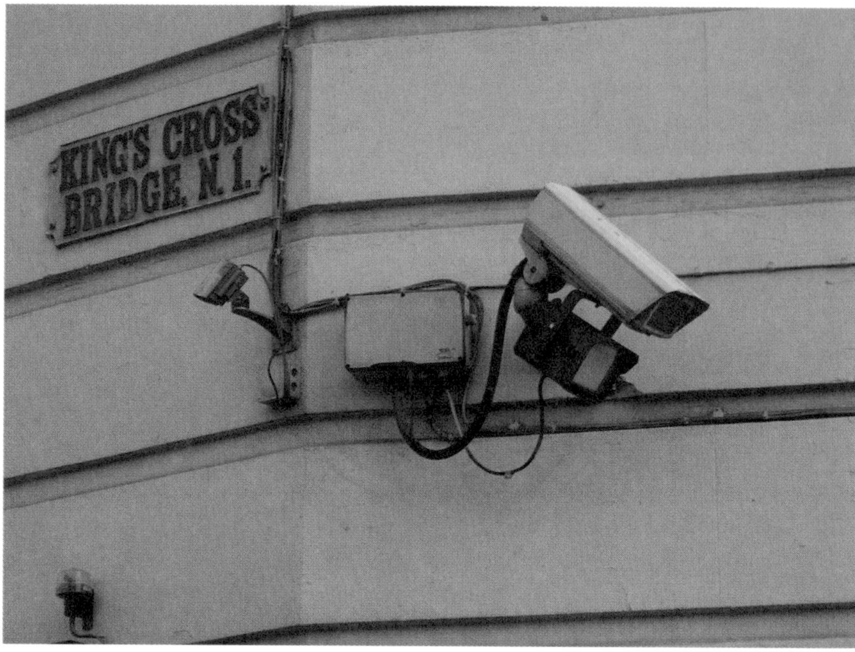


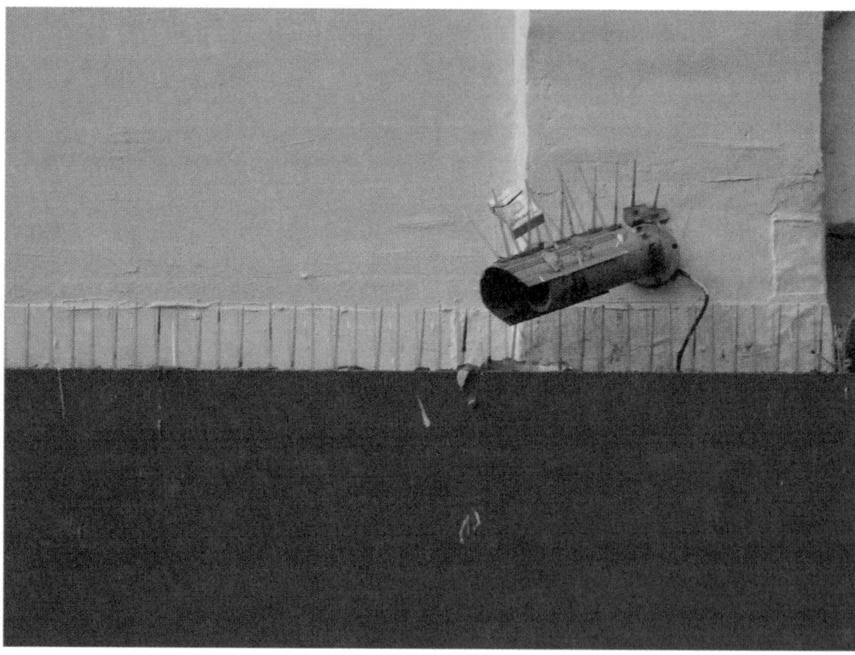

**FIGURES 8.28 AND 8.29**
James Bridle, *All Cameras Are Police Cameras* (2014). Digital photographs. Courtesy of the artist.

The technologically enabled ability to engage in sousveillance is, however, something that many artists have come to utilize in a bottom-up attempt to both combat hegemonic visibility and extend their own ocular capabilities. For graffiti writers in particular, and as discussed in chapter 5, in order to engage in more spatially complex practices, the monitoring and reconnaissance of the activities of authorities is critical. As Erik Hannerz has shown in an analysis of homemade graffiti videos that incorporate not only the process and results of train painting but likewise the sousveillance of authorities that occurs beforehand, these films reveal writers "discussing maps, internal service schedules and blueprints of the transit system" while likewise following them "as they monitor the monitors, hide in bushes, map out and disable cameras, and avoid sensors and alarms" (Hannerz 2022: 7). Yet while the rejection of univeillance is here undertaken for reasons of safety (and, once more, for the sake of the canon), the author likewise argues that the inclusion of this material in the videos helps to define the "adversary but also the playground, its rules, and what is at stake" (p. 2). Rather than being about revealing hegemonic power alone, sousveillance can create a reciprocal relation between writer and rival and thus represent "a sense of individual control and collective cohesion against the security officers" (p. 3). Looking becomes agentic here, not just passively revealing but actively engaging the gaze on one's own terms. The "logic of surveillance" is thus flipped, as Hannerz continues: the writers not only follow the "security officers safely from a distance—while the latter are incapable of detecting both that they are being surveilled and the transgressive movement of the graffiti writer from outside to inside" (p. 8), but the members of the graffiti crew likewise gain power and prestige through eluding and overcoming this prodigious power itself.

Other artists have also utilized visioning techniques as ways to engage with both self and sight. Jill Magid's early work, for example, utilized tools such as a camera hidden in her lipstick (*Lobby 7*, 1999) or in high-heeled shoes (*Surveillance Shoe*, 2000) in an attempt to both make the image mobile and create a more intimate connection to her own body. Yet others have taken this into even more personal territories. In Wafaa Bilal's project *3rdi*, seen in figure 8.30, he surgically implanted a camera into the back of his head via a two-hour medical procedure, setting it to take images automatically every minute of the day for an entire year. Automatically uploading these images along with his GPS coordinates to his website http://www.3rdi.me, the project not only tore down any barrier between private and public, visibility and invisibility, but likewise created images that were simultaneously *by* and *of* him, a self-documentation, as seen in figure 8.31, in which the artist was both present and hauntingly absent at the same time. Yet *3rdi* not only reinforced the overarching new powers of digital surveillance and the ways these track and codify particular "problematic" bodies (especially Iraqi-American ones such as his own), but produced a surfeit of images leading to an unmanageable excess. Here the overabundance of images he produced—the majority of them entirely banal, the majority of them indistinct and blurred—created a glut of data that overloaded any possibility of true capture. Bilal's work thus not only renders surveillant

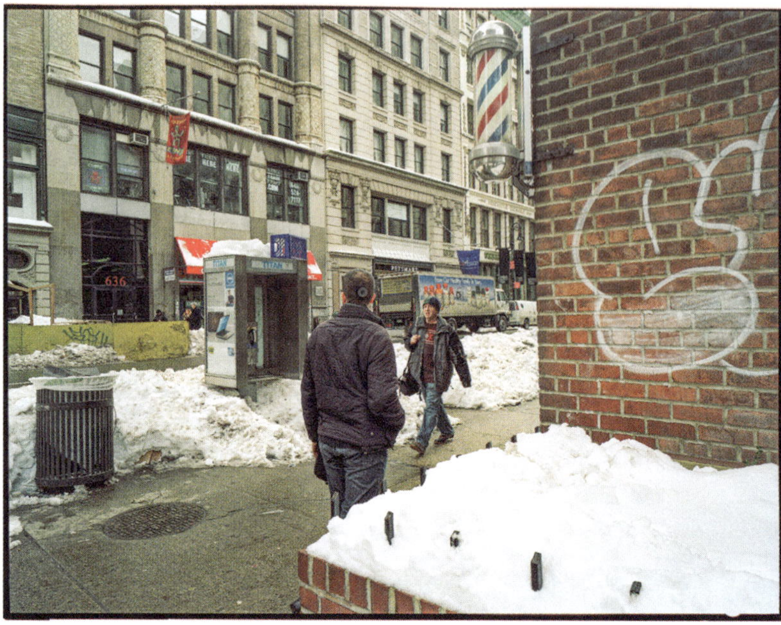


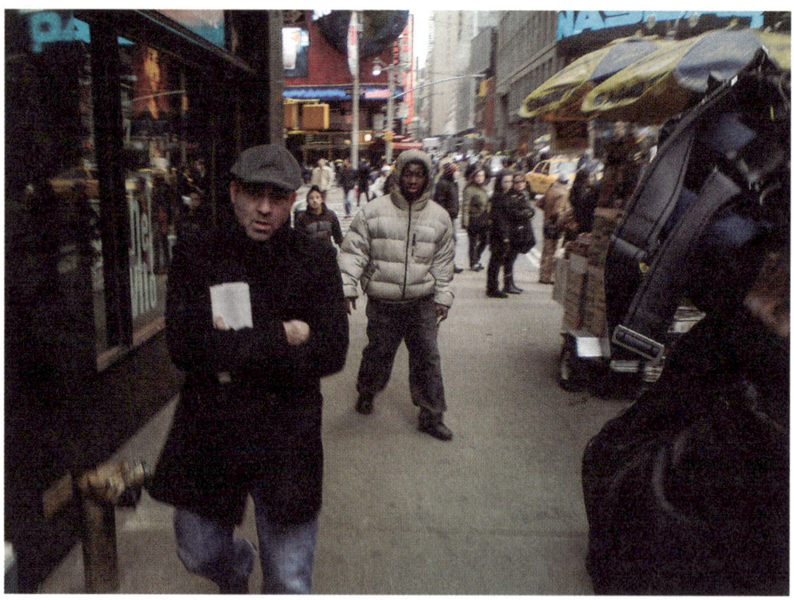

**FIGURE 8.30**
Wafaa Bilal, *3rdi*, 2010–2011. Durational performance. Photo: Ben Pier. Courtesy of Ben Pier and the artist.

**FIGURE 8.31**
Wafaa Bilal, *3rdi*, 2010–2011. Durational performance. Courtesy of the artist.

technologies as both familiar and unfamiliar, but placed them under stress through an equally brutal and everyday act of visioning. Sousveillance here becomes a technique not only of equivalence and safety but of hiding in plain sight, a seeming compliance that camouflages through its generation of *too much*. Like the technique of "subversive affirmation" discussed by Inke Arns and Sylvia Sasse, a strategy of mimesis in which an exaggerated practice of imitation comes to "affirm, appropriate, or consume" hegemonic discourses "while simultaneously undermining them," here Bilal's acts of "pure wastefulness" come to repeat the "aesthetic conditions of totalitarian aesthetics" (Arns and Sasse 2006: 446–447). Fanatical over-identification thus "makes explicit the implications of an ideology and thus produces such elements that may not be publicly formulated in order for an ideology to reproduce itself" (p. 448). A maximalist veillance from below not only can come to create a feeling of ambivalence (of an ambiguous veillance or an *ambi*veillance) by replicating what is already happening yet doing so willingly, but so too maps out the practices and ideologies of contemporary methods of visibility today. It thus reveals an obsessive, violent performance as equally obsessive and violent as the visual culture from which it emerged.

The need to witness contemporary visibility has incorporated not only practices of sousveillance, however, but so too a *meta*-veillance that seeks to see sight itself, to function, as Mann has said, through the "sensing of sensing" (Mann 2016: 1409). In Bridle's *Drone Shadow* project, for example, the artist created a series of 1:1 scale outlines of surveillance drones on the surface of the city, bringing these purposefully invisible artifacts of visibility into the visible human range (as seen in figure 8.32). Seeing drones as a representative of all invisible contemporary technologies, his intervention attempted to "render" this invisibility visible in order to "make it comprehensible," to both point toward its invisibility while simultaneously "pointing out that we always have the capability to see, should we choose to pay attention" (Bridle in Michel 2014). His *Rainbow Plane* project, however, sought to examine not simply the physical technology of seeing but the ways in which these technologies actually *see*. While like his *Drone Shadows*, what was created was a 1:1 outline of an airborne vehicle (here the Gulfstream V); its rainbow pattern recreated a "true 'glitch,' where we see not an error, but a glimpse of how systems really function . . . An aesthetic which reveals not the surface, but the depth of things" (Bridle 2014). The image formed, as seen in figure 8.33, thus recreates the way in which satellite imagery sees—not via photography but rather via recording "electromagnetic radiation in the red, blue, green, and high-resolution panchromatic (black-and-white) bands" (Bridle 2014: n.p.), a technique that, when encountering fast-moving objects such as planes, creates this psychedelic effect. Here we begin to see "how technology sees the world, and thus how technology both obscures and reproduces political intent," while at the same time, as Bridle concludes, acknowledging the way in which "analogous technologies can be used to invert and render visible these relationships" (n.p.).

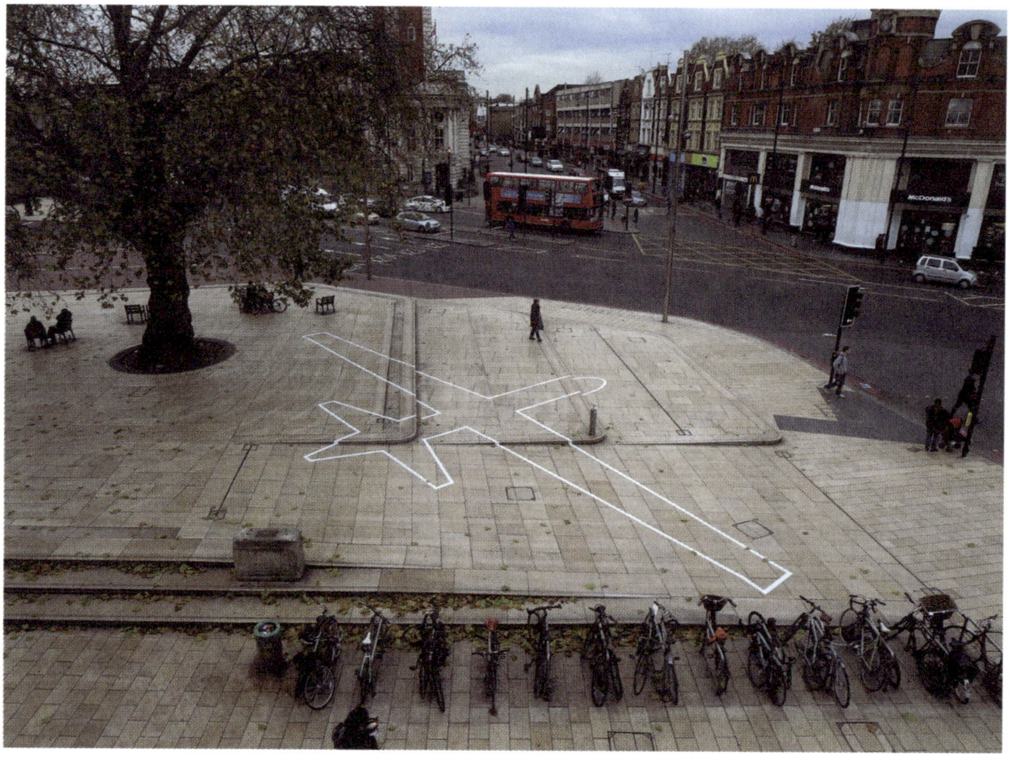

**FIGURE 8.32**
James Bridle, *Drone Shadow 006*, 2013. Public space installation, Windrush Square, London. Courtesy of the artist, in partnership with Britdoc and Picturehouse Cinemas.

This technique of revelation and exposure has also been undertaken by Steve Mann, one of the omnipresent voices in this field whose critical neologisms have helped to structure this chapter. Working since the 1970s to form a series of tools that can make "visible various otherwise invisible physical phenomena"—as seen in the montage from his Augmented Reality Wand[27] in figure 8.34—these can then sense the energy emitted from cameras and microphones, for example, to discern their ability to "see" or "hear" us. Utilizing "Surveilluminescent light sources" that, as seen in figure 8.35, can "glow brightly when within a surveillance camera's field-of-view, resulting in augmented reality overlays that display surveillance camera sightfields" (Mann 2016: 1415), or creating a Sequential Wave Imprinting Machine (SWIN) that "makes visible the otherwise invisible electromagnetic radio waves from a smartphone" (pp. 1414–1415), Mann's augmented visual tools thus show us what happens beyond our traditional scopic powers, enabling us to see what we normally are unable to see. For the

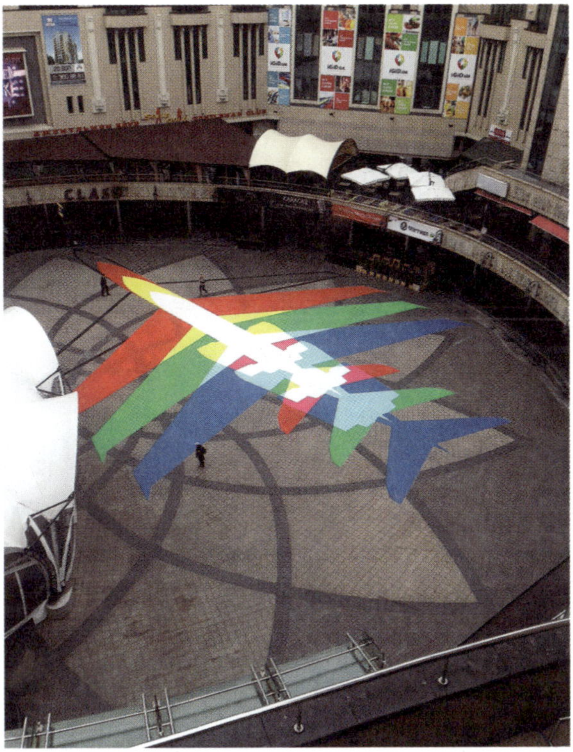

**FIGURE 8.33**
James Bridle, *Rainbow Place 002*, 2014. Public space installation, Kiev. Courtesy of the artist and the PinchukArtCentre.

geographer and artist Trevor Paglen, however, it is not the clarity exposed by Mann but a distortion of vision he aims to reveal, the moments in which we observe (rather than "see") the edges of what we will never truly be able to visually perceive. While his early and celebrated Limit Telephotography works photographed secret military bases and surveillance structures from distances of up to forty miles away (as seen in figure 8.36), creating images that foregrounded the right to veillance while themselves depicting blurry, distorted, otherworldly landscapes, his more recent project, *A Study of Invisible Images* (2017), set its sights on the way our new scopic environment visualizes *us*. Here, Paglen examines how machine visioning interprets and "sees" images—often in ways that surpass our own methods of visualization—a type of sight that, he argues, could lead to the "automation of vision on an enormous scale and, along with it, the exercise of power on dramatically larger and smaller scales than have ever been possible" (Paglen 2016: n.p.). His unsettling image of Frantz Fanon, to return to the philosopher

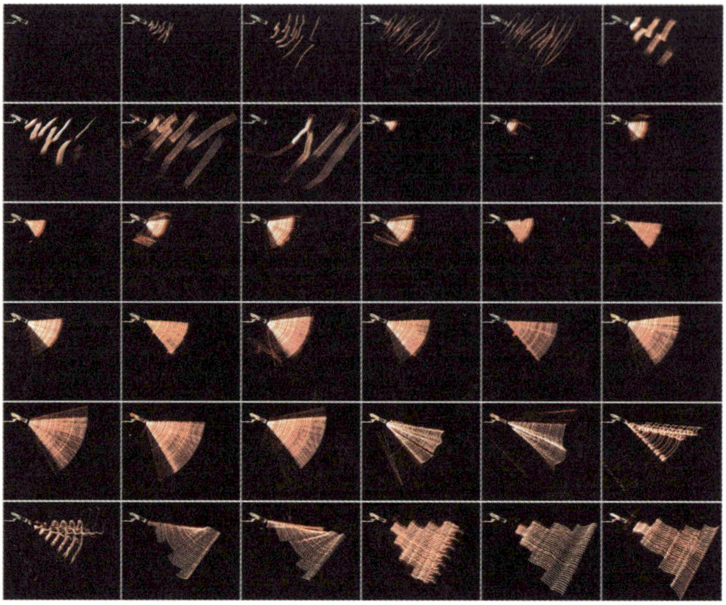

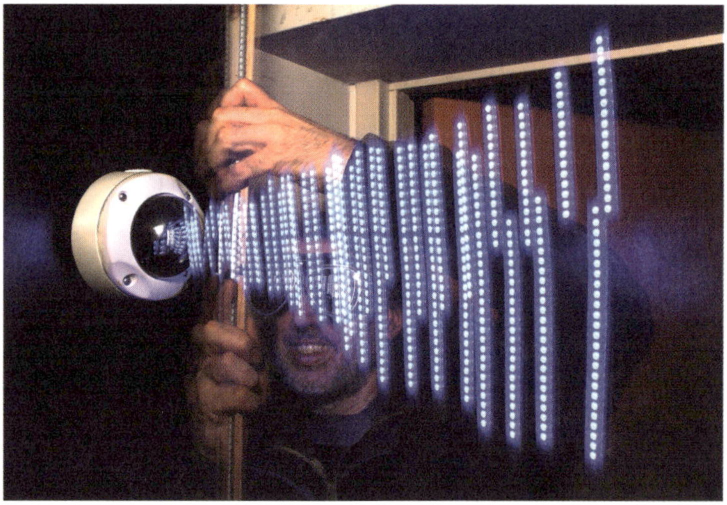

**FIGURE 8.34**

Steve Mann, *Surveillance Study—36 Exposures (Montage)*, 1974. 35 mm film strip, animation of thirty-six exposures. Metavision™ and Metaveillance™ (Veillance of veillance, sensing sensors and sensing their capacity to sense). Courtesy of the artist.

**FIGURE 8.35**

Steve Mann, *Steve Mann with Spaceglasses Demonstrating Surveilluminescence*, 2013. Metaveillogrammetry™ as captured by a Metaveillograph™. Presented at IEEE Conference on Computer Vision and Pattern Recognition, June 23–28, 2014. Courtesy of the artist.

discussed earlier by Browne (see figure 8.37), was in fact produced algorithmically via facial recognition software (to return us to the start of this chapter) that uses the titular "eigenface" technique to classify human faces. The resultant "faceprint," an overlaid collection of found images of Fanon that are averaged out against each other and then subtracted against an averaging of a set of faces held within the system's database (in order to identify the unique facial elements of the individual, or suspect, in question) thus not only forms an image that has never previously existed, but forms a perfect depiction of what Fanon himself termed "control by quantification" (Browne 2015: 6). What Paglen's image thus reveals is a ghostly image and an image of a ghost, an image fixing Fanon as an "object among objects" (Browne 2015: 7), an image digitizing him, reducing him, for purposes of "automation, identification, and verification" (p. 26). Like the now omnipresent facial recognition and surveillance we are each subject to, Fanon is here reduced not merely via the techniques of an overwhelming white gaze, but the techniques of an overwhelming machinic one.

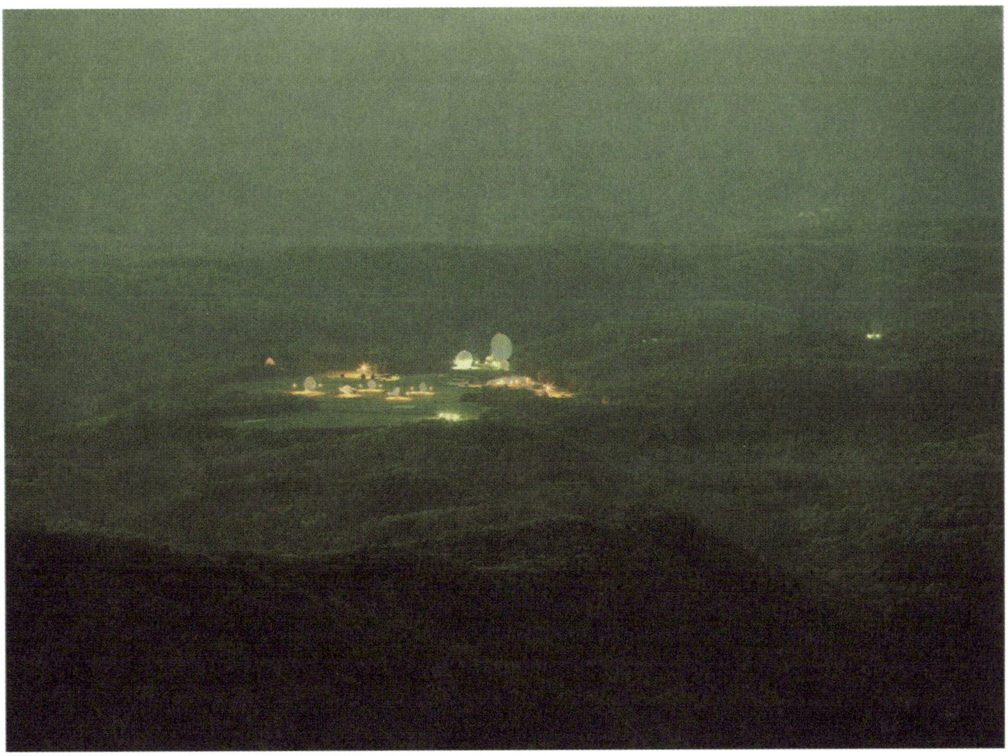

**FIGURE 8.36**

Trevor Paglen, *They Watch the Moon*, 2010. C-print, 36 × 48 in. (91.44 × 121.92 cm). Collection SFMOMA. Courtesy of the artist and Altman Siegel, San Francisco. © Trevor Paglen.

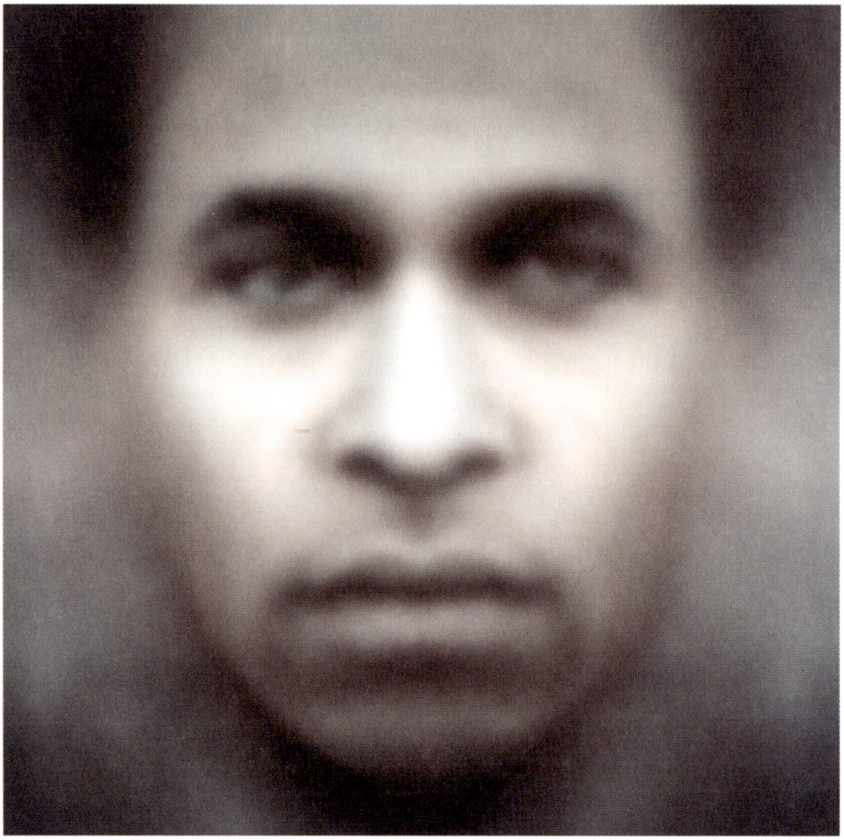

**FIGURE 8.37**
Trevor Paglen, *"Fanon" (Even the Dead Are Not Safe) Eigenface*, 2017. Dye sublimation print, 48 × 48 in (121.92 × 121.92 cm). Courtesy of the artist; Altman Siegel, San Francisco; and Pace Gallery. © Trevor Paglen.

## CONCLUSION *OR* THE RIGHT TO OPA/CITY

So where does all this discussion of veillancing leave us now? What is clear to me is that the overarching visibility of the urban body today, the almost total impossibility of *in*visibility in the city, makes graffiti's continuing existence a monumental act, a monumental achievement in itself. The civilian and surveillance gaze, the omnipresent smartphones and CCTV, the all-seeing-eye of Instagram and AFR, have entirely transformed the act of producing graffiti from just ten, not to say twenty or more, years ago. While graffiti has always toed the line between visibility and invisibility, between that which must be witnessed and that which must remain hidden, the city today has squeezed the width of that line—the gap between the seen and the unseen—into an infinitesimally small state. As such, graffiti's continual existence within this landscape—produced in the face of the algorithmic and digital eye, of the domineering gaze that not only sees us but sees straight through us—reveals a possibility for action outside the domination of the new surveillance. It reveals a form of public action and public speech challenging the visibility trap we are set within.[28]

The controlling visibilities of a city such as London—a city as famed for its AFR as its CCTV—must be understood not simply to restrict but rather to *refashion* the graffiti aesthetic that it co-creates. Rather than the colorful graffiti of Barcelona, the experimental output of Paris, or the typographic verticality of Sao Paulo, the surveillance city that London exemplifies means that a writer's tactics must prioritize not simply speed but likewise efficacy, must prioritize a material visibility and bodily invisibility in the most temporally and physically effective way possible. Surveillance culture in London does not simply reduce the quantity of graffiti, then; it reduces its decorative qualities, increasing the aesthetic of "damage" that must necessarily arise from it: paint stripper and etch, tools that rapidly and permanently burn into a surface, here become tools of stylistic beauty, violent tools working in a parasitic symbiosis with the violence of the city and the violence of surveillance itself. The sheer density of the gaze thus enforces the notorious "ugliness" of London's graffiti (its beautiful ugliness, I should add). Surveillance here thus does create a disciplined body, but not one, as in Foucault's reading, that stands in the service of the state. Discipline here comes from caution, attention, from a way of encountering and surpassing the gaze (whether via hi-vis and a hoodie or the knowledge of how to erase filmic metadata). It comes through a sixth sense[29] encompassing not just seeing but *the sense of being seen*, a scopaesthetic sensitivity to the feeling that one is being watched, whether by a human or machinic eye. The discipline created by graffiti is thus not a docility in which a body is "manipulated, shaped, [and] trained" so as it "obeys [and] responds" (Foucault 1995 [1977]: 136) to the economic imperatives of the state, but one that does so in resistance to the desired utility and coercive obedience the state requires. Visibility thus creates an efficiency enacted against utility, against obedience and the gaze. It creates an aesthetic emergent through the basic necessities of in/visibility in which the need to be both *in* and *out* of sight is met.

As such, what becomes critical here is an understanding of not simply the benefits of visibility or invisibility but rather the asymmetries of in/visibility, the ability of some to be seen when they desire visibility and to be invisible when it is privacy they choose, and yet of others to be invisible when they crave witnessing and visible when it is privacy they require! Visibility is critical to ensure that a political actor's actions and deeds are seen (or critical to ensure one's safety in a space of darkness), while it can also compel us to act in ways other than we desire due to the very knowledge that we are seen. Invisibility, likewise, can form a (safe) space in which we can assemble (rather than *appear*) together in concert (or simply for us to remain invisible from those who may seek our harm) yet can likewise be an area of ostracization in which our voices are compulsorily silenced. Visibility is thus a scale, not a rigid either/or. And while we may doubt, as Peggy Phelan has argued, the potency of visibility as a "source of unity or wholeness," that does not need suggest that "continued invisibility is the 'proper' political agenda for the disenfranchised," nor does it go beyond the false "binary between the power of visibility and the impotency of invisibility" (Phelan 1993: 6).

Rather than the pure transparency of contemporary visibility or the absolute erasure of the concealed, then, it is the Martiniquan philosopher Édouard Glissant's "right to opacity" (Glissant 1997: 189) that can provide us with the critical conceptual frame for this chapter, for a space of in/visibility within the hyper-visible city. For Glissant, the concept of opacity acted not only as a refusal of the enlightenment project of knowledge acquisition that functioned only for the benefit of the colonial power, but as a way of being that could not be reduced "into the preconceived transparency of universal models" (p. 193). Opacity here is thus not simply about obscurity, but instead a resistance to normativity and capture, to the surveillant lights that create an all-too-lucid bodily clarity. It is about a visibility not rejected but obfuscated, an opacity (as seen in figure 8.38) that blurs rather than shrouds. Here, then, visibility can be eluded through using a language incomprehensible to power, a language that is resistant to translation. Like the graffiti monument itself, a monument balanced at the edge of concealment and revelation, a monument that exposes what it must likewise suppress, opacity reveals without necessitating total transparency, retaining a notion of publicity in which privacy still exists, a notion of visibility in which there is *always* still something to hide. Rather than the harsh illumination that blinds, it provides us with that which is visible yet inscrutable, enigmatic, a monument not seeking to illuminate but to hint toward, to warn. The Lefebvrian right to the city, then, the right to speak, to act, and to participate in the city, here becomes refigured via a right to opacity without which these primary rights themselves become impossible. It becomes prefigured by a right to opa/city without which transparency becomes the inescapable mode, a radical opa/city placed at the very edge of the in/visible range.

The graffiti monument thus becomes visible proof of a visible world away from the dangers of visibility. It marks out a presence revealing that which it hides, a visible invisibility that perfectly mirrors the invisible visibilities of the institutional monument, the ability of the monument, as famously discussed by Robert Musil (1986 [1936]), to actively *repel* attention. The power that the institutional monument exudes through its ability to disappear into the background of the urban mise-en-scène—only coming to the fore when being asserted (in times of national need) or being questioned (in times of social unrest)—thus functions much like the invisible hand of what Pierre Bourdieu termed "habitus" (1977). The "indifference of the public to monuments," as Magda Szcześniak and Łukasz Zaremba have described it, thus becomes "proof of the efficaciousness of the monumental form," proof of the "naturalization of the monument and its values" (Szcześniak and Zaremba 2019: 213). While the graffiti monument can thus be understood to reveal what it hides (the body itself), the institutional monument hides what it reveals! It hides its power, its politics, its status as constructed not natural. It

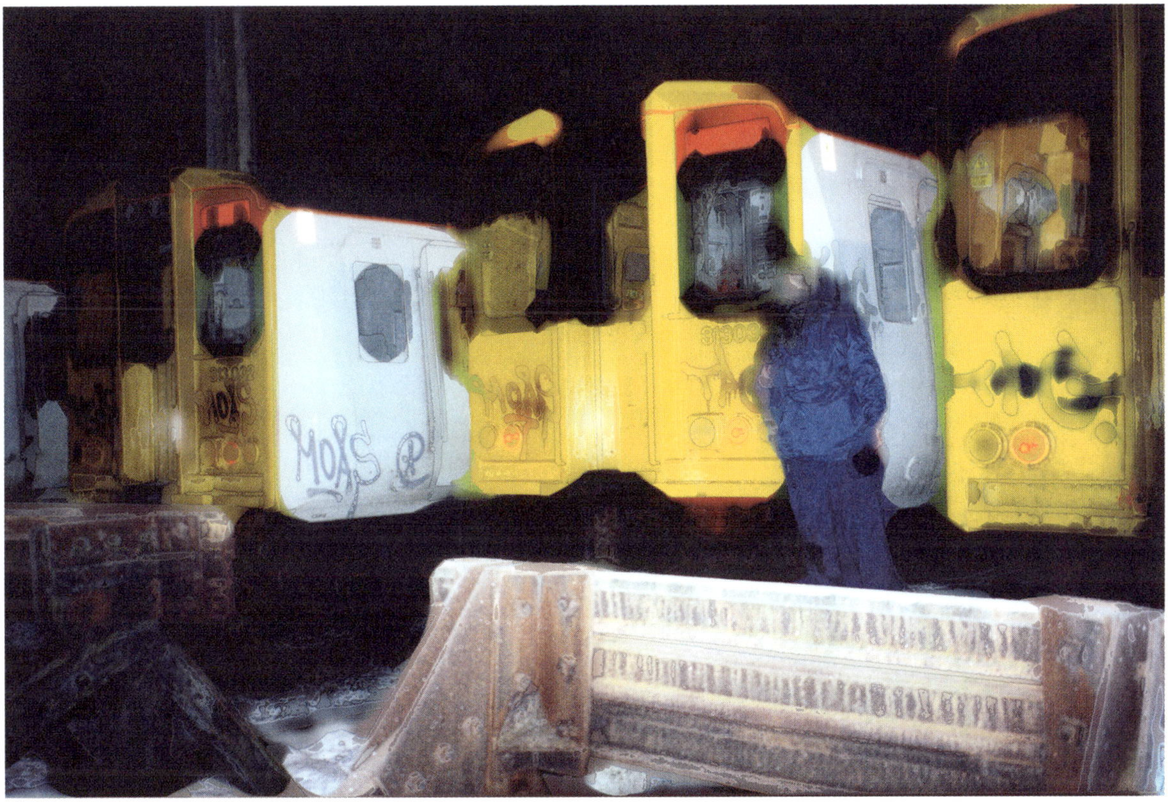

**FIGURE 8.38**
*Post-Panel Tagging*, 2000. Rural England. Photo: Christopher Stead. Digital manipulation: Rafael Schacter. Courtesy of the photographer.

hides its dominance through its mundanity. The graffiti monument, however, brings those at the edge of the city into a visibility that leaves them still unseen. It emerges via a masked revelation, via a thwarting of clarity in which the opaque becomes luminous. Like the subcultures studied by Dick Hebdige, graffiti functions "at the interface between surveillance and the evasion of surveillance" (Hebdige 1983: 86), acting neither as an "affirmation or a refusal" but as a "play for attention and a refusal" (p. 87). It not only "translates the fact of being under scrutiny into the pleasures of being watched" but likewise the "elaboration of surfaces which takes place within it reveals a darker will towards opacity, a drive against classification and control, a desire to exceed" (pp. 86–87). The graffiti monument functions through a form of masking and mimicry in which simulation and suppression come not only to repel visibility but so too to directly engage it. It functions through a masking and mimicry in which the image becomes a tool of communication and a tool of veiling (not veill*ance*) at the same moment.

# 9

# SPECTACULARITY AND TEMPORALITY

Graffiti inhabits a city in which spectacularity dominates, a site of continual conspicuous consumption in which not just space but time is monumentalized. Here, the power of the gaze emerges not just through surveillance but through a way of seeing replicating the principles of the mall and the museum, a gaze in which the city is experienced, as Lefebvre has suggested, through "the image, through publicity, through the spectacle of objects" (Lefebvre 2003: 21). The principal sensorial mode of participation in the city thus comes through observation and consumption rather than engagement or production, the city a "series of displays, an exhibition of objects for sale," the city a site in which the "logic of merchandise" has taken hold (p. 20).

This chapter will explore the city via the two dominant spectacular modes it today appears through: the first, via what is termed the "creative" or the "branded city"; the second, via its "heritage" and "tourist" incarnations. In both cases we will find a city that is "not only transformed into a *site* of consumption" but that "becomes an *object* of consumption" (Lefebvre 2014: 203, my emphasis), a city in which consumption is about not just things but constructed experiences. Moreover, we will find an anachronistic site in which the temporal is flooded by both a backward-looking nostalgia and a forward-looking "utopia." The monumentalizing of the past seen within the official heritage regime in chapter 3 is thus here not only bolstered by the touristification and museumification of the urban realm but set in an anticipatory state in which endless transformation is always the answer and the city is dominated by an overburdened futurity. The fleeting momentariness of the graffiti monument, however, as much as its fundamentally aneconomic and participatory status, will thus be seen to work against the framework of the spectacular city through evading its maximalism as much as using it against itself. Unlike the monumental public art harnessed within the heritage infrastructure, unlike the corporate public art employed as part of the spectacularized infrastructure of contemporary urban space, here the graffiti-monument rejects this frictionless Disneyfication in both direct and indirect ways. The *monument-warning* thus here forms a spectacle acting not as a tool of the monumentalized city but as a tool with which the monumental itself can be ruptured.

## THE CREATIVE/THE BRANDED CITY

The city today is not just a physical space. It is an image curated and marketed as one commodity among a host of competing commodities across the world. It is a site whose survival is seen to rest upon its "creativity," on its status as a "creative" city, and on the economic benefits that that title is assumed to assume. The watershed moment for this practice of city branding is often seen to have emerged with the publication of Richard Florida's *Rise of the Creative Class* in 2002, a treatise transforming our cities into entrepreneurial conglomerates that must sell their charisma to the world. Here, urban regeneration is intrinsically linked to a set of cultural policies that have placed artistic practices at the forefront, policies in which the creative transformation of city is a means to a clear instrumental end. Unless you want your city to go the way of Detroit—the habitually used urban bogeyman—you must build bike paths and creative bohemian quarters, you must support micro-breweries and tech start-ups in order to entice the all-important "creatives" to the new Mecca. Regardless of the numerous critiques placed against the concept (from Hewitt 2011 and Lovink and Rossiter 2007, among many others), the last decades have borne witness to the globally dominating authority of this now ideological norm, the capital C "Creative" takeover of civic public policy.

Of all the ways economic utility is generated within the Creative City, it is place-making (or place-*marketing*) that is the dominant pursuit. Here the spectacular is key, a singular distinction outlining the creative desires of the site. This is the realm of the "starchitects" and Bilbao[1] effects, of the alien architectural presences that litter our cities—from Norman Foster's Gherkin in London (see figure 9.1) to Rem Koolhaas's CCTV building in Beijing—sites in which "uniqueness" is critical. Without your Gehry or your Hadid, without your same-same-unique, can you really compete in the new market of the global elite? Architecture here is thus a trademarked tool for associating goods and origins into one culturally desirable entity. Yet alongside these hard forms of urban branding we also have the soft branding of the Creative City, the realm of flagship cultural festivals (whether on the gargantuan scale of an Olympics or the minor scale of a literary festival) that intertwine site and narrative in one creative package. Culture here thus not only is a "draw" to support the local tourist economy (a ticketed, privatized endeavor) but is affixed to a notion of creativity in which quantitative results rule. In both cases, what is desired is the formation of a city's unique selling point, a competitive cultural strategy (as witnessed in the now ubiquitous city-of-culture contests) that is about investment and finances, public relations and branding. Here one anchors place so as to accrue profit. Here site is a commodity, the city a brand needing brand management to achieve its maximal economic potential.

Yet it is not just the large-scale architectural icons and cultural festivals that are used in the place-making of the Creative City but so too public art in more general. Anish Kapoor and Cecil Balmond's ArcelorMittal Orbit at the London Olympic Park (see figure 9.2) or Kapoor's Cloud Gate at the AT&T Plaza[2] in Chicago are the art equivalents

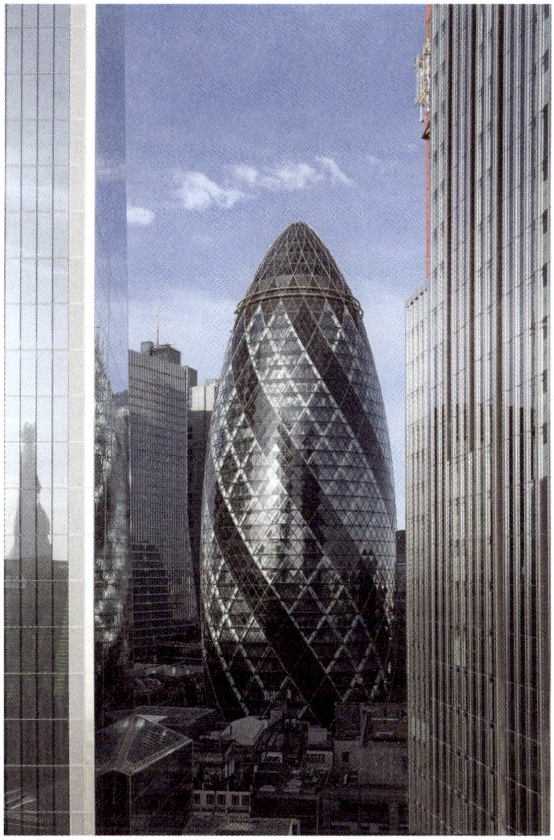

**FIGURE 9.1**
Foster + Associates, 30 St. Mary Axe, seen from the Garden at 120, 2023. Photo: Kallerna. Creative Commons Attribution-Share Alike 4.0 International license.

of our starchitectural designs, sitting at the cross-section of the two genres in fact. Yet our POPS plops work in much the same way, even if at a reduced (financial and physical) scale. The showpiece fountains at Granary Square,[3] its "light architecture" as much as its *IFO*, along with the temporary installations by curatorially selected art and architectural collectives, provide users with spectacular public art that not only looks great on social media but aligns the site with the avant-garde and visually "creative." They provide us with large, colorful installations containing as many bells and whistles as the site's security "ambassadors" themselves, branding the space as one of the future and creative cool. The public art of the Creative City thus must supply landmarks (and landmark events) that can provide context where there is none or reinforce it when there is. It must add value (whether in terms of footfall or social media "interactions")

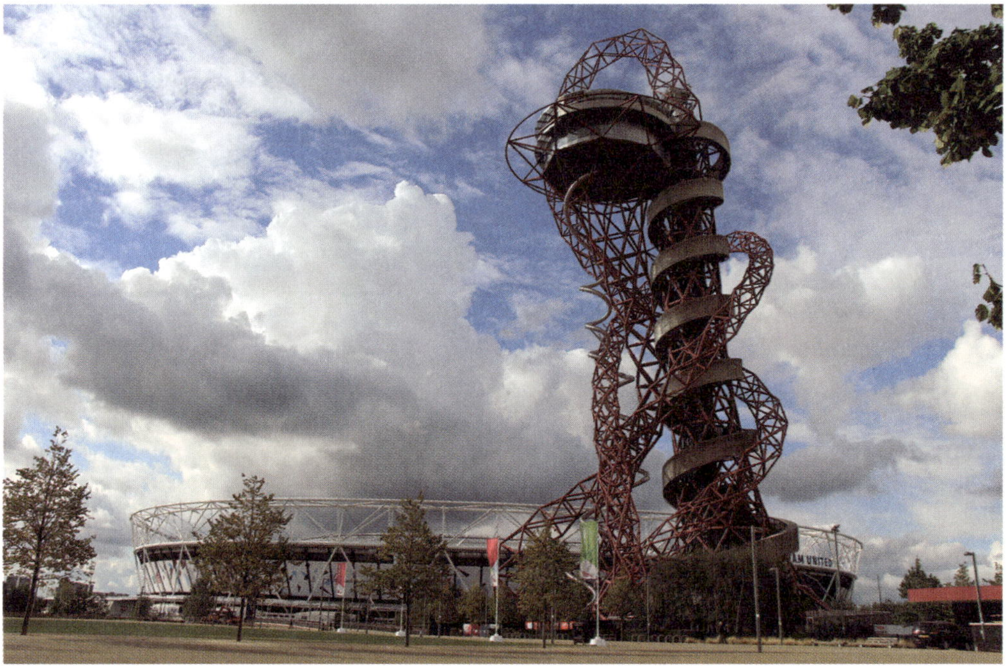

**FIGURE 9.2**
Anish Kapoor and Cecil Balmond, ArcelorMittal Orbit, Queen Elizabeth Olympic Park, London, 2016. Photo: Fred Romero. Attribution 2.0 Generic (CC BY 2.0).

and serve to support rather than critique its surrounds. As such, public art here must follow, as Jonathan Vickery has said, "whatever civic aspirations frame local authority planning," a state of affairs in which "artists are called in, at some appointed stage in the proceedings, and asked to deposit an object or other contribution to a larger strategic process of urban change" (2012: 3).[4] This is not the famous Community Mural Movement seen in the London of the 1980s, part of a grassroots project of municipal socialism supported by the Greater London Council (Benedict et al. 2013), nor the famous *Wall of Respect* produced by the Organization of Black American Culture in Chicago in the 1960s and '70s (Alkalimat, Crawford and Zorach 2017). Rather than social activism and community engagement, here the arts are supported to soften or edify "urban economic development," valued not in themselves, as Jamie Peck has argued, but "as putative economic assets to evolving regimes of urban competition" (Peck 2005: 763–764). Art and culture are here beholden to a form of public funding and private investment in which the goal is always instrumental, part of a process of aspirational development in which the city must be the city of the future if it is to survive at all. And in its pure utilitarianism, in its purposeful spectacularity, public art is here increasingly aligned with the realm of kitsch. Kitsch hides, it veils. Kitsch plunges us into a space that, as Winfried Menninghaus suggested in his analysis of Walter Benjamin, focuses on "instantaneous emotional gratification without intellectual effort," an art of "unadulterated beauty" that "presents no difficulties in interpretation and has absolutely nothing to do with an aesthetics of negativity" (Menninghaus 2009: 41). It presents itself as a simple answer to a complex problem. Shinier! Bigger! More unique!

While the developer-led art projects of plop art were traditionally fronted by the aesthetic of the high arts (seen in an array of Alexander Calders or Henry Moores that litter our urban plazas), of all the aesthetic possibilities available to the Creative City it is graffiti's younger sibling, street art,[5] that has come most strongly to the fore. Much cheaper than an art biennale, and infinitely cheaper than a Guggenheim or a Gormley, what policymakers call the "low-cost high-impact" apparatus of street art is now a dominant visual trope found in contemporary public spaces all over the world. Whether functioning through the system of the street art festival (funded by private developers and/or local councils) or single set-piece installations (organized by place-making organizations and a range of consultants and advisors),[6] the aesthetic of edgy authenticity that street art generates has made it the ultimate delivery system for the Creative City, its semblance of transgression (due to its graffiti roots as much as its superficial referencing of political aesthetics) alongside its site-specific obliviousness working together to shroud any social realities it encounters. Contemporary street art has thus in many ways fallen into the ameliorative trap that Rosalyn Deutsche discussed in terms of the redevelopment projects of the 1980s, functioning in a decorative vein that reproduces "nostalgic images of space that externalize and delegitimate conflict" (Deutsche 1996: xxiv), that creates "harmonious spatial totalities" that merely "decorate . . . the spaces of its display" (pp. 261–262). It provides an image that seems visionary and unconventional while aligning perfectly with the visions and conventions of our contemporary brandscapes. You want authenticity? You want desire? Add street art. You want to put your town, your city (back) on the map? If you paint it they will come. Synthetically simulated through its active employment by property developers and public authorities, artificially stimulated to provide the veneer of edginess and affectation of innovation the Creative City desires, street art is thus used to create the perfect conditions for the "bohemian" hubs these sites require, the edgy grist for the creative mill. In this way, then, the co-optation of street art that has emerged over the last decades has developed not only via the traditional route of the art market but likewise via an intertwined relation to the property market, co-opted not just through selling itself but through selling a (false) notion of place.

There are innumerable case studies that could be recounted here (those of Miami and Manila discussed in Schacter 2014b still entirely pertinent); however, it is the case of Croydon that I want to unpack here. A large commuter town in South London and key transport corridor between the capital and the south coast, Croydon is a diverse urban hub with a large local economy yet habitually placed in a subordinate position to London's central zones in geographic and cultural terms. With easy access to the city yet significantly lower property values, it has been part of numerous art-led regeneration projects since the mid-2000s. "Culture," as council leader Tony Newman said, was thus "at the heart of Croydon's regeneration," and art at the "centre of our plans for our borough's future" (YourCroydon 2016). Street art in particular has been critical to this process. An article published in a major London newspaper in 2016, for example, was headlined "Introducing the New Capital of Street Art . . . Croydon," its subheading informing readers that "Developers want to transform the borough with murals painted by locals" (Davis 2016: n.p.). The author predicted that "the designs will attract Londoners taking their first step on the property ladder," in particular, they claimed, the "ex-office block Green Dragon House" (n.p.). Referring to the flagship site designed by Inspired Homes,[7] the block's developer Martin Skinner[8] suggested that the mural on the building, produced not by a local but by famed UK street artist Ben Eine and seen in

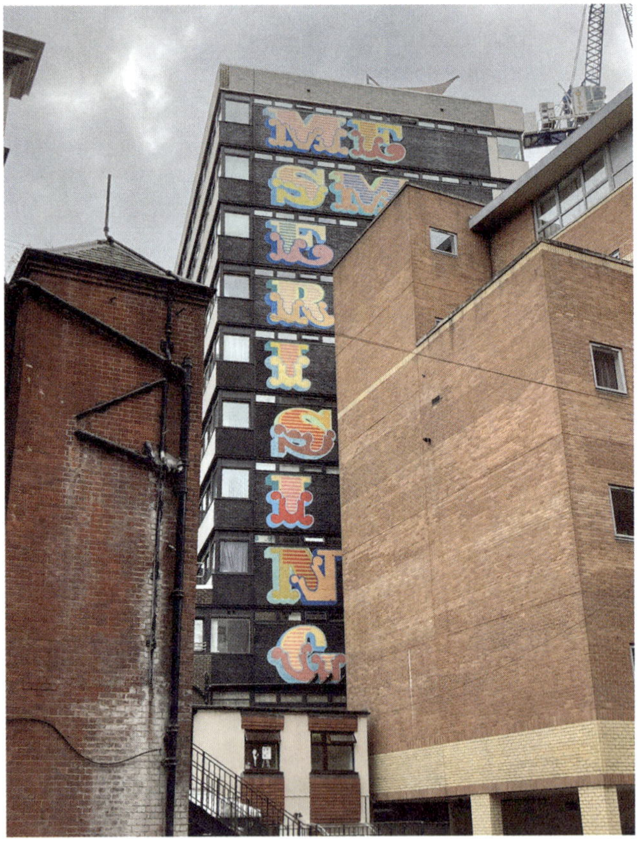


**FIGURE 9.3**

Ben Eine, *Mesmerising*, 2017. Photo: Matt Brown. Creative Commons Attribution 2.0 Generic license.

figure 9.3, "helps to put Croydon on the map once more, inspiring more people to come and live in this buzzing centre of arts, culture, dining and shopping" (DoGoodFactory 2017). Alongside the council and the developer, however, comes the critical third element in this Creative City trifecta, the local street-art guru Kevin Zuchowski-Morrison, who organized the mural (and a print exhibition inside the building) through the vehicle of the local RISE Gallery. Not only given free rein by the council over the newly formed "Croydon Arts Quarter" too (in which the gallery removed the free painting wall[9] and took total control over who could paint where), RISE was also given £60,000 of public funding[10] to institute the "RISE street art festival" in 2018, a project that was, as Oliver Lewis, Croydon Council cabinet member for culture, leisure and sport, claimed, "another big step in changing perceptions of Croydon" (CroydonBID 2018).

Here, then, we see the classic framework for public art in the Creative City: the council, which desperately wants to promote their town and which will go wherever the creative winds flow. The developer who needs council support for their planning permissions, methods for cost-effectively advertising their properties, and increases in the value of the local housing stock more generally. And the gallerist who utilizes public space both to advertise their own roster of artists (the public murals commonly working in concert with private exhibitions of the muralists' studio work) and to develop their own art empire (or art quarter, at the least). Forget my opinions on the "quality" of the murals imposed on the town (as seen in figures 9.4 and 9.5), let alone the top-down imposition of an aesthetic that was almost entirely ignorant of site.[11] Forget the silky ease of consumption and relationship to kitsch. The simulacrum of transgression that this spectacular form of Creative City public art establishes is not simply an insipid but a violent one, mainlining a notion of authenticity into a site to accelerate the process of change: artists arrive (at the behest of capital, not community), ignorant of local circumstances (and too apathetic to inquire), creating the vibrant veneer camouflaging the displacement they generate. The gentrification that Croydon has experienced over the last decade—as documented in *This Is Croydon*[12] by Shane Duncan, for example—the gentrification that the murals, the box-parks, and the creatives' hub have generated, is part of the wider ecosystem that the Creative City produces. The micro-apartments assembled at Green Dragon House are not meant for families, not meant for the current residents of Croydon even. They are meant for young professionals migrating to the area, the public art produced explicitly to bring the new Croydon utopia into fruition. The aesthetic regime employed in the Creative City but is undertaken with a very specific future in mind, a city looking endlessly forward, a city set in an impending time itself spectacularized and maximalized in the same ways as its physical space. Public art is here fastened to a mode of spatial consumption servicing an economic template in which the utopian future is one in which community displacement is a given. Rather than trying to improve amenities for those already in the borough, rather than an equitable future for *them*, it is the dream of Creativity they are working toward, a new Croydon and a new future to come.[13]

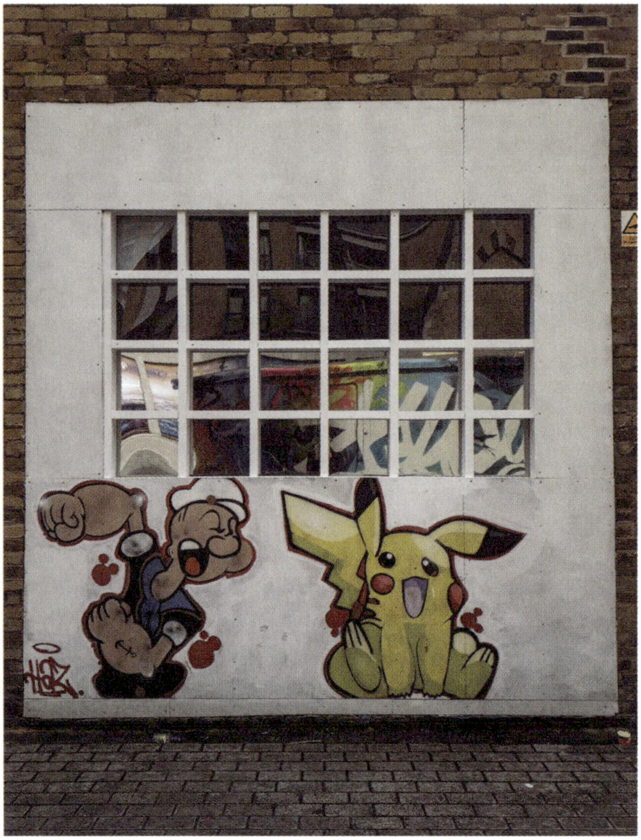

**FIGURE 9.4**
Popeye and Pikachu by Haz, 2018. Photo: Memoirs of a Metro Girl.

And has this future now arrived? Well, sadly, in 2022 Croydon council "declared effective bankruptcy for the third time in two years," petitioning the central government to "write off £1.3bn of debts, including £500m run up through a series of ill-fated commercial investments" (Butler 2022).[14] While this goes a little beyond the issue of street art alone—COVID-19 and a decade of austerity played their part—what remains are a set of policies in which institutionalized public art is seen as a panacea for cities, even while, as Malcolm Miles claimed back in 2005, there is often little "evidence for sustainable benefits to a city's publics" (Miles 2005: 897). Rather than focusing on systemic social improvements, what is instead seen within these sites is a privileging based around "market, not social need" (p. 901) in which the intended "recipients" of these artworks are "rendered passive receivers of culture rather than being empowered to shape cultures" (p. 896). Although strong in rhetoric, then, the true effects of creative

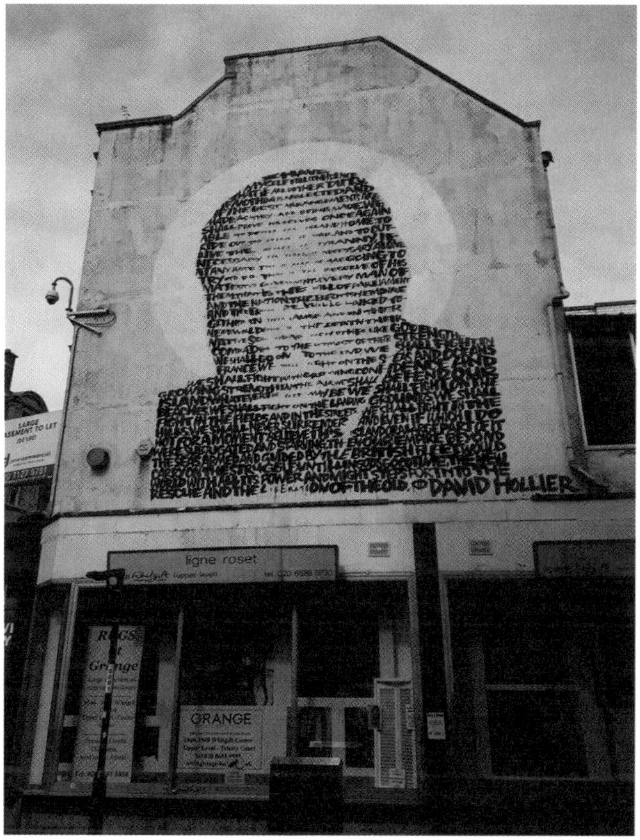


**FIGURE 9.5**
Winston Churchill by David Hollier, 2016. Photo: Memoirs of a Metro Girl.

regeneration, as Loretta Lees and Clare Melhuish have likewise argued, of the "benefits of the arts to economic, social and democratic change," can be seen as not evidentially "robust on any of these measures" (Lees and Melhuish 2015: 255). While arts may in some cases be able to "contribute to place attachment through beautification" and, in other cases, "can raise social or political issues and activate citizens' engagement with the environment," these effects, the authors conclude, "may be peripheral to the underlying structural facts of economic restructuring and deployed simply to mask the realities of social displacement" (p. 252). The neo-muralism of Croydon can thus be seen as a visual indicator of a much larger issue, an aesthetic of seduction founded on displacement, an aesthetic in which murals simply act, in artist and writer Caleb Neelon's expression, as the pupal stage of condos (as seen in figure 9.6). The Creative City trifecta thus further cements the intimate relations between arts and gentrification,

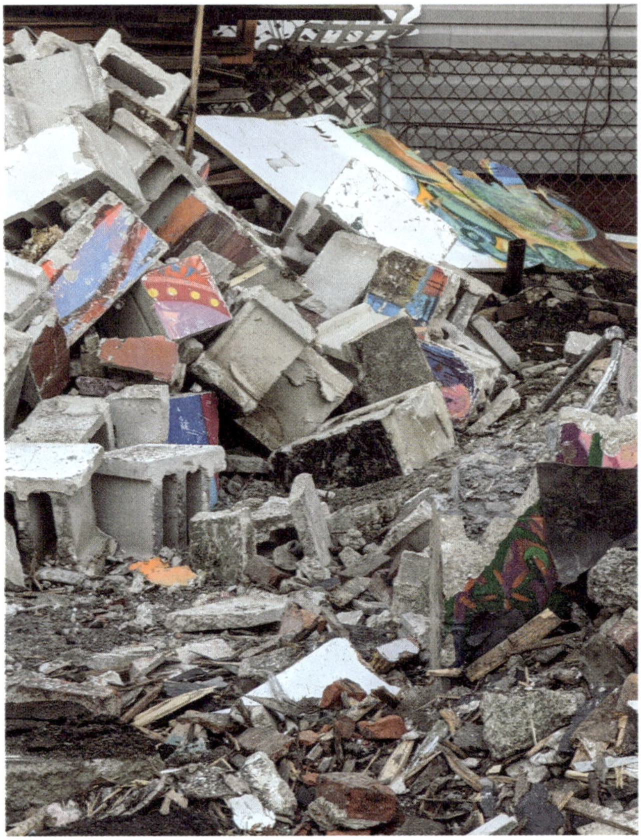

**FIGURE 9.6**
Caleb Neelon, *The Post-Pupal Stage*, 2022. Courtesy of the artist.

something seen through artists' searches for cheap rent (as in New York in the 1970s; see Deutsche and Ryan 1984), through art infrastructure such as the galleries and artist-run spaces (as seen in Los Angeles in the 2010s; see Crisman 2021), let alone through the work of celebrated art bodies such as Philadelphia's Mural Arts[15] or Art Angel[16] in the United Kingdom. As likewise seen in hundreds of other Creative City experiments across the world,[17] "regenerative" public art can never simply be seen to be about renewal. It is about a form of gentrification that, as Tom Slater has argued, is about the "loss of the right to housing suffered by working class people" (Slater 2009: 297), about the "constant fear of displacement among vulnerable renters in particular" (p. 305). Gentrification is thus not simply about improved amenities (and who ever said that amenities were only ever possible via displacement?). It is about the crushing effects of dislocation and displacement that public art is entirely enmeshed within.

While graffiti has remained free from direct Creative City co-optation, it is impossible to deny that it, too, as Sharon Zukin and Laura Braslow have noted, can today be seen to mark out a neighborhood's "cool" character and thus place it on map as an "emerging creative district" (Zukin and Braslow 2011:136). Here, then, graffiti becomes a sign that comes to "attract rather than repel investors" (p. 138), a stepping-stone to the eventual pure white utopia. Yet many graffiti writers can be seen to act in direct resistance to these processes of gentrification and the spectacular aesthetics they parasitically utilize too. Back in Croydon, then, a number of murals produced by the RISE gallery were "defaced" by local graffiti writers over the period of their local dominance, as seen in figure 9.7, for example. "It's a real shame because they could jeopardise everything we're trying to do," Zuchowski-Morrison said in response to one of the graffiti "attacks" (Davies 2015), while on Twitter, Croydon Councilor Tony Newman told his followers, "We're searching CCTV to try & find those who want to destroy our public art you will not succeed" (@TonyJNewman77, February 23, 2015). The "murals," RISE Gallery (presumably Zuchowski-Morrison) added in response, "were modern urban contemporary artworks. The tags were calculated vandalism" (@RISEgalleryuk, February 23, 2015). Setting all of the loaded semantics aside, perhaps the gallery was right. The graffiti *was* meant to deface the murals. Yet could one not also argue that these murals are vandalistic—damaging the environment through what their pigment enables—in a much less superficial yet much more insidious way than the defacing tags? Either way, one can find hundreds, thousands of other cases such as this. "There's so many places where they could tag," said a San Franciscan artist whose mural in that city had been "defaced" by "graffiti vandals." They "could tag a bank, they could tag a fast food restaurant. Those affect people on a daily basis. I don't understand hurting an artist" (Gentile 2022). For the graffiti writer, however, there is no real difference between the mural and the advert, no difference between the mural and a "For Sale" sign (which the murals often really are). They are both selling something, an idea, a future. They both presage their own destruction, the destruction of the mural and its reconstruction as (unaffordable) housing almost always the inevitable result. They both act as a midway point presaging and impelling change, both aesthetic techniques with perlocutionary aims.

Other artists have also used public space to question the ongoing spectacularization of the city. Referencing a particularly British style of pre–*Subway Art* wall-writing in his work, the London-based artist Edwin has focused much of his street output on the relationship between public art and regeneration (as seen in figures 9.8–9.10). Addressing the ways in which "urban" artists have become complicit in ongoing gentrification as much as the manner in which, as Edwin himself said, "commercial muralism" has today become "easily confused with corporate advertising" (Griffiths 2018), Edwin's tongue-in-cheek (yet prophetic) asides written around East London try to reveal what lies below the shiny façade. Yet it is his two-part work seen in figures 9.11–9.13 that for me speaks most perfectly in this context. Here Edwin wrote one of his customary messages not on an empty wall (as per his usual technique) but directly on top of a

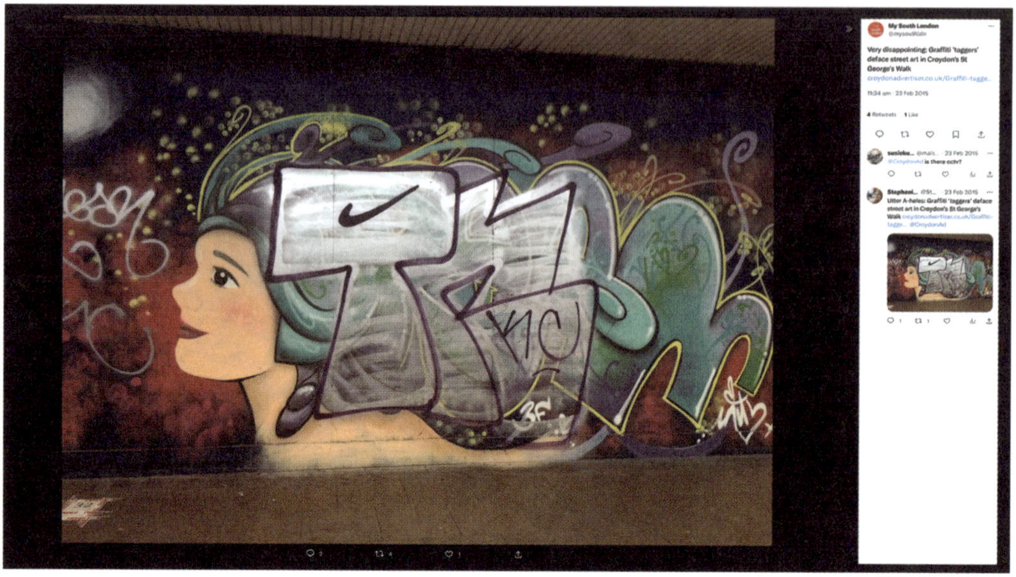


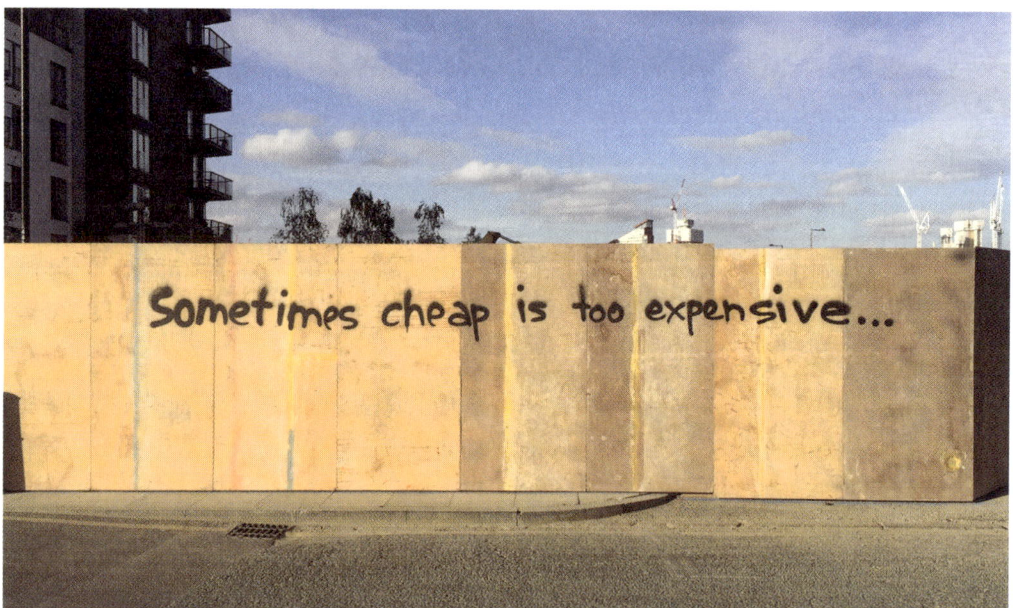


**FIGURE 9.7**
Screenshot of Twitter post by My South London (@mysouthldn): "Very disappointing: Graffiti 'taggers' deface street art in Croydon's St George's Walk," February 23, 2015.

**FIGURE 9.8**
Edwin, *Sometimes cheap is too expensive . . .* , 2016. Courtesy of the artist @thelazyedwin.

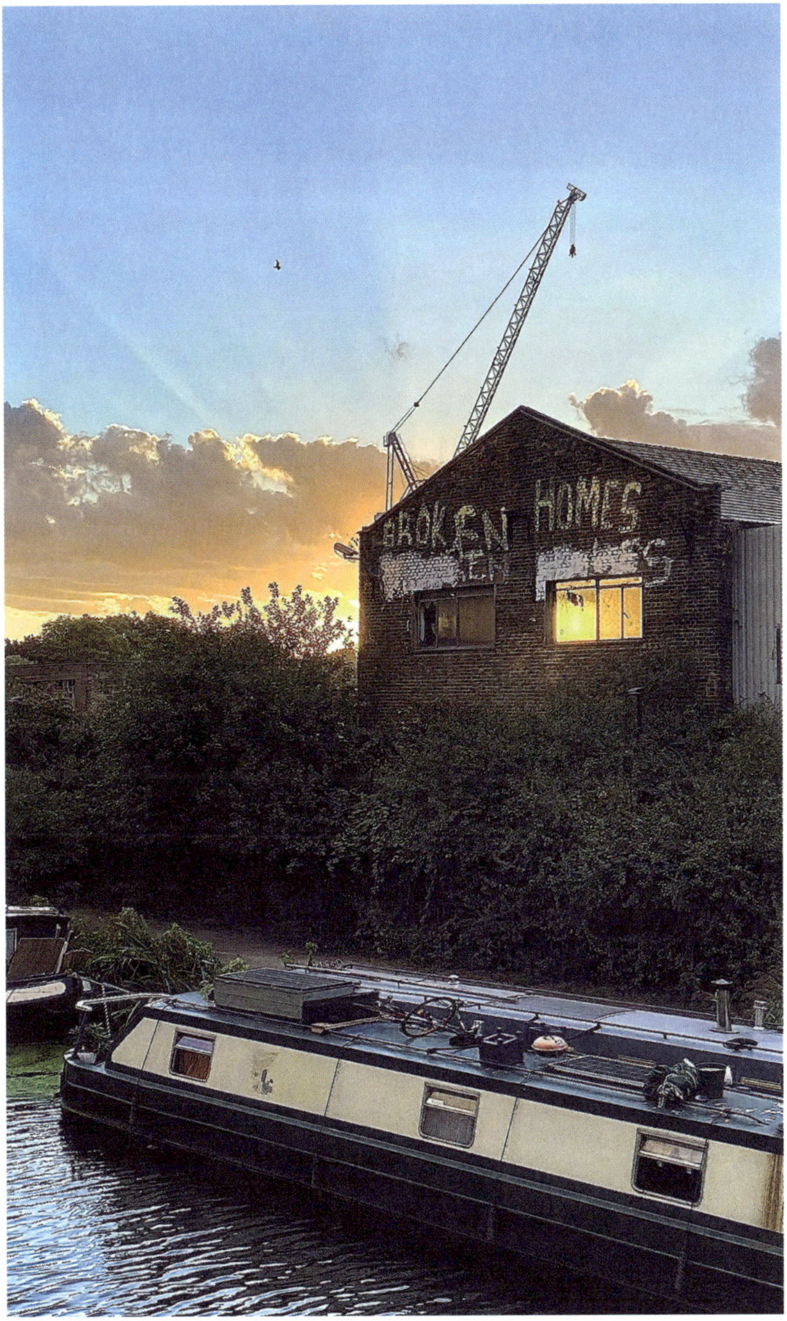


**FIGURE 9.9**
Edwin, *BROKEN HOMES*, 2020. Courtesy of the artist @thelazyedwin.

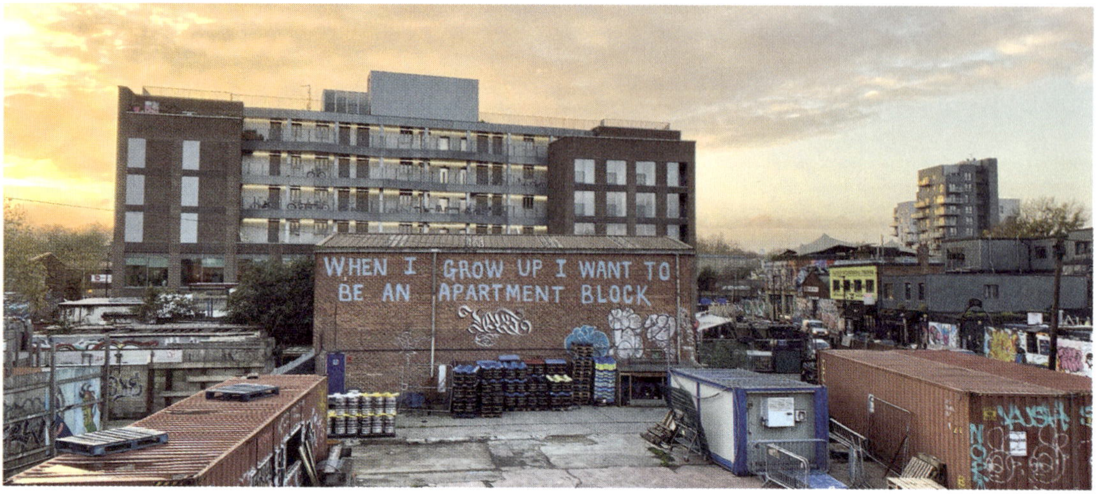


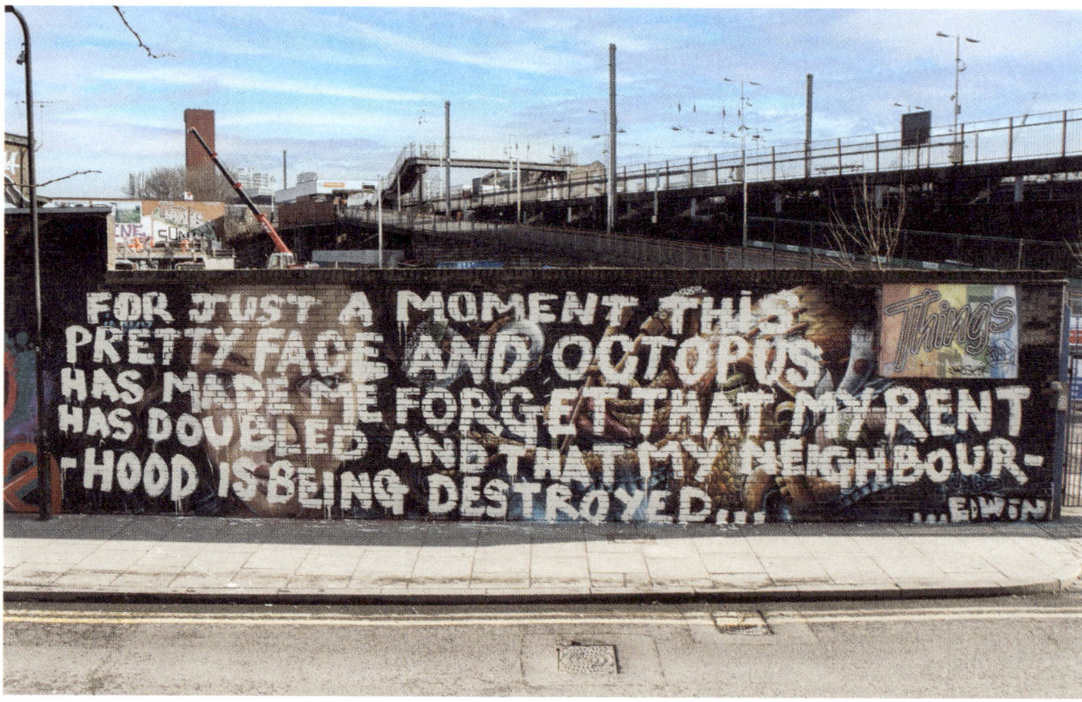


**FIGURE 9.10**
Edwin, *WHEN I GROW UP I WANT TO BE AN APARTMENT BLOCK*, 2022. Courtesy of the artist @thelazyedwin.

**FIGURE 9.11**
Edwin, *For Just a Moment*, 2017. Photo: Fifthwalltv. Courtesy of the artist.

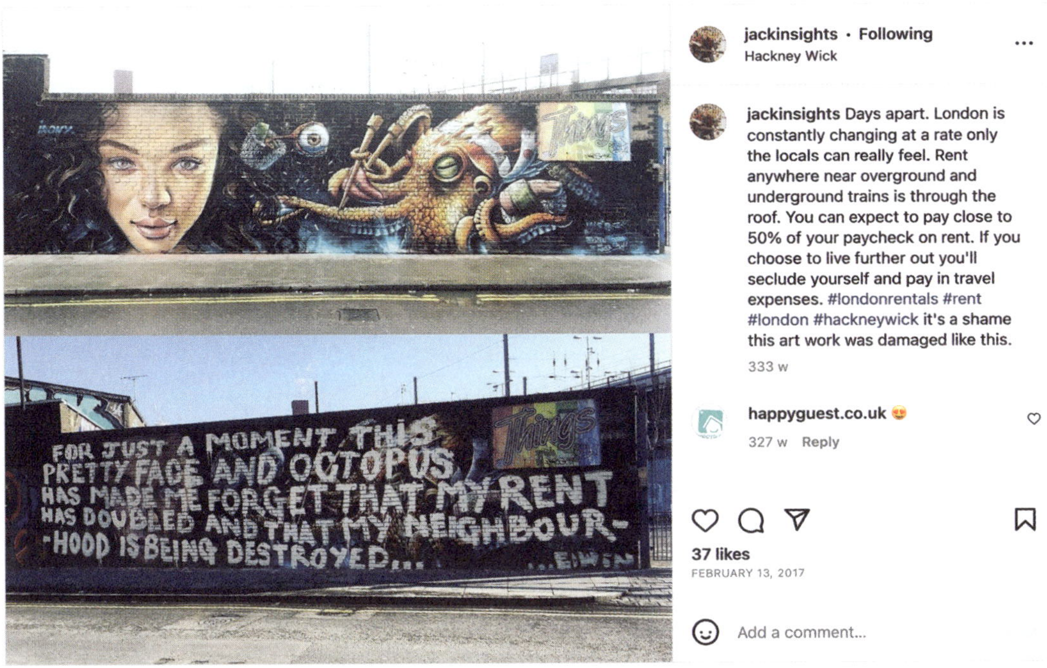


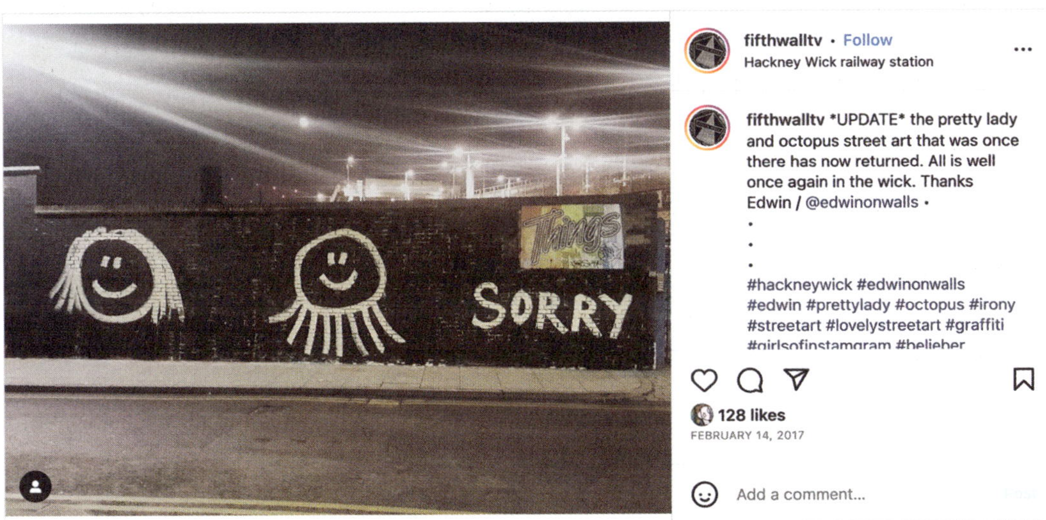


**FIGURE 9.12**

Screenshot of Instagram post by @jackinsights showing original mural beneath Edwin's *For Just a Moment*, February 13, 2017.

**FIGURE 9.13**

Screenshot of Instagram post by @fifthwalltv of Edwin's revision of *For Just a Moment*, February 14, 2017.

street-side street art mural, stating, in white paint-roller and in full caps, "FOR JUST A MOMENT, THIS PRETTY FACE AND OCTOPUS HAS MADE ME FORGET THAT MY RENT HAS DOUBLED AND THAT MY NEIGHBOURHOOD IS BEING DESTROYED." While this (sarcastic) remark seemed fair in itself, in his later amendment the artist blacked out the entire mural, adding a set of purposefully naïve, stick-figure replicas of the original characters, alongside the single word "SORRY." The two stages of Edwin's appropriation thus not only showed *what* the mural masked (increasing property prices) but *how* the mask functioned (through kitsch and the "beautiful"). In a perfectly crude way, the final piece clarifies the utter superficiality of the original, Edwin's condensed depiction revealing the ugly truth beneath the beautiful lie.

In the South Korean artist Jazoo Yang's public project *Dots*, seen in figures 9.14–9.16, however, resistance to the rampant redevelopment of working-class neighborhoods in Busan emerged through a series of house-encompassing interventions. Produced solely with the use of her thumbprint—in a process known locally as *Jijang* and containing the legally binding power of a signature—Yang's work sought to bring focus on the increasing number of communities whose homes were being compulsorily demolished by the thumbprint of others. The buildings on which she worked, by imprinting on them over

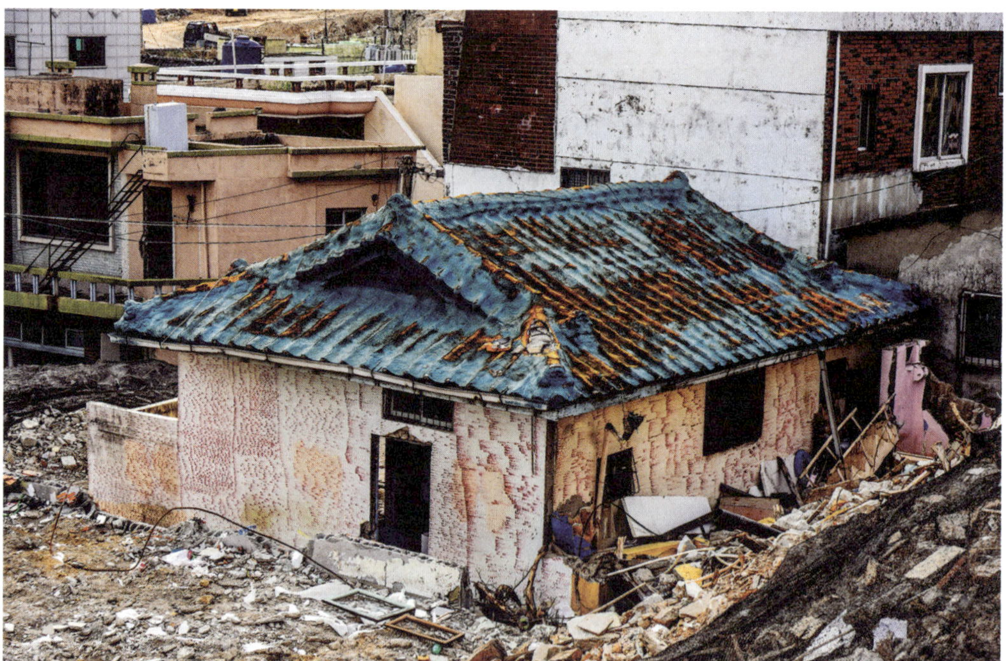

**FIGURE 9.14**
Jazoo Yang, *Dots: Motgol66*, 2015. Photo by Young-moon Ha. Courtesy of the artist.

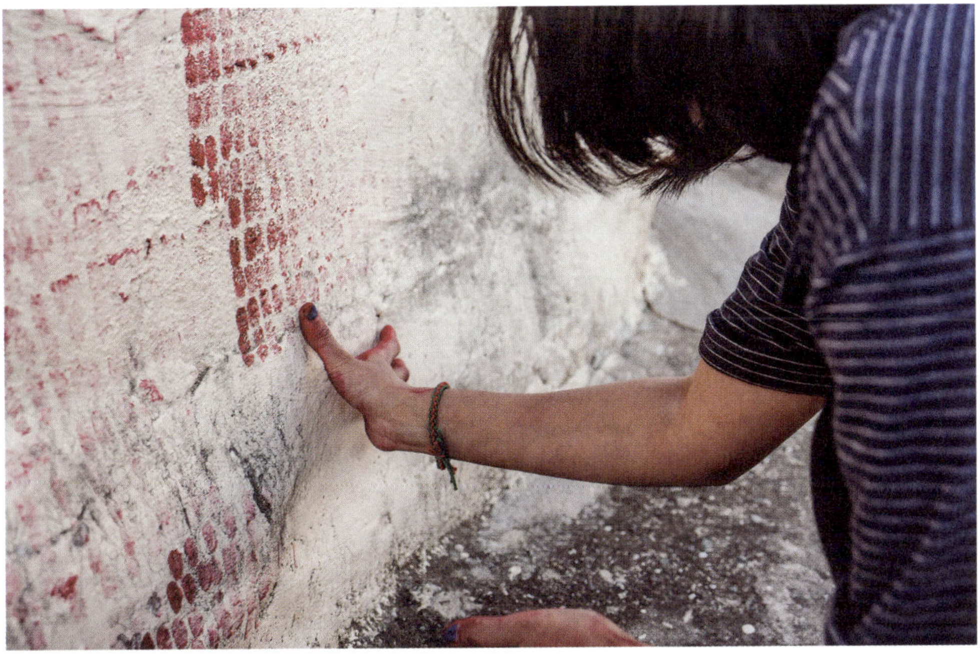

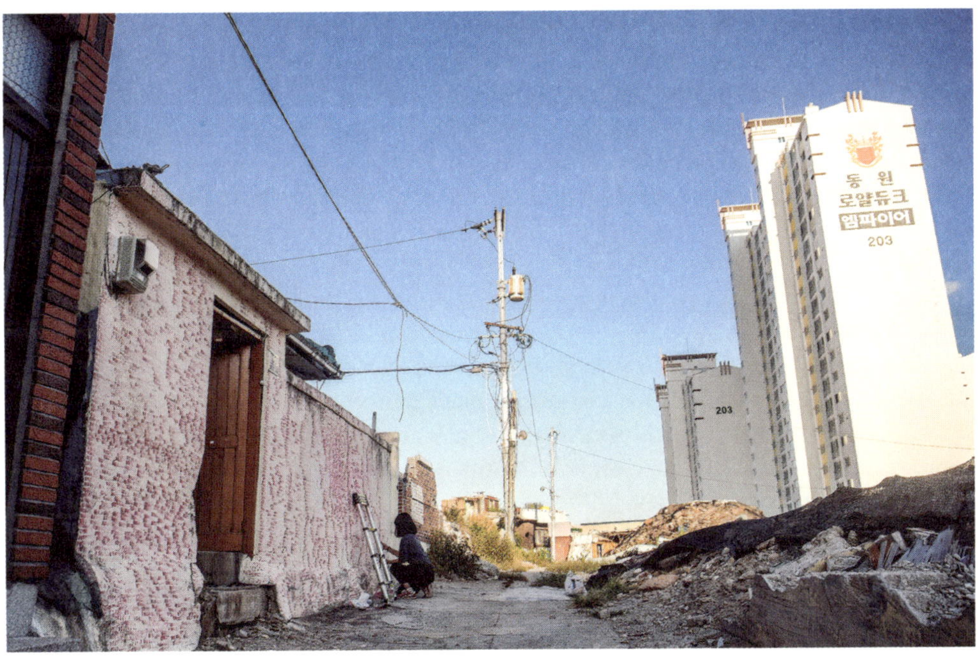



**FIGURES 9.15 AND 9.16**

Jazoo Yang, *Dots: Motgol66*, 2015. Photos by Young-moon Ha. Courtesy of the artist.

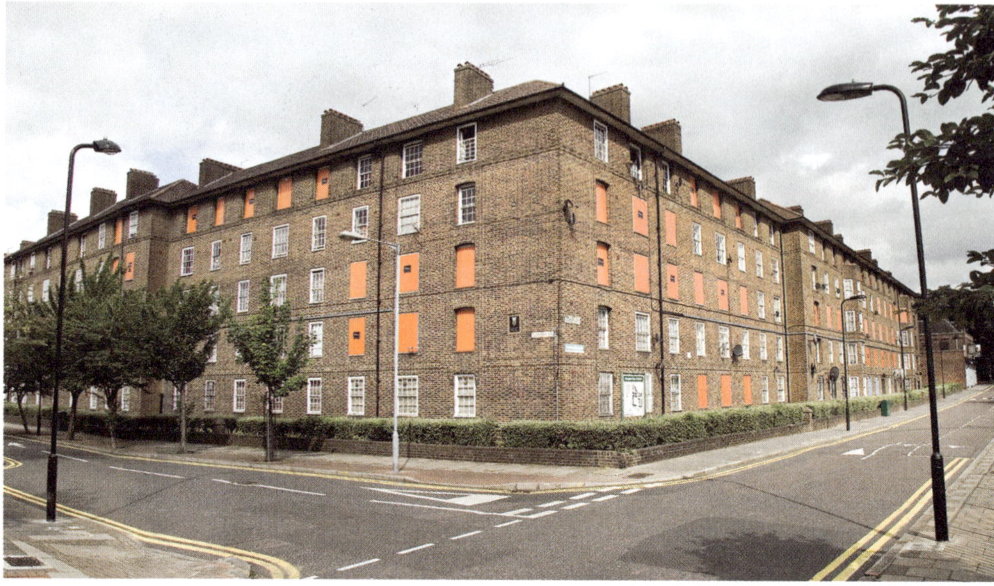

a period of twenty days (during which she received numerous threats from local construction companies), became marked not only with her own personhood but so too with her pledge to record these changes through not only the physical installation but also its ephemeral remainder. In the project *i am here* by Fugitive Images, however, the collective aimed to foreground not just the sites but the people whom these processes of displacement efface. Undertaken at the Haggerston estate in Hackney, London, the project was a reaction to a period of ongoing and purposeful disinvestment by the local council in which, after having decided to demolish the block, they boarded up the windows of the flats with bright orange sheets once the individual properties had been "decanted" (as seen in figure 9.17). As long-time residents of the estate themselves, the collective argued that the "orange boards had turned the façade into a projection screen for people's fears and prejudices around estates, and the people living in them" (Zimmerman and Johansson 2009). As such, and as seen in figures 9.18–9.19, the collective replaced the boards with large-scale portraits of the current and former residents, an intervention in which sixty-seven images were eventually placed over the emptied windows. Attempting to "humanize the façade [and to] complicate and return the gaze of the passers-by," the project thus showed the "faces of ordinary people so often excluded from the visual material produced to market an up-and-coming area by estate agents, developers, private landlords, local councils and other stakeholders" (n.p.). It showed not an image of ruin or of change, but rather the lives of those whom these processes of change had swept away.

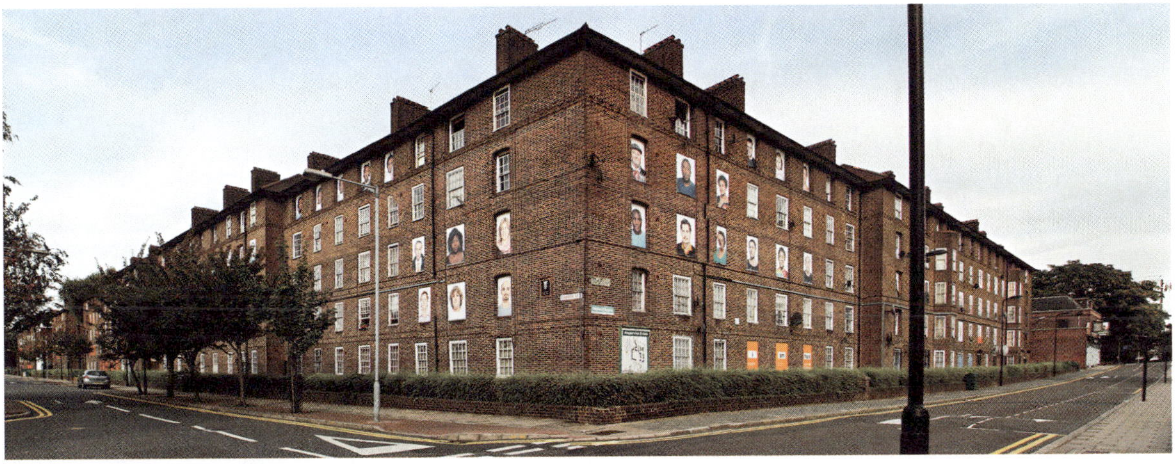

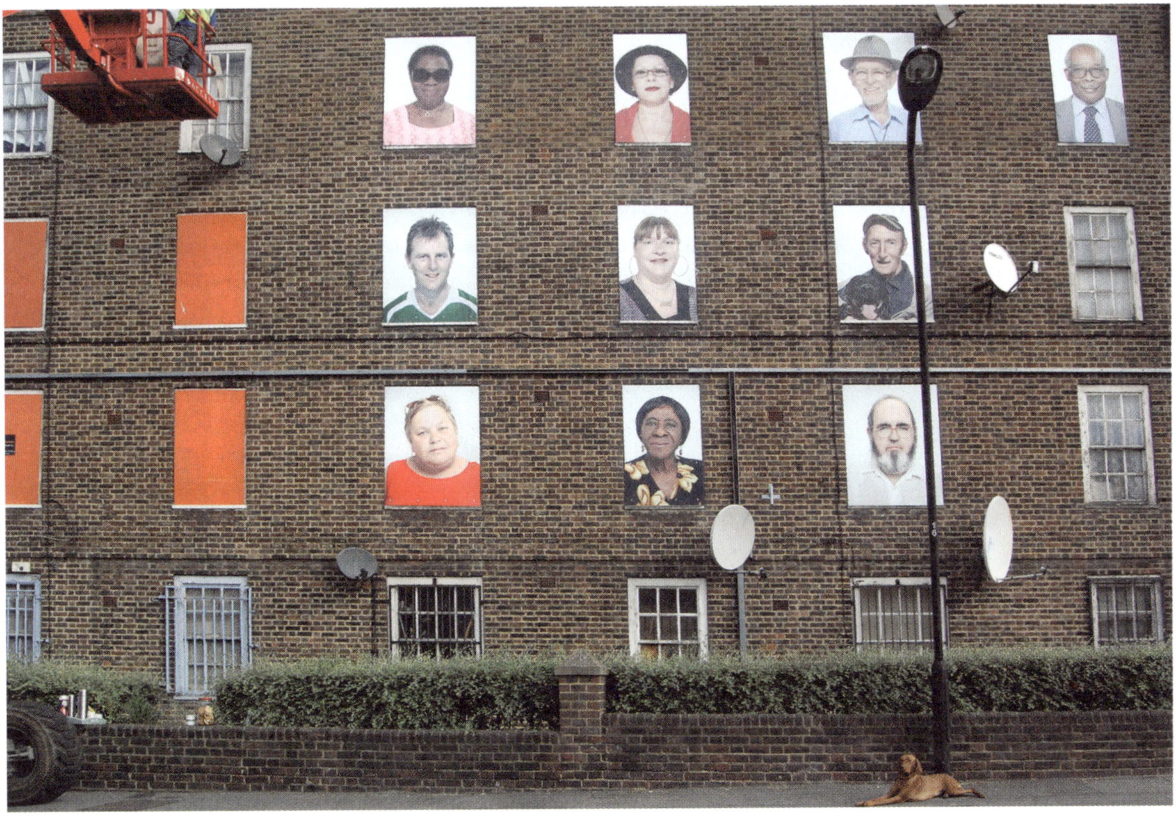

**FIGURES 9.17, 9.18, AND 9.19**

Fugitive Images, *i am here, 2010*. Large-scale public photographic exhibition placing sixty-seven faces over the emptied windows of Samuel House, Haggerston Estate, East London. Courtesy of the artists.

## THE HERITAGE/THE TOURIST CITY

The Heritage City sets itself toward not a cleansed ("creative") future but rather a sanitized past. Here, the practices of the official heritage regime discussed in chapter 3 are transformed from the singularity of monumental objects to the overarching level of the city itself, an act in which, as John Urry has famously explained, almost "everywhere and everything from the past may be conserved" (Urry 1990: 95). A condition emergent from the cataclysmic urban devastation of the twentieth century's world wars, the heritage regime's initial focus on artifacts or buildings developed into a wider management of entire districts and "conservation areas," the state engaging in initiatives to conserve the canonical material heritage that enabled the idea of the imagined nation itself to emerge. While at first the public maintenance of the physical environment was set against private renewal projects in which destruction and reconstruction were the norm, by the end of the century the wider narrative of heritage had become unquestionable. As Melhuish argues, "property developers, urban designers and architects" came to embrace the heritage discourse not only to promote "historic continuity" but likewise to stimulate "place-based regeneration (or place-making), and urban branding" (Melhuish 2022: 17). As such, practices of redevelopment—in particular of the "downtown" and "waterfront" varieties seen in cities across the world—partook in very clear strategies within which memory and materiality became "instrumentalised beyond historic national identity building discourses" and were instead utilized to "facilitate a range of policy purposes" that aimed to produce "profit from property" (pp. 17–18). While often wrapped up in rhetorics of cultural democracy and social amelioration, the heritage regime's focus on the grand narratives of the nation here became seamlessly appropriated by a narrative of regeneration in which our material environments are understood as resources to be exploited for gross domestic product.

The preservative agenda here extolled thus not only functions through a modernist fear of loss but likewise a more contemporary corporate fear of loss of potential profit. As specifically outlined in English Heritage's *National Heritage Protection Plan Framework*, for example, a document described by the then Minister for Culture, Communications and Creative Industries, Ed Vaizey, as "the business plan for the historic environment" (English Heritage 2013: 3), our material environs are today understood as "assets" that need "investment" in order to be maintained (p. 27). Thilan Wijesinghe's essay on the Economics of Conservation written for a ICOMOS, the International Council on Museums and Sites, underscores this perfectly: "funds spent on cultural preservation," he argues, "are essentially developmental in nature, with tangible economic returns" (Wijesinghe 1993: 152), the "value of a cultural monument" being "*directly proportional* to its 'marketability' or its relative standing as a 'marketable product'" (p. 154). The emotional chronicles of a nation are here transformed into more consumptive (rather than identity-based) modes of memory-making in which economic rather than social rationales are at the forefront. As such, even while institutions such as UNESCO have, as Rosemary Coombe argued, begun to bring more attention to "intangible goods, such as ritual, ceremony, poetry, proverbs, foodways, dance, and song" (Coombe 2013: 376), both "tangible and intangible heritage resources" have today become a form of "capital to be developed and marketed" (p. 381), "market ideologies" and "economic returns" becoming the broader heritage norm (p. 378). Permanence here thus becomes not only an ontological and cultural necessity but likewise an economic one.

While the Creative City paradigm focused on ushering in permanent ("creative") residents to the city and on the migration of human capital, the Heritage City is one in which capturing the transient population of leisure-seeking tourists has become the economic holy grail. The figures we're talking about here are, it must be said, mind-boggling. While global tourist numbers in 1950 totaled 25 million, the United Nations World Tourism Organization has estimated that these figures were an estimated 1.5 *billion* in 2019. The tourist industry also accounts for over 10 percent of all jobs across the world today (a total of 333 million) as well as over 10 percent of global GDP (almost $10 *trillion*) (World Travel and Tourism Council 2023). Like the zero-sum game of the Creative City, cities here too are forced to vie with one another to partake in the economic benefits tourism can provide. Heritage here thus becomes implicitly interlinked to a form of leisure in which not just traditional but experiential consumption is key, a form of Disneyfied heritage at the crux of Francesc Muñoz's concept of *urbanalization*. Part of a "standardization of urban landscapes" undertaken for the new "spatial requirements of global tourism" (Muñoz 2017: 79), cities here must re-create themselves to appear "as similar as possible to pre-consumed images promoted by urban branding" (p. 77) while likewise coming to "imitate the urban forms found in shopping malls, festival markets and theme parks, which are themselves based on imitations of city spaces" (p. 79). Difference in the tourist city is thus "used for marketing purposes or . . . torn from the complexity that gave rise to them so they can be packaged within the simplifying discourse of the global order" (Muñoz 2012: 44). Difference is assimilated so as to provide a "sequence of images that are treated as though they were souvenirs," a distinction made "comparable and measurable because the same yardstick is used for interpreting them" (p. 44).[18] The intertwining of the heritage industry with the tourist city flattens out reality to provide easily consumable chunks of the past, simplified packages of culture with all friction (and politics) removed. It thus not only "monumentalizes" but, as Boris Groys suggested, "eternalizes everything that comes within its range," transforming the "relentlessly fluid, incessantly changing urban life into a monumental image of eternity" (Groys 2008: 102).

Like the kitsch of our "creative" cities, nostalgia plays a critical role here, both the vernacular and the traditional coming, as Urry has suggested, to "mingle in a kind of pastiche with play, spectacle and transgression" (Urry 2002: 124). In the United Kingdom, for example, the rapid obliteration of the manufacturing and industrial sectors in the latter half of the twentieth century was accompanied by their almost total integration within the heritage industry, the warehouses and power stations of the Victorian era, for example, transformed into the museums and apartments of today. Granary Square comes to the fore again here, its modes of nostalgic heritization today a leading (and lauded) example of postindustrial urban chic, its tourist-friendly kitsch present in the very name of the site itself. A designation arising from what was called the Granary—a warehouse in the center of the larger Goods Yard complex built by Lewis Cubitt in 1852 and which was central to the industrial transport connections of the United Kingdom—the building now houses the main campus of Central Saint Martins (as seen in figure 9.20), one of the most globally venerated schools of art and fashion, thus suturing the industrial past to a notion of creativity in a similar way to the prototypical Tate Modern conversion.[19] The Western Transit Shed, however, presents us with a mix of office spaces, shops, and restaurants, while the main shopping thoroughfare, Coal Drops Yard (as seen in figure 9.21), provides us with another eponymous link to the site's industrial past and to manual labor in more general (note the metal storage tank, or gas holder, in the background too, now luxury private apartments with penthouse suites starting at £7.4 million). While the core structure of the site has, in line with the Heritage City basics, been "sympathetically preserved," what it provides is simply the industrial finish and contextual branding that these locations necessitate. The buildings around the site as much as its cobbled streets and brick arches thus become a perfectly "authentic" aesthetic asset, one utilized as image while leaving any historic or social interpretation outside the mix. It comes to provide the "content," the backstory that helps to brand the "vibrant shopping space where Londoners and visitors will be happy to shop, share good food, enjoy beauty treats, experience art and cultural events, hang out and maybe even discover a new talent, all while being wowed by London's grand, industrial architecture" (Coal Drops Yard 2020).[20]

The past is the explicit spectacle here, the wow factor accompanying (or impelling) our consumptive and experiential activities, the ahistorical heritage for the frictionless leisure space. What we have is a sanitized site of consumption whose literally superficial materiality is preserved while its social realities melt into air. History (a mainly working-class history) is thus co-opted as image in which the golden past of the industrial age becomes a marketable commodity—with all labor and any sign of contaminated working bodies removed. Selective forgetting is thus here a critical technique (Trouillot 1995); what is left out (most often the history of marginalized social groups) being just as important as what is left in (most often the sentimental narratives of the past). The sublime industrial aesthetic thus not only "leaves industrial ruins completely decontextualized," but, as Stefan Berger has argued, also "suppresses memory cultures associated with capitalism and class," the people who actually lived or worked in these spaces "disappear[ing] from memory in the aesthetic glow radiating from the empty shells" (Berger 2019: 42). Public space thus here becomes a "staged archaeological theme park," a "part of the interiorized commodified spectacle" in which the "divide between the museum in the city and the city as museum has become more porous, if not totally obliterated" (Swyngedouw and Kaïka

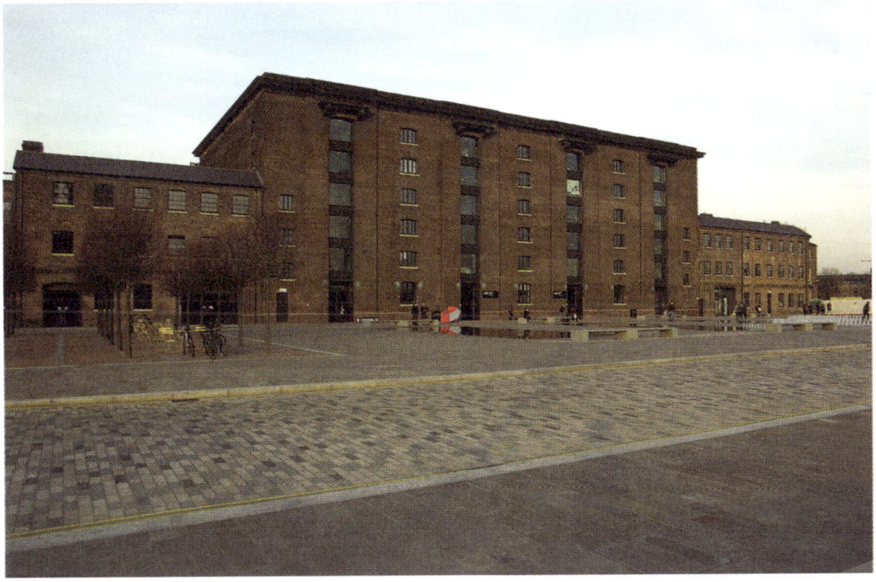

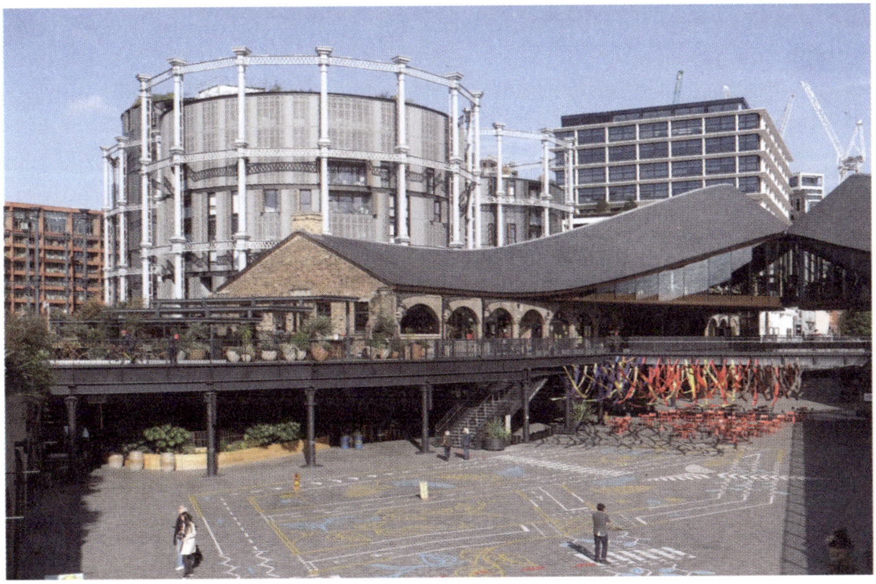

**FIGURE 9.20**
*Central Saint Martins School of Art, King's Cross* by Jim Osley. © Copyright Jim Osley and licensed for reuse under this Creative Commons License.

**FIGURE 9.21**
*King's Cross: Coal Drops Yard* by Jim Osley. © Copyright Jim Osley and licensed for reuse under this Creative Commons License.

2003: 11). Moreover, this porosity is pushed even further through the explicit interweaving of Heritage and Creative City spectacles in sites such as Granary Square. The purposeful manner in which the "Victorian heritage and contemporary architecture collide in an extraordinary canal-side setting," in which the "architecture has been preserved and complemented with dramatic contemporary design" (King's Cross Estate Services 2022: n.p.), begins to show the manner in which these "incongruent landscapes"—as Cecilia Chu describes the relationship between Macau's casinos and its world heritage architecture—come to symbiotically (and symbolically) support one another. Heritage here is thus understood as a "powerful economic asset" encouraging "tourism operators and businesses to convert even more historical places into new forms of 'spectacles' for consumption alongside other attractions of the city" (Chu 2015: 441). Rather than incongruence, then, what we find is a wrapping together of old and new, an industrial aesthetic bestowing not only authenticity but creativity to a site, an aesthetic through which the heritage and branded cities become spectacularly embedded within one another.

Like the usage of street art neo-muralism within the dynamic of the Creative City, the dense power of heritization has come to envelop graffiti's (co-opted) offspring today too, this formerly ephemeral aesthetic becoming harnessed to the creative/heritage dyad and conserved via two juxtaposed techniques. The first, what I term street art's *passive preservation* (Schacter 2019a), emerges not via a process of traditional conservation but rather via the suspension of the images' removal. Whereas any unauthorized image would previously have been erased by local authorities, today the "benefits" of street art—from the tourism it creates let alone the creativity and cool it implies—means that local councils (and their cleaning teams) have come to explicitly distinguish their handling of it from the arch evil that graffiti still presents. As outlined in the *Hackney Graffiti Policy Document* (2016), for example, the council "recognises" that

> some public opinion on what constitutes graffiti has changed and that some "Graffiti" is now considered to be "Street art" and that some members of the community now consider that "Street Art" actually makes a positive contribution to the urban environment. In recognition of this the Council accepts that properly authorised and appropriate street art may be recognised and supported subject to appropriate permissions being sought and granted and subject to that art not being a detriment to local environmental quality.

Albeit with a lot of "some"s (and with a whole range of semantics that could be enjoyably unpacked), here it at least seems that street art contains the ever-present possibility of utility, of value, the ever-present possibility of admission into the world of Art by a community of like-minded citizens. As long as it is "positive" it can be "street art" (and thus preserved), yet if negative it must be "graffiti" (and thus immediately removed). The city here thus marks out the "good" from the "bad" through what it passively chooses *not* to remove. Here, heritage thus emerges through an active passivity, a protection from active destruction if not from passive degradation.

Yet alongside this passive preservation is an active practice of formal restoration. Most famously undertaken in the case of street artist Banksy, here works are "conserved" either through total removal—whole walls being excised from their structures transplanted into "safer" indoor locations—or trapped within "protective" plexiglass (see figure 9.22, for example, in which the framed surround also serves to frame the image as a traditional painting).[21] Allowing the works to remain as tourist attractions while invoking the temporal staticity of the acid-free box, Perspex acts as an attempt to protect the works from damage—from the supposed spite of other artists,[22] from the environmental degradations of the natural world[23]—yet most often acts as a precursor to its inevitable movement from public site to private sale. Here preservation emerges through a classically destructive mode of conservation, a mode in which, like the Philistinic Turks whom Lord Elgin was "protecting" the Parthenon sculptures from, it is the general public who enforce the works' removal into the private sphere (whether they do so illegally as in Elgin's case or not). Grassroots conservationists also play a role here. The UK Reactivation Team, for example, actively maintains and refurbishes works by the French street artist Invader, not only recreating and reinstalling works that have been stolen from the street but conserving and repairing works that had been partly destroyed.[24] In some locations, the newfound monumentality of street art has become part of official heritage schedules too. In Germany, as Samuel Merrill has explored, "works by Klaus Paier have federal protection," while in Australia "murals by both Mike Brown and Keith Haring sit on the state and national heritage registers" (Merrill 2015: 375). Images that present themselves as (lowercased) street art thus come to uphold conventions of stasis so opposed to the transience of their ancestral forms. They thus come in many ways to function as ethnographic objects detached from their social worlds, something to look at and survey rather than that which acts and lives in a living space.

The preservatory mode of street art also begins to hint toward the larger museological turn it is today set within. This comes not simply via the movement of these artifacts from street to museum (as with Banksy's extracted public interventions), but rather through street art enabling a transplantation of the rituals of the museum into the site of the city itself. Here, the image becomes couched not only within the values of conservation but within the modes of connoisseurship, validation, and theatricality more common to the museological realm. Most conspicuously seen in the guided tours that have today become a habitual part of the street art ecology, these tours (as seen in figure 9.23)[25] serve to generate a curatorial authority and narrative fixity coherent with the norms of the museum yet entirely at odds with that of graffiti. Rather than an unmediated relationship between viewer and image, here the works become discursively mediated in the manner of a museum label or exhibition audio guide that, like an image caption, determines how we "read" the image. The tours thus not only

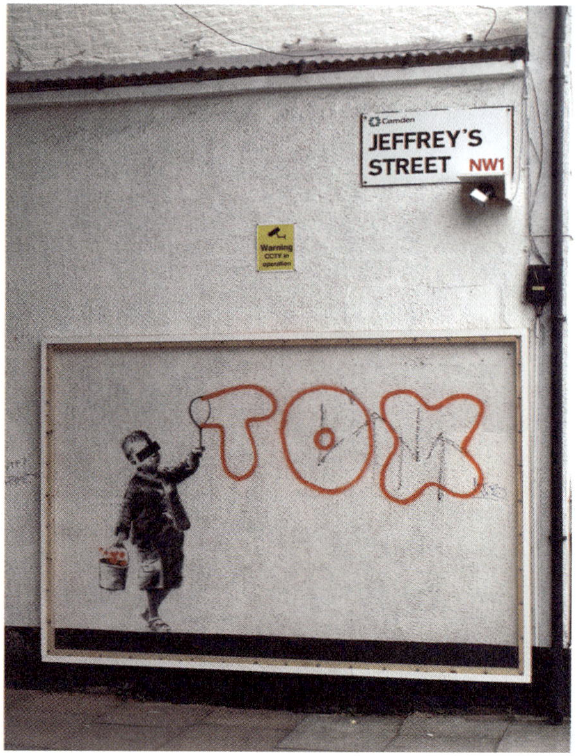


**FIGURE 9.22**
*Banksy*, 2011, Camden, North West London. Photo: Alex Ellison.

"deprive one of the sense of individual discovery" through their "rigid, well-rehearsed, non-collaborative presentation" that allows "little room for contingencies," but, as Sabina Andron has noted in her research on tours in London, likewise create an "imbalanced exchange between a guide and a group of participants" (Andron 2018: 1037). The very structure of the tour thus not only denies any form of participatory engagement with the works, but, through bringing "hundreds, if not thousands of tourists to the area on a weekly basis," leads to the "gradual disappearance of their own material, as new financial interests start setting up camp in the area" (p. 1052). Like the ouroboros, then, the tours eat their own tails (eat their own tourists), each outing not only bringing the last one ever closer but destroying their own content as quickly as they narrate it. The common trope that street art comes to form the "largest museum in the world" can thus here be seen not as a positive notion but as a dangerously conservative one.[26] The city becomes a site in which the controlling rituals of the museum—of walk, don't run and look, don't touch, of consumption, not production—become omnipresent.

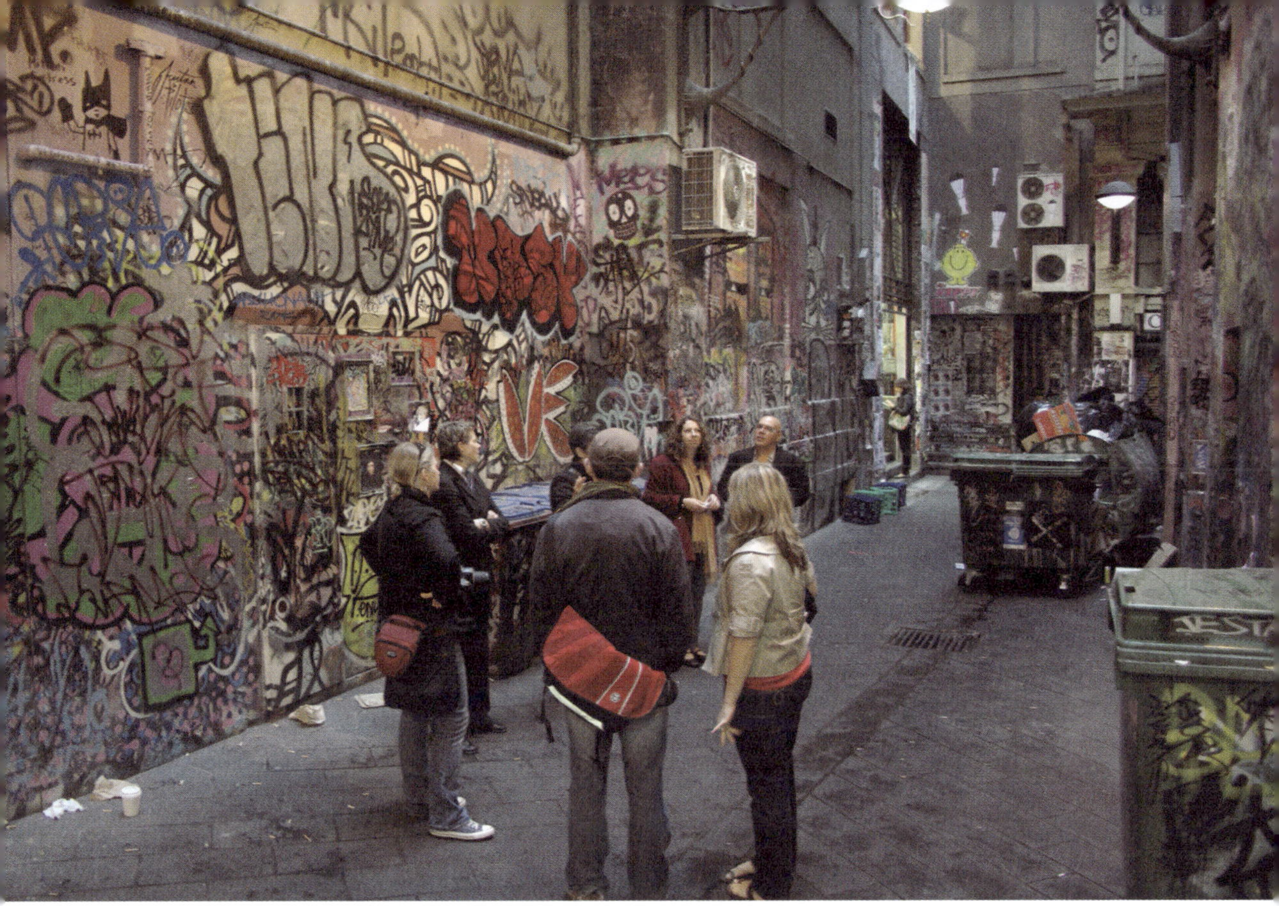

**FIGURE 9.23**
*Street Art—Centre Place, Melbourne (Sadly, Centre Place Is Currently Overtagged!): Melbourne Street Art Tour, October 31, 2008*. Photo: Mike Hauser. Attribution 2.0 Generic (CC BY 2.0).

While street art has been enveloped by both "creative" and "heritage" regimes, graffiti today has become linked to the tourist city too. Here it becomes another unique selling point, the edgy "urban" wallpaper that tourists at "edgy" sites want and expect. In London's Brick Lane, for example, graffiti is a necessity for the "true" experience, while in Park Lane (where we saw James Bridle in the previous chapter) any sign is still genuinely pollutive. While overtly anti-tourist (and anti-Airbnb) graffiti is common in locations where low-cost flights have damaged the rental ecosystem (such as Athens, Berlin, and Barcelona), on the whole graffiti will still persist in these bohemian zones, as they are still frequented by locals. Graffiti, as has already been argued, wants, *needs* to be seen, yet the transient mobility of tourists renders these bodies of little value to the graffiti game. It is not fleeting eyes that are wanted here; it is for public recognition, not wallpaper that these images are formed. Yet, as we saw in chapter 3, graffiti's rejection of the heritage regime is a core tenet of the practice. Graffiti *is* the relentlessly fluid (returning to Groys's terms), *is* that which refuses the eternal. Moreover, its material status (graffiti's physical precarity), its ontological positioning (graffiti's culture of erasure), and its commemorative techniques (graffiti's mnemonical absence) make it a congenitally anti-nostalgic aesthetic. Unlike the museal city frozen in a sentimental yesteryear, graffiti has no time to dwell in the past. That is not to say history is forgotten here—not at all! Legacy is critical. Yet once you are no longer "up," you are no longer in the game. Nostalgia becomes irrelevant when one is engaged in practice, when it is commitment and engagement that counts. Unlike the Heritage City, then, a city in which its material environments rather than performative practices are preserved, here history is not lived-through or longed-for but instead simply recalled.

Still, like graffiti, not all of our public art becomes sucked into the tourist and heritage traps, many artists looking toward the past while still rejecting the dangers of the spectacle. Jochen Gerz's *2146 Stones*, for example (seen in figures 9.24-9.26), a memorial located in Gerz, Austria, rebuffed the dangers of heritization through the production of a monument that remains entirely invisible (as seen, or as not seen, in figure 9.25). Located in a central square in Saarbrücken flanked by a castle used as the Gestapo headquarters during Germany's annexation of Austria, the monument was surreptitiously (and illegally) produced between April 1990 and May 1993, in which Gerz and a group of his students removed 2,146 cobblestones from the square (over one-quarter of the total

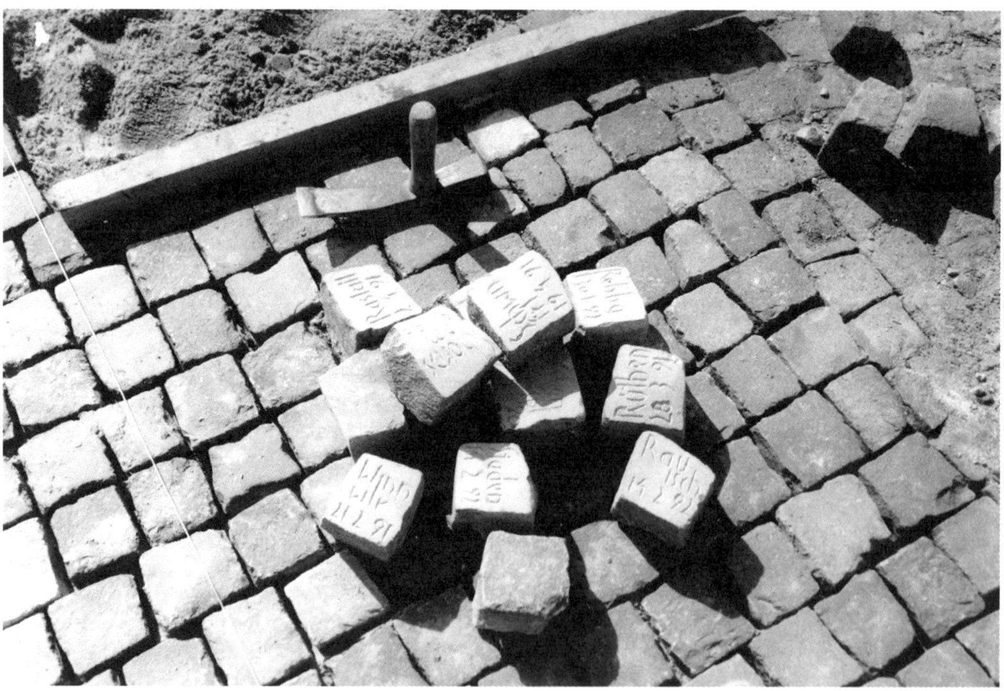

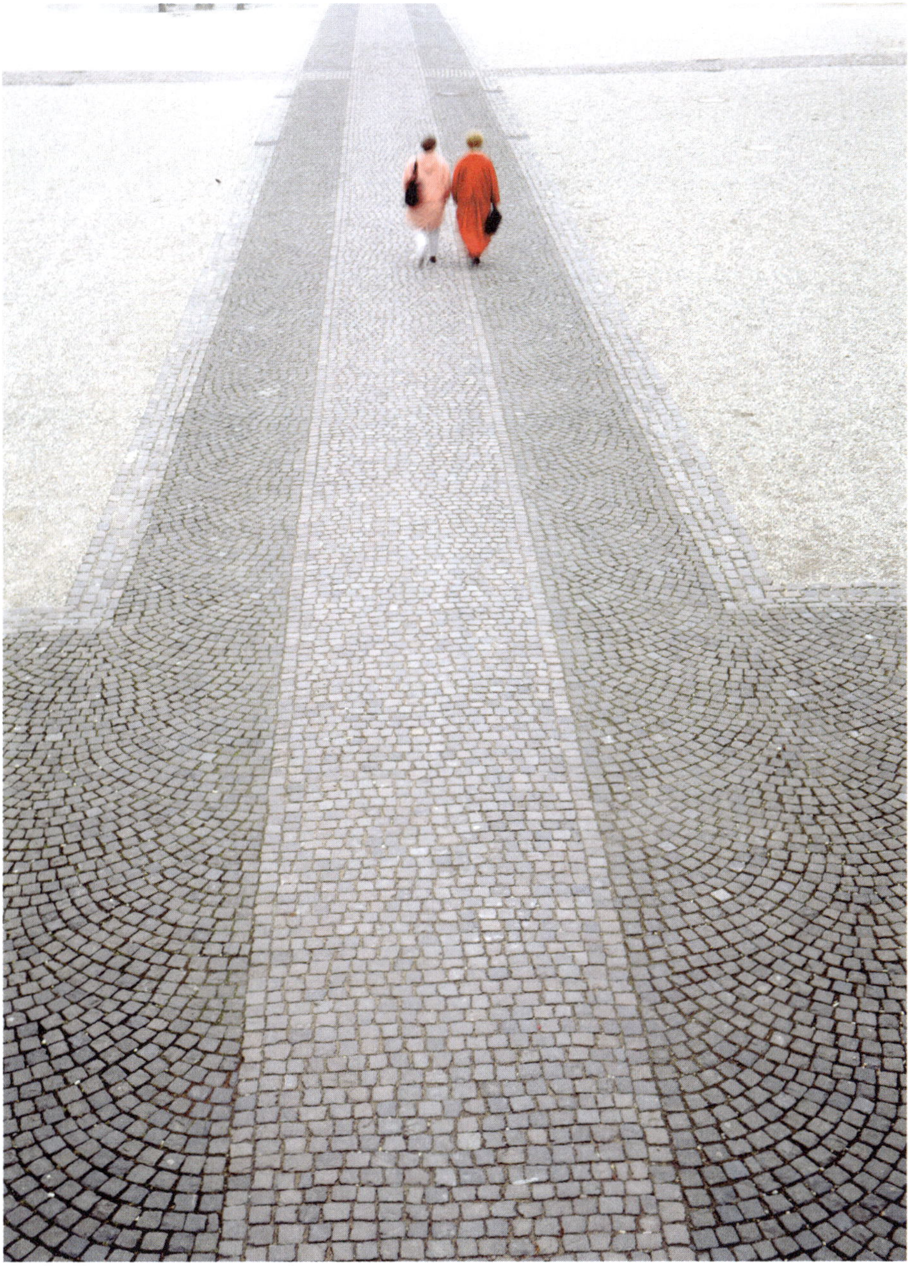

**FIGURES 9.24 AND 9.25**

Jochen Gerz, *2146 Steine—Mahnmal gegen Rassismus/Das unsichtbare Mahnmal (2146 Stones—Monument against Racism/The Invisible Monument)*, 1993. Saarbrücken. 50 × 70 m. 2,146 engraved paving stones. Courtesy of Gerz studio. Photos: Martin Blanke. © Jochen Gerz, VG Bild-Kunst, Bonn 2023.

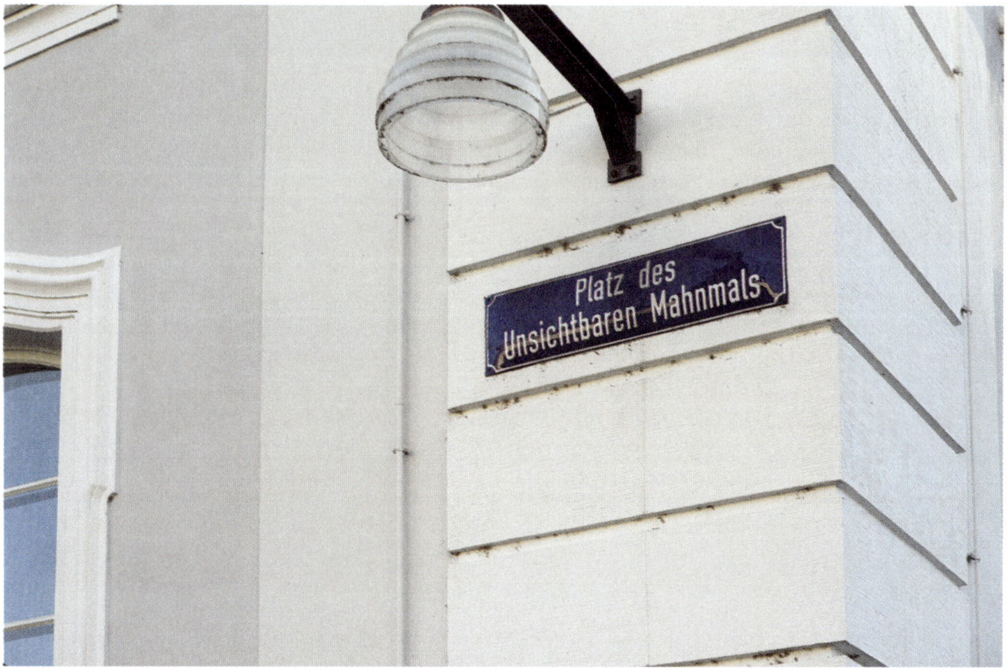


**FIGURE 9.26**
Jochen Gerz, *2146 Steine—Mahnmal gegen Rassismus/Das unsichtbare Mahnmal (2146 Stones—Monument against Racism/The Invisible Monument)*, 1993. Saarbrücken. 50 × 70 m. 2,146 engraved paving stones. Courtesy of Gerz studio. Photo: Roessler. © Jochen Gerz, VG Bild-Kunst, Bonn 2023.

amount) during secret nighttime interventions. Later engraving the stones with the names of Jewish cemeteries that had been destroyed by the Nazis (and in fact producing the most complete list available at that time, comprising 2,146 cemeteries), these were then surreptitiously repositioned in the square with the names placed face-down. Only when the last stone was replaced was the monument "revealed" to the public and later claimed by the city itself (as seen in figure 9.26, in which the sign translates as "the Place of the Invisible Memorial"). Like his *Monument against Fascism* produced with Esther Shalev-Gerz, discussed in chapter 3, Gerz here not only was questioning the dangers of permanent visibility, of a technique of memory-making that makes forgetting the most natural result, but aimed to encourage a more engaged relationship to history: "In my opinion," he said, "the traditional monument was kitsch; it was a horror show after the war. . . . So the invisibility of our monument was like a cure. If you are representing absence you should create absence. That same absence also permits each person to become the author of his/her own memorial work" (Callaghan 2010). Using invisibility, then, not only is memory brought to the fore (a buried memory in which the void becomes made apparent), but the passivity of the spectacle itself is rejected.

In Akay, Rae, and Made's ongoing and multisited series *Private Thoughts for Public Spaces*, however, it was not invisibility but *intimacy* that was targeted. Independently removing pieces of the city's street furniture before transporting them off-site and drilling, etching, or burning texts into them (in a manner parallel to that of Gerz above), the objects were then returned to their original sites to be found by unsuspecting passers-by. Here, however, the engraved texts, as seen in figures 9.27–9.30, were purposively informal and private ones, secrets or confessions that friends or acquaintances had revealed to them, short stories that then became part of the memorial landscape of the city. Here, the visual excess of the street and the urban spectacle (both its sheer scale let alone its aesthetic bombast) was transformed through a purposively minor public art in which the obscured is brought into the light, in which the permanency of the heritage regime as much as its historical heaviness are transformed into something more transitory and intimate. As the artists themselves recount, "we take the most fleeting of all elements in a city—the imagined thoughts in people's heads—and turn them into kinds of memorial plaques. Instead of marking the historical site of a birthplace or a massacre, we choose to remember the places where smaller battles of conscience

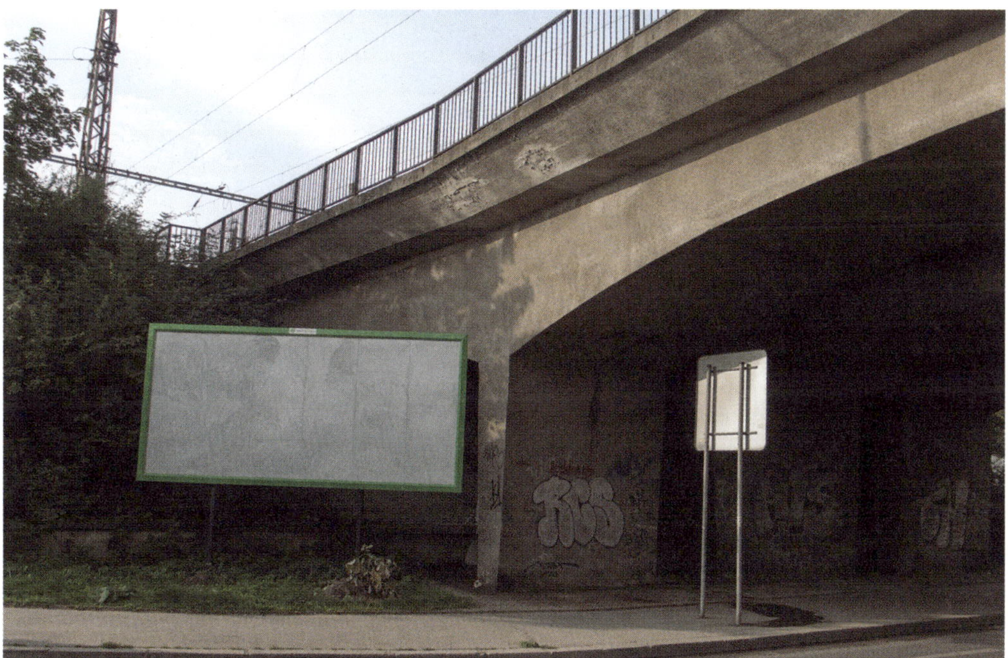

**FIGURE 9.27**
Akay, Rae, and Made, *I'M SO SICK OF THEIR BULLSHIT*, 2009. Inscription on metal. Courtesy of the artists.

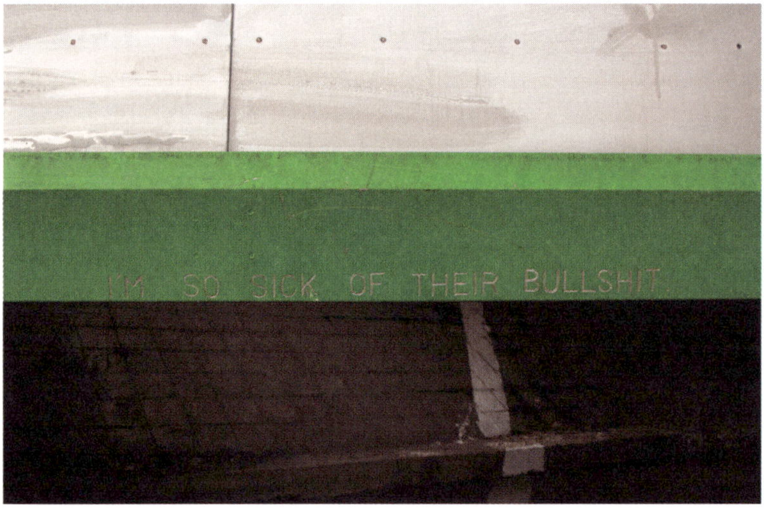

I'M SO SICK OF THEIR BULLSHIT

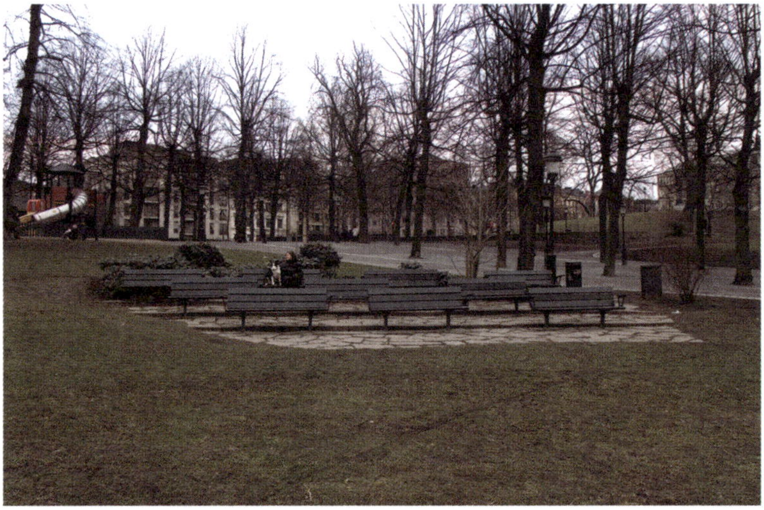

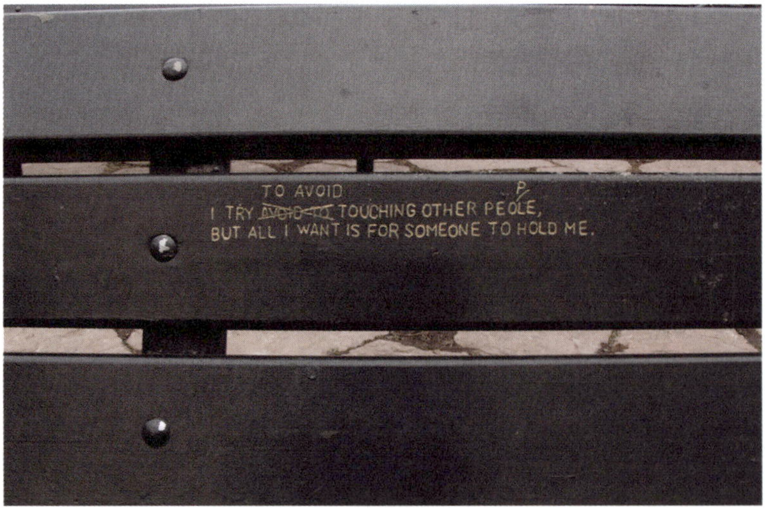

TO AVOID
P
I TRY ~~AVOID TO~~ TOUCHING OTHER PEOLE,
BUT ALL I WANT IS FOR SOMEONE TO HOLD ME.

were possibly fought" (Mudlevel 2011: 270). Purposively autonomous and marginal, the project thus rejects the sanitization of history and the nostalgia of the heritage regime, initiating a non-instrumental, consciously anti-spectacular public art.

In a project situated at the edge of these two previous works, however, Sandra de la Loza's Pocho Research Society of Erased and Invisible History undertook a series of interventions in which sites of "erased or invisible history" in the Los Angeles area were brought into focus via a series of independently installed public plaques (see figures 9.31–9.33). Taking on the role of what she herself termed a "guerrilla historian," and working in particular on the lost heritage of the Latino and indigenous communities in the city, the "invisible monuments" that she installed spoke of sites that had been destroyed by ongoing gentrification and urban transformation, destroyed by a hegemonic narrative in which immigrant communities become excised from the city's official history. Replicating the aesthetic of traditional monumental place markers that themselves come to be understood as "official" history, the project not only smuggled marginalized histories into public space but revealed the gaps and fissures integral to the hegemonic narration of the past. The stories that De La Loza delineated—speaking of the forced displacement of the Mexican community in the construction of the LA Dodgers baseball stadium (in *The Displacement of the Displaced*), of the legendary graffiti writer Daniel "Chaka" Ramos (in *The Triumph of the Tagger*),[27] and of key sites of informal gathering for migrant communities in hostile environments (in *El Otro Ellis*)—not only put the history of the Latino community back on the map, but generate a way of thinking about the past escaping the modality of the nostalgic. What we thus find here, as bell hooks has written, is "a politicization of memory that distinguishes nostalgia, that longing for something to be as it once was, a kind of useless act," and instead extolls a form of "remembering that serves to illuminate and transform the present" (hooks 1989: 17). What we find is a heritage without longing, without elisions: a heritage without the institutionally monumental.

**FIGURE 9.28**
Akay, Rae, and Made, *I'M SO SICK OF THEIR BULLSHIT*, 2009. Inscription on metal. Courtesy of the artists.

**FIGURES 9.29 AND 9.30**
Akay, Rae, and Made, *I TRY TO AVOID TOUCHING OTHER PEOPLE BUT ALL I WANT IS FOR SOMEONE TO HOLD ME*, 2009. Inscription on wood. Courtesy of the artists.

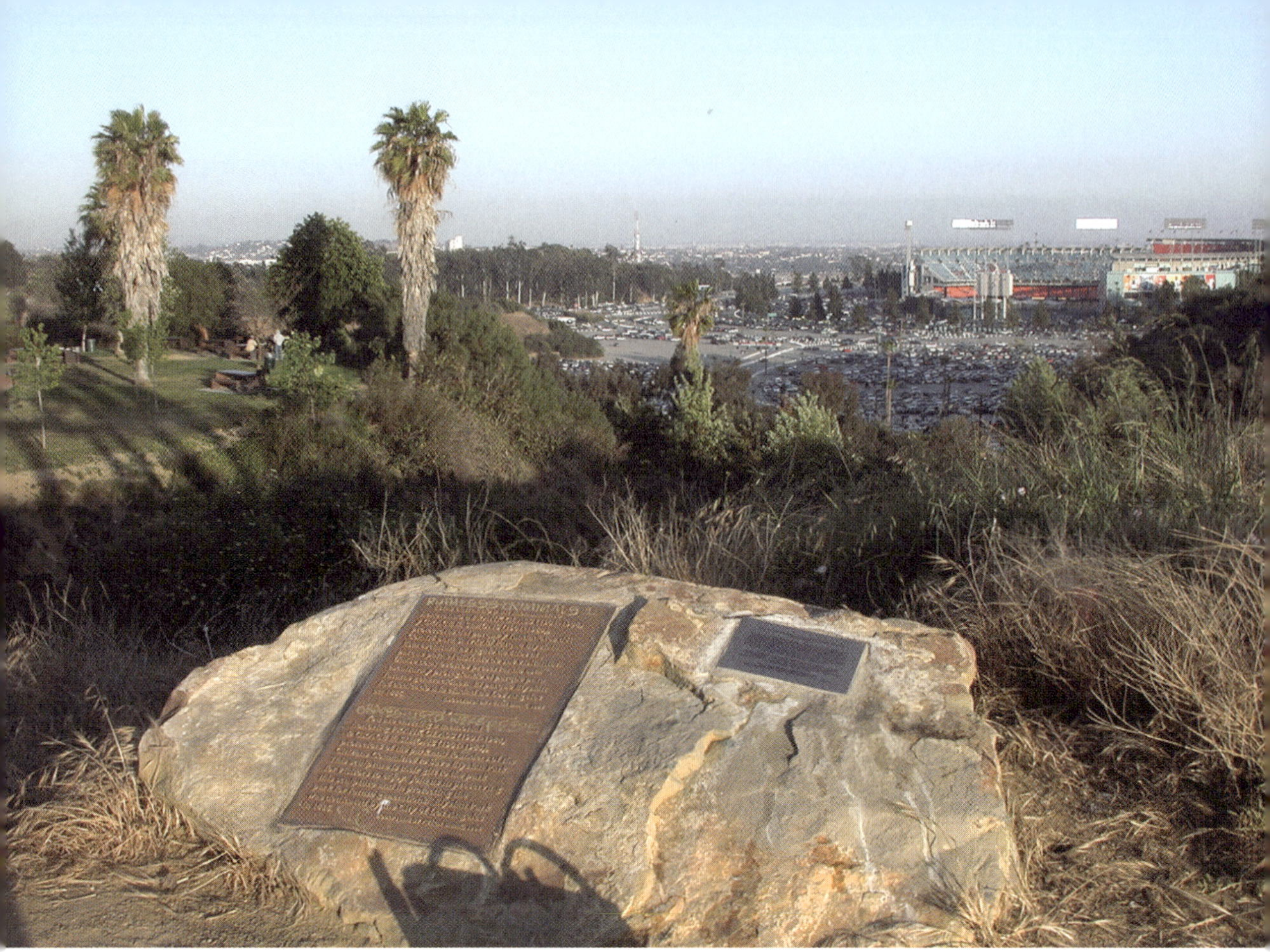

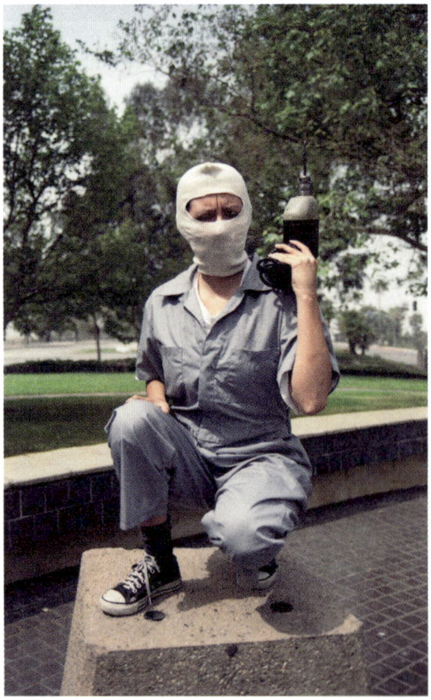

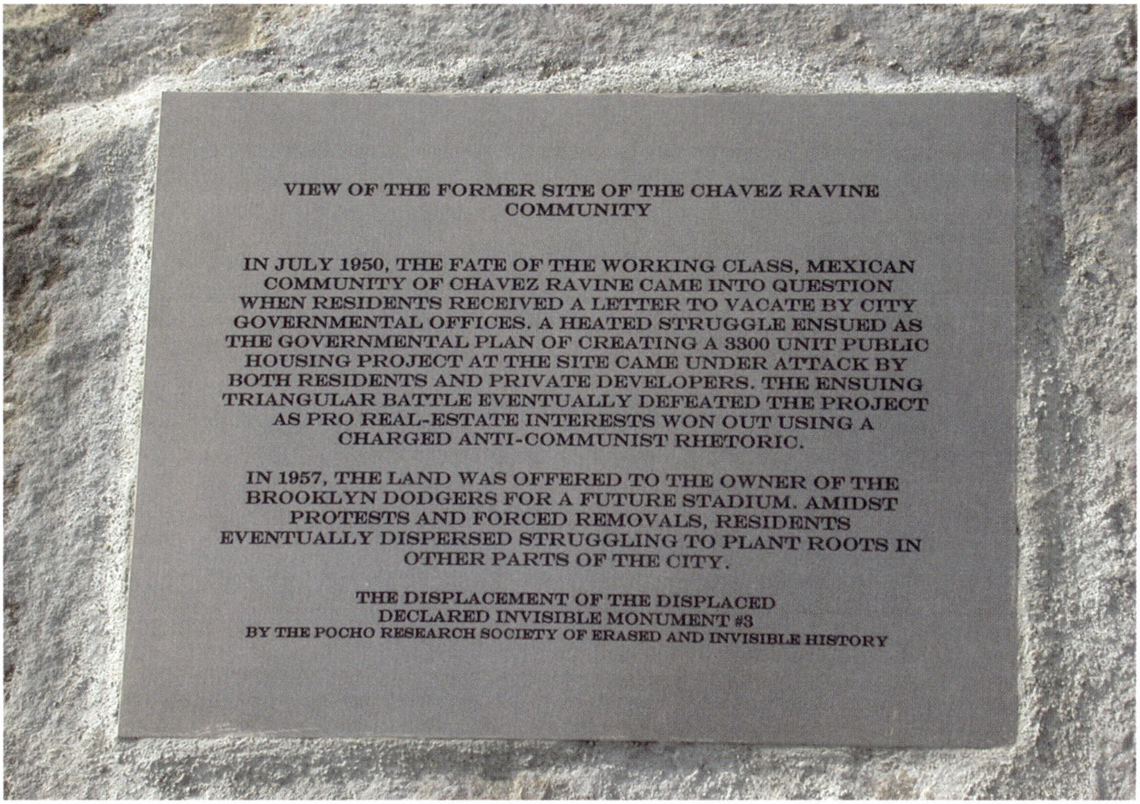


**FIGURE 9.31**
Sandra de la Loza/The Pocho Research Society of Erased and Invisible History, *The Displacement of the Displaced: Declared Invisible. Monument #3*, 2002. Silkscreen on metal. 9 in × 12 in. Courtesy of the artist.

**FIGURE 9.32**
Sandra de la Loza/The Pocho Research Society of Erased and Invisible History, *Untitled*, 2002. Courtesy of the artist.

**FIGURE 9.33**
Sandra de la Loza/The Pocho Research Society of Erased and Invisible History, *The Displacement of the Displaced: Declared Invisible. Monument #3*, 2002. Silkscreen on metal. 9 in × 12 in. Courtesy of the artist.

The spectacular city is thus not only a city that is visually monumental, that craves a Wagneresque, *kolossal* materiality of architectural aliens, place-making muralism, and touristified POPS, but a city that sets itself anywhere but the now. It is a city in which the realities of the present are occluded within a sterilized heritage and regenerative framework, a city that leans on both a nostalgic, dehistoricized past and a kitsch parody of the future. Here only a frictionless, outmoded present dominates, past and future both set in stone, sanitized, monumentalized. Time in the spectacular city thus becomes "'merchandise time' (time for buying and selling, time bought and sold)," becomes regulated, as Lefebvre argued, through a system of "yield and profit," through "programmed leisure," through "habitation as a place of consumption" (Lefebvre 2003: 20). Space too becomes a "network organized for and by consumption," a site in which "pedestrian circulation [is] determined and measured by the ability to perceive store windows and buy the objects displayed in them" (p. 20). Just like the institutional monument, then, these branded, frozen sites work by camouflaging the realities that they create, masking the processes of human displacement via the superficial "benefits" of redevelopment, masking the city in which consumption is the only mode via their nod to history and heritage. The city today is thus not only an increasingly privatized milieu (heritage and creative spaces both), an increasingly surveilled site (branded and tourist spaces unquestionably), but likewise an increasingly spectacularized and anachronized zone. The Creative and Heritage Cities provide us with an urban world in which the entire site replicates the structure of the museum gift shop. It provides us with an overarching urban aesthetic whose ethic is one in which consumption is all.

Participation in the spectacular city is thus formalized and restricted, functioning not through encounter or engagement, or through something said or done together, but through the singularity of the consumptive gaze alone. Opposition here is hence only truly possible through acts commonly deemed illegal (if not on the edge of legality), through acts of graffiti (of course!), yet so too acts of skateboarding and urban exploration, through acts whose creative techniques contradict the economic imperatives of the city and whose methods disrupt urban flow through a nonnormative use of its surface. As in carnival, then, within these non-consumptive urban practices, we find a rerouting of our urban streets and walls, a (mis)appropriation of their purposes that disrupts definitions of public and private. As in carnival, we see marginal techniques that reject the consumptive and pacifying spectacle, a mode of consuming space without contributing to its logic of consumption. As in carnival, we witness a practice through which the city is enveloped in the present and not beholden to a parodic future or past, a performative, participatory, monumental practice countering the monumentalized city itself. Rather than the place-making monuments of our POPS plops, rather than our kitsch neo-muralism or our anachronistic malls-without-walls, it is within practices that are free to undertake, that are architecturally unrestricted, are physically and socially horizontal, multisensorial, durational, that we find that which is outside the Creative City, carnivalized practices revealing the true in the false, that exist for, yet work against. While the interventions of Gerz, Akay, and de la Loza utilized that which is marginal or invisible, then, being against the spectacular does not mean one cannot work in spectacular ways. It means that one cannot be about the "look" and "looking" alone, means that the practices must work not to hide but to reveal, to play on the edge of the seen and the unseen. It means that they must form a participation in which spectatorship alone is disavowed, must create a space of non-consumptive spectacle that disrupts the overwhelmingly consumptive one.

Take Jeremy Deller's public installation *Sacrilege* (2012), for example, an inflatable scale-model sculpture of the United Kingdom's most famous heritage site, Stonehenge, and a work that could at first be seen to be an entirely superficially spectacular one (how could a bouncy castle be anything but!). While at the heritage site itself the stones have been cordoned off since the late 1970s, here participants come to interact with the stones bodily rather than merely staring at them from a distance of fifteen meters. Here spontaneity rather than officialdom reigns (as seen in figures 9.34 and 9.35). *Sacrilege* thus enables a playful, desacralized, celebratory relationship to the nation's collective heritage, a way of engaging with the past in a time outside that defined by our labor, outside that defined by consumption. Like many of Deller's public works, it does not abandon or renounce tradition, but instead takes on a vernacular rather than hegemonic lens on the past, inverting the state's hold over official memory. It engages an English heritage of the margins rather than of the center, a heritage that is open and free for all, a heritage that is about participation, collectivity, joy. Yet it is when one places *Sacrilege* in direct contrast to Stonehenge that Deller's work becomes most effective, when we position the participatory, engaged elation of the former work against the consumptive desiccation of the latter. Take a look at the Stonehenge website, for example:

> An unmissable family day out from £56.60 . . . book your ticket now for the best price and get ready for an unmissable day out at this iconic site . . . Experience the unforgettable atmosphere of the Stone Circle . . . Come face to face with a 5,000-year-old man in the exhibition . . . Step into a Neolithic village and find out if you have what it takes to move a mighty Sarsen stone . . . Get up close to the iconic Stone Circle and take the perfect picture. (English Heritage 2022)

To be clear, these are not hand-picked quotes but the opening copy found on the landing-page of the official website (copy that is hard to say without sounding like a parody of a nineteenth-century showman ).[28] Here, at Britain's most famous heritage site, its most famous monument, we have the ultimate mode of touristification, the ultimate spectacularization of our collective history. Banished from the stones themselves (unless we have paid extra for the VIP "Stone Circle Experience"), we must look on from a distance (having paid our £56.60 first), listening to our official Stonehenge

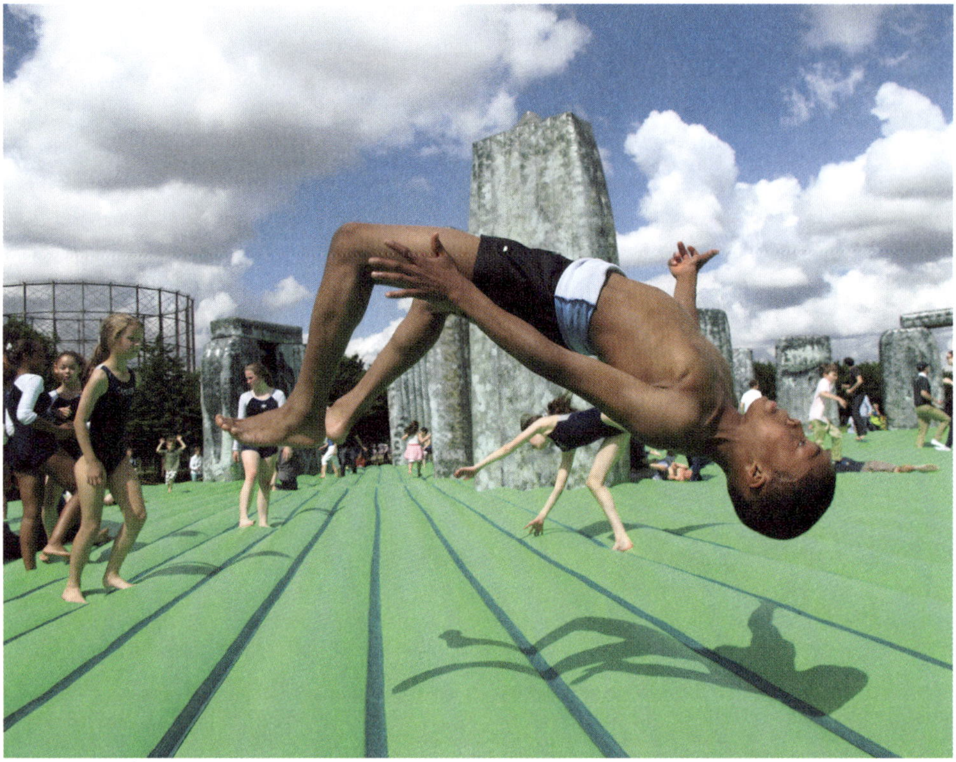

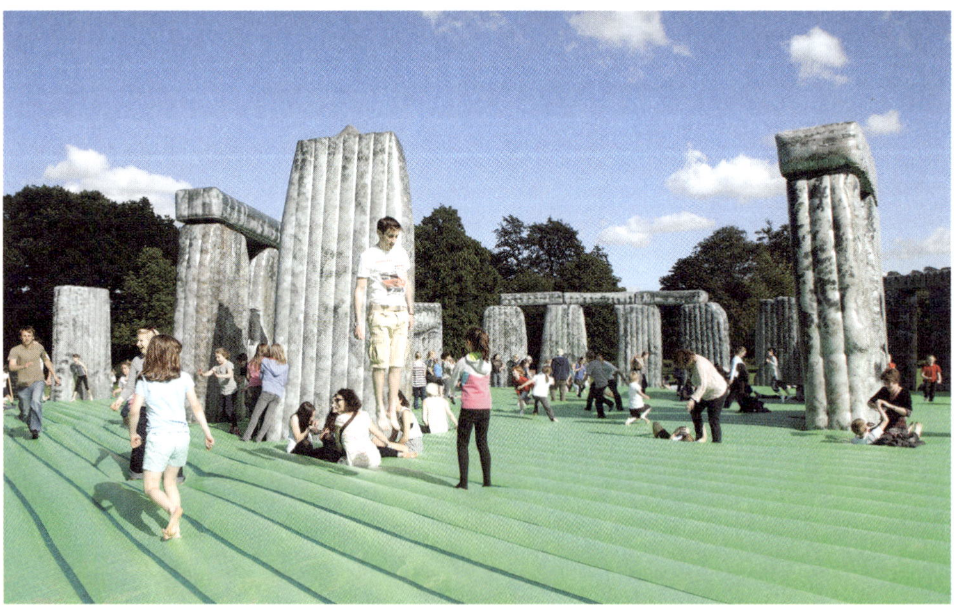

audio guide wearing our official Stonehenge hoodie drinking from our official Stonehenge canteen. Stonehenge, as Barbara Bender wrote over twenty-five years ago, is thus no longer a "'living' space, a meeting-place, a ritual-centre" but rather an icon acting as an "exemplar of past glories" and a "bulwark against the forces of modernity" (Bender 1998: 120). It is a "museum exhibit, a place to be looked at, caught on film" (p. 120), a spectacularized site in which we passively look rather than bodily engage, in which the ultimate mode of Disneyfication now persists.

Like Deller's spectacle rejecting spectacularization, his monument rejecting the spectacular self-aggrandizement of the institutional monument and that rejects the pomposity of statumania and our POPS plops alike, our graffiti-monument too says no, says no through an active engagement and rejection both. Graffiti traces the dangers of both Creative and Heritage Cities, rejects their monumentality, refuses their pacifying aims. As our paradigmatic warning, it cautions us every time it is witnessed, whether overtly so in the worlds of Edwin or implicitly so through the scripted names of countless graffiti writers across the world. It acts as a warning of the cities' increasing privatization, securitization, spectacularization, a warning emerging via a practice that needs not always say because it always does. It acts as a warning that rejects the nostalgic and the kitsch, the large-scale and the permanent, the monologic and the dominant. It acts as a marginal, a carnivalized monument, speaking to the center from the heart of the center itself.

**FIGURE 9.34**
Jeremy Deller, *Sacrilege*, 2012. Greenwich, London. Commissioned by the Glasgow International Festival and the Mayor of London. Courtesy of the artist; Art: Concept, Paris; and the Modern Institute/Toby Webster Ltd., Glasgow. Photo: Jeremy Deller.

**FIGURE 9.35**
Jeremy Deller, *Sacrilege*, 2012. Yorkshire Sculpture Park. Commissioned by the Glasgow International Festival and the Mayor of London. Courtesy of the artist; Art: Concept, Paris; and the Modern Institute/Toby Webster Ltd., Glasgow. Photo: James Hutchinson.

# CONCLUSION

Graffiti is a public artifact, an object existing only via its style, is a time-based form. Graffiti is a text, a practice, a participatory act. Graffiti traces the border between public and private, between the visible and invisible, is positioned in a city in which both time and space are increasingly monumentalized. Yet if this is what this book has said graffiti is (and what graffiti does), what is it that it accomplishes as monument? Well, as our monument-*reminder* we here find a peripheral, agonistic, momentary monument, a monument acting as a visual reminder of a dissensual relation to site, a reminder of the committed practitioners who produced it, a reminder of the inexorability of decay. As the monument-*advice* we find something said, something done, and something that is said and done together, a monument advising us of our right to appear, to claim presence, to participate in the city. And as the monument-*warning*, we find an artifact and practice intertwined with the ongoing privatization, surveillance, and spectacularization of the city, a monument warning us of what are possibly the three most critical issues affecting the public sphere today. The graffiti monument may thus not be the stony, the classical, the permanent monument, not the monological, the elite, the passive monument, not the monument of the state or the monument of the POPS, *yet it is a monument nonetheless*. It is an artifact that reminds, that advises, that warns us. It is an inscription that captivates and attracts our attention. It is a marker of deeds with true urgency for the contemporary urban realm.

The tensions over the institutional monument all across the world today[1] should thus come as no surprise. The basic structure of this traditional form is a densely anachronistic one, its agencies often of a deeply exclusionary nature. The monumental iconoclasm we see today must not, therefore, be understood to be simply about destruction. It is instead a disruption of the means through which we come to think about ourselves and our social and material environments. It is a disruption leading to a new way of engaging with the city, a new way of thinking about its past and future and our role as citizens within it. The war on the institutional monument—a war, it must be said, emergent after decades of discourse that led only to decades of obfuscation[2]—thus starts to reveal the constructed "naturalness" of the urban street, of an architectonic "neutrality" that is entirely partisan. It starts to reveal the dense anxiety of the state in which all signs of its fragility must be displaced, the anxieties of a status quo that fears change above all else.

The war on the *graffiti* monument, however, the institutionally forged iconoclasm in which thousands have been imprisoned (let alone killed[3]) for placing pigment upon substrate (and for a financial quantum of damage whose value has increased literally *ten*fold[4] since the privatization of the train industry), continues unabashed. This is a war that has been categorically lost (as the still burgeoning images, as the institutional exhibitions, as the award-winning books, as the now fifty-year deep history all attest), yet a war that continues to be fought, nonetheless. There is simply too much invested now to stop. There is a multi-billion-dollar industry that needs servicing, an industry that must remove any sight of this contaminant (even if we have now forgotten why it was a problem in the first place). There is an "us" and a "them" that need to be solidified, a virtue signaling in which order must be maintained. The perfectly clean city is still the professed dream, the dream of the entirely privatized, surveilled, spectacularized city, yet the war is not only about this (impossibly) pristine city itself. The war is about a conception of the private that continually shrinks public space. The war is about the domineering nature of the all-seeing city. This war is about the city as site of commercialization, not habitation. The institutional iconoclasm that the graffiti monument faces is thus not just about its illegality but about the fear of what these monumental images prove. It is about the fear of an urban encounter in which economic returns play no part, of a practice in which engagement is productive, not consumptive. It is about the fear of a monument in which marginalized voices and marginalized bodies surface, in which surveillance and the spectacular are evaded, in which a commons appears.

The public monument, be it of an institutional or graffiti variety, is thus an artifact entirely intertwined with the fate and the potential of the contemporary city, with the practices and possibilities of urban citizenship. The more we understand these forms, then, the more we understand their production and consumption let alone their destruction, the more we can understand the cities in which they stand, understand how we come to produce and inhabit our surroundings. And rather than just seeing graffiti as a rejection of monument, it is graffiti as the archetypal reminder, the archetypal advice, the archetypal warning that I hope has now been revealed. Rather than seeing graffiti as an anti-monument, it is graffiti as monument to the marginal and interruptive, to the ephemeral and dialogical, that I hope has become apparent. Rather than seeing graffiti as a counter-monument, it is graffiti as monument to the individual and collective, to participation and presence, graffiti as monument to our right to the city itself that I hope has now been demonstrated in this book.

| | THE GRAFFITI MONUMENT | THE INSTITUTIONAL MONUMENT |
|---|---|---|
| **SITE: POSITION** | ADJUNCTIVE | AUTONOMOUS |
| **SITE: RELATION** | INTERRUPTIVE | ASSIMILATIVE |
| **SITE: DIMENSION** | HUMAN SCALE | COLOSSAL SCALE |
| **SITE: LOCATION** | PERIPHERAL | CENTRAL |
| **STYLE: CANONICAL** | MAXIMUM VISIBILITY | STRUCTURAL INVISIBILITY |
| **STYLE: AGENCY** | OF MAKER | OF THOSE REPRESENTED |
| **STYLE: DISTRIBUTION** | SCALE | SIZE |
| **STYLE: CAPTIVATION** | BECOMING | BEING |
| **TIME: MATERIALLY** | TRANSIENT | DURABLE |
| **TIME: CULTURALLY** | EPHEMERAL | CONSERVED |
| **TIME: MNEMONICALLY** | ABSENT | EVERLASTING |
| **TIME: RELATIONALLY** | DURATIONAL | DISCONTINUOUS |
| **SPEECH: TEXT** | THE NAME | THE HERO |
| **SPEECH: CONTEXT** | THE LINGUISTIC LANDSCAPE | MISE EN SCENE |
| **SPEECH: SUBTEXT** | THE RIGHT TO SPEAK | STATUS QUO |
| **SPEECH: STRUCTURE** | DIALOGICAL/OPEN-ENDED/ILLOCUTIONARY | MONOLOGICAL/DIDACTIC/PERLOCUTIONARY |
| **ACTION: PEDAGOGICALLY** | ACTIVELY PERFORMED THROUGH THE BODY | PASSIVELY DICTATED THROUGH THE BODY |
| **ACTION: FORMALLY** | HUMAN/MARGINAL/OTHER | WHITE/ABLE/MILITARY |
| **ACTION: VISUALLY** | INVISIBLE | HYPER-VISIBLE |
| **ACTION: SENSORIALLY** | IMAGINED/FELT | OCULAR/SEEN |
| **PARTICIPATION: SITE** | MARGINAL | CENTRAL |
| **PARTICIPATION: STYLE** | CARNIVALESQUE/JOYFUL/IRREVERENT | RITUALESQUE/SOMBER/SUBMISSIVE |
| **PARTICIPATION: STRUCTURE** | IMPROVISATION/DURATIONAL | COMPOSITION/ARCHIVAL |
| **PARTICIPATION: RULE** | ASSEMBLAGE/INWARD | APPEARANCE/OUTWARD |

**FIGURE C.1**
The graffiti monument and the institutional monument.

# ACKNOWLEDGMENTS

This book is dedicated to every writer, artist, and member of the graffiti community I have ever spoken with. I am indebted to the knowledge and education each of you have given me. Particular thanks to my friends and interlocutors in Madrid and London who let me into their lives and to the two inspirational (anthropological) big-men in particular, Duncan and Sam. Thanks to all the artists who let me use images of their works and to the galleries and studios that helped arrange this. It is an honor. Much of this book has been silently guided by some of the key theorists of graffiti whose output has influenced mine in an indelible manner. The works of Joe Austin, Craig Castleman, Jeff Ferrell, and Susan Phillips, in particular, were the spark that led to my own research and have each been essential to my understanding of graffiti and the city in equal terms. I hope that this book can contribute to the ground they so critically laid. Thanks also to the graffiti research community who have provided a valued space of intellectual discussion over the last decades, in particular Javier Abarca, Sabina Andron, Konstantinos Avramidis, Edward Birzin, Ricardo Campos, Theo Kindynis, Chandra Morrison, Christian Omodeo, and Mathieu Tremblin, as well as to the four anonymous reviewers whose generous critiques and suggestions were each gratefully received. I also want to thank all my students at UCL, in particular those who took my module "Art in the Public Sphere." Not only did teaching this course help me to develop the arc of this book, but the contributions and critiques of my student collaborators helped to push it further than I ever could have on my own (any mistakes or errors are still, of course, mine).

As with all my outputs, this book has been entirely influenced by my doctoral supervisor, Christopher Pinney, whose writing and encouragement have had a transformative effect on my life. There are no words with which I can thank him sufficiently. Alongside Chris, I also want to thank other key members of the Anthropology Department at UCL; my postdoctoral mentor Susanne Küchler, who has been incredibly supportive during my time as both a student and staff member in the department; Christopher Tilley and Victor Buchli, whose lecture courses on the anthropology of landscape and the anthropology of architecture, respectively, have been key touching points for both my teaching and research since I attended them myself; Haidy Geismar, whose guidance and friendship along with her inspiring work have been invaluable during my time at UCL; Timothy Carroll, for his thoughtful engagement with style; and Charles Stewart, for his consistent ability to offer the right reference at the right time. Thanks to all my fantastic colleagues in the Material Culture subsection too: Rik Adriaans, Kimberly Chong, Ludovic Coupaye, Adam Drazin, Hannah Knox, Elena Liber, Delphine Mercier, Danny Miller, Maria Salaru, and of course Tone Walford. Thank you also to Shannon Ewart, Matteo Fumagalli, Anthony Harris, and Toby Nicholas, for generating such strong camaraderie in the department, as well as to Jonas Tinius, Michal Murawski, Khadija von Zinnenburg Carroll, and Konstantinos Kalantzis for your intellectual generosity and friendship in equal measure. I must also send huge thanks and acknowledgements to my editor, Victoria Hindley, not only for her firm belief in this project but for the subtle yet powerful way she helped mold it into the best version of itself. An equal thanks to the book's associate editor, Gabriela Bueno Gibbs, for her calm advice throughout the process, and to Stephanie Sakson and Deborah Cantor-Adams for their excellent editorial assistance. I must also thank Mel Jordan and the other editors of the journal *Art & the Public Sphere* for letting me use elements of my 2014 article "The Ugly Truth" in chapter 9 of this book.

Finally, I need to thank my parents, without whose support none of this would have been possible, alongside my entire extended family, and in particular, my wife, Diana. Listening to every argument I have made in this book and providing invaluable counterpoints and (brutally) honest assessments at every stage (let alone encouragement and companionship throughout), she has made all of this possible. The last word, though, goes to Malaya. You make every day a better day, and this book ends with the love I shall forever have for you.

# NOTES

## INTRODUCTION

1. The three terms for monument in German—*Mahnmal*, indicating a form of remembrance as urgent warning; *Denkmal*, monument as a space for thought; and *Ehrenmal*, monument as a site of tribute—can be seen as a clear link to these etymological origins.
2. For a historical examination of twentieth-century graffiti, see Austin 2001, Castleman 1982, or Chalfant and Cooper 1984.
3. All translations of Debray's essay are my own.
4. Key publications include Schacter 2008, 2013, 2014a, 2015, and 2019a.
5. Incorporating exhibitions at sites such as London's Tate Modern and Somerset House, my curatorial practice has acted not just as a space for the presentation of previously undertaken research but as a site to conduct research itself. For more on curating and graffiti, see Schacter 2019b.
6. As discussed in Schacter 2017, street art is a practice of image-making originally emerging from graffiti yet that comes to take on a more publicly accessible approach. First emergent in Europe during the 1990s and often focusing on image over text, since the mid-2000s street art has become increasingly commodified and corporatized practice, as discussed in Schacter 2014b and within part III of this book in particular.
7. In *Street to Studio* (2018) I position intermural art as a new genre of art in which the public practice of the artists in question indelibly affected their studio practice while their studio practice simultaneously transformed their street output.

## CHAPTER 1

1. Of all the arguments in this book, this first section leans most heavily on a position made in Schacter 2014a, refined via its movement from an ornamental to a monumental frame, however.
2. The tag, a stylized signature using the writer's chosen graffiti name, is the most common of all graffiti images.
3. In its traditional form, etching has been used since the 1700s, popularized during the Victorian era and utilized most commonly on mass-produced tableware.
4. This autonomy can be revealed through the mass production of many institutional monuments (such as the thousands of Confederacy monuments produced by companies such as Monumental Bronze Co.) which would then be placed anywhere a plinth could fit.

5. Throw-ups depict either a full writer's name or a two- to three-letter contraction of that name (Ok for Oker or Fso for Fatso) in either a single-color outline (a "hollow") or an outline with a different color fill (a "fill-in").
6. It is also worth noting the way in which the Gothic Revivalism of the nineteenth century leads to a seamless movement from Eton to Oxbridge to the Palace of Westminster.
7. Matta-Clark's graffiti series, seen in figures 2.3 and 2.4, alludes to the conceptual links between these subcultural images and his anarchitectural practice—a practice that, like graffiti, was implicitly adjunctive, was often rejected as art, and was habitually produced illegally.
8. See also Abarca 2016, in particular pp. 61–63.
9. While these techniques move beyond normative bodily proportions, they are still integrally linked to the body (one reaching over a building's edge with a paint roller or dancing with a fire extinguisher) and still reveal a specific bodily *performance* if not bodily scale.
10. Joanna Fiduccia's (2022) discussion of Alberto Giacometti's miniature works provides another illuminating study of the power of (the small) scale.
11. The overhead power lines indicate the fact that the tracks are nonelectrified, there being no live "third rail" for writers to worry about. Many trackside environments contain this real danger to life. Here, however, it is commuter and freight trains that provide the writer/interloper with the fatal threat.
12. Sennett's discussion of boundaries and borders will be developed further in the conclusion of chapter 7.
13. For more on territories and "territoriology," see Brighenti and Kärrholm (2022).
14. See Alison Bain (2010) here too.
15. With this said, I do note Bach and Murawski's discomfort with the neoliberal embracement of the peripheral. "Is this decentralising, centrifugal tendency really as absolute, inevitable, or even desirable, as its prophets claim?" (Bach and Murawski 2020: 2).
16. Illegality can also be considered as a negative rather than positive rationale in more general. While many writers do enjoy the feeling of "against-ness" that it produces, issues such as creativity, excitement, sociality, and engagement provide much more compelling and enduring motivations that far supersede illegalities' base singularity.
17. The fences that border tracksides make clear that these zones are illegal to enter, yet outside of key infrastructural points they are left wild, a literal excess.
18. As the writer ESPO put it: "Don't write on houses of worship, people's houses in general, other writers' names, and tombstones. Writing on memorial walls and cars is beef beyond belief" (Powers 1999: 154–155).

## CHAPTER 2

1. It should be noted here that graffiti was a name given to the practice by outsiders. Although largely taken up by the community, the term used prior to this was simply "writing" (and one was a "writer").
2. On the fiftieth anniversary of the article, the artist and graffiti historian Caleb Neelon wrote, "I have yet to talk to any early writer who, as a city teenager in 1971, decided to start writing graffiti because they were reading the NYT, but the word did get around that you just might get famous doing it" (Neelon 2021).
3. The importance of tools on the development of graffiti style cannot be underestimated.
4. Three to six letters also reflects the one to three syllables that make up almost all graffiti names. As a nickname, one's chosen name must first *sound* good. Yet likewise it must be based on letters that *look* good together and enable interesting linkages and combinations.

5. As Clifford Geertz has written within a very different ethnographic context, it is the selection of the moniker that turns "anybodies" into "somebodies" (quoted in Vom Bruck and Bodenhorn 2006: 3).
6. Such as Chalfant's later publication with Jamed Prigoff, *Spraycan Art* (1987) and Charlie Ahearn's legendary feature-film *Wild Style* (1983).
7. A "writers' bench" is a site where writers would meet to observe and critique the graffiti of passing trains and discuss and share sketches.
8. "Not the biggest or the beautifulist but more," as CAP said in *Style Wars*.
9. In the documentary *Kings and Toys* the British artist Prime likewise said: "it's almost like I have agents working for me and I put them in different places round the city, and they stand there and pose for me, and everyone walks by and says 'yeah, that's me, that's Prime'" (Power 1998).
10. Talking about the central E in his name, Delta suggested that it has "a face, a jawbone, eyebrows, mouth and a nose."
11. The subtly of simplicity is likewise often thought to lack "variety" when in truth it simply does "not reveal its variety to certain spectators who are not equipped to see it" (Martin 1983 [1933]: 27).
12. Content that is too clear can thus become too easily commodifiable.
13. As witnessed in what is arguably the most famous painting in the Western canon, Leonardo da Vinci's *Mona Lisa*, ambiguity harnesses our attention, enforces our participation, drags us (kicking and screaming) into the trap of the image.
14. Responding to a question about where he has tagged, 10Foot responded with the following; "Paris, Berlin, NYC, Philadelphia, Buenos Aires, Funchal, Lisbon, Oslo, Copenhagen, Snowdonia, Dublin, Galway, Cork, Waterford, Los Angeles, San Diego, Washington DC, New Orleans, Miami, Monterrey, Mexico City, Guatemala City, Guadalajara, Ajaccio, Milan, Sicily, Corsica, Bari, Tirana, Moscow, Marseille, Rome, Bogotá, Kuwait, Pereira, Quito, Port-au-Prince, Kingston Jamaica, Kingston Surrey, Guildford, Glasgow, San Antonio, Dominican Republic, Havana, Cancún, Panama, Taipei, Bangkok, Tokyo, Okinawa, Kyoto, Osaka. Almost every middle-sized town across the UK from Shaftesbury to Shrewsbury to Grimsby to Burnham-on-Crouch. All the far flung islands . . . Wight, Scillies, Shetlands, Orkneys, Inner and Outer Hebrides. Every state in Mexico" (Ellingham 2023).
15. With that said, I find the "1" of the "10Foot" within the hollow throw-up on the farside wall, for example, as well as the punctuating full stop at the end of the same name, to be particularly pleasurable. While spareness is critical here, even within stylistic spareness a subtle form of animation can still appear.
16. When one writes one's crew name, one becomes author of this name, while the name is more than you yourself. Crew membership is a form of collective ownership and one's self is likewise a divisible part of that crew. Moreover, when writing the names of the deceased or simply putting up the names of crew members or friends, it will most often be clear to other writers *who* did the writing of these names themselves (as the writer's own name will most often be displayed too). Here agency thus becomes split, and what is being produced is both portrait and self-portrait simultaneously.

## CHAPTER 3

1. This attempt to tie a loop between the ancient world and Imperial Britain is monumentally omnipresent. The equestrian statue of George IV positioned alongside Nelson, for example, shows the King not only in a simple Roman cloak but riding bareback and bare-headed (aping the conventions of the Greco-Roman world). Similarly, standing atop St. George's church in Bloomsbury, George IV's ancestor George I can be seen in full Roman toga and sandals.
2. Holzer not only collaborated with canonical graffiti artists such as Lady Pink but her work was strongly influenced by the practice: "I certifiably was inspired by graffiti culture and practice. It was exemplary and effective, and omnipresent in the best possible way" (Holzer in Munsell and Tate 2021, n.p.).

3. Take the neglect of Eduardo Paolozzi's sculpture *Piscator* (1980) at London's Euston station, for example, a work covered in pollution and dirt yet left unrestored as neither the freeholders or leaseholders of the land it sat upon would claim ownership of it!
4. This technique of scratching can also be seen on sites such as the sixteenth-century Palazzo di Bianca Cappello in Florence, whose decorative trompe l'oeil façade was entirely produced via this subtractive method.
5. See Fernando Dominguez Rubio's *Still Life* (2020) for a description of these processes at New York's MoMA.
6. Gandhi and Mandela were being protected not from Black Lives Matter activists but from a fear of right-wing reprisals following the toppling of the monument to Edward Colston in Bristol.
7. From charities such as Keep Britain Tidy, council maintenance teams, local community activists, as much as vigilantes such as New Orleans's Fred Radtke aka the Gray Ghost.
8. For a key text exploring this "legitimate" iconoclasm, see Austin 2001.
9. The often controversial preservation of works by Banksy will be explored in chapter 8.
10. Some of my favorite writers have the "worst" collection of photographs of their own work. One artist featured in this book (who if reading this will definitely know who they are), has literally next to nothing. If I need an image, a third party must come to the rescue.
11. As Merrill has noted, "developments in digital and Internet technologies have seen such records supplemented by a host of graffiti-related websites, online galleries and blogs," part of an "authentic form of grassroots heritage production and curation that should not be overlooked" (Merrill 2015: 383).
12. As Geismar has noted, however, photography too must be understood as an innately "fragile and impermanent medium" (Geismar 2022: 212).
13. To be clear, Dowden was here calling the Black Lives Matter protests a noisy fad.
14. While laws have changed, juries so far seem to disagree with the government line, as seen in the failure of the Crown to successfully prosecute the "Colston Four." Here we can see the dispute between morality and legality in action.
15. Colston's statue was raised more than 170 years after his death at a time when his connections to the slave trade were widely known.
16. The monument was less about Colston and more about the (artificial) creation of a "united" figurehead for the city.
17. Anthony Robben's powerful essay "How Traumatized Societies Remember" argued that for societies that have gone through deep suffering, such as in Argentina following the state terrorism of the late 1970s and early 1980s, official monuments and memorials do not work to cohere citizens or neutralize painful histories but become "extensions, repetitions, and manifestations of social traumas rather than their substitutes" (Robben 2005: 154).

## CHAPTER 4

1. The movement of this maxim from song lyric to supplemental wall text also shows how mutation becomes expansion.
2. It is worth noting that "simply be" is owned by the N Brown Group, whose executive board is conspicuously absent of any members of color.
3. While graffiti itself is often denounced for a perceived anonymity, these images are only anonymous to those who cannot read them. For those internal to the subculture, every image is alive with a very individual personhood.
4. Petro would always say that he could tell a person's character from their pieces, an abductive form of reasoning in which it was in form, not content, that meaning lived.

5. I should note that there is a wide group of artists working in the space of what could be called "conceptual urban intervention"—artists such as Adam Kraft, Akay, Wermke and Leinkauf, Eltono, E. B. Itso, and Oliver Kosta-Théfaine, among many more—who have all come from a graffiti background. The particular mode of intervening within space and testing the normative modes of speech, issues that are subtextually existent while not textually overt in graffiti, are drawn out within these artists' more official practice (discussed further in Schacter 2018).
6. Behind many of the seemingly simple statements made in *Native Hosts* are much larger hidden histories. The work seen in figure 4.17, for example, honors the migration of Native people (including Heap of Birds's parents) from Oklahoma Indian Territory to Kansas (home of the Wichita State University "Shockers" athletic teams) to labor in US military aircraft factories. The text accompanying the work also discusses the importance of the labor unions in supporting Native workers and their shared belief in collective over purely individualistic values. The yellow and black color scheme of the Tawakoni sign likewise mirrors the school hues of the "Shockers" teams while simultaneously hinting toward the "huge natural lands lost across the Kansas Prairie to make wheat farmlands, another form of colonization" (Heap of Birds, personal communication).
7. As per the Hackney Council Graffiti Policy, "the Anti-Social Behaviour Act 2003 confers power on the Council to secure the removal of graffiti, even where the owner does not object to it remaining on their property. In these circumstances the council reserves the right to take formal action against the owner to secure removal and if the owner does nothing then the council may enter the land, clear or otherwise remedy the graffiti and recover the costs from the owner" (Hackney Graffiti Policy Document 2016: 36).

## CHAPTER 5

1. The master-apprentice relationship can be seen to be canonically mandated, being most emotively revealed in the relationship between writers Dez and Trap in *Style Wars* and *Subway Art*.
2. Crews and collectives will thus often contain specific folk experts whose knowledge of preceding writers will be prodigious, spanning cities, countries, decades.
3. Quote from detail, in Bavard [Mosa], *Bulky—Study of the Body in Space (Partition).*
4. Quote from detail, in Bavard [Mosa], *Bulky—Study of the Body in Space (Partition).*
5. "I personally see graffiti as a DIY independent performative practice in urban space. The resulting tags and pieces are the visual trace of an ongoing practice of exploring, searching for autonomy, resisting, exercising, and taking risks without the motivation of financial benefits. To me that's the core value of it" (Matthias Wermke, personal communication).
6. The New York legend Kase2 is a notable canonical exception.
7. Even as a sociological rather than subcultural condition, the male dominance of graffiti is, for me, by far its most problematic aspect. This lack of gender parity has been somewhat transformed since the onset of street art (a lowercased version), whose gray legality has enabled more female participation, which has itself then seeped back into graffiti itself. Yet its gendered nature still broadly remains.
8. I would still suggest, as seen in the following chapter, that a collaborative ethic is a more vital part of the graffiti subculture than the toxic machismo Macdonald discusses.
9. See Iris Marion Young's "Throwing like a Girl" (1980) for a seminal correction of this position.
10. As determined in Monument Lab's *National Monument Audit*, https://monumentlab.com/audit.
11. As found within Art UK's *Sculpture Project*, https://artuk.org/about/sculpture-project.
12. The Mary Wollstonecraft monument by Maggi Hambling is a case in point.

## CHAPTER 6

1. The monument itself, as much as the annual event that enlivens it, is replicated almost exactly at sites all over the United Kingdom as well as its former colonies.
2. The former Leader of the Opposition Jeremy Corbyn was famously criticized for wearing a gray anorak rather than formal black overcoat as he laid a wreath at the Cenotaph at the hundredth anniversary of the end of World War I.
3. Here we can thus not only see the overwhelming concern with "death and immortality" that Benedict Anderson famously noted in monumental culture, but likewise the "strong affinity" between "nationalist [and] religious imaginings" (Anderson 2006 [1983]: 10).
4. I should note that on a more personal scale, the Cenotaph is very effective. The monument was claimed by wider society in an active manner—due in much part to the fact that the majority of the fallen were buried outside the UK at the Western Front itself—and its position directly on the street, its plinth being just centimeters high, as well as its quiet elegance and lack of bombast, generates an intimacy and affinity that works in many ways like a family gravestone.
5. While unpacked in the conclusion of the chapter, it is worth noting that images that feature as we now continue can never come close to replicating the *feeling* of experience. The images are gestures toward, rather than evidence of, the participatory effect.
6. Not only being able to know who is a friend of whom by seeing who writes with whom, this is further exemplified via pieces that share colors (and cans) as seen, for example, in EGS and TRAMA's earlier piece in figure 2.20.
7. I discuss carnival, and the work of Turner and Bakhtin in particular, in more depth in chapter 5 of Schacter 2014a.
8. See Shahak Shapira's YOLOCAUST, for example: https://yolocaust.de.
9. In *Getting Caught*, Rae Mariz perfectly illustrates the restrictions of the image while also condensing the core argument of this chapter into just a few lines: "A picture isn't always worth a thousand words. Sometimes a picture isn't even part of the story. The mostly visual documentation of graffiti history sometimes doesn't even hint at the most interesting part of the culture. Photos will show the evolution of style and technique, maybe. They'll tell you a name, but they won't share the experience of a person and what keeps them going out night after night. . . . The oral histories and legends describe meetings and motivations that are deeper than paint on a surface" (Mariz 2011: 9).
10. While critiqued by the art world in terms of both its political and aesthetic content, the Monument was embraced by many of the Forest Houses' residents. See the article (and the comments) in Kimball 2014 for more.

## CHAPTER 7

1. As Peggy Phelan remarked, "Bowers v. Hardwick [1986] effectively eliminated the notion of privacy for homosexuals: the state is legally permitted to survey and prosecute sodomy between same sex partners, even in their own bedrooms" (Phelan 1993: 106).
2. Those who use the street to advertise wares available elsewhere must then skirt with the dangers of subcultural exclusion through "selling out." This does not mean that zines, prints, books, paintings cannot be sold, simply that the street cannot be used instrumentally to do so.
3. https://www.publicadcampaign.com.
4. https://www.publicadcampaign.com/PublicAccess/Index.html.
5. As Alice Spawls put it, "I noticed, as someone who often couldn't walk without crutches, how many others there were: old and not so old, bent, shuffling, limping, leaning on lampposts or resting at bus stops, waving buses on. There aren't nearly enough bathrooms, rails, benches, ramps or slopes. Nowhere has properly supportive chairs: a moratorium on chairs!" (Spawls 2023: 19).

6. Jos Boys' *Disordinary Architecture Project: A Handy Guide for Doing Disability Differently in Architecture and Urban Design* (2018) is a great corrective (https://disordinaryarchitecture.co.uk) as is the work of the collective *Make Space for Girls* (https://makespaceforgirls.co.uk).
7. Zygmunt Bauman's discussion of the 2011 London riots as riots of "defective and disqualified consumers," in which the inability to consume leads not just to the "absence of pleasure" but to the "absence of human dignity," seems prescient here (Bauman 2011).
8. London's Royal Parks were all originally private hunting grounds, places of restriction given over (only in part) to the "common" man. In comparison, the city's "commons" were implicitly understood to be for collective use (if not collective ownership). While parks are thus traditionally gated, commons have unlimited access. While parks are manicured and obsessively maintained, commons are wilder, feral. While parks delineate a very clear outside and inside, their fencing and nocturnal closure making our appearance there both temporary and indefinite (even as some groups seek to doggedly redetermine this), commons remain porous and open for all.
9. The disquieting use of CCTV and facial recognition at Granary Square will be left for a discussion in the next chapter.
10. "'Pissed Off' is about the fact that in New York City a man doesn't have any public access to relieve himself in a decent manner. There is no way for a gentleman to relieve himself in a gentlemanly way without having to buy a drink. Keeps the rage going" (Hammons 1990 in Schriber 2019: 7).
11. The anti-monumentality of *Pissed Off*, as much as the furtivity of Hammons's work discussed further in chapter 8 (and in a further endnote), goes some way to explaining the lack of images of this legendary intervention here.
12. https://www.greenguerillas.org.
13. See the work of O'Brien, Farrell, and Welsh 2019, for example.

## CHAPTER 8

1. In a memo entitled "Activities in Furtherance of Protecting American Monuments, Memorials, Statues, and Combatting Recent Criminal Violence," the Department of Homeland Security has given guidance on "collecting and reporting on various activities in the context of elevated threats targeting monuments, memorials, and statues," detailing the legal basis for surveilling those threatening to damage (or suspected of damaging) public monuments (Vladeck and Wittes 2020).
2. The private-public (business-police) collaborations such as occurred at Granary Square are increasingly prevalent and a still unregulated activity. See GOV.UK 2021.
3. San Francisco was the first city to have outlawed the use of facial recognition in 2019, and has been followed by many more cities too.
4. The fact that Carnival, an event founded and run by the black community, was chosen for this first AFR experiment is totally unsurprising.
5. See Hill 2020.
6. The focus on China has increased since documentation regarding the mass confinement of the Uighur community has emerged. In 2022, *The Guardian* reported that a Chinese security company was "advertising ethnicity recognition features to British and other European customers, even while it faces a ban on UK operations over allegations of involvement in ethnic cleansing in Xinjiang" (Hern 2022).
7. Renew ORB's press release stated that the technology provides "unparalleled insight into the past behavior of unique devices—entry/exit points, dwell times, places of work, places of interest, and affinity to other devices—and should provide a compelling reach database for predictive analytics (likely places to eat, drink, personal habits, etc)" (Goodin 2013).
8. See James Bridle (2014) on number plate recognition in London.
9. A device developed by the Pentagon, the Jetson Laser Vibrometry System, identifies people via their heartbeats, which it isolates through an infrared laser.

10. I almost never turn my Wi-Fi or Bluetooth off on my (GPS-enabled) smartphone, not wanting to go through the "onerous" labor of having to switch it on when I want to put on my wireless headphones or connect to the web. Laziness is my "opt-in."
11. It is unsurprising that the majority of digital natives have their social-media pages set to private.
12. As Adam Harvey has argued, since "higher performance face recognition algorithms are more marketable, companies have an economic incentive to collect as many faces as possible . . . Among the most common sources cited in face recognition research papers and public face recognition datasets are search results from Google, celebrity photos from IMDB.com, selfies from Instagram, YouTube videos, and Creative Commons licensed images from Flickr. Images obtained online without the consent of the subject are referred to by researchers as 'media in the wild'" (Harvey 2022: n.p.).
13. In London, black men can be stopped and searched just for wearing a jacket (https://www.independent.co.uk/news/uk/home-news/black-man-stopped-warm-weather-police-b2044635.html), while in the United States they can be arrested for sitting in Starbucks (ttps://www.theguardian.com/business/2018/may/02/black-men-arrested-starbucks-settlement).
14. While SUS laws were repealed in 1981, the targeting of black youths continues. During the first months of the COVID-19 lockdown, the Met police stopped and searched *more than a quarter of all black fifteen- to twenty-four-year-olds in London* (Grierson 2020). My italicizing doesn't begin to emphasize how profound this statistic is.
15. There is no proven link (outside of data emergent from those selling surveillance equipment) between CCTV or AFR and crime reduction.
16. Like many households, my own has a surveillance camera outside it, each of the five flats in the building having access to the feed. I admit that knowing my neighbors can hear me when outside the house *does* affect what I say.
17. Cardinal Richelieu's saying—"If you give me six lines written by the hand of the most honest of men, I will find something in them which will hang him"—is the perfect example.
18. "This data is toxic on contact, and it sticks around for a long time: it spills, it leaches into everything, it gets into the ground water of our social relationships and poisons them. And it will remain hazardous beyond our own lifetimes" (Bridle 2015).
19. In 2019 a security team was able to access the security platform "Biostar 2" that the Met Police used to house fingerprint and facial recognition data. These white-hat hackers accessed the records of over 27.8 million people and over one million fingerprint records (which, unlike passwords, last forever)! Frighteningly, they were also able to both add and change data kept on the system.
20. Section 702 of the Foreign Intelligence Surveillance Act (FISA) authorizes the US government to engage in "mass, warrantless surveillance of Americans' and foreigners' phone calls, text messages, emails, and other electronic communications. Information collected under the law without a warrant can be used to prosecute and imprison people, even for crimes that have nothing to do with national security" (ACLU 2017). At the time of writing, Section 702 is still in use in the United States. In 2021 it is believed that the "FBI queried the data of potentially more than 3,000,000 'U.S. persons' without a warrant" (Guariglia 2022).
21. While stalking is an offense with no strict definition in the United Kingdom, it is associated with "following a person, watching or spying on them," the effect of which "is to curtail a victim's freedom, leaving them feeling that they constantly have to be careful." The Crown Prosecution Service (CPS), "Stalking or Harassment," May 23, 2018, https://www.cps.gov.uk/legal-guidance/stalking-and-harassment.
22. As alluded to in the previous chapter, my attempt to gain access to images of Hammons's work led me on an amazing journey from gallery to gallery all the way up to the artist's legendary collector/gatekeeper/manager. Sadly, although perhaps appropriately, Hammons's work thus does not appear visually on these pages. It was a fun chase though.
23. "During a series of telephone conversations I've been having with David Hammons . . . about this country's problematic monuments, he calmly mentioned: 'Sometimes I put clothes on the sculptures.' . . . Then Hammons showed me what he meant, sharing this previously unpublished,

untitled artwork from around 2007. It is exactly what he described: an image of him in a blue sweater and black hat wrapping his red-and-orange scarf around the head of a bronze sculpture of a Black woman standing on the base of the Henry Ward Beecher Monument in Brooklyn's Columbus Park during a snowstorm, an action he says he repeated each winter for five or so years" (Palmer 2020).

24. Rather than the gallery, for Hammons "the only thing that's really going on is in the street; that's where something is really happening" (Hammons in Jones 2011 [1984]: 254).
25. I discussed Adam and E. B. Itso's asylum built within the guts of Copenhagen's Central Station in the early 2000 in Schacter 2015.
26. As the National Rail insignia suggests, the ultimate graffiti camouflage comes through "obtaining" officially branded work clothing matching where one seeks to "work."
27. "When I was 12 years old, back in the 1970s, I mounted an array of lights to a long wand that I could wave through the air in a darkened room while the lights were driven by a wearable amplifier and switching system I built. This allowed me to sense and receive various things and 'display' them on the light stick, so that I could see sound waves, radio waves, and most interestingly, sense sensing itself (e.g. visualize vision from a surveillance camera)" (Mann n.d.).
28. I am conscious of appearing to be writing this while wearing a tinfoil hat, yet the facts available in plain sight (along with the unknown unknowns) make it a tempting choice of headwear. While the true capabilities of contemporary surveillance could be argued to be increasing quantities rather than qualities of data, functional or not its usage to target those already subject to target and to scrutinize those subject to scrutinization, in strategies of preemptive arrest that restrict assembly, are today demonstrably clear.
29. This could be seen as graffiti's seventh sense, following the somatic sixth sense of Marchand (2008), discussed in chapter 5.

## CHAPTER 9

1. Robert Morris is priceless here: "Frank Gehry's Guggenheim Bilbao temple of and to gigantism offers the latest, most up-to-date arena for aesthetic assaults of the awesomely big. Even dinosaurs would get lost in these blimp hangar spaces. Here at last we have Wagner effect architecture specially built for Wager effect art" (Morris 2000: 486).
2. The ridiculous name of artwork in former case and location in latter form part of branding initiatives in which corporate organizations make further inroads into "public" space.
3. Google Maps in fact describes the site as a "public square with dancing fountains."
4. I think it is important to note that the artists working here are not (all) cultural dupes. As Ann Markusen has argued, both Florida's depiction of artists as "inner-city and diversity enthusiasts" and Peck's notion of them as being "locked in competition with each other and abandoning progressive and inclusive agendas" (Markusen 2006: 1935) fail to depict the way artists navigate their worlds. As Markusen says, many are "more self-conscious, critical, and activist that either of these dualities suggests" (pp. 1935–1936), and while they "may be used by developers . . . they are not the architects or chief supporters of private property and land-use practices that favor single-site transformations of land use against community wishes . . . Artists are not the protagonists and lobbyists" (p. 1937).
5. As discussed in Schacter 2017, I distinguish between lower- and uppercased street art, the lowercased as a still independent practice, the upper as a co-opted practice of neo-muralism. This is not to say that muralism is acquisitive itself, but that the majority of its instantiations today are.
6. I should note here that I recently curated a four-year-long mural project in Heerlen, the Netherlands. Organized by a nonprofit organization integrated in the city from the grassroots to the highest political levels, the project had both long-term intent and the means to accomplish this. While COVID-19 was a disruption, the success of the project came not simply from the "quality" of the art

(which of course was a key element!) but from the embeddedness of community involvement. The members of the local neighborhood went on to create their own form of ownership, organizing the photo exhibitions, barbecues, among a series of other communal events; the murals were a fulcrum for wider engagement, not the end point of encounter.

7. *Inspired Homes* focused on "micro-apartments," converting commercial buildings into residential ones to circumvent regulations on minimum size.
8. Skinner died of an overdose in Dubai in 2021 after having been bankrupted and losing his £500 million property empire.
9. "RISE gallery ONLY can allocate this [permission] to you," they stressed on their website, "and submission must be made via this form only."
10. Of this, £45,000 came directly from the Borough and £15,000 from Arts Council England. A further £15,000 came from "The Hub," which seems to be an unidentified organization. It's worth noting that the funding was given to Zuchowski-Morrison after he had been bankrupted, owing tens of thousands of pounds to a company whose plant machinery was used to complete previous public murals. In the same year, the artist Banksy's authentication team issued an unprecedented warning to avoid dealing with Zuchowski-Morrison due to multiple incidents of fraud.
11. "Entirely ignorant" might be unfair. One of Rise's murals in 2016 by American artist David Hollier was a portrait of Winston Churchill made exclusively out of text from the "Fight Them on the Beaches" speech. After criticism of the piece in 2020, Zuchowski-Morrison audaciously claimed that the mural "was not painted to 'iconise' the war-time Prime Minister" but rather to "talk about it and debate to understand each other's opinions" (O'Connor 2020).
12. "I feel like one day I'm going to wake up and it's not going to feel like home anymore," said one of the interviewees. As Marc Fried has famously written, reactions to gentrification and displacement often manifest as loss and are often "intense, deeply felt, and, at times, overwhelming" (Fried 1968: 360).
13. The legendary Jonathan Meades's recent essay on Croydon (2023) could not be more perfect here: "There was also the problem of the snobbery excited by Croydon. Its own councillors despise it, welcome the likelihood of its demolition because the next version is sure to be better: Croydon is a 'brand' forever susceptible to rebrands and rebrands. It is perfectible until it is decided that it is not."
14. Note here that all three members of our trifecta went into bankruptcy.
15. In a statement written in response to critique from architecture critic Inga Saffron, the founder and director of Philadelphia Mural Arts, Jane Golden, praised the work of arch gentrifier Tony Goldman as a "real and inspirational model for the potential in revitalizing communities [that] underscored and reaffirmed the nexus of art and economic development" (Spikol 2012). It seems inconceivable that she was unaware of the displacement faced by the local Latino community due to Goldman's projects. For more, see Camila Álvarez and Natalie Edgar's film *Right to Wynwood*.
16. For the furor surrounding Art Angel's proposed project at the Heygate Estate in London, see the work of anti-gentrification collective Southwark Notes: https://southwarknotes.wordpress.com/heygate-estate/heygate-pyramid-artangel-mike-nelson-and-others-saga.
17. While sites such as Granary Square may not have generated direct displacement due to being built on brownfield or post-industrial sites, they still contribute to what Slater has termed "indirect displacement" in which "conversions elevate rental and sales prices in 'up and coming' areas adjacent to those conversions" (Slater 2009: 305).
18. Guy Debord's definition of tourism as "human circulation packaged for consumption," an "opportunity to go and see what has been banalized," and an industry whose "economic organization . . . already guarantees their *equivalence*" (Debord 2002 [1967]: 45) here comes to fruition.
19. At the newly opened Battersea Power Station in London, the stunning industrial site (which could have been transformed into almost *anything*), today presents us with a Tate Modern sans the art, a Tate Modern cum POPS in which the chain stores and penthouse apartments have replaced any cultural offering at all.

20. Cited without comment: "Built on innovation and creativity, Coal Drops Yard has always been in motion. These Victorian brick viaducts have been the freight rail yards of the industrial revolution, served as film sets, played host to counter-culture artists, and for a decade, hosted some of the biggest rave parties the world has seen. Now reimagined by architect Thomas Heatherwick, the legacy of ideas and hard work that has always been at the heart of Coal Drops Yard continues for a new generation" (Coal Drops Yard 2020).
21. See also Bengtsen 2016 and Hansen 2016.
22. This "spite" is often due to the inauthentic temporality these coverings create, as much as what is deemed as the improper relationship between inalienable art and commerce.
23. Remarkably, the Perspex covers are today understood to generate a trapped humidity that damages the works underneath.
24. In a beautiful twist, some of these re-produced works have been stolen from the street before being sold at auction as original Invaders!
25. A comment on this image from the photographer is worth noting: "Centre Place has been home to some fantastic Street Art but is now full of tagging. Given this, shall remove from the Street Art group!"
26. "The Croydon Rise Festival is a street art festival curated by Monoprixx, Wherethereswalls and Rise Gallery, aimed [*sic*] to become the *largest free open air museum in Europe*" (*Street Art News*, September 23, 2018, my emphasis).
27. "During the late 1980's an invisible army assaulted the city with spraycans transforming bland concrete walls into canvases filled with an explosive language of hard-edged urban forms, radiating color, and an abstract, coded lexicon. The most prolific, the Boyle Heights tagger known as Chaka single-handedly inflicted $30,000 worth of damage to the Southern Pacific Railroad. Triumph of the Tagger. Declared Monument 44. By Pocho Research Society of Erased and Invisible History."
28. I am aware that the Stonehenge media team is trying to find a way to attract people to what is a pretty stationary site. This, however, is surely not it.

## CONCLUSION

1. Alongside the issues of Confederacy monuments in the United States and the toppling of Colston in Bristol, what Abdul Kayum Ahmed (2020) has called "fallism" is of course a truly global affair, famously seen in the Rhodes Must Fall campaign in South Africa as well as in the removal of monuments to Chiang Kai-shek in Taiwan, Leopold II in Kinshasa (and Antwerp), Nelson in Bridgetown, and Gandhi in Accra, among countless other examples.
2. In Bristol, for example, while the "Countering Colston" campaign began to make headway around 2015, the monument had been a cause of deep division in the city from the mid- to late 1990s.
3. The killing (the murder) of Michael Stewart in 1983 in New York after his arrest for graffiti is one of the most famous cases, here due to its later depiction by Jean Michel Basquiat in his masterpiece *Defacement (The Death of Michael Stewart)*.
4. The headlines generated in every case of graffiti prosecution always begin with this financial sum, a sum whose massive inflation leads directly to longer prison sentences.

# REFERENCES


Abarca, Javier. 2016. "From Street Art to Murals: What Have We Lost?" *SAUC—Street Art and Urban Creativity* 2, no. 2: 60–67.

ACLU. 2017. "Warrentless Surveillance under Section 702 of FISA." https://www.aclu.org/issues/national-security/privacy-and-surveillance/warrantless-surveillance-under-section-702-fisa.

Agulhon, Maurice. 1981. *Marianne into Battle: Republican Imagery and Symbolism in France 1789–1880*. Cambridge: Cambridge University Press; Paris: Editions de la Maison des sciences de l'homme.

Ahearn, Charlie, dir. 1983. *Wild Style*. Rhino Entertainment, Submarine Entertainment. 82 minutes.

Ahmed, Abdul Kayum. 2020. "Towards an Emergent Theory of Fallism (and the Fall of the White-Liberal-University in South Africa)." In Jacqueline Bhabha, Wenona Giles, and Faraaz Mahomed, eds., *A Better Future: The Role of Higher Education for Displaced and Marginalised People*. Cambridge: Cambridge University Press.

Ahmed, Sara. 2014. "Atmospheric Walls." *Feminist Killjoys* (blog), September 15, 2014. https://feministkilljoys.com/2014/09/15/atmospheric-walls.

Alkalimat, Abdul, Romi Crawford, and Rebecca Zorach. 2017. *The Wall of Respect: Public Art and Black Liberation in 1960s Chicago*. Evanston, IL: Northwestern University Press.

Ancient Monuments and Archaeological Areas Act. 1979. https://www.legislation.gov.uk/ukpga/1979/46/part/I/crossheading/guardianship-of-ancient-monuments/enacted?view=plain.

Anderson, Benedict. 2006 [1983]. *Imagined Communities: Reflections on the Origin and Spread of Nationalism*, rev. ed. London: Verso.

Anderson, Elijah. 2015. "The White Space." *Sociology of Race and Ethnicity* 1, no. 1: 10–21.

Andron, Sabina. 2018. "Selling Streetness as Experience: The Role of Street Art Tours in Branding the Creative City." *The Sociological Review* 66, no. 5: 1036–1057.

Arendt, Hannah. 1988 [1958]. *The Human Condition*. Chicago: University of Chicago Press.

Arns, Inke, and Sylvia Sasse. 2006. "Subversive Affirmation: On Mimesis as a Strategy of Resistance." In IRWIN, ed., *East Art Map: Contemporary Art and Eastern Europe*. Cambridge, MA: MIT Press, pp. 444–455.

Arte, Anssi. 2015. *Forms of Rockin': Graffiti Letters and Popular Culture*. Aarsta: Dokument Press.

Austin Joe. 2001. *Taking the Train: How Graffiti Art Became an Urban Crisis in New York City*. New York: Columbia University Press.

Austin, J. L. 1962. *How to Do Things with Words: The William James Lectures Delivered at Harvard University in 1955*. Cambridge, MA: Harvard University Press.

Bain, Alison. 2009. "Creativ* Suburbs: Cultural 'Popcorn' Pioneering in Multi-Purpose Spaces." In Tim Edensor et al., eds., *Spaces of Vernacular Creativity: Rethinking the Cultural Economy*. New York: Routledge.

Bach Jonathan P. G., and Michał Murawski. 2020. *Re-Centring the City: Global Mutations of Socialist Modernity*. London: UCL Press.

Bakhtin, Mikhail. 1984 [1965]. *Rabelais and His World*. Bloomington: Indiana University Press.

Bal, Mieke. 1999. *The Practice of Cultural Analysis: Exposing Interdisciplinary Interpretation*. Stanford, CA: Stanford University Press.

Barney, Darin, Gabriella Coleman, Christine Ross, Jonathan Sterne, and Tamar Tembeck. 2016. "The Participatory Condition: An Introduction." In Darin Barney, Gabriella Coleman, Christine Ross, Jonathan Sterne, and Tamar Tembeck, eds., *The Participatory Condition in the Digital Age*. Minneapolis: University of Minnesota Press.

Barthes, Roland. 1977. "The Rhetoric of the Image." In *Image, Music, Text*. London: Fontana.

Barthes, Roland. 1991 [1979]. "Cy Twombly: Works on Paper." In *The Responsibility of Forms: Critical Essays on Music, Art, and Representation*, trans. Richard Howard. Berkeley: University of California Press.

Bauman, Zygmunt. 2011. "The London Riots: Consumerism Coming Home to Roost." *Social Europe Journal*, August 9. www.social-europe.eu/2011/08/the-londonriots-on-consumerism-coming-home-toroost/.

Bell, Catherine. 1997. *Ritual: Perspectives and Dimensions*. New York: Oxford University Press.

Belting, Hans. 2005. "Image, Medium, Body: A New Approach to Iconology." *Critical Inquiry* 31, no. 2 (Winter): 302–319.

Bender, Barbara. 1998. *Stonehenge: Making Space*. Oxford: Berg.

Benedict, Drew, Emma Hart, Dai Jenkins. Dean Kenning, Corinna Till, Owen Hatherley, Laura Liverani, and Work in Progress. 2013. *Reclaim the Mural: The Politics of London Murals*. London: Whitechapel Gallery.

Bengtsen, Peter. 2016. "Stealing from the Public: The Value of Street Art Taken from the Street." In Jeffrey Ian Ross, ed., *Routledge Handbook of Graffiti and Street Art*. London: Routledge.

Berger, John. 1972. *Ways of Seeing: Based on a BBC Television Series with John Berger*. London: British Broadcasting Corporation and Penguin Books.

Berger, Stefan. 2019. "Industrial Heritage and the Ambiguities of Nostalgia for an Industrial Past in the Ruhr Valley, Germany." *Labor* 16, no. 1: 37–64.

Bessa, Antonio Sergio. 2017. "Nothing Works: Gordon Matta-Clark and the Problem of Architecture." In Antonio Sergio Bessa et al., *Gordon Matta-Clark: Anarchitect*. Bronx, NY: Bronx Museum of the Arts, in association with Yale University Press.

Bickford, Susan. 2000. "Constructing Inequality: City Spaces and the Architecture of Citizenship." *Political Theory* 28, no. 3: 355–376.

Birzin, Edward. 2019. "Subway Art(efact)." PhD thesis, Freie Universität Berlin.

Bishop, Claire. 2012. *Artificial Hells: Participatory Art and the Politics of Spectatorship*. London: Verso Books.

Blackwood, Michael, dir. 2005. *Peter Eisenman: Building Germany's Holocaust Memorial*. 58 minutes.

Blas, Zach. 2013. "Informatic Opacity." *The Journal of Aesthetics & Protest*, no. 9. https://www.joaap.org/issue9/9toc.htm.

Blischoff, Paul. 2023. "Surveillance Camera Statistics: Which Cities Have the Most CCTV Cameras?" *Comparitech*, May 23. https://www.comparitech.com/vpn-privacy/the-worlds-most-surveilled-cities.

Bloch, Maurice. 1989 [1974]. “Symbols, Song, Dance and Features of Articulation.” In Maurice Bloch, ed., *Ritual, History, and Power: Selected Papers in Anthropology*. London: Athlone Press.

Blommaert, Jan. 2012. “Chronicles of Complexity: Ethnography, Superdiversity, and Linguistic Landscapes.” Tilburg Papers in Culture Studies, paper 29.

Boulanger, Étienne. 2003. *Work in Progress 2001–2003: Plug-In Berlin*. Nancy: Ministère de la culture et de la communication, D.R.A.C.

Bourdieu, Pierre. 1977. “Structures and the Habitus.” In *Outline of a Theory of Practice*. Cambridge: Cambridge University Press, pp. 72–95.

Bredekamp, Horst. 2018. *Image Acts: A Systematic Approach to Visual Agency*, trans. Elizabeth Clegg. Berlin: Walter de Gruyter.

Brenneis, Donald. 1986. “Shared Territory: Audience, Indirection and Meaning.” *Text* 6, no. 3: 339–347.

Bridle, James. 2014. *All Cameras Are Police Cameras*. Commissioned by the Hayward Gallery. http://shorttermmemoryloss.com/nor/2014/11/07/all-cameras-are-police-cameras.

Bridle, James. 2015. “Big Data, No Thanks.” Blogpost on booktwo.org. November 2, 2015. http://booktwo.org/notebook/big-data-no-thanks.

Brighenti, Andrea Mubi, and Mattias Kärrholm. 2022. *Territories Environments Politic: Explorations in Territoriology*. Abingdon: Routledge.

Browne, Simone. 2015. *Dark Matters: On the Surveillance of Blackness*. Durham, NC: Duke University Press.

Brundage, W. Fitzhugh. 2005. *The Southern Past: A Clash of Race and Memory*. Cambridge, MA: Belknap Press of Harvard University Press.

Brundage, W. 2017. “I’ve Studied the History of Confederate Memorials. Here’s What to Do about Them.” *Vox*, August 18. https://www.vox.com/the-big-idea/2017/8/18/16165160/confederate-monuments-history-charlottesville-white-supremacy.

Buchloh, Benjamin. 2003. *Neo-Avantgarde and Culture Industry: Essays on European and American Art from 1955 to 1975*. Cambridge, MA: MIT Press.

Butler, Patrick. 2022. “Croydon Council Declares Effective Bankruptcy for Third Time in Two Years.” *The Guardian*, November 22. https://www.theguardian.com/society/2022/nov/22/croydon-council-declares-effective-bankruptcy-for-third-time-in-two-years.

Caldeira, Teresa. 1996. “Fortified Enclaves: The New Urban Segregation.” *Public Culture*, no. 8: 303–328.

Callaghan, Mark. 2010. “Speak Out: Invisible Past, Invisible Future: A German’s Alternative Response to the Holocaust.” *Art Times: A Literary Journal and Resource for the Fine and Performing Arts*. Online October; print edition November/December.

Campos, Ricardo, Andrea Pavoni, and Yiannis Zaimakis, eds. 2021. *Political Graffiti in Critical Times: The Aesthetics of Street Politics*. New York: Berghahn Books.

Careri, Francesco. 2017. *Walkscapes: Walking as an Aesthetic Practice*. Ames, IA: Culicidae Architectural Press.

Carmona, Matthew. 2022. “The ‘Public-isation’ of Private Space: Towards a Charter of Public Space Rights and Responsibilities.” *Journal of Urbanism: International Research on Placemaking and Urban Sustainability* 15, no. 2: 133–164.

Casey, Edward. 2007. “Boundary, Place, and Event in the Spatiality of History.” *Rethinking History* 11, no. 4: 507–512.

Cash, John D. 2009. "Negotiating Insecurity: Law, Psychoanalytic Social Theory and the Dilemmas of the World Risk Society." *Australian Feminist Law Journal* 30, no. 1: 87–107.

Castleman, Craig. 1982. *Getting Up: Subway Graffiti in New York*. Cambridge, MA: MIT Press.

Chalfant, Henry, and Martha Cooper. 1984. *Subway Art*. London: Thames & Hudson.

Chu, Cecilia L. 2015. "Spectacular Macau: Visioning Futures for a World Heritage City." *Geoforum* 65: 440–450.

Coal Drops Yard. 2020. "About Us." https://www.coaldropsyard.com/about.

Cohen, Julie E. 2016. "The Surveillance-Innovation Complex: The Irony of the Participatory Turn." In Darin Barney, Gabriella Coleman, Christine Ross, Jonathan Sterne, and Tamar Tembe, eds., *The Participatory Condition in the Digital Age*. Minneapolis: University of Minnesota Press.

Conkey, Margaret. 2006. "Style, Design, and Function." In Christopher Tilley, ed., *Handbook of Material Culture*. London: Sage.

Coombe, Rosemary. 2013."Managing Cultural Heritage as Neoliberal Governmentality." In R. F. Bendix, A. Eggert, and A. Peselmann, eds., *Heritage Regimes and the State*. Göttingen: Göttingen University Press. Retrieved from http://books.openedition.org/gup/348.

Coupaye, Ludovic. 2017. "The Problem of Agency in Art." In Nicholas Thomas and Alison Clark, eds., *Style and Meaning: Essays on the Anthropology of Art—Anthony Forge*. Leiden: Sidestone Press.

Crisman, Jonathan. 2021. "Art and the Aesthetics of Cultural Gentrification: The Cases of Boyle Heights and Little Tokyo in Los Angeles." In Christopher Lindner and Gerard Sandoval, eds., *Aesthetics of Gentrification*. Amsterdam: Amsterdam University Press.

Crossley, Nick. 1995. "Body Techniques Agency, and Intercorporeality: On Goffman's *Relations in Public*." *Sociology* 29, no. 1: 133–149.

CroydonBID. 2018. "RISEfestival: London's Largest International Urban Art Festival Comes to Croydon!" https://croydonbid.com/news/risefestival-london%E2%80%99s-largest-international-urban-art-festival-comes-croydon.

"Croydon Rise Festival." 2018. *Street Art News*, September 23. https://streetartnews.net/2018/09/croydon-rise-festival-aida-wilde-less-homes-4u.html.

Cuauhtémoc, Medina, Jean Fisher, and Russell Ferguson. 2008. *Francis Alÿs*. London: Phaidon Press.

Davies, Gareth. 2015. "Graffiti 'Taggers' Deface Street Art in Croydon's St George's Walk." *Croydon Advertiser*, February 23. https://www.croydonadvertiser.co.uk/Graffiti-taggers-deface-street-art-Croydon-s-St/story-26069062-detail/story.html.

Davis, Barney. 2016. "Introducing the New Capital of Street Art . . . Croydon." *Evening Standard*, September 12. https://www.standard.co.uk/culture/introducing-the-new-capital-of-street-art-croydon-a3342431.html.

de Certeau, Michel. 1984. *The Practice of Everyday Life*. Berkeley: University of California Press.

de Solà-Morales Rubio, Ignasi. 1995. "Terrain Vague." In Cynthia C. Davidson, ed., *Anyplace*. Cambridge, MA: MIT Press.

Debord, Guy. 2002 [1967]. *Society of the Spectacle*. Canberra: Treason Press.

Debray, Régis. 1999. "Trace, forme ou message?" *Les cahiers de médiologie* 1, no 7: 27–44.

Dekeyser, Thomas. 2020. "Dismantling the Advertising City: Subvertising and the Urban Commons to Come." *EPD: Society and Space* 39, no. 2: 309–327.

Department for Culture, Media and Sport. 2010. "Scheduled Monuments: Identifying, Protecting, Conserving and Investigating Nationally Important Archaeological Sites under the Ancient Monuments and Archaeological Areas Act 1979."

Department for Culture, Media and Sport. 2013. "Scheduled Monuments & Nationally Important but Non-scheduled Monuments." https://www.gov.uk/government/publications/scheduled-monuments-policy-statement.

Department of Transport. 2007. *Know Your Traffic Signs: Official Edition*. London: TSO.

Derrida, Jacques. 1979. "The Parergon," trans. Craig Owens. *October* 9: 3–41.

DeSilvey, Caitlin. 2017. *Curated Decay: Heritage beyond Saving*. Minneapolis: University of Minnesota Press.

Deutsche, Rosalyn. 1996. *Evictions*. Cambridge, MA: Graham Foundation for Advanced Studies in the Fine Arts, Cambridge, MA: MIT Press.

Deutsche, Rosalyn, and Cara Gendel Ryan. 1984. "The Fine Art of Gentrification." *October* 31 (Winter): 91–111.

Didi-Huberman, Georges. 2003. "Before the Image, before Time: The Sovereignty of Anachronism." In Claire Farago and Robert Zwijnenberg, eds., *Compelling Visuality: The Work of Art in and out of History*. Minneapolis: University of Minnesota Press.

DoGoodFactory. 2017. "Artist Ben Eine Choses Croydon for His New 10 Storey 'Mesmerising' Mural." June 6. https://www.do-good-factory.co.uk/single-post/2017/06/06/artist-ben-eine-choses-croydon-for-his-new-10-storey-mesmerising-mural.

Douglas, Gordon C. C. 2013. "Do-It-Yourself Urban Design: The Social Practice of Informal 'Improvement' through Unauthorized Alteration." *City & Community* 13, no. 1: 5–25.

Douglas, Mary. 2000 [1966]. *Purity and Danger: An Analysis of Concepts of Pollution and Taboo*. New York: Praeger.

Dowden, Oliver. 2020. *Letter from Culture Secretary on HM Government Position on Contested Heritage*. INT2020/19838/DC. September 22. https://www.gov.uk/government/publications/letter-from-culture-secretary-on-hm-government-position-on-contested-heritage.

Dowden, Oliver. 2021. "We Won't Allow Britain's History to Be Cancelled." *The Daily Telegraph* (London), May 15. https://www.telegraph.co.uk/news/2021/05/15/wont-allow-britains-history-cancelled.

Downey, Greg, Monica Dalidowicz, and Paul H. Mason. 2015. "Apprenticeship as Method: Embodied Learning in Ethnographic Practice." *Qualitative Research* 15, no. 2: 183–200.

Duncan, Shane. 2018. "This Is Croydon." 7 minutes 57 seconds. @Shaneduncan1.

Edensor, Tim, Debora Leslie, Steve Millington, and Norma M. Rantisi, eds. 2009. *Spaces of Vernacular Creativity: Rethinking the Cultural Economy*. New York: Routledge.

Eisenman, Peter. N.d. *Peter Eisenman about the Memorial*. https://www.stiftung-denkmal.de/en/memorials/memorial-to-the-murdered-jews-of-europe.

Ellingham, Miles. 2023. "After Hours with 10 Foot, London's Most Notorious Graffiti Writer." *FT Mag* (London), February 3. https://www.ft.com/content/45a184ee-b7d9-4c16-b1c2-71def32ccf98.

Engin, Isin. 2013. *Democracy, Citizenship and the Global City*. London: Routledge.

English Heritage. 2022. *An Unmissable Family Day Out From £56.60*. https://www.english-heritage.org.uk/visit/places/stonehenge.

English Heritage. 2013. *National Heritage Protection Plan Framework*. https://historicengland.org.uk/images-books/publications/nhpp-plan-framework/nhpp-plan-framework.

Fiduccia, Joanna. 2022. "Scale of the Nation: Alberto Giacometti's Miniature Monument." *Art History* 45, no. 1: 126–156.

Florida, Richard L. 2002. *The Rise of the Creative Class: And How It's Transforming Work, Leisure, Community, and Everyday Life*. New York: Basic Books.

Flusty, Steven. 1994. *Building Paranoia: The Proliferation of Interdictory Space and the Erosion of Spatial Justice*. West Hollywood, CA: Los Angeles Forum for Architecture and Urban Design.

Forge, Anthony. 2017. "Style and Meaning in Sepik Art." In Nicholas Thomas, and Alison Clark, eds., *Style and Meaning: Essays on the Anthropology of Art—Anthony Forge*. Leiden: Sidestone Press.

Forty, Adrian. 1999. "Introduction." In Adrian Forty and Susanne Küchler, eds., *The Art of Forgetting*. Oxford: Berg.

Foucault, Michel. 1995 [1977]. *Discipline & Punish: The Birth of the Prison*. New York: Vintage Books.

Foucault, Michel. 2008. *The Birth of Biopolitics: Lectures at the Collège de France 1978–1979*. Basingstoke: Palgrave Macmillan.

Fried, Marc. 1968. "Grieving for a Lost Home: Psychological Costs of Relocation." In James Q. Wilson, ed., *Urban Renewal: The Record and the Controversy*. Cambridge, MA: MIT Press.

Fusco, Coco. 2001. *The Bodies That Were Not Ours: And Other Writings*. London: Routledge, published in collaboration with inIVA [Institute of International Visual Arts].

Galanakis, Michail. 2013. "Intercultural Public Spaces in Multicultural Toronto." *Canadian Journal of Urban Research* 22, no. 1: 67–89.

Gamboni, D. 2002. "Image to Destroy, Indestructible Image." In Bruno Latour and Peter Weibel, eds., *Iconoclash: Beyond the Image Wars in Science, Religion, and Art*. Cambridge, MA: MIT Press, pp. 88–135.

Geismar, Haidy. 2014. "Drawing It Out." *Visual Anthropology Review* 30, no. 2 (Fall): 97–113.

Geismar, Haidy. 2015. "Anthropology and Heritage Regimes." *Annual Review of Anthropology* 44: 71–85.

Geismar, Haidy. 2022. "Caring for the Social (in Museums)." In Haidy Geismar, Ton Otto, and Cameron David Warner, eds., *Impermanence: Exploring Continuous Change across Cultures*. London: UCL Press.

Geismar, Haidy, Ton Otto, and Cameron David Warner, eds. 2022. *Impermanence: Exploring Continuous Change across Cultures*. London: UCL Press.

Gell, Alfred. 1992. "The Technology of Enchantment and the Enchantment of Technology." In Jeremy Coote and Anthony Shelton, eds., *Anthropology, Art and Aesthetics*. Oxford: Clarendon Press.

Gell, Alfred. 1998. *Art and Agency: An Anthropological Theory*. Oxford: Clarendon Press.

Gentile, Dan. 2022. "'An uncontrollable mess': Taggers Won't Stop Defacing SF Murals." *SFGATE*, February 28. https://www.sfgate.com/sf-culture/article/taggers-are-defacing-SF-murals-16947622.php.

Glissant, Édouard. 1997. *Poetics of Relation*. Ann Arbor: University of Michigan Press.

Gluckman, Max. 1963 *Order and Rebellion in Tribal Africa*. New York: Free Press of Glencoe.

Gombrich, Ernst Hans. 1984. *The Sense of Order: A Study in the Psychology of Decorative Art*. Ithaca, NY: Cornell University Press.

Goodin, Dan. 2013. "No, This Isn't a Scene from *Minority Report*. This Trash Can *Is* Stalking You." *Ars Technica*, August 9. https://arstechnica.com/information-technology/2013/08/no-this-isnt-a-scene-from-minority-report-this-trash-can-is-stalking-you.

GOV.UK. 2021. "Briefing Note on the Ethical Issues Arising from Public-Private Collaboration in the Use of Live Facial Recognition Technology (Accessible)," Biometrics & Forensic Ethics Group, January 21. https://www.gov.uk/government/publications/public-private-use-of-live-facial-recognition-technology-ethical-issues/briefing-note-on-the-ethical-issues-arising-from-public-private-collaboration-in-the-use-of-live-facial-recognition-technology-accessible.

Grabar, Oleg. 1992. *The Mediation of Ornament*. Princeton, NJ: Princeton University Press.

Grabar, Oleg. 2009. *Masterpieces of Islamic Art: The Decorated Page from the 8th to the 17th Century*. Munich: Prestel.

Greenberg, Allan. 1989. "Lutyens's Cenotaph." *Journal of the Society of Architectural Historians* 48, no. 1: 5–23.

Greenfield, Adam. 2013. *Against the Smart City: A Pamphlet. Part I of "The City Is Here to Use."* New York: Do Projects.

Grierson, Jamie. 2020. "Met Carried out 22,000 Searches on Young Black Men during Lockdown." *The Guardian*, July 8. https://www.theguardian.com/law/2020/jul/08/one-in-10-of-londons-young-black-males-stopped-by-police-in-may.

Griffiths, Josh. 2018. "Art Talk: Edwin aka Redwine." *ArtWhore*, May 8. https://artwhorecult.com/art-talk-edwin-aka-redwine.

Grimwood, Gabrielle Garton. 2021. *Contested Heritage: Controversy Surrounding Public Monuments*. No. 9405. Commons Library Research Briefing, December 17. House of Commons Library. https://researchbriefings.files.parliament.uk/documents/CBP-9405/CBP-9405.pdf.

Groth, Jacqueline, and Eric Corijn. 2005. "Reclaiming Urbanity: Indeterminate Spaces, Informal Actors and Urban Agenda Setting." *Urban Studies* 42, no. 3: 503–526.

Groys, Boris. 2008. *Art Power*. Cambridge, MA: MIT Press.

Grünfeld, Martin. 2022. "Culturing Impermanence at the Museum: The Metabolic Collection." In Haidy Geismar, Ton Otto, and Cameron David Warner, eds., *Impermanence: Exploring Continuous Change across Cultures*. London: UCL Press.

Guariglia, Matthew. 2022. "New Surveillance Transparency Report Documents an Urgent Need for Change." https://www.eff.org/deeplinks/2022/05/new-surveillance-transparency-report-documents-urgent-need-change.

Guillory, John. 2016. "Monuments and Documents: Panofsky on the Object of Study in the Humanities." *History of Humanities/Society for the History of the Humanities* 1, no. 1 (Spring): 9–30.

Habermas, Jürgen. 1991 [1962]. *The Structural Transformation of the Public Sphere: An Inquiry into a Category of Bourgeois Society*, trans. Thomas Burger with Frederick Lawrence. Cambridge, MA: MIT Press.

*Hackney Graffiti Policy Document*. 2016. https://hackney.gov.uk/media/2653/Hackney-graffiti-policy/pdf/Hackney-graffiti-policy.pdf?m=636486758376870000.

Hallam, Elizabeth, and Tim Ingold, eds. 2007. *Creativity and Cultural Improvisation*. Oxford: Berg.

Hannerz, Erik. 2022. "Playing in the Yard: The Representation of Control in Train-Graffiti Videos." *Crime, Media, Culture: An International Journal* 19, no. 4.

Hansen, Susan. 2016. "'Pleasure stolen from the poor': Community Discourse on the 'Theft' of a Banksy." *Crime, Media, Culture: An International Journal* 12, no. 3.

Harris, Gareth. 2021. "Keep Problematic Monuments and 'Explain Them,' UK Government to Tell Cultural Leaders." *The Art Newspaper*, February 15. https://www.theartnewspaper.com/2021/02/15/keep-problematic-monuments-and-explain-them-uk-government-to-tell-cultural-leaders.

Harvey, Adam. 2022. *Today's Selfie Is Tomorrow's Biometric Profile*. https://adam.harvey.studio/todays-selfie.

Harvey, Adam. 2023. *CV DAZZLE*. https://adam.harvey.studio/cvdazzle.

Heap of Birds, Edgar. 2004. "Artistic Displacements: An Interview with Edgar Heap of Birds by Nick Blomley." *Environment and Planning D: Society and Space* 22: 799–807.

Hebdige, Dick. 1983. "Posing . . . Threats, Striking . . . Poses: Youth, Surveillance, and Display." *SubStance* 11, no. 4 (issue 37–38: A Special Issue from the Center for Twentieth Century Studies): 68–88.

Hern, Alex. 2022. "Chinese Security Firm Advertises Ethnicity Recognition Technology while Facing UK Ban." *The Guardian*, December 4. https://www.theguardian.com/world/2022/dec/04/chinese-security-firm-advertises-ethnicity-recognition-technology-while-facing-uk-ban.

Hewitt, Andy. 2011. "Privatizing the Public: Three Rhetorics of Art's Public Good in 'Third Way' Cultural Policy." *Art & the Public Sphere* 1, no. 1.

Hill, Kashmir. 2020. "The Secretive Company That Might End Privacy as We Know It." *New York Times*, January 18. https://www.nytimes.com/2020/01/18/technology/clearview-privacy-facial-recognition.html.

Hirschhorn, Thomas, and Yasmil Raymond. 2016. *7 QUESTIONS YASMIL RAYMOND*. https://www.thomashirschhorn.com/7-questions-yasmil-raymond-2016.

Historic England. 2021. *Graffiti on Historic Buildings: Removal and Prevention*. Swindon. Historic England.

Historic England. n.d. "Scheduled Monuments." https://historicengland.org.uk/listing/what-is-designation/scheduled-monuments.

Hobsbawm, Eric. 1995. "Foreword." In Dawn Ades, *Art and Power: Europe under the Dictators, 1930–1945: The XXIII Council of Europe Exhibition*. London: Hayward Gallery.

Holtorf, Cornelius. 2006. "Can Less Be More? Heritage in the Age of Terrorism." *Public Archaeology* 5, no. 2: 101–109.

hooks, bell. 1989. "Choosing the Margin as a Space of Radical Openness." *Framework: The Journal of Cinema and Media*, no. 36: 15–23.

House of Lords, Justice and Home Affairs Committee. 2022. *Technology Rules? The Advent of New Technologies in the Justice System*. March 30. HL Paper 180. Published by the Authority of the House of Lords. https://publications.parliament.uk/pa/ld5802/ldselect/ldjusthom/180/180.pdf.

Howe, Leo. 2000. "Risk, Ritual and Performance." *Journal of the Royal Anthropological Institute* 6, no. 1: 63–79.

ICO. 2022. "ICO Fines Facial Recognition Database Company Clearview AI Inc More Than £7.5m and Orders UK Data to Be Deleted." News, May 23. https://ico.org.uk/about-the-ico/media-centre/news-and-blogs/2022/05/ico-fines-facial-recognition-database-company-clearview-ai-inc.

*Illustrated London News*. 1843. "The Nelson Statue." November 4. https://www.google.co.uk/books/edition/Illustrated_London_News/c3Y5AQAAMAAJ?hl=en&gbpv=0.

Ingold, Tim. 2000. *The Perception of the Environment: Essays on Livelihood, Dwelling and Skill*. London: Routledge.

Ingold, Tim. 2007. "Introduction [Part 1]." In Elizabeth Hallam and Tim Ingold, eds., *Creativity and Cultural Improvisation*. Oxford: Berg Publishers.

Isin, Engin F. 2013. *Democracy, Citizenship, and the Global City*. London: Routledge

Jain, Anil. 2019. "Second Expert Report of Dr Anil Jain." https://www.libertyhumanrights.org.uk/wp-content/uploads/2020/02/Second-Expert-Report-from-Dr-Anil-Jain.pdf.

Jeevendrampillai, David. 2021. *Citizenship Democracy and Belonging in Suburban Britain: Making the Local*. London: UCL Press.

Jefferson, Brian Jordan. 2018. "Predictable Policing: Predictive Crime Mapping and Geographies of Policing and Race." *Annals of the American Association of Geographers* 108, no. 1: 1–16.

Jenrick, Robert. 2021. "Planning and Heritage: Historic Statues, Plaques, Memorials and Monuments." In *Hansard* volume 68, debated on January 18, 2021. https://hansard.parliament.uk/Commons/2021-01-18/debates/2101187000013/PlanningAndHeritageHistoricStatuesPlaquesMemorialsAndMonuments.

Jones, Kellie. 2011. "Interview with David Hammons" in *EyeMinded: Living and Writing Contemporary Art*. Durham NC: Duke University Press.

Joselit, David. 1998. "Voices, Bodies and Spaces: The Art of Jenny Holzer." In David Joselit, Renata Salecl, and Joan Simon, *Jenny Holzer*. London: Phaidon Press.

Kaplan, Caren, and Andrea Miller. 2019. "Drones as Atmospheric Policing: From US Border Enforcement to the LAPD." *Public Culture* 31, no. 3: 419–445.

Kelty, Christopher M. 2017. "Too Much Democracy in All the Wrong Places: Toward a Grammar of Participation." *Current Anthropology* 58, Supplement 15.

Kimball, Whitney. 2014. "How Do People Feel about the Gramsci Monument, One Year Later?" *Art F City*, August 20. http://artfcity.com/2014/08/20/how-do-people-feel-about-the-gramsci-monument-one-year-later.

King's Cross Estate Services. 2022. "Estate Management." https://www.kingscross.co.uk/estate-management.

Kohn, Margaret. 2004. *Brave New Neighborhoods: The Privatization of Public Space*. London: Routledge.

Kraft, Adam. 2023. *Key Notes on the Unruly City: Social, Material, and Spatial Transgressions*. Berlin: A5 Press, in collaboration with Errant Bodies Press.

Küchler, Susanne. 1987. "Malangan: Art and Memory in a Melanesian Society." *Man: A Monthly Record of Anthropological Science* 238.

Küchler, Susanne. 2001. "The Place of Memory." In Adrian Forty and Susanne Küchler, *The Art of Forgetting*. Oxford: Berg.

Küchler, Susanne, and Timothy Carroll. 2021. *A Return to the Object: Alfred Gell, Art, and Social Theory*. Abingdon: Routledge.

Lachmann, Renate. 1988. "Bakhtin and Carnival: Culture as Counter-Culture." *Cultural Critique*, no. 11 (Winter): 115–152.

Lai, Ten-Herng. 2020. "Political Vandalism as Counter-Speech: A Defence of Defacing and Destroying Tainted Monuments." *European Journal of Philosophy* 28, no. 3: 602–616.

Latour, Bruno. 2002. "What Is Iconoclash? Or Is There a World beyond the Image Wars?" In Bruno Latour and Peter Weibel, eds., *Iconoclash: Beyond the Image Wars in Science, Religion, and Art*. Cambridge, MA: MIT Press.

Laurenson, Pip, and Lucy Bayley. 2022. "'Neurosis of the Sterile Egg'—Permanence and Paradox: Museum Strategies for the Representation of Gustav Metzger's Auto-Destructive Art." In Haidy Geismar, Tonn Otto, and Cameron David Warner, eds., *Impermanence: Exploring Continuous Change across Cultures*. London: UCL Press.

Lees, Loretta, and Clare Melhuish. 2015. "Arts-Led Regeneration in the UK: The Rhetoric and the Evidence on Urban Social Inclusion." *European Urban and Regional Studies* 22, no. 3: 242–260.

Lefebvre, Henri. 1991. *The Production of Space*. Malden, MA: Blackwell.

Lefebvre, Henri. 1996 [1983]. *Writings on Cities*. Oxford: Blackwell.

Lefebvre, Henri. 2003. *The Urban Revolution*. Minneapolis: University of Minnesota Press.

Lefebvre, Henri. 2014. "Dissolving City, Planetary Metamorphosis." *Environment and Planning D: Society and Space* 32: 203–205.

Lepecki, Andre. 2016. *Duration*. http://intermsofperformance.site/keywords/duration/andre-lepecki.

Ligon, Glenn. 2004. "Black Light: David Hammons and the Poetics of Emptiness." *ArtForum*, September. https://www.artforum.com/print/200407/black-light-david-hammons-and-the-poetics-of-emptiness-7400.

Lovink, Geert, and Ned Rossiter, eds. 2007. *MyCreativity Reader: A Critique of Creative Industries*. Amsterdam: Institute of Network Cultures.

Lowenthal, David. 2019. "A Sea-Change Rich and Strange." In Hanna B. Hölling, Francesca G. Bewer, and Katharina Ammann, eds., *The Explicit Material: Inquiries on the Intersection of Curatorial and Conservation Cultures*. Leiden: Brill.

Lyotard, Jean-François, and Andrew E. Benjamin. 1989. "The Dream-Work Does Not Think." In *The Lyotard Reader*. Oxford: B. Blackwell.

Macdonald, Nancy. 2001. *The Graffiti Subculture: Youth, Masculinity and Identity in London and New York*. London: Palgrave Macmillan UK.

Macdonald, Sharon. 2006. "Words in Stone? Agency and Identity in a Nazi Landscape." *Journal of Material Culture* 11, nos. 1–2: 105–126.

Macdonald, Sharon. 2009. *Difficult Heritage: Negotiating the Nazi Past in Nuremberg and Beyond*. London: Routledge.

Mace, Rodney. 2005. *Trafalgar Square: Emblem of Empire*. London: Lawrence & Wishart.

Magnet, Shoshana. 2011. *When Biometrics Fail: Gender, Race, and the Technology of Identity*. Durham, NC: Duke University Press.

Mann, Steve. 2013. *Veillance and Reciprocal Transparency: Surveillance versus Sousveillance, AR Glass, Lifeglogging, and Wearable Computing*. 2013 IEEE International Symposium on Technology and Society (ISTAS). http://wearcam.org/veillance/part1.pdf.

Mann, Steve. 2016. *Surveillance (Oversight), Sousveillance (Undersight), and Metaveillance (Seeing Sight Itself)*. 2016 IEEE Conference on Computer Vision and Pattern Recognition Workshops (CVPRW). https://openaccess.thecvf.com/content_cvpr_2016_workshops/w29/papers/Mann_Surveillance_Oversight_Sousveillance_CVPR_2016_paper.pdf.

Mann, Steve. n.d. "XR (eXtended Reality) Wand Built by Steve Mann in the 1970s." http://wearcam.org/surveillancestudy-36exposures.

Marchand, Trevor H. J. 2008. "Muscles, Morals and Mind: Craft Apprenticeship and the Formation of Person." *British Journal of Educational Studies* 56, no. 3: 245–271.

Mariz, Rae. 2011. *Getting Caught*. Stockholm: Toxoplasma Press.

Markusen, Anne. 2006. "Urban Development and the Politics of a Creative Class: Evidence from a Study of Artists." *Environment and Planning A* 38: 1921–1940.

Martin, John. 1983 [1933]. "The Modern Dance." In Roger Copeland and Marshall Cohen, eds., *What Is Dance? Readings in Theory and Criticism*. Oxford: Oxford University Press.

Marx, Gary T. 2005. "Surveillance and Society." In George Ritzer, ed., *Encyclopaedia of Social Theory*. Thousand Oaks, CA: Sage, pp. 816–821.

Massey, Doreen. 1994. *Space, Place, and Gender*. Minneapolis: University of Minnesota Press.

McAuliffe, Cameron, and Kurt Iveson. 2011. "Art and Crime (and Other Things Besides . . .): Conceptualising Graffiti in the City." *Geography Compass* 5, no. 3: 128–143.

McQuarrie, Edward F., and David Glen Mick. 1996. "Figures of Rhetoric in Advertising Language." *Journal of Consumer Research* 22, no. 4: 424–438.

Meades, Jonathan. 2023. "Let's Go to Croydon." *London Review of Books*, April 13.

Melhuish, Clare. 2022. "The Evolving Role of Universities in Framing Critical Urban Heritage Discourse in Regeneration Contexts." In Clare Melhuish, Henric Benesch, Ingrid Martins Holmberg, and Dean Sully, eds., *Universities and Urban Heritage Past and Future: Co-Curating the City*. London: UCL Press.

Menninghaus, Wilfred. 2009. "On the 'Vital Significance' of Kitsch: Walter Benjamin's Politics of 'Bad Taste.'" In Andrew Benjamin and Charles Rice, eds., *Walter Benjamin and the Architecture of Modernity*. Melbourne: Re.press.

Merrill, Samuel. 2015. "Keeping It Real? Subcultural Graffiti, Street Art, Heritage and Authenticity." *International Journal of Heritage Studies* 21, no. 4: 369–389.

Michel, Arthur Holland. 2014. "Interview: James Bridle." https://dronecenter.bard.edu/interview-james-bridle.

Miles, Malcolm. 2005. "Interruptions: Testing the Rhetoric of Culturally Led Urban Development." *Urban Studies* 42, nos. 5–6: 889–911.

Miller, Ivor. 1994. "Creolizing for Survival in the City." *Cultural Critique*, no. 27 (Spring): 153–188.

Ministry of Housing, Communities and Local Government. 2021. *New Legal Protection for England's Heritage*. Press release, January 17. https://www.gov.uk/government/news/new-legal-protection-for-england-s-heritage.

Minton, Anna. 2012. *Ground Control: Fear and Happiness in the Twenty-First-Century City*. London: Penguin Books.

Mitchell, W. J. T., and Barbara Kruger. 1991. "An Interview with Barbara Kruger." *Critical Inquiry* 17, no. 2 (Winter): 434-448.

Mithlo, Nancy Marie. 2004. "'Red Man's Burden': The Politics of Inclusion in Museum Settings." *American Indian Quarterly* 28, no. 3–4: 743–763.

Morris, Robert. 2000. "Size Matters." *Critical Inquiry* 26, no. 3: 474–487.

Mudlevel. 2011. "If That's Grassroots, then We're Mudlevel." In Ben Parry, ed., *Cultural Hijack: Rethinking Intervention*. Liverpool: Liverpool University Press with Jump Ship Rat.

Mumford, Lewis. 1970 [1938]. *The Culture of Cities*. New York: Harcourt, Brace.

Munn, Nancy. 1986. *The Fame of Gawa*. Cambridge: Cambridge University Press.

Muñoz, Franscesc. 2012. "Against Banalising Urban Planning." *Transfer: Journal of Contemporary Culture*, no. 7: 42–47.

Muñoz, Franscesc. 2017. "Urbanalization." *Mark Magazine*, no. 68: 74–79.

Munsell, Liz, and Greg Tate. 2021. "Street Art in the Age of Basquiat: Jenny Holzer and Lady Pink on Streetwise Feminisms, Satanism, and Reaganomics." *ARTnews*, May 6. https://www.artnews.com/art-news/news/jenny-holzer-lady-pink-streetwise-feminisms-satanism-reaganomics-1234591793.

Musil, Robert. 1986 [1936]. "Monuments." In *Selected Writings*. New York: Continuum.

Navarrete-Hernandeza, Pablo, Arielle Vetro, and Paz Concha. 2021. "Building Safer Public Spaces: Exploring Gender Difference in the Perception of Safety in Public Space through Urban Design Interventions." *Landscape and Urban Planning* 214: n.p.

Neelon, Caleb (@calebneelonart). 2021. *50 Years Ago Today*. July 21. https://www.instagram.com/p/CRlv4FhsfQ_/?hl=en.

Noland, Carrie. 2009. *Agency and Embodiment: Performing Gestures/Producing Culture*. Cambridge, MA: Harvard University Press.

Nora, Pierre. 1989. "Between Memory and History: Les Lieux de Mémoire." *Representations*, no. 26 (Spring): 7–24.

O'Brien, Daniel T., Chelsea Farrell, and Brandon C. Welsh. 2019. "Looking through Broken Windows: The Impact of Neighborhood Disorder on Aggression and Fear of Crime Is an Artifact of Research Design." *Annual Review of Criminology* 2, no. 1: 53–71.

O'Connor, Tara. 2020. "Croydon Mural Was Never Meant to Praise Winston Churchill Says Gallery Owner Who Paid for It." *MyLondon*, June 10. https://www.mylondon.news/news/south-london-news/croydon-mural-never-meant-praise-18395903.

Olsen, Bjørnar. 2001. "The End of History? Archaeology and the Politics of Identity in a Globalized World." In Robert Layton, Peter G. Stone, and Julian Thomas, eds., *Destruction and Conservation of Cultural Property*. New York: Routledge.

Osborne, Brian S. 2001. "Landscapes, Memory, Monuments, and Commemoration: Putting Identity in Its Place." *Canadian Ethnic Studies Journal* 33, no. 3.

Paglen, Trevor. 2016. "Invisible Images (Your Pictures Are Looking at You)." *The New Enquiry*, December 8. https://thenewinquiry.com/invisible-images-your-pictures-are-looking-at-you.

Palmer, Daniel. 2020. "A Poignant Take on the Controversy Surrounding Public Monuments." *New York Times Style Magazine*, October 9. https://www.nytimes.com/2020/10/09/t-magazine/david-hammons-monuments.html.

Peck, Jamie. 2005. "Struggling with the Creative Class." *International Journal of Urban and Regional Research* 29, no. 4: 740–770.

Petersen, Jennifer. 2022. *How Machines Came to Speak: Media Technologies and Freedom of Speech*. Durham, NC: Duke University Press.

Phelan, Peggy. 1993. *Unmarked: The Politics of Performance*. London: Routledge.

Phillips, Susan A. 1999. *Wallbangin': Graffiti and Gangs in L.A.* Chicago: University of Chicago Press.

Pinder, David. 2005. "Arts of Urban Exploration." *Cultural Geographies* 12, no. 4: 383–411.

Piper, Keith. 1997. *Keith Piper: Relocating the Remains*. London: Institute of International Visual Arts.

Pitti, Ilaria, Yagmur Mengilli, and Andreas Walther. 2021. "Liminal Participation: Young People's Practices in the Public Sphere between Exclusion, Claims of Belonging, and Democratic Innovation." *Youth & Society* 55, no. 1: 143–162.

Pleasant Grove v. Summum 2009. 555 U.S. ____ 2009. https://www.law.cornell.edu/supct/pdf/07-665P.ZO.

Posener, Jill. 1982. *Spray It Loud*. London: Routledge and Kegan Paul, in association with Methuen.

Power, Michael, dir. 1998. *King and Toys*. 25 minutes. Skiny Films, Channel 4.

Powers, Stephen. 1999. *The Art of Getting Over: Graffiti at the Millennium*. New York: St. Martin's Press.

Rafman, Jon. 2009. "IMG MGMT: The Nine Eyes of Google Street View." *Art F City*, August 12. http://artfcity.com/2009/08/12/img-mgmt-the-nine-eyes-of-google-street-view.

Rawlinson, Kevin. 2019. "ICO Opens Investigation into Use of Facial Recognition in King's Cross." *The Guardian*, August 15. https://www.theguardian.com/technology/2019/aug/15/ico-opens-investigation-into-use-of-facial-recognition-in-kings-cross.

Rendell, Jane. 1998. "West End Rambling: Gender and Architectural Space in London 1800–1830." *Leisure Studies* 17, no. 2: 108–122.

Richards, Thomas. 1991. *The Commodity Culture of Victorian Britain: Advertising and Spectacle 1851–1914*. Stanford, CA: Stanford University Press.

Riegl, Alois. 1982 [1903]. "The Modern Cult of Monuments: Its Character and Its Origin," trans. Kurt W. Forster and Diane Ghirardo. *Oppositions*, no. 25: 21–51.

Riegl, Alois. 1996 [1903]. "The Modern Cult of Monuments: Its Character and Its Origin." In Nicholas Stanley-Price, Mansfield Kirby Talley, and Alessandra Melucco Vaccaro, eds., *Historical and Philosophical Issues in the Conservation of Cultural Heritage*. Los Angeles: Getty Conservation Institute.

Robben, Antonius C. G. M. 2005. "How Traumatized Societies Remember: The Aftermath of Argentina's Dirty War." *Cultural Critique*, no. 59 (Winter): 120–164.

Ross, Sarah. 2008. *InAction*. Insecure Spaces. https://insecurespaces.net/inaction-2008.

Rowlands, Michael. 1993. "The Role of Memory in the Transmission of Culture." *World Archaeology* 25, no. 2: 141–151.

Rowlands, Michael, and Christopher Tilley. 2006. "Monuments and Memorials." In Christopher Tilley, Webb Keane, Susanne Küchler, Michael Rowlands, and Patricia Spyer, eds., *Handbook of Material Culture*. London: Sage.

Rugoff, Ralph. 2000. "Touched by Your Presence: Invisibility in Art." *Frieze Magazine*, no. 50 (January–February). https://www.frieze.com/article/touched-your-presence.

Sampson, Henry. 1874. *A History of Advertising from the Earliest Times: Illustrated by Anecdotes, Curious Specimens, and Biographical Notes*. London: Chatto and Windus.

Savage, Kirk. 2018 [1997]. *Standing Soldiers, Kneeling Slaves*. Princeton, NJ: Princeton University Press.

Schacter, Rafael. 2008. "An Ethnography of Iconoclash." *Journal of Material Culture* 13, no. 1: 35–61.

Schacter, Rafael. 2013. *The World Atlas of Street Art and Graffiti*. New Haven, CT: Yale University Press.

Schacter, Rafael. 2014a. *Ornament and Order: Graffiti, Street Art and the Parergon*. Farnham, UK: Ashgate Publishing.

Schacter, Rafael. 2014b. "The Ugly Truth: Street Art, Graffiti and the Creative City." *Art & the Public Sphere* 3, no. 2: 161–176.

Schacter, Rafael. 2015. "The Invisible Performance/the Invisible Masterpiece: Visibility, Concealment, and Commitment in Graffiti and Street Art." In A. Flynn and J. Tinius, eds., *Anthropology, Theatre, and Development*. London: Palgrave Macmillan.

Schacter, Rafael. 2017 "Street Art Is a Period, PERIOD: or, Classificatory Confusion and Intermural Art." In Konstantinos Avramidis and Myrto Tsilimpounidi, eds., *Graffiti and Street Art: Reading, Writing and Representing the City*. New York: Routledge, pp. 103–118.

Schacter, Rafael. 2018. *Street to Studio*. London: Lund Humphries Publishers.

Schacter, Rafael. 2019a. "From Pollution to Purity: The Transformation of Graffiti and Street Art in London (2005–17)." In C. Tilley, ed., *London's Urban Landscape: Another Way of Telling*. London: UCL Press.

Schacter, Rafael. 2019b. "Curating the Intermural: Graffiti in the Museum 2008–2018." In R. Sansi, ed., *The Anthropologist as Curator*. Abingdon, UK: Routledge.

Schneider, Rebecca. 2011. *Performing Remains: Art and War in Times of Theatrical Reenactment*. London: Routledge.

Schriber, Abbe. 2019. "'Those who know don't tell': David Hammons c. 1981." *Women & Performance: A Journal of Feminist Theory* 29, no. 1: 1–21.

Scott Brown, Denise, Robert Venturi, and Steven Izenour. 1988. *Learning from Las Vegas: The Forgotten Symbolism or Architectural Form*. Cambridge, MA: MIT Press.

Searle, John R. 1980. *Speech Act Theory and Pragmatics*. Dordrecht: Reidel.

Sendra, Pablo, Richard Sennett, and Leo Hollis. 2022. *Designing Disorder: Experiments and Disruptions in the City*. London: Verso.

Sennett, Richard. 1994. *Flesh and Stone: The Body and the City in Western Civilization*. New York: W. W. Norton.

Sennett, Richard. 2017. "The Public Realm." In Suzanne Hall and Ricky Burdett, eds., *The SAGE Handbook of the 21st Century City*. London: SAGE Publications. https://doi.org/10.4135/9781526402059.

Shahvisi, Arianna. 2021. "Colonial Monuments as Slurring Speech Acts." *Journal of Philosophy of Education* 55, no. 3: 453–468.

Sheikh, Simon. 2004. "Planes of Immanence, or The Form of Ideas: Notes on the (Anti-)Monuments of Thomas Hirschhorn." *Afterall: A Journal of Art, Context and Enquiry* 9 (Spring/Summer): 90–98.

Sheller, Mimi, and John Urry. 2003. "Mobile Transformations of 'Public' and 'Private' Life." *Theory, Culture & Society* 20, no. 3: 107–125.

Silver, Tony, director. *Style Wars*. PBS. 1983, 70 minutes.

Slater, Tom. 2009. "Missing Marcuse: On Gentrification and Displacement." *City* 13, nos. 2–3.

Sleiman, Mark, and Randy Lippert. 2010. "Downtown Ambassadors, Police Relations and 'Clean and Safe' Security." *Policing & Society* 20, no. 3: 316–335.

Smith, Neil, and Setha Low. 2013. "Introduction: The Imperative of Public Space." In Neil Smith and Setha Low, eds., *The Politics of Public Space*. London: Routledge.

Solove, Daniel J. 2007. "'I've Got Nothing to Hide' and Other Misunderstandings of Privacy." *San Diego Law Review* 44: 745. GWU Law School Public Law Research Paper No. 289.

Southern Poverty Law Center. 2019. *Whose Heritage? Public Symbols of the Confederacy*. https://www.splcenter.org/20220201/whose-heritage-public-symbols-confederacy-third-edition.

Spawls, Alice. 2023. "Short Cuts: Elective Surgery." *London Review of Books* 45, no. 7 (March): 30.

Spikol, Liz. 2012. "Jane Golden Responds to Inga Saffron's Critique of Murals." *Curbed Philadelphia,* December 8. https://philly.curbed.com/2012/12/8/10297692/jane-golden-responds-to-inga-saffrons-critique-of-mural-arts.

Stavrides, Stavros. 2016. *The City as Commons*. London: Zed Books.

Stejskal, Jakub. 2016. "Art's Visual Efficacy: The Case of Anthony Forge's Abelam Corpus." *Res: Anthropology and Aesthetics* 67–68: 78–93.

Stewart, Charles. 1994. "Review: *An Anthropology of Reading in Ancient Greece*, by Joseph Svenbro and Janet Lloyd." *Man, New Series* 29, no. 4.

Stöckl, Hartmut. 2009. "Beyond Depicting: Language-Image-Links in the Service of Advertising." *AAA: Arbeiten aus Anglistik und Amerikanistik* 34, no. 1: 3–28.

Strother, Zoe. 2002. "Iconoclasm by Proxy." In Bruno Latour and Peter Weibel, eds., *Iconoclash: Beyond the Image Wars in Science, Religion, and Art*. Cambridge, MA: MIT Press.

Svennevig, Jan. 2021. "How to Do Things with Signs: The Formulation of Directives on Signs in Public Spaces." *Journal of Pragmatics* 175: 165–183.

Swyngedouw, Erik, and Maria Kaïka. 2003. "The Making of 'Glocal' Urban Modernities." *City* 7, no. 1: 5–21.

Szcześniak, Magda, and Łukasz Zaremba. 2019. "Paranoid Looking: On De-Communization." *Journal of Visual Culture* 18, no. 2: 209–233.

Takahashi, Melanie, and Tim Olaveson. 2001. "Music, Dance and Raving Bodies: Raving as Spirituality in the Central Canadian Rave Scene." *Journal of Ritual Studies* 17, no. 2: 72–96.

"'Taki 183' Spawns Pen Pals." 1971. *New York Times*, July 21. https://www.nytimes.com/1971/07/21/archives/taki-183-spawns-pen-pals.html.

Thomann-Hanry. n.d. "How to Clean Façades—Cleaning Guide." https://thomann-hanry.co.uk/facade-cleaning-system/how-to-clean-facades.

Thomas, Nicholas. 2001. "Introduction." In Nicholas Thomas and Christopher Pinney, eds., *Beyond Aesthetics: Art and the Technologies of Enchantment*. Oxford: Berg.

Thomas, Nicholas, and Alison Clark, eds. 2017. *Style and Meaning: Essays on the Anthropology of Art—Anthony Forge*. Leiden: Sidestone Press.

Tilley, Christopher. 2004. *The Materiality of Stone: Explorations in Landscape Phenomenology*. Oxford: Berg.

Torre, Susana. 1996. "Claiming the Public Space: The Mothers of Plaza de Mayo." In Jane Rendell, Barbara Penner, and Iain Borden, eds., *Gender Space Architecture: An Interdisciplinary Introduction*. London: Routledge.

Townsend, Anthony M. 2013. *Smart Cities: Big Data, Civic Hackers, and the Quest for a New Utopia*. New York: W. W. Norton.

Trinch, Shonna, and Edward Snajdr. 2017. "What the Signs Say: Gentrification and the Disappearance of Capitalism without Distinction in Brooklyn." *Journal of Sociolinguistics* 21, no. 1: 64–89.

Trouillot, Michel-Rolph. 1995. *Silencing the Past: Power and the Production of History*. Boston: Beacon Press.

Tsing, Anna. 1994. "From the Margins." *Cultural Anthropology* 9, no. 3: 279–297.

Turner, Victor Witter. 1967. *The Forest of Symbols: Aspects of Ndembu Ritual*. Ithaca, NY: Cornell University Press.

Turner, Victor Witter. 1979a. "Frame, Flow and Reflection: Ritual and Drama as Public Liminality." *Japanese Journal of Religious Studies* 6, no. 4: 465–499.

Turner, Victor Witter. 1979b. *Process, Performance, and Pilgrimage: A Study in Comparative Symbology*. New Delhi: Concept.

Turner, Victor Witter. 1983. "Carnival in Rio: Dionysian Drama in an Industrializing Society." In Frank E. Manning, ed., *The Celebration of Society: Perspectives on Contemporary Cultural Performance*. Bowling Green, OH: Bowling Green University Popular Press.

Ugwu, Reggie. 2019. "Kehinde Wiley's Times Square Monument: That's No Robert E. Lee." *New York Times*, September 27. https://www.nytimes.com/2019/09/27/arts/design/kehinde-wiley-times-square-statue.html.

United Kingdom Act of Parliament. 1990. *Entertainments (Increased Penalty) Bill*. https://www.legislation.gov.uk/ukpga/1990/20.

United Kingdom Act of Parliament. 1995. *Criminal Justice and Public Order Act*. https://www.legislation.gov.uk/ukpga/1994/33/contents.

Urry, John. 1990. *The Tourist Gaze: Leisure and Travel in Contemporary Societies*. London: Sage.

Urry, John. 2002. *Consuming Places*. London: Routledge.

Vickery, Jonathan. 2012. *Public Art and the Art of the Public: After the Creative City*. Birmingham: IXIA Public Arts Think Tank.

Vladeck, Steve, and Benjamin Wittes. 2020. "DHS Authorizes Domestic Surveillance to Protect Statues and Monuments." *Lawfare*, July 20. https://www.lawfareblog.com/dhs-authorizes-domestic-surveillance-protect-statues-and-monuments.

Vom Bruck, Gabriele, and Barbara Bodenhorn. 2006. "'Entangled in Histories': An Introduction to the Anthropology of Names and Naming." In Gabriele Vom Bruck and Barbara Bodenhorn, eds., *An Anthropology of Names and Naming*. Cambridge: Cambridge University Press.

Vrasti, Wanda, and Smaran Dayal. 2016. "Cityzenship: Rightful Presence and the Urban Commons." *Citizenship Studies* 20, no. 8: 994–1011.

Warner, Michael. 2002. "Publics and Counterpublics (Abbreviated Version)." *Quarterly Journal of Speech* 88, no. 4: 413–425.

Wigley, Mark. 1993. "White-Out: Fashioning the Modern (Part 2)." *Assemblage*, no. 2: 6–49.

Wijesinghe, Thilan. 1993. "A Proposed Methodology for Measuring the Economic Value of Cultural Monuments." In *Economics of Conservation: Sri Lanka National Committee of ICOMOS for the International Council of Monuments and Sites*. Paris: ICOMOS. https://www.icomos.org/en/resources/publicationall/icomos-bookshop/116-english-categories/resources/publications/292-isc-economics-of-conservation.

Wilson, James, and George Kelling. 1982. "Broken Windows." *Atlantic Monthly* 249, no. 3: 29–36, 38.

Wodiczko, Krzysztof. 1999. *Critical Vehicles: Writings, Projects, Interviews*. Cambridge, MA: MIT Press.

World Travel and Tourism Council. 2023. *Economic Impact Research*. https://wttc.org/research/economic-impact.

Wu Ming. 2016. "Action against the Rich and Powerful Who Take Street Art off the Street." March 11–12. https://www.wumingfoundation.com/giap/2016/03/street-artist-blu-is-erasing-all-the-murals-he-painted-in-bologna/#english.

Young, Diana. 2006. "The Colours of Things." In Christopher Tilley, Webb Keane, Susanne Küchler, Michael Rowlands, and Patricia Spyer, eds., *Handbook of Material Culture*. London: Sage.

Young, Iris Marion. 2020. *On Female Body Experience: "Throwing like a Girl" and Other Essays*. New York: Oxford University Press.

Young, James E. 1992. "The Counter-Monument: Memory against Itself in Germany Today." *Critical Inquiry* 18, no. 2 (Winter): 267–296.

YourCroydon. 2016. "New Post of Creative Director for Croydon Regeneration." March 2. https://news.croydon.gov.uk/new-post-of-creative-director-for-croydon-regeneration.

Zimmerman, Andrea Luka, and Lasse Johansson. 2009. "I Am Here." https://www.fugitiveimages.org.uk/projects/i-am-here/published-in-streetsigns-2010-goldsmiths-i-am-here-some-thoughts-on-site-specificity-and-instrumenta.

Zukin, Sharon. 1995. *The Cultures of Cities*. Oxford: Blackwell.

Zukin, Sharon, and Laura Braslow. 2011. "The Life Cycle of New York's Creative Districts: Reflections on the Unanticipated Consequences of Unplanned Cultural Zones." *City, Culture and Society* 2: 131–140.